Schriften zu Wirtschaftsprüfung, Steuerlehre und Controlling

Reihe herausgegeben von
C.-C. Freidank, Hamburg, Deutschland

In der Schriftenreihe erscheinen ausgewählte, herausragende Dissertationen und Habilitationen aus den Fachgebieten Wirtschaftsprüfung, Steuerlehre und Controlling, die aufgrund ihrer Aktualität, internationalen Ausrichtung, gewählten Untersuchungsmethode und den innovativen Forschungsergebnissen zu neuen wissenschaftlichen Erkenntnissen und einer Bereicherung des einschlägigen Schrifttums führen. Für einen Veröffentlichung kommen sowohl Monographien als auch kumulative Schriftensammlungen in Betracht, die aus den Wissenschaftsdiziplinen der Betriebswirtschaftslehre, des Rechts, der Mathematik oder der Wirtschaftsinformatik stammen und in deutscher oder englischer Sprache abgefasst werden können. Besonders willkommen sind Arbeiten, die einen interdisziplinären Forschungsansatz gewählt haben. Die Entscheidung über eine Aufnahme in die Schriftenreihe wird vom Herausgeber in Kontakt mit dem Betreuer des Dissertations- bzw. Habilitationsprojekts getroffen.

Weitere Bände in der Reihe http://www.springer.com/series/12267

Thomas S. Konrad

Management Control in Public-Private Partnerships

Between International Governmental Actors and the Private Sector

With a foreword by Prof. Dr. Andreas Hoffjan

Springer Gabler

Thomas S. Konrad
Dortmund, Germany

Dissertation Technische Universität Dortmund, 2018

Schriften zu Wirtschaftsprüfung, Steuerlehre und Controlling
ISBN 978-3-658-22867-5 ISBN 978-3-658-22868-2 (eBook)
https://doi.org/10.1007/978-3-658-22868-2

Library of Congress Control Number: 2018948672

Springer Gabler

Printed on acid-free paper

This Springer Gabler imprint is published by the registered company Springer Fachmedien Wiesbaden GmbH part of Springer Nature
The registered company address is: Abraham-Lincoln-Str. 46, 65189 Wiesbaden, Germany

Foreword

In his dissertation, Mr. Konrad analyzes the management control design and reveals critical success factors of strategically oriented public-private partnerships for development between international governmental actors and the private sector. His research work makes a valuable contribution to tackling PPPs from a perspective which truly deserves much more attention, especially in the light of the official promulgation of the so-called Sustainable Development Goals in 2015. The close connection to this global political agenda endorses the dissertation's great practical relevance. Furthermore, the work contributes to enhancing the fundamental scientific basis of accounting-related research on PPPs by addressing a broad range of pertinent management control issues.

The dissertation by Mr. Konrad stands out by an adequately and soundly designed theoretical framework with focus on a clearly delineated target group, namely practitioners. Thus, he conducted interviews with experienced representatives from a variety of multinational corporations, international organizations and development cooperation agencies as part of his international field study. Pertinent professional experience which Mr. Konrad gained prior to his dissertation through different capacities in private sector firms, in the diplomatic service and with the United Nations enabled him to understand, interpret and categorize the experiences and perspectives of this interview partners. In this regard, his research has produced meaningful results and provides recommendations that might be taken into consideration by managerial and operational decision-makers from the concerned stakeholders.

Mr. Konrad has built up his empirical qualitative research on a comprehensive and thorough literature review and anchored his theoretical framework in the school of new institutional economics. Hence, he built a sound basis for the identification of a research gap and the derivation of research questions. His results generate sufficient evidence to answer these questions and therefore to close the identified research gap. Finally, he excelled in the discussion of the results by making a contribution of theory and by providing substantive recommendations to practitioners equally well. That is why I am convinced that this noteworthy thesis will be well-received and enjoy broad recognition by both practitioners and the research community.

Prof. Dr. Andreas Hoffjan

Acknowledgements

At the end of my doctoral project, I would like to express my sincere gratitude to the people who supported me in this endeavour and thank them for their contribution to the successful completion of the present thesis.

First of all, I would like to thank Prof. Dr. Andreas Hoffjan for his close supervision and trustful collaboration. His continuous support and valuable feedback along the entire research project are very much appreciated. Second, special acknowledgements go to Prof. Dr. Liudvika Leisyte for her commitment to assuming the co-supervision. Prof. Dr. Janine Maniora deserves my sincere gratitude for acting as third reviewer.

Moreover, I would like to express my gratefulness to my interview partners from Germany, Italy, Mexico, Switzerland, Turkey and USA. Without their substantive contributions and their willingness to share their manifold and pertinent experiences this research work would not have been possible. In this context, I thank Professor Dr. Bryan Husted from EGADE Business School in Monterrey/Mexico for his valuable feedback on my doctoral project and for his support in establishing contacts with interview partners in Mexico. My three months field research stay there was kindly facilitated by a research grant from the DAAD. Interviews with distinguished representatives from international organizations could be reached through the generous support from Ambassador Peter Thomson from Fiji and Ambassador István Posta from Hungary.

In addition, I am indebted to Prof. Dr. Michael Brandau for his fruitful comments in terms of quality assurance and for being always open to provide wise advice, if required. Patrick Kordus assisted me for several semesters and performed diverse supporting tasks in an excellent manner. Furthermore, I would like to extend my gratitude to my fellow colleagues from the Department of Management Accounting and Control of TU Dortmund University who significantly contributed to creating an enabling environment, characterized by team spirit and strong cohesion, in which I could conduct my doctoral project.

Last but not least, I would like to thank my family, especially my parents Charlotte and Dr. Manfred Konrad, for their enduring and unrestricted support in all my personal and professional endeavours, not only but also during my doctoral studies. For this reason, I devote the present thesis to them.

Thomas S. Konrad

Contents

Foreword ... V
Acknowledgements ... VII
Contents ... IX
List of Abbreviations ... XV
List of Figures ... XVII
List of Tables ... XIX
1. Introduction ... 1
1.1 Motivation and Problem Definition ... 1
1.2 Reasons for the Selected Research Focus ... 4
1.3 Objectives of this Study ... 6
1.4 Structure and Procedure of the Investigation ... 6
2. Basics of Management Control in Public-Private Partnerships ... 9
2.1 Definitions, Differentiations, and Categorizations ... 9
2.1.1 Management Control ... 9
2.1.2 Governance ... 11
2.1.3 Interorganizational/Interfirm Relationships ... 11
2.1.4 Public-Private Partnerships ... 13
2.1.4.1 Typology of PPPs ... 14
2.1.4.2 Reasons for the creation of PPPs ... 18
2.2 Literature Review ... 19
2.2.1 Quantitative Analysis of Reviewed Literature ... 19
2.2.1.1 General Overview ... 20
2.2.1.1.1 Strands of Literature ... 20
2.2.1.1.2 Theoretical Frameworks ... 22
2.2.1.1.3 Methodologies ... 23
2.2.1.1.4 Geographical Scopes ... 24
2.2.1.2 Management control-centered Overview ... 26
2.2.1.2.1 Strands of Literature ... 26
2.2.1.2.2 Theoretical Frameworks ... 27
2.2.1.2.3 Methodologies ... 28
2.2.1.2.4 Geographical Scopes ... 29
2.2.2 Qualitative Analysis of Reviewed Literature ... 30
2.2.2.1 PPP ... 31
2.2.2.2 Joint Venture ... 32
2.2.2.3 Interorganizational/Interfirm Relationship ... 38
2.2.3 PPPs for Development ... 44
2.3 Critical Success Factors ... 49
2.3.1 Extrinsic Factors ... 53
2.3.2 Intrinsic Factors ... 55
2.3.2.1 Intrinsic Factors – Interpersonal CSFs ... 55
2.3.2.2 Intrinsic Factors – Inherent/Structural CSFs ... 56
2.3.2.3 Intrinsic Factors – Procedural CSFs ... 58
2.3.2.4 Intrinsic Factors – General CSFs ... 61
2.3.3 Interim Conclusion ... 62

2.4 Interim Summary and Research Gap ... 62
3. Control Archetypes and Typologies ... 65
3.1 Control Dimensions ... 66
3.2 Control Levels ... 68
3.2.1 Market-based Control Pattern ... 68
3.2.2 Bureaucracy and Hierarchy Control Pattern ... 69
3.2.3 Hybrid Control Pattern ... 69
3.3 Control Mechanisms ... 69
3.3.1 Formal Control ... 69
3.3.2 Informal Control ... 70
3.3.3 Market Control ... 71
3.3.4 Characteristics of Control Mechanisms ... 72
3.4 Joint Venture-specific Control Typologies ... 78
3.5 Control Problems ... 80
3.6 Relationship of Risk and Trust with Control ... 82
3.6.1 Trust ... 82
3.6.1.1 Definition and Relevance of Trust ... 82
3.6.1.2 Dimensions of Trust ... 83
3.6.1.3 Relationship of Trust with Control ... 84
3.6.2 Risk ... 86
3.7 Interim Summary ... 87
4. Theoretical Foundation ... 89
4.1 Actor-centered Institutionalism ... 91
4.1.1 Actor ... 92
4.1.2 Actor Constellations ... 93
4.1.3 Modes of Interaction ... 94
4.1.4 Institutions and Institutional Setting ... 95
4.1.5 Delineation of ACI from Other Pertinent Approaches ... 96
4.2 Transaction Cost Economics ... 97
4.2.1 General Characteristics and Origin of Transaction Costs ... 97
4.2.2 Relationship between Transaction Costs and Management Control ... 99
4.2.3 Behavioral Characteristics ... 100
4.2.4 Transaction Characteristics ... 102
4.2.5 Governance Characteristics ... 105
4.2.6 Other pertinent TCE Characteristics ... 108
4.2.7 Delineation of TCE from Other Pertinent Theories ... 109
4.3 Theoretical Link between ACI and TCE ... 111
4.3.1 ACI-TCE Theoretical Framework ... 112
4.3.2 Forms and Levels of Governance ... 113
4.4 Interim Summary ... 115
4.5 Derivation of the Research Questions ... 115
5. Research Design and Methodology ... 121
5.1 Choice and Definition of the Research Approach ... 121
5.1.1 Characteristics of Qualitative Research ... 121
5.1.2 Characteristics of Field Study Research ... 125
5.1.3 Characteristics of Interview-based Research ... 128
5.2 Methodology of Data Collection ... 130
5.2.1 Sample Selection ... 130

5.2.1.1 Sampling Requirements ... 130
5.2.1.2 Selection of Interview Partners ... 132
5.2.1.3 Sample Composition and Characteristics of the Interviewees ... 136
5.2.2 Interviewing ... 140
5.2.2.1 Conception and Structure of the Interview Guide ... 140
5.2.2.2 Conducting the Interviews ... 144
5.3 Methodology of Data Analysis ... 149
5.3.1 Procedure for Qualitative Content Analysis ... 149
5.3.2 Creation of Categories and Coding Approach ... 150
5.3.3 Quality Assessment of the Methodical Approach ... 153
5.3.3.1 Quality Criteria ... 153
5.3.3.2 Validity ... 154
5.3.3.3 Reliability ... 156
5.3.4 Summary of the Methodical Approach ... 158
6. Results of the Empirical Field Study ... 161
6.1 Basic Characteristics of PPPs for Development ... 161
6.1.1 Characteristics of the Stakeholders Involved ... 161
6.1.2 Characteristics of the Actors Involved ... 164
6.1.2.1 Job Descriptions and Responsibilities ... 164
6.1.2.2 Qualification for PPP Work ... 167
6.1.2.3 Dedication to PPP Work ... 169
6.1.3 Departments Involved and Internal Support ... 170
6.1.4 Decentralization and Local Staff Presence ... 173
6.1.5 Characteristics of the PPPs ... 176
6.1.5.1 Policy Issues ... 176
6.1.5.2 PPP Types ... 179
6.1.5.3 Legal Arrangements and Relationships ... 184
6.1.5.3.1 Types of Contract Arrangements ... 187
6.1.5.3.2 Characteristics of Loose and Tight Contract Arrangements ... 189
6.1.5.4 Duration and Durability ... 190
6.1.5.5 Financial Volume ... 193
6.2 Partnership Setting ... 193
6.2.1 Motivation ... 194
6.2.1.1 Extrinsic Motivation ... 194
6.2.1.2 Intrinsic Motivation ... 198
6.2.2 Objectives ... 199
6.2.2.1 Objectives of PPPs for Development ... 199
6.2.2.2 Mutual Expectations and Goal Alignment ... 202
6.2.2.3 Conflicts of Interest ... 205
6.2.3 Partnership Requirements ... 207
6.2.4 Existence and Characteristics of PPP Strategies ... 208
6.2.5 Contributions ... 210
6.2.6 Partnership Risks ... 215
6.2.6.1 Extrinsic Risks ... 215
6.2.6.2 Intrinsic Risks ... 218
6.2.6.3 Balance between Benefits and Risks ... 220
6.3 Preparation and Implementation ... 222
6.3.1 Partner Selection ... 222

6.3.1.1 Origins of PPP Initiatives 222
6.3.1.2 Previous Experiences 224
6.3.1.3 Characteristics and Selection Procedure 225
6.3.1.4 Selection Criteria 226
6.3.2 Project Phases 228
6.3.3 Preparatory Actions and Planning Quality 232
6.4 Budget and Resource Planning 234
6.4.1 Financing Mechanisms and Equity Ownership Structure 234
6.4.2 Characteristics of Resource Planning 238
6.4.3 Transaction Characteristics 241
6.4.3.1 Specificity of Resources 241
6.4.3.2 Resource Provision Process 243
6.4.4 Resource Efficiency 244
6.4.4.1 Cost Factors 247
6.4.4.2 Cost Reduction 249
6.5 Governance and Control Pattern 250
6.5.1 Governance Structures and Governing Bodies 250
6.5.1.1 Partner-Specific Internal Governance Structures 255
6.5.1.2 Sharing of Responsibilities and Taking of Ownership 256
6.5.1.3 Delegation of Authority 257
6.5.1.4 Level of Complexity 258
6.5.2 Governance Levels 260
6.5.2.1 Decision-Making Processes 261
6.5.2.2 Control Types 262
6.5.2.2.1 Dominant Control 263
6.5.2.2.2 Independent Control 264
6.5.2.2.3 Shared Control 265
6.5.2.3 Categories of Control Mechanisms 266
6.5.2.3.1 Context-Oriented Control 267
6.5.2.3.2 Content-Oriented Control 267
6.5.2.3.3 Consultation-Oriented Control 268
6.5.2.4 Level of integration of Control Systems 269
6.5.3 Level of Cooperation 271
6.5.3.1 Actor Orientations 272
6.5.3.2 Causes and Risk of Opportunistic Behavior 274
6.6 Management Control 277
6.6.1 Behavior and Results Control 277
6.6.1.1 Performance Orientation 278
6.6.1.2 Elements of Performance Measurement 279
6.6.1.3 Benchmark Indicators 281
6.6.1.4 Monitoring 285
6.6.1.5 Reporting and Accountability 289
6.6.1.6 Rules and Guidelines 292
6.6.2 Clan and Social Control 293
6.6.2.1 Control Activities and Communication 293
6.6.2.2 Alignment of Diverging Interests 296
6.6.2.3 Conflict Management 299
6.6.2.4 Networking and Knowledge Management 300

6.6.3 Control Extent and Control Focus ... 302
6.6.3.1 Contractual Controls and Formalization of Management Control Practices ... 303
6.6.3.2 Contractual Safeguardings ... 305
6.6.4 Environmental Factors ... 307
6.6.4.1 Control Challenges ... 307
6.6.4.2 Influences of Organizational Culture ... 309
6.6.4.3 Intercultural Influences ... 314
6.6.4.4 Trust ... 317
6.6.4.4.1 Relationship between Trust and Management Control ... 318
6.6.4.4.2 Trust-building Mechanisms ... 320
6.6.4.5 Management of Control Problems ... 322
6.6.4.5.1 Control Problems and Consequences ... 322
6.6.4.5.2 Risk Management and Control ... 328
6.6.5 Control Effectiveness ... 332
6.6.5.1 Commitment ... 332
6.6.5.2 Contract Compliance and Enforceability ... 334
6.7 Institutional Environment ... 336
6.7.1 Institutional Levels ... 336
6.7.2 Institutional Constraints ... 339
6.7.2.1 Formal Constraints ... 339
6.7.2.2 Informal Constraints ... 341
6.7.3 Role of Governmental Authorities ... 343
6.7.3.1 Support and Impediment ... 344
6.7.3.2 Accountability ... 347
6.7.4 Expansion of PPP Activities ... 348
6.7.5 Influence of Global Institutions ... 350
6.7.5.1 UN and other Global Initiatives and Platforms ... 351
6.7.5.2 Transition from MDGs to SDGs ... 352
6.8 Critical Success Factors ... 355
6.8.1 Extrinsic Factors ... 356
6.8.2 Intrinsic Factors ... 357
6.8.2.1 Intrinsic Factors – Interpersonal CSFs ... 358
6.8.2.2 Intrinsic Factors – Inherent/Structural CSFs ... 361
6.8.2.3 Intrinsic Factors – Procedural CSFs ... 366
6.8.2.4 Intrinsic Factors – General CSFs ... 368
6.8.3 Potential for Improvement of Management Control ... 371
7. Overall Assessment and Discussion ... 377
7.1 Summary of the Research Approach and Central Results ... 377
7.2 Implications for Practitioners ... 379
7.2.1 Recommendations for Management Control Design in PPPs for Development ... 380
7.2.2 Results from the Communicative Validation ... 383
7.3 Conclusions on Theoretical Characteristics of ACI and TCE ... 384
7.3.1 Manifestation of ACI-related Characteristics ... 384
7.3.2 Manifestation of TCE-related Theoretical Assumptions ... 387
7.3.2.1 Behavioral and Transaction Characteristics ... 388
7.3.2.2 Governance Characteristics ... 393

7.3.3 Contribution to and Implications for Management Control Research 395
7.4 Limitations of the Study 398
7.4.1 Specific Limitations related to the Content and to the Selected Theoretical Framework 398
7.4.2 Specific Limitations related to the Methodology Applied 399
7.5 Conclusion and Outlook 401
8. Annex 405
8.1 Complementary Tables 405
8.2 Exemplary Interview Guide (for companies)..415
8.3 Exemplary Description of the Research Study 419
8.4 List of Codes from MAXQDA...421
9. Bibliography...429

List of Abbreviations

AAA	American Accounting Association
ACI	Actor-centered Institutionalism
BOO	Build Own Operate
BOOT	Build Own Operate Transfer
BOT	Build Operate Transfer
CIA	Central Intelligence Agency
CSF	Critical Success Factor
CSR	Corporate Social Responsibility
DAAD	Deutscher Akademischer Austauschdienst
DBFO	Design-Build-Finance-Operate
DBOT	Design-Builde-Operate-Transfer
DCA	Development Cooperation Agency
DFID	Department of International Development
DNA	Deoxyribonucleic Acid
EGADE	Escuela de Graduados en Administración y Dirección de Empresas
ERMAC	Empirical Research in Management Accounting & Control
EU	European Union
EZ	Entwicklungszusammenarbeit
HR	Human Resources
ICC	International Chamber of Commerce
ICT	Information and Communication Technology
IFR	Interfirm Relationship
IJV	International Joint Venture
IO	International Organization
IOR	Interorganizational Relationship
ITESM	Instituto Tecnológico y de Estudios Superiores de Monterrey
JV	Joint Venture
LOI	Letter of Intent
MC	Management Control
MCS	Management Control System
MoU	Memorandum of Understanding
NGO	Non-Governmental Organization
NIE	New/Neo Institutional Economics
ÖPP	Öffentlich Private Partnerschaft
PFI	Private Finance Initiative
PMO	Project Management Office
PPP	Public-Private Partnership
PSC	Public Sector Comparator
R&D	Research and Development
RQ	Research Question
SHCP	Secretaría de Hacienda y Crédito Público
SOP	Standard Operating Procedure
SPAEF	Southern Public Administration Education Foundation
TC	Transaction Costs

TCE	Transaction Cost Economics
UIA	Union of International Associations
UN	United Nations
UNFCCC	United Nations Framework Convention on Climate Change
UNGC	United Nations Global Compact
USA	United States of America
USAID	United States Agency for International Development
VdM	Van der Meer-Kooistra, Jeltje
VFM	Value for Money
VHB	Verband der Hochschullehrer für Betriebswirtschaft e.V.
WEF	World Economic Forum

List of Figures

Figure 1: Structure of the study. 8
Figure 2: Typology of interorganizational and interfirm relationships. 12
Figure 3: Spectrum and types of PPPs. 15
Figure 4: Reviewed articles by journal category. 21
Figure 5: Number of reviewed articles by theoretical framework cluster. 23
Figure 6: Number of reviewed articles categorized by the methodology applied. 24
Figure 7: Reviewed articles classified by geographic focus. 25
Figure 8: Number of MC-centered articles by journal category. 27
Figure 9: Number of MC-centered articles by theoretical framework cluster. 28
Figure 10: Number of MC-centered articles by methodology applied. 29
Figure 11: MC-centered articles by geographic focus. 30
Figure 12: Hierarchy of critical success factors. 52
Figure 13: Extrinsic critical success factors by publication. 54
Figure 14: Interpersonal intrinsic factors by publication. 56
Figure 15: Inherent/structural intrinsic factors by publication. 58
Figure 16: Procedural intrinsic factors by publication. 60
Figure 17: General intrinsic factors by publication. 61
Figure 18: Control archetypes. 66
Figure 19: Theoretical embedding and framework. 90
Figure 20: Actor-centered institutionalism. 92
Figure 21: Combined ACI-TCE theoretical framework. 112
Figure 22: Research questions. 116
Figure 23: Overall research scope. 118
Figure 24: Selection procedure of interview partners. 135
Figure 25: Process of guided semi-structured interviews. 140
Figure 26: Structure of the interview guide. 144
Figure 27: Timeline of the present field study. 145
Figure 28: Elements of qualitative research methodology. 158
Figure 29: Stakeholder types involved in PPPs for development. 164
Figure 30: Overview of typical job responsibilities of the interview partners. 165
Figure 31: Elements of qualification for PPP work. 167
Figure 32: Level of decentralization and local staff presence. 173
Figure 33: Addressed policy issues and purposes of PPPs for development. 177
Figure 34: Types of PPPs for development. 180
Figure 35: Legal relationships between DCAs, IOs, and the private sector. 185
Figure 36: Models of PPP duration. 191
Figure 37: PPP objectives of public and private sectors. 200
Figure 38: Origins and drivers of PPP initiatives. 222
Figure 39: Partner selection procedure. 225
Figure 40: Typical project phases in PPPs for development. 229
Figure 41: Finance structures of PPPs for development. 236
Figure 42: Resource planning and approval procedure. 238
Figure 43: Governance structure – civic association and integrated partnership. 251
Figure 44: Governance structure – multilateral alliance. 252
Figure 45: Governance structure – strategic alliance (direct implementation). 253
Figure 46: Governance structure – strategic alliance (indirect implementation). 254

Figure 47: Characteristics of decision-making processes. 261
Figure 48: Risk of opportunistic behavior. 275
Figure 49: Time-bound monitoring approaches. 287
Figure 50: Reporting lines and frequencies.. 289
Figure 51: Influences of public and private organizational cultures........................... 309
Figure 52: Lifetime- and phase-oriented risk management and control. 328
Figure 53: Overview of different institutional levels. 337
Figure 54: Most frequently mentioned critical success factors................................... 380
Figure 55: Phase-oriented consideration of critical success factors for governance.......
structure and management control design. 381
Figure 56: Approaches to defining and understanding institutions and the......................
institutional environment.. 386
Figure 57: Interconnections between governance and MC and TCE characteristics. 389
Figure 58: Areas of potential future research. 397

List of Tables

Table 1: Excerpt from the UN resolution A/RES/55/2. 5
Table 2: Excerpt from the UN resolution A/RES/70/1. 5
Table 3: Approaches to definition of control. 10
Table 4: Approaches to definition of PPPs. 13
Table 5: Characteristics and classifications of JVs. 17
Table 6: Number of reviewed articles with geographic focus. 24
Table 7: Reviewed MC-related articles regarding PPPs. 31
Table 8: Reviewed MC-related articles regarding JVs and IJVs. 35
Table 9: Reviewed MC-related articles regarding IORs/IFRs. 42
Table 10: Reviewed articles on PPPs for development. 47
Table 11: Terminologies of control levels in extant literature. 68
Table 12: Types of formal and informal control mechanisms. 73
Table 13: Phase-oriented control mechanisms. 78
Table 14: Contractual and managerial controls in JVs. 80
Table 15: Control problems. 81
Table 16: Impact of control and trust upon performance and relational risk. 87
Table 17: Comparison of characteristics of actor constellations and organizations. 94
Table 18: Critical dimensions of the transaction cost economics. 104
Table 19: Contingent factors leading to performance and relational risk. 104
Table 20: Comparison of attributes of the three governance structures. 106
Table 21: Comparison of approaches to governance structures. 106
Table 22: Comparison of TCE vs. agency theory and property rights theory. 111
Table 23: Governance from the perspective of the ACI and the TCE. 114
Table 24: Comparison of quantitative and qualitative research methodology. 123
Table 25: Categories of quantitative and qualitative accounting research. 124
Table 26: Comparative overview of characteristics of different research methods. 127
Table 27: Statistical overview of the making of contact with interview partners. 136
Table 28: Size of the interviewed private sector firms (by number of employees). 137
Table 29: Size of the interviewed IOs (by number of employees). 137
Table 30: Size of the interviewed DCAs (by number of employees). 137
Table 31: Job positions of the interview partners from private sector firms. 138
Table 32: Job positions of the interview partners from IOs. 139
Table 33: Job positions of the interview partners from DCAs. 139
Table 34: Geographical distribution by interview type. 146
Table 35: Interview language used by interview type. 146
Table 36: Overview of interview durations compiled by interview partner type. 147
Table 37: Quality criteria in qualitative research. 154
Table 38: Coefficients of agreement, C_R, of the content analysis. 157
Table 39: Quality assurance actions taken. 159
Table 40: Departments involved and their responsibilities and tasks. 172
Table 41: Governance level per PPP type. 183
Table 42: Directly and indirectly business-related extrinsic motivation factors. 194
Table 43: Expectations of PPPs from public and private sector actors. 204
Table 44: Strict and soft requirements for PPPs. 207
Table 45: Public sector contributions. 212

Table 46: Private sector contributions. 214
Table 47: Overview of extrinsic risks. 217
Table 48: Overview of intrinsic risks. 220
Table 49: Overview of partner selection criteria. 228
Table 50: Direct financial allocations. 237
Table 51: Indirect financial allocations. 238
Table 52: Cost factors. 247
Table 53: Scale-based assessment of actor orientations. 272
Table 54: Elements of performance measurement. 280
Table 55: Overview of qualitative and quantitative benchmark indicators. 282
Table 56: Monitoring actions and foci per monitoring type. 286
Table 57: Social and clan control activities. 294
Table 58: Control problems and countermeasures/reactions. 324
Table 59: Overview of risk management and control measures. 331
Table 60: Extrinsic factors. 357
Table 61: Intrinsic CSFs – Interpersonal factors. 360
Table 62: Intrinsic CSFs – Inherent/Structural factors. 365
Table 63: Intrinsic CSFs – Procedural factors. 368
Table 64: Intrinsic CSFs – General factors. 371
Table 65: Total list of reviewed articles. 408
Table 66: Reviewed journals including number of reviewed articles. 411
Table 67: Reviewed accounting journals without usable results. 412
Table 68: Reviewed articles with mixed method research design by frequency. 412
Table 69: MC-centered articles with mixed method research design by frequency. 413
Table 70: Publications numbered by source. 414
Table 71: Overview on types of actors as per ACI. 414
Table 72: Modes of Interaction. 414

1. Introduction

This doctoral study makes a contribution to the area of accounting research in the context of Public-Private Partnerships (PPPs), placing the focus on Management Control (MC). It investigates empirically characteristics and designs of MC in PPPs for development as well as their critical success factors (CSFs). While these PPPs usually involve and/or affect various stakeholders, such as civil society and national governments, the research focus is narrowed to the collaboration between private sector and international governmental actors in the field of partnerships for development. For the collection of empirical data, semi-structured interviews were conducted with representatives from multinational companies, international organizations (IOs) and development cooperation agencies (DCAs) from different countries. A combined approach of the actor-centered institutionalism (ACI) and the transaction cost economics (TCE) forms the theoretical framework and basis for discussion of the empirical results.

1.1 Motivation and Problem Definition

The role MC plays and should play in organizational contexts has evolved in recent years. This issue was early raised especially by Otley (1994) and Otley et al. (1995), was followed by numerous studies that support the notion that MC as such is and should no be longer restricted to the legal boundaries of individual organizations. Otley et al. (1995) argue that an increasing number of different forms of multi-stakeholder cooperation (e.g. interfirm relationships (IFRs), (international) joint ventures (IJVs/JVs), strategic alliances) demand the enhancement of the theoretical scope of MC research to interorganizational control issues because the applicability of previous theoretical assumptions and concepts from individual organizations to these new and complex ways of collaboration had been questioned (cf. Berry et al., 2009; Donada and Nogatchewsky, 2006; Speklé, 2001; Vosselman and Van der Meer-Kooistra (VdM), 2009). Underlying business activities like the outsourcing of business processes (cf. Langfield-Smith and Smith, 2003; VdM and Vosselman, 2000) or value chain analysis (cf. Dekker, 2003) require the shift towards the adoption of a more interorganizational control focus. Moreover, Berry et al. (2009) bemoan the lack of management accountants' active commitment to adapting, designing and operating contemporary organizational forms on the one hand, and the lack of studies pursuing an integrative approach for analyzing MC on the other hand because the majority of the studies tend to concentrate on selected control variables and aspects. That is why the extant literature was calling for more research about the relationship between resource contributions and the establishment of control practices (cf. Chen et al., 2009), the relevance of trust as informal control mechanism to counteract control issues like uncertainty (cf. Emsley and Kidon, 2007), the results-oriented adaptation and integration of control mechanisms in decision-making processes (cf. Johnson et al., 2002), or different kinds of boundaries and distances and their implications for MC (e.g. in the context of administrational procedures, culture, economic development or geography) (cf. Chen et al., 2009; Groot and Merchant, 2000). In the view of Dekker (2004), there are in general too few articles addressing management accounting and control issues in the different kinds of interorganizational relationships (IORs). While there is a relatively larger share dealing with interfirm relationships and (international) joint ventures, little emphasis has hitherto been placed on PPPs, despite their upsurge in recent years and the serious chal-

T. S. Konrad, *Management Control in Public-Private Partnerships*,
Schriften zu Wirtschaftsprüfung, Steuerlehre und Controlling,
https://doi.org/10.1007/978-3-658-22868-2_1

lenges they imply for MC (cf. Berry et al., 2009; Broadbent and Laughlin, 2005). In general, one has noted insufficient awareness and understanding of the ways in which the new organizational forms should be managed and control activities be designed and performed in order to attain the joint intended outcomes of any kind of IOR. Organizations' lack of access to acquiring relevant skills and competence or the sticking to control concepts traditionally being applied in hierarchical individual organizations complicate the necessary mental shift (cf. Chen et al., 2009; Emlsey and Kidon, 2007). In this vein, several accounting researchers urge the undertaking of more fundamental research on the linkages between central MC elements, namely control mechanisms, control foci and control tightness, their relationships with the institutional environment they are operating in, and on the choices of one or another governance and control structure (cf. Groot and Merchant, 2000; Kamminga and VdM, 2007). For JV-like cooperations, Cäker and Siverbo (2011) additionally recommend to differentiate more clearly between flat horizontal control among partners and rather hierarchic vertical control between the partners and the JV legal entity.

The implications for the justified interest in future research in the area of MC in IORs in general, and in PPPs in particular, are of practical and theoretical nature. Regarding the latter, increasing importance of institutional theories in the context of MC research has been noted (cf. Berry et al., 2009). The TCE has evolved to a leading theoretical framework from the school of new institutional economics (NIE), on the basis of which fundamental control archetypes/typologies were modelled, for instance by Speklé (2001) and, as emphasized by Langfield-Smith and Smith (2003), it was continuously further developed by examinations of the relationship between these archetypes/typologies and control variables, such as risk or trust, for IJVs/JVs and IFRs in particular (cf. Das and Teng, 2001; Meira et al., 2010; VdM and Vosselman, 2000). Much attention was also attached to governance models relying on the TCE and their role for management accounting and control in alliances, networks or outsourcing relationships (cf. Anderson and Dekker, 2005; Dekker, 2008; Nicholson et al., 2006; Richardson and Kilfoyle, 2009). Based on Williamson (1973), an ideal-typical tripartite relationship structure between governance and control has been established, and this can be found concurrently in any kind of IOR (cf. Berry et al., 2009): market-based governance structures (control through competition), hybrid governance structures (control through the creation of alliances, networks and partnerships), and hierarchy-based governance structures (control through authority and power). While Abdul-Aziz (2012) stresses the strong practical relevance of the hybrid form, compared to the rather theoretical nature of market- and hierarchy-based governance, Dekker (2003, 2004) calls for shifting the research focus from discovering the motivations in favour of, or against, one of the three governance forms to analyzing the functioning of management and control of multi-stakeholder cooperations in practice, based on the selected relationship structure. In some cases, principles from theories like the organizational theory, the principal agent theory or property rights theory were used (cf. Appuhami and Perera, 2016; Benito et al., 2008; Emsley and Kidon, 2007). However, only a few articles were dedicated to these theories in conjunction with a focus on PPPs (cf. Appuhami and Perera, 2016; Benito et al., 2008; Jacobson and Choi, 2008; Schepper et al., 2015).

The following characteristics of PPPs and other organizational forms have been highlighted as important challenges and problems for the design, implementation and use of MC. These justify the motivation for the selected research design and scope and will be addressed by the present study:

- PPPs/JVs are complex forms of interorganizational cooperation being composed of two or more actors who face different legal and institutional frameworks (cf. Andon, 2012; Meira et al., 2010; Vosselman and VdM, 2009). Managing those relationships requires MC to go beyond organizational boundaries (cf. Cooper and Slagmulder, 2004; Håkansson and Lind, 2004; Meira et al., 2010). In particular, multinational cooperations, such as IJVs, are complex to manage because they encounter institutional constraints (e.g. economic and political uncertainty) that are unknown in developed countries, and diverging strategic objectives might result from different cultural backgrounds (cf. Li P. et al., 2013; Liu et al., 2014). Managerial competences and the level of trust between partners from different countries might vary as well (cf. Groot and Merchant, 2000). That is why some researchers suggest to adopt in the future more often multi-stakeholder or network perspectives instead of concentrating on one-to-one relationships when analyzing MC issues because the complexities related to control and the alignment of diverging interests tend to be significantly higher (cf. Kamminga and VdM, 2007; Marques et al., 2011).
- The deliberate relinquishment of control of resources, information and responsibilities poses high demands on coordination, control and governance, and potentially raises transaction costs (cf. Berry et al., 2009; Bovaird, 2004; Groot and Merchant, 2000; Nicholson et al., 2006; Trafford and Proctor, 2006). In terms of JVs, complexities for MC result from the arrangements JV partners have to make: 1) sharing of MC of the JV entity, 2) managing the relationship between the JV partners, and 3) aligning the JV's MC with the JV's specific characteristics and conditions (cf. Kamminga and VdM, 2007; VdM and Kamminga, 2015).
- Both qualitative and quantitative performance measurement of PPPs/JVs proves to be difficult and implies significant limitations (e.g. subjectivity and lack of quantitative data, respectively), but also lacks sufficient research attention. Thus, the quantification of costs and risks on a lifecycle basis has been recommended amongst others (cf. Berry et al., 2009; Choi and Beamish, 2004; Giacobbe and Booth, 2009; Liu J. et al., 2014; Merchant and Van der Stede, 2012, p. 742 f.).
- The identification of CSFs is imperative for attaining the goals being associated with partnership engagements, but the lack of evidence was especially bemoaned with respect to factors that make the MC design, implementation and operation successful in IJVs (cf. Babatunde et al., 2012; Berry et al., 2009; Chalos and O'Connor, 2004; Giacobbe and Booth, 2009). Markets are globalizing and former developing countries are evolving to emerging economies, aspects which exert pressure on companies and other actors to seek interorganizational collaboration and to build networks across national borders and institutional boundaries. These partnerships can help to consolidate the individual position in the global competition, but they are complex to manage and often fail. Thus, it is finally crucial to know these CSFs for enabling decision-makers to develop indicators for measuring performance and success (cf. Giacobbe and Booth, 2009; Groot and Merchant, 2000; Li J. et al., 2009; Zhang and Rajagopalan, 2002). In this vein, Li P. et al. (2013) call for looking at IJV's performance not only as a consequence of certain MC mechanisms but for examining the role MC can actively play for performance and success, an approach which is supported by Groot and Merchant (2000).

In summary, this study aims to address the limitations from pertinent extant literature and to therefore contribute to the closure of the identified research gap concerning MC in PPPs for development. Its field research design has been aligned with the approach pursued by Groot and Merchant (2000) who deem the development and refinement of theory more reasonable than proposing and testing of hypotheses, if the existing knowledge about a subject matter is limited like in the present case. Pertinent theoretical perspectives like ethics or moral philosophy that apply to activities related to IORs (cf. Berry et al., 2009) will be disregarded in this study.

1.2 Reasons for the Selected Research Focus

The choice of the research focus is determined by scientific and practice-oriented considerations alike and is placed on PPPs for development. The various categories of these PPPs have been created for addressing different societal needs (e.g. food safety, public health) and for overcoming global challenges (e.g. climate change, poverty eradication), and require moreover (international) collaboration between different actors, such as governments, non-governmental organizations (NGOs), or private sector (cf. Brinkerhoff und Brinkerhoff, 2011; Demirag et al., 2011; Ivanova et. al., 2007; Kolk et al., 2008; Stadtler und Probst, 2012). While partnership engagements between non-governmental actors and companies have been observed since the end of the 20th century already, PPPs involving national governmental actors or IOs started arising in the early 2000s (cf. Kolk et al., 2008; Teisman and Klijn, 2002; Utting and Zammit, 2009). Nevertheless, Kolk et al. (2008) conclude that the overall engagement in PPPs for development remains limited, while Stadtler and Probst (2012) point to the many challenges public and private partners are facing, such as complex partnership settings, ineffective governance, limited previous PPP experience, or, very basically, the potential problems inherent to cross-sector collaboration. The relevance of these issues is fundamentally supported by Rahaman et al. (2010) who put them into a management accounting and control context and emphasize that interorganizational alliances are not confined to for-profit partnerships only. In accordance with other researchers, they argue that several IOs have increased their efforts to encourage the creation of PPPs for development in recent years because the private sector's financial resources and technical competences can help to better implement and more efficiently manage public activities in response to the abovementioned global challenges (cf. Chen et al., 2013; Singh and Prakash, 2010; Sturchio, 2008). These insights do not only justify the scientific interest in the subject matter but also establish a link to the point where a comparison of the United Nations' resolutions A/RES/55/2 regarding the Millenium Development Goals (MDGs) and A/RES/70/1 regarding the Sustainable Development Goals (SDGs) hooks in (Table 1 and Table 2).

MDGs Resolution: United Nations Millennium Declaration (A/RES/55/2)
"20. We also resolve: • (...) • To **develop strong partnerships** with the private sector and with civil society organizations **in pursuit of development and poverty eradication**." "30. We also resolve therefore: • (...) • To **give greater opportunities** to the private sector, non-governmental organizations and civil society, in general, to **contribute to the realization of the Organization's goals and programmes**."

Table 1: Excerpt from the UN resolution A/RES/55/2.
(Source: UN, 2000, p. 5 and p. 8).

SDGs Resolution: Transforming our world: the 2030 Agenda for Sustainable Development (A/RES/70/1)
"60. We reaffirm our strong commitment to the full implementation of this new Agenda. **We recognize that we will not be able to achieve our ambitious Goals and targets without a revitalized and enhanced Global Partnership** and comparably ambitious means of implementation. The revitalized Global Partnership will facilitate an intensive global engagement in support of implementation of all the Goals and targets, **bringing together Governments, civil society, the private sector, the United Nations system and other actors and mobilizing all available resources**."

Table 2: Excerpt from the UN resolution A/RES/70/1.
(Source: UN, 2015b, p. 28).

The wording describing the necessity and extent of public-private cooperation has changed over the 15 years time span between the adoption of the MDGs in 2000 and the entry into force of the SDGs in 2015. In brief, the SDGs stress the indispensability of enhanced PPP activities to achieve overarching development goals, while the MDGs consider PPPs as desirable vehicles. The tightening of the wording reflects an upward shift of PPPs for development on the global political agenda and thereby represents the practical interest in the selected research focus.

In summary, the awareness raised from previous research in conjunction with the global community's call for more and strengthened PPPs for development, voiced through the adoption of the resolutions on the MDGs and SDGs, justifies the placing of the research focus on the collaboration between private sector firms and international governmental actors. The fact that the current magnitude of engagements seems to remain below the desired level, especially from the public sector's perspective, has motivated the present study to scrutinize the operational functioning of these PPPs, namely project management and control, and to identify their CSFs.

1.3 Objectives of this Study

The present study aims to give an overview of the current state of MC in PPPs for development between IOs/DCAs and the private sector on the basis of empirical insights gathered from pertinent concluded and ongoing partnerships. This occurs in the first step by describing their key characteristics to be taken into account by MC. This is followed by an exploration of basic characteristics and MC patterns and designs of PPPs, JVs, and IORs/IFRs in practice as well as the collection of inherent CSFs. The results are then analyzed and discussed by means of theoretical elements of the ACI and TCE (cf. Cäker and Siverbo, 2011; Kamminga and VdM, 2007; Petersen, 2011). Moreover, the empirical results form the basis for the formulation of recommendations that should be considered by decision-makers from public and private sectors in terms of the further development of MC in existing and future PPPs (cf. Appuhami and Perera, 2016; Jacobson and Choi, 2008).

1.4 Structure and Procedure of the Investigation

The pursuance of the abovementioned objectives occurs on the basis of a dyadic research procedure. In the first step, a stocktaking of the existing literature is carried out for enabling pertinent future investigations. For this, a quantitative and qualitative literature review is conducted to critically incorporate extant literature on PPPs, JVs, and IORs/IFRs (cf. Andon, 2012; Broadbent and Guthrie, 2008; Caglio and Ditillo, 2008). Inherent findings identify the research gap which in turn supports the formulation of concrete research questions. In the second step, an international field study with experts from private sector firms, DCAs and IOs is carried out to generate empirical data whose analysis produces new evidence on MC in PPPs, serves the complementation and strengthening of the extant literature, and allows the answering of the research questions in order to contribute to the closure of the identified research gap (cf. Chung, 2016; Groot and Merchant, 2000; Rahaman et al., 2010).

For the literature review, a total of 159 articles published primarily in renowned English language international journals have been systematically analyzed for the period 2000 to May 2017. The commonly applied criteria of analysis in literature reviews also take effect in the present study and comprise the thematic approach, research design including methodology used, geographical scope, strands of literature, and year of publication (cf. Andon, 2012; Broadbent and Guthrie, 2008; Endenich et al., 2011; Gomes et al., 2016; Tang et al., 2010). In addition, a distinction is made between articles dealing with PPPs, JVs or IORs/IFRs, and only those that clearly focus on MC issues enter into the more in-depth qualitative analysis. Besides aspects of MC, emphasis is also placed on the provision of an overview of previously identified CSFs. Through this review, a sound picture of the current state of research on MC in PPPs, JVs and IORs/IFRs can be drawn and a research gap be identified where the present study hooks in. Moreover, it largely provides the input for depicting the manifold characteristics of MC including control archetypes and typologies and for deriving a theoretical framework (cf. Dekker, 2004; Marques et al., 2011; VdM and Vosselman, 2006). These altogether form the basis for step two, namely the empirical field work (cf. Nicholson et al., 2006).

The international empirical field study serves the collection of relevant data for answering the research questions with respect to the selected research subject from accounting, namely MC in PPPs for development (cf. Ahrens and Chapman, 2006; Ferreira and Merchant, 1992; Lillis and Mundy, 2005; Qu and Dumay, 2011). For this purpose, semi-structured interviews are conducted with 28 experts from private sector firms, DCAs and IOs, who have been selected in a targeted fashion with a balanced proportion between public and private sector (cf. Kolk et al., 2008; Rahaman et al., 2010; Stadtler and Probst, 2012). The verbal and written interview data is subsequently transcribed and a system of categories created. This enables the data's coding and a structured content analysis of the empirical results at the end (cf. Bortz and Döring, 2006, p. 341; Kuckartz, 2008, p. 36; Mayring, 2016, p. 89 and pp. 114-117). Due to the hitherto very little evidence on MC in PPPs for development, emphasis is placed on providing a holistic overview of MC design aspects in these partnerships instead of concentrating on selected elements, such as performance measurement or risk management, as has been done by previous studies for other kinds of PPPs, or JVs and IORs/IFRs (cf. Anderson and Dekker, 2005; Langfield-Smith, 2008; Larimo et al., 2016).

The structure of the present study is outlined in Figure 1 and corresponds to one of the suggested publication formats pursuant to Ferreira and Merchant (1992, p. 16). The following Chapter 2 provides first of all definitions of the key words being most important to understand the research subject and scope. Thus, it explains MC and governance and specifies the meaning of PPPs in comparison with the related terms JVs and IORs/IFRs. It continues by giving a quantitative and qualitative overview of the relevant extant literature, discusses MC-centered articles qualitatively and in detail to reveal deficits in this field of research, and derives the research gap on this basis. Chapter 0 takes up the findings from the literature review and works out the various control archetypes and typologies found in PPPs, JVs and IORs/IFRs. It characterizes the identified control dimensions, explains the nexus between control levels and governance structures, and basically differentiates between formal and informal MC mechanisms. Separate subchapters are dedicated to MC aspects which received particular attention in previous research, namely control problems and control specifics in JVs as well as the nexus between risk and trust on the one side and control on the other side. Chapter 4 illustrates the study's theoretical foundation and justifies why a combination of ACI and TCE is suitable for analyzing MC in PPPs for development. Moreover, empirically verifiable assumptions and characteristics are derived from the ACI and TCE and serve as reference framework and basis for discussion of the empirical results in the later Chapters 0 and 7. Chapter 4 concludes with the derivation of the research questions which tackle the research subject from a descriptive, explorative and normative perspective. Chapter 0 connects to the preceding one in the sense that it portrays the selected research design and methodology and explains why they are appropriate for collecting relevant data in response to the research questions. The comprehensive analysis of the empirical results in Chapter 0 is followed by a sound discussion of the results in Chapter 7. Besides a summary of key findings, implications for practitioners are worked out, conclusions on the theoretical assumption are drawn, and the contribution to the ACI and the TCE theory is emphasized. The clear definition of the study's limitations does not only point to its weaknesses but also highlights potential for future investigations in the area of MC in PPPs. Finally, a conclusion and outlook sums up the whole research work and explains why the present research topic prospectively deserves attention by management accounting and control research (Chapter 7.5).

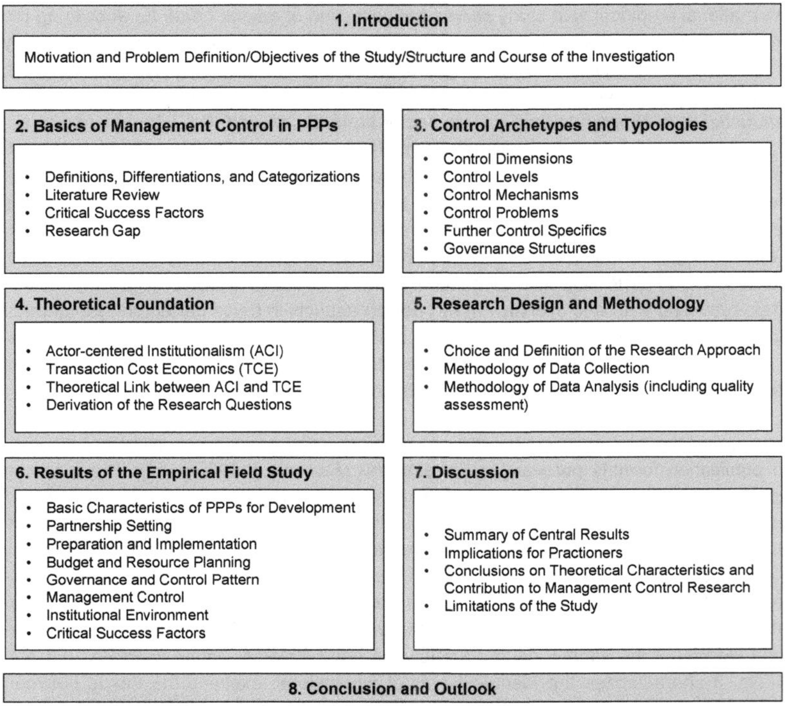

Figure 1: Structure of the study.

2. Basics of Management Control in Public-Private Partnerships

This chapter characterizes first of all the key terms of this study (Chapter 2.1) and then provides a comprehensive literature review (Chapter 2.2), followed by an overview of CSFs revealed by previous studies (Chapter 2.3). Finally, an interim summary in conjunction with the definition of the research gap is presented (Chapter 2.4).

2.1 Definitions, Differentiations, and Categorizations

This chapter defines the key terms Management Control (MC) and Public-Private Partnership (PPP), which are crucial to the present research subject. The term PPP will be differentiated from associated forms of multi-stakeholder cooperation and specified by typologies of PPPs. Explanations of reasons for the creation of PPPs serve for their further characterization. Moreover, this chapter explains commonalities and differences of MC definitions and how MC is interpreted for the purposes of this study. Due to the tight linkages between MC and *governance*, the latter term will also be defined at this early stage.

2.1.1 Management Control

There are multiple approaches for definition of *control* or *MC* in the context of interorganizational relationships (IORs) and their subtypes, including PPPs and Joint Ventures (JVs), which are particular dependent on the control focus. Due to the nature of the present research subject, a few definitions of control or MC are compared in order to reveal differences and commonalities. Keywords are highlighted in bold type (Table 3).

Definition
"Control mechanisms are **organizational arrangements** designed to determine and influence what organization members would do." (Abdul-Aziz, 2012, p. 37)
"Control is defined as influence exercised by the parents over the management of the venture. [...] Control is further conceptualized as a **conduit** through which parents' firm-specific advantages are transferred to the venture." (Choi and Beamish, 2004, p. 202)
"Control, broadly defined, comprises the various policies and procedures that firms use to mitigate different types of risk. Controls **mitigate relational risk** by **changing the incentives for opportunistic behavior**." (Coletti et al., 2005, p. 480)
"...control can be defined as a **means by which a partner's behavior can be influenced** to make it more predictable, thereby decreasing the uncertainty of that behavior and increasing the likelihood that desirable outcomes will be achieved." (Emsley and Kidon, 2007, p. 832)
"Control is the **process or action** by which one entity influences the behavior, process, or output of another entity through the **use of power, authority, and mechanisms**." (Luo, 2007, p. 532)

T. S. Konrad, *Management Control in Public-Private Partnerships*,
Schriften zu Wirtschaftsprüfung, Steuerlehre und Controlling,
https://doi.org/10.1007/978-3-658-22868-2_2

Definition
"...MC as a **purposive process or set of devices and mechanisms**, that through its influence on the behavior of actors within an organization, intends to contribute to the achievement of some pervasive objectives of that organization." (Speklé, 2001, p. 423)

Table 3: Approaches to definition of control.

Despite some differences, the definitions presented in Table 3 do not contradict each other but rather show the diversity of design, purpose and use of *control* or *MC*. These two terms are interchangeably used together with interorganizational controls, which influence the level of governance (bureaucracy, hybrid or market) applied to IORs (cf. Abdul-Aziz, 2012). MCs are essential for IORs, in particular within international settings, as they are characterized by higher complexity and uncertainty. Formal mechanisms, including specific contractual arrangements as well as governance and managerial structures, and informal tools are used to influence actors and their behaviors in a way that is conducive to the achievement of agreed, or at least desirable, outcomes. Control in IORs is dyadic: it focuses on controlling the involved partners and on controlling the IOR as such (cf. Das and Teng, 2001a; Dekker, 2004; Li P., 2013; Luo, 2007; Marques et al., 2011; Speklé, 2001).

MC systems (MCS) comprise the total set of MCs implemented in a partnership and contribute to the building and shaping of IORs as well as to the alignment of interests (cf. Berry et al., 2009). In this capacity, they have different tasks. From a normative perspective, MCSs assume a regulatory function and set boundaries to organizations, comprising different policies (including command structures, if applicable), procedures (e.g. for dispute resolution), and standards (e.g. SOPs). They aim to ensure that decision-makings and partners' behaviors pursue joint rules and strategies as well as to incentivize them to strive for joint partnership objectives. Therefore, uncertainty and opportunistic behavior should finally be reduced (cf. Ahrens and Chapman, 2004; Das and Teng, 2001a; Dekker, 2003; Liu X. et al., 2014; Marques et al., 2011; VdM and Scapens, 2008; Vélez et al., 2008). From an operative perspective, these MC mechanisms serve for monitoring on the one hand (e.g. assignment of duties, rights and responsibilities, incentive setting, performance measurement and rewarding, and sanctioning) and coordination (e.g. assist in organizational learning and planning; provide, share and update information, raise awareness of issues, and contribute to decision-making and problem-solving) on the other hand (cf. Anderson and Dekker, 2005; Vélez et al., 2008). This differentiation between normative and operative tasks can be interpreted as what VdM and Scapens (2008) call a dyadic approach to MCS, namely mechanistic vs. interactive/processual control mechanisms.

MC in general and MCSs in particular are essential to organizations as they can often flexibly react to organizational or strategic changes, by adapting the decision-making process, the tightness of controls, or the proportion between formal and informal controls. MC technologies often build a stable cornerstone in IOR relationships that outlast those changes including joining and leaving of IOR partners (cf. Berry et al., 2009; Chen et al., 2009; Mouritsen and Thrane, 2006). Berry et al. (2009, p. 15) call MCS "socially constructed artefacts" and highlight the informal and social component of MCSs that can trigger better cooperation and increased trust in IORs. Organizational history and culture as well as external environmental factors can fluence them (cf. Marques et al., 2011). However, it should be noted that the concept of MC is rarely perfect. The MC in partnerships is composed of different elements which can be complementary, interrelated, or even conflicting with each other, and which reflect existing processes, structures and MCSs. Implemented MC mechanisms and MCSs are typically the result of a compromise that IOR partners have agreed on (cf. Speklé, 2001).

2.1.2 Governance

Against the background of increasing cooperation between actors from various fields (e.g. agencies, civil society, governments, private firms) at different institutional levels (local, national and international) to tackle policy issues (e.g. related to provision of public services and infrastructure), multi-level governance including multi-stakeholder cooperation gains in importance (cf. Broadbent and Guthrie, 2008; Petersen, 2011; Stadtler und Probst, 2012; Stoker, 1998; Van Kersbergen and Van Waarden; 2004). Although the term *governance* is broadly used in the fields of business, economics and political science, it lacks a sharp and concise definition (cf. Almquist et al., 2013; Rhodes, 1996). However, clear understanding of this term is pivotal because it is tightly related to the design of MC in any kind of multi-stakeholder cooperation.

Stoker (1998) and Van Kersbergen and Van Waarden (2004) argue that governance can take on many different forms, which are between the two cornerstones of hierarchical direction/hierarchy and unilateral action/market and which are closer to alliances and networks in which actors at least partly share common beliefs, concerns, interests and norms. Commonly, one distinguishes between governance levels, market, hybrid and hierarchy (cf. Abdul-Aziz, 2012; Dekker (2004, 2008); Richardson and Kilfoyle, 2009). In this context, Stoker (1998) contends that “Governance refers to a set of institutions and actors that are drawn from but also beyond government” (p. 19), which are acting in an environment where responsibilities for addressing economic and social issues are getting increasingly blurred, and new governance forms are rising, such as self-governing networks (cf. Van Kersbergen and Van Waarden, 2004). Almquist et al. (2013) argue that “...governance deals with the steering and coordination of various actors, often in network-type patterns of collaboration” (p. 479), an approach of definition which is supported by studies of Bevir (2009), Mayntz and Scharpf (1995, p. 62), Teisman and Klijn (2002) and Van Kersbergen and Van Waarden (2004).

Thus, a governance structure forms a framework within which stakeholders interact in different ways with each other and wherein different activities are settled on different governance levels. Analyses of what governance specifically means for MC in multi-stakeholder cooperation and how it is discussed by the theoretical approaches underlying this study follow in the Chapters 3.2 and 4.2.5.

2.1.3 Interorganizational/Interfirm Relationships

In accounting, interorganizational relationships (IORs) and interfirm relationships (IFRs) can be defined as alliances which are composed of operationally and legally independent organizations or entities that coordinate and align acitivites in order to address a broad range of economic, political and social needs. Seeking access to markets, resource sharing and exchanging skills are part of them (Rahaman et al., 2010). To manage complexity and dependencies in IORs and IFRs, control and coordination are necessary. However, design, implementation and uses of MC in these relationships are challenging because MC mechanisms and tools have to overstep organizational boundaries. Hence, there is a need for new forms of coordination and control (cf. Meira et al., 2010; Tomkins, 2001; VdM and Scapens, 2008). In this context, IORs and IFRs including all their subtypes are subject to the three governance levels: hierarchy, hybrid, and market (cf. Abdul-Aziz, 2012; Marques et al., 2011; Vosselman and VdM, 2009). Figure 2 shows a rough typology of IORs and IFRs.

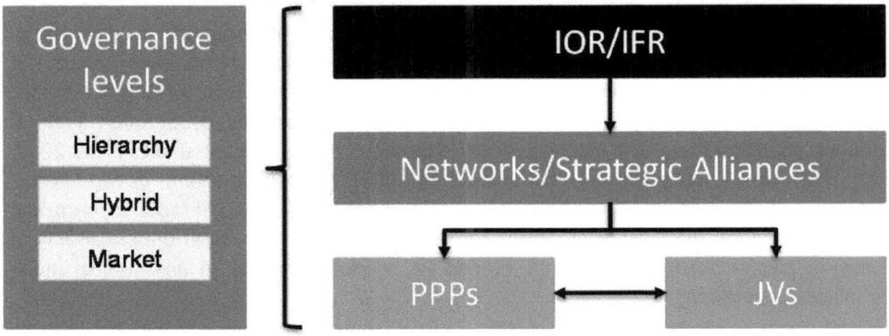

Figure 2: Typology of interorganizational and interfirm relationships.

First level subtypes of IORs and IFRs, which have been numerously mentioned in the literature, are networks and strategic alliances. Second level subtypes, which derive from these, are PPPs and JVs. They are considered as specific forms of networks and strategic alliances (cf. Marques et al., 2011; VdM and Scapens, 2008). In the following, the abbreviation IOR will also cover IFRs, unless the context requires explicit differentiation.

Network relationships can be of formal and informal nature and are characterized by two or more individuals or organizations of any kind that interact voluntarily with each other, share resources, carry out joint activities, and seek for mutually beneficial outcomes. Networks tend to be hybrid forms of governance that leave flexibility to organizations and their participants, but also request commitment (cf. Jones et al., 1997; Richardson and Kilfyole, 2009; Sing and Pradash, 2010). However, there are different levels of networks, which are differentiated by the degree of complexity, ranging from simple dyadic to highly complex relationships with three and more organizations involved (cf. Marques et al., 2011).

By contrast to networks, strategic alliances tend to be less complex and focus on the achievement of joint strategic objectives shared by the involved partners. One differentiates between vertical alliances (e.g. between suppliers and buyers), horizontal alliances (e.g. between competitors), and diagonal alliances (e.g. between firms across industries). Strategic alliances can adopt different forms, such as social-purpose alliance, outsourcing, JV or specific joint activities including joint research or joint product development. What distinguishes both networks and strategic alliances is the durable character of underlying relationships, in which all partners keep their sovereignty (cf. Langfield-Smith, 2008; Miller et al., 2008; Rahaman et al., 2010; Tomkins, 2001).
The aforementioned examples of networks and strategic alliances referred mainly to cooperation between business partners. Connection to the public sector is established by PPPs, which focus on the inclusion of private sector partners in the provision of public services. PPPs are likewise considered as subtypes of IORs in general and of networks and strategic

alliance in particular. In case of hybrid-governed PPPs, commonalities with JVs are significant (cf. Appuhami et al., 2011; Cäker and Siverbo, 2011; Marques et al., 2011; Singh and Prakash, 2010).

2.1.4 Public-Private Partnerships

There are multiple definition approaches of PPPs that vary in particular in dependence of the type of PPP. Due to the nature of the present research subject, a few definitions from accounting/business administration studies and from public administration/public policy literature are compared in order to reveal differences and commonalities. Keywords are highlighted in bold type (Table 4).

Strand of literature	Definition
Public administration/public policy	"...working arrangements based on a **mutual commitment** (...) between a public sector organization with any organization outside of the public sector." (Bovaird, 2004, p. 199)
Accounting/business administration	PPP/PFI is categorized as a proper accounting type (Broadbent and Guthrie, 2008)
Accounting/business administration	"A PPP is an approach (...) for **a more direct control relationship** between the public and private sector than would be achieved by a **simple market-based and arms-length purchase**" (Broadbent und Laughlin, 2003a, p. 334)
Accounting/business administration	"...PPPs can be defined as agreements where public sector bodies enter into **long-term contractual agreements** in which private parties participate in {...} the provision of **infrastructure** (...)." (Grimsey and Lewis, 2002a, p. 248)
Public administration/public policy	"...co-operation between public and private actors with a **durable character** in which actors develop mutual products and/or services and in which **risk, costs, and benefits are shared**". (Klijn and Teisman, 2003, p. 137)
Public administration/public policy	"...form of **structured cooperation** between public and private parties in the **planning, construction and/or exploitation of infrastructural facilities** in which they **share or reallocate risks, costs, benefits, resources and responsibilities.**" (Koppenjan, 2005, p. 137)

Table 4: Approaches to definition of PPPs.

Despite some differences, the definitions presented in Table 4 do not contradict but rather complement each other. No strand of literature-wise difference is noted. Hence, PPPs are long-term oriented and contractually secured forms of public-private cooperation. Dimensions of cooperation are adaptability to changes, information-sharing, problem-solving and restraint from the use of power (cf. Caglio and Ditillo, 2008). Shared costs and benefits, resources, risks and responsibilities are characteristic of PPPs. However, PPPs are usually created for a limited period of time, and all partners maintain their respective autonomy (cf. Singh and Prakash, 2010).

Historically, the concept of PPPs builds on ideas of the new public management. It evolved from the British Private Financing Initiative (PFI) for infrastructure at the beginning of the 1990s. Both approaches aim at increasing the competitiveness, efficiency and effectiveness of public services. This is supposed to be reached by the inclusion of public and private know-how, resources and skills (cf. Appuhami et al., 2011; Benito et al., 2008; Grimsey and Lewis, 2005). Achieving value for money (VFM) is the core objective of PPPs while solving socioeconomic problems is intended likewise (cf. Appuhami et al., 2011; Broadbent and Laughlin, 2003c; Froud, 2003). Typically, PPPs are used to improve public infrastructure services such as education, electricity and water facilities, health care, roads, etc. (cf. Appuhami et al., 2011).

2.1.4.1 Typology of PPPs

Three major components, – the subject matter/purpose, the actors involved, and the type of contract including contractual arrangements –, roughly characterize PPPs. Brinkerhoff and Brinkerhoff (2011) developed a purpose-based taxonomy which clusters PPPs in five groups:

- *Capacity building PPPs*: Private actors help to enhance or build new capacities of public actors through knowledge sharing or transfer, empowering them to provide public services more efficiently and effectively.
- *Economic Development PPPs*: Cross-sectoral partnerships aim at promoting poverty reduction and economic growth at different governmental levels, often with mixed funding. These partnerships are carried out in both developed and developing countries, often as part of corporate social responsibility (CSR) initiatives.
- *Infrastructure PPPs*: Public and private actors jointly finance, build, and run infrastructure works (e.g. electricity and sewage/waste treatment facilities, roads, telecommunications, etc.).
- *Policy PPPs*: Coordinate, design, monitor and promote different public policies at national and/or global or sectoral level.
- *Service delivery PPPs*: Non-public actors deliver public services on the state's behalf. Payment and provision of public services are separated from each other.

In addition, Bovaird (2004) complements this taxonomy by a typology of bases that are underlying PPPs, such as (1) sectoral basis – societal sectors involved (e.g. private sector, civil society); (2) economic basis – PPP is demand-side, supply-side, or mixed demand/supply-side driven; and (3) scope – PPPs are characterized by horizontal, mixed, or vertical relationships between actors involved.

Regarding contractual arrangements, the spectrum of PPPs is manifold. On the one hand, PPPs are governed by public and private stakeholders in equal parts, while in others public or private stakes are dominating. However, PPPs can be clustered by a few major contract forms. A graph created by Gidman et al. (1995) and later on slightly amended by Bennett et al. (2000) and Jamali (2004) is further customized and used in the following in order to give a condensed overview on PPP type categories where PPPs analyzed in this research study might fit in (Figure 3).

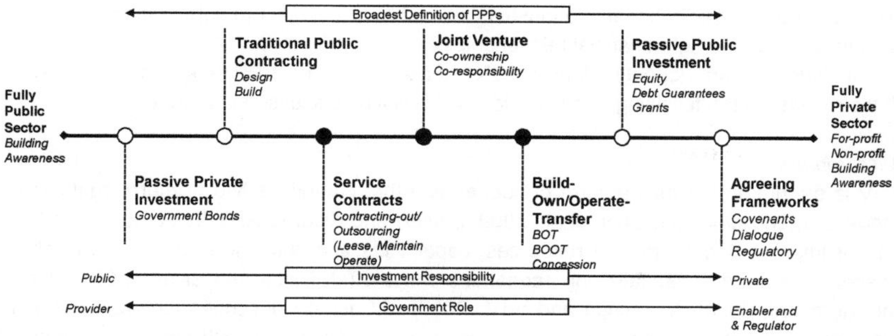

Figure 3: Spectrum and types of PPPs.
(Source: own depiction, based on Bennett et al., 2000; Gidman et al., 1995; and Jamali, 2004)

It outlines seven major PPP types that all fit into the broadest definition of PPPs, ranging from fully public to fully private investment and implementation responsibility. Public authorities assume the role of a provider in case of public sector-biased PPPs and act as enabler and regulator in the opposite case. However, existing pertinent literature usually deals with the three middle types of PPPs (filled nodes), namely Build-Own/Operate-Transfer, JV, and Service Contract partnerships. They are subsequently explained in more detail. The remaining types of PPP in Figure 3 will not be further taken into account. It should be noted that PPPs are not equal to privatizations. Even in cases in which the government is only enabler and regulator without operative involvement, it remains ultimately responsible (Grimsey and Lewis, 2005).

Build-Own/Operate-Transfer

In particular in public infrastructure projects Build-Own-Transfer or Build-Operate-Transfer (both abbreviated with BOT), Build-Own-Operate (BOO), Build-Own-Operate-Transfer (BOOT) are widely used PPP schemes for taking on board private financial resources and know-how. BOT and BOOT agreements stipulate that the private sector partner builds, temporarily owns and/or operates facilities or a service but the property rights are transferred to the public sector partner at the end of contract. By contrast, in case of BOO agreements the private sector keeps ownership of the subject matter of the contract. More complex schemes are Design-Build-Finance-Operate (DBFO) or Design-Builde-Operate-Transfer (DBOT) agreements, which provide concrete output specifications from the private sector (cf. Broadbent and Laughlin, 2004; Budäus and Grüb, 2007; Carbonara and Pellegrino, 2014; Hodge and Greve, 2007). All these schemes have in common that they are framed by diverse concession contracts (cf. Benito et al., 2008; Grimsey and Lewis, 2005).

JVs are the extreme form of ownership shared between public and private sector, in which the private partners participate in management and decision-making activities. However, together with service contracts and build-own/operate-transfer agreements, they differ from traditional contracts by the fact that the private partner is not responsible for asset or service delivery only, but also for appropriate service provision and project management during the contract term (cf. Benito et al. 2008; Grimsey and Lewis, 2005; Tang L. et al., 2010). According to a typology created by Hodge and Greve (2007), BOOT, BOT and sale-and-lease-back

PPPs are loose organizational relationships while JVs are subject to tighter links. What they have in common are tight financial relationships.
To conclude, JVs are not only a form of IOR but also a complex PPP type with hybrid ownership structure. In the following, the specifics of JVs will be discussed in more detail.

Joint Venture
A JV is an interorganizational form of cooperation that comprises two or more legally independent organizations (cf. Chen et al., 2009; Emsley and Kidon, 2007). Its purpose is to facilitate or improve access to new resources, capabilities and customers as well as to share business risks and to capitalize on economies of scale (cf. Cäker and Siverbo, 2011; Groot and Merchant, 2000; Kamminga and VdM, 2007). JV usually describes long-term transactional relationships between the cooperating partners. Their joint activities are commonly executed under the umbrella of a newly established legal entity what makes them distinct from other forms of alliances (cf. VdM and Kamminga, 2015; Zhang Y. and Rajagopalan, 2002). In this context, Langfield-Smith (2008) describes JVs as equity alliances because the JV partners employ an alliance board and implement independent management structures and MC mechanisms in order to exercise control.

JVs are considered as international JVs (IJVs) if they are composed of two or more legally independent partners whereby one of them is headquartered in a country other than the venture's country of operation. Alternatively, JV activities are executed in more than one country to a significant extent (cf. Groot and Merchant, 2000; Johnson et al., 2002). Giacobbe and Booth (2009) as well as Zhang Y. and Li (2001) point out that IJVs are a key strategic management tool, primarily used by multinational firms, for pursuing internationalization strategies and for encountering increasing competition and globalization of markets. IJVs are an option to develop markets, to acquire relevant technological and managerial skills as well as to achieve business targets, which are unlikely to be achieved alone. IJV partners share management and responsibility, risks and benefits, profits and losses and bear capital investment and expenditures. However, due to the voluntary nature of IJV relationships, the participating partners involved are exposed to the risk of opportunism or are prone to behave opportunistically themselves (cf. Zhang Y. and Rajagopalan, 2002). To mitigate such risks the venture contracts stipulate rights and obligations of the partners and their staff involved (e.g. conflict resolution and decision-making processes, financing policies, governance structures, JV venue) and prohibit certain actions such as disclosure of internal corporate information about the JV entity (cf. Groot and Merchant, 2000).

Governance and management control are issues in JVs/IJVs. The partners usually exercise split control over the joint activities and operations, whereby the level of resources provided determines the individual power base to a certain extent (cf. Chen et al., 2009; Choi and Beamish, 2004; Zhang Y. and Li, 2001). The governance and control level applied to the JV/IJV may vary for different reasons, such as partners leaving or newly joining the venture, changing activities or purposes and targets, or changing regulations (cf. Kamminga and VdM, 2007).

In the literature, JVs have been classified by different characteristics such as the equity structure, the degree of internationalization, the origin of resource contribution or the tightness of control. Table 5 gives a brief overview of these features.

Characteristics	Classifications	Source
Degree of internationalization	Matrix-like differentiation between • Domestic JVs/IJVs • Developed/developing countries	Giacobbe and Booth (2009)
Resource contribution	Four types of resource contribution • Different partners provide similar skills and assets • One partner provides the essential assets • Different partners provide complementary skills and assets • Partners' contributions are quite limited	Kamminga and VdM (2006)
Tightness of control	Three types of JVs • Dominant parent JV • Shared management JV • Independent JV	Kamminga and VdM (2007); Zhang Y. and Li (2001)

Table 5: Characteristics and classifications of JVs.

An analysis of the characteristics and classifications of JVs reveals that Giacobbe and Booth (2009) see more challenges and barriers but also more opportunities for IJVs to consolidate their position in global competition. IJVs in developing countries are increasing. In their analysis of the tightness of control, Kamminga and VdM (2007) as well as Zhang Y. and Li (2001) point out that tightness of control determines control processes and decision-making procedures. While in dominant JVs one partner has more power to exercise control and to make decisions, power structures are balanced in shared management JVs. By contrast, the JV management enjoys a high degree of autonomy in independent JVs while the partners do not exert much influence on decision-making and control. In this context, the amount and specificity of skills and assets, which are contributed to the JV entity, determine the partners' decision-making power and control (cf. Kamminga and VdM, 2006). In the following, the abbreviation JV will also cover IJVs, unless the context requires explicit differentiation.

Service Contracts

Service contracts are concluded for those public services, which are outsourced from the public services portfolio and its provision is delegated to external parties. The contracting-out or outsourcing of public services comprises lease or maintenance and operation agreements. In the first case, for instance, the public sector sells public buildings or facilities and leases them back afterwards. By contrast, maintenance and operation agreements stipulate which services are to be specifically provided by the external operator. However, in all cases, the public sector still bears the financial risk, and the government remains the responsible public service provider (cf. Hodge and Greve, 2007; Langfield-Smith and Smith, 2003; Lamminmaki, 2008; Meira et al., 2010; Nicholson et al., 2006).

2.1.4.2 Reasons for the creation of PPPs

In general, there are different instrumental, normative, and strategic reasons why private and public actors enter into PPPs. Such partnerships enable public actors to get access to management and technical expertise, to acquire new competencies and skills, to share complementary resources and to reduce costs. In this way, they aim to increase and improve competitiveness, efficiency, effectiveness, and quality of public services and activities (cf. Appuhami et al., 2011; Benito et al., 2008; Brinkerhoff and Brinkerhoff, 2011; Meira et al., 2010). The nature of PPPs is changing and tends to establish more long-term cooperations instead of mere market-based relationships. That is what in the literature is considered as shift from New Public Management to New Public Governance (cf. Almquist et al., 2013; Bovaird, 2004; Broadbent and Laughlin, 2004; Osborne, 2006; Rhodes, 1996) and what Broadbent and Guthrie (2008) call shift "from public sector provision to the provision of public services" (p. 137) in their study on public sector accounting research. Moreover, they underline the increasing involvement of private sector firms in the provision of public services and consider PPPs as a proper accounting type.

However, PPPs are not a one-sided relation in favour of the public sector. Private firms may capitalize on the insights they gain in the provision of public services and on the influence they may exert upon the design of public infrastructure and policy planning. Moreover, they may raise public awareness for their business. Still, both sides aim at achieving beneficial outcomes and creating transactional value (cf. Dekker, 2004). Concrete joint activities of PPP partners might be policy design and planning, policy coordination, policy monitoring, policy evaluation and review or policy implementation at the policy level or resource mobilization and management (cf. Bovaird, 2004).

With respect to IO-/DCA-related PPPs, different global challenges (e.g. poverty eradication, climate change, terrorism, urbanizations) and other social needs to be addressed require collective action by different actors, including civil society, governments, IOs, NGOs and private sector firms, and trigger the creation of PPPs (cf. Brinkerhoff und Brinkerhoff, 2011; Demirag et al., 2011; Ivanova et. al., 2007; Kolk et al., 2008; Stadtler und Probst, 2012). For instance, education, electricity and water supply, health care, and transport are typical fields of action that all belong to infrastructure. To deliver them is crucial to properly address societal needs (cf. Appuhami et al., 2011; Broadbent and Laughlin, 2004). Finally, PPPs can contribute to achieving economies of scale (efficiency improvement), economies of scope (exploitation of complementary competencies and skills), and to engendering opportunities for mutual learning (knowledge growth) in the provision of public services (cf. Bovaird, 2004). A crucial objective is to finally generate so-called value for money (VFM) in PPP projects, irrespective of the thematic scope (cf. Appuhami et al., 2011; Sciulli, 2008).

Excursus – brief explanation of VFM: Grimsey and Lewis (2002b, p. 109) define VFM as "the effective use of public funds on a capital project, can come from private sector innovation and skills in asset design, construction techniques and operational practices, and also from transferring key risks in design, construction delays, cost overruns and finance and insurance to private sector entities for them to manage". According to Grimsey and Lewis (2005), VFM is determined by competition, performance incentives and measurement, private sector management competencies, length of contract period, and specification of output. To achieve VFM in PPPs, the implementation of an MCS is deemed crucial (cf. Appuhami et al., 2011).

A key indicator used to assess whether a PPP is likely to generate VFM or not, is the so-called Public Sector Comparator (PSC). However, it is not widely used in practice (cf. Carbonara and Pellegrino, 2014; Grimsey and Lewis, 2005; Keating and Keating, 2013).

2.2 Literature Review

This chapter reviews current pertinent literature of 159 articles investigating MC matters in the context of PPPs, JVs and IORs. Several databases (ABI/INFORM Global, EBSCO Business Source Premier, Elsevier/ScienceDirect, Emerald and JSTOR) and Google Scholar were thoroughly searched for articles of interest to this literature review. The search was limited to the time period 2000 to May 2017. These years also encompass the timeframe from the UN Millennium Declaration including the adoption of the Millennium Development Goals (MDGs) on 18 September 2000 to their replacement by the Sustainable Development Goals (SDGs) on 25 September 2015, adopted as part of the 2030 Agenda for Sustainable Development (cf. UN, 2000; UN, 2015a, UN, 2015b). Both resolutions form cornerstones of the world community's political will to promote and enhance partnerships with the private sector.
A PDF of each paper was downloaded and stored in a database including full citation details, established in Citavi. Key words, which were entered into databases, are "management control", "public-private partnerships", "joint venture", and "international organization". In addition, pertinent articles found in the bibliographies of the articles retrieved from databases by key word search have been considered as well. To ensure content quality throughout this thesis, only those journals have been taken into account which obtained an "A+", "A", "B" or "C" ranking grade by the JOURQUAL 3 and/or which were graded by the Academic Journal Quality Guide 2015. The VHB JOURQUAL 3 is a journal ranking provided by the German Academic Association for Business Research (VHB, Verband der Hochschullehrer für Betriebswirtschaft e.V.) while the Academic Journal Quality Guide 2015 is published by the Association of Business Schools (ABS) in the United Kingdom. For a few journals, no VHB or ABS ranking was available. This can be explained by the fact that those journals do not cover business topics in their core. However, they are published by renowned publishing houses such as Emerald or Wiley, and/or are peer-reviewed so that an adequate quality level can be assumed.

This literature review contributes to identifying relevant literature for deeper analysis of MC in PPPs between IOs or DCAs and the private sector, to delineating the topic, and to identifying existing research gaps. The review is divided into two sections. First, a quantitative analysis of the reviewed literature will be given. In the second part, articles, which are relevant to the thematic focus, will be analyzed and discussed in more detail. These articles have in common that they refer to, or place explicit focus on, MC in PPPs, JVs and IORs.

2.2.1 Quantitative Analysis of Reviewed Literature

The quantitative analysis of reviewed literature is twofold. First, in a general overview, all 159 articles, which have been identified as potentially relevant, are subjected to a quantitative analysis. All considered articles are listed in Table 65 (in annex 8.1). Second, a more narrow analysis has been conducted for those articles on PPPs, JVs and IORs in which MC or MC systems form the core research subject, as well as for those that focus on partnerships between IOs or DCAs and the private sector.

2.2.1.1 General Overview

In the following, the different strands of used literature as well as the theoretical frameworks, geographical scopes and methodologies applied in previous articles will be described and analyzed.

2.2.1.1.1 Strands of Literature

The three major strands of literature, “Accounting”, “General Management and International Business”, and “Public Administration & Public Management”, account for 80% of all articles that have been used for the present literature review (Figure 4). The primary search focus was placed on accounting journals. However, with respect to the interdisciplinary nature of the topic, the search also encompassed journals dealing with public administration/public policy, development/non-profit and international business/general management. Since many PPPs are related to infrastructure projects, articles from construction and engineering journals were considered as well, if appropriate. Few articles were gathered from journals related to organizational studies and to the development/non-profit sector. It should be noted that articles of acknowledged MC researchers are not confined to accounting journals only (cf. Anderson and Dekker, 2005; Kamminga and VdM, 2006). That is why a look behind the accounting borders is necessary and appropriate in order to capture relevant literature in its entirety.

To summarize, the relevant journal articles identified have been clustered into seven journal categories: Accounting; Development & Non-profit; Engineering & Management; General Management and International Business; Organizational Studies; Performance & Project Management; and Public Administration & Public Management. The proportion between accounting and non-accounting outlets is 40% vs. 60%.

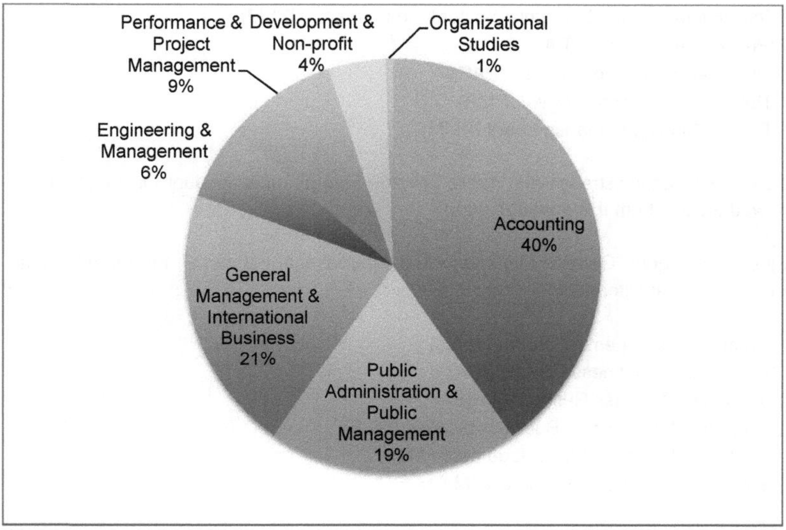

Figure 4: Reviewed articles by journal category.
(in percentage)

In the following are listed those journals of the three major strands of literature from which more than one article has been considered. A listing of all journals including number of reviewed articles, VHB JOURQUAL 3/Academic Journal Guide 2015 ranking and name of the publishing house can be gathered from Table 66 (annex 8.1).

In the journal category "Accounting", the following ten journals provided relevant literature in particular and account for more than 90% of all reviewed articles from this literature strand:

- Accounting, Auditing and Accountability Journal (AAAJ)
- Accounting Forum (AF)
- Accounting, Organizations and Society (AOS)
- Australian Accounting Review (ARA)
- Contemporary Accounting Research (CAR)
- Critical Perspectives on Accounting (CPA)
- European Accounting Review (EAR)
- Journal of Accounting and Organizational Change (JAOC)
- Management Accounting Research (MAR)
- The British Accounting Review (BAR)
-

Further accounting journals, ranked as "A+", "A" or "B" according to VHB-JOURQUAL 3, were scanned for relevant articles, but did not produce usable results. They are listed in Table 67 (annex 8.1).

In the journal category "Public Administration & Public Management", the following journals provided relevant literature:

- International Journal of Public Sector Management (IJPSM)
- Public Administration (PA)
- Public Administration Review (PAR)
- Public Management Review (PMR)
- Public Money and Management (PMM)

These five public administration and public management journals account for about 74% of all reviewed articles from this literature strand.

In the journal category "General Management & International Business", the following journals provided relevant literature:

- European Management Journal (EMJ)
- International Business Review (IBR)
- Journal of Business Research (JBS)
- Journal of International Business Studies (JIBS)
- Journal of International Management (JIM)
- Strategic Management Journal (SMJ)

These five general management and international business journals account for almost 70% of all reviewed articles from this literature strand.

2.2.1.1.2 Theoretical Frameworks

From the 159 papers reviewed, about two thirds employed neither a theory nor any other theoretical framework in their studies. However, some dominance of theories from NIE was noted. The TCE was foremost applied to serve as reference framework, in particular in empirical studies (cf. Anderson and Dekker, 2005; Cäker and Siverbo, 2011; Schepper et al., 2015). Moreover, the TCE has been applied a few times together with organizational theory (cf. Appuhami et al., 2011; Dekker, 2003; Langfield-Smith and Smith, 2003; Marques et al., 2011; and VdM and Scapens, 2008) or agency theory (cf. Emsley and Kidon, 2007). Organizational theory (cf. Chen D. et al., 2009) and agency theory (cf. Poulton, 2012) are also used in a single theory design, and are summarized under "Theories from NIE".

Some other studies enhanced existing research on PPPs, JVs and IORs and/or MC conceptionally or theoretically (cf. Abdul-Aziz, 2012; Li P. et al., 2013; Meschi and Riccio, 2008; Moilanen, 2007). In a few more cases, theories from social sciences, e.g. exchange theory (cf. Johnson and Korsgaard, 2002) and boundary-spanning theory (cf. Luo, 2007), or microeconomics, e.g. game theory (cf. Zhang Y. and Rajagopalan, 2002), were used. The distribution of articles per theoretical framework cluster is shown in Figure 5.

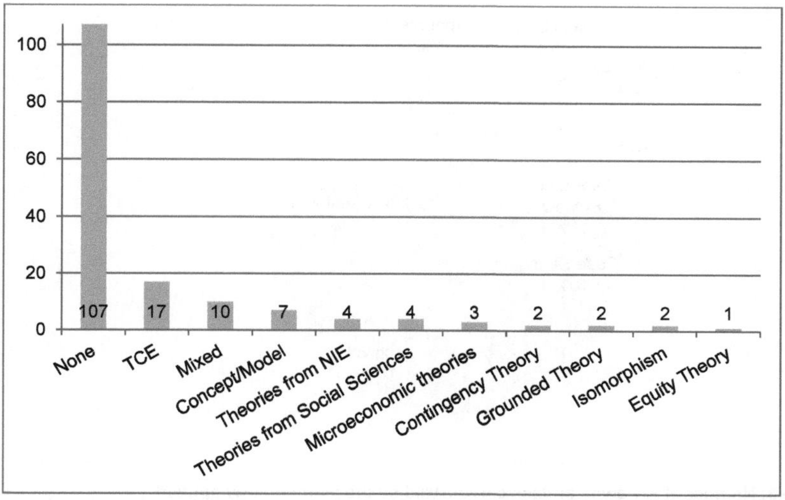

Figure 5: Number of reviewed articles by theoretical framework cluster.

In summary, the TCE and theories from NIE in general have been widely used in research on PPPs, JVs and IORs and/or MC, predominantly in empirical studies. However, the absence of a theoretical framework even in numerous empirical studies is striking. Reasons for that could not be identified from the affected studies themselves.

2.2.1.1.3 Methodologies

From the 159 reviewed articles, 90 are empirical studies vs. 69 non-empirical studies. Hence, clear dominance of one of these approaches in terms of research on PPPs, JVs and IORs cannot be seen.

The same pattern can be observed in the methodology that is applied in these studies (Figure 6). At first glance, no methodology is dominant, except mixed methods, which reach 33 percent share. Only the survey (cf. Chan, 2010a/2010b; Cheung et al., 2012) and the archival design (cf. Carbonara and Pellegrino, 2014; Stafford et al., 2010) have significantly more than ten percent share. However, an in-depth review of the methodologies included in the category "mixed methods" leads to more differentiated results (Table 68 in annex 8.1). In 41 out of 53 studies with a mixed method design, interviews were carried out, while in all reviewed field studies interviews were used for data collection (cf. Nicholson et al., 2006; Reeves, 2008). Moreover, conceptual developments and the use of archival data from corporate documents and databases were part of mixed method designs as well (cf. Boersma et al., 2003; Burke and Demirag, 2015; Henjewele et al., 2013; Yang et al., 2013).

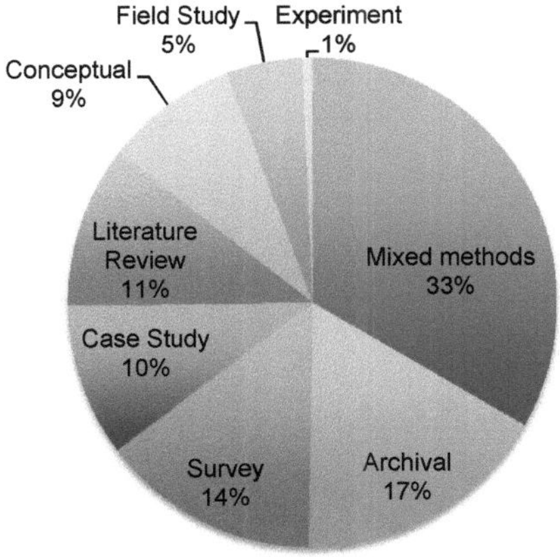

Figure 6: Number of reviewed articles categorized by the methodology applied.

In summary, although no methodology is clearly dominant, an empirical research design including interviews has been widely used in previous research on PPPs, JVs and IORs. Thus, a research design that allows interviews as means of data collection is appropriate for further exploring this field of research.

2.2.1.1.4 Geographical Scopes

From the 159 reviewed articles, 91 have a specific geographic focus. The geographic scope embraces single country, two-country, multi-country, or continent/regional perspectives. Only 14 articles make any kind of reference to IOs. Table 6 outlines the geographic scope of those articles, which include any geographic focus in their analyses.

Single-country	Two-country	Multi-country	Continent/regional
68	10	10	3

Table 6: Number of reviewed articles with geographic focus.
(Note: For this analysis, Australia is considered as a country only)

The dominant geographic scope is the single-country perspective, by which PPPs, JVs and IORs are analyzed within one country. Cross-border studies were undertaken in particular if matters of IJVs and PPPs formed the research object. However, only in a few articles, the geographic research scope was extended to two countries or more. The reasons for narrow geographical foci are probably diverse. Besides individual research interests, the comprehensiveness and complexity of international studies including necessary resources could explain the dominance of single-country studies. When looking at the methodologies chosen, it is striking to see that about half of the two-country and multi-country studies carried out surveys. These are less costly than field-based interviews. When looking at the 68 empirical studies with specific geographic focus, it is conspicuous that 32 out of them opted for undertaking interviews as part of either a field study or mixed methods design (cf. Demirag et al., 2012; Loosemore and Cheung, 2015; Kamminga and VdM, 2006). Thus, there is no evidence for the dominance of one type of geographical scope that is commonly adopted for the analysis of international PPPs, JVs and IORs; the same applies to the chosen research design and method for studies with specific geographic focus.

Figure 7 displays all countries and groups of countries, which have been in scope two or more times. The remaining countries and groups of countries are summarized under "others".

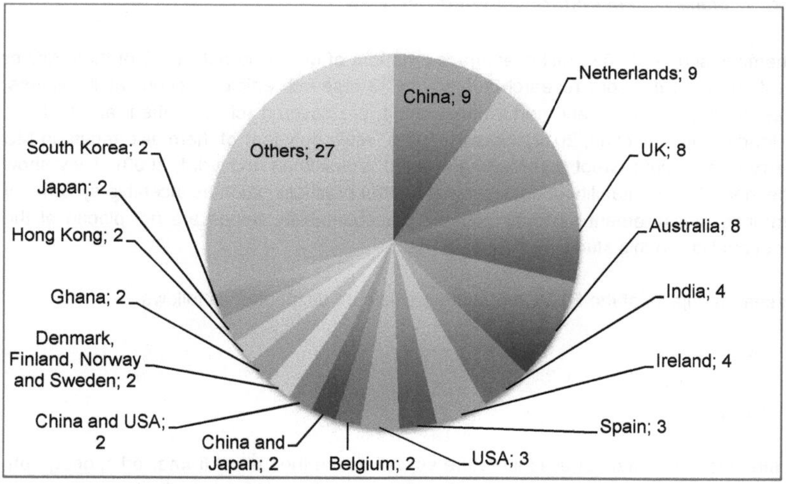

Figure 7: Reviewed articles classified by geographic focus.
(Depicted by number of countries and groups of countries)

Previous research on PPPs, JVs and IORs has hitherto placed geographic focus on so-called BRICS countries[1], first and foremost China, and on Western European countries as well as on Australia and USA. Some of them are also found in multi-country combinations and under "others". Figure 7 shows that extant literature concentrated in particular on anglophone countries, which could be explained by the fact that the concept of PPPs enjoyed increasing attention in public debate about public financing in Australia and in the UK. In the latter, PPPs are politically highly accepted and usually operate as PFIs, a concept, which was developed by the British government in the 1990s and gained increasing importance from the beginning of the 2000s (cf. Broadbent and Laughlin (2003c, 2004); Grimsey and Lewis, 2005; Osei-Kyei and Chan, 2015). Moreover, many renowned authors originate from anglophone countries (cf. Andon, 2012). The geographic research interest in China can be explained by its increasing importance for and influence on the global economy as well as by the role that PPPs and JVs play for the country's economic and infrastructure development

[1] BRICS countries comprise the states of Brazil, Russia, India, China and South Africa. The abbreviation "BRICS" has been invented by the US-American Investment Bank Goldman Sachs (cf. O'Neill, 2001).

(cf. Chalos and O'Connor, 2004; Chan et al., 2010a). Apart from that, the Chinese authorities began allowing more private sector participation in the provision of public services from the early 2000s, which raised researchers' interest in analyzing Chinese PPPs (cf. Osei-Kyei and Chan, 2015).

To summarize, the extant literature on PPPs, JVs and IORs leaves abundant scope for related research at national or international level, including intercultural aspects that may play a role for success and failure as well as for the design of such forms of cooperation.

2.2.1.2 Management control-centered Overview

The thematic scope of 102 articles embraces matters of MC while only in 50 of them MC or MC systems form the core research subject. In 33 research articles, accountability issues, such as good governance and performance audit, are covered (cf. Broadbent and Guthrie, 2008; Martin and Halachmi, 2012; Watson, 2003), while only four of them also focus on MC (cf. Berry et al., 2009; Groot and Merchant, 2000; Vosselman and VdM, 2009). They show that the idea of accountability underlies many control practices, such as incentive systems or performance measurement systems. However, accountability issues are not placed at the center of analysis in this study.

The research objects of the 50 MC-centered articles are distributed as follows:

- PPPs: 4
- JVs: 21
- IORs: 25.

Next, the different strands of used literature as well as the theoretical frameworks, geographical scopes and methodologies applied in the 50 core papers will be described.

2.2.1.2.1 Strands of Literature

From the 50 core articles on MC in PPPs, JVs and IORs, 35 have been published in accounting journals (Figure 8). This makes evident that the research on these forms of cooperation is foremost anchored in the field of accounting, followed by journals dealing with general management and international business topics. Journals from others than these two journal categories play no important role for MC analyses, in spite of some reference to MC.

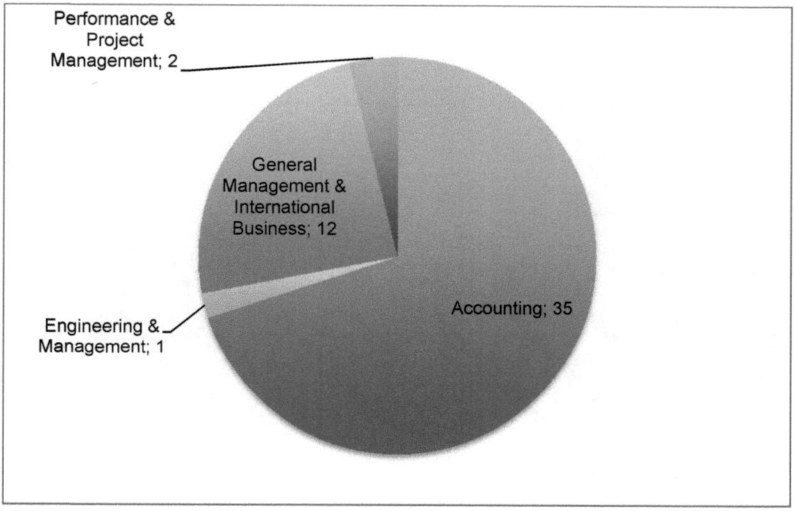

Figure 8: Number of MC-centered articles by journal category.

2.2.1.2.2 Theoretical Frameworks

Figure 9 outlines the distribution of articles per theoretical framework cluster for the 50 core papers on PPPs, JVs and IORs. The results align with those from the general overview where the categories "none", "TCE", "Mixed", and "Concept/Model" are dominating as well. All mixed theoretical frameworks include the TCE (cf. Emsley and Kidon, 2007; Meira et al., 2010). In conjunction with that, Organization Theory is applied in most cases (cf. Appuhami et al., 2011; Dekker, 2003). Other theories from microeconomics or social sciences as well as contingency theory and isomorphism have rarely been used in the context of MC in PPPs, JVs and IORs.

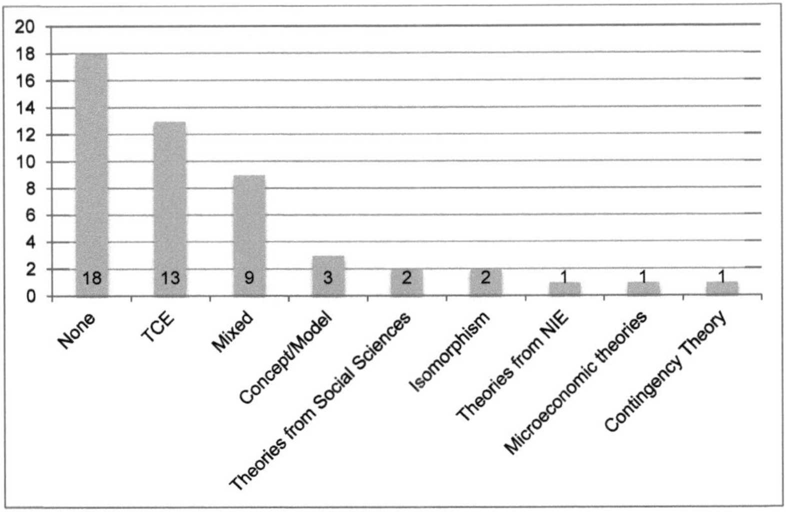

Figure 9: Number of MC-centered articles by theoretical framework cluster.

To summarize, in accordance with the results from the general overview the TCE and theories from NIE in general form an appropriate theoretical framework for research on MC in PPPs.

2.2.1.2.3 Methodologies

From the 50 MC-centered articles, 38 are empirical studies vs. 12 non-empirical studies. Hence, a clear dominance of empirical studies in terms of research on PPPs, JVs and IORs and/or MC can be noted. Compared to the general overview, a mixed- method design can be stated as clearly dominant, followed by a survey design (Figure 10). However, an in-depth review of the methodologies included in the category "mixed methods" leads to more differentiated results (Table 69 in annex 8.1). In 21 out of 25 MC-centered studies with a mixed-method design, interviews were carried out, in all cases as part of a single- or multiple-case study design. It should be noted that interviews were part of all field studies as well (Nicholson et al., 2006; Rahaman et al., 2010). Like in the general overview, conceptual developments and the use of archival data from corporate documents and databases were part of mixed-method designs, too (cf. Abdul-Aziz, 2012; Boland et al., 2008; Kamminga and VdM, 2007).

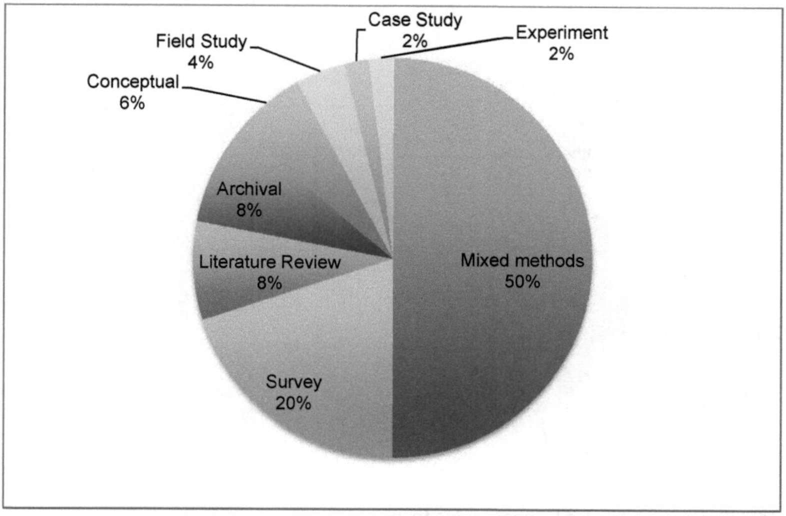

Figure 10: Number of MC-centered articles by methodology applied.

To summarize, empirical research designs including interviews were at the forefront of methodological approaches in previous MC research on PPPs, JVs and IORs. Hence, using an empirical research design is appropriate to also explore MC in PPPs between IOs/DCAs and the private sector.

2.2.1.2.4 *Geographical Scopes*

From the 50 MC-centered articles, 28 have a specific geographic focus. The geographic scopes embrace single-country, two-country, or continent/regional perspectives. Thereof, only Rahaman et al. (2010) make reference to IOs. Figure 11 displays all countries and groups of countries, which appeared within this scope two or more times. The remaining countries and groups of countries are summarized under “others”.

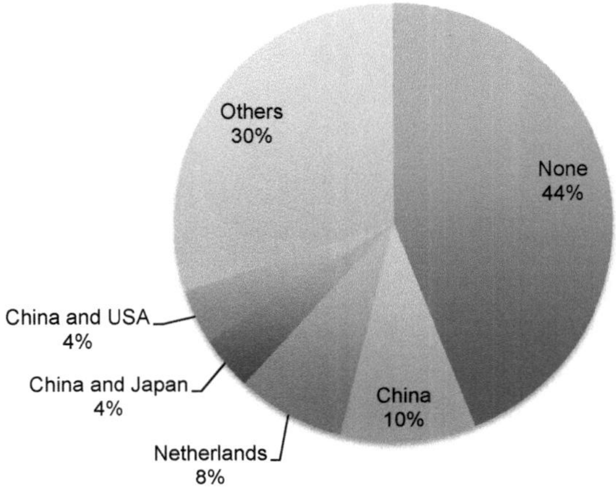

Figure 11: MC-centered articles by geographic focus.
(Percentage of countries and groups of countries)

Previous research on PPPs, JVs and IORs with emphasis on MC has hitherto placed the geographic focus on China and on selected Western countries such as Japan, Netherlands and USA (cf. Chalos and O'Connor, 2005; Chen D. et al., 2009; Dekker, 2008; Li P. et al., 2013). Some of them also find themselves in another country combination under "others" again.

To conclude, the extant literature on PPPs, JVs and IORs with focus on MC leaves abundant space for related research at national or international level.

2.2.2 Qualitative Analysis of Reviewed Literature

Extant research has dealt with MC in PPPs, JVs and IORs in various studies which are distinguished by the research questions including research scope, geographical scope, research design, and by the extent to which reference is made to a theoretical framework. As the present study explicitly focuses on MC in PPPs, JVs and IORs, only those studies are considered which put MC in the center of their analysis, or which are at least strongly related to that. The subsequent qualitative literature review briefly presents the 50 MC-centered studies pertinent to the research topic, clustered by their research scope (PPP, JV, or IOR) (Table 7 to Table 10).

2.2.2.1 PPP

Four articles explicitly discuss MC issues in PPPs (Table 7).

Study	Research design	Theoretical framework	Geo-graphical scope	Results
Abdul-Aziz (2012): Control mechanisms exercised in Malaysian housing public-private partnerships.	Mixed methods	Concept/ Model	Malaysia	Both hybrid and bureaucracy governance archetypes have been found in transactions, including corresponding control mechanisms
Appuhami et al. (2011): Management Controls in Public-Private Partnerships: An Analytical Framework.	Conceptual	Mixed	None	Elaboration of a conceptual framework of control archetypes and control strategies to handle (behavioral) risk in PPPs
Appuhami and Perera (2016): Management controls for minimising risk in public-private partnerships in a developing country: Evidence from Sri Lanka.	Mixed methods	Mixed	Sri Lanka	Project phase-oriented adaptation of MC to different kinds of risks; dominant use of bureaucratic control which is complemented by trust-based control to a significant extent
Kivilä et al. (2017): Sustainable project management through project control in infrastructure projects.	Mixed methods	None	Finland	Sustainable project management pursues a holistic control approach that goes beyond mere indicator-based project control and links a project to its institutional environment

Table 7: Reviewed MC-related articles regarding PPPs.

In line with MC typologies of several Dutch scholars and with respect to Malaysian housing PPPs, Abdul-Aziz (2012) examined first what control mechanisms (formal/informal) were implemented to ensure contract compliance, and second, which interorganizational governance scheme is most closely related to housing PPP transactions. He distinguishes between three project phases (exploratory, contract, and execution) and discusses to what level of governance (market, hybrid, hierarchy) belong the formal and informal control mechanisms applied to the transactions in each phase. In line with the tripartite governance level as outlined by Abdul-Aziz (2012), Appuhami et al. (2011) speak of "control archetypes" and replace 'hybrid' by 'clan' and 'hierarchic' by 'bureaucratic' control. Against this background, they discuss two control strategies, namely trust-based strategies and performance evaluations, with respect to how VFM of PPPs can be increased by appropriate MC systems. Appuhami and Perera (2016) extend the discussion on appropriate governance and MC structure to a developing country and name the three project phases according to Abdul-Aziz (2012) slightly differently, but basically agree (selecting, building, operating). Finally, Kivilä et al. (2017) conclude that project management is sustainable when it pursues a holistic control approach where the governance structure links the internal project control with the institutional environment, such as rules and regulations or external stakeholders.

2.2.2.2 *Joint Venture*

The subsequent 21 articles discuss MC issues in JVs or IJVs (Table 8).

Study	Research design	Theoretical framework	Geo-graphical scope	Results
Boland et al. (2008): Designing management control in hybrid organizations: The role of path creation and morphogenesis.	Mixed methods	Iso-morphism	None	Development and implementation of MC systems at the joint venture and project levels are crucial for hybrid governance forms in the construction, gas and oil industries
Cäker and Siverbo (2011): Management control in public sector Joint Ventures.	Mixed methods	TCE	Sweden	Vertical control packages: affected by competence and goodwill trust; parent differences and parent diversification Horizontal control packages: affected by calculative, goodwill, and system trust; parent differences; quality achievement
Chalos and O'Connor (2004): Determinants of the use of various control mechanisms in US–Chinese joint ventures.	Survey	None	China and USA	Many control sets are influenced by specific asset investments and partner knowledge Different views on control mechanisms between Chinese and US JV partners
Chalos and O'Connor (2005): The Perceived Effect of Accounting Controls on U.S. - Chinese Joint Venture Transaction Costs and Performance.	Survey	None	China and USA	Transactions costs compromise performance Managerial and contractual controls diminish adverse impacts of transaction costs and positively influence JV performance
Chen D. et al. (2009): Parent contribution and organizational control in international joint ventures.	Survey	Theories from NIE	China	Property-based contribution → process and output control Knowledge-based contribution → social and process control Control practices differ between

Study	Research design	Theoretical framework	Geo-graphical scope	Results
				local and foreign firms
Choi and Beamish (2004): Split management control and international joint venture performance.	Mixed methods	TCE	South Korea	Split control outstrips other approaches No dominance of one MC type
Emsley and Kidon (2007): The Relationship between Trust and Control in International Joint Ventures: Evidence from the Airline Industry.	Mixed methods	Mixed	None	Information from behavioral, output and social controls contribute to competency trust (operational level) and goodwill trust (executive level) building Competency trust proved to be easier to destroy than goodwill trust
Giacobbe and Booth (2009): Controlling International Joint Ventures: An Investigation of Australian Parent Partners.	Survey	None	Australia and other countries	Australian parent partners apply a limited number of controls with more formalized control structures in many cases
Groot and Merchant (2000): Control of international joint ventures.	Mixed methods	Contingency Theory	Netherlands	IJV specific causal factors influence three elements of MC in IJVs: control mechanisms; control focus (broad vs. narrow); and control tightness
Johnson and Korsgaard (2002): Perceived fairness, decision control, and commitment in international joint venture management teams.	Survey	Theories from Social Sciences	Canada and USA	IJV management teams demonstrated more commitment to the IJV than to the parent firms Strong positive nexus between organizational commitment, procedural justice and strategic decision control
Kamminga and VdM (2006): Parents' contribution and management control of joint ventures.	Mixed methods	TCE	Netherlands	International character of IJVs strongly impacts on MC
Kamminga and VdM (2007): Management	Mixed methods	None	None	Case studies confirmed tripartite model of control patterns: con-

Study	Research design	Theoretical framework	Geo-graphical scope	Results
control patterns in joint venture relationships: A model and an exploratory study.				sultation-based; content-based; and context-based Institutional environment strongly impacts on JV controls
Larimo et al. (2016): Performance measurement choices in international joint ventures: What factors drive them?	Survey	TCE	Denmark, Finland, Norway and Sweden	Cultural distance, level of trust and the firms' motivations to create an IJV influence the choice of performance measures which moreover vary by project phases. While previous target country experiences impact upon the choice of performance measures, past IJV experiences do not.
Li J. et al. (2009): Control, collaboration, and productivity in international joint ventures: theory and evidence.	Archival	None	China	Achievement of balance between collaboration benefits and control determines optimal scheme of IJV ownership structure
Li P. et al. (2013): The characteristics and dynamics of management controls in IJVs: Evidence from a Sino-Japanese case.	Mixed methods	Concept/ Model	China and Japan	Overall MC structure is built at the JV's beginning A split and tight control style is applied and an unequal control extent identified that does not reflect the 50:50 equity structure
Liu X. (2014): A Meta-analysis of factors leading to management control in international joint ventures.	Archival	None	China	Main factors determining MCs in IJVs: resource contribution; equity share; trust; and strategic importance to the IJVs
Luo (2007): Private control and collective control in international joint ventures.	Survey	Theories from Social Sciences	China	Collective and private controls are neither predetermined nor exogenous but influenced by the partners' relationships and by the transactional environment Bargaining power symmetry; cultural, relational, and social links; goal congruity; operational

Study	Research design	Theoretical framework	Geo-graphical scope	Results
				integration; and resource complementarity contribute to reducing private control by individual parties
Mantecon et al. (2016): The Control and Performance of Joint Ventures.	Archival	None	USA and other parts of the world	Contractual arrangements related to decision-making rights promote cooperation between JV partners and JV performance, especially in the event of power imbalance between the partners
VdM and Kamminga (2015): Joint venture dynamics: The effects of decisions made within a parent company and the role of joint venture management control.	Mixed methods	None	Europe and Asia	JV MC cemented the JV relationship Central management's insufficient knowledge about the value of social aspects for the JV relationship (e.g. considering local values and norms, exchanging information in face-to-face contacts, and trust), tight control of the JV partner and strong bargaining power produced complex dynamic processes If decision-makers lack sufficient previous JV experience, their decisions can lead to unintended effects and therefore to complex dynamic processes
Zhang Y. and Li (2001): The control design and performance in international joint ventures: a dynamic evolution perspective.	Mixed methods	None	China	The more autonomy a MC system leaves to IJV partners, the better they perform Evolvement of IJV control designs from shared management, to dominant parent types towards independent parent types over time
Zhang Y. and Rajagopalan (2002): Inter-partner credible threat in international joint ventures: An infinitely repeated prisoner's dilemma model.	Mixed methods	Micro-economic theories	China and Japan	Inter-partner credible threat is able to address coordination cost concerns and appropriation concerns together in IJVs

Table 8: Reviewed MC-related articles regarding JVs and IJVs.

There are different motivations to enter into JVs, and partners associate different objectives with such cooperation. Groot and Merchant (2000) identified four main groups of objectives: 1) cost reduction (e.g. achieving economies of scale, getting access to cheap foreign labor forces), 2) getting access to technological expertise and knowhow, 3) getting access to new markets (e.g. strengthening intercultural skills, avoid trading barriers), and 4) risk reduction (e.g. mitigating political risk, sharing business risk). In the light of these categories, Giacobbe and Booth (2009) revealed in their study about Australian IJVs that growth and profit were for both the Australian and the international partner the highest motivation to enter into an IJV. The same applies to risk sharing. While Australian companies aim at expanding to new markets with related products, learning and knowledge exchange are among the five most important factors of the international partners who originate mostly from emerging and developing countries. Whatever are the reasons for entering into a JV, for the JV's success it is crucial that partners formulate clear strategic objectives which provide guidance to the JV activities (cf. Chalos and O'Connor, 2005).

In accordance with Kamminga and VdM (2006), Johnson et al. (2002) have shown in their study on commitment, decision control and perceived fairness in IJVs teams, that the international character of IJVs strongly influences control. They argue that different national backgrounds including cultural values, language and management styles strengthen existing conflicts of interest within IJV entities, between parent partners and managers, but also among parent partners. In addition, they revealed that differences in previous experiences, decision-making authority and length of job tenure can impact upon managers' commitment to and individual identification with the IJV. The findings from Larimo et al. (2016) in the context of performance control confirm the influence cultural aspects have but are more ambivalent regarding the importance of previous experiences. Their results support the idea that previous experiences from the JV's target country influence the choice of performance measures. Still, they did not find enough evidence for assuming that previous JV experiences matter. In this vein, Langfield-Smith (2008) argues that different views on control systems and divergent organizational cultures can lead to conflicts. The parent partners significantly determine decision control within IJVs and therefore influence the venture's performance. JV performance implies that JV managers are generally satisfied with the JV's performance outcome (cf. Choi and Beamish, 2004). Thus, Kamminga and VdM (2007, 2015) emphasize that parent firms should choose appropriate control tightness in response to uncertainty, in order to promote effective decision-making and venture performance. Yet, the choice of control tightness should be done in the light of the parent firms' bargaining power and the specific JV relationship characteristics.

Trustful personal relationships between individuals, especially managers, are important elements of MC in JVs and are crucial for conflict resolution, effective decision-making or knowledge-sharing and learning. High staff turnover is harmful to this (cf. VdM and Kamminga, 2015). Cäker and Siverbo (2011) add that strong mutual trust is conducive to the implementation of interorganizational MCs. Trust is a phenomenon that is more rarely observed in JVs than in hierarchical forms of IORs because JV partners cannot mutually issue commands and instructions so that they need to trust each other to some extent (cf. Emsley and Kidon, 2007).

The research on MCS applied in JVs is still at its infancy (cf. Groot and Merchant, 2000). Apart from trust and intercultural aspects, these authors identified a few more factors that influence control of JVs in particular: Diverging partners' JV objectives lead to more comprehensive control, except if the JV serves product diversification only. Moreover, partners that possess special or critical competences are likely to exercise more and tighter control. The same applies to JVs from which parents expect good performance within a short period of time (cf. Cäker and Siverbo, 2011). However, JV MC has to attune itself to the JV's characteristics. A mismatch can impair the JV relationship (cf. VdM and Kamminga (2007, 2015)).

Split MC, or the extent to which control over JVs should be shared, and the impact of shared control upon JV performance are ongoing issues (cf. Choi and Beamish, 2004). In empirical studies, Choi and Beamish (2004) and Li P. et al. (2013) revealed that split MC leads to better JV performance. They argue that control should be split in a way so that it matches with the complementary skills and resources provided by the partners. Hence, each partner maintains control of activities which are related to his skills and resources. Those who provide more or more important resources and skills would have control over the JV accordingly. Zhang Y. and Rajagopalan (2002) also support a shared MC structure for JV and argue on a game-theoretic basis that credible inter-partner threat can make JV control more effective and therefore reduce coordination costs and mitigate control problems.

The matter of shared MC touches the issue of JV ownership structure and is usually constrained by legal and contractual requirements. However, the ownership structure is crucial for the venture's design. Those partners, who bring in certain performance-improving, inimitable and scarce capabilities and resources, including managerial expertise, possess a higher bargaining power and are likely to influence the ownership structure to their favour, leading to imbalanced shared JV control. Cultural and linguistic advantages and information asymmetry regarding financial, operational, proprietary, or relational information can accentuate this effect, which is dominant in emerging and developing countries where a partner joins from a developed region (cf. Chalos and O'Connor, 2005; Chen et al., 2009; Giacobbe and Booth, 2009; Li J. et al., 2009; Mantecon et al., 2016). However, Li J. et al. (2009) point out that balanced collaboration and control between partners require comparable levels of ownership stakes. They contend that an equitable ownership structure increases the partners' feeling that they make valuable contributions to the venture and therefore impact positively upon the achievement of objectives. In turn, such a positive feeling enhances the partners' mutual commitment to the JV, prevents disengagement, and promotes knowledge transfer and enhancement. Still, JV control structures may evolve and vary in time. However, Mantecon et al. (2016) figured out that suitable contractual arrangements promote cooperation and JV performance even if there is power imbalance between the JV partners in terms of decision-making and voting rights. Zhang Y. and Li (2001) in their empirical study on Chinese IJVs found that the MC design development followed a path of increasing autonomy. While MC was shared at the beginning, one parent partner was dominant later on, while at the end control was exercised independently.

In addition, Chen et al. (2009) underline that the capabilities and resources contributed by one partner significantly influence which other partners feel attracted to enter the JV and which governance structure is finally chosen. They distinguish between intangible knowledge-based (e.g. know-how, skills, managerial and technical competencies) and tangible property-based resources (e.g. brands, financial capital, patents and physical assets, all based on clear property rights). While property rights, rules and contracts protect the latter one, complexity or tacitness build barriers around knowledge-based resources.

2.2.2.3 *Interorganizational/Interfirm Relationship*

The subsequent 25 articles discuss MC issues in IORs or IFRs (Table 9).

Study	Research design	Theoretical framework	Geo-graphical scope	Results
Anderson and Dekker (2005): Management control for market transactions: The relation between transaction characteristics, incomplete contract design, and subsequent performance.	Survey	TCE	None	Hazard-related supplier and transaction characteristics are positively linked to four types of MC Positive relationship between costs of contracting and contract terms on legal recourse, after-sales service and assignment rights
Berry et al. (2009): Emerging themes in management control: A review of recent literature.	Literature Review	None	None	Research gaps identified: Little research on ICTs and their impact upon MC capability and design; little attention has been paid to control and culture; control and gender; control and risk; and control and sustainability
Caglio and Ditillo (2008): A review and discussion of management control in interfirm relationships: Achievements and future directions.	Literature Review	None	None	Research gaps identified: Management accounting and control mechanisms and identification of MC problems and related solutions in parity-based alliance settings; Accounting and trust-building serve tackling moral hazard and opportunism in alliances
Coletti et al. (2005): The effect of control systems on trust and cooperation in collaborative environments.	Experiment	None	None	Strong MC system can contribute to enhancing trust among collaborating partners Increased levels of trust are positively related to the level of cooperation among partners
Das and Teng (2001a): Trust, control, and risk in strategic alliances: An integrated framework.	Conceptual	None	None	Control, risk and trust are three dimensions in strategic alliances, which are interlinked by specific relationships
Dekker (2003): Value chain analysis in interfirm relationships: a field study.	Mixed methods	Mixed	None	It is necessary to manage appropriation concerns and coordination requirements in IFRs TCE and Organizational Theory form useful frameworks to provide explanations of the empiric observations

Study	Research design	Theoretical framework	Geo-graphical scope	Results
Dekker (2004): Control of inter-organizational relationships: evidence on appropriation concerns and coordination requirements.	Mixed methods	TCE	None	Coordination of tasks and management of appropriation concerns are two major control problems in IORs Little empirical evidence of control mechanisms applied in IORs
Dekker (2008): Partner selection and governance design in interfirm relationships.	Survey	TCE	Netherlands	Dependence, coordination requirements and appropriation concerns affect the governance design in IFRs Formal governance, partner experience and partner selection mitigate adverse effects of interfirm control problems
Dekker (2016): On the boundaries between intrafirm and interfirm management accounting research.	Literature Review	TCE	None	Research gaps identified: Limited prior management accounting research in intrafirm and interfirm relationships 1) the alignment of actions and interests of boundary spanners, 2) interrelations between both relationship types and 3) the use of intrafirm MC mechanisms
Donada and Nogatchewsky (2006): Vassal or lord buyers: How to exert management control in asymmetric interfirm transactional relationships?	Mixed methods	Mixed	None	Lord buyers primarily apply market-based control, blended with some bureaucratic- and social-based control Vassal buyers can reduce transaction risk by social-based control only Relational behaviors between partners are suitable strategies to reduce adverse effects of mutual dependence
Langfield-Smith (2008): The relations between transactional characteristics trust and risk in the start-up phase of a collaborative alliance.	Mixed methods	TCE	Australia	High transaction frequency, high behavioral and environmental uncertainty and high asset specificity are characteristics of the examined alliance Composition of the alliance's control package: Social, output, and behavior controls The control package leads to trust-building and risk mitigation

Study	Research design	Theoretical framework	Geo-graphical scope	Results
Langfield-Smith and Smith (2003): Management control systems and trust in outsourcing relationships.	Mixed methods	Mixed	None	The transaction parties and environment adopted a trust-based control pattern Main elements of the MC design: Social controls; outcome controls; and (goodwill) trust
Marques et al. (2011): The use of management control mechanisms by public organizations with a network coordination role: A case study in the port industry.	Mixed methods	Mixed	Portugal	Mixed-type networks: public organizations in a network coordinator role apply MC mechanisms to assess the contributions to network performance of the involved organizations and their motivations to cooperate
Meira et al. (2010): Management controls and interfirm relationships: a review.	Archival	Mixed	None	Prevailing form of IFRs: outsourcing and supply chain Prevailing theoretical approach: TCE (trust as theoretical issue in many studies)
Moilanen (2007): Knowledge translation in management accounting and control: A case study of a multinational firm in transitional economies.	Mixed methods	Concept/ Model	None	Accounting information alone does not enable MC to work in countries of the former Soviet Union, due to personal networking structures and common business traditions. Personal contacts are crucial to making MC effective
Mouritsen and Thrane (2006): Accounting, network complementarities and the development of interorganisational relations.	Mixed methods	None	None	Controls engender predictability and durability in horizontal networks MC mechanisms help to constitute networks' boundaries Trust is a form of accountability and a problematizing devise that underlies MC system instead of being a MC mechanism itself
Nicholson et al. (2006): Transaction costs and control of outsourced accounting: Case evidence from India.	Field Study	TCE	India	Identified MC practices and mechanisms mitigate negative effects of potential uncertainty and opportunism: contractual incentives; physical arrangements in the center; security standardization and standards; utilization of ICT
Rahaman et al. (2010): Accounting for social-	Field Study	None	Ghana	To govern social-purpose alliances the balancing of three

Study	Research design	Theoretical framework	Geo-graphical scope	Results
purpose Alliances: Confronting the HIV/AIDS pandemic in Africa*				(inter-)related tensions is required: Coercive and enabling uses of accounting; differential costs of control; and global control and local flexibility
Richardson and Kilfoyle (2009): Accounting in markets, hierarchies and networks: The role of accounting in the transnational governance of postal transactions.	Case Study	TCE	None	Remedial transaction costs can induce failure of governance structures Networks are a specific governance form which enable embedded organizations to continue to exist as independent hierarchies and to interact with each other Networks and bilateral contracts are governance mechanisms which can reduce and even eliminate accounting, when transactions shift from a market-based governance mechanism to another
Van der Stede (2003): The effect of national culture on management control and incentive system design in multi-business firms: evidence of intracorporate isomorphism.	Survey	Iso-morphism	Belgium	Corporate-level effects influence the specifics of MC and incentive systems in foreign business units more than the consideration of local conditions → management styles of foreign business units align with those exerted in the parent company MC and incentive systems are adapted to national business culture
VdM and Scapens (2008): The governance of lateral relations between and within organisations.	Mixed methods	Mixed	None	Lateral relations are characterized by minimal structures (technical, social, institutional, economic) and by a package of combined governance/MC practices (hierarchical, market-based and relationship) Feature of lateral relations: cooperation and competition; exchange of knowledge and information sharing; flexibility; shifting and shared leadership roles; standardization
VdM and Vosselman	Mixed	TCE	Nether-	Model of MC structures of IFRs

Study	Research design	Theoretical framework	Geo-graphical scope	Results
(2000): Management control of interfirm transactional relationships: the case of industrial renovation and maintenance.	methods		lands	(three MC patterns and contingency factors) Cultural, historical, institutional and strategic factors are very important for the design and functioning of the MC structures
VdM and Vosselman (2006): Research on management control of interfirm transactional relationships: Whence and whither.	Literature Review	TCE	None	Editorial paper that outlines in particular aspects and types of IFRs and the relationship between control and trust against the background of the TCE
Vélez et al. (2008): Management control systems as inter-organizational trust builders in evolving relationships: Evidence from a longitudinal case study.	Mixed methods	None	None	MC systems directly create trust and facilitate conditions that promote trust MC systems have a coordinating and supervisory function that helps to prevent trust from harmful suspicions Result and action controls enhance mutual trustworthiness between partners and create goodwill-based trust and competence
Vosselman and VdM (2009): Accounting for control and trust building in interfirm transactional relationships.	Conceptual	None	None	A governance structure, negotiated and agreed upon by participating parties is imperative for effective control mechanisms Control practices are related to accountability instruments (e.g. cost management systems, financial incentive systems, performance measurement, and target costing), which incentivize and constrain behavior regarding reconciliation of interests Trust plays an important role in interfirm transactional relationships → Trust contributes to producing control while excess control damages trust if it overcompensates for legitimate adverse behavioral expectations

Table 9: Reviewed MC-related articles regarding IORs/IFRs.

Extant MC-related literature on IORs or IFRs has particularly dealt with the role that accounting plays for these interorganizational forms of cooperation, and with implications it has for control going beyond single organization boundaries. Trust has been an issue as well.

In a field study about social-purpose alliances in Ghana, Rahaman et al. (2010) discussed which forms of governance those alliances may adopt, and how these are matched with control mechanisms. They identified three ways through which accounting promotes governance in IORs: 1) accounting is a means to determine the composition of participants in an alliance, and the requirements for participation, 2) accounting can help to implement standardized business practices, and 3) accounting is an important factor for keeping an alliance stable because participants have to provide auditable financial information, which facilitates internal and external control and evaluation (e.g. about misuse of resources) and encourages participants to comply with the interests and the strategic vision given by the stakeholders. Thus, accounting is a tool to influence and control people's behavior, to provide stakeholders with financial and non-financial information on the likely behavior of partners involved in the IOR including resulting output. Furthermore, accounting is supposed to help establishing shared beliefs and values, to ensure reciprocity among partners and to align different interests of the partners involved. Therefore, control problems and potential solutions will be identified, and the fear of opportunistic behavior, resulting from reasonable adverse behavioral expectations, will be addressed. Typically, accounting is of formal control nature and comes along with formal incentive mechanisms, such as performance measurement or financial incentive programs (cf. Caglio and Ditillo, 2008; Vosselman and VdM, 2009).

Two streams of literature on MC in IORs or IFRs have been identified. The first one deals with the identification of influence factors upon the use of MCSs, while the second one focuses on consequences which may result from the use of different MCSs. Both streams have in common that they build on organizational theory or TCE (cf. Berry et al., 2009; Caglio and Ditillo, 2008; Marques et al., 2011). However, Dekker (2004) emphasizes that the scope of MC activities has been extended and goes beyond legal boundaries in the case of IORs or IFRs. In addition, Dekker (2003) points to two major difficulties in this context: 1) selecting suitable control mechanisms from an available set of MCs in order to effectively control and manage interdependencies between IOR or IFR partners, and 2) applying the same or different control mechanisms as those applied in intra-firm coordination. His literature review from 2016 reveals that by today there is still much research potential left to investigate appropriate management accounting and control mechanisms for IFRs (cf. Dekker, 2016). Moreover, on the basis of his empirical results, Dekker (2003) argues that governance arrangements tend to become more comprehensive when asset specificity, dependence between partners, task interdependence and transaction size increase. However, prior collaboration experience between partners can reduce the use and extensiveness of governance provisions, lead to leaner controls and therefore lower transaction costs (cf. Dekker, 2008; VdM and Vosselman, 2006). In this context, Das and Teng (2001a) analyze which control mechanisms are appropriate for different types of IORs. While many other authors often think in governance level terms, they distinguish between three types of equity structures, minority equity alliance (one or more partners acquires equity shares), non-equity alliance (no equity provision), and JV (owned by two or more partners).

As in the case of JVs, cultural aspects have been identified as influence factor upon MCSs in IORs (cf. Van der Stede, 2003). This author revealed that differences in MCSs emanate from the corporate level rather than from specific local conditions, which the local business unit may assert. To make the MCS working effectively, he argues that the control mechanisms have to match with the shared societal values of the cultural environments by which the organizational and individual members are controlled.

With their conceptual work on IFRs, Vosselman and VdM (2009) aim at contributing to the discussion on the links between accounting, control, and trust. In their view, trust and control are not simply complements or substitutes, but interaction takes place between them. They conclude that accounting can support exercising of control and trust-building, both being required for goal attainment and for keeping positive behavioral expectations. Trust itself also comes from the institutional environment and frames the governance structure of the underlying transactional relationship. Coletti et al. (2005) argue that a MCS can increase the level of trust among partners, given that the MCS is able to engender visible cooperation between them. They indicate feedback-based performance reports as a control mechanism to make collaboration visible, and therefore to create trust which can positively impact upon MCS in turn. In reference to strategic alliances, Das and Teng (2001a) argue that control and trust are tightly interrelated with risk so that an accurate understanding of the relationship between both of them is crucial for appropriate risk management in such cooperations. In accordance with this view, VdM and Scapens (2008) recall that conventional MCSs designed for intra-organizational control are not flexible enough and inappropriate for IORs as they may compromise the autonomy of the partners involved and therefore impede trust-building. However, Caglio and Ditillo (2008) and Vélez et al. (2008) agree that the nexus between trust and MCSs in IORs is complex as trust proved to be difficult to implement in practice. Thus, this issue deserves further consideration and is still open to debate.

2.2.3 PPPs for Development

The structured literature search has produced 14 articles that deal with PPPs between public development actors and the private sector (Table 10). While they all have in common a nexus with IOs or DCAs, they strongly vary by thematic focus, research design and geographic focus, falling in quite different journal categories. While half of them has been published in journals that are assigned to the "development & non-profit" category, the remaining ones spread over accounting, general management & international business, and public administration & public management. This underlines the interdisciplinary character of PPPs in the strategic and sustainable development context, and has encouraged public and private practitioners, such as Khoday (2007), Sturchio (2008) and Utting and Zammit (2009), to discuss their experiences about the usefulness as well as strengths and weaknesses of these partnerships.

Study	Research design	Theoretical framework	Geographical scope	Results
Chen et al. (2013): Public-private partnerships for the development of disaster resilient communities.	Case Study	Grounded Theory	None	Means to ensure coordination and alignment between partners: 1) social and relational capital, 2) economic, organizational and social mechanisms

Study	Research design	Theoretical framework	Geo-graphical scope	Results
				Mix of formal and informal controls should be geared to the levels of complexity and uncertainty of a partnership's activities Critical and important success factors of disaster management PPPs: 1) social capital, 2) high degree of institutionalization, 3) alignment of incentives among private and public partners, and 4) technological progress
Khoday (2007): Mobilizing market forces to combat global environmental change: Lessons from UN? Private sector partnerships in China.	Archival	None	China	Persisting lack of effective implementation of international frameworks on biodiversity and climate change (e.g. UN conventions) Hesitancy and lack of knowhow to implement market-based mechanisms, sustainable financing mechanisms (e.g. eco-compensation)
Kolk et al. (2008): Business and partnerships for development	Mixed methods	None	Netherlands	Partnerships between firms and NGOs more common than PPPs because of different views between public and private sector Partnerships are very often strongly linked to a firm's core activities and sector or deal with supply chain issues
Martin and Halachmi (2012): Public-Private Partnerships in Global Health: Addressing Issues of Public Accountability, Risk Management and Governance	Archival	None	None	PPPs help to leverage technological, human and financial resources that would be unavailable to broad public if governments acted alone
Poulton and Macartney (2012): Can Public–Private Partnerships Leverage Private Investment in Agricultural Value Chains in Africa? A Preliminary Review.	Archival	Principal-Agent Theory	Africa	PPP mechanisms classified by principal-agent models: 1) extension contracts (moral hazard/hidden action), 2) challenge fund (adverse selection), and 3) guarantee fund (moral hazard/hidden information) Challenge funds tend to encourage investments with large so-

Study	Research design	Theoretical framework	Geo-graphical scope	Results
				cial returns
Rahaman et al. (2010): Accounting for Social-Purpose Alliances: Confronting the HIV/AIDS Pandemic in Africa	Field Study	None	Ghana	To govern social-purpose alliances the balancing of three (inter-) related tensions is required: Coercive and enabling uses of accounting; differential costs of control; and global control and local flexibility
Reed and Reed (2009): Partnerships for Development: Four Models of Business Involvement	Conceptual	None	None	Four types of partnerships, differing by their degree of social control: conventional Business (weakest); corporate social responsibility; corporate accountability; and social economy (highest)
Richter (2004): Public–private partnerships for health: A trend with no alternatives?	Archival	None	None	PPP are not necessarily innovative and positive but often also imply high risks Measures to be taken: identify conflicts of interest; establish and institutionalize clear and effective policies and procedures, which put the public interest at the heart of all kinds of public-private cooperation
Samii et al. (2002): An Innovative Public–Private Partnership: New Approach to Development.	Case Study	None	India	Creating an universal scheme for technical assistance of UN organizations UNIDO's innovative capacity is restricted by scarce resources, limited experiences and mandate, bureaucratic structure and processes. Innovations happen randomly and are typically driven by individual dedication
Schäferhoff et al. (2009): Transnational Public-Private Partnerships in International Relations: Making Sense of Concepts,	Literature Review	None	None	Possible trade-off between broad stakeholder participation and adequate policy formulation Meaningful stakeholder participation can be undermined by

Study	Research design	Theoretical framework	Geo-graphical scope	Results
Research Frameworks, and Results.				resource constraints and underrepresentation of concerned stakeholders Lack of effective mechanisms to hold decision-making boards accountable
Singh and Prakash (2010): Public–Private Partnerships in Health Services Delivery.	Mixed Methods	None	India	The dominant role of governments in networks is based on their control and authority over information and resources → governments strongly rely on formal mechanisms for PPP coordination Horizontal coordination, public managers' ability to manage IORs effectively, social capital and trust are crucial for effective governance of networks
Stadtler and Probst (2012): How broker organizations can facilitate public–private partnerships for development.	Mixed Methods	None	None	Broker organizations can perform a crucial role as mediators, learning catalysts or conveners during partnership implementation, helping to overcome partnering problems and challenges
Sturchio (2008): Business engagement in public programs: the pharmaceutical industry's contribution to public health and the millennium development goals.	Case Study	None	None	PPPs are mechanisms that allow making progress in tackling challenges in the public health sector and therefore to contribute to attaining the MDGs
Utting and Zammit (2009): United Nations-Business Partnerships: Good Intentions and Contradictory Agendas.	Literature	Review	None	The UN's way of partnering with transnational cooperations should shift from a kind of "best practice learning" to an approach that includes more "critical thinking"

Table 10: Reviewed articles on PPPs for development.

The study of Rahaman et al. (2010) is the only one dealing with MC at its core and having an explicit linkage to PPPs with IOs, although they speak of interorganizational alliances in this context. Furthermore, Chen et al. (2013) and Singh and Prakash (2010) make reference to MC in their studies on disaster resilience building and public health services delivery. Both of them consider the building of social capital as crucial for enabling effective and successful partnership coordination and management. They emphasize that by nature partnerships are less a matter of technical design but a social construct. Thus, the MC design should be geared to the building of social capital and to the alignment of interests and incentives between partners because higher social capital can reduce transaction costs (TC) in partnerships. For this reason, they advocate for a highest possible degree of informal control in PPPs. However, they acknowledge that natural and external influence factors, such as complexity, uncertainty or government's power, limit the flexibility of partners to freely choose formal and informal control mechanisms and usually lead to more formal control.

Reed and Reed (2009) make the bridge from a MC to an ethical perspective on PPPs. Along with Schäferhoff et al. (2009) and Utting and Zammit (2009), they question the usefulness of transnational development PPPs in general, focusing mainly on partnerships between UN organizations and private sector firms. Reed and Reed (2009) take up the critical voices that blame business partnerships for serving individual corporate interests only and for creating business-driven regulatory and policy regimes which both together adversely impact on sustainable development. To cluster development PPPs by societal benefit, they developed a concept that distinguishes four types of partnerships including approaches to development and globalization. These range from conventional business with a neo-liberal approach and weak social control to social economy partnerships seeking for alternative forms of globalization that are accompanied with strong social control. Even more critical are Schäferhoff et al. (2009) who mourn imbalanced participation of concerned stakeholders and lack of accountability. In this context, Utting and Zammit (2009) dun for more critical thinking about the logics and forces behind the increasing number of PPPs established with UN organizations and call for benchmarking them against their development impact and their contribution to fundamental UN goals.

Regardless of the thematic focus, whether this may concern delivery of public health goods (cf. Martin and Halachmi, 2012; Richter, 2004), market-based development financing and investment (cf. Khoday, 2007; Poulton and Macartney, 2012), or technical assistance services (cf. Samii et al., 2002), these authors all consider the provision of clear and effective policies and procedures including a reliable political framework, efficient processes with a minimum of bureaucratic burdens and a high degree of cooperative behavior as key for successful partnership implementation that satisfies all actors involved. To improve the resource endowment of PPP projects, Khoday (2007) and Poulton and Macartney (2012) call for more market-based financing mechanisms, such as eco-compensation or challenge funds. However, lack of enabling environment (e.g. unreliable economic environment, lacking contract enforcement, and protection of property rights), entry barriers (e.g. lacking access to technical knowhow or market information, high risks and fixed costs) and coordination failures (e.g. absence of instruments to enforce commitments, information asymmetry, lack of trust) create major sources of market failure in the present context, according to Poulton and Macartney (2012) and in line with the findings by Khoday (2007) and Martin and Halachmi (2012). Richter (2004) contends that PPPs are not necessarily innovative, a view that is supported by Samii et al. (2002) who criticize that bureaucratic procedures, lack of resources and skills and limited mandates hamper the innovative capacity of UN-dependent PPPs where innovation emanates all too often from individual commitments.

On the basis of interviews, Kolk et al. (2008) and Stadtler and Probst (2012) analyzed for multiple cases characteristics and differences of PPPs for development. Kolk et al. (2008)

differentiate between private-nonprofit, public-private, and tripartite partnerships, and find that PPPs are less common than private-nonprofit cooperation, while Stadtler and Probst (2012) mainly discuss the role of federal agencies of development cooperation (e.g. CIDA, USAID), non-profit membership organizations (e.g. World Economic Forum), and IOs (e.g. UNDP, UNIDO) as kind of brokers in facilitating PPPs for development. While Kolk et al. (2008) find that companies hold the view that corporate interests always prevail in partnerships, with the public sector being in a weaker position, Stadtler and Probst potentially see public sector actors and non-profit actors in a broker role, acting as conveners, learning catalysts or mediators, where they help to overcome partnering challenges and problems (e.g. lack of mutual understanding and trust, limited partnership implementation experience). However, from both publications it can be concluded that the respective skills, competences and capacities are decisive in each individual partnership regardless of whether cooperation occurs on eye-level, or one partner is more powerful and can better enforce individual interests.

2.3 Critical Success Factors

Determinants and mechanisms that are crucial for making PPP or JV projects a success or a failure, so-called critical success factors (CSFs), have enjoyed increasing research interest since the 2000s. In line with the literature review on MC in Chapter 2.2.1.2, Western countries and selected emerging countries, in particular China, were in the focus of previous research. This is concluded from the systematic literature review on CSFs for PPP projects published by Osei-Kyei and Chan (2015) for the period 1990-2015, and by the present study's subsequent analysis for publications from the year 2000 until 2017.

Following Rockart (1982), Babatunde et al. (2012, p. 215) define CSFs as the "few key areas of activity in which favourable results are absolutely necessary for a manager to reach his/her goals". Chou and Pramudawardhani (2015) and Osei-Kyei and Chan (2015) make reference to Rockart in their definitions of CSFs as well, and emphasize that it is vital for decision-makers to take into account the model of CSFs for management measures, a model which has been used for management purposes in PPP projects since the 1970s.

This chapter intends to identify, display and structure CSFs of PPPs, JVs and IORs that have been revealed in studies published since 2000. For the search of relevant literature, the same databases and quality requirements as used for the literature review in Chapter 2.2 have been applied. Key words, which were entered into the search engines, are "critical success factors", "success factors" and "factors of success", in combination with "public-private partnership", "joint venture" or "interorganizational relationship". Results from this search, but also selected articles from the literature review which have a different focus but touch upon or partially cover the issue of CSFs, will be taken into account for the subsequent analysis. In spite of the comprehensive search for publications on CSFs in PPPs, JVs, and IORs, the compilation of CSFs in this study might not be all-embracing and fully inclusive because only a limited amount of findings from existing literature can be captured. This can be explained through the fact that relevant studies, such as those by Dekker (2004, 2008), Groot and Merchant (2000) or Langfield-Smith (2008), neither refer explicitly to CSFs nor do they include the afore-mentioned key words.

In total, 36 articles have been reviewed. Obstacles to PPPs, as they are named in some pertinent studies, will be considered because they are simply CSFs with negative sign, and their inclusion gives a more holistic picture of CSFs in extant literature.

In many previous studies, CSFs were displayed in large tables, ranked by their citation frequency by their importance, and/or by authors (cf. Babatunde et al., 2012; Chan et al., 2010a; Chou and Pramudawardhani, 2015; Osei-Kyei and Chan, 2015). However, many factors are inherently linked with each other, which is not evident in some of the previous studies. Thus, the CSFs identified through the literature search for this study have been grouped into self-defined clusters and categories. Similar to Gupta et al. (2013), a factor hierarchy will be set up to structure the numerous CSFs collected from existing literature (Figure 12). In a first step, success factors and obstacles will be split up by factor typology, extrinsic or intrinsic (cf. Mota and Moreira, 2015). While extrinsic factors usually have to be accepted as exogenously given by PPP decision-makers, they are responsible for recognizing intrinsic factors and to address them through appropriate management measures in order to facilitate successful PPP implementation. In this study, extrinsic factors will be categorized as economic, legal/political and social, an approach, which is supported by the studies of Chan et al. (2010a), Chou and Pramudawardhani (2015), and Mota and Moreira (2015). Following their idea of creating factor groups, this study clusters intrinsic factors twofold, in four major categories (interpersonal, procedural, inherent/structural, general) and several sub-categories. Factors assigned to the three categories of the extrinsic factors are moreover split up into success factors and obstacles. The same differentiation is undertaken for the intrinsic factors on the sub-category level. Both major categories and sub-categories are self-defined.

On the basis of the reviewed publications, 119 CSFs have been identified. From these, 94 factors are intrinsic and 25 factors are extrinsic. Not all factors, which make an exclusive reference to one specific sector or field of activity (e.g. infrastructure) and are not potentially applicable to other areas, have been taken into account for this study. Still, many of the identified CSFs result from studies on infrastructure projects. Differently named factors with the same meaning have been merged to avoid redundance and statistical biases with respect to the citation frequency. However, by contrast to Osey-Kyei (2015) who considered only those factors, which were mentioned in at least two publications, all identified factors will be listed in this study. The reason for this is that through the exploratory nature of this study some of the seldomly identified CSFs might be confirmed and should therefore not be excluded from consideration from the outset.

All extrinsic and intrinsic factors have been assigned to the category they match with best. Subsequently, overviews of the different extrinsic and intrinsic CSFs will be provided (Figure 13 to Figure 17). The publications are numbered by their respective source (Table 70 in annex 8.1). Moreover, CSFs are ranked by the accumulated number of times they have been identified by previous publications. If CSFs are equally mentioned they have been listed in alphabetic order.

Across all categories, seven CSFs have been found which were mentioned ten or more times in the reviewed publications: appropriate risk allocation; commitment; competitive, efficient and transparent procurement process; favourable/stable macroeconomic environment; strong governmental and political support; favourable legal framework; lack of trust. Although the individual relevance of these seven factors may vary from project to project, from project stage to project stage, and from sector to sector, they are likely to impact upon most PPPs, JVs, and IORs.

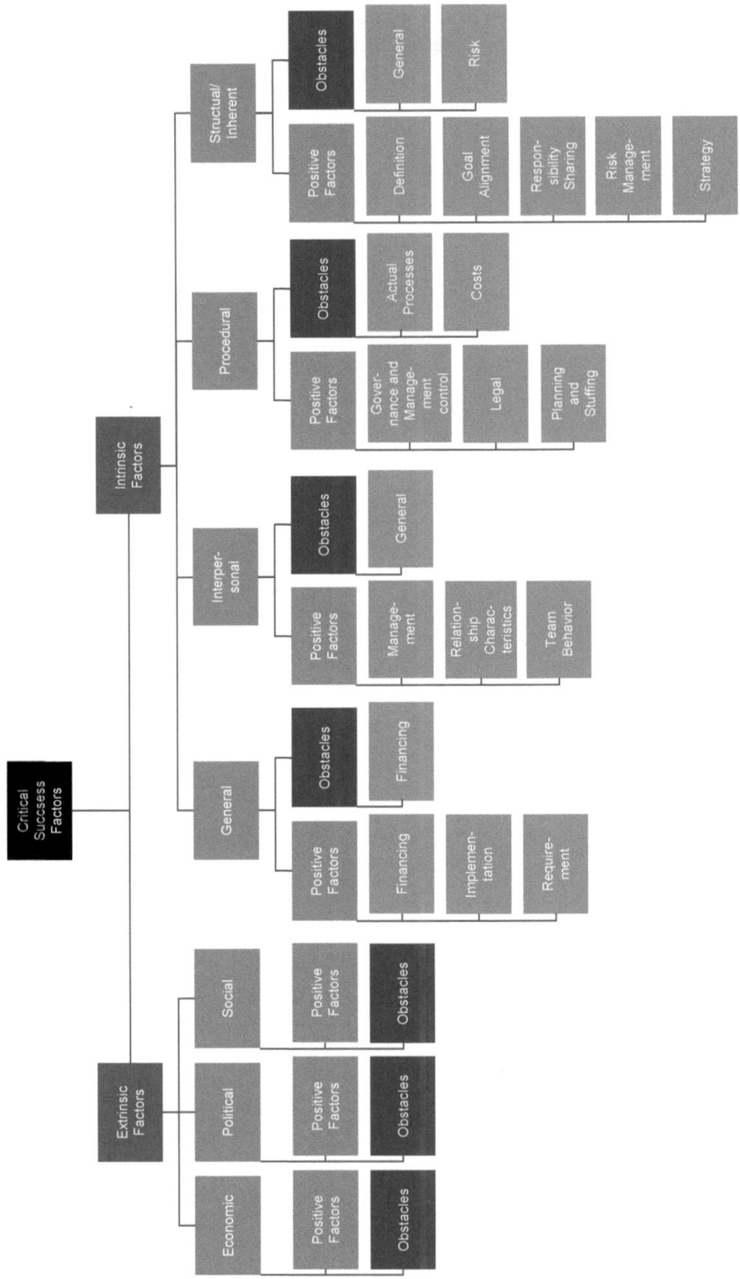

Figure 12: Hierarchy of critical success factors.

2.3.1 Extrinsic Factors

Extrinsic factors have been divided into the three categories economic, legal/political, and social. This procedure is in line with studies from Chan et al. (2010a), or Mota and Moreira (2015), who similarly grouped CSFs into these categories. An enabling and macroeconomic environment that is underpinned by reasonable economic policy measures is crucial for attracting private sector entities to enter into partnerships with public actors because economic risks for long-term cooperation eminate from inflation or interest rate (cf. Almarri, 2017; Hwang et al., 2013; Mota and Moreira, 2015). This goes hand in hand with the availability of conducive financial markets, which are not adversely affected by such economic influences but provide the platform to match supply and demand for financial resources needed for PPP projects (cf. Chan et al., 2010b; Li B., 2003). Moreover, the level of the government's involvement and support, which influences the risk-sharing proportionalities between public and private actors, and the legal framework are particularly important for the conclusion of joint cooperations (cf. Babatunde et al., 2012; Osei-Kyei and Chan, 2015). Absence or lack of well-established legal framework conditions for PPPs impede the creation and effective implementation of partnership projects, in particular, if they are limited to traditional client-contractor models (cf. Chan et al, 2010b). Apart from economic, legal and political aspects, acceptance of a PPP by the general public and its societal support are crucial for its long-term success (cf. Li B. et al., 2005a; Zhang X., 2005). Taken together, the extrinsic factors decide about how strong private sector entities feel encouraged and attracted to commit to the provision of public services in concert with public actors. A complete overview of extrinsic factors is given in Figure 13.

	Publication numbers:	1	2	4	5	7	12	13	14	15	16	22	23	25	26	27	32	33	Total
Extrinsic factors																			
Economic	**Success factors**																		
	Favourable/stable macroeconomic environment	x	x	x		x	x	x	x			x	x		x	x	x		12
	Available financial market	x	x	x		x	x	x				x	x			x	x		10
	Sound economic policy	x	x			x	x	x				x	x			x	x		9
	Favourable investment environment						x			x								x	3
	Obstacles																		
	Lack of competition				x		x												2
Legal/Political	**Success factors**																		
	Strong governmental and political support	x	x	x		x	x	x		x		x	x		x	x	x		12
	Favorable legal framework	x	x			x	x	x			x	x	x		x	x	x		11
	Government involvement by providing guarantee/ government support	x	x	x		x		x				x	x		x	x	x		10
	Good governance	x	x			x	x	x				x	x			x	x		9
	Stable political environment/system			x			x		x						x	x			5
	Judicious government control			x			x		x										3
	Obstacles																		
	Lack of well-established or inadequate legal/regulatory frameworks				x		x												2
	Confusion over government and evaluation criteria											x							1
	Country risk													x					1
	Excessive restrictions on participation											x							1
	Lack of clear government objectives and commitment						x												1
	Lengthy delays because of political debate											x							1
	Low credibility of government policies						x												1
Social	**Success factors**																		
	Societal support	x	x			x		x				x	x			x	x		8
	Stable social environment			x			x		x										3
	Community outreach						x			x									2
	Consideration of environmental, safety and health responsibilities										x								1
	Obstacles																		
	Public opposition				x		x												2
	Lack of flexibility				x														1
	National cultural differences													x					1

Figure 13: Extrinsic critical success factors by publication.

2.3.2 Intrinsic Factors

In the following Chapters 2.3.2.1 to 2.3.2.4 will be presented the different kinds of intrinsic factors pursuant to the self-defined hierarchy of CSFs in Figure 12.

2.3.2.1 Intrinsic Factors – Interpersonal CSFs

The interpersonal intrinsic factors describe how stakeholders, in particular managers and operative personnel of PPPs, should behave and deal with each other to make partnership implementation successful. In extant literature, interpersonal CSFs refer mainly to team behavior and collaboration as well as to characteristics, which account for a good relationship between PPP partners. Others refer to what should be expected from managers to lead a PPP in a good direction.

Long-term commitment and assuming responsibility by both public and private partners in a joint partnership is one combined factor, which has been mentioned by several previous studies (cf. Babatunde et al., 2012; Leiringer, 2006; Osei-Kyei and Chan, 2015). Commitment is what Johnson et al. (2002, p. 1143) define as "...the belief in and acceptance of organizational goals and values, a willingness to exert effort on behalf of the organization, and a desire to maintain organizational membership". They found that establishing fair and transparent decision-making processes is essential to achieving stakeholders' commitment to the PPP and towards the other partners. Commitment positively impacts on partners' credibility, which in turn forms a good basis for prospective partnerships and potentially attracts new partners (cf. Almarri, 2017; Mota and Moreira, 2015). By contrast, lack of commitment or commitment symmetry are serious threats to successful partnership implementation and may lead to the lack of trust, which is considered as one of the major impediments in interpersonal relationships, such as PPPs (cf. Gupta et al., 2013; Jamali, 2004; Langfield-Smith and Smith, 2003; Trafford and Proctor, 2006). The level of trust influences the choice of MC mechanisms applied to the PPP and is relevant for determining the potential or actual risk of opportunistic behavior by PPP partners, which harms a PPPs overall performance and successful implementation (cf. Dekker, 2004; Langfield-Smith, 2008; Langfield-Smith and Smith, 2003). A higher level of trust strengthens interpersonal ties, eases coordination and negotiation and reduces TC (cf. Zhang Y. and Rajagopalan, 2002). A complementary factor to build and promote trust is open, honest and effective communication (cf. Glagola and Sheedy, 2002; Jacobson and Choi, 2008). Thus, the analysis of the interpersonal intrinsic factors reveals that they are highly complementary and can mutually reinforce each other. A complete overview of interpersonal intrinsic factors is given in Figure 14.

		Publication numbers:	1	2	3	4	7	8	9	11	12	13	15	16	17	19	20	21	22	23	27	28	29	30	31	32	35	Total
Intrinsic factors - interpersonal																												
		Success factors																										
Interpersonal	Management	Direction and good leadership																			x			x				2
Interpersonal	Management	Incentives											x										x					2
Interpersonal	Management	Top management commitment													x													1
Interpersonal	Relationship Characteristics	Commitment (and responsibility of public and private sector)	x	x	x		x		x		x	x	x					x	x	x	x					x		13
Interpersonal	Relationship Characteristics	Open, honest and effective communication and trust							x		x		x	x							x		x	x				7
Interpersonal	Relationship Characteristics	Fairness and respect									x		x	x														3
Interpersonal	Relationship Characteristics	Attitude											x										x					2
Interpersonal	Relationship Characteristics	Expectation of excellence							x				x															2
Interpersonal	Relationship Characteristics	Respecting goals of other participants							x				x															2
Interpersonal	Relationship Characteristics	Taking responsibility							x				x															2
Interpersonal	Relationship Characteristics	Decisions are reached in a participative way																						x				1
Interpersonal	Relationship Characteristics	Good partners' relationship				x																						1
Interpersonal	Relationship Characteristics	Partners have adequate confidence in each other's cooperation																							x			1
Interpersonal	Team Behavior	Collaborative working and sharing resources			x				x				x					x										4
Interpersonal	Team Behavior	Teambuilding											x										x					2
Interpersonal	Team Behavior	Willingness to compromise/collaborate									x		x															2
Interpersonal	Team Behavior	Willingness to improve processes			x								x															2
Interpersonal	Team Behavior	Relationships are cooperative rather than competitive																						x				1
Interpersonal	Team Behavior	Work together in teams																						x				1
		Obstacles																										
Interpersonal	General	Lack of trust			x				x		x		x	x		x	x					x	x	x				10
Interpersonal	General	Potential and risk of opportunistic behaviour by one or more partners and exploitation of a dependance relationship						x		x						x	x										x	5
Interpersonal	General	Partners spend too much of their time discussing and lose sight of the important business issues								x																		1

Figure 14: Interpersonal intrinsic factors by publication.

2.3.2.2 Intrinsic Factors – Inherent/Structural CSFs

The inherent/structural intrinsic factors describe overarching challenges and problems of PPPs which are inherent to PPPs' nature, which need to be addressed by high-level stakeholders and managers rather than by operational staff, which can be countervailed by appropriate project internal procedures to a limited extent only, and/or which might not be solved shortly. In extant literature, alignment of project partners' individual objectives, responsibility sharing, effective risk management and strategy building have been identified as major categories of CSFs and obstacles alike.

A baseline condition for successful PPP project implementation is goal alignment that implies shared goals on the one hand and consideration of partners' individual benefits and objectives on the other hand (cf. Babatunde et al., 2012; Chou and Pramudawardhani, 2015; Li B. et al., 2005a; Hardcastle, 2006; Tang W. et al., 2006). As part of an overall strategy, goals and targets of PPPs should be clear to each stakeholder from the outset in order to promote effective collaboration and efficient resource allocation as well as to capitalize on the skills and competences of the respective private and public partners (cf. Jamali, 2004; Osei-Kyei and Chan, 2015; Trafford and Proctor, 2006). Furthermore, shared goals should come along with shared authority between public and private sector partners (cf. Chou and Pramudawardhani, 2015; Li B., 2003; Yuan et al., 2009), based on clear role and responsibility assignment (cf. Chan et al., 2004; Gupta et al., 2013, Jacobson and Choi, 2008), because otherwise operational risks may result (cf. Hwang et al., 2013). In this context, appropriate risk allocation is the success factor, which has been mentioned most often in this intrinsic factor category (cf. Almarri, 2017; Babatunde et al., 2012; Chan et al., 2010a; Li B. et al., 2005a; Osei-Kyei and Chan, 2015). Chou and Pramudawardhani (2005) and Hwang et al. (2013) emphasize that diligent and reasonable risk identification and allocation should be executed at an early stage of project implementation and be reflected by the contractual arrangements. The reason for this is that coherent risk management proved to be one of the most vital factors of success or failure of PPPs. Obstacles, which have not yet been mentioned often in extant literature but which might also affect PPPs between private sector firms and IOs or DCAs, are for instance lack of experience and suitable skills, cultural and geographical distance or organizational complexity. By nature, they are strongly inherent in partnerships projects where public and private entities are coming together. Usually, those obstacles cannot be removed in the short run, but can be overcome through repeated collaboration in the long run (cf. Chan et al., 2010b; Chen D. et al., 2009; Li B., 2003; Zhang Y. and Rajagopalan, 2002). A complete overview of inherent/structural intrinsic factors is given in Figure 15.

		Publication numbers:	1	2	4	5	6	7	10	11	12	13	14	15	16	19	20	21	22	23	26	27	29	30	32	33	35	Total
Intrinsic factors - inherent/structural																												
Inherent/Structural		**Success factors**																										
	Defi-nition	Clear boundaries													x													1
		Mission and objectives																						x				1
	Goal Alignment	Multi-benefit objectives	x	x				x				x							x	x					x			7
		Sharing common goals							x					x									x					3
		Clear (delineation of) targets and goals													x							x						2
		Clear shared expectations							x					x														2
		Each of the partners' objectives will be met								x																		1
	Responsibility Sharing	Shared authority between public and private sectors	x	x				x				x	x						x	x					x			8
		Clear roles and responsibilities						x			x		x	x								x						5
		Shared responsibility between public and private sectors			x						x		x															3
	Risk Management	Appropriate risk allocation and sharing	x	x	x			x			x	x	x	x					x	x	x	x			x	x		14
		Risk awareness									x			x														2
		Risk transfer												x				x										2
		Improved risk profile											x															1
	Strategy	Specific plan/vision									x			x														2
		Business diversification			x																							1
		Strategy formation																						x				1
		Strategy implementation																						x				1
		Obstacles																										
	General	Lack of suitable skills and experience				x							x						x									3
		Differences in partners' objectives and orientations														x	x											2
		Distance from their subsidiaries (e.g., in terms of culture, administration, geography and economy					x																					1
		Lack of (coherent) alliance strategies																						x				1
		Organizational complexity																									x	1
	Risk	High level of risk associated with alliances														x	x											2
		High risk relying on private sector																	x									1
		Misallocation of risks				x																						1

Figure 15: Inherent/structural intrinsic factors by publication.

2.3.2.3 *Intrinsic Factors – Procedural CSFs*

The procedural intrinsic factors describe how project internal procedures should be designed and practiced to make partnership implementation successful. Compared to the inherent/structural CSFs, the procedural CSFs concentrate less on the broad lines of PPPs but on their operational implementation. In extant literature, procedural CSFs refer mainly to the customized design of governance and MC mechanisms and processes and to accurate planning and staffing of PPPs. Legal frameworks act as supporting elements of PPP's specifics with respect to efficient and effective implementation because poor actual processes and high costs hamper project internal procedures and therefore form major obstacles.

Coming from the corner of infrastructure PPPs, numerous authors touched upon governance issues of PPPs and highlighted the importance of competitive, efficient and transparent procurement processes to be implemented in partnership projects (cf. Almarri, 2017; Hardcastle et al., 2006; Li B. et al., 2005a; Osei-Kyei and Chan, 2015). However, this notion can also be transferred to the investigated PPP projects in this study and be extended to project internal processes in general. The reasons are mainly the strong requirement for competitive and transparent procedures to meet compliance rules and anti-bribery laws, in particular from the public sector's side in terms of partner selection and tendering, and all stakeholders' call for value for money and efficient use of resources (cf. Babatunde et al., 2012; Gupta et al., 2013; Jamali, 2004). These approaches go along with diligent and realistic assessment of benefits and costs that result for each partner involved (cf. Babatunde et al., 2012; Chou and Pramudawardhani, 2015; Li et al., 2005a; Yuan et al., 2009). Clear contract documents including adequate dispute or problem resolution mechanisms serve for the achievement of compliance and the overcoming of procedural challenges and disagreements between project partners (cf. Chan et al., 2004; Glagola and Sheedy, 2002; Jacobson and Choi, 2008; Langfield-Smith and Smith, 2003). All these financial, legal and procedural implications of PPPs should be addressed by effective trust-building and risk-reducing MC mechanisms that are underlying partnership operations. Thus, MC forms a CSF itself (cf. Chan et al., 2010a; Langfield-Smith, 2008; Langfield-Smith and Smith, 2003; Li P. et al., 2013). A complete overview of procedural intrinsic factors is given in Figure 16.

		Publication numbers:	1	2	3	4	5	7	9	10	12	13	14	15	16	19	20	22	23	24	26	27	29	30	32	Total
Intrinsic factors - procedural																										
		Success factors																								
Procedural	Governance and Management Control	Competitive, efficient and transparent procurement process	x	x		x		x			x	x	x					x	x		x	x			x	12
		Thorough and realistic cost/benefit assessment	x	x				x				x						x	x						x	7
		Effective and suitable management control systems in place				x										x	x			x						4
		Appropriate governance structures														x	x									2
		Consistent Monitoring													x							x				2
		Monitoring of the partnering process			x									x												2
		Subcontractor involvement			x									x												2
		Financial accountability																				x				1
		Measureable output performance													x											1
		Specific reporting and record keeping requirements													x											1
		Streamline approval process																				x				1
		Strong central structure at the level of central administration													x											1
	Legal	Creation of conflict resolution strategy and implementation of a dispute/problem resolution mechanism			x					x				x									x			4
		Clarification of contract documents						x					x								x					3
		Reasonable relaxation of contract requirements								x				x												2
	Planning and Staffing	Appropriate project identification and planning including clear project brief and client requirements				x																x				2
		Expert advice and review									x			x												2
		Selection of a reliable and competent partner							x													x				2
		Middle managers to develop plans for joint activities																						x		1
		Operational personnel, who carry out the day-to-day work of the alliance																						x		1
		Top management to develop broad goals and monitor progress																						x		1
		Obstacles																								
	Actual Processes	Lengthy negotiation processes					x						x					x								3
		Poor transparency in diverse process, such as concessionaire/ project partner selection									x				x											2
		Complex decision making									x															1
		Poor risk management									x															1
		Reduction of the project accountability																x								1
	Costs	High participation costs											x					x								2
		High project costs																x								1
		High transaction costs					x																			1

Figure 16: Procedural intrinsic factors by publication.

2.3.2.4 *Intrinsic Factors – General CSFs*

The general intrinsic factors address cross-cutting issues that do not clearly fit into one of the three other intrinsic factor categories. They range from details on the financial endowment and stability of PPPs to fundamental questions regarding the way of project implementation and related requirements.

On the financial side, Chan et al. (2010a) and Zhang X. (2005) stress the importance of the economic viability of PPP projects, which should go along with a solid financial basis including a viable percentage of equity and solvent private sector partners (cf. Gupta et al., 2013; Jacobson and Choi, 2008; Osei-Kyei and Chan, 2015; Tang W. et al., 2006). Before implementation, the project's technical feasibility and questions on technology transfer should be clarified (cf. Almarri, 2017; Babatunde et al., 2012; Yuan et al., 2009). A basic prerequisite of PPPs is that there is the necessity or demand to realize them (cf. Gupta et al., 2013; Osei-Kyei and Chan, 2015). Openness towards innovation by the public sector and the provision of innovative technologies by the private sector partners are conducive in this context (cf. Chan et al., 2004; Osei-Kyei and Chan, 2015). Other repeatedly underlined requirements for successful PPP projects are a well-organized public agency on the one hand and strong private sector partners on the other hand (cf. Chou and Pramudawardhani, 2015; Hardcastle et al., 2006; Hwang et al., 2013; Li B. et al., 2005a; Osei-Kyei and Chan, 2015; Yuan et al., 2009). A complete overview of general intrinsic factors is given in Figure 17.

		Publication numbers:	1	2	3	4	5	7	11	12	13	14	15	22	23	26	27	29	32	33	36	Total
Intrinsic factors - general																						
		Success factors																				
General	Finan-cing	Economic viability				x				x			x			x				x		5
		Equity											x			x		x				3
		Sound financial package								x			x							x		3
	Implemen-tation	Project technical feasibility	x	x				x			x			x	x							6
		Technology transfer				x									x				x			3
		Environmental impact of the project															x					1
	Requirement	Well-organized public agency	x	x				x			x	x		x	x		x		x			9
		Innovation			x								x				x					3
		Strong private consortium	x					x							x		x					4
		Necessity for the project								x							x					2
		Better value for money										x										1
		Compatibility skills of the involved parties															x					1
		High level of know-how from both partners														x						1
		Obstacles																				
	Financing	Financial capacity of the private sector								x							x				x	3
		Expected debt paying ability of the project								x											x	2
		Difficulties in seeking financial partners					x															1
		Disagreements about cost allocations							x													1

Figure 17: General intrinsic factors by publication.

2.3.3 Interim Conclusion

From the extant literature it can be concluded that multiple interlinked and mutually reinforcing extrinsic and intrinsic factors impact upon PPP projects and are vital for their successful implementation or failure. Many factors, such as commitment, costs, financing, risk allocation or trust can be success factors and obstacles at the same time, depending on how they are managed and pronounced in the different PPP projects. Each PPP is individual and can face different challenges and be subject to different limitations, such as number and types of stakeholders involved, complexity of the addressed issue, available financial and non-financial resources, geographical scope, etc. Thus, each PPP project is affected to varying degrees by the identified CSFs and requires management decisions that are customized to its specific needs and circumstances. Further CSFs will be explored by this study. Although this chapter differentiates between extrinsic and intrinsic factors for analysis purposes, in practice decision-makers should take them into account alike.

2.4 Interim Summary and Research Gap

The present, systematic literature review reveals that research on MC in PPPs, JVs, and IORs is generally strongly rooted in accounting literature, followed by articles published in general management/international business and public administration/public management journals. However, only four of the MC-centered articles explicitly focus on PPPs while much more of them deal with JVs, which are both sorts of IORs that have been studied under that term by numerous articles as well. When the focus is narrowed to business partnerships for development, involving internationally operating public actors, such as IOs and DCAs, which are at the center of analysis in this thesis, that picture further changes. Only four out of 159 reviewed articles analyze those kinds of PPPs against the background of MC issues, and only Rahaman et al. (2010) place explicit focus on MC. Thematically related, existing literature mainly reviews and assesses from a business ethics (cf. Reed and Reed, 2009; Utting and Zammit, 2009) or general management (cf. Kolk et al., 2008; Stadtler and Probst, 2012) perspective, without making reference to MC. However, the fact that pertinent MC issues of PPPs, JVs, and IORs are discussed from diverse perspectives, by different types of journals and by means of very diverse practical examples, shows and underlines the interdisciplinary character of PPPs, which should be also considered for the design of the empirical part of this research study.

In general, there is no clear dominance of the empirical approach vs. the non-empirical one, concerning research design and methodology. This picture changes with respect to the MC-centered studies about three quarters of which are empirical. Pursuing a mixed methods approach in half of them, interviews form the dominant method to collect data, followed by surveys. In all MC-centered field study-based articles researchers carried out interviews. Thus, interviews seem to be an appropriate mechanism to generate empirical data for this research study.

Across all reviewed studies 67%, and from the MC-centered studies 36%, apparently have not applied a theoretical framework and discussed their findings on the basis of such. However, among those studies that used one, the TCE turned out to be the dominant theoretical framework applied, in particular in MC-related research, either standing alone or combined with other theories from NIE. This evidence is in line with the findings of Meira et al. (2010) who recommend adopting organizational and social theories, such as institutional or actor-network theories, instead of neo-classical economics, as a framework to study IORs. That is why the TCE forms an appropriate theoretical framework to this research study, irrespective of its use as single reference framework or in a combined manner with another theoretical approach.

Most studies with specific geographic focus have analyzed PPPs, JVs, and IORs in anglophone western countries and in the so-called BRIC states, especially China. Some pursued a comparative approach with either a binational or multinational focus. Thus, PPPs, JVs, and IORs are not only implemented at international level but raise and also deserve research interest by the global management accounting and control research community. Moreover, this literature shows that there is abundant potential to gather MC-related experiences with PPPs, JVs, and IORs from many other parts of the world, in particular from Africa, Asia, Europe and Latin America.

In conclusion, there is very little empirical and theory-based research on strategic PPPs for development from a MC perspective. No study has been found that explicitly focuses on MC in PPPs between the private sector, IOs and/or DCAs. The present study aims to close this research gap.

3. Control Archetypes and Typologies

This section gives an overview of archetypes and types of controls which have been discussed in the literature and applied to previous empirical studies, particularly on IORs including PPPs and JVs. “Control archetypes can be defined as a characteristic, discrete configuration of control devices that is descriptively and theoretically representative of a significant group of observable management control structures and practices” (Speklé, 2001, p. 427). Speklé underlines that control archetypes differ with respect to costs and benefits, efficiency and problem-solving capacity. Synonymously used terms are control typology or control taxonomy (cf. Caglio and Ditillo, 2008; Chalos and O'Connor (2004, 2005)). The research on different control archetypes is roughly marked by the following elements:

- Control dimensions (control extant/tightness, control mechanisms and control focus),
- Control levels,
- Control mechanisms (formal vs. informal) and
- Environmental factors (e.g. culture and control problems)

In addition to these elements,

- JV-specific control typologies and
- The relationship of risk and trust with control

have been particularly discussed by previous literature.

In the following, the different control archetypes including their complements will be analyzed in more detail and their interdependencies explained. The basis for this discussion forms Figure 18, which shows how the control dimensions, the types of control mechanisms, the control levels as well as environmental factors are linked to each other. A more detailed analysis of these elements follows in the subsequent chapters.

T. S. Konrad, *Management Control in Public-Private Partnerships*,
Schriften zu Wirtschaftsprüfung, Steuerlehre und Controlling,
https://doi.org/10.1007/978-3-658-22868-2_3

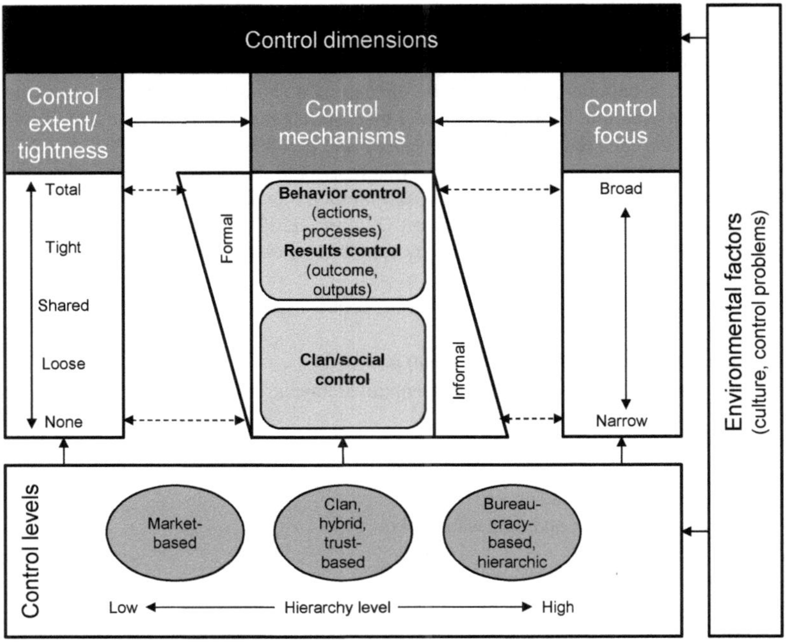

Figure 18: Control archetypes.
(Source: following Giacobbe and Booth (2009) and based on Abdul-Aziz (2012); Appuhami et al., 2011; Caglio and Ditillo, 2008; Das and Teng, 2001a; Dekker, 2004; Donada and Nogatchewsky, 2006; Groot and Merchant, 2000; Kamminga and VdM, 2007; Langfield-Smith, 2008; Langfield-Smith and Smith, 2003; Li P. et al., 2013; Liu X. et al., 2014; VdM and Vosselman, 2000).

3.1 Control Dimensions

The extant literature, primarily from JV research, has identified three control dimensions,

- control mechanisms,
- control extent/tightness and
- control focus,

which broadly characterize the MC mechanisms implemented in different kinds of IORs and which are interrelated with each other. Three major control levels and environmental factors, such as the relationship between control and culture and control problems, influence them (cf. Cäker and Siverbo, 2011; Geringer und Hebert, 1989; Giacobbe and Booth, 2009; Groot and Merchant, 2000; Kamminga and VdM, 2007; Li P. et al., 2013).

Control mechanisms are devices through which control is exercised (cf. Li P. et al., 2013). Typically, they are differentiated by formal and informal controls. Their extents and uses vary with the control tightness and the control focus applied. The tighter control is exerted and the more comprehensive the control focus taken is, the more use is made of formal controls. By contrast, loose control extent and narrow control focus imply the use of informal control. However, hybrid modes including a combination of formal and informal controls are common and particularly used in JVs. Clan, personnel and social controls are characteristic for informal controls while behavior and results control represent formal control mechanisms (cf. Berry et al., 2009; Cäker and Siverbo, 2011; Das and Teng, 2001a; Ouchi, 1979). Outcome controls can be both, formal and informal (cf. Langfield-Smith and Smith, 2003). The different types of control mechanisms will be discussed in Chapter 3.3.

Control extent or tightness describes the degree to which actors control one another, or to which parents exercise control in e.g. JVs (cf. Cäker and Siverbo, 2011; Li P. et al., 2013). This degree ranges between two extreme dichotomous variables; total control, which usually goes along with strong formal control mechanisms, and no control of any kind. However, extant literature provides more support to the continuous variables of loose, shared and tight control (cf. Giacobbe and Booth, 2009). Groot and Merchant (2000) point out that tighter control is often accompanied by significant punishments or rewards, linked to the achievement or non-achievement of (often short-term) objectives, whereas Kamminga and VdM (2007) consider determination of control tightness as less evident as it may be assumed. They argue that exercising tight controls can diminish flexibility of JVs and be applied in a direct, indirect or subtle manner. They contend that high control complexity in JVs typically is accompanied by loose control tightness while tight control is applied to JVs with medium and little control complexity requirements. However, whether controls are tight or not is also a matter of perception. If one partner or party is entitled to approve or make key decisions, control might be perceived as tight by those who do not have these rights and power (cf. Groot and Merchant, 2000). Determinants of the degree of control tightness in IORs are for instance the desired level of certainty in JVs or environmental factors, such as the level of uncertainty and information asymmetry. Factors like the ownership of critical resources or technology or the possession of crucial knowledge of business and operational processes enable those partners to implement a tight control regime (cf. Giacobbe and Booth, 2009; Kamminga and VdM, 2006; Li P. et al., 2013).

Control focus refers to the latitude and scope of control. A broader focus means that all or at least many activities and processes are subject to informal and/or formal control mechanisms while under a narrow focus control is confined to a limited range of critical processes and activities (cf. Cäker and Siverbo, 2011; Giacobbe and Booth, 2009; Li P. et al., 2013). To measure control focus, Giacobbe and Booth (2009) suggest setting the number of managers deployed to a JV relative to the number of partners involved. Analogous to control tightness, Kamminga and VdM (2007) contend that the control focus depends on the level of control complexity. They state that in case of little to medium control complexity the control focus is placed on activities and output while relationship aspects and input enjoy more emphasis if control complexity is high. In the same vein, Chalos and O'Connor (2004) argue that diverging control foci of partners vary with their respective relative knowledge, impacting on control tightness accordingly. Hence, like for the control extent/tightness aspects that are difficult to balance, compensate or eliminate in the short to medium run, such as an IOR's complexity and basic conditions like partners' skills and competences, strongly influence the control focus that should be adjusted to an IOR's specific activities and processes.

3.2 Control Levels

Extant literature differentiates between three discrete levels of control, which are strongly rooted in TCE where they are considered as levels of governance (Williamson (1996, 1999)). For the control levels, different terms are used. However, they have roughly the same meaning, but their foci slightly differ. The different control levels themselves range from low to high hierarchy levels. The chosen control level regime determines the control dimensions.

Control levels	Representative studies
Market (governance) Bureaucracy (governance) Hybrid (governance)	Abdul-Aziz (2012); Berry et al. (2009); Speklé (2001)
Market Bureaucratic Clan	Appuhami et al. (2011); Håkansson and Lind (2004); Liu X. et al. (2014); Ouchi (1979)
Market-based pattern Bureaucratic-/Hierarchical-based pattern Alternative pattern	Caglio and Ditillo (2008); Speklé (2001)
Market-based pattern Bureaucracy-based pattern Trust-based pattern	Donada and Nogatchewsky (2006); Langfield-Smith and Smith (2003); VdM and Vosselman (2000)

Table 11: Terminologies of control levels in extant literature.

Despite different terminologies used for the three control levels, Table 11 makes obvious that there is more or less consensus among researchers about the meaning of the two extreme control types, market-based and bureaucratic or hierarchical control pattern. Bureaucracy and hierarchy are used synonymously in this context. Concerning control levels between these extremes, the discussion is more diverse, ranging from hybrid governance to clan control and alternative and trust-based control pattern. These control levels are not mutually exclusive but can be used interchangeably or simultaneously (cf. Berry et al., 2009; Mouritsen and Thrane, 2006). Subsequently, the three discrete control levels will be briefly explained. Their strong linkages with TCE will be explained in the theoretical framework of Chapter 4.

3.2.1 Market-based Control Pattern

Under a market-based control regime, competition between different organizations creates control (cf. Berry et al., 2009; Williamson, 1973). Hence, market mechanisms exercise the control function (cf. Abdul-Aziz, 2012). If these are working efficiently and effectively, no formal control mechanisms, such as detailed contracts or institutional factors (e.g. norms, values), are required for achieving control. Otherwise, hierarchy or hybrid control patterns are appropriate (cf. Caglio and Ditillo, 2008; Langfield-Smith and Smith, 2003; Speklé, 2001).

3.2.2 Bureaucracy and Hierarchy Control Pattern

Under a bureaucracy or hierarchy-based control regime, the exercising authority and power creates control, followed by evaluation and surveillance. The latter are combined with straight administrative means of control, such as incentive-setting and monitoring. Social controls including trust play a secondary role (cf. Abdul-Aziz, 2012; Berry et al., 2009; Langfield-Smith and Smith, 2003; Speklé, 2001; VdM and Vosselman, 2000; Williamson, 1973).

3.2.3 Hybrid Control Pattern

Under a hybrid-based control regime, control is exercised less formal and rigid. Those regimes are often applied to different types of IORs where partners or networks assume rather informal control functions (cf. Berry et al., 2009; Williamson, 1973). In this context, social controls and outcome controls play a major role for achieving control objectives as they reduce the need for formal contracts and can exert a risk-reducing impact (cf. Abdul-Aziz, 2012; Langfield-Smith and Smith, 2003). Trust is seen as a crucial element for achieving control in hybrid governed IORs (cf. Cooper and Slagmulder, 2004; Tomkins, 2001; VdM and Vosselman (2000, 2006)). Due to the comprehensive discussion regarding the relationship of control with trust and risk, a separate analysis follows in Chapter 3.6.

3.3 Control Mechanisms

In this section, different formal and informal control mechanisms will be discussed for the three discrete control levels and further clustered by typical lifecycle phases of IORs including subtypes. The predominant view in organizational research is that all MCS are composed of formally written and informally unwritten controls (cf. Langfield-Smith, 2008). The tripartite splitting of control mechanisms originates from research on organizational control, depending on what type of control is aimed at influencing in an IOR context (e.g. asset protection, uncertainty reduction) (cf. Chen et al., 2009; Speklé, 2001).
The analysis of types of control mechanisms in this chapter proceeds tripartite. First, formal and informal control mechanisms will be briefly defined. Second, the different formal and informal control mechanisms including their characteristics will be outlined. In the third step, concrete, phase-oriented control activities and measures will be listed. In addition, a short analysis of the TCE-oriented view on control mechanisms follows in the theory part of this study in Chapter 4.2.2.

3.3.1 Formal Control

Two modes characterize formal control, which is also labelled as hierarchic or bureaucratic control. Either actions (behavior control) or the results (outcomes or output) of these actions (results, outcome or output control) are measured. Behavior control is supposed to ensure that processes are working properly and actions are taken compliantly. By contrast, results control (also called outcome or output control) focuses on reliable and accurate performance measurement (cf. Cäker and Siverbo, 2011; Das and Teng, 2001a; Langfield-Smith and Smith, 2003). The use of formal controls is typically based on formal policies, procedures and rules and goes along with tight contractual obligations (cf. Das and Teng, 2001a; Dekker, 2004). Exercising formal control requires that managers in crucial positions, such as controllers, know important interorganizational processes, have access to relevant data and are able to measure outcomes and outputs (cf. Chen et al., 2009). In general, outcome control is assumed to be appropriate when output is precisely measurable but task programmability is low while behavior controls are suitable in the reverse case (cf. Langfield-Smith, 2008; Langfield-Smith and Smith, 2003).

- *Results control* aims at motivating decision-makers (e.g. managers) to pursue and meet strategic objectives and goals (cf. Cäker and Siverbo, 2011; Chalos and O'Connor, 2004; Groot and Merchant, 2000). These control mechanisms determine outputs to be achieved by the IOR including its partners and require implementing monitoring mechanisms for precise performance measurement (cf. Dekker, 2004). This enables decision-makers to pay attention to key performance measures. A drawback is that this close monitoring leaves little margin for preferring long-term targets over short-term objectives (cf. Das and Tang, 2001a).
- *Behavior control* aims at monitoring and directing behavior and processes with respect to achieving intended results, based on proper actions that comply with predetermined behavior (cf. Cäker and Siverbo, 2011; Chalos and O'Connor, 2004; Dekker, 2004; Langfield-Smith, 2008). Suitable boundaries are set for behavior (cf. Emsley and Kidon, 2007). That is why behavior control is also called process control (cf. Das and Teng, 2001a). The inclusion of behavior and process control mechanisms in IOR contracts requires a high degree of behavior observability. Otherwise, the involved stakeholders are unlikely to ensure effective control (cf. Chen et al., 2009).

3.3.2 Informal Control

This form of control is based on the idea that a common culture, organizational norms, customs and values contribute to increasing goal congruence and to the alignment of individual interests among participating partners. Two informal control mechanisms are social and clan control, which have both been used synonymously in previous studies (cf. Das and Teng, 2001a; Langfield-Smith, 2008; Liu et al., 2014). Informal control is linked to the development of trustful relationships as well as to informal systems and cultures, which evolve over time, adopt a self-regulation character and can engender some familiarity among partners (cf. Dekker, 2004; Emsley and Kidon, 2007). The meaning of culture in the context of MC is not that clear. In their study on emerging themes in MC, Berry et al. (2009, p. 12) formulated three propositions about the nexus between control and culture:

(1) Culture is dominated by control; it is up to managers to build, choose or design an organizational culture.
(2) Culture is control; the establishment of cognitions, norms or values influences the entire organization. If necessary, control can reconstitute and maintain culture.

(3) Culture dominates control; social control mechanisms decisively influence control procedures and structures. Intercultural-bound different control practices have been identified in diverse countries.

Hence, this tripartite nexus between culture and control underlines the complexity that national and organizational culture can imply for MC and therefore influence how extensively informal controls are used in an organization. Complementary to culture is trust, or the degree of trust, that influences the extent to which formal controls are necessary in order to ensure contract compliance and to prevent opportunism. Hence, trust can assume a pivotal coordination function in IORs with more informal and social control structures, where output measurability and understanding of transformation processes are low, and where tasks are not precisely specified (cf. Das and Teng, 2001a; Dekker, 2003; Kamminga and VdM, 2006; Langfield-Smith, 2008).

Social control (or clan control) can be found in all organizations but to different degrees. Social control does not predetermine any desired output or appropriate behavior, but aims at contributing to consensus-building among members as well as developing shared beliefs, norms and values, which are accompanied by commitment to the joint activities. In contrast to formal controls, social control cannot be simply designed but evolves over time and is influenced and shaped by different social activities (cf. Das and Teng, 2001a; Emsley and Kidon, 2007; Langfield-Smith and Smith, 2003; Ouchi, 1979). The existence of social mechanisms and channels is a prerequisite for that (cf. Chen et al., 2009).

3.3.3 Market Control

This form of control can be applied across all phases of a typical IOR lifecycle. Market control is neither formal nor informal because it is based on market mechanisms and is not applicable in bureaucratic/hierarchic or hybrid control patterns. However, it plays a major role at the early stage of a partnership and is mainly applicable to transactions of non-specific but standardized assets (cf. Appuhami et al., 2011). Market-based transactions are usually executed repeatedly and show high output measurability and high task programmability (cf. Langfield-Smith and Smith, 2003). Hence, if one party behaves opportunistically, the betrayed party can easily switch to another supplier, what makes market participants replaceable by one another. Uncertainty is low and alternative partners are numerous so that detailed contracts are not necessary (cf. Langfield-Smith and Smith, 2003).

In general, no special control mechanisms are required insofar the implemented market mechanisms are working effectively (cf. Abdul-Aziz, 2012). Still, a few market control mechanisms are typically employed and commonly comprise financial and output control, which are based on quantifiable and measurable market and accounting data (cf. Liu et al., 2014).

3.3.4 Characteristics of Control Mechanisms

On the basis of the explanations of formal, informal and market control, Table 12 displays characteristics of these different types of control, categorized by control mechanisms and control levels.

Control mechanism	Control level	Characteristics	Reference
Market control			
Market	Market	• Behaviors of control actors • Minimize relational risk	Appuhami et al. (2011)
Formal control			
Behavior/action/process control	Bureaucratic, hierarchic	• Behavior surveillance/Monitoring of ongoing behaviors • Promote desirable and prevent undesirable actions • Reduction of opportunistic behavior and inherent risk • Requires commitment to and compliance with specific actions, policies and procedures, as per contract • Requires specification of processes and behaviors	Chen et al. (2009); Groot and Merchant (2000); Langfield-Smith (2008); Li P. et al. (2013)
Results/outcome/output control	Bureaucratic, hierarchic	• Creating awareness of mutual expectations • Measuring target achievement and rewarding outcomes • Minimizing performance risk (based on performance measurement standards) • Outcome-based performance measurement (e.g. product and service quality, net profit, sales) • Requires explicit goal-setting and outcome targets/requirements • Setting performance incentives • Strengthening goal con-	Appuhami et al. (2011); Cäker and Siverbo (2011); Chalos and O'Connor (2004); Chen et al. (2009); Dekker (2004); Groot and Merchant (2000); Langfield-Smith (2008)

Control mechanism	Control level	Characteristics	Reference
		gruence	
Informal control			
Clan/social control	Hybrid, trust-based	• Aligning diverging goal preferences and partner interests • Appropriate for IORs where parties are tightly collaborating • Balance contractual shortcomings if contracts for controlling long-term IORs are insufficiently detailed • Based on social interactions • Cultural control (e.g. peer control, socialization processes, strengthening social ties) • Ensure ability and willingness to perform and encourage staff to perform well • Influencing embedded values of the controlled parties • Managing and reducing risk from human behavior (e.g. appropriation concerns; relationship and performance risk) • Personnel control (e.g. expatriate staffing, staff appointments) • Promoting trust as well as shared beliefs and values • Requires a lot of communication and interaction through organizational activities • Requires selection of trusting personnel and specified training measures	Appuhami et al. (2011); Cäker and Siverbo (2011); Chalos and O'Connor (2004); Chen et al. (2009); Das and Teng (2001a); Dekker (2004); Groot and Merchant (2000); Langfield-Smith (2008); Li P. et al. (2013); Liu X. et al. (2014); Marques et al. (2011)

Table 12: Types of formal and informal control mechanisms.

Table 12 shows that pertinent MC literature concentrates on formal and informal control while explicit market control mechanisms play a minor role. Among formal and informal control, the characteristics of control mechanisms are manifold but generally have one important commonality: They assume an active and a passive function at the same time. For instance, behavior control mechanisms monitor behavior of IOR partners and therefore try to prompt them to undertake only actions that are in line with the underlying partnership contract. Still, if processes are not specified and the level of commitment by the involved parties is low, behavior and process control lack effectiveness. In terms of results and output control, clearly defined benchmarks form the basis for reasonable measurement of target achievement. In case of informal control, clan and social control mechanisms try to promote commitment, harmony, motivation and trust in a partnership. However, aspects like intrinsic motivation to move the partnership forward together and frequent communication between partners are imperative to make informal controls working.

Usually, PPPs, JVs and IORs projects divide into different phases, ranging from preparatory and initial activities to follow-up measures after project completion. On the basis of the characteristics shown in Table 12, the subsequent Table 13 lists phase-dependent and phase-independent control activities and measures that are typically applied in IORs including subtypes, according to extant literature. The phase-dependent control activities and measures are split in those, which are carried out before contract conclusion or at an initial stage, and those that are applied during execution and implementation. By contrast, the phase-independent activities and measures are time-independent and of phase-overarching nature. A further classification is undertaken by means of the control levels. This approach follows procedures adopted by Abdul-Aziz (2012), Appuhami et al. (2011), Caglio and Ditillo (2008), Dekker (2004), Langfield-Smith and Smith (2003), Liu et al. (2014) as well as VdM and Vosselman (2000) in previous studies on MC.

	Market-based control pattern	Bureaucracy-/Hierarchy-based control pattern	Clan-/Hybrid-/Trust-based control pattern	References
Phase-dependent control activities and measures				
Ex-ante: Exploratory/Contact/Contract phase	• Competitive bidding (to ensure compliance) • Market control (e.g. accounting and financial data) • Specification of output controls (e.g. bids, budget control)	• Behavior controls (e.g. preparation of audit and PPP guidelines, planning, programmes, regulations, rules and SOPs; implementation of authority structures, laws and regulations, meetings, negotiations) • Develop specific selection criteria • Elaborate specific written contracts • Results (e.g. bids, budgets, financial proposals, goal- and incentive-setting, design/technical/quality specifications)	• Establishing a system of trust (including aligning culture, history of previous contracts, localness) • Outcome and social controls • Partner selection (based on competence, interaction, reputation, sincerity, trustworthiness) • Risk allocation between parties and risk-sharing attitude	Abdul-Aziz (2012); Appuhami et al. (2011); Caglio and Ditillo (2008); Chen et al. (2009); Dekker (2004); Langfield-Smith and Smith (2003); Van der Stede (2003); VdM and Vosselman (2000)

	Market-based control pattern	Bureaucracy-/Hierarchy-based control pattern	Clan-/Hybrid-/Trust-based control pattern	References
Ex-post: Execution/Implementation phase	• Competitive bidding upon occasion (due to high switching costs) • Output controls (evaluation and assessment of output regarding e.g. delivery time, quality and quantity)	• Behavior and output monitoring • Behavior controls (e.g. communication with parent partners, degree of delegated decision-making, implementation of authority structures, organizational structuring, policies, procedures, regulations and rules, specified tasks/activities) • Bonds and guarantees • Involvement of local partners • Operational, process, strategic control • Results controls (e.g. budgets, performance goals/targets, rewarding, service standards, specifications as per contract)	• Leadership by example (senior management practices appropriate attitudes, leadership style and rituals) • Outcome and social controls (evolving over time) • Place loyal and qualified staff in key operative positions • Trust-building and -developing activities (e.g., cooperative working behavior, ceremonies, culture, informal negotiations/meetings, partner development, risk- and information-sharing, rituals, social events) • Trust can result from friendship, reputation, or former contractual relationships	Abdul-Aziz (2012); Appuhami et al. (2011); Caglio and Ditillo (2008); Cäker and Siverbo (2011); Chalos and O'Connor (2004); Chen et al. (2009); Chenall (2003); Dekker (2004); Giacobbe and Booth (2009); Groot and Merchant (2000); Langfield-Smith (2008); Langfield-Smith and Smith (2003); Liu X. et al. (2014); Marques et al. (2011); Van der-Meer-Kooistra and Vosselman (2000); Van der Stede (2003)

	Market-based control pattern	Bureaucracy-/Hierarchy-based control pattern	Clan-/Hybrid-/Trust-based control pattern	References
Phase-independent activities and measures				
Contract	• No detailed contract (due to standardized output and activities) • Market mechanisms are dominant • Period of contract: rather short-term	• Detailed contract (rather long-term, including elements on dispute resolution, performance evaluation, payment mechanisms, reporting, specific contract terms, renewal and termination of contract) • Hostage arrangements	• Flexible and non-specific contract that evolves over time • Period of contract: rather long-term	Abdul-Aziz (2012); Appuhami et al. (2011); Cäker and Siverbo (2011); Caglio and Ditillo (2008); Langfield-Smith (2008); Langfield-Smith and Smith (2003)
Dispute resolution	• Formally institutional-based (e.g. application of intellectual property rights and contract law)	• Formally agreed procedures, based on contract	• Informally (e.g. by discussions and negotiations)	Abdul-Aziz (2012); Appuhami et al. (2011); Dekker (2004); Marques et al. (2011)
Focus	• Competitive bidding • Market prices linked to standardized outputs and activities	• Approval processes • Laws • Policies • Procedures • Regulations • Rules • Staff policy (selection, training, specification of individual roles)	• Beliefs • Codes of conduct • Common agreements • Culture • Norms • Socialization • Values	Appuhami et al. (2011); Berry et al. (2009); Chen et al. (2009; Langfield-Smith (2008); Langfield-Smith and Smith (2003); Liu et al. X. (2014); Marques et al. (2011)

	Market-based control pattern	Bureaucracy-/Hierarchy-based control pattern	Clan-/Hybrid-/Trust-based control pattern	References
Monitoring	• No particular monitoring	• Creating a board of directors • Detailed reporting (e.g. budgetary) • Direct intervention • Formal meetings and negotiations • Rigid performance targets • Staff surveillance	• (frequent) informal meetings and discussions • Personal consultations • No detailed reporting	Appuhami et al. (2011); Caglio and Ditillo (2008); Cäker and Siverbo (2011); Dekker (2004); Langfield-Smith (2008); VdM and Vosselman, 2000

Table 13: Phase-oriented control mechanisms.
(Clustered by control levels)

Across the three control levels, phase-dependent controls serve to prepare the best possible setting for successful partnership project implementation at the ex-ante stage before contract conclusion. All three levels have in common that there are determined objectives, outputs and/or results to achieve while they differ by their qualitative and quantitative characteristics. In a market-based and hierarchy-based control pattern, MC activities depend more on rather formal agreements including clearly measurable and quantifiable benchmarks, while hybrid patterns evolve over time and allow more flexible assessment of goal achievement. At the ex-post stage, which comprises the actual project implementation, a comparison of the control activities and measures per control level reveals that hierarchy-based and hybrid-based control patterns provide more diverse tools to address complexities and different, long-term oriented types of partnerships. Those patterns place emphasis on the creation of common normative bases that underlie partnerships where all involved partners act together in a collaborative manner, while market-based control patterns promote competition and measure performance mainly by means of efficiency indicators. The little importance that market-based control attaches to monitoring underlines its strong output orientation and is a major difference compared with the two other control patterns, which endorse continuous monitoring during partnership implementation.

3.4 Joint Venture-specific Control Typologies

The literature review revealed that 21 out 50 MC-centered articles specifically refer to JV partnerships. The fact that PPPs are often based on hybrid forms of cooperation underlines the importance that MC evidence from JVs has for PPPs. Complex organizational and contractual structures are characteristic for JVs and form bigger challenges to MC than hierarchy- or market-based forms of cooperation. For this reason, this chapter discusses control typologies that specifically occur in JVs.

Three major control types have been identified for JVs: 1) dominant, 2) independent, and 3) shared control. For IJVs, it is further distinguished between dominant control exercised by the domestic partner or by the foreign partner (cf. Chen et al., 2009; Choi and Beamish,

2004; Li P. et al., 2013; Zhang Y. and Rajagopalan, 2002). The practical implications are as follows:

1) *Dominant control*: one dominant parent partner actively "manages the JV as if it was a wholly owned subsidiary" (Li P. et al., 2013, p. 249) and makes decisions alone. The other parents remain rather passive. The dominant partner aligns control measures and JV activities with own goals. Overarching bodies, such as the board of directors being composed of executive representatives from each parent partner, play a ceremonial rather than a managerial role. In IJVs either the foreign or the local partner exerts dominant control.
2) *Independent control*: managers from one parent partner can make decisions independent from any other parents and exercise control alone. No separate legal JV entity is created.
3) *Shared control*: all parent partners actively manage and control the JV, and managers sent to the board of directors are endowed with influence and decision-making authority.

These control types can be further split up into three categories of control mechanisms which are also either formal or informal, but consider JV-specific characteristics: 1) *Context-oriented control* is typically applied to JVs with a high level of control complexity and comprises informal and culture-based control measures (e.g. strong emphasis on team work, low hierarchy between parent partners' representatives and JV staff). Control tightness is loose. 2) *Content-oriented control* is typically applied to JVs with a low level of control complexity and includes tight formal control measures. Parent partners directly intervene in decision-making and JV activities through the board of directors and the JV's management. 3) *Consultation-oriented control* is typically applied to JVs with a medium level of control complexity and includes tight formal control measures. These controls are process-oriented and enable parent partners to exert control from afar. They use reporting requirements to exert impact upon decision-making processes and planning. For this reason, close personal consultations are necessary in order to coordinate and harmonize complementary contributions and/or diverging interests (cf. Giacobbe and Booth, 2009; Kamminga and VdM, 2007; Meira et al., 2010).

With specific focus on TCE, Chalos and O'Connor (2004, 2005), Firth (1996), Geringer and Hebert (1989), Mjoen and Tallman (1997) and Zhang Y. and Rajagopalan (2002) list a few contractual and managerial controls, which are redundant with or complement behavior, output or social controls from extant literature but have a particular reference to JVs (Table 14).

Controls	Characteristics
Contractual controls	
Accounting safeguards	This mechanism serves for the protection of the partner's core assets and competences and aims to increase venture performance.
Board of directors appointment	The implementation of a shared board aims to diminish partner's TC. Through the board partners intend to implement their particular interests and objectives.
Equity shareholding	Protection of partner assets through equity

Controls	Characteristics
	ownership where majority ownership is linked to performance.
Managerial controls (formal/informal)	
Communications	Communication between partners enhances understanding of mutual SOPs and promotes better performance and technology transfer. Means of good communication are feedback and frequent reporting, which help to create a common understanding about performance expectations and to make the actions-results nexus transparent.
Delegated managerial decision rights	Different kinds of decision-making responsibilities, such as operational or strategic decisions, are delegated from upper levels (e.g. board of directors) to lower levels (middle managers).
Managerial incentives	Managers are rewarded on the basis of their performance. Therefore, they will be motivated to perform and to act in the interest of the JV partner objectives.
Planning and budgeting systems	Budgeting and planning are crucial for financial and operational performance being interlinked with each other. Actual-to-target results reveal information about performance. Joint budgeting and planning of partners promote information sharing and are pivotal for monitoring the achievement of JV performance targets.

Table 14: Contractual and managerial controls in JVs.

The package of contractual and managerial controls that is applied to JV depends particularly on factors, such as differences of parent partners (including goals, management styles, national and organizational cultures), which can cause information asymmetry, the bargaining of partners or the level of trust (cf. Cäker and Siverbo, 2011; Kamminga and VdM, 2007; Liu et al., 2014; Zhang Y. and Li, 2001).

3.5 Control Problems

In extant organizational research literature, several control problems have been identified in IORs including subtypes, and potential solutions have been discussed accordingly. Those underlying problems exert influence upon the choice of control level (or governance level) and on design and implementation of formal and informal control mechanisms (cf. Caglio and Ditillo, 2008; Marques et al., 2011). Table 15 displays four major control problems and their roots.

Control problem	Reasons
Appropriation concerns	Opportunistic behavior of the partners in conjunction with asset specificity, transaction frequency and uncertainty engenders appropriation concerns. If uncertainty is high, parties might be tempted to behave opportunistically and to accept losses at expense of the other parties and therefore to harm the cooperative relationship.
Coordination requirements	Partners have to coordinate activities and resources of the cooperation as well as to mutually adapt. This also includes fair sharing of investments, risks and benefits. Hence, coordination is a complex task when external and internal surrounding factors such as the level of interdependence and uncertainty are high.
(Inter-)dependence	If one partner is unilaterally dependent from another one, there will be an uneven power advantage in favour of the one partner. Thus, the one partner is in a stronger position to determine the control design and to exert control, at expense of the other partner.
Partner experience	Partner experience describes the level of familiarity that cooperating partners gained during previous joint activities, and which can influence the choice of the control or governance level. Repeated interactions and learning usually contribute to strengthening interorganizational ties and to dealing better with complexities and challenges of sharing control and management with other parties. If there are no other control problems, partner experience is not an issue. Otherwise, high partner experience can mitigate other control problems or increase them when partner experience is low. An extensive control level is usually chosen when the control problems are high in total, and vice versa.

Table 15: Control problems.
(Source: Caglio and Ditillo, 2008; Dekker (2003, 2004, 2008); Giacobbe and Booth, 2009; Marques et al., 2011; Mouritsen and Thrane, 2006; Speklé, 2001; VdM and Vosselman, 2006)

To deal with emerging control problems in IORs, Dekker (2004, 2008) proposes to carefully select cooperation partners and to design and implement a suitable governance structure, which facilitates managing interdependent activities and interaction between partners, a key task of coordination (cf. Marques et al., 2011). Mouritsen and Thrane (2006) underpin that higher initial investment in selecting a good partner will lower the need for using formal controls, which can be replaced by alternative mechanisms, such as trust, instead. Therefore, they expect a reduction of the heaviness of appropriation concerns and coordination requirement problems. In other words, opportunistic behavior is less likely to emanate from socially embedded activities or transactions (cf. VdM and Vosselman (2000, 2006)). A high level of partner experience fosters the creation of social embedding and therefore alleviates adverse influences from the three other control problems. If an IOR's control problems are high the level of partner experience is likely to influence MC and governance design, otherwise its impact is rather low because it is less relevant (cf. Dekker, 2008). Compared to the three other control problems, partner experience is not only related to knowhow but also to trust and evolves on a long-term basis. Thus, lack of partner experience cannot be tackled in the short-run and therefore forms a particular challenge to MC.

3.6 Relationship of Risk and Trust with Control

This chapter addresses the particular relationship of risk and trust to which has been pointed at an early stage in Chapter 1.1 already and specifies the different kinds of trust and risk which were raised by the extant literature.

3.6.1 Trust

This subchapter describes first of all the meaning of trust in the context of MC before it provides then an overview of the different dimensions of trust. In a third step the actual relationship between trust and control is illustrated.

3.6.1.1 Definition and Relevance of Trust

In the context of control, trust means "...having confidence that one's expectations will be realized." (Langfield-Smith and Smith, 2003, p. 284), and "...expectations about the likelihood of having a desirable action by the trusted partner" (Donada and Nogatchewsky, 2006, p. 266). Emsley and Kidon (2007, p. 833) also consider trust as "...the psychological state of accepting vulnerability on the basis of positive expectations of the intentions of another's behavior". In this context, Langfield-Smith and Smith (2003, p. 284) add that these positive expectations imply "...adopting a belief, without having full information to confirm that belief." but through which uncertainty can be absorbed and behavioral risks be reduced. Trust can even increase the predictability of the others' behavior (cf. Kamminga and VdM, 2007). Coletti et al. (2005, p. 481) emphasize that trust is not equal to trustworthiness. They consider trustworthiness "...as an innate personal characteristic reflecting one's preference for upholding some norm of behavior, regardless of economic incentives" while trust is "...one's perception of another's trustworthiness". Hence, the level of trust reflects the degree of reliability of the trustee (cf. Vélez, 2008).

Das and Teng (2001a) call trust a "multilevel phenomenon" (p. 255), which occurs at organizational, personal and interorganizational level, both nationally and internationally, and depends on personal and cultural contextual variables within an enabling environment. It can help to cut down costs (e.g. monitoring and coordination costs) in IORs, in particular when the level of interdependence between partners is high and coordination is crucial, like in hybrid relationships. Trust can promote the dissemination of information, which is for instance highly relevant for accounting, and therefore facilitates less detailed contracts, which are otherwise costly in terms of monitoring and enforcement (cf. Berry et al., 2009; Kamminga and

VdM, 2007; Meira et al., 2010; Tomkins, 2001; VdM and Vosselman, 2000; Vosselman and VdM, 2009).

Trust is a dynamic instead of static development process, which evolves over the lifetime of IORs, fostered by continuing interactions between cooperation partners including joint organizational processes and activities. Moreover, trust results from, and may help to promote, mutual adaption and learning, which are vital for a strong and durable relationship, for instance through advocacy for each other's objectives and knowledge exchange (cf. Langfield-Smith, 2008; Langfield-Smith and Smith, 2003; VdM and Vosselman, 2000; Vélez, 2008).

3.6.1.2 Dimensions of Trust

In extant literature, there are three dimensions of trust mainly discussed, as formulated by Sako (1992) and adopted in many MC studies with respect to IORs (cf. Dekker, 2004; Donada and Nogatchewsky, 2006; Emsley and Kidon, 2007). These are competence trust, contractual trust, and goodwill trust.

Competence trust: This form of trust relates to the expectation of one partner regarding appropriate managerial and partnering competences as well as technical ability of the other partner(s) to perform joint activities (cf. Cäker and Siverbo, 2011; Donada and Nogatchewsky, 2006; VdM and Vosselman, 2000; Vélez, 2008). Competence trust is rather robust because abilities and competences do not get easily lost. Moreover, the operational performance is easy to measure and to observe what makes partner's competences and abilities quite transparent. That is why little information is needed to build competence trust, but the threshold for destroying it is high (cf. Emsley and Kidon, 2007).

Contractual trust: This form of trust relates to the assumption that the other partner complies with written and unwritten agreements and underlies ethical codes, such as honesty, loyalty or reciprocity (cf. Donada and Nogatchewsky, 2006; Langfield-Smith and Smith, 2003; VdM and Vosselman, 2000; Vélez, 2008). Just as well as in case of competence trust the institutional environment can promote trust through different mechanisms, such as legal regulations or the certification of the partners' business activities (cf. Langfield-Smith and Smith, 2003).

Goodwill trust: This form of trust relates to the confidence that the other partner contributes to the establishment of mutual interests and objectives and complies with them, even if possibilities of opportunistic behavior arise. So, it is expected that the other partner avoids harmful practices but performs even more than formally agreed (cf. Cäker and Siverbo, 2011; Donada and Nogatchewsky, 2006; VdM and Vosselman, 2000; Vélez, 2008). Moreover, team and individual trust as well as the implementation of joint dispute resolutions promote the development of goodwill trust. Moral characteristics of goodwill trust are dependability, integrity and responsibility (cf. Das and Teng, 2001a). Emsley and Kidon (2007) argue that goodwill trust is difficult to establish and requires a high amount of goodwill-related information. They consider it as fragile as it heavily relies on the alignment of partner's individual interests, which are not set in stone. However, goodwill trust can be useful to overcome information asymmetry (cf. Langfield-Smith and Smith, 2003). Little information about non-compliance or betrayal can induce the destruction of goodwill trust. Das and Teng (2001b) and Langfield-

Smith (2008) established a connection between trust and risk. They contend that goodwill trust impacts upon the partners' perception of relational risk while performance risk is subject to their appraisal of competence trust. At least, it is likely to minimize both types of risk (cf. Appuhami et al., 2011).

Besides goodwill trust and competences trust, Cäker and Siverbo (2011) have identified four more forms of trust in JVs. They further differentiate between horizontal vs. vertical trust, calculative trust and system trust. In case of *horizontal trust*, parent partners trust each other so that less contractual safeguarding is needed (e.g. against competence spill over). By contrast, *vertical trust* means that parent partners trust the JV entity or company, so that a lower level of MC is needed (e.g. because of the JV entity's or company's good performance). *Calculative trust* refers to a situation without incentive to leave the JV partnership or to act opportunistically because of lacking alternatives and high opportunity costs. Thus, parent partners trust each other, knowing that all parties benefit most if they collaborate. *System trust* (alternatively: institutional trust) results from formal institutions and informal rules (e.g. legislative matters and national culture) that establish a society's socio-economic system and set incentives to JV partners to abide by these legal and societal framework conditions. However, despite the further classification of trust by Cäker and Siverbo (2011), horizontal trust bears some proximity to goodwill trust while vertical trust, calculative trust, and system trust result from rational motivations like the JV's performance and clear incentives that are linked to competency trust. To conclude, these four forms of trust serve for more differentiated analyses of trust in IORs and complement the interpretations of goodwill and competency trust.

3.6.1.3 Relationship of Trust with Control

Trust is an informal control mechanism that can contribute to the reduction of coordination costs and to the mitigation of behavioral risks including opportunism. Thus, from a higher level of trust a higher overall control level can result. On the other hand, controls can promote and enhance trust-building through monitoring or information sharing. The higher the level of trust the fewer formal control mechanisms are necessary, which are moreover more costly to implement and to enforce than trust (cf. Abdul-Aziz, 2012; Cäker and Siverbo, 2011; Dekker (2003, 2004); Liu et al., 2014; VdM and Vosselman, 2006). Thus, when costs of hierarchic or market control mechanisms are high, trust can be an efficient alternative as part of a hybrid governance structure (cf. VdM and Vosselman, 2006). Shared values and high social tightness can be used alternatively to minimize the required level of control (cf. Luo, 2007). Langfield-Smith and Smith (2003) hold the view that trust is required to attain control if the measurement of output and activities does not sufficiently produce accurate and reliable results. In addition, increasing trust can positively influence the level and nature of cooperation between partners (cf. Coletti et al., 2005). Ex-ante trust is often a factor that influences decisions with respect to cooperation partner selection (cf. Liu et al., 2014).

Different researchers, such as Kamminga and VdM (2006), Langfield-Smith and Smith (2003) or Nooteboom et al. (1997), have enhanced the TCE by the influence factor *trust* as a potential carrier of control between partners in IORs. It is considered as particularly important for those IORs that are exposed to significant risks and for which risk management is vital (cf. Das and Teng, 2001b; Langfield-Smith, 2008; Sako, 1992).

Berry et al. (2009) have elaborated four different approaches about the relationship between trust and control:

1) Trust as an alternative to control (cf. Dekker, 2003),
2) Effective MCS can contribute to trust-building (cf. Seal et al., 1999),
3) Control practices and structures themselves can be bodies of trust (cf. Mouritsen and Thrane, 2006) and
4) Some control practices presume trust as a necessary requirement (cf. Cooper and Slagmulder, 2004).

With respect to competency and goodwill trust, and with respect to the control dimensions or mechanisms, Emsley and Kidon (2007) argue that at the operational level behavioral, output and social control deliver relevant information to build competency trust. By contrast, goodwill trust generates relevant information through social control mainly at the executive level (e.g. board of directors or steering committee). In practice, goodwill-related information can hardly be produced by output or behavioral controls because information about e.g. practices intended to harm the other parties' interests cannot be considered as an output, and contracts, which are affecting goodwill trust and are supposed to control behavior, can manage uncertainties only to a limited extent.

However, there are also critical voices regarding the impact of trust upon control, saying that the relationship between both is too complex for drawing clear conclusions. Albeit extant literature has revealed either a complementary or a substitutive relationship between control and trust along the lifetime of IOR relationships (cf. Berry et al., 2009; Caglio and Ditillo, 2008; Vosselman and VdM, 2009), some authors are uncertain about whether trust is a proper control type or not. For instance, Emsley and Kidon (2007) and Tomkins (2001) argue that it would be illogical to consider trust as a control because the motivation behind promoting trust in relationships is to avoid using controls, so to use trust instead of control. On the other side, formal control, if excessively used, may harm the level of trust and therefore adversely impact upon durability and stability of the IOR (cf. Vélez, 2008; Vosselman and VdM, 2009). It is probably hard to determine the demarcation line between excessive and conducive use of formal control. However, the view of Neu (1991) and Ring & Van de Ven (1994) that even the use of contracts can be perceived as distrust, is not shared by others (e.g. Vélez, 2008).

A quote from Vosselman and VdM (2009, p. 269) summarizes the discussion about the relationship between control and trust: “control needs trust, and trust needs control”. Thus, it does not matter whether control creates trust, destroys trust, or trust enables control, as outlined by Cäker and Siverbo (2011), because control and trust are mutually dependent and do not stand in an either/or-relationship with each other. Moreover, Mouritsen and Thrane (2006) and Vosselman and VdM (2009) argue that control and trust both pursue common objectives, namely the absorption of opportunistic behavior and related behavioral uncertainty as well as durable relationships and predictable actions. They point out that trust gains importance in case of its absence. Thus, if opportunistic behavior is expected in the future but trust is absent, a strong potential replacement of formal control is not available. That is why Cäker and Siverbo (2011) and Mouritsen and Thrane (2006) warn to consider formal control and trust as two separate alternatives. If formal control and trust crowd out each other, the achievement of their common objectives could be harmed.

3.6.2 Risk

In extant literature on the different types of IORs, especially PPPs, notable attention has been paid to the concept of risk because it is considered as pivotal for understanding and analyzing how those relationships are operating (cf. Broadbent et al., 2008; Froud, 2003). On a meta level, Li B. (2003) and Li B. et al. (2005c) differentiate between *macro, meso* and *micro risk*. Macro risks are typically exogenously given and range from economic, political and legal to natural risks, whereas meso and micro risks are endogenous and refer to a specific PPP project. While meso risks are project-related (e.g. in terms of design, financing or operation), micro risks emanate from the stakeholders involved and from the relationships between them. Li B. et al. (2005c) see the major reason for the existence of micro risks in the nature of public and private sector partners. While the private sector usually is profit-driven, the public sector bears social responsibility and has to provide and maintain public services. Other studies on PPPs that have followed this tripartite division of risk are those by Hwang et al. (2013) and Chou and Pramudawardhani (2015) who adopt an integrated focus on risk factors and on the so-called CSFs. In line with Li B. et al. (2005c), they summarized macro, meso, and micro risk under "risk allocation", which they consider in turn as an important CSF of PPPs.

In their analytical study on MC in PPPs, Appuhami et al. (2011) emphasize that PPPs are a sort of IORs, and they define risk (or alternatively *behavioral risk*) as the sum of all possible adverse consequences, which emanate from the "unexpected behavior of individuals" (p. 65) and substantially affect the objectives of IORs in this context. In accordance with Coletti et al. (2005) and with Das and Teng (2001a), they further distinguish between *performance* and *relational risk*. In general, both types of risk deal with uncertainties regarding the cooperation between partners and the organizational performance (cf. Das and Teng, 2001a). However, entering into an IOR presumes that partners are willing to accept these behavioral risks, including uncertainty, to some extent. Positive expectations towards behavior are crucial for making partnerships successful (cf. VdM and Vosselman, 2009).

Performance risk refers to "...the probability that collaboration objectives will not be achieved despite the full cooperation of the partners" (p. 480), which mainly results from market forces like demand fluctuations and competition (Coletti et al., 2005). A core objective of many IORs is to share risks among partners. This shared risk is a kind of performance risk (cf. Das and Teng, 2001a).

Relational risk refers to "...the probability that collaboration objectives will not be achieved because of lack of cooperation" (Coletti et al., 2005, p. 480). This type of risk results from an IOR's formation and inherent incentives to behave opportunistically. However, previous research revealed that formal control mechanisms have been applied to mitigate this risk (cf. Coletti et al., 2005; Das and Teng, 2001a).

The consequences that performance and relational risk entail for IORs depend significantly on how risk is perceived, so that Das and Teng (2001a) differentiate between actual and perceived risk. They propose that two factors, namely control and trust, determine perceived risk. Even if the actual risk is not reduced, trust can reduce the perceived risk through the creation of positive behavior expectations. The role of control in this context is to influence behavior, to make undesirable outcomes less likely and therefore to reduce actual risk in an

IOR. Appuhami et al. (2011) argue that behavior control impacts upon relational risk, output control focuses on performance risks while trust is supposed to mitigate both types of risk alike. Table 16 displays several combinations of control mechanisms with competency and goodwill trust, and shows where these can moderate or lower relational and performance risk and where those remain high.

	Behavior Control	Output Control	Social Control
Goodwill trust	*Low* Relational risk *High* Performance risk	*Moderate* Relational risk *Moderate* Performance risk	*Low* Relational risk *Moderate* Performance risk
Competency trust	*Moderate* Relational risk *Moderate* Performance risk	*High* Relational risk *Low* Performance risk	*Moderate* Relational risk *Low* Performance risk

Table 16: Impact of control and trust upon performance and relational risk.
(Source: Das and Teng, 2001a, p. 267)

Following the interpretation of Das and Teng (2001a), both relational and performance risks are perceived high if there is neither control nor trust in a partnership. So, most combinations of control and trust lower the risks to a moderate or low level. Given that the relationship between two partners A and B is marked by goodwill trust where both of them can rely on not being betrayed by the other party, relational risks are moderate to low, regardless of the chosen control type. However, behavior control is not suitable to mitigate performance risks because it is less compelling than output or social control, and its impact is harder to measure. Yet, behavior control is useful to reduce relational risk for both competency and goodwill trust while social control contributes to lower performance and relational risk.

To conclude, the more trust is competency-based the better control can reduce performance risk, with output and social control being most effective. No control type can reduce relational risk below performance risk. By contrast, goodwill trust feeds off close and trustful relationships between partners, so that relational risk can be better reduced than performance risk, with behavior and social control being most effective. No control type can reduce performance risk below relational risk.

3.7 Interim Summary

MC in IORs varies by control dimensions that are adjusted to the chosen control level being used to manage or govern any kind of partnership. Previous studies drew clear linkages between control levels, control extent or tightness, control dimensions and mechanisms, and control focus. Concerning the control levels, the existing literature demonstrates broad consensus on the tripartite structure although strongly TCE-oriented studies discuss those control levels more from a general governance perspective. Control mechanisms primarily divide into formal and informal controls while market control is treated separately because of its exclusive alignment towards market mechanisms. For this reason, market control is usually not used in IORs that do not want to rely on market mechanisms only, whereas formal and informal control mechanisms can be combined quite individually, depending on the involved partners' preference for a more hierarchic or hybrid control pattern. The suitability of the chosen control level and the effectiveness of the employed control mechanisms depend particularly on how well their respective characteristics are considered for the control design and finally are practiced by the involved partners. By virtue of their hybrid nature, JVs are more complex than hierarchy- and market-based partnerships so that the literature developed JV-specific control types, which comprise a mix of formal and informal contractual and managerial controls. Different control problems can undermine the effectiveness of MC and threaten an IOR's successful implementation so that they should be anticipated and considered by the MC design as far as possible. Risk and trust are two complex impact factors that influence MC to different extents, depending on the actual control level and mechanisms. Hitherto, previous literature discussed the influence and handling of risk and trust primarily with respect to hierarchic and hybrid control levels. However, the concepts of risk and trust presented in this chapter remain quite theoretical.

To conclude, concerning PPPs between IOs/DCAs and the private sector, the present study should figure out if the control levels are in practice as discrete as they are in theory, how the control dimensions are actually designed, and what formal and informal control mechanisms are used in this context, taking into account environmental influence factors. The four typical control problems in IORs derived from previous studies should be analyzed and enhanced for PPPs between IOs/DCAs and the private sector. Moreover, the empirical part of this study should help to figure out what kinds of trust occur in PPPs between IOs/DCAs and the private sector, identify inherent risks, and reveal how MC can promote trust as well mitigate and deal with risks.

4. Theoretical Foundation

In the present study, two approaches from the school of new institutional economics (NIE), **actor-centered institutionalism (ACI)** and **transaction cost economics (TCE)**, have been used in a combined manner to analyze and characterize the embodiment of accountability, governance and control mechanisms which apply to PPPs between IOs and the private sector. In practice, NIE approaches, and TCE in particular, revealed to be important providers of frameworks for understanding phenomena in management accounting and control (cf. Anderson and Dekker, 2005; Boland et al., 2008; Covaleski et al., 2003; Dekker, 2004; Richardson and Kilfoyle, 2009; Scapens, 1994; Vosselman, 2002). The reason for using two theory concepts is that dual or multiple theoretical perspectives proved to facilitate more exhaustive analysis, if coherently applied, while single theoretical approaches often provide limited understanding of phenomena and the complexities associated with the research object (cf. Appuhami et al., 2011; Donada and Nogatchewsky, 2006; Emsley and Kidon, 2007; Meira et al., 2010). On a macro level, the ACI approach contributes to characterizing the types of actors and institutions being involved in PPPs with IOs/DCAs as well as the ways of interaction by which PPPs are carried out, including the level of governance and partnership. On a micro level, the TCE contributes to capturing incentives, motivations, resources and skills of the individual and composite actors being involved in PPPs between IOs/DCAs and the private sector, based on theoretical assumptions. MC mechanisms play a role for both levels because both macro factors (e.g. cultural and institutional norms and values, political situation) and micro factors (e.g. organizational life, specific interests of participating organizations) affect PPPs at different levels, from project initiation to contractual arrangement, implementation and project conclusion. MC mechanisms are supposed to absorb and equilibrate diverging effects of these macro and micro factors and therefore to make PPPs more efficient and effective as well as to contribute to contract compliance (cf. Ball and Craig, 2010; Demirag et al., 2012; Nicholson et al., 2006; Otley et a., 1995; VdM and Vosselman, 2000).

In the following section will be explained why the ACI approach and TCE are considered as appropriate to explore the present research topic. Furthermore, delineation from other theoretical frameworks/theories from the area of new institutionalism, which have been particularly applied to analyzing PPPs in the past, will be briefly discussed.

The NIE evolved from the schools of neo-classical theory and institutional economics. It has been established as a multi-disciplinary approach and is used in different areas of social sciences (including organization theories, political science, and public policy). Moreover, it forms a further development of the neoclassical theory while remaining between a framework and a theory (cf. Baudry and Chassagnon, 2010; Mayntz and Scharpf, 1995, p. 41; North, 1986; Scapens, 1994; Scharpf, 1997, p. 41). Decisively shaped by Oliver E. Williamson in the 1970s, its roots trace back to Ronald H. Coase whose articles *The Nature of the Firm* (1937) and *The Problem of Social Costs* (1960) form the starting point of NIE considerations and who brought up the idea that TC exist on markets where cooperation between actors and exchange of goods and services take place (cf. Coase, 1998; North, 1990, p. 11 f.; Williamson, 2010). The institutional economics approach goes back to Hamilton (1919) in particular, who deems institutional economics a theory, which sharply distinguishes from neo-classical economics. In contrast, the NIE approach considers neo-classical ideas but takes a

T. S. Konrad, *Management Control in Public-Private Partnerships*,
Schriften zu Wirtschaftsprüfung, Steuerlehre und Controlling,
https://doi.org/10.1007/978-3-658-22868-2_4

critical view on fundamental but restrictive assumptions, such as the rational maximizing economic actor who acts on the basis of complete and perfect information (cf. Baudry and Chassagnon, 2010; Mayntz and Scharpf, 1995, p.41; Scapens, 1994; VdM and Vosselman, 2000; Vosselman, 2002). It has been criticized that the interplay between costs and characteristics of transactions is ignored by neo-classical theory (cf. Anderson et al., 2000; Sartorius and Kirsten, 2005).

The NIE does assume that cooperations are marked by bounded rationally acting actors and information asymmetry which both cause TC. Moreover, it recognizes that institutions influence economic, political and social behavior of actors wherefore they play a considerable role for society. In this context, a normative, rule-setting and trust-building capacity is ascribed to institutions (cf. Covaleski et al., 2003; Mayntz and Scharpf, 1995, p. 41; Menard and Schirly, 2005, p.1; North, 1990, p. 12). The idea of the existence of TC was later on elaborated by Williamson (1990) to formulate the TCE theory.

Further formative representatives of the school of NIE are Armen Alchian, Kenneth Arrow, Steven Cheung, Harold Demsetz, Douglass North, and Elinor Ostrom (cf. Coase, 1998; Klaes, 2000; Menard and Shirley, 2005, p.1; Richter and Furubotn, 2003, p. 39; Williamson, 1990, p. 21).

Figure 19 shows origins of the NIE in a graphic scheme and outlines associated frameworks/theoretical approaches and theories. The school of NIE forms the theoretical perspective from which PPPs between IOs/DCAs and the private sector will be analyzed.

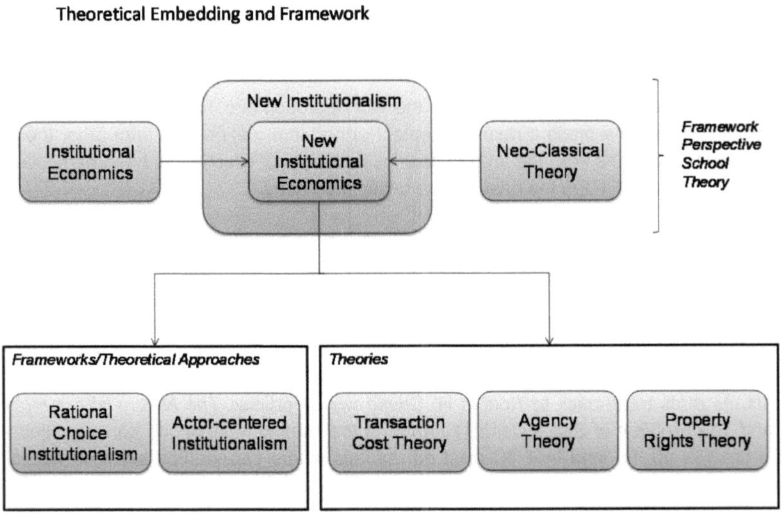

Figure 19: Theoretical embedding and framework.

(Source: own depiction, based on Coase, 1998; Hall and Taylor, 1996; Hamilton, 1919; Kim and Mahoney, 2005; Mayntz and Scharpf, 1995, p. 41; Menard, 2005; Menard and Shirley, 2005, p.1; North, 1986; North, 1990, p. 11 f.; Ostrom, 1994; Richter and Furubotn, 2003, p. 39; Scapens, 1994; Scharpf, 1997, p. 41; Vosselman, 2002; Williamson, 1990; and Williamson, 2010)

4.1 Actor-centered Institutionalism

The actor-centered institutionalism approach was developed by two research scholars from the Max Planck Institute for the Studies of Societies, namely Fritz Scharpf and Renate Mayntz, who aimed to provide a platform for analyzing problems of organization and governance between and among societal actors and institutions (cf. Mayntz and Scharpf, 1995, p. 39). Their motivation arose from the assumption that there is need for explanation of policy and social phenomena, which form the outcome of combined interactions between different actors (collective, corporative and individual) who are subject to the institutional context within which their interactions take place (cf. Scharpf, 2000, p. 17).

Along with similar approaches, such as Institutional Analysis and Development (cf. Ostrom et al., 1994) or the Actor-System-Dynamics approach (cf. Burns et al., 1985), the ACI approach brings paradigms from economic and sociological theories together to achieve greater coherence between actual political interactions, actors involved, institutional context, and theoretical perspectives (cf. Scharpf, 2000, p. 73 f.).

However, Mayntz and Scharpf (1995, p. 39) underline that the ACI approach should not be considered as a theory but rather as a heuristic device because it is not designed for specific research subjects. With respect to the ACI approach, Scharpf (2000, p. 75 f.) highlights in which sense an approach differs from a theory. He argues that theories must come along with theoretically justified but empirically verifiable assumptions, while approaches only provide some guidance to find explanation for certain research problems. That is why Scharpf (1997, p. 38) defines the ACI as a framework, which "...emphasizes the influence of institutions on the perceptions, preferences and capabilities of individual and corporate actors and on the modes of their interaction."

Scharpf (2000, p. 75 f.) contends that actors, institutions and their constellations as well as research interests are too diverse and too specific to formulate universal assumptions, which are universally applicable to research subjects. This issue is noted by Scapens (1994) as a general characteristic of institutional approaches.

The ACI approach aims to explain relationships between actors and institutions including interests, norms and rules, which drive them. Moreover, it intends to analyze impacts of actors' capabilities and orientations, actor constellations and modes of interaction upon actions and behaviors of actors (cf. Heinze, 2012, p. 56; Scharpf, 1997, p. 43 f.). Hence, the ACI tries to provide a tool to analyze actors and their actions as well as institutional settings in an inclusive instead of a fragmented manner (cf. Mayntz and Scharpf, 1995, p. 46). Coming from the corner of political science, the ACI approach assumes that policy decisions result from deliberation and negotiation processes of actors (stakeholders) who are influenced by different institutional settings. Thus, determining factors are actors themselves including their characteristics, actor constellations and institutions (cf. Petring, 2007; Scharpf, 1997, p. 38). Figure 20 shows the ACI approach in the form of a chart, where bold frames highlight its core elements. Using these elements, the PPPs reviewed in this study will be characterized from a macro perspective.

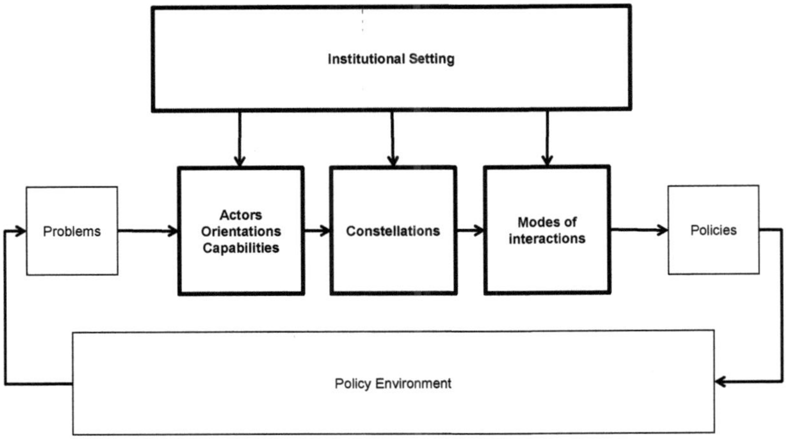

Figure 20: Actor-centered institutionalism.
(Source: Scharpf, 1997, p. 44)

In the following paragraph, the ACI will be briefly delineated from another pertinent approach, the Rational Choice Institutionalism (RCI), and ACI core elements will be defined. These are actor, actor constellation, and modes of interaction as well as institution/institutional setting. Certain actor constellation and chosen modes of interaction produce specific interactions together. Due to their complexity and multidimensionality, both terms will be regarded separately (cf. Scharpf, 1997, p. 72).

4.1.1 Actor

The ACI approach according Mayntz and Scharpf (1995) and Scharpf (1997), distinguishes between individual, collective and corporate actors (Table 71 in annex 8.1). These are differentiated according to actions they take, purposes they have, resources they dispose of, and decisions they make (cf. Mayntz and Scharpf, 1995, p. 50; Scharpf, 1997, pp. 54-57). Scharpf (1997, p. 37 and p. 43) notes that actors can moreover be characterized by "specific capabilities, specific perceptions, and specific preferences" they have, and which the surrounding institutional setting can influence. All individual actors are part of corporate actors, forming organizations. These organizations can include political bodies (e.g. political parties, public agencies), economic bodies (e.g. firms, trade unions) or social bodies (e.g. churches, NGOs) (cf. North, 1996, p.9). The existence of corporate actors depends on their individual members (cf. Mayntz and Scharpf, 1995, p. 50; Scharpf, 1997, p. 39). Empirically, no major differences between the categories of collective and corporate actors were noted but rather dominance of the corporate actor (cf. Coleman, 1974, p. 44; Kenis and Schneider, 1987; Scharpf, 1997, p. 58). Hence, a more detailed focus does not seem to be necessary, and the category of the collective actor including its sub-categories will be disregarded in the present study.

Individual actors: in organizations, they perform concrete and operative work, which is prescribed through instructions, norms and rules by higher corporative actors. However, individual actors have a significant influence upon corporative actors because it depends upon their individual interests and capabilities how efficiently, effectively and successfully actions are performed, for instance project work. This might be difficult to measure because they enjoy some freedom of action (cf. Mayntz and Scharpf, 1995, p. 50 f.). Individualistic actions that are not in harmony with corporate interests can result from this (cf. Scharpf, 1997, p. 61 f.). Hence, organizations are subject to intrinsic risk of opportunistic behavior (opportunism) by individual actors.

Corporate actors: Coleman (1974, p. 44) calls the corporate actor "...a corporative body with its own power to act, thanks to the transferal of members' rights and resources to this unit". Therefore, control over resources shifts from the individual to the corporate actor. About resources can be decided in a hierarchical manner or by majority. Individual members subject themselves to the interest and objectives of the corporate actor (e.g. by employment contract). By bundling resources, the corporate actor pursues a corporate self-interest that can harmonize, but does not necessarily do so, with the individual interests of the individual members. However, individual actors are likely to pursue their own interests, trying to realize them within the corporate body. Among those interests are control over resources, freedom of power, and physical well-being (cf. Coleman, 1974, p. 44; Kenis and Schneider, 1987; March and Simon, 1976, p. 87; Mayntz and Scharpf, 1995, p. 49). Corporate actors are typically firms, government ministries, IOs, political parties, or unions. Some of them are created and mandated by governmental decisions or institutional rules, such as IOs (cf. Mayntz and Scharpf, 1995, p. 49; Scharpf, 1997, p. 39 and p. 61).

Having said that, the question of whether and how *corporate actors* differentiate from *organizations* may arise because both typically are some kind of social and legal entity, such as firms or political parties. Some NIE and organization theorists even argue that such entities are *institutions* (cf. March and Simon, 1976, pp. 7-9; Mayntz and Scharpf, 1995, p. 40); North, 1990, p. 6; North, 2005, p. 22; Vanberg, 1982, p. 32). While the term *institution* is more controversially discussed and will be regarded in Chapter 4.1.4, no crucial difference is noted between *corporate actors* and *organizations* that are pertinent to the use of the ACI approach in this research study.

4.1.2 Actor Constellations

Mayntz and Scharpf (1995, p. 44) describe the concept of actor constellations as characteristic of highly specialized and complex societal sectors in which different actors come together to find solutions to existing policy problems. Those problems cannot be resolved by single (author's note: individual and corporate) actors unilaterally. Moreover, single actors do not have determinative power over policy outcomes. Therefore, the level of provided resources and plurality among actors matter for actor constellation. Each actor puts in particular capabilities, outcome expectations, perceptions, specific orientations and strategy options, which go along with certain monetary or non-monetary payoff aspirations. These are not necessarily compatible with each other because levels of trust, actor's abilities, motives and power may vary (cf. March and Olsen, 1989, p. 43; Scharpf, 1997, p. 69).

The actor constellations can be further characterized by the following actor orientations:

- *hostile* (loss of others equals own gain)
- *competitive* (delta of own and another's gain matters)
- *egoistic-rational* (the own gain only matters)
- *co-operative* (common gain matters)
- *altruistic* (own gain does not matter)

They are supposed to contribute to describing relationships between actors and to outlining actors' incentives and motivations to pursue an actor constellation (cf. Mayntz and Scharpf, 1995, p. 57; Scharpf, 1997, pp. 61-66; Scharpf, 2000, pp. 148-153). Thus, actor constellation "...describes the level of potential conflict, but it does not yet include information about the mode of interaction through which that conflict is to be resolved..." (Scharpf, 1997, p. 72). Here, the question of how *actor constellations* differentiate from *organizations* may arise. Table 17 outlines some core differences and commonalities of actor constellations and organizations.

Characteristics	Actor constellations	Organizations
Actor composition	Individual and corporate	Individual and corporate
Legal situation	One or more legally independent entities/corporate actors	One legally independent entity/corporate actor
Nature of collaboration	Diverse actor orientations	Co-operative behavior (individual members subject themselves to the organization's interests and objectives despite individual economic aspirations

Table 17: Comparison of characteristics of actor constellations and organizations.
(Source: Mayntz and Scharpf (1995, p. 44 and pp. 60-62))

4.1.3 Modes of Interaction

The institutional setting builds the frame within which actors interact with one another in different constellations and in different modes. So-called *arenas* form spaces within which interaction between actors take place. Based on the institutional setting, responsibilities and tasks are assigned to the different actors in these arenas in order to facilitate some kind of division of labor with respect to common policy problem solving. In TCE, the modes of interaction are discussed under the heading of *governance* (cf. Boland et al., 2008; Covaleski et al., 2003; March and Olsen, 1989, p. 1 and p. 26; Mayntz and Scharpf, 1995, p. 48 and p. 60; VdM and Vosselman, 2000). As this term is broadly discussed in practice, a separate paragraph will be dedicated to make it better tangible in the context of the ACI approach (Chapter 4.3).

According to Scharpf (1997, p. 93), the modes of interaction can be categorized in:

- *hierarchical direction,*
- *majoritarian voting,*
- *negotiated agreements and*
- *unilateral action.*

All of these modes are accompanied by contractual agreements or commitments in order to resolve coordination problems and potential conflict among actors, which may cause distrust and raise TC (cf. Scharpf, 1997, p. 70 and p. 93). The categorization by Scharpf (1997) is supported by March and Olsen (1989, p. 156) who express similar ideas by mentioning "bargaining, coalition formation, exchange, and the exercise of power" as forms of converting individual interests into common interaction. With respect to the institutional setting, the modes of interaction imply different levels of institutional capacity and structure. In case of unilateral mode of interaction, little or even no institutional structure does exist. By contrast, the other three modes of interaction come along with more complex and demanding institutional arrangements and structures, which compel actors to commit and comply with agreements, norms and rules. Hence, the different modes of interaction diverge in their compatibility with different institutional settings (cf. March and Olsen, 1989, p. 28; Mayntz and Scharpf, 1995, p. 46 f. and p. 61; Scharpf, 2000, p. 92; Table 72 in annex 8.1).

4.1.4 Institutions and Institutional Setting

The term *institution* basically has two fundamentally different meanings, which reflect its heterogeneous use among new institutionalist theorists:

1) Mayntz and Scharpf (1995, p. 40), Ostrom (2005, p. 824) and Vanberg (1982), p. 32) point out that institutions are often considered as social, organizational, or legal entities (e.g. firms, political parties, public agencies, etc.) among scholars, such as Van Kersbergen and Van Waarden (2004). However, they rather advocate a second and more broadly recognized definition.
2) North (2005, p. 22) defines institutions as "...rules of the game – both formal rules, informal norms and their enforcement characteristics", which "...form the incentive structure of a society, and the political and economic institutions, in consequence, are the underlying determinants of economic performance" (North, 1994, p. 359). Humans make use of institutions in recurring situations, for instance for creating business strategies for which rules and norms form institutional boundaries (cf. Ostrom, 2005, p. 824).

Reflecting on the aforementioned definitions of institutions, Williamson (1996, p. 4 f.) concludes that they "mainly operate at the level of the institutional environment, the so-called rules of the game" (macroanalytic perspective) while he takes a microanalytic perspective and focuses on the "institutions of governance" (hierarchies, hybrids and markets), as he calls them. Thus, he takes the institutional environment as exogenously given and is more concerned with institutions of governance in terms of individual transactions. Based on Williamson (1979), Vosselman and VdM (2009) conclude that institutions build a form of governance structure, and the corresponding institutional environment embodies contractual arrangements, at least with respect to interfirm transactional relationship.

To avoid conceptual confusion between ACI and TCE, the term "institutions of governance" will subsequently be represented by synonyms such as "levels of governance", "governance levels" or "governance structure" when referring to this tripartite categorization of governance. Regardless the different definitions, the origin of institutions should be clear. The creation of institutions results from interaction of human individuals who have produced rules, norms and strategies, independent of whether these were installed democratically or not. Institutions can evolve and vary cross-nationally and over time. Division of labor and increasing specialization within society are considered as driving forces behind this (cf. North, 1986; North, 1990, p. 6; Scharpf, 1997, p. 39 and p. 41).

Institutions assume a function of control and direction, which refer to allocation of power and resources, definition of accountability and responsibility and exercise of power. They aim to provide guidance and structure to human interactions and to reduce uncertainty among them (cf. Mayntz and Scharpf, 1995, p. 40; North, 1990, p. 6; O'Toole, 1995; Richter and Furubotn, 2003, p. 7 f.). In spite of the strong societal role institutions play, they just form a frame within which actors act, the so-called *institutional setting*. This institutional setting has a norm-setting character and influences actors' personal expectations, perceptions and preferences with respect to policy. It includes rules and regulations established by regulatory and governmental bodies at a higher level as well as those set up by organizations themselves at a lower level (e.g. conditions of employment, contracts). However, it cannot finally determine actors' concrete actions or outcomes of interaction (cf. Boland et al., 2008; Mayntz and Scharpf, 1995, p. 49; O'Toole, 1995; Scharpf, 1997, p. 36; Schulze, 1997; VdM and Scapens, 2008; Vosselman and VdM, 2009).

Scharpf (1997, p. 46 f.) proposes four clusters of institutional settings: 1) anarchic minimal institutions, 2) networks, regimes and joint-decision systems, 3) associations, constituencies and representative assemblies, and 4) hierarchical organizations and the government, which are supposed to affect the modes of interaction.
Moreover, these clusters reflect institutional arrangements, which facilitate or make the different modes of interaction more difficult. For instance, hierarchic organizations, such as governmental entities, enable both hierarchic and consensus-oriented interaction, depending on their institutional arrangements while networks and joint-decision systems are not designed for a hierarchic mode of interaction but rather for negotiations or majoritarian decisions (Table 72 in annex 8.1)

4.1.5 Delineation of ACI from Other Pertinent Approaches

Another approach, which is broadly discussed in NIE, is the RCI. Being strongly rooted in the neo-classical theory, it starts from the premises that individual actors are considerably utility-oriented, that they know their utility functions, that they have a clear preference order of options, and that they dispose of almost complete information (cf. Hall and Taylor, 1996; March and Simon, 1976, pp. 129-131; O'Toole, 1995). Altogether, this is supposed to enable individual actors to make a rational choice between different available options (author's note: for instance between entering into a PPP or conducting a project on their own). These premises are observed critically by notable new institutional economists who argue that decision-making is used to be more complex in practice because preference orders of options are not that clear, and information is imperfect. Therefore, actors are supposed to be inhibited in making completely rational choices or decisions (cf. March and Simon, 1976, pp. 129-131; North, 1990, p. 9; Richter and Furubotn, 2003, pp. 192-193; Simon, 1959).

However, the most striking difference between the ACI and the RCI approach is that the RCI considers institutions as means being used by individual actors to maximize their personal utility, whereas the ACI assumes institutions to form a defined setting within which individual actors are acting (cf. Hood, 1990; Mayntz and Scharpf, 1995, p. 52; Scharpf, 1997, pp. 63-65). In other words, the ACI approach identifies actors and institutions as two societal mechanisms that interact as equals. Due to the more practice-oriented premises, the ACI will be part of the theoretic basis of this explorative research study, while the RCI will not be further taken into account. With respect to practical applicability of the ACI approach, Scharpf (1997, p.38) underlines that interaction-oriented policy research requires use of empirical data and should be carried out on a case-by-case basis. In this context, the literature review in Chapter 2.2 revealed several empirical studies on PPPs that deal with different public policy issues, while Petersen (2011) is the only one found that uses the ACI as theoretical framework.

4.2 Transaction Cost Economics

The transaction cost economics (TCE) is rooted in the school of NIE. It was founded by Ronald Coase and later on substantially developed by Oliver Williamson (both obtained the Nobel Prize in Economics) and has evolved to an important approach in the field of organizational and behavioral science (cf. Baudry and Chassagnon, 2010; Coase, 1998; Goshal and Moran, 1996; Maher, 1997; Oxley, 1997; Pessali, 2006; Reeves, 2008; Richardson and Kilfoyle, 2009; Speklé, 2001; Williamson, 1990). The idea of the existence of TC was early raised by Coase (1937 and 1960) who argued that TC, insomuch they are significant, determine the organization of economic activity and help to understand how economic transactions are governed (cf. Maher, 1997).

4.2.1 General Characteristics and Origin of Transaction Costs

Followed by Sartorius and Kirsten (2005), Williamson (1996; p. 379) defines a transaction as "the microanalytic unit of analysis in transaction cost economics", which "occurs when a good or service is transferred across a technologically separable interface". TC are associated with difficulties, frictions and problems in economic organization, and they are, broadly spoken, the operating costs of the economic system (cf. Arrow, 1969, p. 48). In other words, the parties involved in a transaction bear incurring TC, which are equal to the losses caused by these difficulties, frictions and problems and to the resources spent in order to prevent, mitigate and reduce those losses. This approach to TC underlies most TCE-based accounting studies (cf. Richardson and Kilfoyle, 2009). TC arise from economic exchanges of resources between transaction partners that occur in a socio-economic environment for which costly information, incomplete contracts and imperfect enforcement of agreements are assumed. Moreover, TC arise if the economic value of services and goods is difficult to gauge. If there are distrust and lack of information between the contracting parties the true value of transaction is hard to measure. The amount of TC also varies with experience and knowledge of the actor involved in the transaction. Transactions that are executed for the first time usually cause higher TC than recurring ones (cf. Ouchi, 1980).

In organizations, TC incur for maintaining governance structures, which are underlying specific transactions. Moreover, properties of human action and behavior influence the amount and extent of TC (cf. Vosselman, 2002). The two main behavioral assumptions of the TCE, *opportunism* and *bounded rationality*, which are associated with frictions in transactions, are not only drivers of TC but also help to understand rationalities behind transactions. Based on this, the TCE does moreover believe in incompleteness of contracts (cf. Klaes, 2000; Nicholson et al., 2006; Ouchi, 1980; Pessali, 2006; Richardson and Kilfoyle, 2009; Speklé, 2001; VdM and Vosselman, 2000; Williamson, 1996, p. 56; Williamson, 1999). Due to the cross-cutting nature and importance of these two assumptions for the whole TCE, they will be discussed separately and in more detail in Chapter 4.2.3. Depending on the attributes of specific transactions (e.g. one-off vs. recurring transaction), different forms of governance structure are implemented. In this regard, the TCE contributes to explaining choices of governance structures and how these are embedded into institutional framings (cf. Dekker, 2004; Krause, 2014; Reeves, 2008; Richardson and Kilfoyle, 2009). Covaleski et al. (2003) add that socio-political backgrounds of transactions should be considered for the choice of governance structure.

Transactions costs can be differentiated into ex-ante costs and ex-post costs, for which the time of contract conclusion forms the reference point (cf. Williamson, 1996, p. 379). Thus, TC typically incur by initiation of transactions (e.g. for search and collection of information), by negotiation and decision-making processes as well as by monitoring and enforcement of contractual arrangements, including sanctioning (cf. Langfield-Smith, 2008; North, 1990, p. 27; Reeves, 2008; Richter and Furubotn, 2003, p. 41). The amount of TC impacts upon conduction and organization of economic activities (cf. Mouritsen and Thrane, 2006; North, 1990; Pessali, 2006; Richter and Furubotn, 2003, p. 40). However, Baudry and Chassagnon (2010) emphasize that TC are not static but they evolve and vary along with organizational learning and knowledge growth of the involved actors. Moreover, they argue that Williamson was notably influenced by organization theory, prompting him to promulgate four major concerns, which can cause problems within organizations and therefore produce higher TC:

- Authority and hierarchy in organizations,
- Intra-organizational conflicts,
- Atmosphere within organizations, and
- Dynamics in organizations.

These concerns are expressed with respect to firms for which internal organization is noted as a source of frictions and conflicts (cf. Baudry and Chassagnon, 2010). However, the occurrence of TC is not confined to business and economics only, but the TCE is applicable to public policy issues as well (cf. Williamson, 1996, p. 27 and p. 84). For instance, Williamson (1999) distinguishes between six transaction types in the public sector: infrastructure, judicial, procurement, redistributional, regulatory and sovereign. One linking element between business and public sector are PPPs. Their lifecycle roughly splits up into an ex-ante exploratory/contract phase and an ex-post execution/implementation phase (Chapter 3.3.4). Using the TCE, Appuhami et al. (2011) have shown in their analytical framework for MC in PPPs that different contingent factors of the TCE, such as opportunism and bounded rationality, apply to PPP projects at different phases and to varying degrees. Hence, before and during the implementation of PPP projects incur TC that should be considered when the governance structure and MC are designed.

To summarize, the TCE is a generalist-oriented approach that finds application in numerous fields of economics (e.g. economic development, public finance) and business administration and management (e.g. finance, marketing, strategy), but also in social sciences (e.g. political science, sociology) or public policy (e.g. corporate governance, regulation). It contributes to better understanding of contractual arrangements, of coordination and governance of economic activities, and also helps to find a suitable MC design for different kinds of interorganizational cooperation (cf. Appuhami et al., 2011; Kim and Mahoney, 2005; Reeves, 2008; Williamson, 2010). Thus, the analysis of the general characteristics and of the origin of TC confirms the suitability of TCE to serve as theoretical framework for PPPs, JVs, and IORs, as revealed by the literature review in Chapter 2.2. In the following, the linkages of TCE to MC in IORs, JVs and PPPs and different, pertinent characteristics, elements and implications of the TCE will be explained, with particular view to accounting.

4.2.2 Relationship between Transaction Costs and Management Control

In accordance with Williamson (1996, pp. 103-105; 1998; 1999; 2010), many researchers from accounting and organizational sciences emphasize the importance of theoretical aspects from TCE for MC, particularly in IORs, and how this can be aligned with underlying governance structures (cf. Adler, 2001; Anderson and Dekker, 2005; Dekker, 2004; Kamminga and VdM, 2007; Marques et al., 2011; Speklé, 2001; VdM and Vosselman, 2000, Vosselman, 2002). In this context, VdM and Vosselman (2000) and Vosselman (2002) assume that all transactional relationships contain some MC mechanisms. Besides bounded rationality and opportunism, which both form challenges to MC (cf. Nichsolon, 2006), Dekker (2004) identified two control problems in IORs, coordinating tasks and managing appropriation concerns, which need to be tackled by appropriate MC systems in order to decrease TC (cf. Marques et al., 2011, Vosselman and VdM, 2009). Suitable remedies to achieve that task are formal and informal control instruments (cf. Cäker and Siverbo, 2011; Dekker, 2004; Langfield-Smith, 2008; Chapter 3.3):

- Formal controls: These rather hierarchical controls (e.g. incentivizing, monitoring, sanctioning) are equivalent to what Williamson (1996, pp. 103-105) called "administrative controls" in the TCE context, and they are particularly instrumental to hierarchic governance structures.
- Informal controls: In IORs, in which often more than two actors with different interests and strategies execute transactions, the MC systems needs to be complemented by informal or social controls (e.g. atmosphere, social norms and values, trust) in order to govern transactions efficiently and effectively and to reduce uncertainty (cf. Dekker, 2004; Ghosal, 1996; Marques et al., 2011; Tomkins, 2001).

The choice of control types depends on the level of control required for protecting the transaction sufficiently. In fact, formal control mechanisms are more expensive than their informal complements, which operate at low-cost. However, if the required level of control allows doing so, preference will be given to informal controls because formal control always causes some distrust, which can be harmful to interorganizational transaction relationships between two or more partners (cf. Dekker, 2004). Hence, if the two control types complement well each other, a positive atmosphere can be created, contributing to the reduction of TC, as stated by Baudry and Chassagnon (2010). In this way, the TCE can help to identify TC, and based on that provide guidance on finding an optimal interorganizational governance structure including a suitable balance between formal and informal control (cf. Sartorius and Kirsten, 2005).

Speklé (2001, p. 438) concludes in his literature-based study that "TCE is about understanding the match between activities to be controlled and control structures" and helps to characterize transactional activities and to identify an appropriate underlying governance structure. He emphasizes the importance, which TCE ascribes to economic efficiency as "a genuine survival condition" (p. 426), a maxim to be pursued in order to avoid structural maladaptation and waste of resources and a determinant for arranging control systems in transactional relationships. On a micro level, he underscores the dependence of organizational effectiveness and success from the contributions of individuals working for them. He argues that MC structures can be interpreted as means to resolve incentive setting and contract enforcement problems that are associated with these contributions. Covaleski et al. (2003) strongly endorse Speklé's position by underlining the role that MC plays in protecting transactions against risks, such as opportunistic behavior. However, they note that MC goes beyond being a mere contributor to achieving transactional efficiency and effectiveness. They emphasize that control structures can help to integrate individuals within and between organizations and to improve organizations' operational working processes and therefore diminish TC. Concretely, TC reflect misalignment between transaction characteristics and the contract structure, which is why they undermine the organizational performance in PPPs, JVs and IORs (cf. Anderson and Dekker, 2005; Chalos and O'Connor, 2005). Based on empirical evidence, they suggest the implementation of accounting-oriented contractual and managerial controls to counteract the adverse impacts of transactions costs upon performance and to help matching governance structure with transaction characteristics.

4.2.3 Behavioral Characteristics

Bounded rationality

The behavioral assumption, bounded rationality, is considered as a key factor affecting economic interaction and organization (cf. Pessali, 2006). To operate efficiently and effectively, organizations and their actors attempt to act rationally. However, in practice they face some institutional and environmental constraints and influences, such as information asymmetries including incomplete and imperfect information. For this reason they act within cognitive boundaries including limited cognition and foresight (cf. Covaleski et al., 2003; Reeves, 2008; Williamson, 1987). In this context, Williamson (1987) emphasizes that intentional rational behavior is compromised by these constraints and influences, so that bounded rationality should not be set equal to irrational behavior. He argues that actions which are not carried out rationally can be explained by uncertainty among organizations and by complexity of the subject matter and of environmental factors. Still, complexity and uncertainty remain ill-defined terms (cf. Pessali, 2006).

The TCE assumes that different actors and organizations conclude agreements and contracts, and exchange with each other resources which are unavoidably subject to incomplete and imperfect information. Consequently, they are exposed to increased risk of opportunistic behavior and exploitation if one party capitalizes on information advantages to the detriment of the other one (cf. Dekker, 2004; Froud, 2003; Reeves, 2008; Williamson, 1996, p. 377 f.; Williamson, 1998). That is why in practice management accountants, controllers and others may make decisions and conclude incomplete contracts, which include errors, gaps and omissions. In summary, bounded rationality is problematic for two reasons, in two ways:

- Before contract conclusion: Bounded rationality inhibits actors to write complete contracts, which include all pertinent information.
- After contract conclusion: Due to incomplete contracts actors do not have all pertinent information available, wherefore their actions and decisions are subject to bounded rationality.

Nevertheless, the TCE ascribes foresighted capacities to rationally acting individuals and organizations that incorporate experiences as well as perceived and anticipated hazards into their strategic planning and contractual calculus in order to ease adverse effects of complexity and uncertainty (cf. VdM and Kamminga, 2015; VdM and Vosselman, 2000; Williamson, 1998). Mitigation of adverse impacts from different kinds of complexity (e.g. complex decision-making, organizational complexity) and different reasons of uncertainty (e.g. lack of trust, risks) proved vital for making PPPs, JVs and IORs successful (cf. Gupta et al., 2013; Zhang Y. and Rajagopalan, 2002; Chapter 2.3). Thus, Vosselman (2002) concludes that actors tend to act rationally and to make rational decisions but still remain constrained by complexity and uncertainty.

Opportunism

Besides bounded rationality opportunism is one of the two key behavioral factors that is assumed to affect transactions and to be pivotal to benefits and costs of different governance modes (cf. Covaleski et al., 2003; Maher, 1997; Richardson and Kilfoyle, 2009). Thus, Williamson (1998, p. 31) considers opportunism as "...an unflattering attribute...", which is "...nonetheless basic to the logic of organization". And Ghosal (1996, p. 17) defines opportunism as "...a stronger form of the self-interest assumption of motivation that is common to economics and other social science disciplines", which "...includes calculated efforts to mislead, deceive, obfuscate, and otherwise confuse..." (Williamson, 1996, p. 378) and that can cause market failure and threaten the existence of organizations in the worst case. Williamson (1973, p. 317) points out that opportunism results from efforts "...to realize individual gains through a lack of candor or honesty in transactions". By invoking opportunism as a risk for transactions, Covaleski et al. (2003) see two major purposes that are pursued:

- Strengthening stakeholders' awareness for the danger of opportunistic behavior as a result of incomplete and imperfect contracts and
- Motivating stakeholders to take preventive actions in order to identify, explain and mitigate opportunism-related hazards.

However, Baudry and Chassagnon (2010) argue that opportunism neither is an objectively given property nor do individuals behave opportunistically at all times. Opportunism is to a greater degree influenced by some soft factors, such as individuals' attitudes, commitment or "favourable or unfavourable assessment of the specific transaction partner, the group or the organization", which may vary over time (Ghosal, 1996, p. 21). The prevention and mitigation of opportunism including corresponding risk reduction proved crucial for making PPPs, JVs, and IORs successful (cf. Dekker, 2004; Groot and Merchant, 2000; Chapter 2.3). To protect transactions against the opportunistic behavior by contracting parties including breach of contract, the choice of the level of governance (hierarchy, hybrid, or market) and the design of contracts, which should be as complete as possible, are deemed crucial to ensure fair and equitable sharing of revenues of investments. The governance level most appropriate to prevent opportunism needs to be decided case-by-case (cf. Dekker, 2004; Ghosal, 1996; Maher, 1997; Speklé, 2001; VdM and Vosselman, 2000).

However, besides contract design and level of governance, also management accounting and control fulfill an important function in preventing opportunism and in reducing corresponding hazards (cf. Richardson and Kilfoyle, 2009; Vosselman and VdM, 2009). They are moreover important factors to make PPPs, JVs, and IORs successful (cf. Chan et al., 2010a; Langfield-Smith, 2008; Li P. et al., 2013; Chapter 2.3). Kamminga and VdM (2007) contend that the risk of opportunistic behavior in transactions depends on its control complexity. The higher the control complexity of a transaction, the higher the inherent risk of opportunistic behavior, and vice versa. For instance, control complexity in JVs is high because of information asymmetry among the participating parties and a great deal of tacit knowledge, which is inherent to this hybrid form of governance.

Levels and types of control potentially suitable and appropriate for transactions have been broadly discussed. Hierarchical control forms, such as monitoring, incentivizing or sanctioning, may impede opportunistic behavior effectively on the one hand, but can also cause opposite effects on the other hand, if actors feel encouraged to behave more opportunistically than without these control measures and to exhaust given possibilities. In brief, it is impossible to implement comprehensive formal control structures and credible control-based threats which would perfectly prevent actors from behaving opportunistically (cf. Ghoshal, 1996; VdM and Vosselmann, 2009). In this context, VdM and Vosselman (2000) present the idea of "social embeddedness" of transactions, which implies that formal control structures come along with social control mechanisms such as trust in order to build durable and stable transactional relationships and to reduce TC. Thus, in spite of the negative connotation the term "control" may have, MC can even be a carrier of trust- and relationship-building for PPPs, JVs, and IORs, because MC can prevent opportunism, if complementary formal and social control mechanisms are in place. The use of appropriate MC systems and technologies can help to provide information more responsively and timely and therefore contribute to diminish information asymmetry, which is a driving factor of opportunism in transactional relationships (cf. Krause, 2014; Marques et al., 2011; Mouritsen and Thrane, 2006; Vosselman and VdM, 2009; VdM and Vosselman, 2000).

4.2.4 Transaction Characteristics

Besides the two main behavioral assumptions of the TCE approach, there are three related critical dimensions that facilitate specification of transactions and determination of inherent TC on the one hand, but are concurrent drivers of them on the other hand. This duality challenges the designing process of MC in the sense that clear identification of the extent of these critical dimensions and interdependencies between them is required before suitable control mechanisms can be defined for one particular transaction or for a set of transactions (cf. Chen D. et al., 2009; Dekker, 2004; Kamminga and VdM, 2007; Langfield-Smith, 2008; Nicholson, 2006; Speklé, 2001; Vosselman, 2002; Williamson, 1979):

- Degree of asset specificity,
- Uncertainty (including complexity), and
- Frequency of the transaction.

While uncertainty is mainly an issue of bounded rationality, asset specificity is considered as decisively influencing opportunism. Asset specificity "...concerns the ability of assets involved in a transaction to be put to alternative uses should the contract be prematurely terminated" (Covaleski et al., 2003, p. 420). In brief, the greater the degree of asset specificity, the higher the risk of opportunism because the contracting party is less able to alternatively use the asset or to seek for an alternative transaction partner. Hence, the degree of asset specificity and the risk of opportunism are positively related with each other (cf. Baudry and Chassagnon, 2010; Covaleski et al, 2003; Reeves, 2008; VdM and Vosselman, 2000). The following Table 18 defines these three critical dimensions and outlines some of their characteristics.

Critical dimension	Definition	Characteristics
Degree of asset specificity	• "Degree to which investments in physical or human assets are transaction-specific or idiosyncratic" (Vosselman, 2002, p. 140) • "... degree to which resources dedicated to a transaction can be redeployed in other transactions without loss of value or high cost (Dekker, 2008, p. 918) • "...degree to which investments associated with the transaction are specific to the parties involved" (Reeves, 2008, p. 972) • Other examples: dedicated assets, reputational capital, location or site specificity	• Rising asset specificity increases risk of opportunistic behavior → Need for more elaborated governance structure (hybrid or hierarchic) or accounting-based monitoring mechanisms to protect the transaction and to ensure contract compliance • Intermediate level of asset specificity typical for JVs (hybrid governance level) • Investments of high asset specificity suffer from high loss of their value if the related transaction relationship terminates • The greater the asset specificity, the lower the opportunities to use the asset for alternative purposes → risk of holdup and opportunistic behavior rises
Uncertainty	• "Extent to which the desired contributions (author's note: to the trans-	• If uncertainty rises, risk of incomplete contracts increases as well.

Critical dimension	Definition	Characteristics
	action) are amenable to ex ante programming" (Speklé, 2001, p. 427) • "Degree of specifiability of intended performance and predictability of (the influence of) the environment within which the contract is to be executed" (Speklé, 2001, p. 421)	• The higher the uncertainty, the higher the complexity because more complex governance structures are needed → Implies rising TC • Reasons for uncertainty: e.g. external factors (disturbances; environmental complexity; technological changes), internal factors (complexity of and unfamiliarity with tasks; difficulties in anticipating the partners' actions and intentions)
Frequency	• Indicates if a transaction is executed once only, occasionally or recurrently	• The higher the frequency and volume of a transaction, the more likely a more elaborated governance structure is needed.

Table 18: Critical dimensions of the transaction cost economics.
(Source: own depiction, based on Chen D. et al., 2009; Covaleski et al., 2003; Dekker, 2008; Kamminga and VdM, 2007; Kim and Mahoney, 2005; Langfield-Smith, 2008; Maher, 1997; Speklé, 2001; Vosselman, 2002; Williamson (1979, 1998))

Previous TCE-based studies on IORs discussed in particular the transaction characteristics including behavioral assumptions before the background of risk because performance and relational risks can cause TC in partnerships. Especially, information asymmetries, incongruent goals of the partners and unique asset investments made by the partners have been inferred as sources of risk (cf. Chalos and O'Connor, 2005). In this context, Appuhami et al. (2011) have revealed several contingent factors that can engender performance and relational risk, while not all factors lead to these two types of risk likewise (Table 19).

Contingent factors	Performance risk	Relational risk
Asset specificity	✔	✔
Bounded rationality	✔	✔
Opportunism	✕	✔
Transaction frequency	✔	✔
Uncertainty	✔	✔

Table 19: Contingent factors leading to performance and relational risk.
(Source: in reference to Appuhami et al., 2011)

Opportunism is the single factor which refers to relational risk only. Moreover, Appuhami et al. (2011) have shown that opportunism and bounded rationality are the only factors which equally exist under regimes of market, bureaucratic/hierarchic and clan/trust-based control, while the other contingent factors are low, medium or high pronounced.

In summary, the degree of asset specificity, the degree of uncertainty and complexity inherent to transactions, as well as the frequency by which specific transactions are executed, determine and influence the amount of TC, and also the choice of the appropriate governance structure and of suitable control mechanisms to be implemented. The management of performance and relational risks further increases the complexity to design the governance structure and MC. Together, they are supposed to ensure contract compliance to a maximum, to mitigate adverse effects of bounded rationality, and to prevent opportunism in PPPs, JVs and IORs (cf. Abdul-Aziz, 2012; Appuhami et al., 2011; Dekker, 2008; Kamminga and VdM, 2007).

4.2.5 Governance Characteristics

The cornerstone of governance of transactions and of related contractual arrangements form the three governance structures of hierarchy, hybrid, and market according to Williamson (1991), a view that is also shared by the accounting research community (cf. Dekker, 2004; Håkansson and Lind, 2004; Kamminga and VdM, 2007). MC-related characteristics of these governance structures have been discussed in Chapter 0 while this chapter focuses on specific transaction cost-related governance characteristics.

Each transaction underlies a contract that is aligned with a certain governance structure. Based on the specificities of the transaction and of the corresponding TC, the choice of one alternative governance structure is made. Governance structures can be highly specific, semi-specific or non-transaction specific (cf. Maher, 1997). Their specificity depends on the three critical dimensions and on certain attributes, which are ascribed to them accordingly (Chapter 4.2.4). However, according to Oxley (1997), transactions can differ by governance characteristics in the following way:

- The more parties are involved in a transaction, the more likely a hierarchical governance structure is chosen.
- If transactions are executed cross-boundary and multi-nationally, a more hierarchical governance structure is likely to be chosen.
- If transaction partners are grouped as alliances and JVs, a less hierarchical governance structure is likely to be chosen (often a hybrid form).

Williamson (1996, p. 105) ascribes certain attributes to contracts and transactions, depending on the choice of governance structure (Table 20). Three attributes require some short definition:

- *Incentive intensity*: Measures the degree, to which the benefits and net receipts (negative and positive) are associated with efforts and investments made by one party and as stipulated by contract (cf. Williamson, 1996, p. 378).
- *Administrative controls*: Means control mechanisms (e.g. monitoring, sanctioning) which apply to transaction execution and contract compliance and protect the transaction against risks, such as opportunistic behavior (cf. Covaleski et al., 2003; Williamson, 1996, p. 104).
- *Contract law*: Rigidity and strength of rules and norms included in contracts in order to enforce contractual arrangements. (cf. Williamson, 1996, p. 27).

Attributes	Governance Structure		
	Hierarchy	Hybrid	Market
Incentive intensity	Weak	Semi-strong	Strong
Administrative controls	Strong	Semi-strong	Weak
Contract law	Weak	Semi-strong	Strong
Risk of adverse effects from incomplete contracts	Low	Medium	High

Table 20: Comparison of attributes of the three governance structures.
(Source: adapted from Williamson (1996, p. 105; 1999))

On the basis of these definitions, Table 20 leads to the following considerations:

- The more hierarchic the governance structure is, the lower is the risk of adverse effects emanating from incomplete contracts. By contrast, in hybrid or market governance structures contractual arrangements must be designed sharper and more concise in order to reduce risk of incompleteness.
- The more market-based a transaction is, the higher is incentive intensity because parties' individual benefits and receipts are strongly associated with individual efforts and investments made than they are in hierarchic structures. To ascertain fair incentive intensity, contracts must be stronger as well.
- The four attributes are complementary and not conflictive to each other. For instance, in the case of an alliance or JV, which is governed in a hybrid mode, incentive intensity is semi-strong, so that the rigidity of the contract law behaves accordingly, and softer monitoring mechanisms are implemented (cf. Williamson, 1996, p. 105).

Typically, for unilateral contractual arrangements (e.g. contracting-out, licensing agreements) less hierarchical governance structures are chosen, while bilateral cooperation (e.g. cross-licensing agreements or technology sharing) or equity-based alliances (e.g. JVs) require stronger control mechanisms and stronger contract law (cf. Oxley, 1997).

Arguing from a management accounting and control perspective and following Ouchi (1980), Håkansson and Lind (2004) and VdM and Vosselman (2000) modify the tripartite governance structure of Williamson (1973, 1990, 1996) and apply a more social norm-oriented approach (Table 21).

Governance structure *(according to Williamson (1973, 1990, 1996))*	Governance structure *(according to Håkansson and Lind (2004), Ouchi (1980) and VdM and Vosselman (2000))*
Hierarchy	Hierarchical coordination/Bureaucracy-based pattern
Hybrid	Clan coordination/Trust-based pattern
Market	Market coordination/Market-based pattern

Table 21: Comparison of approaches to governance structures.
(Source: Håkansson and Lind, 2004; Ouchi, 1980; VdM and Vosselman, 2000).

Ouchi (1980) considers the three governance structures as mediating or control mechanisms for transactions which help to form prices of transactions and to determine value of contributions made by involved parties. While the two approaches do not significantly differ with respect to the poles of governance structures, Håkansson and Lind (2004), Ouchi (1980) and VdM and Vosselman (2000) advocate a more social norm-oriented perspective in case of hybrid governance structures, such as applied for JVs. Speklé (2001) also builds his strong TCE-oriented perspective on MC on Williamson's interpretation (1993a). He differentiates between competition-based market control and several hierarchical or hybrid control mechanisms (arm's length control, boundary control, exploratory control, and machine control) (cf. Nicholson et al., 2006). Although these archetypes follow the tripartite governance structure and control levels (market, hierarchy, and hybrid) and refer to the control archetypes (e.g. explanation of action and results control) as proposed by Giacobbe and Booth (2009) and Donada and Nogatchewsky (2006), as presented in Chapter 0, there are two pivotal differences: first, Speklé's governance structures and control archetypes refer to an organizational, but not to an interorganizational context (cf. VdM and Vosselman, 2006). The latter uses to be more complex, so that governance and MC need to be adjusted accordingly. Second, a tight TCE-oriented perspective alone, as per Speklé, ignores informal control mechanisms, such as clan or social control, and therefore limits the possibilities of designing a hybrid governance structure (cf. Dekker, 2004). Thus, several studies, which applied TCE from a broader perspective, have proven these informal control mechanisms to be crucial for controlling IORs including subtypes, (cf. Appuhami et al., 2011; Caglio and Ditillo, 2008; Das and Teng, 2001a; Dekker, 2004; Kamminga and VdM, 2007; Langfield-Smith, 2008; Liu et al., 2014). For this reason, their perspective on TCE will be used in the present study to analyze governance structures and MC in PPPs between IOs/DCAs and the private sector while the tight TCE-oriented approach developed by Speklé (2001), and later adopted by others (cf. Nicholson et al., 2006; Vosselman, 2002), will not be further considered.

To conclude, the increasing organizational complexity and coordination efforts that are coming along with the upsurge of interorganizational cooperations, such as alliances, JVs, and strategic partnerships (cf. Håkansson and Lind, 2004), promote trust-based clan coordination to become an appropriate hybrid governance form for transactional relations of such cooperations (cf. Berry, 1994; Ouchi, 1980; VdM and Vosselman, 2000). Although trust is not acknowledged to be a deployable social control mechanism per se, it helps to make implemented governance structures and controls more effective, in particular if asset specificity and interdependencies between involved parties are high. This goes along with clan coordination, another social mechanism, which builds governance structures on common beliefs, traditions and values. Inherent to this form of coordination is clan control, which follows the idea that strong corporate culture induces higher organizational commitment (cf. Håkansson and Lind, 2004; Kamminga and VdM, 2007; Ouchi, 1979; VdM and Vosselman, 2000). In the context of clan control, Ouchi (1979, p. 76) evokes two more transaction characteristics to be added to the TCE framework, *knowledge of the transformation process* and *output measurability of transactions*. Both factors serve to measure if, and to which extent, desired organizational performance was achieved. In Ouchi's sense, this means that in the best case scenario both the de facto measurability of behavior and the output and accountant's ability to undertake that performance measurement are high, wherefore they determine how effectively an organization can be controlled and which governance structure is suitable for that. However, regardless of the chosen governance structure, a high need for information usually is predominant among the parties involved in a transaction and management accounting affair, and control is deemed a contributor to meeting this need (cf. Håkansson and Lind, 2004).

4.2.6 Other pertinent TCE Characteristics

In addition to the TCE-related two behavioral assumptions, the three critical dimensions, and the different governance characteristics, which all together dominate discussions about MC design and governance structure setting in the context of PPPs, JVs and IORs, there are some more TCE characteristics that have been raised by a few studies only, namely atmosphere, mundane vs. opportunistic TC, and relational characteristics. Their inclusion contributes to enhancing the theoretical framework through which findings from the empirical part will be analyzed. Thus, these characteristics are briefly explained:

Atmosphere
With respect to interaction within organizations, Baudry and Chassagnon (2010) highlight the impact that atmosphere can have on transactions. Williamson (1993b, p. 135) argues that "...atmosphere refers to interactions between transactions that are technologically separable but are joined attitudinally and have systems consequences". Three main factors are assumed to influence the atmosphere within organizations: the settlement of disputes, the structure of incentive systems, and the manner in which work is controlled (cf. Baudry and Chassagnon, 2010).

Mundane vs. opportunistic transaction costs
Together with Baldwin (2007), Richardson and Kilfoyle (2009) suggest to distinguish between so-called mundane and opportunistic TC. They criticize that to date accounting literature allegedly is predominantly oriented towards Oliver Williamson's TCE approach and his ex-post contractual focus on the costs of opportunistic behavior (opportunistic TC). Instead, they advocate considering the costs of contract design (e.g. contract negotiation and renegotiation, monitoring of contract quality), which incur primarily ex-ante, prior to contract conclusion, and which are often underestimated (Krause, 2014). That is what they call mundane costs. In brief, Richardson and Kilfoyle (2009, p. 943) define mundane TC as "costs associated with defining, measuring and compensating for transactions".

Relational characteristics
Besides the previously mentioned three critical dimensions, the JV literature discusses four relational characteristics associated with the TCE (cf. Kamminga and VdM, 2007; VdM and Kamminga, 2015):

1) Parental differences
2) Bargaining power,
3) Information asymmetry, and
4) Trust.

While trust has already been discussed in Chapter 3.6.1, some attention should be paid to the remaining three characteristics:

Parental differences: Parents are independent organizations (e.g. firms) involved in a JV. They may differ because of the motivations and strategic interests for entering into a JV and because of their individual characteristics (e.g. corporate and national culture, management practices). All these attributes together are called parental differences. Depending on the strength of differences and on the complexity of the JV, MC mechanisms need to be designed in a more or less rigid and sophisticated manner (cf. Kamminga and VdM, 2007; Parkhe, 1991).

Bargaining power: This term describes the power position of a parent partner to exercise control over the JV partnership and therefore to influence the MC mechanisms being implemented. As stated in Chapter 3.3, controls mechanisms serve to assure contractual arrangements that are complementary to the underlying governance structure. Hence, the more bargaining power a parent partner possesses, the more this partner can impact on control mechanisms and decision-making. In consequence, this parent partner gains in power to determine transactional outcome (cf. Cäker and Siverbo, 2011; Kamminga and VdM, 2015).

Information asymmetry: Asymmetrically distributed information between the JV management and the JV's parents usually complicates control of the JV. Typical reasons for information asymmetry are intercultural differences, diverging expertise and knowledge of the parents and JV management, or geographical distance between the JV and its parents. The more pronounced these factors are the more likely tight control mechanism are implemented; they go along with diminished autonomy and flexibility for the management and pose particular challenges to them in highly uncertain environments where quick decision-making and prompt adjustment to new situations are crucial (cf. Kamminga and VdM, 2007).

4.2.7 Delineation of TCE from Other Pertinent Theories

The agency theory and the property rights theory form further important research branches of the NIE sciences besides the TCE (cf. Kim and Mahoney, 2005; Menard, 2005; Richter and Furubotn, 2003, p. 39). All these theories have been widely applied in the social sciences, ranging from accounting and economics to political science or strategic management, and have in common that they touch the issue of contractual arrangements with respect to relations between individuals/individuals, individuals/organizations and organizations/organizations (cf. Kim and Mahoney, 2005; Menard, 2005; Richter and Furubotn, 2003, p. 39). Thus, this chapter explains how the TCE distinguishes from the agency theory and the property rights theory, and why the TCE is more suitable than the two other theories to underlie the analysis of MC in PPPs between IOs/DCAs and the private sector.

Although all three theories consider transactions as part of economic organization, it is only the TCE itself which concentrates on the smallest unit of analysis from a holistic perspective, namely the transaction (cf. Williamson, 1996, p. 58). By contrast, the property rights theory takes an institutional view, according to which transactions are tightly bound by norms and contractual arrangements, which do not facilitate ex-post amendments because contracts are assumed to be complete once they come into effect. The MC scope is narrowed to property rights compliance by the parties involved in the transaction (cf. Grossman and Hart, 1986; Kim and Mahoney, 2005; Richter and Furubotn, 2003, p. 407).

The agency theory follows a market-based approach, which disregards potential hierarchies that are framing transactions. It focuses on incentives of individuals (e.g. individual persons, individual firms, and individual organizations) and on the maximization of their benefits and interests assuming complete contract settings from the outset. Just like TCE, the agency theory assumes that transactions including contractual arrangements are subject to information asymmetry. Agency theorists regard individuals as actors that rather compete than collaborate with each other, and usually pursue individual instead of common goals. Although need for control is accentuated in the light of risk of opportunistic behavior, MC mechanisms are usually based on selected quantitative elements which are particularly oriented toward monetary benchmarks while organizational achievements such as trust-building or social capital formation are ignored (cf. Budäus and Grüb, 2007; Håkansson and Lind, 2004; Kim and Mahoney, 2005; VdM and Vosselman, 2000; Williamson, 1987).

By contrast, the TCE places problems of economic organization and inefficient outcomes in the center of transaction analyses. Moreover, the TCE strongly favours an ex-post perspective on downstream TC which occur after conclusion of contracts as a result of incomplete contracts, a core assumption of the TCE. The choice of suitable governance forms (hierarchic, hybrid or market) is deemed crucial to reduce TC. MC mechanisms contribute to effectively implement different governance forms. Due to the broad range of possible governance forms, which can vary between the two poles of hierarchy and market, and with respect to the focus on issues of economic organization, the scope of MC in this study is not confined to a specific MC design. What matters is the appropriateness of the MC types chosen (cf. Kim and Mahoney, 2005; Williamson, 1998).

Table 22 summarizes the core characteristics of the three theories that have been compared and discussed before.

	Transaction cost economics	Property rights theory	Agency theory
Unit of analysis	Transaction	Institution	Principal-agent contract
Focal dimension	Various types of asset specificity	Property rights	Incentives
Contractual focus *Assumption:*	Contracts are always incomplete	Incompleteness of contracts is avoidable	Risk of incomplete contracts is diminishable
Response:	Choice of (ex post) governance mechanism	Ex-ante property rights allocation and ex-post distributional conflicts	Ex-ante incentive alignment. Monitoring mechanisms
Scope in Management Control issues	Focus on MC in its entirety	Focus on control from property right ownership perspective	Focus on selected (primarily quantitative) elements of MC
Central problems of	Bounded rationali-	Externalities, un-	Information asym-

	Transaction cost economics	Property rights theory	Agency theory
economic organization	ty, information asymmetry, opportunism, and asset specificity	clearly defined and difficult to enforce property rights, vested interests	metry, risk aversion (by agents)
Nature of interaction	Cooperation	Tendency to competition	Competition

Table 22: Comparison of TCE vs. agency theory and property rights theory.
(Source: own depiction, following Kim and Mahoney (2005) and based on Demsetz (1967); Grossman and Hart, 1986; Linder, 1999; Menard, 2005; Richter and Furubotn, 2003, pp. 39-41 and p. 407; Speklé, 2001; Williamson, 1996, pp. 56-58; Williamson, 1998)

In relation to the subject matter of this thesis, Petersen (2011) outlines that the PPP concept has evolved from mere forms of contracting-out and privatization to a stage where priority is given to a more collaborative approach in order to overcome characteristic shortcomings of PPP relationships underlying an agency theoretical design, in particular information asymmetry (which implies "hidden characteristics", "hidden action" and hidden information") and opportunistic behavior. However, in accordance with the observations of Petersen (2011), Linder (1999) contends that partnerships, such as PPPs, are more in the nature of cooperation than of competition, a characteristic that is ascribed to the TCE. Insights from pertinent previous new institutional research on networks, organizational behavior and partnerships support this view (cf. March and Simon, 1976; Van Kersbergen and Van Waarden, 2004). Due to the tight assumptions that accompany the agency theory and the property rights theory, which disregard hybrid organizational patterns of partnerships and may not adequately capture complexity of PPPs between IOs/DCAs and private sector firms, it will be refrained from using them as a theoretical framework for the present study.

4.3 Theoretical Link between ACI and TCE

The motivation to build a bridge from the ACI to TCE emanates from the founders of the ACI approach, Mayntz and Scharpf (1995, p. 41). They assume bounded-rational actors who cause TC due to their omnipresent susceptibility to opportunistic behavior. Institutions are assumed to potentially reduce TC and to facilitate governance forms of interaction and transaction that range from pure hierarchy to pure market. The institutional setting or institutions perform a standard-setting capacity and manifest some boundaries, guidelines and governance structures including rules and norms in IORs, and they influence organizational practices (cf. Covaleski et al., 2003; Krause, 2014; North, 1986; Speklé, 2001; VdM and Vosselman, 2000; Vosselman and VdM, 2009). Institutions adopt a regulatory function and are supposed to minimize TC, e.g. by setting incentive structures, and therefore increase economic efficiency, at least in theory (cf. North, 1986).

In terms of PPPs, the discussion about governance concepts contributes to aligning the elements of the ACI approach with the TCE. A structured governance framework forms the basis for MC activities in PPPs, which are by nature complex forms of interorganizational cooperation (cf. Andon, 2012). Complexities of any kind not only prove to be critical for PPPs' success in general, but also create challenges for the design of MC (cf. Gupta et al., 2013; Kamminga and VdM, 2007; Meira et al., 2010; Speklé, 2001; VdM and Kamminga, 2015; Zhang Y. and Rajagopalan, 2002). In consistence with Appuhami et al. (2011), Donada and Nogatchewsky (2006), and Emsley and Kidon (2007), who used a second NIE approach besides the TCE in order to better analyze and understand the complexities associated with their research object, the ACI and the TCE will serve in a combined manner as theoretical framework for the empirical analysis of MC in PPPs between IOs/DCAs and the private sector. While Petersen's (2011) is the only identified empirical study on PPPs based on the ACI, hitherto no other study has been found that used ACI and TCE both together in order to analyze any kind of IORs. Thus, the current study is also supposed to enhance extant literature by using an unprecedented dual theoretical approach from NIE.

4.3.1 ACI-TCE Theoretical Framework

On the basis of Figure 21 this chapter outlines how the theoretical elements of the ACI approach and the TCE mesh with one another.

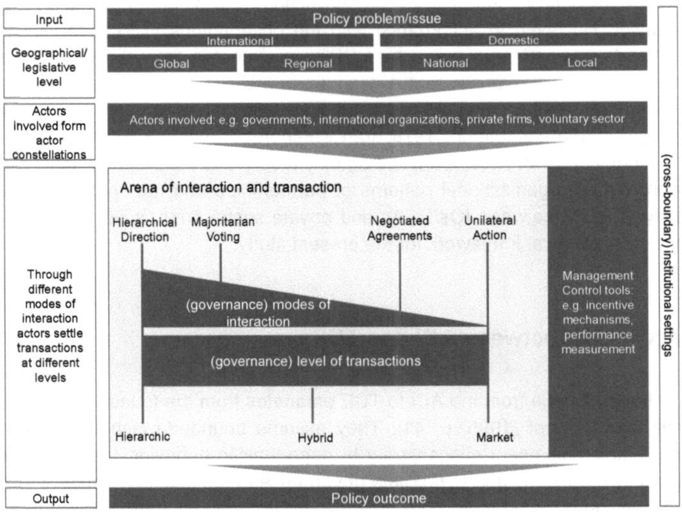

Figure 21: Combined ACI-TCE theoretical framework.
(Source: own depiction, based on Mayntz and Scharpf (1995, p. 62); Rhodes, 1996; Scharpf, 1997, p. 46 f.; Stoker, 1998; Van Kersbergen and Van Waarden, 2004)

The core of the combined ACI-TCE theoretical framework forms the so-called "arena" of interaction and transaction. Various actors with various backgrounds therein come together in various constellations and as part of various organizations in order to tackle policy issues and problems at various geographic and legislative levels (cf. March and Olsen, 1989, p. 43;

Mayntz and Scharpf, 1995, p. 44; Scharpf, 2000, p. 17; Scharpf, 1997, p. 69). Policy issues and problems form input factors for interactions and transactions in these arenas. The institutional environment sets boundaries to the whole process, from policy problem identification to policy outcome, while MC mechanisms enable coordination of the interactions and transactions on the basis of the chosen governance structure.

From a macro-perspective, institutions embrace and influence the processing of a policy problem/issue from its beginning (input) to its outcome (output) as they frame the arenas within which individuals and organizations interact with each other and execute transactions. Both interaction and transaction underlie existing governance structures, which are substantially influenced and shaped by the institutional setting. To enforce on a micro-level the boundaries, guidelines and governance structures, which are set to individuals and organizations, many researchers from the accounting field promote MC practices and tools as appropriate means of implementation, regardless of the chosen governance form (cf. Adler, 2001; Mouritsen and Thrane, 2006; Scapens, 1994; VdM and Vosselman, 2000; Vosselman and VdM, 2009).

MC is seen as a means of solution that anticipates and prevents organizational problems, such as bounded rationality and opportunism, and that promotes legitimacy of transaction. Moreover, MC has a transparency- and trust-building capacity that support collaboration and smooth operation within and among individuals and organizations (cf. Kamminga and VdM, 2007; Mouritsen and Thrane, 2006; Vosselman and VdM, 2009). Richardson and Kilfoyle (2009) suggest that MC systems form a key element of governance structures and vary in line with the nature of transactions (cf. Anderson and Dekker, 2005; Kamminga and VdM; Speklé, 2001; Vosselman and VdM, 2009). In brief, MC systems can be customized and flexibly adapted to the characteristics of transactions, irrespective of the underlying governance structure (hierarchy, hybrid or market) and the institutional setting they are embedded in.

4.3.2 Forms and Levels of Governance

Mayntz and Scharpf (1995, pp. 60-62) emphasize in their work that modes of interaction and institutional settings are predominantly discussed among scholars under the key term “governance”, taking particular reference to the TCE approach (cf. Covaleski et al., 2003; Dekker, 2004). Despite this awareness neither Mayntz and Scharpf (1995) nor Scharpf (1997) discuss modes of interaction and institutional settings when considering governance. However, this term should be briefly discussed because of the role it plays in connecting the ACI approach and the TCE with each other as well as in characterizing forms of MC in PPPs.

Coming from a public policy-oriented angle of the ACI by Scharpf, the four modes of interaction represent four different governance levels. Complementary to the ACI's modes of interaction, the TCE approach by Williamson yielded three governance levels of transaction,

- Hierarchic,
- Hybrid and
- Market

upon which numerous researchers have drawn in their studies on the governance role of management accounting and control with respect to IORs including PPPs and JVs (cf. Anderson and Dekker, 2005; Berry et al., 2009; Chen D. et al., 2009; Cooper and Slagmulder, 2004; Covaleski et al., 2003; Dekker, 2004; Håkansson and Lind, 2004; Kamminga and VdM, 2007; Richardson and Kilfoyle, 2009; VdM and Vosselman, 2000; Vosselman, 2002; Vosselman and VdM, 2009). Hence, governance modes of interaction and governance levels of transaction have in common that they range between two extreme forms of governance, hierarchic and non-hierarchic governance, wherefore conceptual cornerstones are marked. Table 23 compares the different governance modes/levels from the ACI and the TCE approach and displays implications they have for coordination and steering of various actors, according to the definition by Almquist et al. (2013).

Governance levels		**Governance forms**	**Cooperation levels**
Modes of interaction (ACI)	Levels of transactions (TCE)		
Hierarchical Direction	Hierarchic	Governance through power and authority	Cooperation and partnership strongly limited
Majoritarian Voting	Hybrid	Governance through alliances and networks → strongly consensus-oriented	Cooperation and partnership e.g. in the form of PPPs and JVs
Negotiated Agreements			
Unilateral Action	Market	Governance through competition	Cooperation and partnership strongly limited

Table 23: Governance from the perspective of the ACI and the TCE.
(Source: own depiction, based on Berry et al. (2009); Caglio und Ditillo, 2008; Chen D. et al., 2009; Covaleski et al., 2003; Dekker, 2004; Jamali, 2004; Håkansson and Lind, 2004; Kamminga und VdM, 2007; Koppenjan und Enserink, 2009; Mayntz und Scharpf, 1995, p. 57 and pp. 60-62; Merchant und Van der Stede, 2012, p. 14; Richardson and Kilfoyle, 2009; Scharpf, 1997, p. 93; VdM and Vosselman, 2000; Vosselman, 2002; Vosselman and VdM, 2009; Williamson, 1996, p. 378)

Critics may argue that levels of governance are not as discrete as Table 23 may let assume (cf. Miller et al., 2008; Speklé, 2001). In terms of long-term oriented, hybrid governance alliances and networks can adopt multiple forms of cooperation (cf. Richardson and Kilfoyle, 2009). However, the steering of PPPs or JVs is likely to tend to one of the governance levels indicated in Table 23. Thus, a further subdivision of governance levels does not appear to be conducive to the empirical part of this thesis and to its thematic scope.

Moreover, discussions about governance are conducted sector-oriented, differentiating in particular between corporate governance in the private sector and good governance/public accountability in regarding public entities (cf. Almquist et al., 2013; Rosenbaum and Shepherd, 2000; Stoker, 1998; Van Kersbergen and Van Waarden, 2004; Woods, 2000). However, in-depth discussions about forms of governance will be disregarded with respect to the scope of the present study. To conclude, the theoretically founded modes of interaction and levels of transactions can be summarized under the term "governance" and form the vehicle through which ideas of governance will be incorporated in this thesis.

4.4 Interim Summary

The literature review in Chapter 2.2 has shown that theories from NIE, in particular TCE, represent suitable theoretical frameworks for studies on MC in PPPs, JVs, and IORs, which have been published in renowned accounting journals. Several pertinent studies pursued a combined theoretical approach, using the TCE together with interdisciplinary approaches or theories from social sciences (cf. Appuhami et al., 2011; Dekker, 2003; Donada and Nogatchewsky, 2006; Emsley and Kidon, 2007; Meira et al., 2010; VdM and Scapens, 2008). These studies did this in order to enable a better understanding of the complexities related to the multi-stakeholder character of PPPs, JVs, and IORs, as well as to facilitate a more thorough analysis that is built on a solid theoretical basis. In terms of PPPs, public and private actors enter into cooperation in different constellations at different geographical levels in order to provide a broad spectrum of public services of common interests. Partnerships can encounter diverse institutional settings and vary by the way actors collaborate with each other as well as by the mode of interaction which is formalized by underlying contractual agreements. Thus, the basic structure and the multi-stakeholder character of PPPs reflect the theoretical elements of the ACI, as defined by Scharpf (1997) amongst others.

To address practical MC issues, such as governance and contract design or performance measurement and monitoring, the TCE has built the theoretical framework in a series of studies on PPPs, JVs and IORs (cf. Anderson and Dekker, 2005; Choi and Beamish, 2004; Covaleski et al., 2003; Dekker, 2004; Jacobson and Choi, 2008; Kamminga and VdM, 2007; Meira et al., 2010; Richardson and Kilfoyle, 2009; VdM and Vosselman, 2000) and is dominant in identifying MC patterns and explaining MC systems in various types of partnership. In conjunction with some governance and relational characteristics, bounded rationality, opportunism, asset specificity, frequency and uncertainty form the major attributes of the TCE that help to characterize PPPs, JVs and IORs as well as to identify and anticipate inherent organizational difficulties, frictions and problems. To improve organizational performance, reduce TC and promote partnerships' success, these challenges need to be overcome and the impact of transactions costs be reduced. To achieve this, a tripartite approach, that is composed of either a market-, hybrid- or hierarchy-based governance structure framed by a suitable contract design including formal and informal controls, typically underlies all kinds of partnerships. In this context, numerous previous investigations applied a field study design to analyze MC in PPPs JVs and IORs on the basis of the TCE (cf. Dekker, 2003; Jacobson and Choi, 2008; Nicholson et al., 2006; Schepper et al., 2015).

To conclude, the use of ACI and TCE as a coherent theoretical approach is appropriate to empirical research on MC in PPPs established between IOs/DCAs and the private sector. A field study design represents a reasonable way to explore these PPPs.

4.5 Derivation of the Research Questions

In this chapter, pertinent research questions, underlying this research study, will be worked out and answered through the evidence and findings from the empirical field study. These questions are derived through integration of the research gap that has been identified in the structured literature review and the theoretical framework underlying the present study; they are supposed to address MC in PPPs between IOs or DCAs and private sector firms in a way that helps to close the inherent research gap.

Following a coherent research process (cf. Kromrey, 2009, pp. 70-73), the research questions split up into a tripartite structure that facilitates describing and assessing MC in PPPs between DCAs/IOs and the private sector. Consequently, four research questions have been developed to conduct this process (Figure 22). While the descriptive section (RQ1) serves to identify key characteristics of the PPPs under review, which MC should take into account, the explorative will generate new evidence for MC research by analyzing these PPPs against the background of the theoretical framework (RQ2.1 & 2.2). Both the descriptive and the explorative research questions will rest upon empirical data collected from the field study. In the normative section (RQ3), the actual scientific added value of this study will be generated by merging existing and newly generated evidence on MC in PPPs. However, for the sake of applicability of the theoretical framework for different PPPs and the qualitative field study-based research approach of this study, the research questions are not too narrowly formulated to maintain flexibility and open-mindedness. The reason is that too detailed and specified research questions may cause ex-ante biases of the empirical findings to be generated and therefore simply lead to confirmations of preconceived conclusions (cf. Endenich, 2012, p. 47; Ferreira and Merchant, 1992, p. 5).

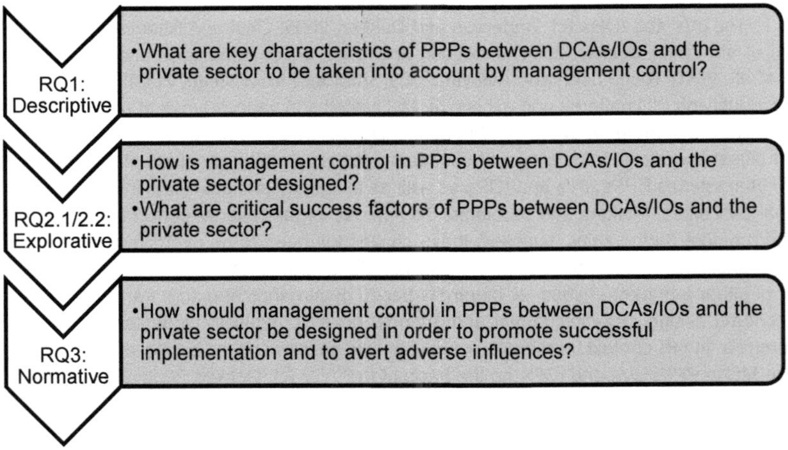

Figure 22: Research questions.

Following an institutional economic approach, awareness of a partnerships' underlying structure, as well as of internal and external influence factors that are setting some framework conditions, needs to be raised at the outset. This implies the identification of the actors involved on the inter- and intraorganizational level, the constellation they are acting in, their skills and competences but also their motivation for the partnership and environmental factors, which all together may influence partners' actions and behavior and therefore have implications for MC (cf. Heinze, 2012, p. 56; Petring, 2007; Scharpf, 1997, p. 38 and p. 43 f.). In addition to this, the TCE brings in the notion that contract design (cf. Anderson and Dekker, 2005; Reeves, 2008), resource allocation and financing (cf. Schepper et al., 2015) characterize a partnership formally, but also the interaction between partners is therefore strongly relevant for understanding MC. The matter of contract design and financing bridges to two more elements, namely risks and risk allocation (cf. Chung and Hensher, 2015; Demirag et al., 2012; Hwang et al., 2013), as well as the level of trust between partners (cf. English and Baxter, 2010; Langfield-Smith, 2008), which do not only form characteristics of partnerships, but whose identification is also relevant for determining the degree of formal MC (cf. Broadbent and Laughlin, 2008; Froud, 2003).

Thus, having clear awareness of the key characteristics of a partnership paves the way for understanding why MC is designed and practiced in a certain way and for assessing it against the theoretical framework (cf. Brandau, 2010, p. 38; Broweleit, 2014, p. 174 ff.; Gerdes, 2011, p. 3). From these considerations results

> **RQ1: What are key characteristics of PPPs between DCAs/IOs and the private sector to be taken into account by management control?**

The second research question, split up into two subquestions, actually forms the core of analysis of MC in PPPs. It is dedicated to the stocktaking of how MC is designed in PPPs between DCAs/IOs and the private sector, what control mechanisms are applied and why (RQ2.1). This is done against the backdrop of different kinds of CSFs that are crucial for making PPPs successful, or otherwise can lead to failure, and that MC should address (RQ2.2).

Anderson and Dekker (2005) build a linkage between the theoretical background of this study, characteristics of PPPs and MC. Seen from the TCE side, and with a focus on market transactions, they consider resource exchanges and interaction between different partners as contractually based transactions. Basically, they assume that transactions and partners have certain characteristics which are potentially in tense relationship with the contractual agreements. Thus, in PPPs, MC should be designed in a way that contract compliance is promoted and alignment between the partners' different characteristics is achieved. In other words, alignment of MC with the actors and with the subject matter of the PPP is essential. Moreover, the MC design of a partnership needs to consider and address different control topics in theory and in practice. Among those are, in particular, alignment and harmonization of diverging interests, budget and resource control, conflict management and prevention, organizational culture and governance structure, performance management and measurement including monitoring, risk management, and strategic control (cf. Berry et al., 2009; Cäker and Siverbo, 2011; Kamminga and VdM, 2007; Liu J., 2014; Pothukuchi et al., 2002; Van der Stede, 2003). However, the challenge to design MC appropriately is not confined to the PPP as an organizational and/or legal entity between two or more partners because environmental influences and the institutional framework have to be considered likewise (cf. Boland et al., 2008; Meschi, 2005). From these considerations results

> **RQ2.1: How is management control in PPPs between DCAs/IOs and the private sector designed?**

The cross-cutting nature of MC in PPPs becomes evident when the CSFs of PPPs, JVs and IORs are analyzed in a systematic way, as done by Chan et al. (2010a) or Osei-Kyei and Chan (2015). While only a few articles explicitly (cf. Chan et al., 2010a) or implicitly (cf. Langfield-Smith, 2008; Langfield-Smith and Smith; Li P. et al., 2013) mentioned effective and suitable MC itself as CSF of PPPs or associated forms of cooperation, many more studies deem several elements of MC crucial for partnerships' successful implementation, which are categorized under "Governance and Management Control" in Figure 16. In addition, numerous studies identified different kinds of partnership characteristics as important CSFs, such as clear and effective contracts (cf. Jacobson and Choi, 2008; Mota and Moreira, 2015), commitment (cf. Glagola and Sheedy, 2002; Li B. et al., 2005a), conducive team behavior (cf. Chan et al., 2004; Jacobson and Choi, 2008) or responsibility sharing (cf. Chou and Pramudawardhani, 2015; Hwang et al., 2013). The understanding of different partnership characteristics as CSFs and the awareness of many other external and internal factors that might impact more strongly or weakly on partnerships are not only critical for successful partnership implementation but also need to be taken into account for the design of MC. Hence, the matter of CSFs of PPPs builds linkages between RQ1 and RQ2.1, as well as between theory and practice. Thus, to understand the design of MC including the challenges and the problems that it is facing in PPPs between DCAs/IOs and the private sector, CSFs need to be identified through the field study. From these considerations results

RQ2.2: What are critical success factors of PPPs between DCAs/IOs and the private sector?

As shown in Figure 23, the overall research scope and analysis approach is based on a combined theoretical framework, composed of ACI and TCE, and on findings from previous PPPs, JVs and IORs in terms of MC and CSFs, which have been carved out in the literature review. The evidence gained from that explains the reasoning for the research questions RQ1, RQ2.1 and RQ2.2 and will help to answer them in a structured manner. With respect to the identified research gap, the focus will mainly be placed on PPPs between private sector firms and IOs, and also between private sector firms and DCAs (cf. grey shaded areas in Figure 23) but partnerships between all three of them will be considered too (cf. grey dotted area in Figure 23).

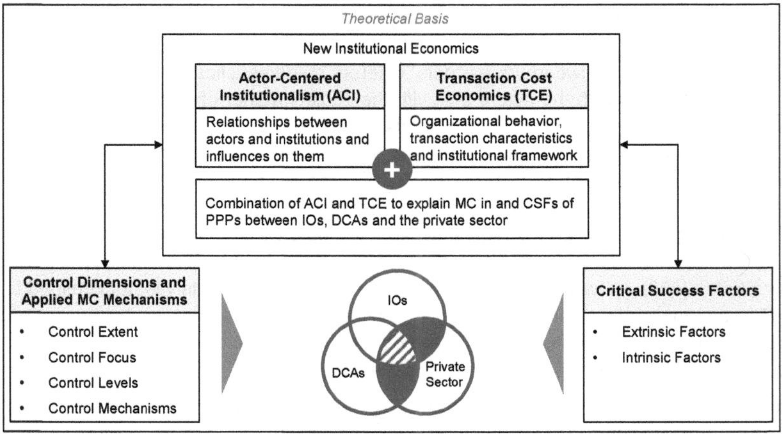

Figure 23: Overall research scope.
(Source: own depiction, following Broweleit (2014))

Previous studies revealed different kinds of partnerships between diverse public and private partners that enter into joint cooperation at local, regional, national and international level. Moreover, these partnerships face particular challenges and are subject to divergent external and internal influences (cf. Andon, 2012; Broadbent and Laughlin (2003a, 2004); Chou and Pramudawardhani, 2015; Jamali, 2004; Meira et al., 2010; Torres and Pina, 2001). That is why MC design in PPPs varies, and a broad range of different CSFs has been identified for them (cf. Berry et al., 2009; Osei-Kyei and Chan, 2015). The choice of formal and informal MC mechanisms occurs individually, and previously identified CSFs may apply in the same vein, acquire another weight, or new factors may become relevant (cf. Appuhami et al., 2011; Groot and Merchant, 2000; Jacobson and Choi, 2008). Thus, results from previous research are transferable to PPPs between DCAs/IOs and the private sector only to a limited extent and do not provide a sufficient basis for recommendations on how to design MC in such PPPs. From these considerations results

RQ3: How should management control in PPPs between DCAs/IOs and the private sector be designed in order to promote successful implementation and to avert adverse influences?

Through synthesis of existing knowledge from pertinent previous studies with the findings from the field research of this study the identified research gap on MC in PPPs will be closed and therefore scientific added value be generated. To this end, the present research questions serve as benchmarks for analysis of the empirical results. In order to prepare the ground for this analysis, the motivations for the chosen research design and the methodological approach will be explained in the subsequent Chapter 0.

5. Research Design and Methodology

The empirical part of the present thesis is based on semi-structured interviews that are embraced by a qualitative field study research design and have been subjected to content analysis. In the subsequent chapters, the basics of the chosen research design and methodology will be explained at first. This is followed by detailed descriptions of how data has been collected and analyzed and is completed by a quality assessment of the methodological approach used in the course of this field study. A brief summary concludes this chapter.

5.1 Choice and Definition of the Research Approach

The choice of a research approach should be aligned with the research focus, the evidence and current knowledge from extant literature and the theoretical basis of the research subject. Moreover, the nature of the research topic and the access to data deserve consideration at an ex-ante stage. Finally, the research approach should be fit for purpose, thus be designed in a way to provide the best possible basis and framework conditions for answering the research questions (cf. Brandau, 2010, p. 41; Cooper and Slagmulder, 2004; Endenich, 2012, p. 156). A fundamental decision to be taken by the researcher in this context is whether a qualitative or a quantitative design is more suitable to answer the research questions. While quantitative research is typically based on standardized, numerical information, qualitative research uses verbalized data and experiences (cf. Bortz and Döring, 2006, p. 295 f.; Broweleit, 2014, p. 169). The literature review revealed the small number of studies that hitherto had dealt with MC in PPPs for development and the low level of theoretical foundation of many studies. In this case qualitative and interview-based research is suitable to form and refine theories and theoretical approaches and it enables researchers to explore complex or unknown phenomena, processes and relationships (cf. Donada and Nogatchewsky, 2006; Endenich, 2012, p. 156; Håkansson and Lind, 2004; Lillis and Mundy, 2005; Chapter 2.2.2).
In the following, the methodological elements of the qualitative field study design, based on semi-structured interviews, and the reasons for choosing it will be explained, in conjunction with its delimitation from other potential research designs, methodologies and methods.[2]

5.1.1 Characteristics of Qualitative Research

In recent years, qualitative research has evolved into a fundamental research approach, established and used by diverse scientific disciplines in social sciences including business administration. Due to its application-oriented and pragmatic nature, qualitative research basically claims to identify and describe the social reality of individuals and organizations as well as to draw attention to interpretative patterns, processes and structural characteristics. Compared to these research strategies, which usually work with large-scale samples as part of objectivistic and rather standardized methodological concepts, qualitative research differs by

[2] According to Ahrens and Chapman (2006, p. 821), methodology means the "general approach to studying research topics" (qualitative vs. quantitative) while methods comprise "specific research techniques" (e.g. interviews, surveys).

T. S. Konrad, *Management Control in Public-Private Partnerships*,
Schriften zu Wirtschaftsprüfung, Steuerlehre und Controlling,
https://doi.org/10.1007/978-3-658-22868-2_5

often better and closer access to the research subject and to the phenomena under investigation. Hence, the generic term *qualitative research* describes different research perspectives, which are characterized by their theoretical reference framework, methods of data collection, methods of data analysis and fields of application (cf. Bortz and Döring, 2006, p. 304; Flick et al., 2013, pp. 14-19; Mayer, 2013, p. 22 f.; Moll et al., 2006, p. 376). Qualitative research methods facilitate the provision of "...detailed descriptions of events, situations and interactions between people and things providing depth and detail" (Patton, 1987, p. 301) and to explore "complex, interdependent issues" (Wright, 2004, p. 57). In this context, Flick et al. (2013, p. 19) distinguish between three research perspectives: 1) access to subjective viewpoints, 2) description of processes in the context of social situations, and 3) hermeneutical analysis of deep-set structures.

Due to growing environmental complexity, accounting research pays increasingly more attention to qualitative research methodologies: "The complexity of [...] environment and the more prominent role attributed to accounting has resulted in an increase in the use of qualitative methodology based on its ability to provide fresh and interesting insights to the way that accounting interacts with its environment" (Moll et al., 2006, p. 375). In Chapter 4.3 it is shown that MC in PPPs, JVs, and IORs is subject to different kinds of complexities. The research approach of the present study matches the first perspective according to Flick (2013) in terms of the methods of data collection (semi-structured guided interviews) and data analysis (coding and qualitative content analysis) but also integrates elements of the second perspective concerning the fields of application. The reason is that individuals who work for different organizations will be requested to share their experience and tacit knowledge from implementation of PPPs for development.

For a long time, quantitative-positivistic approaches dominated social sciences research whose quality was benchmarked by their methodological proximity to the natural sciences. Critical voices started complaining about partially simplifying theoretical assumptions in quantitative models, which lack sufficient proximity to reality and neglect contextual factors, social activities and subjective perspectives. On this basis, qualitative research emerged (cf. Bortz and Döring, 2006, p. 302; Broweleit, 2014, p. 170; Lamnek and Krell, 2010, p. 6 ff.). Table 24 compares key characteristics of quantitative and qualitative research methods.

	Quantitative Research Methodology	Qualitative Research Methodology
Scientific discipline orientation	Natural sciences	Social sciences
Epistemological implications and consequences	• Separation of • Theory validation	• Integration of • Theory development and refinement
Understanding of methods	• Hard methods: standardized • Large sample size • Random sampling	• Soft methods: non-standardized • Single cases or limited sample size • Theoretical sampling •
Scope	Identification of cause-and-effect relationships	Identification of regularities of action and interaction (action

	Quantitative Research Methodology	Qualitative Research Methodology
		and interpretative patterns)
Research logic	• Deduction (induction) • Analytic/abstract • Objectifyable results matter • Emphasis on replicability • Generalizability • Hypothesis testing	• Induction • Holistic/specific • Subjectivity matters • Emphasis on singularity • Type identification • Hypothesis generation
Analysis and evaluation	• Measure and explain • Statistical methods	• Understand and describe • Interpretative analysis

Table 24: Comparison of quantitative and qualitative research methodology.
(Source: based on Broweleit (2014, p. 171), Lamnek and Krell (2010, p. 268 f.))

It shows that quantitative research intends to measure and explain identified cause-and-effect relationships and to derive a theory from statistical evidence (deduction), while qualitative research aims at understanding, describing and interpreting empirical findings that might allow drawing conclusions on the existence of regularities and therefore lead to theory development and refinement (induction).

To clarify the practical meaning of either a qualitative or a quantitative research approach, Maxwell (2013, p. 31) differentiates these categories as follows: "Quantitative and qualitative researchers tend to ask different kinds of causal questions. Quantitative researchers tend to be interested in whether and to what extent variance in x causes variance in y. Qualitative researchers, on the other hand, to ask how x plays a role in causing y, and what the process is that connects x and y". He contends that qualitative research is particularly suitable if the focus is placed on learning from the perspective of participants of a research study and if the following goals are pursued (p. 30):

- "Understanding the meaning, for participants in the study, of the events, situations, experiences, and actions they are involved with or engage in."
- "Understanding the particular contexts within which the participants act, and the influence that this context has on their actions."
- "Understanding the process by which events and actions take place."
- "Identifying unanticipated phenomena and influences (...)."

In this sense qualitative research provides more flexibility to adjust the research design to and to focus on individual specifics of study participants and therefore to reveal unanticipated relationships and phenomena. Compared to quantitative research it does not need to strictly follow a predetermined set of procedural rules to ensure correct execution of the research (cf. Atkinson and Shaffir, 1998). Basic characteristics of the research subject and relevant influence factors to be considered will be identified by means of "What"-questions, thus establishing a baseline for the analysis. To understand complexities and interdependencies between processes and actions, as well as to explain certain phenomena, "How"-questions serve to explore those relationships, and "Why"-questions help to find adequate explanations (cf. Endenich, 2012, p. 159; Lillis and Mundy, 2005, p. 127 ff.; Moll et al., 2006, p. 377; Wright, 2004, p. 57). With specific reference to accounting, Ryan et al. (2002, p. 41 ff.) developed three categories of quantitative and qualitative accounting research: critical, interpretive, and mainstream (Table 25).

Category	Characteristics
Critical	• Qualitative • Subjective perspective • Analyzes actions within a broader social context • Focuses on the societal role of accounting in terms of issues, such as conflict, dominance and exercise of power • Follows a radical humanist approach, using social theories by critical theorists like Foucault, Habermas, Latour and Marx
Interpretive	• Qualitative • Subjective perspective • Analyzes actions within a broader social context • Objective representation of reality is impossible because of individuals' inability to fully understand the phenomena and complexities affecting the research subject • Interpretative approach is based on commonalities of experience from the research subjects • Explores the interaction between accounting and its environment as well as with other organizational processes • Intends to reveal prospects for changing or modifying accounting practices and therefore to improve everyday operations ("...accounting practices are not natural phenomena..." (Moll et al., 2006, p. 381))
Mainstream	• Quantitative • Objective perspective • Generalization and prediction of cause-and-effect relationships • Only measurable and observable phenomena are considered as meaningful

Table 25: Categories of quantitative and qualitative accounting research.
(Source: based on Covaleski et al. (1996); Hopper and Powell (1985); Moll et al. (2006, p. 381 f.); Ryan et al. (2002, p. 41 ff.); Smith (2015, p. 145 f.))

The present study pursues an interpretative approach because the research questions help to analyze PPPs for development within a broad social context that includes the institutional environment, and they aim at revealing potential changes and modification for MC, based on identified commonalities of experience among different PPPs. Concretely, the research questions RQ1 and RQ2.2 are supposed to identify MC-related key characteristics and CSFs ("what"), while RQ2.1 and RQ3 aim at producing new evidence on the current design of MC in PPPs for development and finding starting points for further development of MC in the light of identified CSFs ("how"). Implicitly, the research question are targeted on understanding why MC in PPPs is designed in a certain way, and why certain factors are particularly important to make PPPs successful (Chapter 2.3).

Previous research on international management issues supports the interpretative approach because it has shown that quantitative research methods seem to face up to limits when research subjects are examined that are subject to complex phenomena with low level of structuration and therefore limited opportunities for statistical analysis (cf. Covaleski et al., 1996; Endenich, 2012, p. 158; Mayring, 2016, p. 10). While "hard" aspects like price or transaction volume can be quite easily mapped by statistical models, "soft" aspects, such as diverging interests, political and social objectives, relationships between business partners, are not only difficult to approximate by measurable parameters, but are often even more important for complex business relationships (cf. Wright, 2004, p. 50). Based on his study on MC, performance measurement and partner selection in IJVs, Parkhe (1993, p. 231) criticizes the current dominance of quantitative research although alone it fails to enable an integrated research perspectives on such complex IORs. He points to the fact that "hard" quantitative research methods have been used to analyze and explain "soft" factors or phenomena like opportunism and trust-building (cf. Endenich, 2012, p. 159). The literature review on CSFs of PPPs, JVs, and IORs underlines this notion because important factors like partners' commitment, existence of a favourable legal framework or societal support for a partnership are difficult to capture numerically and to include in a statistical model accordingly (Chapters 2.3.1 and 2.3.2.1).

To conclude, a qualitative research design is more suitable than the use of quantitative research methodology for the present research study. It facilitates analyzing and understanding characteristics, MC design and inherent influence factors as well as the underlying processes of managerial and operational activities of complex IORs like PPPs for development. Moreover, in the sense of Maxwell (2013), the wording of the research questions underscores the explorative nature of the present study, which aims at explaining MC phenomena in PPPs for development, based on theoretical elements of the ACI and the TCE, but no theory validation by hypothesis testing. In line with previous studies on MC in PPPs, JVs and IORs, the present study aims to further develop and refine the ACI and the TCE but does not claim to develop "...a theory that is universally true [...] each theoretical model has to be open to refinement or, ultimately, rejection" (VdM and Vosselman, 2000, p. 54).

5.1.2 Characteristics of Field Study Research

Field research emerged around the end of the 19th century in the area of ethnology; it was subsequently used, developed and extended to business by the Chicago School in particular, and received rising attention by management accounting and control from the mid-1980s. This development went along with first meta-studies and surveys on diffusion and benefits of field research (cf. Ahrens and Dent, 1998; Bortz and Döring, 2006, p. 337; Covaleski et al., 1996; Ferreira and Merchant, 1992; Merchant and Van der Stede, 2006; Young, 1999).[3] The trends towards more field research in accounting emanated from a call of leading accounting researchers who advocated for more field studies in order to better understand context and

[3] The so-called "Chicago School" is rooted in social sciences and was motivated by doing applied research close to reality and society. In this context, the Chicago School is seen as a catalyst of qualitative research in social sciences including economics (cf. Endenich, 2012, p. 157).

institutional environment in which accounting activities take place (cf. Hopwood, 1983; Dekker, 2016; Kaplan (1984, 1986); Merchant and Van der Stede, 2006). They argued that field research enables researchers to better recognize environmental changes, such as new technological progress or external global economic and political influences. Thus, accounting-related field research is about exploring interdependencies of accounting with organizational processes and life, while less emphasis is placed on accounting techniques but more on the meaning and role of "accounting in use" (Ahrens and Dent, 1998, p. 3). However, field research in accounting is still at its beginning, but pertinent studies increasingly reach placement in leading accounting journals. The literature review of the present studies has shown that it also plays an important role for empirical MC-related research in PPPs, JVs, and IORs. This makes clear that field study-based research has been established as a generally accepted means of doing research in accounting (cf. Endenich, 2012, p. 161; Lillis, 1999; Smith, 2015, p. 146 f.; Young, 1999; Chapter 2.2.1.2.3).

Field research can be qualitative, quantitative, or a mix of both. It can combine multiple research methods to collect data for generating enough research evidence that either bolster one another or triangulate (e.g. archival data, document analysis, internal corporate records, interview data or observations) (cf. Ahrens and Chapman, 2007; Atkinson and Shaffir, 1998; Merchant and Van der Stede, 2006; Smith, 2015, p. 152 f.). From this approach use has been made, so that besides interview data, documents provided by interview partners and field were considered. However, field studies remain predominantly associated with qualitative research where interviews and observations form primary methods of data collection (cf. Ferreira and Merchant, 1992; Ryan et al., 2002, p. 154). In this vein, Ahrens and Chapman (2006, p. 821) define qualitative field studies as follows: "Qualitative field studies collect data in the domain 'field' and employ 'qualitative' methodology". Doing qualitative field research is an empirical procedure that is first of all "...about studying phenomena in their natural setting" (Atkinson and Shaffir, 1998, p. 41), which promotes "the generation of relevant theory" and serves for "refining existing theory "(Merchant and Van, 2006, p. 118 f.). Thus, field research is used to be based on profound explanatory and theoretical concepts like institutional theories and MC concepts, to explain phenomena in accounting (cf. Ahrens and Chapman, 2006). Therefore, field study research has proved to be an important pillar in the portfolio of methods employed in accounting research, which concentrates on analyzing how individuals or groups of people execute management accounting and control activities for achieving organizational objectives (cf. Ahrens and Dent, 1998; Atkinson and Shaffir, 1998; Ferreira and Merchant, 1992). Thus, field studies are particularly suitable to explore complex and not well understood accounting issues and practices that are embedded in sensitive organizational settings because relevant data are often not publicly accessible, or survey study results are likely to be subject to significant response biases. Field studies are distinguished by their in-depth focus on real-world phenomena that enable researchers to gain a comprehensive and profound understanding of different environmental, individual and organizational factors, which might impact management accounting and control in terms of design, implementation and performance. Moreover, field study research is characterized by personal interaction between researcher and study participants, being usually more open-minded than rather rigid frames like experiments or surveys, and allows clarifying open questions on the short way. Therefore, field study research creates opportunities to gain substantive and unanticipated insights and provides a good basis for trust-building. The latter is a crucial aspect for studies dealing with sensitive topics where the researcher's persuasiveness is required to acquire study participants. Nonetheless, this proximity turns into a drawback if the required cooperation is not forthcoming or sustainable and generally implies the risk of observational biases. Furthermore, field studies are typically resource-intensive ventures with regard to time and money (cf. Endenich, 2012, p. 164 f.; Ferreira and Merchant, 1992; Merchant and Van der Stede, 2006; Young, 1999). However, field studies are quite helpful for creating "usable knowledge" (p. 118) in practice-oriented fields like accounting where practicioners take a problem-centered rather than a paradigm-focused perspective on accounting issues and phenomena, because for them it matters what is likely to work in practice (Merchant and Van der Stede, 2006).

Two major alternative methods to field studies for conducting field research in accounting are case studies and surveys (cf. Abernethy et al., 2001; Ahrens and Chapman, 2006; Atkinson and Shaffir, 1998; Chua et al., 2007; Dekker, 2016; Ferreira and Merchant, 1992). This fact is endorsed by the results from the literature review for MC-centered empirical studies (Chapter 2.2.1.2.3). Through a comparative analysis of respective key characteristics, Lillis and Mundy (2005) undertook a systematic delineation of field studies from case studies and surveys (Table 26), serving as benchmark of the field research in the present study.

	Single Case Study	Multiple Case Study	Field Study	Survey
Research scope	Exploration of the nature of (unknown) phenomena and structures	Comparison of the nature of phenomena in different contexts	Examination of theoretical concepts	Testing of causal relations and of the validity of existing theories
Level of complexity	High	Medium	Medium	Low
Research purpose	Analysis of specific phenomena	Comparison of specific phenomena	Further development and refinement of theoretical concepts and constructs	Statistical generalizability
Sampling procedure	Non-random	Non-random	Non-random	Random
Sample size	Small	Small	Medium	Large
Measurement accuracy	Low	Low	Medium	High
Analysis method	Qualitative	Qualitative	Qualitative/Quantitative	Quantiative

Table 26: Comparative overview of characteristics of different research methods.
(Source: following Boehle (2014, p. 219); Brandau (2010, p. 40); Ferreira and Merchant, 1992; Lillis and Mundy (2005, p. 130))

Both case study and field study research are useful to explore accounting research topics for which empirical evidence is limited (cf. Lillis and Mundy, 2005; Vaivio, 2008; Yin, 2014, p. 12). They enable researchers to analyze complex accounting phenomena and therefore overcome a major limitation of surveys, which by nature cannot deal with in-depth issues (cf. Abernethy et al., 2001). In particular at an early stage of knowledge in a certain area, the development and refinement of theories are more paramount than hypothesis testing, which presumes a solid level of knowledge (cf. Groot and Merchant, 2000). Renowned accounting researchers with focus on complex IOR and JV constructs emphasize that case and field studies enabled them to study MC issues in a real-life context, and to identify and specify control mechanisms in those partnerships. It helped them to uncover influence factors upon MC and to find explanatory approaches for interactions between stakeholders within an organizational context. Therefore, they have been in a position to develop and refine theories like TCE in the context of IORs and JVs (cf. Berry et al., 2009; Dekker (2003, 2004); Emsley and Kidon, 2007; Ferreira and Merchant, 1992; Kamminga and VdM (2006, 2007); VdM and Vosselman, 2000). Thus, it is reasonable to conduct a field study to research on PPPs for development because this topic is not yet well explored from a MC perspective, but ACI and TCE have been used already in previous studies on PPPs, JVs, and IORs where the present study can rely on.

In accounting research, sample sizes of field studies are typically rather small, as compared to surveys, but should not form a researcher's primary concern because no statistical significance of the results is envisaged (cf. Ferreira and Merchant, 1992; Kaplan, 1984; Roslender and Hart, 2003). The same applies for case studies (cf. Cäker and Siverbo, 2011). While case studies often comprise a small one-digit number of research subjects, the sample size of field studies typically ranges between 12 and 36 research subjects or interview partners (cf. Abernethy and Lillis, 1995; Brandau, 2010; p. 40; Guest et al., 2006; Lillis, 1999; Lillis and Mundy, 2005; Merchant and Manzoni, 1989; Roslender and Hart, 2003), although there are also numerous studies remaining below or going beyond this range (cf. Helfferich, 2011, p. 175; Kvale, 2007, p. 44; Lamnek and Krell, 2010, p. 351; Müller F., 2013, p. 156). To provide some guidance on determining an appropriate sample size, Kvale (2007, p. 43) recommended: "Interview as many subjects as necessary to find out what you need to know. In qualitative studies, the number of subjects tends to be either too small or too large. If the number of subjects is too small, it is difficult to generalize and not possible to test hypotheses of differences among groups or to make statistical generalizations. If the number of subjects is too large, there will hardly be time to make penetrating analyses of the interviews". Hence, for field studies an adequate sample size is reached if a further extension does not generate more material findings.

5.1.3 Characteristics of Interview-based Research

Within qualitative research and for field studies in particular are interviews the dominant method of data collection. They serve the studying of complex organizational or social phenomena from different theoretical angles. Even in quantitative studies they are often used for pilot purposes in order to collect preliminary input data for designing a survey later on (cf. Ferreira and Merchant, 1992; Qu and Dumay, 2011). There exist diverse interview types that distinguish by different dimensions, such as interview purpose, level of guidance, degree of differentiation or types of interviewees and interview questions (cf. Bortz and Döring, 2006, p. 238; Lamnek and Krell, 2010, p. 303).

The extant literature distinguishes amongst others between *biographic*, *clinical*, *expert*, *narrative* or *problem-centered* interviews. These are not always clearly distinct from each other, but can be roughly clustered into structured, semi-structured or unstructured interviews, being either more open or more closed (cf. Helfferich, 2011, p. 36; Hopf, 2013, p. 351 ff.;

Lamnek and Krell, 2010, p. 307 ff.; Mayring, 2016, p. 67; Qu and Dumay, 2011). While in closed interviews wording and order of the questions including the possible answers are predetermined, open interviews allow interviewers to flexibly adapt the interview questions to the specificities of the interviewee who can respond freely and in his/her own words (cf. Bortz and Döring, 2006, p. 315; Boucoiran, 2010, p. 81). Qu and Dumay (2011) contend that structured interviews serve the examination of facts (neopositivist perspective), while unstructured interviews concentrate on meaning (romanticist perspective). Semi-structured interviews are cross-cutting and explore the "social construction of situated accounts" (p. 239 f.), taking a localist view. Regardless of the selected degrees of structuration, interviews enable researchers to enter into interviewees' private social environment and to gather their individual expectations, perceptions and views of a certain research subject (e.g. MC in PPPs for development). In case of semi-structured interviews, each additional interview contributes to the continuous triangulation of previous findings and allows the researcher to develop his/her own understanding on the research subject in an open-minded manner (cf. Ahrens and Chapman, 2006; Qu and Dumay, 2011; Vélez et al., 2008).

Semi-structured interviews form the dominant method in qualitative research. Their popularity results from the flexible and comprehensible manner in which they can be undertaken in order to reveal important but often concealed aspects of organizational and human behavior (cf. Alvesson and Deetz, 2000, p. 194; Kvale and Brinkmann, 2009, p. 27; Qu and Dumay, 2011). Their use is moreover popular for collecting data on MC or international management research, often in terms of cross-national studies (cf. Ahrens and Chapman, 2004; Atkinson and Shaffir, 1998; Endenich, 2012, p. 167 f.; Ferreira and Merchant, 1992; Lillis and Mundy, 2005; Roslender and Hart, 2003; 2.2.1.2.3). These interviews are usually theory-based and show a medium level of standardization. The underlying interview guides usually cover different themes to be addressed during the interview but allow researchers to pose predefined questions in a flexible manner. Furthermore, additional spontaneous questions help to ensure common understanding of the given answers and to deepen issues, which have not been anticipated during interview guide preparation but arise situationally. Morever, semi-structured interviews promote the collection of unbiased responses because interviewees are free to decide about the comprehensiveness and the level of details of their explanations, or even to refuse answering certain questions (e.g. for secrecy reasons) (cf. Boucoiran, 2010, p. 81 f; Patton, 2009, p. 342; Qu and Dumay, 2011). Hence, the confidentiality of interview data in terms of use and disclosure needs to be assured in writing (cf. Helfferich, 2011, p. 190 ff.). Potential drawbacks of semi-structured interviews are on the one hand that relevant topics remain unconsidered if the interviewer detaches too much from the interview guide to further deepen thrilling explanations from the interviewee. On the other hand, there is the risk of deferral of important ideas from the interviewee, if the interviewer sticks too much to the guide and is unable to flexibly combine and shift interview questions, and therefore counteracts the flow of conversations (cf. Boucoiran, 2010, p. 82 f.; Lillis, 1999). Nonetheless, closed or open-ended and standardized interviews would thwart both the explorative nature of the present study and the gathering of the diversity and specifics of PPPs for development. Thus, the benefits of rather open and guided, semi-structured interviews outweigh the drawbacks, so that this technique will be applied in the present study.

5.2 Methodology of Data Collection

The data collection forms a core element of field study research and is inseparably linked to the procedures of sampling and interviewing in the case of interview-based qualitative research (cf. Kaya, 2009; p. 49; Lamnek and Krell, 2010, p. 173 f.). Several decisions regarding the sample composition including requirements and the selection of interview partners have to be made in a diligent manner (cf. Flick, 2014, p. 154 ff.; Qu and Dumay, 2011; Vaivio, 2008). In this sense, this chapter describes the operationalization of the chosen research approach which was defined and justified in the previous Chapter 5.1.

5.2.1 Sample Selection

The identification and the making of access to pertinent stakeholders of PPP projects forms a major challenge and a critical step for the whole research process because the selection of appropriate interview partners ("experts") with relevant experience sets the basis for generating meaningful research results. Moreover, the acquisition of interview partners is a time-consuming task and concurrently a key variable that is hard to influence. Previous experiences have shown that the experts' availability is usually limited due to many priority commitments from the daily business. Thus, the researcher has to bring reasonable arguments which convince and prompt the mainly unknown experts to participate in his/her study (cf. Bogner et al., 2014, p. 27; Endenich, 2012, p. 183; Ferreira and Merchant, 1992; Gläser and Laudel, 2010, p. 117; Smith, 2015, p. 67). In this sense, the researcher has to duly analyze potential organizations and interview partners who could contribute to answering the research questions formulated in Chapter 4.5. This requires the definition of clear selection criteria. The contacting of concrete companies, DCAs and IOs needs to be aligned with these criteria accordingly (cf. Finger, 2014, p. 110).

The following sub-chapters will explain what requirements have been laid down for the sampling, how the selection of interview partners proceeded, and what are the characteristics of the finally selected interview partners including the organizations and partnership projects behind them.

5.2.1.1 *Sampling Requirements*

For the purpose of selecting the sample, qualitative research methods do not claim to produce results that can be generalized and be transferred to a broader global context but gear towards the answering of the research questions. Thus, the sampling requirements should also be determined in this spirit. Relevant questions to answer in this context are (cf. Bogner et al., 2014, p. 35; Gläser and Laudel, 2010, p. 117; Smith, 2015, p. 67):

- Who has relevant information?
- Who is likely to be in a position to share relevant information in a concise manner?
- Who is likely to be willing to share information?
- Who of the potential interview partners is accessible and available?

Basically, there is no general definition of how experts may be characterized. Usually, it behooves the researcher's individual research interest to determine who is an expert. That is why there are no universal guidelines for the determination of sampling requirements (cf. Boehle, 2014, p. 224; Bogner et al., 2014, p. 10 f.). These range from clearly measurable demographic variables (e.g. age, gender, profession) to rather pragmatic characteristics, such as the experts' availability and willingness to participate or minimum relevant experience and knowledge required by the researcher. Finally, the selection of interview partners is an intentional process where it is up to the researcher to decide for each individual case who is an expert whose competences make him eligible for acting as interview partner in support of answering the research questions (cf. Bogner et al., 2014, p. 34 f.; Eisenhardt, 1989; Merkens, 2013, p. 292 ff.). However, in general terms, one can say that experts differ by having pertinent experience and specialized knowledge about certain subject matters within a certain social context, which strongly overlap with the researcher's research scope. Interviews form a means to access and gather these experiences and knowledge (cf. Gläser and Laudel, 2010, p. 11 f.). Limited resoures in terms of time and money do moreover affect the feasiblity of data collection and therefore confine the circle of potential interview partners from the outset (cf. Lamnek and Krell, 2010, p. 351).

To ensure that interview partners have sufficient expertise, the following sampling requirements have been applied to the search of experts for the present study:

- Interview partners work either for a company, a DCA or an IO.
- Interview partners have either PPP-specific project coordinator/manager experience or external/senior experience on PPPs for development in general.
- Interview partners have an academic background.
- Job experience and organizational affiliation should preferably amount to a minimum of two years in total.

It is important to gather both operational and management experiences from experts at different career levels for understanding the multi-stakeholder character of PPPs and for obtaining a holistic picture from ways of PPP implementation. Restrictions concerning education level and job experience help to establish some homogeneity within the sample. To be considered, PPPs had to fulfill the following requirements, unless the interview partners did not take a PPP-independent perspective (e.g. senior level) because in this case they were dropped as not applicable:

- PPP was created from the year 2000,
- PPP is of strategic nature for the involved organizations (CSR aspects play a minor role),
- PPP has been in existence for a minimum of two years.

All organizations were required to perform international activities, other than PPPs, as part of their business activities. Using the number of employees as selection criterion, companies additionally had to have a workforce of at least about 1.000 members. This lower bound is supposed to limit the range between larger and smaller entities and therefore to ensure a certain degree of comparability (cf. Eschenbach et al., 2007, p. 353; Kieser and Walgenbach, 2007, p. 325). For DCAs and IOs, there was no need to set these additional conditions because by nature they have in common to be embedded in national governmental structures, to work globally and/or to be driven by member states at international level, differing primarily by their field of activity. Hence, due to the exploratory nature of the study as well as with respect to the diversity and internationality of PPPs between DCAs/IOs and the private sector, no restrictions have been set for the following characteristics of partnership project, organization and interview partner:

- Subject matter of the PPP,
- Geographical focus of the PPP,
- Nationality of the interview partners,
- Specialist background and departmental affiliation.

Still, restrictions applied for the national origin of companies and DCAs. Finally, Germany, Mexico and Switzerland have been considered for this study because these countries have a lot in common in terms of economic, legal and political framework conditions. All three states are constitutionally designed as federal republics that are composed of federal states (Germany and Mexico) or of cantons in case of Switzerland. Using the ICC Open Market Index[4] from 2015 as an indicator, their economic openness was steadily increasing in the last five years being on average or above that index compared to the rest of the world (cf. Finger, 2015, p. 9 and p. 18). Moreover, these countries have in common that their respective legal systems rest on the civil law code (cf. CIA, 2016). In addition, both Germany and Mexico enacted their first legal PPP frameworks in the middle of the 2000s to promote public-private cooperation. In Germany, this happened on the basis of the adoption of the so-called ÖPP-Beschleunigungsgesetz[5], which came into force on September 8th in 2005 (cf. Bundesgesetzblatt, 2005). One year before, the European Union (EU) released its "European Union Rules on Public-Private Partnerships" (cf. World Bank, 2016). Mexico provided initial guidance to PPPs on the basis of the "Acuerdo por el que se establecen las Reglas para la realización de proyectos para prestación de servicios", published by the Mexican Ministry of Finance (SHCP) on April 9th in 2004 (SHCP, 2004). However, a final legal framework for PPPs in general was adopted by the Mexican parliament several years later, on January 16th in 2012, called "Ley de Asociaciones Público Privadas" (cf. World Bank, 2016). For Switzerland, no specific guidelines and rules could be found. By comparison, IOs are by nature globally acting entities so that setting restrictions on their national origin would not have been reasonable. Although the present thesis is clearly not a comparative study, the consideration of the experiences from stakeholders from more than one country mitigates potential country-specific biases. The selected sampling requirements are equal or similar to those used in previous field studies (cf. Berding, 2011, p. 88 ff.; Brandau, 2010, p. 47 f.; Choi and Beamish, 2004; Johnson et al., 2002; Rahaman et al., 2010).

5.2.1.2 *Selection of Interview Partners*

The selection of interview partners for the present study pursues mainly a so-called "purposeful sampling" approach where experts are selected non-randomly by ex-ante determined criteria, based on publicly available information about the potential interview partner and on

[4] The Open Market Index is published on a biennial basis by the International Chamber of Commerce (ICC), headquartered in Paris/ France.

[5] ÖPP (=Öffentlich Private Partnerschaft) is the German term for PPP.

the researcher's knowledge about the subject matter. To gain experts that are hard to identify from outside, and to attain a sufficient number of interview partners, contacts established through the so-called "snowball procedure" were additionally considered (cf. Bogner et al., 2014, p. 35; Finger, 2014, p. 111 f.; Merkens, 2013, p. 291 f.; Patton, 2009, p. 230 f.).

Based on defined sampling requirements, companies, IOs and DCAs to contact were selected and potential contact channels for approaching them were checked. For reasons of research efficiency, building a kind of basic population that serves as starting point for structured search for suitable interview partners was tried in the first step. Thus, private sector companies were only considered if they were listed in their major national stock market indices. This approach relies on the underlying assumption that larger, stock-listed companies are more likely to enter into PPPs with IOs or DCAs because their business is more international-oriented and they are economically in a better position to afford resources for such partnerhips. Moreover, private sector companies were potentially eligible if they were active members of the United Nations Global Compact (UNGC).[6] This criterion results from the idea that companies commited to the UNGC principles are potentially open to also engage in PPPs for development with different stakeholders. DCAs were considered if they originate either from Germany, Mexico or Switzerland and maintain joint operations with partners from at least one of the other countries. Among the IOs only those were eligible that are listed in the Yearbook of International Organizations database of the Union of International Associations (UIA)[7]. In the second step, diligent online research was done for those companies, DCAs and IOs that met the aforementioned selection criteria, to check whether they maintain any PPP activities that match with the research focus of the present study. If so, those organizations were taken into account for further selection and finally considered if they also met the sampling requirements from Chapter 5.2.1.1. In the third step, it was verified if the personal network, composed of personal relationships with the United Nations and with senior researchers from the Department of Management Accounting and Control of TU Dortmund University (Germany) and from the EGADE Business School of the ITESM[8] (Mexico), could help to make contact to the selected organizations because getting access to potential interview partners is one of the major obstacles for qualitative field research (cf. Bogner et al., 2014, p. 37 f.; Helfferich, 2011, p. 175 f.). Using personal networks proved to ease establishing contact because support from renowned institutions is a trust-building mechanism, which gives some ex-ante credibility to the researcher's enquiry and increases the likelihood to get a positive or even any answer from the contacted organization (cf. Bruns and Mc Kinnon, 1993; Helfferich, 2011, p. 175 f.; Moll et al., 2006, p. 385). Asking previous interview partners

[6] UNGC: The United Nations Global Compact is a voluntary initiative that envisages to create an inclusive, people-centered and sustainable global economy. It allows different kind of companies (e.g. public and private sector firms, big and small and medium-sized enterprises) to contribute to the achievement of the SDGs by signing an agreement with the UN. By doing this, companies commit to align their business activities and practices in future with the ten UNGC principles, which stipulate ecologic and social basic standards. For keeping active their membership, companies have to submit an annual progress report on how they integrated these principles into their business operations. However, these agreements do not include any legal enforcement mechanisms (cf. Arevalo and Fallon, 2008: Williams. 2014).

[7] UIA: The Union of International Associations (UIA), founded in 1907, is a Brussels-based documentation centre and research institute, which enjoys associate and consultative status with a few UN entities. It publishes amongst other the Yearbook of International Associations, a comprehensive encyclopedia, giving an overview of ten thousands of active and inactive intergovernmental and international non-governmental organizations (http://www.uia.org/; http://www.uia.org/yearbook).

[8] Escuela de Graduados en Administración y Dirección de Empresas (EGADE) of the Instituto Tecnológico y de Estudios Superiores de Monterrey (ITESM), Campus Monterrey, Mexico.

to use their networks for supporting the present research study revealed to be an effective acquisition channel as well. However, this approach can lead to biased results, for instance, if the selected experts do not reflect the typical population of the research subject. To diminish the risk of so-called "informant bias", induced by this kind of snowball effect, not more than one provided contact has been accepted per interview partner. Moreover, the provided contact had to represent the perspective of another stakeholder, different from the facilitator. The conduction of pretests and the presence of more than one interview partner during interviews further relieve informant bias effects (cf. Doty and Glick, 1998; Finger et al., 2014, p. 111 f.; Hurrle and Kieser, 2005; Patton, 2009, p. 230 ff.). Thus, personal networks can contribute to opening doors, which would otherwise remain closed, but the researcher must be aware of limitations in terms of generalizability of the results. In case of no existing direct or indirect contact to a selected organization, free acquisition was required. The career networks LinkedIn and Xing served as contact channels in this context. Once concrete contact persons had been identified, they were usually contacted by email or via the messenger services of LinkedIn and Xing, and only in a few cases by phone if the other two options were not available. This approach helps to make sure that potential interview partners receive all relevant information in a condensed manner and relieves pressure on answering promptly (cf. Bogner et al., 2014, p. 35; Gläser and Laudel, 2010, p. 161 f.). Thus, for each organization to contact, a two-sided PDF document was prepared that briefly described study objectives, research questions, thematic background, and methodology including sample requirements. Moreover, it proactively highlighted how organizations can contribute to the study, what benefits they can expect from participating, and why their experience would form an asset (see exemplary brief description in annex 8.3). This individualized two-sided document was designed in the organization's respective corporate language and sent out together with a cover letter. The contact persons were offered more detailed information about the research study and the interview conditions during a preliminary phone call. This occasion was supposed to foster mutual understanding of the subject matter, clarify open questions from both sides, and finally figure out if there is sufficient thematic overlap (cf. Gläser and Laudel, 2010, p. 162 f.). Given an interview enquiry was positively received, and not rejected or not replied to after repeated requests, a preliminary call was arranged. If this was positive, an interview date was set up. In some cases, where the thematic overlap was quite obvious from the beginning and strong interest in participating was demonstrated by the potential interview partner, the preliminary call was skipped and an interview date directly arranged. Based on the information gathered from publicly available online sources, from first email communication and from the preliminary call, individualized interview guides were prepared and provided to the interview partners prior to the actual interview, usually about two weeks in advance. This procedure contributed to building trust and reducing uncertainty on the interviewee's side, in particular in those cases, where interview partners had to ask their supervisors for permission to give an interview. Moreover, interview partners were enabled to better prepare themselves for the interview. However, disadvantages of providing the interview questions prior to the actual interview are difficulties deviating from the interview guide and receiving less spontaneous answers. Still, most interview partners asked to obtain the questions beforehand and appreciated this concession made to them (cf. Bogner et al., 2014, p. 30 f.; Demirag et al., 2012). It should be noted that in practice tight time budgets inhibited most interview partners from studying the interview questions in advance, although they actually had the will to do so. Figure 24 shows the before described selection procedure of interview partners.

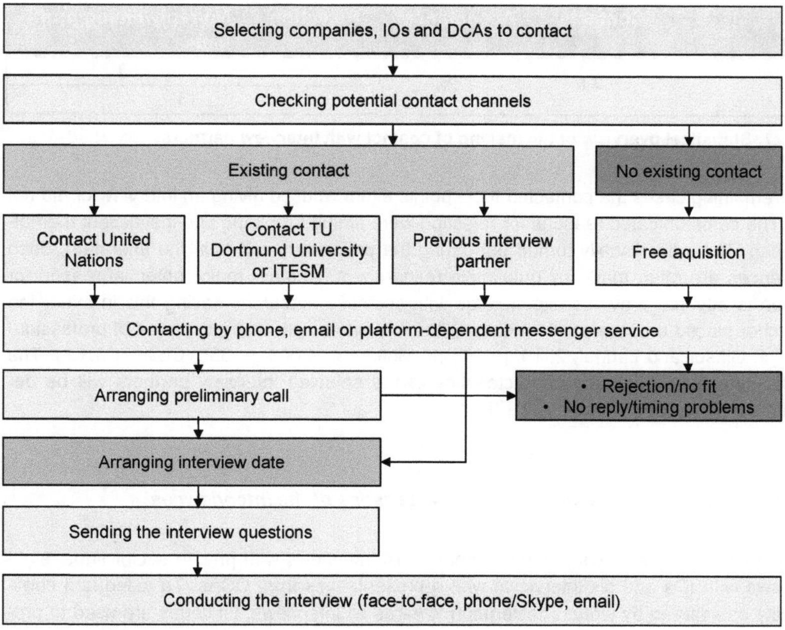

Figure 24: Selection procedure of interview partners.

Finally, from 41 potential interview partners contacted in total, 68.3 % agreed to an interview. Thus, 28 inteviews with 32 people could be arranged. This success rate is above the average usually reached in field study research (cf. Ferreira and Merchant, 1992; Moll et al., 2006, p. 385). Moreover, the total number of interviews fits well into the range which is generally considered as appropriate for field studies. It was unlikely that more interviews would have yielded essential new findings. When falling marginal utility of each additional interview was noted, data collection was terminated (cf. Acar et al., 2008; Smith, 2015, p. 67; Chapter 5.1.2). Most interview contacts were provided by other contacts, made either by TU Dortmund University, by EGADE Business School, by the UN or by previous interview partners (cf. Brandau et al., 2014; Ferreira and Merchant, 1992). A few contacts were established by personal contacts and through free acquisition (Table 27). All interview partners were working actively in their respective organizations at the time of the interview, so that the interviews were conducted during the regular working time, except for one case. This applies at least for the personal and telephone- or Skype-based interviews.

	Contacts	Acceptance	Rejection	No reply/timing problems
Personal contacts	3	3	-	-
Provided contacts	35	22	4	9
Free acquisition	3	3	-	-

	Contacts	Acceptance	Rejection	No reply/timing problems
Total	41	28	4	9
			13	

Table 27: Statistical overview of the making of contact with interview partners.

In the remaining cases the contacted focal points either refused giving an interview or did not reply. The communicated reasons for rejection were timing problems and insufficient thematic overlap. The latter usually turned out during the preliminary call or in the aftermath. Such experiences are often made by qualitative researchers. Another major potential reason for rejection is adverse previous experiences with scientific research. Having this in mind, the researcher placed emphasis on conducting the interviews with a strong sense of professionalism (cf. Gläser and Laudel, 2010, p. 163 ff.; Moll et al., 2006, p. 385; Chapter 5.1.3). The sample composition and the characteristics of the selected interview partners will be described in the following Chapter 5.2.1.3.

5.2.1.3 *Sample Composition and Characteristics of the Interviewees*

The sample of 28 interviews in total comprises 14 interviews with private sector firms, eight interviews with IOs and six interviews with representatives from DCAs. To safeguard confidentiality as assured by written declaration towards all interviews, ID codes are used to protect anonymization of the names of organizations and persons but still to make them classifiable (cf. Demirag et al., 2012; Mayer, 2013, p. 46; Silverman, 2010, p. 30). In this context, demographic, industrial and other descriptive statistical data, such as number of employees, annual turnover, number of locations worldwide or job experience in number of years, have been raised and categorized (cf. Lillis, 1999). These data have been gathered from publicly available sources and will be subsequently presented to the best extent possible, determined by the confidentiality requirements, so that origin and context of comments and statements quoted in Chapter 0 are comprehensible, but without making any organization or person identifyable (cf. Mayer, 2013, p. 46).

The proportion between interview partners from private sector firms and public entities, i.e. IOs and DCAs, is balanced (Table 28 to Table 30). Most of the interviewed companies have tens of thousands of employees and are doing business across the globe, either just distribution and/or even with own production plants. More than half of them are active in more than 50 countries with origins in Germany, Mexico and Switzerland. They belong to diverse industries, covering the fields of energy, finance, food, health, technology, and transport in the broader sense. Further specifications cannot be made for preserving anonymity.

ID code	Number of employees	ID code	Number of employees
CO1	> 10,000	**CO8**	> 50,000
CO2	> 50,000	**CO9**	> 50,000
CO3	> 50,000	**CO10**	< 1,000
CO4	> 10,000	**CO11**	> 50,000
CO5	> 50,000	**CO12**	> 10,000

ID code	Number of employees	ID code	Number of employees
CO6	> 50,000	**CO13**	> 50,000
CO7	> 50,000	**CO14**	> 10,000

Table 28: Size of the interviewed private sector firms (by number of employees).
(Source: annual reports, corporate webpages)

The interviewed IOs have in common that they all belong to the UN System[9] but are diverse in terms of size and scope of activities. Half of them employed more than 5,000 people around the world while the remaining ones had less then 1,000 employees at the time of the interview. There was no ex-ante restriction set to organizations from the UN System, but the UN in its entirety is the leading multilateral institution in terms of PPPs for development. Thus, the population of potential PPPs selected for analysis mainly consists of partnerships with the participation of any UN organization (cf. Khoday, 2007; Reed and Reed, 2009; Stadtler and Probst, 2012).

ID code	Number of employees	ID code	Number of employees
IO1	< 1,000	**IO5**	> 5,000
IO2	> 5,000	**IO6**	> 1,000
IO3	> 5,000	**IO7**	> 5,000
IO4	< 1,000	**IO8**	< 1,000

Table 29: Size of the interviewed IOs (by number of employees).
(Source: annual reports, webpages of the organizations)

Like the IOs, the interviewed DCAs conduct PPP projects with global outreach, some of them maintaining own offices abroad. Still, by contrast to the IOs, their PPP activities are not subject to the decisions of a number of member states but are mainly influenced by the development policy interests of their respective home country's national government.

ID code	Number of employees	ID code	Number of employees
DC1	> 5,000	**DC3**	> 5,000
DC2	> 5,000	**DC4**	< 1,000
DC5	> 5,000	**DC6**	n/a

Table 30: Size of the interviewed DCAs (by number of employees).
(Source: annual reports, webpages of the agencies.)

The interviewees from companies vary by current job position, length of stay in this position, pertinent previous professional experiences and fields of study (Table 31). While nine interviews referred to concrete partnerships with IOs or DCAs, only two interview partners reported overarching partnership experiences. Most of them held leadership positions at the time of the interview and bore the main responsibility for the partnership from their company's side. Moreover, most of them had both operational and management experiences alike, enabling them to comment on MC in their partnerships from different perspectives. The diversity

[9] UN System: The UN System goes beyond the six main UN Organs (General Assembly, Security Council, Economic and Social Council, Trusteeship Council, International Court of Justice, Secretariat) and comprises numerous affiliated funds, programmes and specialized agencies (http://www.un.org/en/about-un/index.html).

of the job positions of the interview partners reflects the manifold opportunities to anchor the organizational lead for partnership implementation, regardless of the lack of sample representativeness. Some positions go along with a certain public visibility (e.g. CO1, CO3, CO7, and CO11), whereas others are more strongly related to internal operational work (e.g. CO5, CO8, and CO10).[10] Except for CO3, partnership work accounted for a significant but not for an exclusive part of the interviewees' task portfolios. On average, corporate interviewees had slightly more than four and a half years of work experience in their current position. Eight of them could rely on ten or more years of experience in different duties with their respective company. In two cases, they had worked for an IO or DCA before, thus knowing their counterparts' perspectives in the partnership very well. Their academic backgrounds strongly varied, ranging from degrees in natural sciences to culture and language studies. Still, about half of them held a degree in business administration or economics or had done some postgraduate business studies.

ID code	Job position	ID code	Job position
CO1	1) Vice President 2) Corporate Communications Manager	**CO8**	Senior Researcher
CO2	Program Manager	**CO9**	1) Vice President 2) Finance Manager
CO3	Director of Partnerships	**CO10**	1) Regional Sales Manager 2) Product Development Manager
CO4	Director Governmental Affairs	**CO11**	Head of CSR
CO5	Research Manager	**CO12**	Director Market Development
CO6	Senior Political Advisor	**CO13**	1) Director of Sustainable Development 2) Section Head
CO7	Head of CSR	**CO14**	Social Innovation Advisor

Table 31: Job positions of the interview partners from private sector firms.

Compared to the corporate interviewees, the job profiles of interview partners from IOs distinguish more clearly between operational duties (IO2, IO4, IO5, and IO7) and management positions (IO1, IO3, IO6, and IO8) for PPP implementation (Table 32). Two of them were high-ranked diplomats with longstanding experience in multilateral diplomacy, thus assessing the implementation of PPPs from diverse perspectives. With the exception of one person, all interview partners from IOs were expatriates at their current duty station. In this context, most of them were working at their organization's headquarters at the time of the interview. On average, the interviewees from IOs relied on almost three years of work experience in their current position, while all of them had a minimum of three and a half years of experience in working within the UN System. Half of them gained professional experiences in diverse industries in the private sector before. Their academic backgrounds ranged from business administration/economics and law to political sciences and natural sciences.

[10] For confidentiality reasons, some of the job positions have been amended or shortened. Still, the changes do not distort the nature of the respective job position.

ID code	Job position	ID code	Job position
IO1	Inspector	**IO5**	Partnership Specialist
IO2	Compliance and Risk Management Officer	**IO6**	Chief of Partnerships
IO3	Director of Partnerships	**IO7**	Consultant
IO4	Associate Strategic Planning Officer	**IO8**	Program Coordinator

Table 32: Job positions of the interview partners from IOs.

For job positions of interview partners from DCAs, more homogeneity has been noted, as compared to companies and IOs. All of them had gained experiences from different partnerships at different job levels in their career, enabling them to perform a variety of tasks. Thus, there is no clear distinction between management and operational duties, rather they have to cover both (Table 33). All of them performed a strong project management and coordination role in PPP work. On average, the interviewees from DCAs had almost four years of work experience in their current position, while most of them could rely on much more years of experience in working with their respective organization. Their academic backgrounds ranged from business administration/economics to political sciences and natural sciences, thus being as diverse as those of interviewees from companies and DCAs.

ID code	Job position	ID code	Job position
DC1	Global Coordinator	**DC3**	Project Manager
DC2	Project Manager	**DC4**	Senior Project Manager
DC5	Sub Project Manager	**DC6**	Sub Project Manager

Table 33: Job positions of the interview partners from DCAs.

Concerning the PPPs as such, it can be said that in 17 out of 28 interviews the questions were answered with reference to specific PPP projects, while in the remaining cases interview partners reported about their general PPP experiences. All partnerships were of strategic nature for the involved organizations, being pertinent to the respective industries and their core activities. Thus, the underlying topics of the PPPs were as diverse as the number of industries whereas the geographical focus of partnership activities was placed particularly on African countries. In terms of duration, the PPPs ranged from a minimum of three years up to more than ten years in total, while all of them were created after the year 2000, mainly at the end of the last decade and later. Moreover, the vast majority of them are still ongoing.

To conclude, the sample requirements as defined in advance were met. This applies for organizations, interview partners and PPPs alike. Across all three groups of interview partners, it was noticed that more than half of the interviewees held degrees in business administration/economics or related fields of study, therefore having certain professional proximity to MC in PPPs.

5.2.2 Interviewing

Against the background of the selected interview technique, this section will explain the conceptualization of the semi-structured interview guide as well as characteristics of conducting interviews which should follow a flexible but still structured process (cf. Mayring, 2016, p. 69 ff.; Smith, 2015, p. 141). At this early design phase of interview-based field studies, researchers have to make many decisions, concerning the target group of interview partners, sample size or data analysis method amongst others (cf. Qu and Dumay, 2011).

First of all, researchers must acquire sufficient expertise in the relevant thematic areas being addressed during the interviews in order to collect substantive and meaningful interview data being conducive to the research purposes. This includes the clear definition of the research scope and of the problems and issues to be covered by suitable interview questions. This work has been mainly covered by the literature review and by the analysis of MC issues in previous PPPs, JVs and IORs (Chapters 2.2.1 and 2.2.2). Based on this, the interview guide is designed and subjected to a pilot stage, before the actual interviews are undertaken (Figure 25).

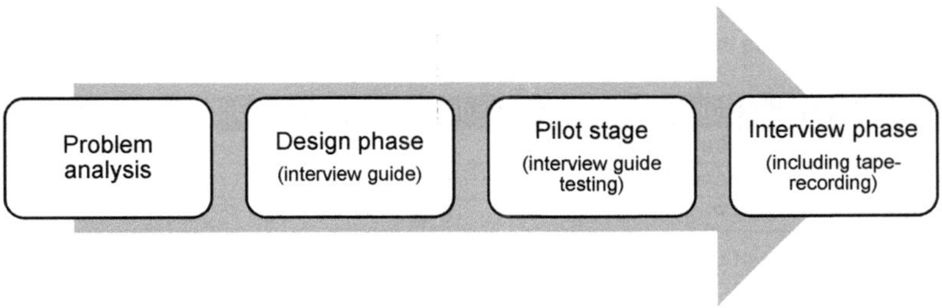

Figure 25: Process of guided semi-structured interviews.
(Source: based on Mayring (2016, p. 71))

5.2.2.1 *Conception and Structure of the Interview Guide*

The interview guide of this study has been designed from existing knowledge on MC in PPPs, JVs and IORs; it is supposed to ensure full addressing of the pertinent subject areas and completeness of the collected data as well as to promote comparable procedures during each interview. Comparable interview guide structures moreover facilitate data analysis at a later stage (cf. Endenich, 2012, p. 174; Gläser and Laudel, 2010, p. 142 ff.; Helfferich, 2011, p. 180; Lillis, 1999; Patton, 2009, p. 343). Furthermore, semi-structured interview guides help to structure the study's terms of reference and provide orientation to the researcher during the actual interview. This does not imply that all questions need to be posed in all interviews in the same order with the same wording because interview guides can be used in a rather flexible manner to promote the dialogue between interviewer and interviewee instead of an interrogation-like situation. Thus, interview guides form a mechanism of methodological and substantive preparation for data collection that has accomplished its main duty once concrete interviews are taking place (cf. Bogner et al., 2014, p. 27 f.; Lillis, 1999; Smith, 2015, p. 141). For the structuration and wording of concrete interview questions, empirical social researchers recommend considering a few basic rules. The interview guide should be clustered into cohesive subject areas, which are logically attuned to one another, but can be flexibly moved if required by the conversational situation. Concise and specific questions should fit into a coherent line of argumentation. The amount of interview questions should be adjusted to the scheduled interview duration and leave enough time buffer to deepen pertinent aspects and to prevent the impression of just ticking off a checklist (cf. Bogner et al., 2014; p. 29 f.; Gläser and Laudel, 2010, p. 146 f.; Helfferich, 2011 p. 180; Smith, 2015, p. 143 f.). Interview questions should not include double negative clauses, judgmental wording, or be of suggestive nature (cf. Diekmann, 2016, p. 479 ff.).

Basically, it is legitimate to customize the interview guide to each type of interview partner (cf. Gläser and Laudel, 2010, p. 117). In this vein, the present study distinguishes between experts from companies, DCAs and IOs. However, not only the types of interview partners differ but also each PPP is different in terms of scope, size and stakeholders involved. Moreover, the interview partners are distinct by their job positions and specific personal experiences. For instance, senior staff or executives who are responsible for several projects at the same time can better explain general experiences with PPPs from an overarching perspective while regular project staff is in a position to share experiences from daily operations. Moreover, distinctive language aspects of each organizational type and the academic background of the concrete interview partner including previous professional experiences should be considered for the concrete wording, given that this information is available prior to the interview. On an individual level, the meaning of MC and inherent elements, for instance, is likely to be clear to an economist while somebody with natural sciences background might struggle with it. As IOs are organs of global politics being characterized by strong cultural diversity, their entire oral and written communication is by nature quite diplomatic and differs from business language in companies on the organizational level. Keeping these specifics in mind, the wording of the written interview questions should reflect to some extent the corporate language of the respective interview partner to prevent ambiguities and to build trust upfront through linguistic proximity but without compromising their meaning. Besides, the interviewer's knowledge base and interview experience grow by each additional interview and can entail continuous modifications of the interview guide. Thus, it is common that for each interview partner an individual interview guide is designed, where it is more about making rewordings or slight modifications of the order than on eliminating entire subject areas. This matters in particular for complex organizational and management issues (cf. Bogner et al., 2014, p. 30 f.; Bortz and Döring, 2006, p. 253; Gläser and Laudel, 2010, p. 150 ff.; Patton, 2009, p. 346; Qu and Dumay, 2011).

In the present study, individual interview guides have been prepared for each interview partner. First, a generic interview guide for companies has been designed closely in line with the key elements of the ACI and TCE as well as with the control archetypes/typologies and CSFs identified in previous studies (Chapters 0 and 4). This has been modified for IOs and DCAs in a second step. Still, their structure is basically identical and differs by a few questions only. For German or Spanish native speakers, the interview guides were translated into German or Spanish accordingly while the starting point was the English version. This related additional workload is justified by the aspiration to enable interviewees to speak in their native language and therefore reduce adverse impacts of linguistic obstacles potentially affecting the quality of content (cf. Bogner et al., 2014, p. 44 f.; Bortz and Döring, 2006, p. 253; Kruse et al., 2012, p. 32 ff.; Resch and Enzenhofer, 2012, p. 81). The translation from English to German has been undertaken by the author of this study, while for the conversion from English to Spanish native Spanish-speaking researchers from EGADE Business School in Monterrey/Mexico were consulted to ensure correct translation. At the end of the design phase, the draft interview guide was subjected to a pretest for improving its soundness and for eliminating ambiguities concerning the instructions and questions. Three pretest interviews were carried with one senior researcher from a university, one management accountant from a company, and one project manager from a DCA. However, none of these three pretest interviews was considered for the final sample (cf. Brandau et al., 2014; Johnson et al., 2002; Kamminga and VdM, 2007; Smith, 2015, p. 134 f.). Their recommendations were considered for amendments as well as for further refinement and slight modifications of the interview guide, such as changing the order and wording of interview questions (cf. Mayring, 2016, p. 69).

At the outset, a brief description of the research subject and information concerning anonymity and confidentialty of responses as well as answering the questions are provided. Then follows a short definition of MC to ensure common understanding between interviewer and interviewee about the meaning of that pivotal term in the context of PPPs for development (cf. Finger, 2014, p. 125; Gläser and Laudel, 2010, p. 142 ff.; Patton, 2009, p. 346; Smith, 2015, p. 142 f.).

The interview guide is clustered into six thematic sections (Figure 26) that will serve as headings for preparing specific questions. This proved to be a suitable design for interviews of one to two hours. While the interviewees' version is about three and a half pages long, the one of the interviewers extends to approximately five pages, containing several additional questions, which can occasionally be raised if the actual questions did not generate sufficient knowledge or clarity. This amount of text corresponds to what is recommended by qualitative social research (cf. Bogner et al., 2014, p. 28 f.). At the beginning, the interviewee is kindly requested to briefly introduce and to mention some facts and figures about the organization and the partnership in focus. The latter is skipped if the interviewee speaks from a partnership-independent, overarching perspective. This depends on experience and position of the interviewee and is clarified prior to the actual interview. In the first thematic section, interviewees are moreover asked to explain the overall strategy that their organization pursues in terms of cooperation with public or private sector partners, respectively. This information allows the interviewer to capture some overall framing conditions and to better assess how PPP activities and/or a concrete partnership is embedded in an organization and from what perspective the interviewee is narrating. Thus, the first questions help to collect information important for the further course of the discussion, and they serve to set an impulse to induce a smooth and open dialogue (cf. Helfferich, 2011, p. 181).

The thematic sections 2 to 4 are strongly derived from the conceptual and theoretical fundamentals of this study, as worked out in Chapters 2, 0 and 4, where theory is translated into interview questions. While the sections 2 and 3 are particularly linked to the TCE, the questions in section 4 derive from the ACI. For this reason, the issue of MC also lies primarily in these three sections, despite its cross-cutting nature (cf. Kamminga and VdM, 2007; Nicholson et al., 2006). The thematic section 2 initiates a rather open discussion on motivations to enter the partnership and on the overall partnership setting in terms of joint or diverging objectives and expectations. To better understand the starting point, it is also important to be informed about the major project phases and to learn how the organization including involved staff prepared for their PPP (cf. Mouritsen and Thrane, 2006; Nicholson et al., 2006). Moreover, this section addresses critical issues in PPPs, namely contributions, costs, financing and risk, which are potential drivers of TC and need to be addressed by suitable MC mechanisms (Chapter 4.2). The subsequent thematic section 3 forms the main chapter in terms of MC. First, data are collected on project management and organization including monitoring in order to get an overview of the governance structure and governing bodies (e.g. steering committee, project team, geographic distribution of staff), and to get an idea of how the different stakeholders involved are interlinked with each other and whom they are accountable to in terms of reporting. Furthermore, performance measurement in the context of benchmarks for goal achievement is analyzed as well as experiences on the level of compliance and commitment towards underlying contractual arrangements enquired. The section concludes with questions on experiences concerning the influence of diverse cultural aspects, the level of trust and the coping with MC challenges or problems during partnership implementation (cf. Nicholson et al., 2006). The fourth thematic section takes an ACI perspective and deals with institutional influences on the partnership as well as with the experiences made regarding interaction and collaboration between stakeholders. In the first part, interviewees are asked to describe the legal, political and social environment in the country(ies) of PPP implementation and how supportive governmental authorities behaved in this context. The second part concentrates on the characterization of decision-making processes and conflict ability in the light of potentially diverging interests and objectives. At the end, interviewees obtain the opportunity to qualitatively assess the overall collaboration and behavior of the actors involved.

The CSFs follow in thematic Section 5. This topic is put at the very end because it is supposed to encourage interviewees to reflect on their partnership experiences just shared during the interview. They are asked to summarize what factors contributed to making a concrete partnership successful or are generally conducive to prosperous PPP implementation. The interview guide concludes with final questions on desires for the future the interviewees might have for MC in ongoing or upcoming partnerships, conditions and incentives for extended partnerships, and what impacts they expect for the transition from the MDGs to the SDGs in their respective PPP activities. Besides, interviewees are encouraged in this section to add any relevant aspects that have not been explicitly asked before but which they deem important.

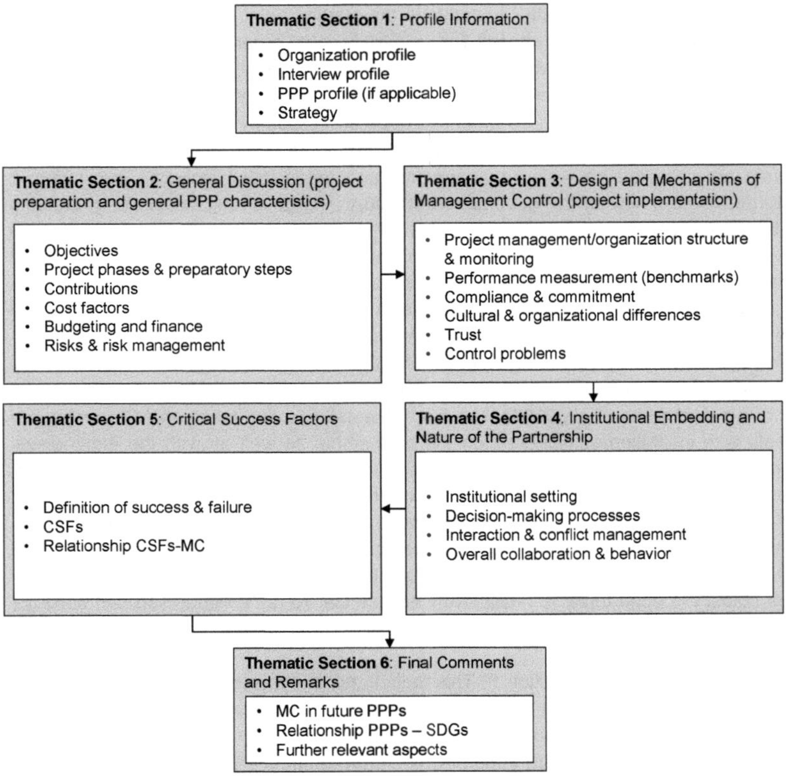

Figure 26: Structure of the interview guide.

In line with Chapter 5.1.3, the interview questions are mainly designed as "what/which" and "how" questions to gather findings and explore relationships. "Why" questions are not included in the written interview guide because they need to be posed spontaneously in dependence of the interviewee's specific answers to the "what/which" and "how" questions. An exemplary interview guide for companies is attached in annex 8.2.

5.2.2.2 Conducting the Interviews

The preliminary work for conducting interviews commenced in July 2015 with the development of a draft interview guide for companies, conceptually based on control archetypes and typologies as well as on theorerical elements of the ACI and TCE. The timeline is depicted in Figure 27. An amended version for IOs was prepared at the same time. The interview guide was subjected to the three pretests in October 2015 and revised on the basis of the comments and recommendations received by the test interviewees (previous Chapter 5.2.2.1).

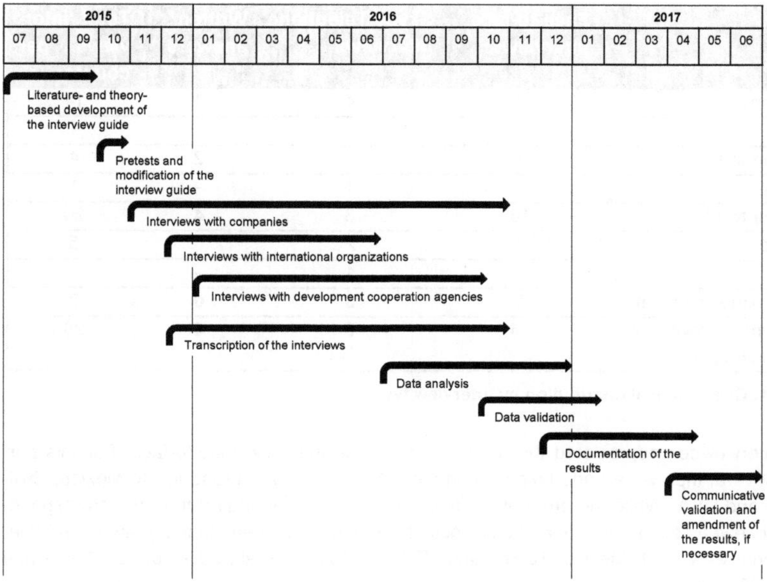

Figure 27: Timeline of the present field study.

The interviews took place between November 2015 and October 2016 and were mainly conducted either face-to-face or by Skype/telephone. For internal compliance and timing reasons, a few interview partners were only willing to answer interview questions in writing. In the first step, face-to-face interviews were communicated to all interviewees as preferred platform, despite high costs in terms of time and money, in particular for travelling abroad. These burdens are not only valuable because of the signal of appreciation sent to the interviewee, but allow the interviewer to better understand complex issues, to better take control of the conversation, and to build a level of trust that would not be reached by the other interview types. Those tele-interview forms imply a higher risk of loss of information (cf. Ferreira and Merchant, 1992; Gläser and Laudel, 2010, p. 153 f.; Kaya, 2009, p. 52). However, finally the interviewee's convenience mattered for the choice of interview type. Interviews should be carried out as single interview whenever possible, because many questions ask for personal experiences and assessments, making the interview situation intimate to some extent. In the presence of other colleagues, interviewees are potentially less open. Still, if interview partners were of the view that colleagues could make valuable complementary contributions, their presence should be welcomed and always accepted. That is why individual face-to-face interviews evolved to be the preferred interview form by researchers in the field of accounting (cf. Gläser and Laudel, 2010, p. 154 ff.; Lamnek and Krell, 2010, p. 316; Moll et al., 2006, p. 387). The interviews were conducted with partners from Germany, Italy, Mexico, Switzerland, Turkey and USA. In terms of nationalities, the cohort was even more diverse. Personal face-to-face interviews were set up only in Germany, Mexico, Switzerland and USA. The geographical distribution and the interview language classified by interview type are shown in Table 34 and Table 35.

	Face-to-face interviews	Skype/Telephone interviews	Written answers	Total interviews per country
Germany	9	4	1	14
Italy	-	-	1	1
Switzerland	1	1	2	4
Turkey	-	1	-	1
Europe total	**10**	**6**	**4**	**20**
Mexico	3	2		5
USA	2	1	-	3
North America total	**5**	**3**	**0**	**8**
Total interviews per interview type	**15**	**9**	**4**	**28**

Table 34: Geographical distribution by interview type.

Most interviewees appreciated the option of doing the interview face-to-face. For this purpose, several trips were undertaken within Germany. Journeys abroad led to Mexico, Switzerland and USA. While the preference for written answers emanated from the corresponding interviewees alone, budget and time restrictions mattered when planning Skype and telephone interviews with Mexico, Turkey and USA (cf. Bogner et al., 2014, p. 35; Gläser and Laudel, 2010, p. 153).

	Interview language		
	English	German	Spanish
Face-to-face interviews	5	8	2
Skype/Telephone interviews	4	4	1
Written answers	3	1	-
Total	12	13	3

Table 35: Interview language used by interview type.

Most interview partners were German native speakers, and, thus, most interviews were done in German. However, English and Spanish were used in three different situations: 1) interview partner was an English or Spanish native speaker, 2) English or Spanish was the only language fluently spoken by both interviewee and interviewer, or 3) English or Spanish formed the dominant business language, making it easier for interviewees to talk about the subject matter in English or Spanish than in any other language.

At the beginning of each interview, the research purpose was briefly explained again, and the interviewees were updated about the progress status of the empirical field research. To give them a better idea of how their response will fit into the research context, the type of interview partners (companies, IOs and DCAs), the branches they cover, and the geographical scope were roughly depicted. Before starting, interviewees were asked for permission to use a digital recording device for ensuring accurate and complete gathering of all information and knowledge shared. Moreover, this course of action allows the interviewer to dedicate full attention to the interviewing process, without being diverted by taking notes, and therefore enables him to handle the interview guide in a flexible way if necessary (cf. Bogner et al., 2014,

p. 37 f. and p. 59 f.; Gläser and Laudel, 2010, p. 157 f.; Mayer, 2013, p. 47; Patton, 2009, p. 380; Rahaman et al., 2010). To address confidentiality concerns, each interviewee was issued a confidentiality declaration which states the measures undertaken to maintain confidentiality in terms of anonymization, transcription and disclosure. Interviewees were assured that neither their name nor their organization's name or any other identifying information will appear in the later thesis. Anonymizations were carried out as far as necessary. These strict principles apply to transcription and disclosure accordingly. The confidentiality declaration was signed by the interviewer under the eyes of the interviewees. Assuring and maintaining confidentiality is not only a requirement of good scientific practice but in fact a strong trust-building mechanism that encourages interview partners to share sensitive information with the interviewer, which cannot be disclosed unfiltered but is important to understand the context and special circumstances of PPPs and their stakeholders (cf. Bogner et al., 2014, p. 89 f.; Irvine, 2003; Patton, 2009, p. 408; Qu and Dumay, 2011; Silverman, 2010, p. 30 f.; Smith, 2015, p. 142 f.). Usually, the available time frame for the interview was agreed in advance, either during the preliminary call or by email. Still, interviews are time-consuming and form additional effort for interview partners who usually have high workloads and need to somehow align an interview with their tight schedules. These circumstances impact on the time available for field research, regardless of thematic overlap and personal interest (cf. Bogner et al., 2014, p. 37 f.; Gläser and Laudel, 2010, p. 153). Thus, the interviewees were kindly asked to reconfirm the agreed time frame for enabling the interviewer to prioritize interview questions in case of less time available than actually expected. To make sure that all relevant organizational issues were covered prior to the interview, the interviewer used a checklist. On overall average, interviews lasted 1:10h while the median duration is 1:09h. These very similar lengths of time indicate that there are generally no major biases in terms of interview duration, except for the interview with CO11[11]. Table 36 gives an overview of durations of interviews conducted with the different types of interview partners.

In absolute numbers or hh:mm	Companies	IOs	DCAs	Total
# of interviews (abbreviation)	14 (CO1-CO14)	8 (IO1-IO8)	6 (DC1-DC6)	28
# of interview partners	18	8	6	32
Total duration	16:01	4:26	7:25	27:52
Mean duration	1:14	0:53	1:14	1:10
Median duration	1:11	0:44	1:10	1:08
Standard deviation	0:22	0:20	0:14	0:22
Minimum duration	0:11[11]	0:39	1:00	0:11
Maximum duration	1:51	1:33	1:42	1:51

Table 36: Overview of interview durations compiled by interview partner type.[12]
(in hours)

[11] The eleven minutes long interview stands out from the others because it went along with the observation of a 90 minutes meeting session in which CO11 and IO8 were involved. The observations have been summarized in a note of two pages. Open questions were clarified by a follow-up interview in the aftermath. The second shortest interview among company representatives was done with CO9 and took 1:00h.

[12] The times indicated in this table refer to personal and skype-/ telephone-based interviews only.

The face-to-face and Skype-/telephone-based interviews were tape-recorded and transcribed verbatim; all interviewees granted permission to do so. In the aftermath of each interview, a short protocol was prepared for recording any noteworthy aspects of the interview procedure and follow-up matters (e.g. interest in research results, specific disclosure requirements, time pressure) (cf. Gläser and Laudel, 2010, p. 192; Patton, 2009, p. 383 f.). Additional data were collected from a variety of digital and written documents provided prior or after the interview, such as annual or company reports, internal guidelines, organizational charts. These additional sources helped to complement verbatim interview data, an approach also pursued by other accounting researchers (cf. Abernethy et al., 2001; Kamminga and VdM, 2007; Nicholson et al., 2006; Rahaman et al., 2010).

Upon completion of the data collection and the transcription of interviews, the so-called "communicative validation" was undertaken in the period May to June 2017. An overview of the central results in the format of a PowerPoint presentation was sent to the interview partners for seeking feedback. They were kindly invited to comment their views on the provided selection of central results in written or to discuss by phone/Skype the findings made by the researcher. This mechanism helps to increase the validity of collected data and results (cf. Flick, 2014, p. 495). A more in-depth explanation of this procedure follows in Chapter 5.3.3.3 while the outcome of the communicative validation will be presented in Chapter 7.2.2.

In the aftermath of each verbal interview, a short memo that summarizes pros and cons of the conservation was prepared. Such memos contribute to better understanding the conditions under which the respective interviews took place and the comments and statements have been made. Extant literature on content analysis strongly recommends preparing such memos as they also help to better interpret the interview results and are thus considered important for the validity assessment of the results (cf. Bogner et al., 2014, p. 43; Bortz and Döring, 2006, p. 311 f.; Chapter 5.3.3.2).

The researcher has noted positively that all interview partners showed themselves interested in receiving the research results and most of them were basically open to participate in the communicative validation. The researcher faced mostly a pleasant discussion atmosphere, which was characterized by openness and willingness to share PPP experiences. Though each interview was quite individual by nature, the interview guide could still be implemented as intended in the vast majority of cases. Moreover, the communication with the interview partners was generally smooth so that in some cases appointments could be arranged promptly. Several interviewees offered proactively to make contact with other stakeholders involved and declared to be available for follow-up questions. The good overall level of experience in multi-stakeholder dialogues among the experts eased the interviews additionally.

Major challenges associated with the interviews were time pressure and temporary interruptions caused by incoming phone calls or by an earthquake simulation once in Mexico. In a few cases, the interview guide could not be processed as expected on the one side, or responses were little detailed and given rather reactively on the other side. Both scenarios required the researcher to conduct the discussion very actively. In very few situations, interviewees seemed to be representing an official position instead of sharing their own view. Moreover, it would have been conducive for some questions if the interviewees had possessed more experiences in each other's sector, either private or public sector. However, none of the aforementioned challenges impaired any interview in the way that it would need to be excluded from the sample because in total the pros strongly outweigh the cons.

5.3 Methodology of Data Analysis

The social sciences and related disciplines face the challenge that the existing methodical literature does not provide comprehensive and generic guidelines for systematic analysis of complex, verbal interview data (cf. Mayring, 2015, p. 10; Kvale and Brinkmann, 2009, p. 181). Thus, there is usually no other step in qualitative research which shows higher intransparency than the analysis and interpretation of interview data (cf. Naderer and Balzer, 2011, p. 407). Hence, a transparent analysis procedure is required to generate robust results and to draw meaningful conclusions from the interview records and transcripts. In this context, qualitative content analysis proved to be an acknowledged method in accounting in order to systematically scrutinize comprehensive textual datasets, such as interviews, and therefore to extract relevant information for answering the research questions (cf. Beck et al., 2010; Endenich, 2012, p. 191; Gläser and Laudel, 2010, p. 46; Henke, 2016, p. 137; Smith, 2015, p. 108 f.). "Content analysis aims to reduce the raw data to manageable amounts for analysis" (Beck et al., 2010, p. 207), and allows to draw "replicable and valid inferences from texts (or other meaningful matter) to the contexts of their use" (Krippendorff, 2004, p. 18). For this purpose, a system of categories needs to be built by means of which the interview data are coded in a systematic way. So-called Qualitative Data Analysis (QDA) software can support the categorization and coding process and contribute to improving the overall quality and transparency of the content analysis (cf. Kuckartz, 2010, p. 97; Schmidt, 2013, p. 455).

5.3.1 Procedure for Qualitative Content Analysis

At the outset, the tape-recorded expert interviews have to be transcribed literally and completely. This step is imperative to facilitate a comprehensive and meaningful analysis of the interviews and to produce reasonable findings in support of answering the research questions (cf. Bortz and Döring, 2006, p. 341; Broweleit, 2014, p. 203; Lamnek and Krell, 2010, p. 356). Transcription ensures first the full textualisation of verbal data, and allows second the interpretation of statements within a specific context including the identification of linkages between them (cf. Maxwell, 2013, p. 112; Mayring, 2016, p. 89). Indeed, the preparation of transcriptions is a time-consuming but crucial step in qualitative research, which is still without alternative: "Difficult and time-consuming though transcription is, there really is no satisfactory alternative to recording and fully transcribing qualitative research interviews" (cf. King, 1994, p. 25). Hence, transcribing the interviews represents the only way textualising them concisely and accurately, without impairing the data quality by premature interpretations (cf. Broweleit, 2014, p. 203; Kvale and Brinkmann, 2009, p. 177 ff.; Silverman, 2010, p. 239 ff.).

In the present study, the transcribing of interviews usually was done promptly after interview conduction to prevent piling up of workload which would delay final content analysis and could become a discouraging task (cf. Maxwell, 2013, p. 104 f.; Moll et al., 2006, p. 389). Computer-assisted transcription was performed by using the software "f4" (cf. Kuckartz et al., 2008, p. 29). In practice, there are different transcription approaches and rules which are not universally applicable or suitable so that the transcription procedure should finally be aligned with the specific research interest and the information needed for data analysis (cf. Gläser and Laudel, 2010, p. 193; Silverman, 2010, p. 212). That is why Flick (2014) recommends doing transcriptions only as precise and as much as necessary for answering the questions underlying the research (p. 379 f.). Given the fact that this study places emphasis on content and aims to gather substantive information, there is no need to document in the transcripts emotional states of the interview partners or minor disturbances that happen during interviewing (e.g. incoming phone calls that are shortly responded) because they have no relevance for the later content analysis. In this vein, diligent smoothing with respect to orthography and language style accompanied the transcription of interview conversations, but without compromising or reducing content and meaning of phrases (cf. Bortz and Döring, 2006, p. 312; Gläser and Laudel, 2010, p. 193; Kuckartz et al., 2008, p. 27; Kvale and Brinkmann, 2009, p. 182; Mayring, 2016, p. 91). To ensure complete and literal transcription in the best possible way, the corresponding protocols were subjected to a quality check by listening them once again (cf. Kruse et al., 2012, p. 36; Lamnek and Krell, 2010, p. 368; Schmidt, 2013, p. 449). The requirement to ensure anonymity and confidentiality is of particular importance for the transcription because selected quotations from the transcript protocols will be used for the presentation of the results obtained by empirical findings in Chapter 0. Thus, any information that could make persons or organizations identifiyable has been anonymized. The names of interviewees and organizations have been replaced by the respective ID codes as assigned in Chapter 5.2.1.3 (cf. Endenich, 2012, p. 190; Flick, 2014, p. 380; Gläser and Laudel, 2010, p. 194).

The aforementioned transcription rules apply to all interviews, regardless of the language of conversation used. All interviews have been analyzed in their original language to prevent misinterpretations or linguistic biases caused by translation. However, statements made in German and Spanish language interviews that are considered for the presentation of the results and discussion will be translated into English to make all results universally understandable for the research community. Thus, these statements will appear in original language and as translation, while the latter will be written in smaller font size. To address the inherent risk of significant biases between original sentence and its translation, the following rules will apply (cf. Endenich, 2012, p. 190 f.; Wettemann, 2012, p. 102 f.):

- Translate as exactly as possible, but without compromising the meaning of the original text,
- Do not paraphrase,
- Add clarifying explanations and comments in footnotes, if appropriate (e.g. in case of metaphors and sayings).

For resource reasons in terms of time and money, only the German- and Spanish language statements, considered for citation in Chapter 0, have been translated, but not the entire transcripts (cf. Schlichting, 2013, p. 155).

5.3.2 Creation of Categories and Coding Approach

The database of the content analysis comprises the written answers and transcripts from 28 interviews, internal documents provided by the interview partners (e.g. guidelines, partnership-related documents), and external, publicly available documents gathered by the researcher (e.g. annual reports, CSR reports, guidelines, PPP pamphlet) (cf. Baumgarth and Koch, 2009, p. 155; Moll et al., 2006, p. 390). In total, the transcripts comprise 612 pages, with an average of about 25 pages (verbal interviews only), and are therefore within the typical range of pages per transcript (cf. Kuckartz, 2010, p. 30).[13]

For the qualitative content analysis and coding of interview data in the present study, a multi-stage procedure according to MAYRING will be used, which relies on different analysis techniques. First of all, there are three basic, complementary forms of interpretation that are independent from each other and are not executed consecutively: *summarization*, *explication*, and *structuration*. It is up to the researcher to decide which analysis technique is most suitable to facilitate the answering of the research questions in the best possible way, based on the given data (e.g. documents, notes, and transcripts). Of course, it can also be a combination of two or all three techniques (cf. Henke, 2016, p. 137; Mayring, 2015, p. 67), which can be defined as follows:

- *Summarization* aims to reduce the total amount of data generated by tape recording and to cut off unnecessary information by focusing on essential statements (e.g. by bundling or removing of redundant comments). Substantial content shall be preserved.
- *Explication* aims to enrich unclear text passages with additional information which improve the understanding by explanation and interpretation.
- *Structuration* aims to filter certain aspects from the data, to assess the data by means of certain benchmarks or to categorize them on the basis of ex-ante determined criteria. Therefore, a so-called system of categories will be worked out which undergoes an iterative, inductive procedure to enhance and refine it in order to improve its suitability at the end.

On the basis of the structuration technique, the system of categories has been deductively derived in the first step (cf. Demirag et al., 2012; Früh, 2011, p. 73; Kromrey, 2006, p. 326). Before improving the system of categories inductively in the second step, the interview data have been summarized in the sense that non-relevant paragraphs have been omitted. However, given the fact that all interviews followed clear semi-structured interview guides, almost all obtained information was usable, and no interview had to be left out because of insufficient meaningfulness. Only in a few cases interview partners provided additional sources of information, which basically confirmed or specified verbal comments made during the actual interview. To avoid misunderstandings, once something was unclear, the interviewer kindly asked for clarification on the subject matter. Thus, document-based explications were only needed in very few cases.

The design of the system of categories, which comprises main and sub-categories, basically follows the order of the research questions and is aligned with the structure of the interview guide. While the main categories were derived from the research questions and the interview guide, sub-categories were developed and refined in an iterative manner during the coding procedure. Categories are also called codes. Coding means the assignment of appropriate

[13] Transcript format: for this, apply the same format criteria as for the regular text body (Font type: Arial; font size: 11; line space: 1.5; page margin: left 4cm, top/bottom/right 2cm each).

analysis units (single words, sentences, text passages) to main and sub-categories. After the coding of about 50% of the total textual interview data, the system of categories was benchmarked against consistency, logic and relevance for the underlying research questions. Only minor changes were necessary in the sense that categories were merged, split or renamed. Hence, the hitherto coded data were adapted to the revised system of categories and the remaining 50% were coded accordingly. Thus, a comprehensive system of categories was designed that enables the researcher to structure an unstructured mass of information and thereby filter out relevant aspects that serve the answering of the research questions (cf. Kuckartz, 2008, p. 12, 36 ff.; Mayring, 2016, p. 105 and pp. 114-117). Due to the iterative development process no test run for the system of categories was necessary at the end (cf. Gläser and Laudel, 2010, p. 201; Henke, 2016, p. 138).

The system of categories (or list of codes) itself is structured in eight meta categories which are further subdivided in up to five levels of sub codes, depending on the degree of granularity of the obtained information. The eight meta categories are as follows: Basics, Partnership Setting, Preparation and Implementation, Budget and Resource Planning, Governance and Control Pattern, Management Control, Institutional Environment, and Critical Success Factors.

Categories can be classified by type or coding family (cf. Flick, 2014, p. 395 f.; Kuckartz, 2016, p. 41 f.; Maxwell, 2013, p. 156 f.). While the *Basics* meta code comprises fact-based categories, such as number of involved stakeholders, job position of the interview partner, PPP types or legal framework of the PPP, the remaining meta codes contain analytical, content-related, and evaluative categories. The meta codes *Partnership Setting* and *Preparation and Implementation* contain statements which are assigned to categories that deal amongst others with the origin of a PPP, motivation, objectives, requirements, strategies or project phases and are therefore part of the C-Family (causes, consequences, conditions), the Strategy-Family and of the Identity-Family (identity, external/self-perception). *Budget and Resource Planning*, *Governance and Control Pattern* and *Management Control* belong more likely to the Culture-Familiy, the Consensus-Family, the Interaction-Family and the Process-Family because they focus on management and operational governance and control procedures and mechanisms between the different stakeholders involved in a partnership. In this context, aspects such as different (organizational) cultures, norms and values and diverging interests play a role for the design of formal and informal MC process and structures, which form the basis for any kind of interaction between the partners involved. The *Institutional Environment* and *Critical Success Factors* categories are of overarching nature and cannot be assigned to a specific coding family.

Formal categories, such as interview duration, interview language, geographical distribution of the interviews, and lengths of transcript have already been presented in Chapter 5.2.2.2. In total, 2,660 codings have been assigned to the inductively developed system of categories, which comprises 162 categories (8 meta codes, 154 sub codes) (annex 8.4).

The software tool MAXQDA 12 supported the designing of the system of categories and the coding procedure. This program allows assigning single word, sentences or text passages to defined categories and to flexibly merge, split, shift or subordinate them and therefore strongly eases the inductive iteration process of the system of categories. Still, the software only facilitates the operative implementation of the coding method, but is not involved in the actual data analysis and interpretation (cf. Flick, 2014, p. 462; Kuckartz, 2016, pp. 177-185; Maxwell, 2013, p. 116 f.). Hence, a granular system of categories has been developed, which helped to condense and structure the comprehensive interview data and is supposed to support a differentiated presentation and discussion of the results, building on the theoretical framework and the research questions.

5.3.3 Quality Assessment of the Methodical Approach

Regardless of the research topic and the chosen methodology, the assurance of quality is pivotal for any research design. However, compared to quantitative research, qualitative research methodologies face the challenge to agree on a common standardized quality assessment approach, which goes along with specific and universal quality criteria (cf. Flick, 2014, p. 487 f.; Przyborski et al., 2010, p. 35). In the following, quality criteria typically used in qualitative research will be presented, and it will be explained how they are applied to the present research work.

5.3.3.1 Quality Criteria

Considering basic quality principles from quantitative research, four major quality criteria have been established in the qualitative context and aim to ensure a representative and reliable data collection as well as valid results (cf. Bortz and Döring, 2006, p. 326; Broweleit, 2014, p. 218; Flick, 2014, p. 487 f.). These four quality criteria are *external validity*, *internal validity, objectivity,* and *reliability*, which all together form essential requirements of field studies (cf. Atkinson and Shaffir, 1998; Kvale and Brinkmann, 2009, p. 242; Lamnek and Krell, 2010, p. 134 ff.; Rössler, 2010, p. 195). **External validity** means the requirement that research results can also be transferred to research objects other than the present ones, for instance on kinds of PPPs other than PPPs for development. By contrast, **internal validity** requires that results be unambiguous, causally interrelated with each other and clearly interpretable. For instance, in order to attribute certain MC challenges or problems to concrete causes or influence factors (cf. Bortz and Döring, 2006, p. 53; Lamnek and Krell, 2010, p. 134; Smith, 2015, p. 34). **Objectivity** means to ensure that research results are as far as possible unbiased by the researcher himself and requires to transparently indicate any subjective influence factors. **Reliability** is based on objectivity and requires that data analyses can be replicated without leading to major differences. In this sense, valid results require reliability of the applied research method (cf. Broweleit, 2014, p. 223; Lamnek and Krell, 2010, p. 149 f.; Rössler, 2010, p. 195). Table 37 shows a selection of appropriate review mechanisms that allow to verify if and to which extent the quality criteria are met.

Criteria	Requirement	Review	Review Mechanism (examples)
External validity	Generalizability/transferability of the results	Representative sampling	• Communicative validation • Targeted sampling

Criteria	Requirement	Review	Review Mechanism (examples)
Internal validity	Authenticity/credibility of the research design	Unambiguity of the results	• Communicative validation • Triangulation
Objectivity	• Confirmability of the results • Impartiality of the researcher	• Standardization of research methods • Transparency	• Detailed disclosure of the research process • Use of standardized research methods
Reliability	Accuracy, auditability and reliability of the measurement and results	• Pretest • Independent testing	• Replicability • Stability

Table 37: Quality criteria in qualitative research.
(Source: based on Atkinson and Shaffir (1998); Broweleit (2014, p. 219); Flick (2014, p. 506); Kuckartz, 2016, p. 202; Kvale and Brinkmann (2009, p. 242); Rössler (2010, pp. 195-198); Wrona (2006, p. 208))

In summary, validity and reliability form two fundamental quality criteria that are applicable to the analysis of interview data (cf. Mayring, 2016, p. 140) and being considered as more crucial than objectivity for qualitative research (cf. Lamnek and Kell, 2010, p. 137). However, the issue of objectivity has been addressed by duly documenting the research process and presenting it in a transparent manner. The Chapters 5.2.2.1 and 5.2.2.2 show the timetable of the data collection, the interviewing process and by means of which criteria interview partners have been selected and interviews were conducted. The disclosure of the semi-structured interview guide and of the systems of categories underlines that the data collection and data analysis followed a structured procedure (Chapters 5.3.1 and 5.3.2). The subsequent Chapters 5.3.3.2 and 5.3.3.3 will explain the measures by which data validity and reliability have been assured for the present research.

5.3.3.2 Validity

Validity has a twofold meaning, validity of the applied methodical instruments and validity of the results. The former ones are valid if they enable the researcher to collect and analyze data as intended. Results are valid insofar as they reflect the reality to a reasonable extent (cf. Krippendorff, 2004, p. 313; Kvale and Brinkmann, 2009, p. 246). It should be reiterated that the main focus of qualitative research is not placed on fully generalizable and statistically representative results. Still, the diligent selection of diverse interview partners and the systematic analysis of the interview transcripts contribute to achieving an appropriate level of *external validity* of the research results and to making these results generalizable to some extent (cf. Flick, 2014, p. 522 f.). That is why the targeted sampling approach was chosen, going along with minimum requirements imposed on the selected interview partners and on the examined PPPs. Moreover, the relatively comprehensive field research and the use of mainly "how" and "what" questions in the interview guide, enriched by "why" questions during the interviews, prevented the present research work from only documenting MC in PPPs, but helped to gather experience-based knowledge that basically improves the external validity of the results (cf. Kuckartz, 2014, p. 168 f.; Yin, 2014, p. 48).

Validity of qualitative research can be measured by means of different criteria. The most important one is **consensual validity**, which basically means that several researchers and persons involved in or affected by the research project agree on the relevance and the credibility of the research method and the research results. Approaches to demonstrate consensual validity are communicative validation and argumentative validation (cf. Bortz and Döring, 2006, p. 328). **Communicative validity** is given if there is consensus between the researcher and the research subjects on the research design and on the results interpretation (cf. Flick, 2014, p. 495; Kvale and Brinkmann, 2009, p. 253 ff.; Mayring, 2016, p. 147). That is why communicative validation is a mechanism to measure both external and internal validity. To achieve **internal validity** pretests were undertaken to make sure that the interview questions are reasonsable and understandable to the interview partners. The preliminary phone calls with the interviewees helped to establish a common understanding of the research object and to clarify open questions from both sides (Chapter 5.2.1.2). To reach **external validity** all interviewees were contacted once again and asked to give feedback on the empirical results in order to validate the researcher's analyses and interpretations (Chapter 5.2.2.2). With respect to the logical order of the research work, the results of the communicative validation will be discussed in Chapter 7. **Argumentative validity** is a mechanism of *external validation* and means that there is consensus between the researcher and fellow colleagues or other researchers who are in the capacity to validate the research results (cf. Bortz and Döring, 2006, p. 328; Lamnek and Krell, 2010, p. 140). In this context, continuous dialogue with senior accounting researchers about the suitability of the selected methodology has taken place, and their critical comments and recommendations were considered during the realization of the research project. Additional feedback was drawn from internal doctoral meeting sessions at TU Dortmund and EGADE Business School as well as from the 2015 ERMAC Conference in Vienna, and from the 2016 AAA Government and Nonprofit Section Midyear Meeting in Arlington (USA) where this research project was presented at both an early and an advanced stage.

Internal validity was moreover promoted by the assurance of strict confidentiality of the interview conversations so that many interview partners felt encouraged to speak more frankly and to share with the researcher information which cannot be quoted in Chapter 0, but is still valuable to know for the analysis and interpretation. Furtherrmore, the tape-recording and transcribing of the interviews ensured the accuracy and completeness of the obtained information. The interview memos contain positive and negative aspects about each verbal interview and therefore provide an additional help for the analysis of the validity of results (Chapter 5.2.2.2). The same holds true for memos created in MAXQDA and attached to the different codes in the system of categories (cf. Kuckartz, 2010, p. 134; Mayring, 2016, p. 105; Patton, 2009, p. 446). Inconsistencies and uncertainties were clarified during the interviews by means of documents and data supplied by the interview partners. However, given the diligent selection of interview partners, the structured interviewing process, and due to the comprehensive amount of interview data, no additional data triangulation was undertaken (cf. Flick, 2014, p. 519 f.; Lamnek and Krell, 2010, p. 142; Mayring, 2016, p. 147 f.).

5.3.3.3 *Reliability*

Content analysis requires quality assurance of the data analysis process. In this context, an appropriate level of *reliability* of the analysis procedure and of the results is crucial and is benchmarked against the key criterion *consistency*. Thus, neither the repetition of the coding procedure at various points in time nor the alternation of the coder should lead to any significant differences in results in order to avoid considerable inconsistencies. Here, *intracoder reliability* and *intercoder reliability* form the two dominant indicators to approach the overall level of reliability (cf. Krippendorff, 2004, p. 214-216; Mayring, 2016, p. 141; Rössler, 2010, p. 197). Their determination requires the definition of coding rules to ensure the intersubjective comparability of the coding results. These results correspond to the system of categories including the related specifications and key questions. Moreover, impartiality and independence of the second coder is pivotal to avoid any subjective influences (cf. Gläser and Laudel, 2010, p. 2010; Krippendorff, 2004, p. 215; Mayring, 2016, p. 118; Chapter 8.4). How these two indicators are determined for the present study will be explained in the following:

- *Intracoder reliability* measures the concordance of two or more separate coding procedures by the same coder at different points in time. A high degree of agreement between both coding procedures indicates a high level of stability of the analysis (cf. Himme, 2009, p. 487 f.; Rössler, 2010, p. 198).
- *Intercoder reliability* measures the concordance between the researcher and a second coder in terms of the coding of the interview data, applying the same coding rules in the present case of the interview transcripts. A high degree of agreement between both coders points to a high level of objectivity and therefore improves the reliability of the methodical elements and of the results (cf. Gläser and Laudel, 2010, p. 210; Mayring, 2015, p. 64).

The existing content analysis literature produced different quantitative indicators for the measurement of reliability. Despite some weaknesses, the coefficient of agreements according to Ole Holsti is used for the calculation of intracoder and intercoder reliability. It became established because of its easy determination and interpretation. That is why it will be also used in the present research work (cf. Früh, 2015, p. 187; Krippendorff, 2004, p. 245; Mayring, 2015, p. 127 f.; Rössler, 2010, p. 202). Weaknesses of Holsti's approach are inaccuracy resulting from multiple coding of analysis units and insufficient familiarity of additional coders with the subject matter. However, the very detailed system of categories and a diligent selection of the second coder counteract these weaknesses (cf. Früh, 2015, p. 183-188; Chapter 8.4). The coefficient of agreement is defined such that it can assume a value between 0% and 100%. It is calculated as follows (cf. Bortz and Döring, 2006, p. 196; Holsti, 1969, p. 140):

$$C_R = \frac{2 * M}{N_1 + N_2}$$

Parameters:

- C_R: coefficient of agreement of the coding procedure
- M: number of matches of codings between the first and the second coding procedure by one coder (intracoder) or by two different coders (intercoder)
- N_1: number of matches of codings resulting from the first coding procedure
- N_2: number of matches of codings resulting from the second coding procedure

For the determination of the **intracoder reliability**, all transcripts have been coded and categorized twice with a time interval of about two months while the second coding includes an additional iteration step. The coefficient of agreement between the first coding and the second coding amounts to C_R = 85.11%. The number of codes Z slightly increased from 2,663 to 2,671 codes. Based on the list of codes from the second coding, each category was subjected to an iterative consistency check to make sure that all codings were assigned to the most suitable category. Special emphasis has been placed on categories with very few codings and on double codings (cf. Kuckartz, 2008, p. 83 ff.). As a consequence, some codings were reassigned or removed, and a few categories were merged or dissolved. That is why C_R between the second coding and the iteration step decreased to 76.35%. The final number Z of codes amounts to 2,660 units. However, the major adjustments of the system of categories were made in the transition from the first to the second coding procedure. Thus, it is reasonable to reduce biases and inconsistencies in the results by including an additional iterative coding step as was done by previous accounting researchers who pursued a multi-stage coding procedure (cf. Demirag et al., 2012; Li P. et al., 2013; Wrona, 2006, p. 205). For the required minimum of C_R, there is no single accepted value. Still, Früh (2015, p. 185 f.), Kuckartz (2016, p. 210), Rössler (2010, p. 204) and others recommend a threshold of C_R = 75% or 80% for assuming a very good level of reliability, depending on the complexity and the amount of data material which both are high in the present research work. In summary, due to the high intracoder reliability, stability and reproducibility of the results of this study can be assumed.

For the determination of the **intercoder reliability,** a senior management accounting researcher was consulted and asked to code seven randomly selected interviews, which corresponds to 25% of all interviews (cf. Krippendorff, 2004, p. 215). This is an appropriate size for the sub-sample, given that Wimmer and Dominick (2006, p. 167) recommend to encode 10-25% of the total data material, Kaid and Wadsworth (1989, p. 208) suggest only 5-7%, and Rössler (2010, p. 203) urges to do at least 200-300 codings, which corresponds to 7.5-11% of the codings of the present work. The random selection was carried out by using Microsoft Excel.[14] The coding by the second coder resulted in C_R = 78.14%, and occurred on the basis of the system of categories which was developed out of the first iterative step by the researcher. This coefficient value exceeds the required minimum and allows assuming a high level of objectivity of the results. The coefficients of agreement for both intracoder and intercoder reliability have been calculated by means of a corresponding analysis function in MAXQDA (cf. Mayring, 2015, p. 120; Table 38).

Reliability	Field Study	Required minimum
Intracoder	85.11% (76.35%)	• 75%: Früh (2015, p. 185 f.), Klenke (2008, p. 102), Monette et al. (2013, p. 208)
Intercoder	78,14%	• 80%: Krippendorff (2004, p. 288), Rössler (2010, p. 204)

Table 38: Coefficients of agreement, C_R, of the content analysis.

[14] Random sampling: The selection of interviews coded by the second researcher comprises the interviews CO6, CO7, CO9, DC4, IO3, IO5, and IO7.

5.3.4 Summary of the Methodical Approach

This chapter illustrates the motivation and the reasons for the use of a qualitative interview-based research design for an exploratory international field study on PPPs for development. In detail it explains the elements of the actual methodical approach and shows what quality assurance mechanisms were applied to counteract potential limitations, risks and weaknesses of this approach (Figure 28). The choice of this research design is determined by the nature of the research problem and the identified research gap. Consequently, and aligned with the underlying research questions, the present research approach focuses more on exploring descriptive, explorative and normative characteristics of MC in PPPs for development from a few PPP projects than on gathering quantifiable metrics from a large-scale sample. Hence, it represents more an in-depth than an in-breadth analysis.

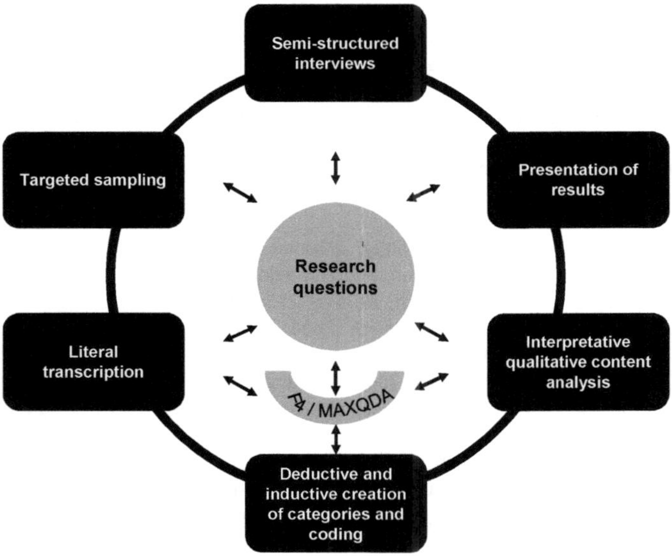

Figure 28: Elements of qualitative research methodology.
(following Kuckartz (2016, p. 45), Müller N. A. (2016, p. 164))

The targeted sampling of private sector firms, IOs and DCAs was followed by semi-structured interviews with 32 interview partners from 28 entities where the proportion of public and private sector origin is balanced. The data collection phase extended over one year and embraces interviews with experts from six different countries, while the geographic focus is placed on Germany, Mexico and Switzerland. The interview transcribing in English, German and Spanish happened software-supported by the F4 programm while the creation of categories and the entire coding procedure was done by means of MAXQDA. Both the design of the interview guides and the data collection as well as the content analysis were aligned with the conceptual basics (Chapter 0), the theoretical framework (Chapter 4.3) and the research questions (Chapter 4.5), continuously accompanied by common quality assurance mechanisms in qualitative research (Table 39).

Criteria	Research Design	Data Collection	Data Analysis
External validity	• Minimum requirement for interview partners • Targeted sampling	-	Communicative validation of the results with the interview partners
Internal validity	• Communicative validation • Focus on the research subject • Pretests	• Request for clarification during the interviews in case of inconsistencies or uncertainty • Triangulation (double-checking of interview statements with provided documents)	Transcript validation before starting the coding
Objectivity	Documentation of the research process	Standardized research methods (e.g. semi-structured interview guide, selection procedure of interview partners)	Standardized research methods (e.g. single system of categories for all interviews)
Reliability	-	-	• Intracoder reliability • Intercoder reliability

Table 39: Quality assurance actions taken.
(Source: following Broweleit (2014, p. 226) and Wrona (2006, p. 208))

The application of the four quality criteria has demonstrated that the chosen research design including its methodological elements is suitable for addressing the research questions from Chapter 4.5 on MC in PPPs for development so that valid and reliable results can be produced. The results of this empirical field study are presented and discussed in-depth in the following Chapter 0.

6. Results of the Empirical Field Study

This chapter presents the findings and results from the empirical field study, which will be accentuated by key statements quoted from the 28 interviews. The general structure of the presentation follows the thematic areas according to the interview guide. It begins with a descriptive overview of the basic characteristics of the analyzed PPPs for development (Chapter 6.1) and continues with the analysis of partnership settings (Chapter 6.2). Both serve the answering of research question RQ1. The chapter on preparation and implementation of partnerships (Chapter 6.3) guides to the explorative analysis of the interview data. It continues with the examination of budget and resource planning processes (Chapter 6.4), governance and control patterns (Chapter 6.5), followed by a comprehensive study of implemented MC mechanisms and reasons for that (Chapter 6.6), and concludes with an analysis of the relevance of the institutional environment for PPP implementation (Chapter 6.7). All these explorative chapters respond to research question RQ2.1. In the final Chapter 6.8 is given an overview of extrinsic and intrinsic CSFs as well as the potential for improvement going along with them. Therefore, this chapter replies to the explorative research question RQ2.2 and exposes first ideas for the development of existing and future PPPs in the sense of RQ3. The structure and naming of the respective subchapters are strongly aligned with the sub-codes pursuant to the system of categories as defined in annex 8.4. Most chapters and subchapters conclude with a brief summary.

References are indicated in brackets after quotations. Statements quoted from CO1, CO9, CO10 and CO13 furthermore distinguish between first and second speaker. The acronyms can either stand for the interviewee or for the entity he or she is representing. Quotations from German and Spanish interviews are followed by analogous English translations, and are written in brackets and smaller font size. For a few quotations, sources will not be indicated because of their very critical nature that demands the application of an increased secrecy level. Thus, the origin of the affected quotations is marked by "n/a" (not available) instead of a regular acronym.

6.1 Basic Characteristics of PPPs for Development

Although the present work places its focus on the axis of the private sector and IOs/DCAs, many partnerships are composed of more types of stakeholders and are embedded in complex multilateral frameworks. Thus, this chapter will give an overview of the different stakeholder types and people involved as well as of the fundamental characteristics of the PPPs for development included in the sample of the present study. It serves the answering of **research question 1.**

6.1.1 Characteristics of the Stakeholders Involved

Both public and private sector organizations maintain partnership relationships with several stakeholder types that vary by the respective subject matter or policy issue they deal with, which can be broad. Hence, both (inter-)governmental actors and the private sector enter

T. S. Konrad, *Management Control in Public-Private Partnerships*,
Schriften zu Wirtschaftsprüfung, Steuerlehre und Controlling,
https://doi.org/10.1007/978-3-658-22868-2_6

into partnerships with other public and private entities, which are potentially very different from them and shed different lights on the same centre of interest. This comprises amongst others academic institutions, NGOs, and philanthropic foundations that contribute very differently to these partnerships and are involved in them to varying degrees. Moreover, actors like DCAs and IOs are by nature more closely bound to national public stakeholders because governments confer mandates to them and use to be their main customers.

> *Beteiligte Partner, die wir haben, das ist jetzt ein Spektrum von verschiedenen Dingen. Wir haben entweder Verträge mit Regierungsorganisationen oder Nichtregierungsorganisationen. (CO1-1)*
> (Involved partners we have, that is a wide range of things. We have contracts with either governmental organizations or non-governmental organizations.)

> *I mean, we have now the four kinds of non-state actors where NGOs, private sector entities, philanthropic foundations, academic institutions cooperate. We have partnerships with all of them. (IO3)*

On the operational level, DCAs and NGOs often have a strong stake in the PPP implementation, depending on contextual factors like individual capacities and local conditions. By contrast, academic institutions assume more an advisory function while philanthropic foundations often act as financiers of comprehensive global projects, for instance in the health area. Moreover, many PPPs often act under the umbrella of global platforms or alliances like the Business Call to Action or the Vaccine Alliance GAVI.

> *So, in some national projects we do have NGOs as implementing partners or certain components as well. So, it could be implemented through a NGO as well. I'm not sure to what extent. I have a feeling that it's not a huge amount of them and it probably depends a little bit on the country context as well as what the capacity of our office or of the other partners is and the situation in that sense. I would say that there are lots of kinds of partnerships, in that sense that we work with [DCA Partner] or [DCA Partner] to advance joint goals in a country, implementing the projects. (IO7)*

> *Und dann eben ganz in dem Sektor tätige private Partner [...]. Dann gibt es da quasi auch so Sektor-Organisationen, Dachorganisationen, dazu gehört jetzt z.B. die [globale Plattform der zugrunde liegenden PPP]. Das ist quasi eine Industrie-Assoziation, die sich vornimmt, den Sektor zu stärken. (CO8)*
> (And then private partners being active in this sector [...]. Then there are also kind of sector organizations, umbrella organizations where the [global platform underlying the PPP] belongs to, for instance. That is more or less an industry association that intends to strengthen the sector.)

The involvement of stakeholders and the development of PPPs often follow an evolutionary path. Thus, partnerships increase over time in terms of number of members, range of activities and geographical focus. However, this requires openness and willingness from all partners to accept new ideas and to develop together continuously. In particular, the public side often pushes the opening of a partnership for more and different types of stakeholders who are interested in the policy issue covered by the PPP and who can contribute to achieving its objectives, regardless of the organizations' size or specific business segment.

> *Im Programm sind auch mehr Partner dazugekommen, sehr viel mehr NGOs. Wir waren Gründungspartner und haben uns natürlich über viele Partner gefreut. Jetzt kommt mit Sicherheit von Ihnen die Frage: Warum jetzt nur zwei privatwirtschaftliche [...]? Aber hier war zum einen die [IO Partner] dahingehend uns gegenüber fair, aber [IO Partner] wollte das eben auch für jeden öffnen. (CO4)*
> (The program was also joined by more partners, much more NGOs. We were founding partners and of course we were happy about many new partners. Now certainly comes up your question: Why only two private sector firms [...]? But on the one hand the [IO partner] was fair to us in that sense, but the [IO partner] actually wanted to open it for everybody.)

> *Y esta asociación pues se constituye como una plataforma interinstitucional donde se relacionan actores del sector público, del sector privado, académico, financiero y todos los demás, personas o empresas relacionadas con la [manera de producción de energía]. (DC6)*
> (Well, and this is constituted as an interinstitutional platform where actors from public sector, private sector, academia, finance and all the other people or firms related to the [mechanism of energy production] get in touch with each other.)

> *Es sind große globale Player wie [privater Partner] dabei [...]. Wir haben Firmen wie [privater Partner] dabei, wirklich ganz großer deutscher Mittelstand. Dann aber auch relativ kleine Unternehmen, die dann aber alle gesagt haben: "Unabhängig von unserer Größe und dessen, was wir produzieren, haben wir alle ein Ziel. Und das ist eben nachhaltiges [Primärprodukt]." Und da haben sie sich zusammengeschlossen. (DC2)*
> (There are global players like [private sector firm] on board [...]. We have firms like [private sector firm] on board, really very big German medium-sized companies. But then also relatively small firms which all have said: "Regardless of our size and of that what we are producing, we all have one goal. And that simply is sustainable [primary product]". And then they joined together.)

While the involved stakeholder types are rather clear, drawing conclusions on the typical magnitude of these PPPs in terms of the number of involved stakeholders and people is much more difficult. The number of stakeholders varies from two partners in smaller PPPs to over 20 to 40 in larger ones, and can comprise even hundreds if the different partners are linked to each other under the umbrella of a global platform. This range also reflects the PPPs considered for the sample. However, the figures tend to fluctuate especially in larger PPPs, making it difficult even for present members to clearly have in mind all current partners.

> *Also die letzte Zahl, die ich gestern gesehen hatte, war 39. Es schwankt aber auch ein bisschen und kommt daher, dass von der alten Initiative in die [Rechtsform der neuen Initiative] nicht alle Mitglieder mit rüber getreten sind. Es sind neue dazu gekommen. Wir sind gerade dabei, das tatsächlich nochmal zu erheben, aber es sind tatsächlich um die 40. (DC2)*
> (Well, the most recent figure, which I have seen yesterday, was 39. It fluctuates a bit and results from the fact that not all members converted from the old initiative to the [legal form of the new initiative]. Currently, we are gathering it again but we actually have around 40.)

> *Mittlerweile, wenn ich jetzt bei der Task Force teilnehme, sind es [privater Partner] und [CO4] und die restlichen 20 Leute, wir sind 25, kommen irgendwie von [...] überall her. (CO4)*

(Meanwhile, when I join the Task Force there are [private sector partner] and [CO4] and the remaining 20 people, we are 25, and come from [...] everywhere.)

In summary, Figure 29 gives an overview of the previously described stakeholder types involved in PPPs for development.

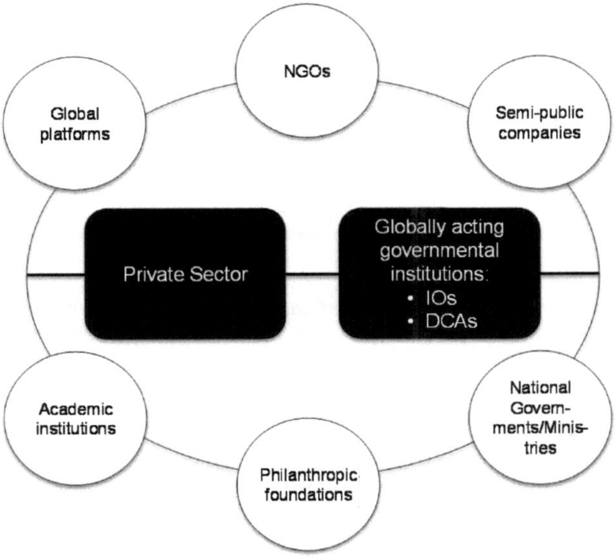

Figure 29: Stakeholder types involved in PPPs for development.

6.1.2 Characteristics of the Actors Involved

This chapter gives an overview of the current job profiles and responsibilities of the interviewees, of their skills and previous experiences that qualify them for PPP work. Moreover, the overall level of individual but also organizational dedication to the PPP work and the presence of local staff at the places of implementation of the respective PPPs will be analyzed.

6.1.2.1 Job Descriptions and Responsibilities

While in Chapter 5.2.1.3 was given an overview of the job positions of the interview partners, this chapter shows specific responsibilities associated with executive and operational capacities (Figure 30). Despite similar or even identical job descriptions, the actual task portfolio can differ significantly or vary over time. Moreover, an overlapping of duties, which are typically rooted at the executive or strategic rather than at the operational level, has been noted.

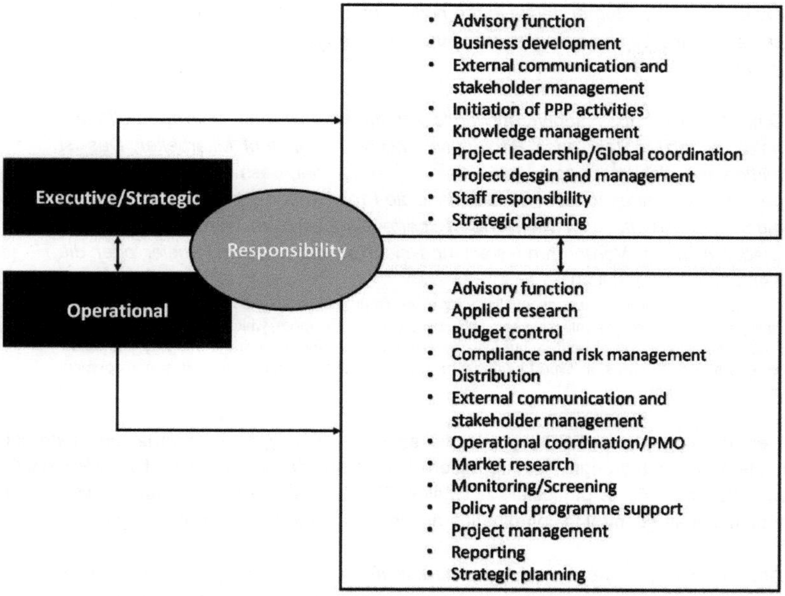

Figure 30: Overview of typical job responsibilities of the interview partners.

The key term is **responsibility** in this context. While the formally defined sphere of responsibility of a certain job position is associated with executive or operational duties, the actual task portfolio, and therefore the indirect responsibilities, might vary a lot. In particular, project manager and coordinator roles are rather unspecific so that the actual job responsibilities and decision-making power heavily rely on factors like internal hierarchies or organizational size. Activities like business development, general project management or strategic planning can be either executive or operational, depending on how and by whom they are performed, and if the persons concerned have staff responsibility or not. These phenomena seem to apply for the private sector, IOs and DCAs alike. For instance, CO1-1, CO14, DC5 all hold responsible positions in the respective hierarchies of their organizations, differing by academic background and years of PPP experiences, but having in common that their roles vary between operational and executive tasks, depending on the project stage and changing priorities. They are in charge of the initiation, extension, planning and implementation of PPPs, but also assume staff responsibility if required.

> *Initiator, Verantwortlicher, und teilweise auch Arbeitender. (CO1-1)*
> (Initiator, responsible person, and partially also operationally working person)

> *And my responsibilities include developing new business models for the company and scaling up the current social business initiatives, also developing social business initiatives. And also managing some partnerships where [CO14] is ally or part of global networks [...]. And more specifically in the part of the developing new social business initiatives, [...] my main activities include market research,*

exploring new customer paints in the bottom-up pyramid segment, where [CO14] can add value by combining its core business with social issue or an environmental issue. (CO14)

Das heißt, ich habe Hauptverantwortlichkeit für ein gewisses Projektportfolio und hatte bis letztes Jahr auch Personalverantwortung für fünf Mitarbeiter. Das ist mittlerweile nicht mehr so, was nichts damit zu tun hat, dass es da irgendwie Ärger gegeben hätte, sondern einfach dass die Projektarbeit oder, ich sage mal, die eigentliche Arbeit, auch wieder als Experte eingesetzt zu werden, mittlerweile wieder mehr im Vordergrund steht und nicht so der Wissenstransfer oder die Personalführung. (DC4)
(That means, I have the main responsibility for a certain project portfolio and also had staff responsibility for five employees until last year. This is not like that any more, which has nothing to do with happening of any kind of trouble, but just the actual project work or, I say it this way, the actual work to be employed as an expert has now more priority than knowledge transfer or management of human resources.)

Moreover, the operational PPP work is influenced by the types of internal and external stakeholders and by the degree of internationalization and decentralization of the PPP activities, as stated by IO7. In particular, in smaller PPP teams, the task portfolio ranges from budget planning and control to coordination and leadership task, as described by DC5:

And currently, as mentioned, our angle is more on the policy and programme support. So, it is both, global level, senior management support, but also supporting our different country offices, re-join units, other headquarter units, on working with the private sector across different thematic topics. So, it covers quite a range of issues. (IO7)

Pues, tengo tareas de dirección, de gerencia, de coordinación, manejo de presupuesto, de diseño, de programas, de proyectos como [Nombre de la PPP]. Y bueno, tengo también un equipo a cargo [...]. (DC5)
(Well, I have tasks in management, leadership, coordination, budget management, project design, programme management of projects like [PPP name]. And well, I also have to take care of a team [...].)

Often, the job responsibilities and specific positions evolve over time because people climb up the career path in their respective organizations, such as CO4 who originates from a strongly operative and technical area. He moves within a field of tensions that he faces as consequence of the multiple expectations diverse stakeholders place on him. Externally, his role embraces elements of an ambassador and stakeholder of his corporation pushing him in an executive position while internally his role is rather operational and is linked to strong accountability towards the upper management:

Also die Position als solche heißt "Director Governmental Affairs". [...]. Bei [Wettbewerber] wird es auch Politik-Abteilung oder Lobby-Abteilung genannt, aber es ist eben die Tätigkeit, dass man mit Externen kommuniziert und jetzt das Unternehmen gegenüber externen Stakeholdern repräsentiert, die nicht Kunden oder Lieferanten sind. Dazu gehören vorwiegend Politiker und Verbände. Der Job beinhaltet dann auch Verbandsarbeit, Verbandsmitarbeit, aber eben auch direkte Politikerkontakte und bei mir im Speziellen die Aufgabe [CO4] in der [Name der

> *PPP], [...], zu vertreten [...]. Und meine Rolle, wie ich vorher sagte, ich repräsentiere [CO4]. Das ist ein bisschen divergent. Einerseits stark im Operativen, da ich aus dem operativen Geschäft komme [...]. Und so habe ich halt auch sehr viel Technik-Background bzw. operativen Background, den ich dort einbringen kann. Aber andererseits repräsentiere ich eben auch [CO4], wenn wir dann bestimmen, wo [Anmerkung: in der PPP] geht die Reise hin, was muss man als nächstes beachten, sodass hier auch strategische Fragen dann von mir beantwortet werden. (CO4)*
>
> (Well, the position as such is called "Director Governmental Affairs". [...]. [Competitors] call it political section or lobbying department but the actual duty comprises the communication with external people and to represent the company towards external stakeholders that are not clients or suppliers. Part of that are primarily politicians and associations. The job also embraces work in associations, but also the maintenance of direct contacts with politicians, and in my specific case it is the task to represent [CO4] in the [PPP name]. And in my role, as I just said before, I am representative of [CO4]. That is a little divergent. On the one side, strongly operational because I am coming from the operational business. Thus, I also have very much technical background or operational background that I can bring in there. But, on the other side, I also represent [CO4]. Hence, when we determine where [remark: in the PPP] the path is leading to, what we have to consider next, then strategic questions will be answered from my side as well.)

Hence, from the 32 interviewees no clear job profile for PPP managers could be derived because the actual duties vary too much, and the proportion of operational versus executive tasks can change over time even for the same job position, and it depends very much on the involved stakeholders. This applies at least to private sector firms, DCAs and IOs alike.

6.1.2.2 *Qualification for PPP Work*

In line with the diversity of the job responsibilities, there is neither a unique way of how people came into their position nor exist clear sets of skills and competences they acquired to qualify for PPP work. In most cases, it is rather a mix of qualifications the interviewees adopted during their respective careers, based on academic studies, previous professional experiences, training on the job and advanced training (Figure 31).

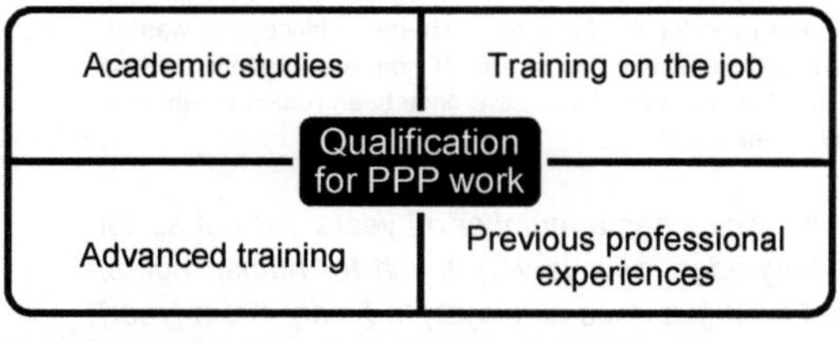

Figure 31: Elements of qualification for PPP work.

While most of them did rather general academic studies like business administration, law, medicine or natural sciences, a few of them like DC4, DC5, and CO13-1 already paved the way for their later professional careers through pertinent postgraduate studies in agricultural and energy economics or public administration because they discovered their special interest in development issues at an early stage:

> *Also ich habe mich schon während dem Studium sehr früh auf das Thema Entwicklungsfinanzierung konzentriert. Es war also kein Zufallsprodukt, dass ich bei der [DC4] in diesem Bereich gelandet bin. (DC4)*
> (Well, I already focused on the matter of development financing at an early stage of my studies. So, it did not happen by coincidence that I ended with [DC4] in this area.)

> *Yo soy economista. Y tengo una especialidad en economía ambiental y ecológica [...]. (DC5)*
> (I am an economist. I have a specialization in environmental and ecological economics [...].)

> *Tengo una carrera Bachelor en economía con un minor en finanzas y aparte hice otra carrera en finanzas y banca. Después hice una maestría en Public Policy. Entonces, mi formación siempre ha sido hacia temas de estrategia y finanzas. (CO13-1)*
> (I have a bachelor in economics with a minor in finance and apart from that I did another career in finance and banking. After that I did a master in public policy. Hence, my education has always been oriented towards strategy and finance topics.)

Others like CO3 and IO6 got to know the perspectives from other stakeholders they are nowadays working with together in PPPs. Both of them deem their previous professional experiences very valuable for their current work because the insights in diverse organizational cultures enable them to better understand and manage multi-stakeholder collaboration. These interorganizational experiences seem to facilitate the daily PPP work and are obviously appreciated by both the private and the public sector as employers. However, the majority of the interview partners never worked for another stakeholder type.

> *Und habe bei allen relevanten Stakeholdern irgendwann mal in irgendeiner Form gearbeitet, also bei der UN, bei der [...] Foundation, bei Unternehmen und sogar beim [zuständigen Ministerium]. Insofern war das schon eine relativ gezielte Ausrichtung auf Multistakeholder-Social-Impact-Arbeit, und ich muss auch gestehen, dass dieser Lebenslauf und auch die Erkenntnisse, die man sammelt, wenn man mal in anderen Organisationskulturen verankert war, sehr wichtig für die Arbeit sind. (CO3)*
> (And I have been working for all relevant stakeholders in some form for some time, so for the UN, for the [...] foundation, for companies, and even for the [ministry in charge]. Hence, this was already a relatively targeted orientation on multi-stakeholder social impact work and I have to confess that this curriculum vitae and also the insights you gain, if you have once been rooted in other organizational cultures, are very important for the work).

> *Well, I was working for a company, which has a [number of] years track of social values [...]. So, always very cutting-edge, always very much for human rights, development [...]. So, I was hired from [previous employer] in [year]. From [year] we had a very structured sustainability strategy. So, that had to do with the core business, so sustainability in the supply chains and also with a part that was related to social impact. And within the social impact side of the story what I developed was partnerships with the UN. Also because of this experience, this was very important when I was recruited by [IO6]. (IO6)*

Others like CO5, DC2 and IO5 had worked before on the same or similar topics like that the PPP is dealing with, but in other not partnership-related departments. Thus, their technical knowledge qualifies them for the PPP work. Additionally, they acquired necessary skills through training on the job or in project control and project management courses. CO3 and CO5 emphasize that in their PPPs structured training programmes are set up in order to provide all operational staff with the relevant skills and competences needed for the PPP implementation. The trainings are customized to the specific local conditions that staff members are facing in the target countries. In summary, the career paths of the 32 interviewees are very individual so that no typical qualification profile for PPP work can be drawn from their CVs.

6.1.2.3 Dedication to PPP Work

Dedication can be manifold in this context and does not only refer to the labor time people afford for their actual work, but it can also mean passion or intrinsic motivation. For the vast majority of the analyzed PPPs applies that partnership work is only one part of the people's task portfolio, and only very few people are employed full-time for that. If so, they undertake site visits when necessary, but still work most time from afar at headquarters level. One reason is that the workload does not incur steadily but in phases, for instance for training sessions and meetings abroad, as stated by CO10-1:

> *Genau, es ist auch nicht kontinuierlich, dass man sagt: Ich habe jetzt jeden Tag oder jede Woche was zu tun. Mal ist es drei Wochen ruhig, weil es einfach auch dauert, bis man Prozess- oder Projektschritte implementiert. Dann kommt es mal wieder geballt, dass man sich einen Tag nur damit beschäftigt. Das ist wirklich phasenabhängig. (CO10-1)*
>
> (Exactly, it is not continuously such that one could say: I have something to do every day or every week. Sometimes, it remains silent for three weeks because it simply takes time until process or project steps are implemented. Then, it comes concentrated so that you deal one single day only with that. That is really in phases.)

Another aspect of dedication to PPP work is passion or intrinsic motivation. CO7 reports that employees often approach her after natural disasters and present ideas of how the company could contribute to providing relief to the affected countries and people. Although any kind of help is not necessarily equal to a PPP such an attitude among employees towards social responsibility forms a good basis for PPP work in general. At the individual level, CO8 describes the overlap of personal interests in development issues and private sector interests as the core dimensions of his work. His dedication results from the view that huge amounts of investments and resources as well as specific knowhow are required to tackle these issues and that private sector engagement is needed for that. In his role, he envisages to figure out how to align the resolution of development issues with private sector interests and resources. The dedication of both CO8 and CO13-2 results from the fact that their respective companies enabled them to pursue their own ideas or to develop visions for PPP work:

> *Y cuándo me invitaron aquí a la [CO13], yo estaba un poco renuente por lo que significaba el cambio. Sin embargo conozco al director que me invitó [...]. Y él fue que me dijo que prácticamente podemos hacer la [CO13] otra cosa, hacer algo diferente y a mí me llamaba mucho la atención el tema de desarrollo social. Esto era algo que me llamaba la atención pero no me gusta como se hace. En-*

tonces, él me hizo una oportunidad interesante. Entonces, esto es como llego aquí a [CO13]. (CO13-2)

(When they invited me to come here to the [CO13] I was a little bit reluctant to what the change would mean. Still, I know the director who invited me [...]. And it was him who basically told me that we can make [CO13] something different and the matter of social development called my attention a lot. That was something that called my attention, but I do not like how they do it. Hence, he made an interesting offer to me. So, that is how I came here.)

At the corporate level, CO14 strategically pursues the enhancement of existing PPPs and the creation of new PPPs by exploring matters of joint interest between them and the national government in particular. Hence, PPP engagement can be either individually or organizationally driven, but the level of intrinsic motivation and personal interest people have for this kind of interorganizational work makes the difference.

On the side of the scale up of the current social initiatives, I am looking for new partners or new customers by exploring the public policy and trying to develop a new partnership with the government, because for the majority or for the initiative, I am very focussed on public concerns or on basic services or basic rights. So, the government is very engaged with these topics. (CO-14)

6.1.3 Departments Involved and Internal Support

The type and number of departments and other internal actors involved in the implementation of a PPP, besides the department or unit in charge, varies by the level of managerial and operational power the latter is equipped with and by stakeholder type. While the interviewed companies anchored their PPP activities either in the CSR department or in an independent unit at headquarter level, DCAs and IOs seem to be more flexible in delegating the main responsibility to their staff at local level. However, the final authority also remains with the head office.

Das heißt, wir sind ein Unternehmensbereich und eine Geschäftseinheit und keine karitative oder auch kein Öffentlichkeitsarbeitsteil des Unternehmens. (CO3)

(This means that we are a corporate division and a business unit, rather than a beneficient or public relations section of the company.)

That one is usually conducted by the initiating unit. So, if the partnership is initiated by the country office, then the country office connects with the regional office and somebody with the global one [...]. Then there is an office that independently reviews what you put together and clears the due diligence. (IO5)

Given the business orientation of the private sector they involve and seek support from core business-related departments and units like business development, production, R&D and sales. Moreover, they place emphasis on proper communication towards external stakeholders like the general public but also towards internal stakeholders throughout the organizational structure, such as local sales or technical staff who finally assume an important part of the operational PPP implementation on-site. Often public and private partners develop small-scale products being customized to local conditions, such as health-care products or specific technology so that technical experts, R&D and production planners need to be closely consulted during the PPP implementation. In this context, several private sector interviewees highlighted the role played by the compliance department, which is closely linked to the legal department and is in charge of monitoring that the PPP implementation and production activities are compliant with e.g. environmental, health or labor standards. All public and private actors attach very much importance to an appropriate contract design and an acceptable level of legal certainty so that no PPP can be commenced without prior approval from the legal office. Moreover, the CSR departments in private sector firms are at least continuously informed about ongoing PPP activities, insofar they are not in charge themselves, because of the thematic proximity of CSR work and PPPs, which can be congruent.

DCAs and IOs maintain some central units at HQ level, which support local level activities while the operational lead remains on-site. For instance, DC2 maintains a kind of inhouse consulting team that provides the project team with methodical and technical questions. Both DC2 and IO6 run special sections that deal with stakeholder management but are not involved in operational PPP work:

> *Dann habe ich eine Einheit, die für die direkte Kooperation und Zusammenarbeit mit unterschiedlichen Auftraggebern verantwortlich ist. Also in meinem Fall dann das [zuständige Ministerium], das eigentlich die ganze Fachexpertise sozusagen hat. Worauf legt denn dieser spezielle, spezifische Auftraggeber einen spezifischen Blick? (DC2)*
> (Then I have a unit which is responsible for the direct cooperation and collaboration with different clients. In my case that is the [ministry in charge], which actually has the whole technical expertise. What does this specific client place emphasis on?)

> *In order to have supporters here in [IO6]. We're kind of proposing programmes, but the programmes are given to us by the technical division or by the local offices. (IO6)*

> *[…] quite often, we have our human rights specialists or might have our environment specialists or extractive sector specialists or communication specialists […]. So, usually we do have quite a bit of project management support from regional and headquarters level where they try to help the different offices to set meaningful target indicators. (IO7)*

Like in case of IO5, the due diligence at the beginning of a partnership and the review at the end are often centralized by IOs in order to ensure compliance and impartiality in the assessment. Table 40 summarizes the involved departments including their responsibilities and tasks named by the interview partners, without any claim on completeness.

Department	Responsibility/task	References
Business development	• Business case development • Commercialization of PPP work	CO4, CO7
Communication	• External communication • Internal communication	CO1, CO3, CO5, CO11, IO6, IO7
Compliance	• External compliance requirements • Internal compliance requirements	CO1, CO4, CO9
CSR	• Coordination of CSR activities	CO3, CO11

Department	Responsibility/task	References
Finance	• Budgeting	CO5, CO9, DC2
Government/policy	• Policy analysis	CO4, IO6
Human resources	• Staff selection and approval	DC2
Inhouse consulting	• Methodical expertise • Technical expertise	DC2, DC3
Legal/contract	• Contract design • Contract enforcement	CO1, CO5, CO7, CO9, DC3, IO3
Procurement	• Harmonization of procurement processes	CO4
Production/technical division	• Customization • Expert advice • Feasibility check • Production planning	CO1, CO4, CO5, CO7, CO9, IO6, IO7
Research and development	• Applied science and product development	CO4, CO5, CO8
Review and evaluation	• Due diligence • Independent review	IO5
Sales/external structure	• Inclusion of sales staff and other local staff in PPP implementation	CO3, DC3
Stakeholder management unit	• Customer relationship management	DC2, IO6

Table 40: Departments involved and their responsibilities and tasks.

The level of internal support is not necessarily indicated by the number of departments or people involved but rather means the moral support that implementers receive internally from their management and decision-makers. Low internal visibility and wrong perceptions of what the PPP work actually is about form obstacles to internal support, in particular in private sector firms.

> *[...] also in der [CO9] sind wir immer noch ein, sagen wir mal, "exotisches Team". Also für uns wäre es natürlich gut, wenn dieses ganze Thema insgesamt mehr Visibilität hätte, dann würden wir davon auch vielleicht profitieren eine höhere Aufmerksamkeit zu haben [...]. Vielleicht ist das Thema generell noch einfach so ein bisschen in den Kinderschuhen, diese Branche ist noch nicht etabliert wie andere Bereiche innerhalb des [Produktbereichs]. Von daher ist einfach noch sehr viel im Fluss. (CO9-1)*
>
> ([...] well within (CO9) we are still an, let us say, "exotic team". So, for us it would be good if this topic had more visibility because then we might benefit from having increased awareness [...]. Maybe it is just that this topic is generally still in its infancy, this business area is not yet established like other fields within the [product area]. Thus, there is very much still flowing.)

> *Aber wir hatten vielmehr manchmal das Problem, intern zu verdeutlichen, dass das kein CSR-Projekt ist, sondern dass wir da ein Geschäftsmodell sehen, was sich jetzt nach und nach auch bewahrheitet. (CO8)*
>
> (Sometimes we rather had the problem to make internally clear that this is not a CSR project, but that we see a business model behind it, a fact that comes true progressively.)

In summary, the level of internal support can be of either operational or managerial nature, and for IOs and DCAs this means operational support from central departments or units and less approval from the top management because PPP engagement is part of the mandate of many of these organizations. By contrast, internal support in private sector firms seems to rely quite much upon the top management's awareness and understanding of PPPs including the business opportunities they can imply. As CO10-1 stated, the acquisition of management support is a tedious step that is not done from one day to another but results from a process of change of mindset.

6.1.4 Decentralization and Local Staff Presence

The degree of decentralization and internationalization of PPP work, as well as the extent and kind of local staff used in the target countries of PPP implementation, differ between private sector, DCAs and IOs and depend very much on their respective existing global presence (Figure 32).

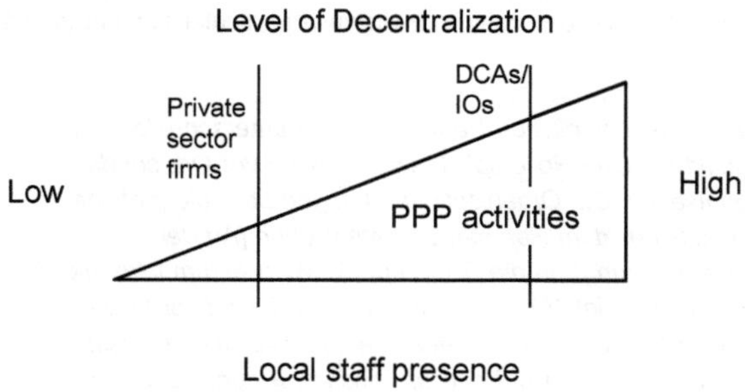

Figure 32: Level of decentralization and local staff presence.

By mandate, IOs and DCAs are active globally and in this sense they are able to run PPPs at local, regional and global level because many processes are decentralized and preference is given to country level ownership if no overarching interests of the organization or concerns speak against it. The reason is that PPPs are very individual and often designed in a way to tackle very specific local policy issues so that local actors know best how to address them.

> *So, the partnerships will vary. There are those that are at global level. There are those that are at regional level, and there are those that are at country level [...]. So, it really varies from sector to country, from country to country, depending on the project. (IO5)*

> *[...] the partnerships that are ongoing here are not kind of managed and finalized only by the headquarters. But there are very interesting ones I am finding out that are finalized by the local offices and regional offices. Now, [IO6] does not have a structure like [UN organization] or other agencies that have their local committees. The local committees of [UN organization] will do fundraising but they will*

also start partnerships with local private sector. Now, [IO6] doesn't have this but [IO6] has its regional and local offices that also finalize and sign partnerships. So, that is an interesting dimension because sometimes big brands are kind of hooked first at the local level and then at the international level. (IO6)

[...] we do have a very decentralized process [...]. If it's a purely country level project and with national or even international partners who have an office in the country, they are not anyhow high risk, sort of good reputation, obvious partnering benefits and so on. Usually, the country level takes the decision on those on its own. They sometimes might consult with us or the regional bureau but those kinds of simple policy dialogue, these kinds of a little bit more informal partnerships happen all the time without any further engagement of other units, just the country office. (IO7)

Private sector firms tend to build their PPP engagement on existing presence abroad, such as production sites or sales and distribution structures. In general, they do more of their PPP work remotely than IOs or DCAs are used to do. So, all PPP activities usually emanate from the HQ, but can expand and cascade down locally in dependence of the local conditions and the level of complexity. Moreover, it would be costly to build up a particular local organizational structure only for the PPP.

Wir müssen hier zwischen unterschiedlichen Partnerschaften unterscheiden. Bei dem Thema, wo das Produkt mit eine Rolle spielt, sind wir nicht vor Ort, sondern wir verkaufen an die Organisation. Die Organisationen bringen über die [nationalen Ministerien] im Land das Produkt im Rahmen der öffentlichen [Art der Versorgung] über ihre [Behördeneinrichtung] an die [Zielgruppe], wenn es um [Produkte] geht. Da sind wir nicht mit im Spiel. Wo wir mit im Spiel sind, sind solche Projekte, die unter dem Stichwort "Education Awareness" laufen. Die sind ja wesentlich anspruchsvoller im Managing. Auch bei den [politischen Fragen] geben wir das sozusagen in die Hände der [IO Partner]. Mit dem [IO Partner] sprechen wir darüber: Welche Mengen braucht ihr? Wann braucht ihr die Mengen? Wo gibt es sozusagen aus eurer Sicht noch Verbesserungsmöglichkeiten, wo wir mit unterstützen können? Aber vor Ort sind wir nicht. (CO1-1)

(We have to distinguish between different partnerships. For issues where the product plays a role we are not on-site but we sell it to the organization. When it is about [products], the organizations provide the product to the [target group] via the [national ministries] and the [public authority] in the country as part of the public [type of service]. There, we are not part of the game. But we are part of the game in those projects that are run under the heading of "Education Awareness". Those are much more challenging to manage. Also in case of [policy issue] we hand this over to the [IO partner]. With the [IO partner] we speak about: Which quantity do you need? When do you need the quantity? Where do you see possible improvements where we can support you? But we are not on-site.)

And especially in other countries, where we can transfer what we are doing and what is working here in Mexico and start working in other countries, where we have operations. (CO14)

Regarding the local staff presence, one differentiates between short-term/long-term temporary international staff and permanent local staff. Private sector firms like CO3 or CO9 maintain distribution or manufacturing and service centers throughout the world. Both of them state that they do not have German or other international staff permanently deployed to the African countries where they implement their respective PPP projects, but that permanent local staff is charged to interact with public and other stakeholders on-site as part of their task portfolio. In their main capacity they often work as relationship managers, sales agents or technical experts. Insofar there is not yet physical presence in certain countries, the companies tend to involve their local business-related staff in neighbouring countries or in regional centers in the operational PPP work rather than investing in new local presence, in particular when it is about politically difficult places. Another option observed is keeping international staff permanently on-site but on a rotating basis, as done by CO8. To strengthen this long-lasting presence they also hire working students from volunteer programs, which are designed to bring young and qualified people together with firms working in the context of international development cooperation. Still, most of the interview private sector firms send their PPP staff at least for a few days or weeks to the countries of implementation in order to monitor the progress and to have face-to-face conversations and consultations with local stakeholders, which are crucial to maintain and nurture relationships with them.

> *[...] wir haben einige feste Mitarbeiter. Dann greifen wir aber auch auf die Kollegen in den Ländern und in den Regionen zu, die für [Unternehmensbereich] arbeiten [...]. Also wir haben ja in den Ländern auch Mitarbeiter, die jetzt nicht für dieses Projekt eingestellt worden sind, aber das sind unsere [CO3 Mitarbeiter]. Die verkaufen am Montagmorgen [Produkt] und dann gehen sie nachmittags ins Ministry of [PPP Fokus] und nehmen am [Name der PPP]-Meeting teil. (CO3)*
> ([...] we have a few permanent employees. But then we also fall back upon colleagues in the countries and in the regions who work for the [business unit] [...]. But we also have employees in the countries who have not been hired for this project but they are [CO3 employees] and Monday morning they sell [product] and in the afternoon they go to the Ministry of [PPP focus] and participate at the [PPP name] meeting.)

> *Also wir haben das alle Vollzeit begleitet, aber nicht immer vor Ort. Aber es waren bei uns immer Leute vor Ort. (CO8)*
> (Well, we all have accompanied this full-time but not always on-site. Still, there have always been people from us on-site.)

By political missions and mandates DCAs and IOs maintain comprehensive local staff presence, in particular in developing countries, and often have established long-standing networks with local stakeholders where private sector firms have hitherto no access to, but which they open for them to facilitate PPPs. In this context, they also collaborate with other international actors like chambers for foreign trade or national embassies. Together with their network partners, DCAs and IOs employ private sector specialists in different countries to support the establishing of PPPs and accompany the foreign firms during the PPP implementation.

> *Es gibt auch von der [DC3] verschiedene Experten, sage ich mal, oder Kollegen, die in den verschiedenen AHKen sitzen, in den Auslandshandelskammern in den Ländern, und die dort zu dem Thema "Zusammenarbeit mit der Wirtschaft" beraten, so mit dem öffentlichen Bereich. Es gibt außerhalb noch verschiedene Units, also auch in unseren Partnerländern, also wir haben so eine Art Business Development Unit auch in [Zielland 1] oder auch in [Zielland 2], wo auch Kollegen speziell als Ansprechpartner oder so eine Art Erst-Ansprechstelle eingesetzt werden, um Anfragen aus der Wirtschaft [Anmerkung: zu bearbeiten]. (DC3)*

(There are also different experts or colleagues from [DC3] who are located in the different AHKs, in the chambers for foreign trade, and who provide consultancy on the matter of "Cooperation in the Economy", so with the public sector. Apart from that there are still different units, also in our partner countries, so that we have a kind of business development unit in [target country 1] or also in [target country 2], where colleagues are employed as special contact persons or a kind of first point of contact for [remark: handling] enquiries from the private sector.)

Some offices also have better capacity at the country level. They have private sector specialists already in place, who are used to working with the private sector. (IO7)

To summarize, it is more the public sector that maintains a decentralized organizational structure and permanent local staff presence in countries of PPP implementation while the private sector tends to use either its existing sales and distribution structure or to dispatch employees for a short period of time.

6.1.5 Characteristics of the PPPs

This chapter will analyze the characteristics of the PPPs considered for this study and cluster them by commonalities and differences in terms of their purpose, design and legal framework. A view on the duration, durability and financial volume will round off the analysis. It should be added that the present chapter does not claim to portray all kinds of existing PPPs including their respective characteristics, but reports only on those which have been identified from the empirical sample.

6.1.5.1 Policy Issues

The different PPPs analyzed in this study have been created to address diverse policy issues related to the broad fields of infrastructure and sustainable development. The eight main longitudinal thematic areas comprise amongst others PPPs in the areas of **disaster management** including disaster risk reduction and prevention, **energy consumption and production**, **microfinance** and **sustainable investment**, **food supply**, **health, decent housing** conditions and **clean water supply**. In complement to this, each PPP has a cross-sectional purpose (Figure 33).

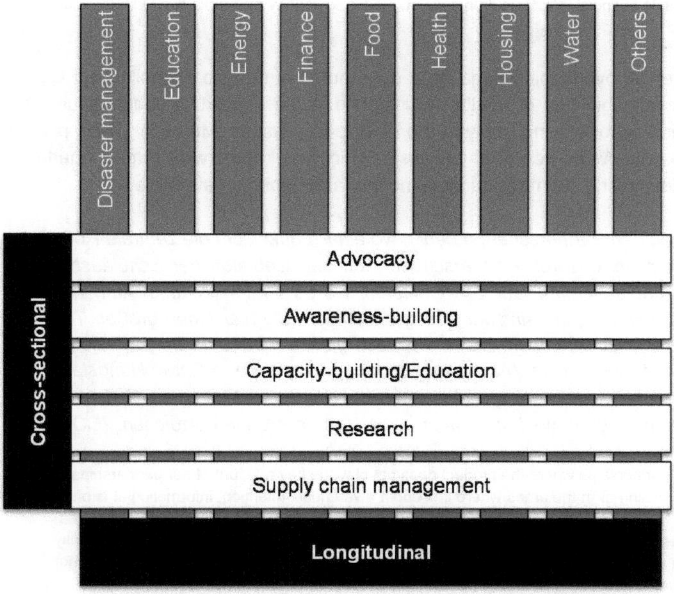

Figure 33: Addressed policy issues and purposes of PPPs for development.

PPP partners advocate for joint interests or values, they create awareness of policy issues and invest in capacity-building and education for enabling the beneficiaries of the PPP to help themselves and to contribute to solving policy issues, such as malnourishment or environmental pollution. In several PPPs the private sector partner undertakes applied research on issues of food supply or health care using the knowhow from its actual business activities. Moreover, it supports public actors in making supply chain processes of firms in developing and emerging economies more efficient and sustainable. IOs promote such engagement by offering frameworks and proven concepts for structured public-private cooperation.

> *The mechanism uses investments in public goods and a supportive policy framework to incentivize and scale up responsible private investments in food and agriculture value chains, benefitting smallholder farmers by giving them access to secure markets, technology and services, and other rural people by creating off-farm jobs along value chains and across the larger rural economy. (IO4)*

> *Wir haben uns von Anfang an nicht auf […] Finanzmanagement […], sondern wir haben uns eher auf Prozesse fokussiert. Wir haben gesagt: "Wenn wir irgendwie die wirtschaftlichen Prozesse unterstützen und dabei erfassen, dann haben wir eine höhere Wahrscheinlichkeit, vermutlich zuverlässige Finanzkennzahlen zu haben, als wenn wir irgendjemandem da ein Accountingsystem hinstellen, was nicht verwendet wird. (CO8)*
> (From the beginning we did not focus on finance management […] but we focused rather on processes. We said: "If we somehow support and capture the economic processes, we are likely to

have more reliable financial indicators than if we set up for somebody an accounting system which will not be used.)

Education is somehow overlapping because it does not only refer to schooling but also to education and capacity-building of adults, for instance in the context of health issues, because education is key for solving many of the other policy issues. Moreover, firms provide their products or knowhow for free or at low costs, which would otherwise remain unattainable for people in developing countries because neither affordable nor available.

Wenn man jetzt an Partnerschaften denkt, wo ein Produkt nicht die zentrale Rolle spielt, sondern bei unseren Partnerschaften auf den Gebieten der Schulausbildung oder Schulerziehung, auf den Gebieten, wo es um Awareness, Aufmerksamkeit, Information geht, sind wir häufig diejenigen, die hier einen großen Teil der Finanzierung übernehmen, weil wir einfach glauben, dass derartige Projekte notwendig sind. Denn ohne Wissen und Bildung können Sie in Entwicklungsländern Dinge nicht wirklich erfolgreich umsetzen. Wenn die Menschen dort nicht wissen, worum es geht, wird man auch keine Verbesserungen erreichen. (CO1-1)

(If you think of partnerships where the product does not play the key role, but of our partnerships in the fields of schooling or in the areas where it is about awareness, attention, information, it is often us who bear a large portion of the financing, because we simply believe that such projects are necessary. The reason is that without knowledge and education you cannot implement things really successfully in developing countries. If the people there do not know what it is about, you will not achieve improvements.)

Compared to the private sector that usually focuses on one specific thematic area related to its core competences, IOs and DCAs tend to tackle all issues, both longitudinal and cross-sectional, that are covered by their mandate. For instance, IO5 and IO7 cover issues of accountability and governance, which are cross-sectional issues referring to specific thematic areas:

There are companies that can align for example to social issues, to issues of governance, to issues of accountability and gender issues. So, it depends on the thematic focus. [IO5], fortunately or unfortunately, is very broad because our role is more coordination. We are not focusing on one thematic issue. So, we are working on quite broad issues. So, the social, the economic and the people part is all inclusive and of course, we have the resilience. We are not humanitarian per se but we are actually engaged in building back after the crisis, not the immediate response but the resilience thereafter, which is really integrated in development [...]. (IO5)

[...] our biggest portfolio is around governance and environment-related initiatives. (IO7)

[IO8]-programmes focus mostly on our four areas. One is education, the others are migration and media and youth. (IO8)

In summary, different policy issues can be tackled for manifold purposes by a broad range of possible public-private actor constellations. It seems that both public and private actors are quite open-minded so that they cover many different issues by their work and are willing to go even beyond their core business or core activities if a partnership is promising.

6.1.5.2 PPP Types

This chapter analyzes the different types of PPPs for development for the present interview sample, based on the typology of PPPs in Chapter 2.1.4.1. In line with typologization approaches by Bovaird (2004), Brinkerhoff and Brinkerhoff (2011), and Kamminga and VdM (2006), seven determinants have been identified that characterize PPPs and therefore contribute to typing them: **legal framework**, **policy issue and purpose**, **governance level**, **resource contributions**, **financing mechanism**, **level of practical orientation**, and **mandate**. These determinants do not apply likewise to all PPPs, but do so to varying extents. In the following, the diverse PPP types allocated in Figure 34 will be discussed in the light of these determinants. In addition, Table 41 gives an overview of the typical governance levels per PPP type.

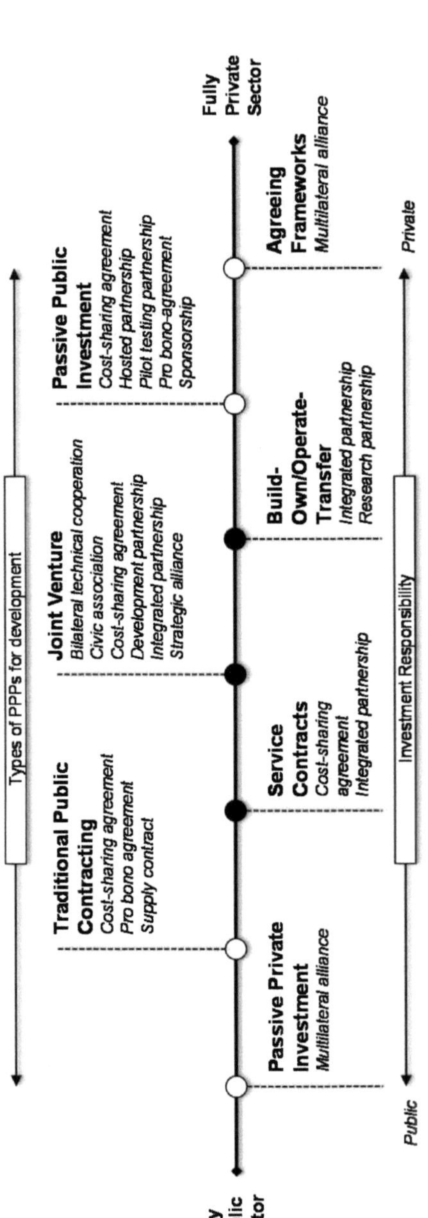

Figure 34: Types of PPPs for development.

- **Bilateral technical cooperation**: This type of PPP is usually applied by DCAs, which implement in line with their government's interest partnership projects with local stakeholders in a target country. Such partnerships are governed in a hybrid manner where the financial burdens are shared. Compared to development partnerships, the DCAs enjoy a higher degree of freedom in bilateral technical cooperations.

  [DC5] es parte de los trabajos de cooperación técnica bilateral entre los países. Como no recibimos dinero extra para esta actividad, no tenemos que pedirle permiso al [responsable ministerio nacional]). (DC5)

  ([DC5] is part of the bilateral development cooperation work between the two countries. As we do not receive additional money for this activity, we do not have to ask the [national ministry in charge] for permission)

- **Civic association**: DC6 characterized her partnership as a non-profit association, legally framed in a kind of separate legal entity where public and private actors are matching complementary skills and resources to address the policy issue of joint interest. Thus, civic associations are usually governed in a hybrid and therefore JV-like manner.
- **Cost-sharing agreement**: In this kind of PPP, IOs seek to share costs for development projects at local, regional and global level but usually keep the lead. The investment responsibility can rest primarily with either the public or private sector, but it can also be equally shared. The implementation of certain project parts is delegated or outsourced to the private sector while the latter rarely assumes an equal role in the partnership. Cost-sharing agreements are typically subordinated to a kind of umbrella agreement.

  [...] umbrella agreement, then at a country level, at a regional level they want to do a specific project. Then they do a cost-sharing agreement. (IO5)

- **Development partnership**: This term was mentioned by several interview partners, but it is a generic rather than a specific one for those PPPs that are governed in a more hybrid manner.
- **Integrated partnership**: According to DC1, these are partnerships in which private sector partners assume specific tasks or cooperate for specific tasks whenever suitable. Depending on the extent of collaboration the lead remains with the DCA, or the governance is shared with the private sector in a hybrid manner.
- **Multilateral alliance**: These are usually large-scale partnerships at global level, composed of two-digit or even three-digit numbers of members. When it is about standardization or norm-setting, the governance level usually is hierarchic and the IO has a strong leadership role due to the mandate given by the member states. By contrast, IOs provide global discussion platforms for implementing PPPs and support the private sector in the initiation of different kinds of operational projects at local level. In this case, the private sector assumes the major investment responsibility.

  So, the [UN organization] is doing this effort to invite private companies, especially the national companies doing this in social innovation and to combine their strengths in the market with social and environmental issues. So, they are able to reach new markets and create new affordable solutions for low income segments worldwide. (CO14)

  We have the [PPP name]. [...] business is invited to belong to this platform, and through this platform they are encouraged to have an inclusive approach in the way they are doing business. So, it's called "inclusive business approach". That means that when they do business they are thinking of the end-users, they are thinking of the whole chain, of those who buy their products, those who consume, those who produce, those who market, those who are their employees. So, they are thinking of everybody of the value chain in their business, and thinking of their needs, of their benefits, [...]. (IO5)

- **Pilot (testing) partnership**: This kind of partnership is usually implemented at local level and addresses a certain policy issue only partially but paves the way for a larger roll-out at a later stage. Foreign private sector firms assume the major investment responsibility and inherent business risks and enable local stakeholders to get involved without major efforts. That is why the private sector typically takes the lead in these partnerships.

Eine andere Form der Partnerschaft, die wir auch angeboten haben, das war quasi so etwas "light". Das haben wir dann ein "Tester-Agreement" genannt. Da waren die Aufwände von Seiten des Partners nicht so groß, sondern die Auflage war: "Ihr dürft [das Produkt] von uns quasi kostenfrei, mit bestimmten Auflagen nutzen. Und ihr verpflichtet euch [das Produkt] tatsächlich zu nutzen und uns über die Ergebnisse der Nutzung zu berichten." (CO8)

(Another form of partnership that we also offered was a kind of "light". We called that a "tester agreement". Thus, the efforts from the partner's side were not that big, but the condition was: "You are allowed to actually use [the product] for free under certain conditions. And you commit to really use [the product] and to report to us about the results from the use.)

- **Pro bono agreement**: This is a mechanism primarily used by IOs to acquire cash and in-kind resources as well as knowhow. Private sector firms are given the opportunity to contribute to the IO's development work by providing technology, their products or knowhow in terms of human resources to the IO for free. Usually, the governance level remains hierarchic and leadership rests with the IO if the pro bono contribution is more a kind of donation. However, it becomes market-oriented the more the private sector partner is involved in the operational implementation.
- **Research partnership**: Applied research projects aim to develop concrete solutions for very specific issues in areas such as energy, health or nutrition. Both CO1 and CO5 emphasize that the public and private sectors usually jointly finance these partnerships, often fed from funding programmes by national governments or supra-national institutions like the European Union. Moreover, the companies often have to commit themselves to transfer the research results partially to the public, or even fully if they do not aim to capitalize on their research findings.
- **Sponsorship**: Similar to pro bono agreements, sponsorships allow the private sector to make voluntary contributions to specific development activities of IOs, which are usually related to the core business of the respective company. The difference is that they are typically confined to cash or in-kind contributions.
- **Strategic alliance**: Such an alliance can be created if two or more partners, at least one public and one private one, have very complementary resources and joint interests which can be strategically achieved through a partnership at the best. Thus, a JV-like strategic alliance with a hybrid governance structure is often formed, and the investment responsibility is shared. Strategic alliances are long-term and large-scale oriented and often result from previous temporary cooperations.

Eine strategische Allianz ist es dann, wenn es mindestens in zwei Ländern mit mindestens zwei privaten Partnern ist. (DC1)

(It is a strategic alliance if it is in at least two countries with a minimum of two private partners.)

- **Supply contract:** Private sector firms assume a supplier role if the public sector needs specific input, usually in terms of physical products, and pays for that, but the companies are not involved in the operational implementation. Thus, this kind of PPP corresponds to the traditional public contracting, and the governance structure is hierarchic.

PPP type	Governance level
Bilateral technical cooperation	Hybrid
Civic association	Hybrid
Cost-sharing agreement	Hierarchic, hybrid
Development partnership	Hybrid
Integrated partnership	Hierarchic, hybrid, market
Multilateral alliance	Hierarchic, market
Pilot-testing partnership	Market
Pro bono agreement	Hierarchic, market
Research partnership	Market
Sponsorship	Market
Strategic alliance	Hybrid
Supply contract	Hierarchic

Table 41: Governance level per PPP type.

Apart from the formal typification of PPPs being accompanied by certain contractual elements, CO5 points to the level of practical orientation as one determining factor of the nature of PPPs:

> *Und ansonsten gibt es halt wirklich von den Arten der Partnerschaften mehr praxisorientierte und weniger praxisorientierte Partner. Also so eine [UN-Organisation], [...] ist nicht unbedingt auf Implementierung spezialisiert. Das ist eher politisch motiviert, oft, und so ein bisschen Framework-orientiert, während die [DCA] schon sehr Hands-on [...] ist. (CO5)*
>
> (And besides there are really more practically oriented and less practically oriented partners among the types of partnerships. Well, such an [UN organization] [...] is not necessarily specialized for implementation. That is often politically motivated and as such a kind of framework-oriented while the [DCA] is [...] actually very hands-on.)

However, this statement should be seen in a broader context. IOs in general, and UN organizations in particular, are endowed with diverse mandates that determine whether their focus of work is placed more on defining and setting international norms or on operational development work. Those mandates result from negotiations between the member states of the respective IOs and impact directly or indirectly on the PPP activities of the IO. While the implementing IOs work very much operationally and interdisciplinarily at local level, the norm-setting ones are often specialized agencies which act rather at global level in the determination of worldwide norms and standards, for instance in the fields of aviation, communication, health, labor or public finance. Compared to that, DCAs are usually subject to the interests of their national governments or at least embedded in one main national context only. Thus, the number of stakeholders from the public side is lower than for IOs and the baseline situation therefore less complex for public-private cooperation. The legal framework and contractual design represents not only a few PPP types, like for cost-sharing agreements or supply contracts, but is an important determinant for characterizing the other PPP types as well.

6.1.5.3 Legal Arrangements and Relationships

This chapter gives an overview of how different PPP partners are legally related to each other and of the kind of legal frameworks and contracts used to form a basis for PPP activities. Moreover, it will describe characteristics of the different legal arrangements, whether they are tight or loose, and how the interview partners interpret them. Farther-reaching contractual relationships, which the interviewed PPP stakeholders maintain from their side, for instance with subcontractors, will not be described and discussed because of the given research focus (Chapter 1.2).

Three major forms of legal relationships between DCAs, IOs and the private sector have been identified (Figure 35). The first form is a **direct relationship** where a contractual arrangement is concluded between one or more private sector partners and one public partner. In large partnerships, such as multilateral alliances, more than one public partner is often involved. Examples include PPP initiatives and platforms established by several UN organizations or by DCAs that jointly collaborate on their government's behalf. Still, there is usually one lead institution from the public sector's side. The second form is an **indirect relationship through a third-party stakeholder**. Often this applies to PPPs where DCAs implement joint projects with the private sector on their national government's behalf and receive funding for that from the responsible ministry. The nexus between DCA and the ministry corresponds to a customer-contractor relationship. While a direct legal relationship still exists between private sector and DCA in this case, the national government's involvement has legal implications and therefore also connects private sector and DCA indirectly with each other.

> *Das [Name der PPP] ist erstmal ein Auftrag. Als [DC2] haben wir einen Auftrag aus dem [auftraggebenden Ministerium], der konditioniert und daran gebunden ist, dass die Privatwirtschaft oder jetzt dieser [Art der PPP] ebenfalls einen signifikanten, finanziellen Beitrag leistet. (DC2)*
> (The [PPP name] is first of all a contract. As [DC2] we have an order from the [client ministry], which is conditioned and bound by that the private sector or now this [PPP type] also makes a significant financial contribution.)

In another case, the bureaucratic obstacles to conclude a binding contract between the private sector firm and a development bank prompted the two main stakeholders to involve a NGO as third-party stakeholder and to endow it with a strong legal capacity. Still, they do not feel compromised in their actual partnership work.

> *Tiene dos contratos, uno con la [CO13] y otro con el Banco. ¿Cómo y porqué llegamos a esto? Una [nota: razón] es que es muy difícil llegar a subir a un ente como el Banco, que forma parte de otra organización. Entonces, el tema administrativo era tan complejo que se decidió quedar en un acuerdo de buena voluntad, en un acuerdo no vinculante. Sin embargo los recursos si están legalmente*

vinculados a través de la agencia ejecutora que es [nombre del NGO]. Entonces, [CO13] tiene un contrato con [nombre del NGO], [nombre del banco de desarrollo] tiene un contrato con [nombre del NGO] y lo que hacemos es hacer una coordinación. Es decir que estemos viendo que tenemos cada uno [nota: de los socios] en los contratos y que sea una planeación conjunta. Y aunque tengamos contratos separados, por lo menos se vea como uno solo. (CO13-2)

(It has two contracts, one with the [CO13] and another one with the Bank. How and why did we get there? One [remark: reason] is that it is very difficult to approach an entity like the Bank, which is part of another organization. Hence, the administrative matter was so complex that it was decided to remain with a voluntary agreement, a non-binding agreement. Still, the resources are legally related through the executive agency, which is [NGO name]. So, [CO13] has a contract with [NGO name], [name of the development bank] has a contract with [NGO name], and what we do is making a coordination. This means that we see each of [remark: the members] in the contracts and that the planning is done jointly. And although we have separate contracts, we see it at least like a single one.)

The third form is an **indirect relationship through a separate legal entity**, which has been applied for instance by CO9, DC6 and IO3. Although no clear pattern has been drawn from these three cases, in which situations a separate legal entity is created, it seems that financial and governance aspects play an important role for actors from both public and private sector. CO9-1, DC6 and IO3 made clear that the governance structure of their PPPs is completely separated from the governance structure of their respective organizations so that legal links are established by agreements or contracts.

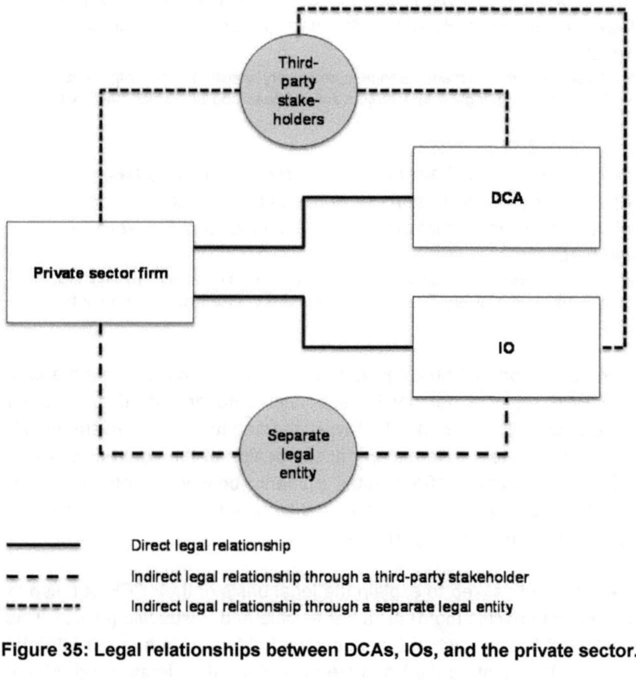

Figure 35: Legal relationships between DCAs, IOs, and the private sector.

The choice and design of the legal arrangement for a PPP is closely aligned with the PPP type. However, in particular the public sector often enters the foregoing PPP negotiations with standard templates for legal arrangements that are often customized later on, whether it is about an actual contract or not. Sometimes the institutional environment influences the contract design in the sense that the mandates of IOs and DCAs leave little margin to consider specific needs of the private sector partners.

> *Also diese Verträge gibt es als Standard und, je nach Projekt, manche Klauseln müssen unter Umständen auch angepasst werden. (DC3)*
> (Well, we have these contracts in a standard (remark: version) and some provisions have to be adjusted perhaps, depending on the project.)

> *Sometimes we might draft a new project for the initiative. So, it really depends on the type of the partnership and the interests between the two or more partners. So, it depends. Some are more strategic, some are less strategic, and then we select the right kinds of contractual modalities and ways to work around it. (IO7)*

In line with these two statements made by DC3 and IO7, two private sectors voice the need to keep contractual arrangements, whether they are loose or tight, somehow flexible so that unexpected developments can be considered during the course of the project:

> *Es gibt vertragliche Vereinbarungen, die schon auch im Detail ganz bestimmte Dinge regeln. Es muss dabei immer die Freiheit existieren, entsprechend zu adjustieren, wenn Themen bei einem Projekt auftauchen, die so vorher nicht vorhersehbar waren. (CO1-1)*
> (There are contractual agreements which already arrange in detail very specific things. There must always be the freedom to adjust accordingly if in a project some issues pop up which have not been predictable.)

> *Ich bin persönlich ein großer Fan [...] einer differenzierten Betrachtung zwischen harten und weichen Normen [...]. Und wenn der Konsens brüchig ist, das Thema im Grunde floating, dann muss man dem auch durch entsprechend flexiblere Regeln Rechnung tragen. (CO3)*
> (Personally, I am a big fan of [...] taking a differentiated view on tight and soft norms [...]. And if the consensus is fragile, so the matter is basically floating, then you have to take that into account by more flexible rules accordingly.)

In other words, initially concluded contract arrangements shall support and promote the successful implementation of PPP projects but not impede later amendments if all relevant stakeholders deem that necessary. Besides the PPP type, the financing mechanism including resource contribution is an important determinant for the design of the contract arrangements. For instance, DC3's organization differentiates primarily between contracts where both public and private sector make cash contributions and those where individual contributions from each side (e.g. in-kind) are set off against each other.

The interview partners were not only asked to explain the legal basis of their PPP but also to assess whether it is rigorous and specific (tight) or rather flexible and unspecific (loose). This query resulted in the question of how an actual formal contract differs from a rather informal kind of agreement, such as a letter of intent (LoI) or a memorandum of understanding (MoU), and in what situations which modality is chosen. Even among IOs there seem sometimes to exist different views on the definition of contracts. While most IOs, DCAs and private sector stakeholders do not consider MoUs as real contracts, IO7 defines MoUs together with cost-sharing and pro bono agreements as "formalized contractual frameworks". However, as soon as money or other tangible and intangible resources are exchanged or transferred between PPP stakeholders formal contracts will be concluded. These go beyond mere declarations of intent, not least because of accountability and compliance requirements set by the institutional environment.

> *So, you have [...] the very stringent [remark: agreements, where the partners] cannot even produce their product without signing that contract because they don't receive the [product name] over the ones [...] anything, which involves money has a contract. We wouldn't do any transfer of money or goods. We wouldn't accept any resources without a contract and without being fully transparent of what we do with it. And then you have others, which are more based on a MoU, which are loose consultations, which are accepting somebody for hearings. (IO3)*

> *But with a MoU you cannot transact anything. You cannot exchange resources. You cannot exchange expertise or anything. (IO5)*

In summary, there exists a huge variety of legal arrangements in PPPs for development, which are often individualized and therefore hard to clearly classify. However, the following two subchapters will carve out types of contract arrangements observed in the empirical sample and name some characteristics that determine a contract's tightness.

6.1.5.3.1 Types of Contract Arrangements

In the following will be described the different contractual arrangements that underlie the analyzed PPPs. This list does neither claim to include all kinds of contracts of PPPs for development nor to be legally precise, but it rather summarizes the interview partners' interpretations of the legal basis of their PPPs. Some of them are equal to a PPP type.

- **Consortium agreement**: This contract type typically applies to large-scale, multilateral PPPs with numerous stakeholders that result from public tenders and clearly determine the respective rights and obligations. Based on an operation plan this includes for instance the financial contributions to be made by each party involved. Hitherto consortium agreements were applied in partnerships with both DCAs and IOs as well as with the EU.

  > *[...] Konsortialverträge, wo alle Partner unterschrieben haben, und das waren zum Teil an die 20 Stück. Dementsprechend waren die Vertragsverhandlungen auch etwas komplexer und langwieriger bzw. die PPP-Verträge, die wir dann auch mit einer [DCA] z.B. hatten, die waren dann bilateral. (CO5)*
  > (Consortium agreements that were signed by all partners, and these were partly up to 20. Thus, the contract negotiations were more complex and lengthy while the PPP contracts that we also had with DCA, for instance, were bilateral.)

- **Cooperation agreement**: In particular, DCAs conclude this kind of contract with private sector firms. DC1 and CO10 stated that cooperation agreements are actual contracts which are much more binding than MoUs but leave enough flexibility to adjust over the course of a PPP.
- **Cost-sharing agreement**: see PPP Types (Chapter 6.1.5.2).
- **Letter of Intent**: By such a rather loose agreement one or more partners declare their interest or intention to conclude an actual contract at a later date. Like a MoU, a LoI can build the basis for partnership negotiations.

  Häufig startet eine Partnerschaft mit einem Letter of Intent oder einem Memorandum of Understanding, um sozusagen die Basis zu bilden, auf der man die Verhandlungen dann führt. (CO1-1)

  (A partnership often starts with a Letter of Intent or a Memorandum of Understanding to build the basis for the negotiations.)

- **Management agreement**: This contract type mandates a partner to assume certain managerial functions in a joint partnership and therefore formalizes duties and responsibilities. In the present case, it was applied for a PPP based on a separate legal entity.

  Also, wo wir als externer Dienstleister des [Name der PPP] das Mandat haben, bestimmte Aufgaben eines [Funktionsbeschreibung] auszuüben. Das heißt, wir sind dann zumindest, formell ausgedrückt, der Agent, und [Name der PPP] ist der Principal. (CO9-2)

  (Well, where we as external service provider of the [PPP name] have the mandate to exercise certain tasks of a [functional description]. This means that at least formally we are the agent, and [PPP name] is the principal.)

- **Memorandum of Understanding**: The term MoU is often synonymously used for LoIs so that in practice there does not seem to be a big difference. While both are typically non-binding agreements, a MoU is usually concluded between several partners who declare their interest or intention to perform certain activities or and/or to conclude an actual contract at a later stage. Hence, a MoU is the most basic legal partnership form together with the LoI.

  For a basic partnership, [remark: it] would be a Memorandum of Understanding. So, this one would include the non-financial collaboration, intentions for collaboration. (IO5)

  You go from general cooperations and so there is a Memorandum of Understanding, which is a general sort of contract. It's not a contract. It's a Memorandum of Understanding where you say that you want to cooperate with x or z. (IO6)

- **Pro bono agreement**: see PPP Types (Chapter 6.1.5.2).
- **PPP contracts**: Large DCAs doing a lot of PPP work have standardized PPP contracts that are either adopted by the private sector partners or customized if necessary, as stated by DC3 amongst others. Strategic alliances often are also based on these contracts which additionally require a proven business case behind the project, according to CO3.
- **Secrecy agreement**: This contractual element is a mechanism to bridge the transition phase from a MoU to an actual contract to ensure that the safety interests of the involved stakeholders are met at all times. Thus, it is often accompanied by a LoI or a MoU.

Begleitet wird das in vielen Fällen auch mit einem Secrecy Agreement, weil wir ja möglicherweise in den Verhandlungen auch vertrauliche Daten austauschen, die möglichst innerhalb der Gesprächspartner bleiben sollen. Es wird dann ein Vertrag abgeschlossen. (CO1-1)

(This is accompanied in many cases by a Secrecy Agreeement because during the negotiations we possibly exchange confidential data that should remain with the dialogue partners as far as possible. Then a contract will be concluded.)

- **Subcontract/Supply contract**: In PPPs with a dominant public sector or where third party stakeholders are involved, the IOs, DCAs and the private sector might all altogether be in a sub-contractor or supplier role. For instance, in one case, an IO was subcontractor from a national government, the DCA subcontractor from the IO and the private sector from the DCA.

  Also vertraglich ist [IO] immer Auftragnehmer, dann vom [nationalen Ministerium] letztendlich in dem Fall. Und wir sind der Unterauftragnehmer. Das ist einfach ein ganz normales Auftraggeber-Auftragnehmer-Verhältnis. (DC4)

  (Well, contractually [IO] is always the contractor, from the [national ministry] at the end. And we are the subcontractor. This is a normal client-contractor relationship.)

Except LoIs and MoUs, all aforementioned legal arrangement types can be considered as actual contracts. Other mentioned contract forms could not be specified as clearly as the previous ones, and so they have not been considered for this discussion.

6.1.5.3.2 Characteristics of Loose and Tight Contract Arrangements

Rather loose MoUs are preferably used at high level to somehow formalize a general partnership between two or more public and private actors while actual contracts come into play for implementing projects.

Usually, at the corporate level, partnerships are made between [IO4] and another entity through "memoranda of understandings". At the project level, there are many other agreements between the government who is implementing the [IO4] financed project and the private sector in a particular country. Overall, also these agreements should fall under certain legal obligations. (IO4)

But also when implementing the project level, the contractual design can be rather informal, if this is required for the operational work or partnership activities. For instance, DC4 underlines that the actual implementers and project managers need to have some flexibility in terms of the budget use while IO7 explains that tight agreements are not reasonable for strongly dialogue-oriented PPPs. It seems that partnerships with DCAs generally tend to be subject to more formal contracts, while for IOs this depends very much on whether it is about an implementing partnership or not, as well as on existing or previous cooperation experiences, for instance as supplier.

The contractual frameworks can sometimes be rather informal, kind of flexible when it comes to advocacy and policy dialogue, for example, it is not really a strong partnership necessarily, but it can be some level of loose partnership in a way. So, those are more informal. (IO7)

> *Also der Härtegrad ist bei IOs weicher als dieser [Name der DCA]-Vertrag. Der [Name der DCA]-Vertrag ist relativ hart, aber auch nicht so knallhart wie ein Liefervertrag. Das liegt in der Natur der Sache [...]. Die [Anmerkung: IOs] wollen auch jederzeit im Grunde eine Opt-out Möglichkeit haben, falls ihnen ein Reputationsschaden entsteht. Also wenn man nicht gerade irgendwie im Procurement-System drin ist und man procured irgendwelche Produkte, [Anmerkung: dann geht das] bei den Partnerschaften [...] in der Regel nur auf Memorandum Basis [...]. (CO3)*
>
> (Well, the degree of hardness is softer for IOs than this [DCA name]-contract. The [DCA name]-contract is relatively tough but also not as tough as a supply contract either. It is in the nature of things [...]. The [remark: IOs] basically want to have an opt-out opportunity at all times, if they suffer reputation damage. So, if you are not actually in the procurement system and you procure any products, [remark: then it works] for the partnerships [...] usually on memorandum basis only [...].)

If neither a formal contract nor an informal MoU can be reached, commitment-based contract-replacing mechanisms form a resort. CO5 told from UN-private sector cooperation workshops including quarterly calls and meetings that replace any kind of contract arrangement but cannot be considered as real partnership either. Another option is the membership model for partnerships that rest on separate legal entities. As DC5 reported, partners are members, they sign a letter of commitment and pay a membership fee. In return, they obtain a membership certificate but no contractually stipulated rights and obligations. Thus, this PPP model works only if all partners take their commitments serious.

Tight contracts are characterized by clear conditions that determine everybody's rights and obligations including contributions to make. Moreover, tight contracts are legally binding and often comprise sanctioning and contract enforcement rules. Stakeholders set milestones and monitor the PPP implementation including the appropriate use of resources, which are determined for specific purposes.

> *Even when we support the [IO] or [PPP name], we know exactly what the money is going to be used for. So, we always make sure we only get into contracts, when we know that we really get our hands on the project to a certain extent. And the fund is for that project, not a general support. (CO7)*

By nature, some types of contract arrangements are looser or tighter than others, but in summary it seems that the legal bases of PPPs are designed as formal as necessary but as flexible as possible. Moreover, it depends on the risk aversion of the stakeholders involved and on the legal requirements set by governments.

6.1.5.4 Duration and Durability

This chapter aims to analyze aspects and factors that influence the duration and durability of the sample's PPPs, which were all created after the year 2000 and lasted at least three years and are partially still ongoing (Chapter 5.2.1.3). The formal duration of PPPs is closely related to the contract arrangement while the actual one is often not foreseeable from the outset. Moreover, most interview partners emphasized that they are strongly interested in maintaining long-term partnerships. However, public actors like DCAs and IOs in particular often have clear guidelines that limit the duration of PPP contracts to a certain maximum number of years. Four different models of PPP duration were identified from the interviews (Figure 36).

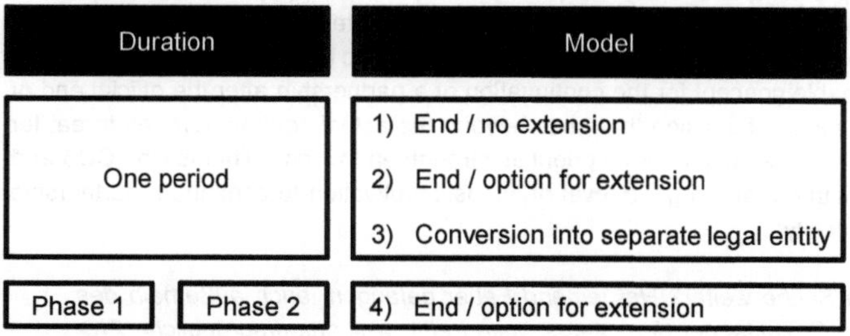

Figure 36: Models of PPP duration.

In the first model, the duration of PPPs is limited by fixed end dates and without option for extension, while in the second model this option is given. In particular, in very long lasting partnerships the contract renewal tends to be a merely formal act although the legal department has to verify this every time again. Insofar as the organizations' internal rules and guidelines do not provide the option for limited or unlimited extension, the conversion of the PPP into a separate legal entity forms an alternative third model. In some cases the PPP implementation is divided into phases from the beginning, which in turn mark two terms instead of one coherent period. Typically, one period lasts between two and five years while phases take about two to three years. However, the contract durations can vary quite a lot and are moreover determined by the purpose of the PPP, the complexity of the underlying policy issue and the PPP type.

> *Die Laufzeiten für die Verträge sind unterschiedlich. Das können 3 Jahre sein, das können 5 Jahre sein, dann immer mit der Option zu verlängern [...]. Wenn das Projektende definiert ist und das Ganze ist nicht in zwei Jahren machbar, dann macht man es halt in fünf Jahren. Dann dauert der Vertrag, also dann ist das Vertragsende nicht so definiert, sondern der Vertrag endet mit Abschluss des Projekts. Also da gibt es auch, was die Rechtsabteilung angeht, genug Juristen, die sich genau mit Kooperationen dieser Art auskennen. (CO1-1)*
> (The terms of the contracts are different. That can be three years, that can be five years, always with the option to renew [...]. When the project end is defined and the whole thing is not feasible within two years, then you simply do it within five years. Then the contract lasts, well, then the contract end is not defined so well, but the contract ends with the conclusion of the project. So, concerning the legal department, there are enough lawyers who know this kind of cooperations very well.)

> *The range is so broad. I mean, the [PPP name] and [PPP name] were both incubated in [IO3]. They started in [IO3], they matured into an own legal entity [...]. Some of them are really long-term and sustainable. Some of them are short-term because they should be short-term. You resolve a problem on a project-level and then it's done. Some of them don't work. So you have all kinds. (IO3)*

Important factors that influence the durability are contract compliance, flexibility, and commitment including motivation. An extreme scenario of insufficient contract compliance is its infringement, for instance corruption. This phenomenon occurred in one of the analyzed PPPs and finally led to its termination. Given the fact that partnerships evolve over time and that obstacles and problems are rarely completely anticipated, the partners' flexibility to accept adjustments to changing framework conditions and to extend the duration or to renew the contract, if necessary, strengthens the durability. Both public and private sector recognize the lack of a sustainable concept for the continuation of a partnership after the official end of contract and the absence of a vision that goes beyond the actual contract term as threat for the durability of PPPs. Changing internal priorities strengthen this risk. That is why CO5 and DC2 consider commitment and a good level of intrinsic motivation to continue a partnership as crucial for its durability:

> *Wer treibt die Sache weiter? Hat jemand Feuer gefangen, auch außerhalb des ursprünglichen Projekts, der den Status weitertreibt, weil das ursprüngliche Projektteam dann erstmal seine Aufgabe erledigt hat und sich verläuft? Es gibt neue Projekte. Die Leute werden anders eingesetzt. Und wenn dann niemand die Sache weitertreibt, dann verläuft es sich. Und dann wird es auch nie offiziell beendet, aber keiner macht es halt weiter. Also das ist so ein Phänomen, das habe ich öfters erlebt. (CO5)*
>
> (Who pushes on these things? Did somebody catch fire, also outside the actual project, and promotes the status, because the actual project team has accomplished its duty for the time being and disperses? There are new projects. The people are employed elsewhere. And if nobody continues the thing, then it disperses. And then it will never be officially concluded, but nobody carries on. Well, that is a kind of phenomenon, which I often experienced.)

> *Letztendlich sind […], ich sage mal ganz ehrlich, korrupte Strukturen aufgetreten, dass man dann beispielsweise sagte: "Naja, […] erstmal müssen wir irgendwie das Ganze formell ins Leben rufen. Da brauchen wir 20.000 Dollar von euch und dann werden wir hier eine große Feier organisieren. Und dann werden aus allen möglichen [Büros des lokalen Partners] Leute eingeflogen, um über das Projekt informiert zu werden, und die Leute werden dann natürlich auch nur im 5-Sterne-Hotel hausen und nur mit Allowances […]." Also da wurde dann sehr früh klar, da geht es nicht ganz mit rechten Dingen zu. Dann wollte man von uns wiederum noch 50.000 Dollar haben, um Autos für diese Project Units zu kaufen, um dann auch das Monitoring in den [Büros des lokalen Partners] machen zu können. So war dann die Argumentation. Und da haben wir natürlich irgendwann gesagt: "Also, jetzt reicht es." (n/a)*
>
> (Finally, there […], I will be very honest, arose corrupt structures, so that they said for instance: "Well, […] first we have to officially start the whole thing. Therefore we first of all need 20,000 Dollar from you and then we are going to organize first a big party. And then people from all [offices of the local partner] will be flown in, to be informed about the project. and of course, the people were only accommodated in five star hotels and only with allowances […]." Thus, it became clear at an early stage that something goes wrong. Then they wanted another 50,000 Dollar from us to buy cars for these project units, in order to be able to do the monitoring in the [offices of the local partner]. So, that was argumentation. And at one point we obviously said: "Well, that is enough.")

To prevent the early termination of PPPs or the withdrawal of partners, CO1-1 recommends concentrating on a small number of projects while IO7 urges to select partners carefully.

> *Wir haben auch kein Projekt vorzeitig abgebrochen, sondern die Projekte, die wir machen, haben wir zu Ende geführt. Und da sage ich immer: "Weniger ist mehr.*

Lieber zwei Projekte richtig als zehn anzufassen und dann auf einmal zu spüren, dass man wahrscheinlich nur fünf oder vier zu Ende bringen kann."(CO1-1)
(We never terminated a project prematurely, but the projects we carry out, we concluded them. And I always say: "Less is more. It is better to really tackle two projects instead of ten and then to feel that you can conclude probably only five or four.")

Of course, sometimes there are also cases where there are just challenges in the project implementation and the partner may withdraw. I know maybe one or two cases like that [...]. Usually, we do also recommend that our offices would define at least exclusionary criteria of the risk assessment before they start discussing with the company. (IO7)

In summary, the duration of PPPs depends mainly on external factors like individual internal PPP rules and guidelines that have to be taken for granted, and on unpredictable events which might promote or hinder an extension of the partnership activities. By contrast, the durability relies more on the individual behavior of the involved stakeholders and people as well as on their ability and willingness to really engage with each other.

6.1.5.5 Financial Volume

To characterize the size of PPPs for development, the interview partners were asked to share the financial volume of their partnership with the researcher or to indicate at least an approximate value. However, due to confidentiality reasons, most interview partners did not feel in a position to comment on that. In general the financial volume of the analyzed PPPs ranges between a few hundred thousand euros and a two-digit million amount. Still, most partnerships seem to dispose of a low to medium one-digit million amount, which is raised by both public and private sector. Especially in partnerships with DCAs, there exist budget caps for certain PPP types while IOs seem to be more flexible in this regard, depending on the amounts national governments and private sector partners are willing to contribute. In PPPs that are divided into phases, the budget is usually linked to each phase and not allocated for the whole time period.

6.2 Partnership Setting

This chapter analyzes diverse fundamental characteristics of the settings of PPPs for development and therefore serves the answering of **research question 1**. It illuminates extrinsic and intrinsic motivation factors behind PPP engagements and reveals the diverse expectations and objectives public and private actors pursue. Moreover, it shows fundamental requirements these actors impose on any kind of partnership and the contributions public and private sector typically make. Finally, this chapter is dedicated to extrinsic and intrinsic risks, which the interview partners perceive as project-specific or inherently linked to PPPs.

6.2.1 Motivation

Each company, DCA or IO pursues diverse interests through a partnership that motivates it to get engaged. This chapter distinguishes between extrinsic and intrinsic motivations of actors to engage in PPPs. Extrinsic motivation means that the willingness to enter into partnership was raised by external factors, which can be related to either the actual business or the institutional environment, for example in the context of changing norms and regulations. Intrinsic motivation factors are more loosely connected to, but not isolated from, the actual business of companies, DCAs and IOs, and are rather driven by internal aspirations and endeavours. Hence, extrinsic and intrinsic motivations are not mutually exclusive, and the boundaries between them sometimes become blurred.

6.2.1.1 Extrinsic Motivation

Hard directly business-related and softer indirectly business-related factors explain what a stakeholder motivates to engage in PPPs for development. Table 42 provides an overview of them.

Directly business-related	Indirectly business-related
Complementation of resources	Corporate social responsibility
Doing core business	Image and reputation
Fulfillment of the mandate	Reduction of environmental impact
Lobbying	
Market development	
Securing resources	

Table 42: Directly and indirectly business-related extrinsic motivation factors.

The overall awareness is that both public and private sector need each other to cope with changing requirements in a complex and globalized world that is moreover facing fundamental challenges like climate change, which are threatening humanity's existence. In this vein, there seems to be broad consensus among the interviewees that no party can resolve these issues alone.

> *Die Ausgangsmotivation ist, dass [Fokus der PPP] im Grunde nur als öffentlich-private Partnerschaft funktioniert. Also, das ist eines der Geschäftsfelder oder auch eines der entwicklungspolitischen Felder, bei denen der Staat keine [Produkte] herstellt, aber gesunde [Produkte] an Armutszielgruppen ohne staatliche Rahmen nicht geliefert werden, weil Armutszielgruppen [...] [Anmerkung: diese Produkte] mangels Wissen und mangels Erkennbarkeit nicht nachfragen. (CO3)*
> (The original motivation is that [PPP focus] works basically only as PPP. So, that is one of the business segments or also one of the development policy areas where the state does not produce any [product], but healthy [products] are not delivered to poverty target groups without public framework because the poverty target groups [...] do not demand [remark: these products] due to lack of knowledge and awareness.)

The key thing about the Sustainable Development Goals is that they are universal. It's applying to developing and developed countries and there is a lot of emphasis on engaging the private sector because to achieve these goals we cannot do it with the public sector alone. We also need to have integration of the private sector. The HOW is the issue. I think the WHY is clear to everybody. (IO5)

Directly business-related motivational factors stand for **core business**, **complementation of resources**, **fulfillment of the mandate**, **lobbying**, **market development**, and **securing of resources**. Engaging in PPPs predominantly belongs to the **core business** of DCAs and IOs rather than to activties of private sector firms. These public actors partially fund their work by profit-oriented projects with the private sector, or are **requested by mandate** to seek PPP engagements in order to promote the achievement of their organizational objectives, such as the SDGs.

Welche Erwartungen, warum haben wir das gemacht? […]. Wir sind [Rechtsstatus der DCA], das sich über Aufträge finanziert. Also von daher suchen wir natürlich immer nach Aufträgen, und da gab es einen Auftrag, wo wir gesagt haben: "Der […] überschneidet sich mit unseren [Art der Ziele], Steigerung der Nachhaltigkeit, etc." (DC2)

(Which expectations, why did we do that? […]. We are [legal status of the DCA], which is financed by projects. That is why we are obviously always looking for projects, and there was a project where we said: "That one […] overlaps with our [type of objectives], improvement of sustainability, etc.")

Mainly because previously people did perhaps not look on the private sector so positively or there was not such an easy marriage. But now I think […] *what is going on around the SDGs. The public sector, the governments, are realizing they need the private sector […], let's say, to reduce the carbon emissions, for example, […]. The governments cannot do it alone. So, I think there is a shift in the way business is done and that is only going to help us, at least to work better in my opinion. (IO5)*

In this context, CO8 emphasizes the motivation to align business and development cooperation interests but adds the importance of economic sustainability of large-scale PPP projects. He explains that more CSR-oriented, not-for-profit projects can only be financed on a small-scale by private sector firms. Moreover, both public and private sector entities seek **to complement resources** and to benefit from each other's strengths and competences. While private sector firms mainly look for networks, the public sector aspires to acquire additional financial and in-kind resources as well as to get access to specific technical knowhow.

Allerdings haben wir als kleiner Mittelständler zwar so ein kleines Netzwerk vor Ort. Wir haben aber nicht das Netzwerk zu den entsprechenden Regierungsautoritäten, was z.B. [Name des öffentlichen Partners] hat. (CO10-1)

(Indeed, we as a small medium-sized company do have a kind of small network on the ground. But we do not have the network to the corresponding governmental authorities, which, for instance, [name of the public partner] has.)

[…] una de las cosas que hemos visto en las alianzas es que las complementamos con los socios […]. O sea creo que una de las cosas que hemos buscado

> *en nuestras alianzas es que cada uno de los socios pone algo en la mesa que común, conjunto nos hace más fuerte que cada quien por su lado. (CO13-1)*
> ([...] one of the things we have observed in the alliances is that we complement with the partners [...]. That is why I believe that one of the things we have been looking for in our alliances is that each partner is putting something on the table, which makes us stronger together than each one for himself.)

> *With respect to the UN, all organizations are open to cooperation with the private sector and are engaging in different types of partnerships with business, especially in a time of shrinking budgets, with the possibility to generate additional resources as well as in-kind contributions and different more efficient forms of management. (IO1)*

Another aspect, particularly affecting the business activities of private sector firms, is the institutional environment. Private actors tend to actively influence the setting of norms and standards in a way that institutional boundaries and therefore TC are reduced. The exertion of influence on public decision-makers is often called "**lobbying**". Despite the negative connotation of this term, the consequences of lobbying are not necessarily negative in the development context. For example, PPPs aiming to standardize elementary goods across borders and to make them more efficient can contribute to decreasing TC for business and society alike, insofar as lower production costs are passed on to the consumers. Moreover, the environment can benefit from technology with lower use of energy. On the other hand, governmental pressure to enact a law if the private sector does not seek collaboration with the public sector to address certain policy issues can stimulate the creation of PPPs.

> *[...], dass wir die Länder, Ländermärkte, Regionenmärkte mit dieser Initiative so vorbereiten, dass wir eben unsere Produkte dort, am besten standardisiert, verkaufen können. (CO4)*
> ([...], that we prepare the countries, country markets, region markets through this initiative in a way that we can actually sell there our products, preferably standardized.)

> *Und wir versuchen dann auch an der internationalen Meinungsbildung teilzunehmen, welche regulatorischen und politischen Rahmenbedingungen wir brauchen, um eben die CO2-Emissionen [...] zu senken, wie man Klimaziele effizient erreichen kann. (CO6)*
> (And we also try to participate in formation of opinions, which regulatory and polical framework conditions do we need, in order to reduce [...] the CO2 emissions, how we can achieve the climate goals efficiently.)

> *In [Land XY] ist das Ganze durch die Regierung getrieben, die gesagt hat: "Wenn ihr Unternehmen nicht mitmacht, kriegt ihr halt ein Gesetz." Da waren die Unternehmen ganz schnell dabei. (DC2)*
> (In [country XY] the whole thing has been driven by the government that said: "If you, the companies, do not join in, you simply get a law." And then the firms got involved quickly.)

Most private sector firms communicated very openly that one of their major motivations is **market development**. In some cases the firms implementing partnerships in certain countries are hitherto not active there at all or just at a very low level. Through their DCA and IO partners they get access to local public and private actors which are otherwise harder to reach. Moreover, market entries are costly and associated with certain risks. Thus, PPPs form a kind of laboratory environment that enables private companies to dare a light market entry with a clear timeframe and relatively inexpensive withdrawal options, depending on the extent of engagement.

Die [CO5] hat […] für die [verantwortliche Abteilung], die sich dieser öffentlich-geförderten Projekte bedient, ganz klar als Zielvorgabe ausgesprochen, dass man neue Märkte erschließt, mit einem drei bis fünf-Jahres-Horizont. Sprich, man geht in solchen öffentlich geförderten Projekten Themen an, die noch nicht ausgereift genug sind, um ein 100%-Invest der [CO5] heute schon zu rechtfertigen. Und deswegen war die Zielvorgabe ganz klar: "Versucht euer Bestes, Prototypisches auszuprobieren. Und mit dem Ziel, in drei bis fünf Jahren ein kommerziell verwertbares Produkt daraus zu generieren." (CO5)
(The [CO5] has […] cleary stated for the [department in charge], which operates these publicly funded projects, to develop new markets with a time horizon of three to five years. In other words, you tackle topics in such publicly funded projects, which are not yet mature enough to justify a 100% investment by the [CO5] already today. And that is why the objective was very clear: "Try your best, try out prototypical things. And with the target to produce a commercially usable product within three to five years.")

Another fundamental motivation is the **securing of resources**. Climate-related phenomena like drought and flooding or environmental pollution can threat the access to raw materials for manufacturing companies, for example. That is why some private sector firms are engaged in partnerships that serve the environmental protection and the sustainable use of raw materials. A healthy environment secures access to input factors for production, a fact which in turn is important for business continuity.

El agua es un tema primordial. […] vemos […] grandes riesgos: Porque físicamente ya no hay agua. O sea en el espacio geográfico se acaba el agua, se agota. Porque socialmente [nota: si] […] las comunidades no tienen agua, nosotros no vamos a tener agua. (CO13-1)
(Water is an essential topic. […] we see […] big risks: Because physically there is no water anymore. This means that in the geographic space the water ends, exhausts. Because socially [remark: if] […] the communities do not have water, we will not have water.)

La única cosa que agregaría […] es la continuidad operativa de nuestros negocios. (CO13-2)
(The only thing I want to add is the operative continuity of our business.)

Indirectly business-related are **CSR**, **image and reputation**, and **reduction of environmental impact**. Most private sector firms emphasize the aspect of **CSR** as one main motivational factor for their PPP engagement, even if the actual CSR department was not in charge of that.

Unsere Motivation ist getragen von der Kultur, […] dass wir Verantwortung übernehmen wollen. […] glauben wir, dass wir als Unternehmen auch eine gesellschaftliche Verpflichtung haben. (CO1-1)
(Our motivation is driven by the culture […] that we want to assume responsibility. […] we believe that we as a company also bear some social responsibility.)

Ja, CSR hat auch immer zugetroffen. Also unsere CSR-Abteilung war immer sehr glücklich über unsere Projekte. (CO8)

(Yes, CSR has also always mattered. So, our CSR department was always very happy about our projects.)

Some firms, such as CO1, CO2 and CO4, explain their feeling of social responsibility by the awareness of the **environmental impact** of their business, and they emphasize their motivation to reduce this impact through partnerships. Another factor motivating firms to engage in PPPs is the improvement of their image and reputation.

Ja, es ist für uns schon immer so eine Art Leuchtturm-Projekt für Projekte dieser Art gewesen. Auch wenn wir nicht viele haben, aber dort haben wir gezeigt, wir können auch unter schwierigen naturräumlichen, teilweise auch sozialen Bedingungen solche Projekte dann umsetzen. (CO6)

(Yes, it has always been a kind of flagship project for this type of projects. Although we do not have much of them, we could show there that we can also implement such projects under difficult natural and partially also social conditions.)

In summary, the diverse statements from public and private sector interviewees demonstrate that questions of economic survival, the pursuance of individual business interests to meet corporate objectives or political interests to fulfill mandates being set to IOs and DCAs by national governments explain the extrinsic motivation to engage in PPPs for development.

6.2.1.2 Intrinsic Motivation

Despite the dominance of extrinsic motivational factors for PPP engagement, particularly from the private sector side, some intrinsic motivation has also been noted, at both individual and organizational level. On the one hand proactivity and personal interest in development issues are a source of engagement, which can result in an actual partnership if it coincides with the business interests.

[...] es gab auch Menschen, die ein persönliches Interesse daran hatten, sowas voranzutreiben. Da hing auch das Herzblut [...] an dem Thema. Aber natürlich war das auch ein Thema, wo die [...] beteiligten Personen das Gefühl hatten, dass da noch Bedarf ist, oder da ist der Markt noch nicht so weit entwickelt und gäbe es auch Potential [...], da Produkte aufzusetzen, die einfach neu sind und auch den Bedürfnissen unserer Kunden entgegenkommen. (CO9-1)

([...] there were also people who had a personal interest in driving something like that. There was also put one's heart [...] in that topic. But of course, that was also a topic where the [...] people involved had the feeling that there is demand or that the market is not yet developed that much und that there is also potential to set up products, which are simply new and also correspond to the needs of our clients.)

On the other hand, little economic benefit and restrained communication of the own PPP work might also be an indicator of intrinsic motivation, as practiced by CO7:

Quite many international organizations are surprised. Many corporate organizations do [type of PPP work] because they want to use it for their communications, they want to put it on their websites, they want to show big numbers [...]. And we try, you can say it is an arrogance from [CO7] to say, "We do this because we want to help and we do not want to publish it". So, that is a totally different ap-

proach. And when we talk to the international organizations, they say, "Oh, you should give us so much money. We put your logo on our website. We can send you materials. You can use it for public relationships." And we say, "No, we do not want that." And so quite often they are surprised and say, "Why do you not want it? That is what everybody wants." And we say, "No, we do not want it because we want to see the people on the ground helped, but we are not going to show this [remark: PPP work] now on our website that like it is the biggest thing." The biggest thing at [CO7] is the [product] which is proved every day. (CO7)

In summary, the statements by CO7 and CO9-1 show that intrinsic motivation in conjunction with passion may form a veritable source of energy to bring joint public-private projects forward and [may] result in a particular level of risk appetite needed to enter in certain PPP projects.

6.2.2 Objectives

This chapter gives an overview of general objectives public and private sectors pursue in joint PPPs. It does moreover analyze what expectations stakeholders place in partnerships, whether objectives are of strategic nature or not, and what conflicts of interest the actors might face.

6.2.2.1 Objectives of PPPs for Development

While in Chapter 6.2.1 the fundamental motivational factors for PPP engagements have been gathered, this chapter displays diverging and overlapping objectives that public and private sectors pursue in the partnerships on scope. Furthermore, it tries to figure out to which extent awareness of mutual objectives exists among partners. Figure 37 compares the objectives that have been formulated by the interviewees for their respective partnerships. However, this overview does neither claim to be fully inclusive nor mean that private sector objectives cannot also be public sector objectives and vice versa. The intersection contains objectives, which either both public and private sectors mentioned, or which result from the awareness of mutual objectives.

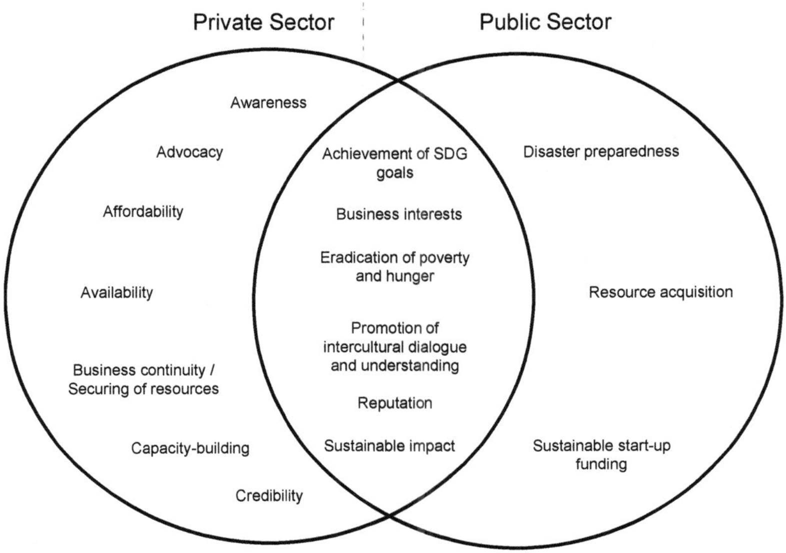

Figure 37: PPP objectives of public and private sectors.

On the private sector side, companies promote **awareness-building** and **advocacy** for certain policy issues as well as for achieving **affordability** and **availability** of their products and services for the target groups.

> *Sie haben [...] Awareness, Advocacy. Also das Thema bewusst machen und das Thema erklären und weitergeben. Sie haben das Thema Availability, indem man was zur Verfügung stellt [...]. Und was natürlich insbesondere die Partner interessiert, ist das Thema Affordability. (CO1-1)*
> (You have [...] awareness, advocacy. So, to become aware of the issue, to explain it and to pass on. You have the matter of availability, by providing something [...]. And what interests the partners in particular is the matter of affordability.)

Sometimes the PPPs objectives strongly overlap with the fundamental motivation of practising partnerships. In case of CO13, the securing of water access is pivotal for ensuring **business continuity** in the long-run so that this extrinsic motivation is also strongly reflected in the PPP objectives. That is why CO13 invests in **capacity-building** of local key stakeholders who have to support the PPP implementation for making it successful. The same approach is pursued by CO2, which therefore meets its public partner's objective of disaster preparedness:

> *Y por último el [nombre de la PPP] atiende al tema regulatorio, sobre todo a la capacitación de los tomadores de decisiones. (CO13-1)*
> (And finally the [PPP name] addresses the regulatory issue, in particular the capacity-building of decision makers.)

> *Ziel der Partnerschaft ist es, [Fokus der PPP] und ihr Personal im Katastrophenschutz zu schulen, in Katastrophengebieten schnelle Hilfe zu leisten und [...] zu steuern, um die humanitäre Hilfe zu verbessern. (CO2)*
> (The partnership's objective is to train [PPP focus] and its staff in disaster control, to provide and [...] to control quick assistance in disaster areas for improving the humanitarian aid.)

Another objective proclaimed by CO6 is building **credibility** for its own sustainability endeavours through PPP projects. This aspect is strongly related to **reputation**, and **image-building**, which private sector firms do not only communicate frankly but the public sector also recognizes and accepts, insofar as the benefits from joint partnerships are fairly shared with the beneficiaries. In the same vein, DC4, IO2, and IO5 also say openly that the improvement of the **resource endowment** forms an important objective for the public sector, to fund either its own or third-partner development activities:

> *So I guess, for the UN it is definitely about the monetary support, which motivates to get engaged with PPPs, while for the latter it might be more about reputation and establishing a main actor role in development work. (IO2)*

> *Depending on the partnership, some of them are more keen on having strategic, core business-related benefits from it, which is fine for us as long as it benefits the communities and it's not unfair competition or any of that. It's not that we are against core business benefits [...]. A lot of them do want to put it in their CSR activities or they want to see it in press releases about our common project or they want to have like a little bit of an objective mediator between them and the community, helping in advancing community development projects. So, there are very different reasons why they engage. (IO7)*

> *So, there are two kinds of objectives. One has to do with a specific goal for the initiative, so we share with [UN organization], what we are going to do in order to achieve this goal and what we need if it is a case, so that [UN organization] perhaps can figure out how to help us to achieve this goal. And the second purpose, which is more related with the partnership in general, is to obtain exposure, globally. [...] we are pursuing the social impact, we are pursuing the equilibrial point, the economical revenue, which is not similar like the traditional businesses. (CO14)*

Hence, appropriate alignment of mutual objectives paves the way for making a sustainable impact and for the achievement of SDG goals, such as the eradication of poverty and hunger, which also private sector firms like CO3 and CO9 consider as one of the key challenges. While the key objective of the private sector remains business interest, the matching of complementary resources is something both share alike. The awareness of each others objectives exists on both side although it seems that the public sector has at least clearer ideas of the private sector's objectives than viceversa, whether theses ideas are correct or not.

> *Unsere Partnerschaft dient dazu, die Stärken des öffentlichen Sektors und unsere spezifischen Stärken zu vereinen. Einerseits verfügen wir über die [...] Kompetenz und die finanziellen Ressourcen, unsere Projekte durchzuführen, andererseits erhalten wir das regionale, anwendungsbezogene Wissen der einzelnen Länder, in denen wir agieren mit Hilfe der [IO Partner]. Dies ermöglicht uns, uns*

vor Ort noch stärker zu engagieren und uns zu profilieren. Demnach gibt es sehr viele Interessensüberschneidungen zwischen dem privaten und öffentlichen Sektor, die wir nutzen möchten. (CO2)

(Our partnership serves to unite the strengths of the public sector and our specific strengths. On the one hand, we dispose of the [...] competence and the financial resources to implement our projects, on the other hand, we receive regional, practical knowledge from the different countries in which we act with support of the [IO partner]. This enables us to engage even stronger on-site and to build an image. Thus, there are many overlappings of interest between the private and public sector, which we want to use.)

Das ist schon ganz klar [...] die privaten Partner machen es nicht nur alleine aus Social Responsibility, sondern die möchten schon einen Business Case haben. (DC1)

(This is very clear [...] the private partners do not act for social responsibility only, but they also want to have a business case.)

In summary, the nature of the objectives, and therefore of the analyzed PPPs, is mainly strategic. This does not apply to those PPPs being explicitly set up as strategic alliances. If private actors pursue business interests, or public actors promote the achievement of the SDG goals to fulfill their mandate, there is always a strategic component. Private sector firms aim to pave the way for later large-scale market entries and to enhance their distribution potential. The advocacy for standardized rules and norms across countries for inducing market changes and the securing of access to raw materials, what CO13-1 calls "strategic intent" of the PPP engagement, are clearly strategically motivated but do not run counter to public sector's objectives, insofar they have sustainable impacts. In this sense, both public and private sectors also align their partner selection strategically and choose those partners that are most helpful in achieving their own objectives. However, one interview partner also made negative experiences and warns of little effective partnerships that do not guarantee a long-term orientation.

From the projects that I could observe, achievements are formulated to be more tangible and only up to a medium term at most. Quick fixes or quick wins seem to be focused on, while long term objectives are being neglected. (IO2)

6.2.2.2 Mutual Expectations and Goal Alignment

This chapter discusses expectations public and private stakeholders set each other in their PPPs, deals with questions of how these can be harmonized, and also gives examples of disappointments and unfulfilled expectations. In general, expectations deviate from objectives in the sense that they are rather implicit and not declared as clear targets. However, they can be overlapping. In this context, both public and private sectors emphasize the importance to reflect their own, the partners' and the beneficiaries' interests in order to design PPPs inclusively:

Man muss Werte und Effizienz zusammenbringen und man muss das in einem synergetischen Puzzle machen, wo für beide Seiten etwas drin ist. Und man muss für das Unternehmen immer die Frage beantworten: What's in it for us? Und das muss man nicht nur finanziell beantworten, das muss man in aller Breite

> *beantworten […]. Wie kann ich ein Projekt so aufsetzen, dass es im Grunde die Interessen der Partner, die Interessen der People und die Interessen der Company im breitesten Sinne entwickelt? (CO3)*
> (You have to align values and efficiency and you have to do that by a synergetic puzzle where something is in for everybody. And for the company you always have to answer the question: What's in it for us? And you do not have to answer that financially only but in breadth […]. How can I set up a project in a way so that it does basically develop the partners' interests, the people's interests and the company's interests?)

> *So, when we come together we are not just thinking as [IO5] or as government, but we also look at the view of the others. What do they think? How do they want to do it? What is their approach? So, it's really needed to bring together the different approaches […]. Then you have better results as compared as you are just doing things in your own way. (IO5)*

Underlined by examples, Table 43 gives an overview of major expectations expressed by public and private interview partners.

Expectation	Interview partner	Example
Achievement of common goals/ Existence of common interests	CO1, CO2, CO6, IO8	*Und auf dem Gebiet arbeiten wir ausschließlich mit der [UN-Organisation] zusammen, weil wir einfach glauben, dass hier mit der [UN-Organisation] viele Dinge gesichert sind, […] im Sinne der Qualitätssicherung und auch im Sinne der Verteilung im Land. (CO2)* (And in this area we exclusively cooperate with the [UN organization] because we believe that with the [UN organization] are many things assured, […] in the sense of quality assurance and also in the sense of distribution in the country.) *[…] you might think that the private sector and the United Nations may have different goals and it is true. […] mostly private sector is driven by profit and growth and the UN is mostly driven by poverty eradication, and this is more or less the final goal, but […] there is common interest in having more stable societies, more diverse societies. And this is where the partnership and other partnerships were created, really playing on this common interest of both […]. (IO8)*
Clear com-muni-cation of expectations and predictability	CO2, CO5, IO6	*[DCA]-Partnern. Die haben immer gerne gehört, wenn man klar gesagt hat: "Wir wollen hier Marktanteile gewinnen. Wir wollen hier Geschäfte machen." Mit einem CSR-Projekt konnte man da nicht so viele Sympathien gewinnen. (CO5)* ([DCA] partners. They always liked to hear if you clearly said: "We want to gain market share here. We want to make business here. You could not gain much sympathy by a CSR project.) *For example, I have very clear in mind that the private sector has an expectation for communicating […] in partnerships. It's important. On the other hand, the United Nations has its own policies on this. So, these expectations sometimes don't*

Expectation	Interview partner	Example
		meet. But if you want to develop these partnerships you need to find a common ground. Sometimes, it's difficult for the private sector to find partnerships and programmes that are really related and impacting the business. (IO6)
Mutual benefit	DC3, IO4	*Und das ist halt immer so diese Balance: Entwicklungspolitischer Mehrwert und auch kommerzielle Interessen. (DC3)* (And actually it is always this kind of balance: development of political value added and also commercial interests)
Professional competence and commitment	DC2, DC4, CO4, CO14	*[...] the expectation from [CO14] is money and I think the expectation from the [UN organization] is more our experience or contribution and our commitment regarding [...]. (CO14)*

Table 43: Expectations of PPPs from public and private sector actors.

Other expectations that have been expressed are the clear delineation from commercial activities (CO2, CO7) and the hope to gain awareness from the private sector for own development activities (DC2).

The anticipation of mutual expectations and the alignment of particular interests are not an easy task, as they are both causes of dissatisfaction and uncertainty and therefore potential drivers of TC. Thus, it takes time and it is important to take time to get to know each other, as stated by CO10-1:

> *Die [DCA] hat die Erwartungen von uns und wir haben die Erwartung von der [DCA], bis wir dann gegenseitig verstanden haben, wie wir beide funktionieren. Dann haben wir uns aufeinander eingespielt und konnten unsere Erwartungen angleichen. Aber es war doch tatsächlich so, dass ich mit ganz anderen Erwartungen reingegangen bin und die [DCA] auch mit ganz anderen Erwartungen. (CO10-1)*
>
> (The [DCA] places expectations on us and we have the expectation of the [DCA], until we have understood each other how we both are working. Then we have attuned to one another and could align our expectations. But it was indeed such that I entered with very different expectations, and the [DCA] also did this, yet with very different expectations.)

Disappointments and unfulfilled expectations were voiced by DC4, CO7 and CO14. For instance, DC4 expects more input from his partners and more value for money with respect to the huge budget approved by the contracting government, input in the sense of manpower and technical competence. By contrast, CO14 gained in some situations the feeling that private companies behave as "fancy attendees" at events hosted by DCAs or IOs where they are expected to share their knowledge, but the public sector does not equally show interest in their expectations. The alignment of goals and expectations is not only difficult in the event of clear communication but also in the opposite. DC2 reports that in their partnership many private sector firms delegate authority to the public partner without having clear expectations, but still expect their interests to be represented:

> *"Wir machen einfach bei euch mit und ihr dürft auch in unserem Namen sprechen." Da gibt es ganz viele unterschiedliche Erwartungshorizonte, Interessen-*

gemengengelage, die man auch gar nicht so ganz genau zusammenfassen kann. (CO2)
("We simply join you and you are also allowed to speak on our behalf." There are many different expectations, situations of conflicting interests, which you cannot really summarize.)

That is why the management of expectations is crucial, not only between partners but also within each participating organization. CO14 recommends to not set expectations too high from the beginning but to allow expectations developing gradually:

[...] I managed the expectation internally. So, I would rather not create the expectation that a relationship with [UN organization] will allow us to work in field or to a scale up in a faster way the things that we were doing. So, that was my particular expectation. And so I managed the relationship and I am like a boundary spanner from both sides, so from the [CO14]' side I communicate what I think is more realistic. (CO14)

In summary, there is basically enough overlap between the interests of public and private sector so that mutual expectations can be met in many situations. However, this requires that all partners involved respect their counterparts' objectives and demonstrate serious interest in reaching an agreement acceptable to everyone.

6.2.2.3 Conflicts of Interest

In the present context of PPP objectives, the term *conflicts of interest* will be discussed with reference to difficulties in harmonizing public and private sector interests, legal implications and incentive conflicts. Conflicts of interests are an issue that both public and private sector face alike in either an active or passive role, in particular if the actors involved are accountable to different stakeholders with different interests. DC2 reports from a partnership where his organization assumes a coordinating project management office (PMO) function. Thus, he is accountable to the partners involved. On the other side, DCAs also often work for-profit and pursue business interests.

Als [PMO] muss ich natürlich neutral beraten [...]. Auf der einen Seite bin ich [DC2]-Mitarbeiter und versuche unseren Umsatz zu steigern. Auf der anderen Seite muss ich da alle Mitglieder glücklich machen. Das sind aber solche Rollenverständnisse und Rollenkonflikte, die relativ häufig auftreten, qua deren, wie wir verfasst sind und wie wir auch arbeiten. (DC2)
(As [PMO] I have to advice neutrally of course [...]. On the one side, I am [DC2] staff and try to increase our revenue. On the other side, I have to make all members happy. These are such a kind of understandings and conflicts of roles, which happen relatively often, given our setup and also our way of working.)

Thus, there exists a business-driven conflict. Taking the same line, CO4 adds that between them and third-party stakeholders involved, such as NGOs, the fundamental objectives are sometimes so divergent making it actually impossible to avoid and settle conflict of interests. A mandate-driven conflict situation was reported by IO5. While IOs need the support from national private sector firms to implement the SDGs and therefore to fulfill their mandate, financial dependencies from large donor countries might prompt IOs to collaborate with their companies also in areas others than partnerships and therefore infringe internal compliance directives:

> *[...] we already have good relationships with the governments where we work. So, I think there is opportunity to increase this collaboration. At the same time the donor governments, governments like Germany for example, they are giving core resources to [IO5]. They want to promote companies from Germany also to work with us, maybe from the procurement angle. (IO5)*

This issue was generally summarized by IO1 and applies particularly for norm-setting institutions, according to IO3. It is further exacerbated if member states do not succeed in aligning their interests well and therefore leave IOs behind with blurred mandates for PPP work:

> *A growing challenge is posed in the context of PPP by the United Nations twofold role as framework provider and facilitator to promote partnerships (owing to its "convening power", neutrality and integrity) and also as implementer, notably in developing countries. (IO1)*

> *[...] we have the challenge that we are probably one of the agencies with most partnerships, but we are certainly also the agency with [remark: a strong] normative mandate. And therefore, [...] we have to engage but we have to be engaged with caution. And that [remark: challenge] leads also to the negotiation process, where some countries first came from the idea we need to engage more [remark: in PPPs] and other countries came from the idea we need to protect better, from conflict of interests and other undue influences. (IO3)*

A situation of bounded rationality do stakeholders face if mutual incentive structures are not clear, which in turn is a potential cause of conflicts of interests, as stated by CO13-1:

> *Pero sobretodo entender la estructura de incentivos [...] es lo que se vuelve como complejo porque normalmente no es tan claro. O sea hay ciertos incentivos que son visibles, por ejemplo todos queremos estar con el medio ambiente pero luego empiezan los incentivos de cada una de las organizaciones a jalarlos a diferentes lugares. (CO13-1)*
>
> (But especially understanding the incentive structure [...] is something that gets complex because normally it is not so clear. That means that there are certain incentives visible, for instance that we all want to be with the environment, but then begin the incentives of each organization to pull it to different places.)

In another case, CO4 seconded own staff for a certain period to an IO. He explains that clear contract arrangement and strict compliance prevented conflict of interests:

> *[...] sie muss eben dann auch definitiv unterschreiben, dass sie nicht für [CO4] arbeitet, sondern das war alles vertraglich, genau geregelt, dass sie für [UN-Organisation] arbeitet und auch [CO4]-Interessen auch nicht von ihr zu vertreten sind, sondern sie hat nur [UN-Organisation]-Interessen zu vertreten. Um da in keine Compliance-Bredouille zu kommen, haben wir es auch gar nicht erst versucht. (CO4)*

([...] she has definitely to confirm that she does not work for [CO4], all that was contractually arranged in detail, that she works for [UN organization] and [CO4] must not be represented by her either, but she only has to represent [UN organization] interests. In order not get into compliance trouble, we did not even attempt it.)

In summary, the reasons for and the extent of conflict of interests can be manifold but clear communication of interests and objectives, awareness of incentive structures, clear contracts, commitment and strict compliance can contribute to avoiding or at least mitigating this phenomenon.

6.2.3 Partnership Requirements

Public and private sector actors place strict and soft demands on partnerships that must or should desirably be met, regardless of the concrete partner. Thus, these requirements are not equal to selection criteria applied to the concrete partner selection (Chapter 6.3.1.4). Table 44 gives an overview of strict and soft requirements.

Strict requirements	Soft requirements
Control structure	Commercial benefit
Cost and funding restrictions	Excellent reputation
Development focus	Geographical proximity
Limited subcontracting	Leadership
No service provision to the private sector	Private sector involvement
Private sector involvement	Societal benefit
Transparency	Specific expertise
	Strategy alignment

Table 44: Strict and soft requirements for PPPs.

On the hard requirements side CO1-1 emphasizes the need of **transparency** in terms of project planning and budget monitoring. A complementary element of this is the existence of a **control structure**, which DC2 demands for each partnership. Both public and private sector also set very specific requirements in terms of maximum share of **administration costs** at the overall budget and **funding** mechanisms. To ensure efficient project implementation CO7 sets strict conditions to the number of contract partners:

Also wir hatten die Maßgabe, Minimum 40 % der eigenen Kosten als öffentliche Subventionierung einzuwerben. Maximal waren das dann 50 %. (CO5)
(Well, we had the condition to acquire a minimum of 40% of the own costs as public subsidiary. There was a maximum of 50%.)

How much in the percentage of the programme is going to be used for the administrative part? And we do not go above 15 %. If it is more than 15 %, we would not work with them. [...] we do not do third party contracts because it is always tedious, the interest can really deviate. So, we only partner with one organization at a given time. (CO7)

CO8 explains that public tenders for PPPs require or at least explicitly desire private sector involvement while CO13-1 and DC5 both acknowledge that PPPs should have **commercial and social benefits** alike:

> *A nivel corporativo una de las cosas que nosotros hacemos para que las inversiones sean sostenibles, es que tiene que ser de interés para la sociedad y de interés para la compañía. Esto es lo que hace que realmente sean sostenibles y estratégicas. (CO13-1)*
>
> (One thing we do at corporate level is that the investments are sustainable, that is they have to be in the interest of the society and in the interest of the company. This is what makes them really sustainable and strategic.)

However, IO7 clearly states that despite the legitimacy of inherent business interests, the **achievement of development objectives** prevails:

> *But, of course, it's always very clear that the number one priority is the development objectives and communities. So, in some cases we have said "Fine, we can see what are the entry points for exclusive business, for example". But it's very clear that we are not a trade promotion agency or we do not benefit one country only and at the cost of developing countries in that sense. (IO7)*

As soft requirements, IO6 mentions moreover specific expertise and CO6 notes the willingness to take leadership while CO8 points to the necessity of fit between the partners' particular **strategies**. Moreover, CO3 raises the idea that the **geographical proximity** of national DCAs, compared to IOs, is sometimes a decisive requirement:

> *Und ich denke auch die Nähe der Partner zueinander ist irgendwo entscheidend, weil [...] die Kapazität im Vergleich zur Aufgabe ist natürlich beschränkter bei diesen globalen Organisationen. Das heißt die "Person pro Quadratmeter Problemzone" plus die Ressourcen, die dafür zur Verfügung stehen, ist natürlich verschwindend gering bei der UN im Vergleich zu [...] anderen Organisationen, die [...] in bestimmten Ländern arbeiten. (CO3)*
>
> (And I think the proximity of the partners to each other is somehow decisive because [...] the capacity compared to the task is naturally more limited in these global organizations. That means the "person per square meter problem zone" plus the resources that are available for that are dwindling small in the UN, compared to other organizations, which [...] are working in certain countries.

In summary, public and private partners impose diverse strict and soft requirements on PPPs, which do not necessarily apply to all PPPs alike but can be combined.

6.2.4 Existence and Characteristics of PPP Strategies

Chapter 6.2.2.1 revealed that PPPs are often of strategic nature. Still, this does not imply that these partnerships follow clear overall strategies. Thus, this chapter will show to which extent PPP strategies actually exist among public and private actors and what the elements of them are. While most DCAs and IOs, in particular the large ones, seem to have or at least develop an explicit and clear strategy at the central level, the situation on the private sector side is more fragmented.

> *[...] the [IO5] Strategic Plan [...]. It [is] really much aligned to the SDGs. So to say, there is not only need to build on what we have but even to increase more how we work with the private sector or with private partners. (IO5)*

> *So, we are now designing the new strategy and the strategy will be that global partnerships have to be dealt with by headquarters because they have a number of dimensions. (IO6)*

While a few companies consider sustainability activities including PPPs as core element of their corporate strategy, several interview partners reported to be at the very beginning of PPP activities so that these are neither part of a corporate strategy nor does a separate strategy exist for them.

> *Nachhaltigkeit ist dort wesentlich mehr als zuvor, nicht nur Teil der Strategie, sondern Kern der Strategie. Also das Unternehmen sieht Nachhaltigkeit als den Treiber von Innovation und Weiterentwicklungen. (CO3)*
> (Sustainability is much more than before not only part of the strategy but core of the strategy. Thus, the company sees sustainability as the driver of innovation and development.)

> *[...] um offen und ehrlich zu sein, also wir sind uns nicht bewusst, dass es eine Gesamtstrategie gibt, die jetzt das Senior Management formuliert hat und dann von den einzelnen Abteilungen umgesetzt wird. (CO9-1)*
> ([...] to be frank and fair, we are not aware of the existence of an overall strategy that has been formulated by the senior management that has to be implemented by the different departments.)

> *Una estrategia global, particular por parte de [CO13], no existe. O sea que creo que hay una intención estratégica de hacerlo pero no hay nada articulado [...]. (CO13-1)*
> (A global strategy, particularly from the part of [CO13] does not exist. This means that I believe that there is a strategic intention to do that but there is nothing articulated [...].)

Others, like CO10 declared their interest in designing a strategy, or in defining the way to deal with public actors rather as an approach or a guideline, such as CO7 and CO14. Hence, insofar as stakeholders have recognized the strategic nature of PPPs, and even if there is no explicit PPP strategy, partnerships can still be an element of overall corporate or organizational strategies. Concerning the respective objectives, the private sector's strategic orientation is mainly guided by **strategic market positioning,** while the public sector tends to align its PPP strategies with the **achievement of the SDGs**:

> *In unserem Fall sollte man [...] Kosten- und Qualitätsführer in [Produktkategorie] sein, sonst wird man sich wahrscheinlich nicht in großem Umfang an der Entwicklung bestimmter Marktstrukturen beteiligen können [...]. (CO3)*
> (In our case you should be [...] cost and quality leader in [product category], otherwise you are unlikely to be able to participate in the development of certain market structures on a large scale.)

I see that private sector work cuts across the whole strategic plan to some extent. I think the more significant outcomes from the strategic plan are especially the ones [...] dealing with inclusive and sustainable growth, number one and also number seven, which are on the development debates and actions, prioritizing poverty and inequality and exclusion. (IO7)

Moreover, CO9 and CO4 underline the achievement of **unique selling points** and the creation of **networks** as important elements of the strategies behind PPPs while in case of CO11 the PPP activities are subject to the company's CSR philosophy. On the public sector's side, IO6 places strong emphasis on the attachment of a **communication plan** to each partnership to create value for money and build awareness while IO5 names **inclusive business** and **resource mobilization** as core elements of her organization's PPP strategy.
The ways stakeholders implement their strategies and tackle PPP work are quite manifold. This applies in particular to the partner selection on the private sector's side.

We look out for innovative, best-in-class projects that can be done. So, we do not do what everybody else is doing. We try to find modern, innovative projects that make a long-lasting impact. So, that is our approach. (CO7)

Entonces, la filosófia que hemos tenido es aplicar herramientas del sector privado a problemas sociales. Esto es como la forma en que [CO13] y nosotros abordamos los temas [...] que estamos muy enfocados en eficiencia y eficacia. [...] estamos buscando alianzas sobre todo con sectores que nos complementen, en el entendido que tiene [CO13] de que si ayuda solucionar el problema social, ayudamos el enfoque estratégico de la compañía. (CO13-1)
(Well, the philosophy we have is applying tools of the private sector to social problems. It is like the way [CO13] and we tackle the issues [...] and we are very much focused on efficiency and effectiveness. [...] we are looking for alliances, particulary with sectors complementing us, in the understanding that [CO13] has that if we help to resolve the social problem, we support the strategic focus of the company.)

However, an element that CO14, DC5, and most others consider as strategic to build a basis for partnership work is the identification of relevant stakeholders and the creation of common platforms where they can get together. In summary, the private sector has also recognized the strategic character of PPPs for development and considers them in many cases in the overall corporate strategy. Still, exclusive strategies on PPPs seem to barely exist on the private sector side, at most strategies on collaboration with the public sector in general.

6.2.5 Contributions

This chapter compares the different kinds of contributions public and private stakeholders make to joint partnerships, their specifics, and how they complement each other. Contributions can be classified into three major pillars: **skills and competences**, **financial** and **in-kind**. Pursuant to the frequent mention, both public and private stakeholders seem to consider skills and competences as their major contribution to PPPs or as the major input factor provided by their partners. However, all three kinds of contributions are strongly related to each other and therefore hard to clearly differentiate so that the different contributions are allocated to the most suitable pillar. All partners provide at least some staff members (in-kind) who bring in some skills and competences. Financial contribution in the present context refers to kind of cash or non-cash funding, which is provided additionally to any other material and personnel expenses.

Skills and competences in the public sector context means in particular the provision of its global network but also specific expertise in the implementation of PPPs for development under difficult cirumcstances in developing and emerging countries. IO2 and IO8 highlighted the credibility UN organizations enjoy due to their development activities around the globe and this paves the way for approaching local public and private stakeholders in terms of PPP initiatives. Moreover, the UN System possesses pertinent experiences in different areas of action and can thereby provide customized policy advice to private sector firms collaborating with them. DC1 and DC5 emphasize the existing project management and other methodical competences of DCAs wherefore they can contribute to preparing private sector firms for development engagements on the ground and take the project lead where appropriate. The self-perception of DCAs and IOs coincides with the external perception by private sector firms which unanimously confirm the public sector's coordinator and facilitator role on the ground as its dominant contribution to joint PPPs.

> *Kontakt ist [...] ein gutes Stichwort. Wenn man jetzt auf der Makroebene arbeitet, also wo es auch notwendig ist, dass man regierungsnah arbeitet oder mit verschiedenen Ministerien in dem Ort, dann bietet die [DC3] [...] irgendwo ihr Netzwerk an [...]. Diese Kontakte haben jetzt in der Regel die Leute aus der Privatwirtschaft nicht so [...]. Dann die Regionalexpertise, dadurch dass unsere Kollegen meistens auch schon über mehrere Jahre in den Projektländern arbeiten, kennen sie die lokalen Gegebenheiten, die Märkte, aber auch die Kultur und haben da auch nochmal ein anderes Netzwerk, einen anderen Zugang zu den Menschen. Das sind also diese Dinge, die sehr, sehr interessant sind für die Privatwirtschaft. Auf der anderen Seite lässt sich das gut mit z.B. sehr spezieller, technischer Expertise aus der Privatwirtschaft vereinbaren, die wir nicht haben. Wenn es z.B. darum geht [...] eine bestimmte Technologie anzuwenden, die einfach sehr speziell ist und dieses Unternehmen ist vielleicht sogar der Hersteller dieser Technologie oder Anbieter, dann würde natürlich dieser auch die Expertise bei Trainings z.B. anbieten. (DC3)*
>
> (Contacts is [...] a good keyword. If you work at the macro level, where it is necessary to work closely to the government or with different ministries at this place, then the [DC3] somehow offers its network [...]. People from the private sector usually do not have these contacts. Then the regional expertise, given that our colleagues mostly work for several years already in the project countries, they know the local conditions, the markets, but also the culture and also have another kind of network, another access to the people. These are the things, which are very very interesting for the private sector. On the other side, this can be well-combined with very specific technical expertise from the private sector, which we do not have. When it is e.g. [...] about using a certain technology that is basically very specific and this company is maybe even the producer or supplier of this technology, then it would offer this expertise also in trainings, for instance.)

An overview of public sector contributions is given in Table 45.

Kind of contribution	Contributions	References
Skills & competences	• Contracting of third-party (local) stakeholders • Coordination of diverse governmental authorities • Coordination of product- and quality-related standard-setting • Credibility • Expertise in facilitating project implementations on the ground • Integration of expertise across the UN System • Methodical competences in project control and process management • Monitoring of local activities and stakeholders (e.g. compliance with regulations and quality assessment of locally produced basic goods) • Policy advice • Project management on the ground • Training of internal staff and of private sector actors in specific topic areas (e.g. agriculture, energy, health) • Training of private sector actors in customizing their products to development needs	CO3, CO13, DC1, DC3, DC4, IO2, IO8
Financial	• Cash provision by national governments	CO4
In-kind	• Labor time/staff provision	CO5, DC5

Table 45: Public sector contributions.

The perception of the private sector's contributions is more diverse. DC2 and IO5 underline that for them the actual kind of contribution matters less than the existence of awareness of certain policy issues and the willingness of the private sector to contribute to resolving them:

> *Wir haben auch viele Mitglieder, die nichts mitbringen oder relativ wenig mitbringen und die diese [Name der PPP] dann zum Aufbau ihrer eigenen Expertise brauchen. Und das auch sehr klar sagen: "Ich kann mich nirgendwo so richtig einbringen. Ich weiß ja gar nicht so viel und ich komme einfach immer, um zu zuhören und zu lernen." (DC2)*
>
> (We also have many members who contribute nothing or bring in relatively litte und who need this [PPP name] for building their own expertise. And who also clearly say: "I cannot really contribute anywhere. Actually, I do not know that much but I always join in to listen and to learn.")

> *So, just belonging to this platform, being a member, and conducting your business differently already has an impact on the SDGs. In this case you are not giving money to [IO5]. It's just the way you conduct your business that makes like the community a better place. (IO5)*

Moreover, some public actors stress the broad range of options to handle private sector contributions. The needs and capacities of the different local and international stakeholders, whether they are formal partners or just involved and affected as local authorities or beneficiaries, are manifold. The example of IO7 shows that a good portion of flexibility and open-mindedness can bring together diverse actors in diverse actor constellations and enable them to bring different kinds of contributions into a joint partnership:

> *In a lot of the partnerships the company actually doesn't give us money. So, it can be that the company provides something completely different. They can provide an innovative technology or they can provide their key expertise or something like that. So, it really depends a lot on the partnership and also on the resources that are available [...]. For example, some countries have a legislation that they [remark: the companies] have to put certain percentage into community level development or so on and they might come to us saying: "We need to do something in this community for X amount of money and it's not our core business and we are not development experts. Can you help to work with the community?". So, in those kinds of partnerships it might be 100% coming from the company. In other cases it can be zero coming from the company. So, it really depends. (IO7)*

However, in general the private sector's core contribution is the provision of business competences in accompany of diverse financial and in-kind contributions being applied to development-related policy issues. This circumstance is summarized by CO13-1 who also points to the option of contributing through an experience-based, evolutionary process:

> *El conocimiento que hemos adquirido en estos temas ha sido más práctico. O sea no habemos aprendido a la hora que lo hemos estado haciendo. Digo que hemos preparado la gente con algunos cursos pero no es una formación de cada carrera sino que simple y sencillamente tratamos de aplicar un pensamiento estructurado y herramientas del negocio a problemas sociales [...]. Es poder ver las cosas desde otro enfoque. Es decir, para nosotros no hay cosas intocables que así se han hecho toda la vida y entonces no las cuestionamos. Esto creo que ha sido una ventaja. [...] nosotros aportamos dos cosas: El tema de recursos, o sea hay una aportación económica [...] nosotros aportamos este conocimiento de negocio, de cómo gestionar cosas, de cómo controlar la alianza. (CO13-1)*
>
> (The knowledge that we acquired in these topics has been more practical. That means that we did not learn shortly what we are doing. I say that we have prepared the people in some training courses, but it is not training for each person's career, but we simply apply a structured way of thinking and business tools to social problems. It is the ability to see things from another angle. This means that for us there are no intangible things that have been done this way for the whole life and that is why we do not question them. I believe that this has been an advantage. [...] we contribute two things: the matter of resources, which is an economic contribution [...] we contribute this business knowhow, of how to manage things, of how to control the aliance.)

The contributions made by private sector firms are not unconditional and are often subject to internal guidelines or external rules and laws. On the financial side, most companies link their funding to specific in-kind contributions or project activities, e.g. the purchase of technologies or organization of events. Donations are made rather small-scale while granted credits and loans are by nature bound to strict conditions. While some organizations like IO3 and IO5 bemoan the very small percentage, one-digit or even below one percent, to which amounts their income from private sector resources, some private sector firms like CO7 and CO14 clearly state that they do not finance public entities on principle:

> *I mean [CO14] has put financial resources in, you know, NGOs or global platforms that are very, very related with public entities, but at the end [CO14] is not putting money in any public entity. (CO14)*

In the context of discount prices for certain products, CO4 remarks that in some partnerships private sector firms are not even allowed to offer them below production costs, for instance, if the PPP results from a public tender. On the staff side, some firms seconded staff to public organizations for some time as a sort of in-kind contribution (e.g. CO4 and CO7).
An overview of private sector contributions is given in Table 46.

Kind of contribution	Contributions	References
Skills and competences	• Business process engineering/modeling • Communication and public relations competences • Conceptual knowledge • Creation of business plans • Knowledge in supply chain management • Methodical expertise • Product-related trainings • Provision of expertise to local stakeholders (e.g. engineering, health, transport) • Quality assessment • Technical consulting during conceptualization and implementation • Understanding of business processes	CO2, CO3, CO4, CO5, CO14, DC1, DC2, IO7
Financial	• Donations • Financial contributions for distribution and logistics • Financial contributions for meetings and workshops • Granting of credits/loans • Product-related funding • Project-related funding	CO1, CO3, CO6, CO7, CO9, CO10, IO7, IO8
In-kind	• Conference and workshop materials • Discount prices for certain products (e.g. for basic goods, health products) • Expenditures related to capacity-building and trainings • Labor time/staff provision • Travel expenditures	CO1, CO2, CO3, CO4, CO5, CO9, CO10, DC3, IO7

Table 46: Private sector contributions.

In summary, it matters that the different resources complement each other in a target-oriented manner, where both public and private sector bring in what they can afford and do best.

> *It can be in cash, it can be in-kind, it can be in expertise, it can just be in the processes the way things are done. So, just kind of complementing each other to catalyze the development. (IO5)*

In this context CO2 remarks that the complementarity of resources should go along with the need to involve all relevant stakeholders, those who formally establish partnerships, those who set the institutional environment, such as local and national governmental authorities, and those who shall benefit from the partnership. CO3, CO4 and CO10-1 add that private sector firms, which are actually competitors, still must strongly collaborate in PPPs for making the complementarity of resources really effective.

6.2.6 Partnership Risks

This chapter describes risk factors and how the interview partners assess the balance between benefits and risks in their partnerships. In this context, CO1 distinguishes between extrinsic project-associated risks and intrinsic project risks. Approaches to managing and controlling risks will be discussed in Chapter 6.6.4.5.2.

6.2.6.1 Extrinsic Risks

Extrinsinc project-associated risks are external influence factors that threaten or at least hamper the implementation of partnerships and that the partners involved have no or just very little influence on. The extrinsic risks are classified by their nature, economic, environmental, political, and social/societal. While **environmental risks** seem to play a minor role, the **economic risk** of insufficient demand for the PPP-related products or services concerns both the public and the private sector, as stated by CO5 and DC1. In general, not only **political risks**, such as civil wars, riots or other violent conflicts are triggers of major concerns of all actors, but also changes of government being accompanied by potentially changing institutional environments can obstruct partnership work. CO14 adds that for his company's PPP activities political risks including corruption are higher at country level than in the cooperation with IOs:

> *Grundsätzliche Risiken sind politische Risiken, d.h. man sucht sich ein Land aus oder identifiziert ein [...] Zielland. Dann kann es sein, dass man von dort grünes Licht von den wesentlichen Stakeholdern bekommt, aber dann Beteiligte wechseln und das Interesse an der Zusammenarbeit erlischt. (CO3)*
> (Fundamental risks are political risks. Thus, you select a country or identify a [...] target country. It can be that you receive the green light from the essential stakeholders but then parties concerned change and the interest in cooperation lapses.)

> *Und ich denke, die Risiken waren da, wirklich in der Lage zu sein, alle sozialen Umweltrisiken in Afrika, die es gibt, oder Impacts, die es gibt, abzuschätzen, ab-*

zuwägen und auch zu kontrollieren. Und ich glaube, da war von Anfang an klar, dass die [CO9] jetzt nicht die Kernkompetenz in diesem Bereich hat. (CO9-2)
(And I think there were risks to be really in a position to assess, weigh up and also to control all social environmental risks or impacts that exist in Africa. And I believe that it has been clear from the beginning that [CO9] does not have the core competence in this sector)

The risk-level. [...] for instance here in [target country], we partner with many government entities [...]. And those projects are very risky, because [...] the change of the government or the bureaucracy or the people from these government entities are doing something which is not correct to do. You know, we face different risks, when we work with public entities here in [target country], [remark: while] in the case of the international organization or global organization [...], we do not see relevant risks. (CO14)

On the **social/societal** side, the risk of reputational damage was stressed by the public sector in particular. This risk does not only result from potential failures or adverse impacts on environment and society caused by the PPP implementation, but seems to be much more driven by internal and external reservations towards public-private cooperation.

Da ist auch das [zuständige Ministerium] nach den Erfahrungen von [Name einer PPP], die einfach massiv von NGOs, [...] zu Recht oder zu Unrecht kritisiert wurden, unheimlich vorsichtig geworden. [...] es ist teilweise auch schon sehr viel Polemik dabei, aber das ist, was das [zuständige Ministerium] auch fürchtet. Also dass einfach in der [...] Öffentlichkeit steht: "Hier, Entwicklungshilfegelder für [Firmenname], unmöglich" oder sowas. Wobei das natürlich nicht stimmt, dass Gelder irgendwie an die gehen oder sowas. Aber so wird es dann im öffentlichen Interesse, im öffentlichen Bild wahrgenommen. (DC1)
(After the experiences from [PPP name] the [ministry in charge], which has been massively criticized by NGOs [...] rightly or wrongly, got more prudent. [...] there is partially a lot of polemics, which the [ministry in charge] also fears. That to the [...] public is simply communicated: "Here, development aid funding for [company's name], impossible!" or something like that. Although this is actually not true that money goes to them but that is how it will be perceived by the public.)

Das ist natürlich unsere Reputation, mit wem wir überhaupt von den Privaten oder dass wir überhaupt mit den Privaten zusammenarbeiten. Da gibt es unterschiedliche Meinungen von Kollegen, Kolleginnen, aber auch insgesamt mit Leuten, die in der Entwicklungszusammenarbeit (EZ) tätig sind. Die sagen ganz klar: "Unser Auftrag ist es eben, einen Mehrwert für die Menschen [...] zu gewährleisten oder auch gerade für Gruppen mit geringeren Chancen, und der Private macht doch eigentlich das Gegenteil. Und den dürfen wir nicht auch noch supporten." Also das ist so ein bisschen Schwarz-Weiß-Malerei. (DC3)
(Of course, this is our reputation with whom we actually collaborate from the privates or that we collaborate with them at all. There exist different opinions among colleagues but also in general from people who are working in development cooperation. They clearly say: "Our mission is to ensure value added for the people [...] or in particular for marginalized groups while the private does actually the opposite. And we should not support them." So, that is a kind of black-white thinking.)

In this context, CO14 points to the risk of failing in communicating properly to the public about the motivation of the PPP activities. This applies in particular if public and private sector directly collaborate in countries with low public trust in governmental authorities:

The first risk from my perspective is to communicate to the general public the opposite things that we want to communicate. And to be more specific, it is because [CO14] is running an initiative with social purposes and some public resources have been allocated to this initiative. People might think, especially when there is no public contest: "Why is [CO14] not participating in a public contest to get this project?" or "If the government has these public resources to reduce these poverty levels in this specific community, why did the government not grow up a public contest?" (CO14)

In summary, CO8 concludes that there are dozens of potential extrinsic risks which are finally hard to control and may need to be accepted as given. Table 47 gives an overview of them:

Es gibt tausende externe Einflüsse: Eine Firma kann pleitegehen. Es kann ein Bürgerkrieg ausbrechen. Es kann einfach die zuständige Person in Schwangerschaftsurlaub gehen. Es ist nicht alles so vorhersagbar. (CO8)
(There are thousands of external influences: A company can go bankrupt. Civil war can break out. The responsible person takes pregnancy leave. All this is not predictable.)

	Interview partners	CO1	CO3	CO4	CO5	CO6	CO7	CO8	CO9	CO10	CO12	CO14	DC1	DC3	IO1	IO2	IO3	IO4	IO7	Total
Extrinsic risk factors																				
Economic	Lack of demand (for product, service)				x								x	x						3
	Bankruptcy of partners							x												1
Environmental	Natural disasters								x											1
	PPP-related adverse impacts on the environment					x														1
Political	Civil war/ conflicts/ riots	x	x					x						x					x	5
	(Unexpected) change of goverment/ government is not in place		x									x		x					x	4
	Political risks in general					x				x	x									3
	Corruption											x								1
	Political sensitivity of the subject matter																		x	1
	Strikes	x																		1
Social/ societal	Reputational damage					x							x	x	x	x	x	x		7
	Staff shortage/ turnover (e.g. due to dismissal, pregnancy, termination); Loss of knowledge due to staff turnover		x				x												x	3
	Lack of awareness-raising/ Failure in communicating to the public											x	x							2

Table 47: Overview of extrinsic risks.

6.2.6.2 *Intrinsic Risks*

Intrinsic project risks are internal influence factors which threaten or at least hamper the implementation of partnerships, but for which the partners involved bear responsibility and which can be mitigated. The intrinsic risks are classified by their nature, internal management, interorganizational/interpersonal and other general factors. Like extrinsic political risks, **internal management risks** exist primarily due to uncertainties resulting from changes of decision-makers whose interests and objectives are often hard to anticipate. Staff shortage or turnover going hand in hand with the loss of knowledge is the only identified risk being extrinsic and intrinsic alike because it can be driven by the affected person himself (extrinsic) or result from management decisions (intrinsic).

> *Es gibt immer interne Managementrisiken, dass mal ein Vorgesetzter wechselt und entweder Budgetkürzungen vornehmen könnte oder vielleicht einfach die Zusammenarbeit in Frage stellt. Das sind Risiken, die sich bei uns jetzt nicht materialisiert haben, aber die generell nicht zu unterschätzen sind. Kernpersonal wechselt, ist ein Risiko, was sich auf [DCA Partner]-Seite leider öfter mal realisiert hat, dass auch Wissensträger [Anmerkung: verloren gehen], das ist halt oft sehr spezielles Wissen in solchen Partnerschaften, wenn man jetzt gemeinsam eine Strategie, ein Konzept, Milestones und einen Actionplan erarbeitet hat [...]. (CO3)*
>
> (There are always internal management risks that a supervisor changes and either prompts buget cuts or simply questions the cooperation in general. These are risks which did not materialize in our case, but which should generally not be underestimated. Core staff changes, that is a risk, which regrettably happened several times on the [DCA partner] side, that also knowledge carriers [remark: get lost], often there is very specific knowledge in such partnerships, if you have elaborated a joint strategy, a concept, milestones and an action plan [...].)

Bureaucracy and the lack of commitment, compliance and perseverance to undergo also difficult project phases and to accept uncertainties are seen as major risks burdening **interorganizational** but also **interpersonal relationships** between the actors involved. Moreover, a link is seen between commitment and staff turnover.

> *Wir haben [...] die letzten zwei Jahre extrem viele Wechsel gehabt und wir hatten damals klar ein Commitment, [...] auch ein CEO-Commitment und es ist halt immer sehr, sehr schwierig hier. Das will ich als internes Risiko eben sagen. Die Leute immer wieder von neuem zu überzeugen, wenn sie wieder gewechselt haben, dass das [Anmerkung: PPP] sicherlich nicht heute oder morgen den Umsatz umbringt, lieber Business-Unit CEO, sondern wahrscheinlich auch nicht übermorgen, aber es ist halt eine Investition in die Zukunft. (CO4)*
>
> (In the last two years [...] we have had quite a lot of changes and at that time we had a clear commitment, [...] also a CEO-commitment and it is actually always very very difficult here. I want this to be mentioned as internal risk. To convince the people again and again, if they have changed, that the [remark: PPP] will surely not generate the revenue today or tomorrow, dear business unit CEO, but probably the day after tomorrow either, but it is just an investment for the future.)

> *The key risk, as I said before, is the bureaucracy. You know that it costs money. Number two: [...]. The people change all the time, so it is not like a company where you have to talk about employee retention and you make sure that the*

partner sees the same employee for two years. They do not care. You come back, they have changed. (CO7)

Das zweite Risiko ist, was immer in einer großen Firma passiert, und auch überhaupt in großen Organisationen, man ist abhängig von Politik. Es gibt natürlich unfassbar viele vertragliche Verpflichtungen, aber letztlich, wenn ein Unternehmen sich entscheidet, es macht fortan etwas anderes, dann ist das ein Risiko für so ein Projekt. Und es kann so ein Projekt auch theoretisch beenden. Ist bei uns nicht passiert, aber theoretisch ist es ja möglich. (CO8)

(The second risk is, what always happens in a big company, but also in general in big organizations, that you depend on politics. Of course, there are incredibly numerous contractual obligations, but finally, if a company decides to do something else, then this is also a risk for such a project. And theoretically, it can terminate such a project. This did not happen in our case, but, indeed, it is theoretically possible.)

In the context of commitment, CO4 describes a situation where over a longer period he paved the way for a meeting between his CEO and high-level representatives from an IO while the latter decided shortly to send only low-level delegates. If the meeting had finally taken place, the CEO would probably have been very much upset. Thus, mutual commitment is essential for receiving management support. Other risks mentioned in this category are different kinds of corruption, the lack of confidentiality and loyalty as well as the lack of proper communication.

[...] Vertraulichkeit nicht gewahrt wird [...]. Und da sehe ich bei der [DCA Partner] eine höhere Loyalität gegenüber einem Unternehmen aus dem eigenen Staat, als es vielleicht bei einer Internationalen Organisation der Fall ist, wo man im Grunde ja diese loyale Rückbindung nicht in dem Maße hat, dass man sich immer zwei Mal im Leben begegnet. (CO3)

([...] confidentially is not maintained [...]. And there I see a higher loyalty from the [DCA partner] towards companies from the same country, compared to an international organization, where you basically do not have this kind of loyal reconnection that much, that you meet at least twice in life.)

The key risk, the main risk, is a problem of communication. The possibility of not understanding expectations [...]. (IO6)

Several interview partners like CO5 and DC5 point to the risk of selecting partners that finally do not prove to be suitable or to perform in the expected manner, which in turn diminishes the implementation quality of the PPP. Moreover, CO3 and CO4 stress the risk of conflicts of interests, even during project implementation, where other partners begin to pursue opportunistic interests. This applies in particular if competing companies are involved in the same partnership dealing with innovative technologies. CO4 calls this "Risiko der Konkurrenzbeteiligung" (risk of competitors' participation). Thus, CO3 appeals finally to consider partnerships as a kind of innovation process with a fair balance between shared benefits for all and the protection of the innovator's intellectual property. Table 48 gives an overview of the intrinsic risks.

	Interview partners	CO3	CO4	CO5	CO7	CO8	CO10	CO11	CO14	DC2	DC3	DC5	IO1	IO2	IO5	IO6	IO7	Total
Intrinsic risk factors																		
Internal management	Fundamental questioning of the partnership	x	x			x												3
	Staff shortage/ turnover (e.g. due to dismissal, pregnancy, termination); Loss of knowledge due to staff turnover	x			x												x	3
	Budget cuts	x																1
Interorganizational/ interpersonal	Bureaucracy				x			x	x									3
	Non-compliance/ breach of contract arrangements/ lack of perseverance		x			x				x								3
	Communication and mutual understanding											x				x		2
	Favoritism, nepotism and other undue activities and influences												x	x				2
	Confidentiality and loyality	x																1
General	Partner selection/ implementation quality		x	x		x									x			4
	Non-achievement of targets (common and individual)	x				x			x									3
	Budget overrun				x		x											2
	Conflict of interests	x	x															2
	Financial stability of the private sector partners										x						x	2
	Timing	x														x		2
	Innovation risks	x																1

Table 48: Overview of intrinsic risks.

6.2.6.3 Balance between Benefits and Risks

Before discussing the balance between benefits and risks of PPPs for development, it should be noted that the analysis of extrinsic and intrinsic risk factors has revealed manifold risk perceptions so that no clear definition of risk can be concluded from this. The vast majority of the interview partners assess their PPPs hitherto as well-balanced in terms of benefits and risks. However, there are also some critical voices or others that highlight some specifics of their assessment. On the IO side, the opinions range from very positive to very negative, thus from questioning PPPs at all to some kind of risk appetite if a partnership seems to be promising. It shows that experiences with PPPs and expectations of them vary quite a lot within the UN system.

> *[...] can you give me concrete results of joint partnerships where the private sector partnership had a concrete measurable impact? [...] there are a few such concrete exceptions, but most of corporate social responsibility partnerships are*

nice talk and window dressing. I don't say all but much of them are [...]. Which organization has more than five percent income from private sector? (IO3)

The benefits outweigh the risks. But still, there is a plan in place on how you are going to mitigate the risks and manage them in the process of implementing the partnership. (IO5)

So, we do also enter to rather high-risk partnerships when it makes sense, and the partnership does add value to the community or the development outcomes that we want to achieve. (IO7)

The DCA interview partners assess their previous PPP experiences unanimously positive. DC6 has not identified any risks so far and sees the main benefit of PPPs in enabling public and private sector to get together and to discuss issues of common interest. Given the fact that many DCAs deal with the PPPs on behalf of their national governments, the economic pressure to self-sustain is limited because continuous funding is assured, and business risks from failed PPPs are therefore low for DCAs, according to DC3. Insofar as input and output are shared in a balanced manner, DC1 considers PPPs as a risk-mitigating mechanism for both sides:

Und da sieht man eben auch ein bisschen den Charakter von dieser [Art der PPP]. Die [Anmerkung: privaten Firmen] würden es alleine eben nicht machen, weil das Risiko zu hoch ist [...]. Und man achtet auch von vorne herein darauf, [...] dass es ausgewogen ist. [...] wenn man jetzt ein Vorhaben hätte, wo es um [Fokus der PPP] geht, da würde das [zuständige Ministerium] ohnehin von vornherein sagen: "Lieber nicht, da ist uns das Risiko zu hoch." (DC1)
(And there you also see a little bit the character of these [PPP type]. The [remark: private firms] would not do it all alone because the risk is too high [...]. And from the beginning you pay attention to, [...] that it is balanced. [...] if you had a project what is about [PPP focus], the [ministry in charge] would say straight away: "Better not, the risk is too high.")

Private sector firms balance benefits and risks and align their engagement to the results of their risk assessments. However, they also voice that some risks simply have to be accepted, but careful partner selection can reduce them.

Und wenn Konkurrenten im Grunde da reinspielen, wird man sich überlegen, wo und in welchem Umfang man investiert, wenn das auch gegebenenfalls dann eigenes Risiko und ander' Leut's Chance ist sozusagen. (CO3)
(And if competitors are involved, you will think about where, and to which extent, you invest if your own risk potentially is other people's benefit.)

The biggest challenge with large organizations is the bureaucracy. So, you lose a lot of time and time is money. And the second thing, because of the bureaucracy you lose a lot money on administrative costs because, you know, this goes to this one and goes to that one and so on. These are the key challenges that you will have with the large organizations. On the other hand, you have a better chance to have a good collaboration in the sense that they are international, they are recognized, they know what they are doing and all that. So, this is the price you pay. [...] it is easier to work with them because they are big. And you do not have to worry about non-compliance and all those things, because they are an internationally recognized organization. (CO7)

In summary, awareness of risks, risk assessment and the early taking of measures to prevent and mitigate them enable stakeholders to design PPPs for the benefit of all.

6.3 Preparation and Implementation

This chapter describes the preparation and implementation of PPPs for development and considers their origins and previous experiences of the interview partners. It analyzes characteristics of the partner selection and the selection procedure itself as well as the planning quality of preparatory actions. A core element of this chapter is the analysis of typical project phases into which PPP implementation is divided. The present chapter serves for answering **research question 2.1**.

6.3.1 Partner Selection

This subchapter analyzes in the first place from whom and from where PPP initiatives emanate and to which extent previous experiences have already existed. Following this, the partner selection procedure including selection criteria will be presented.

6.3.1.1 Origins of PPP Initiatives

The majority of PPPs for development is created upon initiative of either public or private sector actors and is driven top-down, bottom-up, or result from existing networks. In some cases, third-party actors like NGOs or local communities approached firms seeking their skills and resources to address certain policy issues, as stated by DC1 and IO7 (Figure 38).

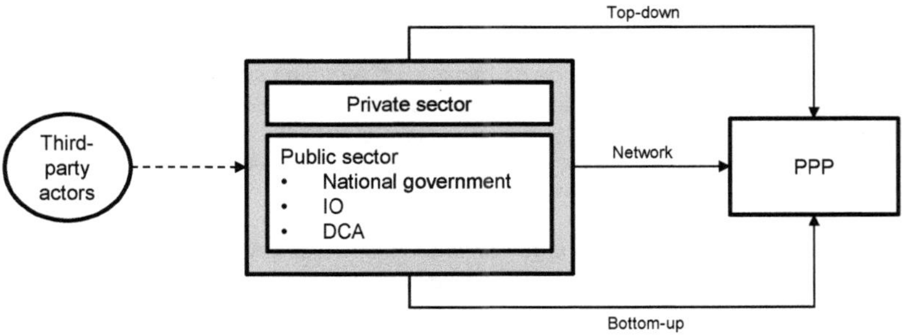

Figure 38: Origins and drivers of PPP initiatives.

Moreover, the origin of partnerships is closely related to the type of PPP. For example, strategic partnerships are more likely driven top-down by governments, but also by private sector heads, while other kinds of PPPs can also result from the initiative of individuals, thus being bottom-up. This experience has been made by CO7, CO10 and IO1 amongst others:

> *Strategic partnerships are often initiated with the help and policy support of the "central authority", while project partnerships usually evolve in a highly decentralised fashion. (IO1)*

Public sector-driven PPPs often result from public tenders by national governments which use supranational institutions (e.g. EU), IOs, or their DCAs to channel their willingness to establish partnerships, as reported by CO6 and DC4. In this context, DC3 remarks that they receive applications from mainly national firms with relevant core business and only few international ones. In addition, DC2 points to the fact that DCAs are often requested by governments to develop suitable measures for addressing certain policy issues. For instance, if they are charged to elaborate concepts for the promotion of renewable energies, the formation of PPPs is one option to fulfil this requirement. According to CO5, private sector firms doing applied research on technologies, which is relevant for development, also call for tenders, and seek public support for getting access to target groups in developing countries. Stakeholders from IOs underlined that national public actors and private firms jointly approached them while they themselves rarely take the initiative. By contrast, DC5 stresses that her local office enjoys autonomy to initiate certain PPP types proactively and independently from the head office.

> *We don't do that much of cold-calling. So, quite often it's the company who approaches us. [...] or that we identify kind of an area of mutual interest, which is the starting point. [...]. Lately, some governments who have more right-wing agenda and more kind of thinking that they need to advance their national private sector together with their development agenda. Some of them have approached us and asked for ideas how we could work to benefit also their national private sector. But, of course, it's always very clear that the number one priority is the development objectives and communities. [...] in some of the community development initiatives, it's actually been the community who comes to us with the private sector company and says that "We want your project management expertise and support in building the community capacity in managing those kinds of projects.". (IO7)*

Networks are another enabler of PPPs. Thus, IO7 stresses that they often met partnering firms already before, on other occasions, e.g. through their advocacy work for certain development issues, while others like CO5 systematically invest in networks, using them as vehicles to establish contacts with potential PPP partners:

> *Ab da war klar, dass man da auch jemanden in Brüssel braucht. Man braucht jemanden in Berlin. Man hat Beziehungen gepflegt und hat natürlich auch schon ein Netzwerk an Partnern gehabt und ausgebaut. Und dann kam man entweder selbst mit einer Idee auf und hat Partner dafür gesucht oder die Partner, die schon [CO5] kannten, oder auch neue Partner kamen auf uns zu und haben uns gebeten, unsere Expertise für dieses und jenes Projekt miteinzubringen. Das war also beidseitig entsprechend der Fall. (CO5)*
>
> (From then on, it has been clear that you also need somebody in Brussels. You need somebody in Berlin. You nurtured relationships and, of course, we already had a network of partners that we ex-

tended. And then, either you came up with an idea or you searched for a partner for that, or the partners, which [CO5] already knew, or also new partners, approached us and asked us to bring in our expertise for this or that project. This was both-way the case.)

In summary, PPPs emerge in different ways, leading to different actor constellations and face diverging institutional environments, which in turn depend also on what kind of public actors are involved. Thus, it depends on the actor constellation. Furthermore, it seems that both public and private sectors take initiative for joint PPPs alike.

6.3.1.2 Previous Experiences

Most public actors already had previous PPP experiences, often longstanding ones in different areas of activity. They practice knowledge management to some extent so that they can capitalize on previous experiences for future partnerships. In particular, DCAs seem to be very structured in this regard. Both DC1 and DC3 report from databases, which they maintain to store historic data about past partnerships, and they know which internal departments to contact if more detailed information is needed:

> *[...] wir haben ja ein Datensystem, was wir auch viel und gut nutzen, was uns natürlich dabei hilft, erstmal zu schauen, wenn der Erstkontakt besteht: Was gab es überhaupt schon alles mit diesem Partner? Das lässt man sich dann erstmal anzeigen, dass man da gut informiert ist und weiß, was da schon in der Vergangenheit gelaufen ist, sprich mit dieser Firma. (DC3)*
> ([...] we do have a data system which we use quite a lot, and which helps us to look, once first contact has been established: What did we already do together with this partner? You ask for an overview for demonstrating that you are well-informed and that you know what already happened with this company in the past.)

Also, DC4 and DC5 state that they build on such internal networks. The matter of networks is key in this context. Large corporations, such as CO1 and CO5, emphasize the longstanding and trustful relationships, which they built over years with several public actors through other activities in research or policy consultations before. This eases the initiation of new joint activities like PPPs for development. However, most private sector firms are rather at the beginning of their experiences with this kind of PPP. Some of them like CO3 or CO7 gained experiences from two or three pertinent partnerships while for CO4, CO10 or CO13-1 it is the first one:

> *Con organismos internacionales creo que sería la primera [nota: alianza] y más [...] es la primera donde está formalmente establecido una alianza y tiene una visión de largo plazo. (CO13-1)*
> (I believe it is the first [remark: partnership] with international organizations and moreover [...] it is the first one where a partnership is formally established and has a long-term vision.)

Others, like DC4 and CO14, report from failed PPPs or from others which finally did not happen. What they conclude is that previous experiences are helpful, whether they are positive or negative. At least, they help to define realistic expectations and objectives for future partnerships.

6.3.1.3 Characteristics and Selection Procedure

The partner selection can occur quite differently between public and private sector organizations but also among each of them. Still, their selection procedures show some commonalities so that the analysis of the partner selection at an aggregated level is appropriate (Figure 39).

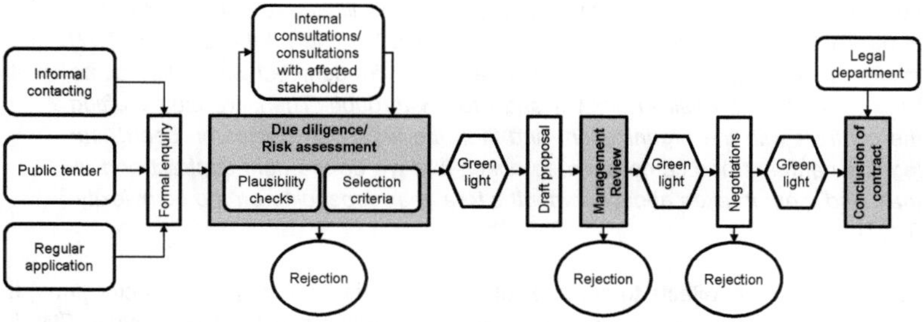

Figure 39: Partner selection procedure.

As shown in Chapter 6.3.1.1, PPPs can have diverse origins. However, whether they result from informal network-based consultations or formal applications and public tenders, all of them undergo a formal enquiry in the first place. Based on that, all interviewed stakeholders subject potential partnerships and the respective partners to a due diligence including risk assessment. For this purpose, they usually apply plausibility checks and predefined selection criteria.

> *Usually, we do also recommend that our offices would do at least exclusionary criteria of the risk assessment before they start discussing with the company. If they start negotiating with a company who has a subsidiary that manufactures controversial weapons, for example, it's a wasted discussion in that sense because we just don't go that way. So, to save everybody's time and efforts we usually do run that first stage of the risk assessment, even before entering into discussions, to also prevent any wasted time from either side in that sense. And if we do need to turn down any partners we try to do it quite politely. (IO7)*

Moreover, they often consult internal stakeholders, such as departments with technical or regional skills, who would be either affected by the PPP activities or possess pertinent experiences being helpful for making the partner selection. IOs sometimes go a step further and also include in their decision-making the views of the potential beneficiaries.

> *Sometimes, we do organize national or local level dialogues with the civil society organizations, before we enter into a partnership to start already with their consent in a way that it makes sense for the issue or that kind of a thing. In a way [remark: there are] also the stakeholder's response mechanisms, that we have in place, so that there is a transparent, standardized process of raising a concern if you have one. (IO7)*

Insofar as a PPP idea successfully passed the first assessment at operational level, a proposal is prepared and submitted to the respective management boards. Even in relatively decentralized IOs, the central management prefers to have the final say before a PPP is officially launched on the organization's official behalf, as stated by IO6. Given that the management boards of all partnering actors give their approval, the official negotiations begin and end with the conclusion of the contract or other kinds of legal arrangements, for which all parties usually involve their legal departments.

> *I will present that to the head of the CEO office who will then take it and present it to the CEO. And based on that, they can say "Yes" or "No". If the CEO of [CO7] thinks, "that is something [CO7] would be like to be identified with", they come back to me with a positive answer and I follow through. Then, we start drafting the contract with the organization, and then the legal part comes on board, our legal department and compliance, to check that we do the right contract and all that. And then, it takes about six months to a year depending on the complexity. (CO7)*

This statement by CO7 reflects to some extent the answers of other private sector firms. It shows that the partner selection procedure can be a lengthy and tedious process. Still, it should be noted that this procedure usually varies once a PPP is initiated and new partners or members want to join. In this case, a partnership's governing bodies in place take responsiblity for the partner selection.

> *Claro que existe un proceso en el cual dentro del [nombre del órgano rector] se presentan las peticiones para asociarse. Y el [nombre del órgano rector] en su conjunto delibera si es pertinente o no que esta persona o esta empresa pueda ser socio de [nombre de la PPP]. (DC6)*
>
> (Of course, there exists a process where the requests for membership are presented to the [governing body name]. And the whole [governing body name] deliberates whether it is pertinent or not that this person or that company can be partner of [PPP name]).

In summary, it seems that all the partner selection procedures are multi-stage processes sharing numerous commonalities across different PPP types. Thus, the process stages do not seem to really differ between different PPP types. Still, this chapter does not presume to be representative for any kind of partnership.

6.3.1.4 Selection Criteria

In the following will be described which criteria public and private actors apply to their partner selection. This analysis is distinguished from Chapter 6.2.2.3 in the sense that selection criteria are applied to concrete potential partners rather than to PPPs in general. Table 49 gives an overview of hard and soft selection criteria which have been mentioned by the private sector, DCAs and IOs. Hard selection criteria affect the fundamental interests and objectives of stakeholders and are sometimes even stipulated in some internal rules and guidelines or set by mandate. This usually makes them non-negotiable. Across sectors there is agreement that mutual goals must be compatible, that the risk assessment must be positive, and that each involved party makes a significant contribution. For example, several IOs strictly exclude private firms whose business areas are imcompatible with their mandate. In this vein, IOs mostly benchmark private sector partners against core minimum values and ethical standards. Still, unless it is not about companies from tobacco or arms industry, for instance, these criteria remain rather soft. In the context of compatibility, the private sector strongly emphasizes the need to match complementary resources. Others link approval to positive results from non-binding feasibility studies. However, even alledged trivial criteria take effect. While IO5 acknowledges that the company size often is an issue, thus preference is given to larger companies because small and medium-sized companies are harder to handle, CO3 points to the relevance of cultural distance, language, loyalty and reliability:

> *Und da sehe ich bei der [Name der DCA] eine höhere Loyalität gegenüber einem Unternehmen aus dem eigenen Staat, als es vielleicht bei einer internationalen Organisation der Fall ist, wo man im Grunde ja diese loyale Rückbindung nicht in dem Maße hat, dass man sich immer zweimal im Leben begegnet [...]. Wir waren uns ziemlich sicher, dass [Name der DCA] ein sehr verlässlicher Partner sein wird. Das hat auch kulturelle Gründe. Man spricht die gleiche Sprache. Es hat logistische Gründe. Man ist [XY] km voneinander entfernt, das heißt die Abstimmung funktioniert auch besser. (CO3)*
>
> (And there I see a higher loyality by the [DCA name] towards a company from the same country as compared to the case of an international organization, where you basically do not have this loyal relationship, that you always meet twice in a lifetime [...]. We have been pretty sure that [DCA name] will be a reliable partner. There are also cultural reasons. You speak the same language. There are logistical reasons. You are [XY] km away from each other. Thus, the coordination works better.)

However, partner selection is sometimes also quite pragmatic. DC6 explains that her PPP entity, established in the field of advocacy, is very open and little restricitve so that almost every public or private sector actor, whether big or small, can become partner insofar as his business is pertinent for addressing the underlying policy issue.

	Interview partners	Private	Public		Total number of times mentioned
			DCA	IO	
Selection criteria					
Hard	Goal alignment	x	x	x	3
	(Minimum) commercial or financial contribution	x	x	-	3
	Positive risk assessment	x	x	x	3
	Clear policy of non-engagement with certain actors (e.g. arms industry)	-	-	x	2
	Marketability	-	x	-	2
	Availability of infrastructure (e.g. access to banking and telecommunication)	-	x	-	1
	Clear commercial interest of the private sector partner	-	x		1
	Financial stability of the company (creditworthiness)	-	x	-	1
	Immediate compliance with self-commitment	-	x	-	1
	Limited number of PPPs per partner	-	x	-	1
	No business interests only	-	x	-	1
	No funding of third parties	x	-	-	1
	No support of individuals	x	-	-	1
	Political stability in target countries	-	x	-	1
	Profitability	x	-	-	1
	Public interest	-	x	-	1
Soft	Complementarity of resources/compatibility	x	-	-	4
	Alignment with core values and ethical minimum standards/ alignment with mandate	-	-	x	2
	Feasibility	x	x	-	2
	Company size	-	-	x	1
	Cultural distance	x	-	-	1
	Demonstration of serious interest in the subject matter	-	x	-	1
	Geographical distance	x	-	-	1
	Impact on beneficiaries	-	x	-	1
	Language	x	-	-	1
	Loyalty	x	-	-	1
	Political relevance of the subject matter	-	x	-	1
	Reliability	x	x	-	1

Table 49: Overview of partner selection criteria.

In summary, partner selection is a rather static procedure if hard criteria apply while it becomes quite dynamic and flexible if soft criteria prevail. Especially public actors seem to fall back primarily to hard selection criteria while the private sector is more open to using soft criteria in a pragmatic manner.

6.3.2 Project Phases

This chapter analyzes whether PPPs follow recognizable paths, and if so, in what typical phases they are structured. Moreover, it describes the reasons for existing structure patterns. Due to the diverse specifics of each analyzed PPP, and given that the present work is not a multiple case study, the analysis of project phases occurs at an aggregated level.

In Chapter 3.3.4 it has been shown that extant literature on PPPs broadly differentiates between an **exploratory** and an **execution period**, which are separated from each other by the conclusion of contract. Such a strict differentation was indeed noted for several PPPs of the present sample as well. There are five major phases, **preparation**, **initiation**, **design**, **implementation** and **conclusion**, which are divided over these two periods (Figure 40).

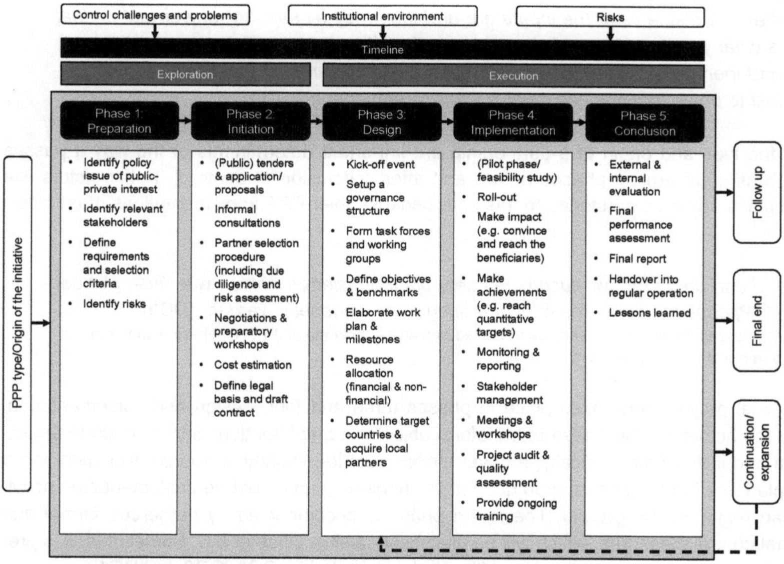

Figure 40: Typical project phases in PPPs for development.

Conclusion of contract in the present context means any kind of formalization of joint PPP activities, whether it is legally binding or not (Chapter 4.2.7). The contract-drafting and signing phase marks the transition from initiation to design where a PPP takes shape and becomes concrete. Usually, a smooth transition to the third phase tends to take place because many elements of the actual design phase use to be predetermined in phase one and phase two. Moreover, both public and private actors tend to broadly clarify their mutual objectives and interests before doing anything concrete. Driven by mandate or requirements from the national governments, DCAs and IOs often apply strict minimum funding requirements or selection criteria. Those should be clear prior to conclusion of contract because they are hard to negotiate at a later stage. Thus, the decisions made in phase one and phase two set directions to the design and implementation and determine the degrees of flexibility and freedom of the operative actors involved. However, this ultimately depends on the fundamental PPP approach. Little binding PPPs, based on looser contractual arrangements (e.g. MoUs) or long term-oriented partnerships (e.g. strategic alliances), leave more flexibility to designing the partnership and to making adjustments during implementation, or even to changing the partnership's focus, if desired by all parties (see previous statements by CO1 or CO3 in Chapter 6.1.5.3). By contrast, this flexibility is limited in the event of more hierarchic, fixed term PPPs (e.g. public tenders or supply contracts), which imply specific conditions being set by one party. This point was stressed by CO12 from his experiences as contractor in infrastructure PPPs:

> *[...] the [public partners] have been very specific with their designs. So, they are controlling those because they are afraid that a PPP-team will come in, did the [PPP focus] so much that it will not work [...]. And they literally go through, and they will define what the inputs are and then they all say: "Whatever that is, that is what you have to use." You can specify different inputs if you can justify them, and then go through a godly amount of quality insurance and quality testing [...], just to prove that you can meet a small design change. (CO12)*

Thus, the type and origin of a partnership are important determinants of the way it passes through different project phases before and after conclusion of contract. Public actors like DCAs place some cornerstones to this path because their PPP implementations often follow routines.

> *[...] und da haben wir auch einen sehr standardisierten Ablauf, wie diese [Art der PPP] geplant oder vorbereitet und dann auch umgesetzt werden. (DC3)*
> ([...] and there we have a very standardized procedure, how these [PPP type] are planned or prepared and then implemented.)

The actual project work takes place in phases three and four, design and implementation, where the actors involved need to transform objectives and intentions into a concrete project design and into action. Basically, a governance structure, staffing, resource allocation and a work plan need to be agreed upon quite at the beginning, even before implementation activities can begin on the ground. The fourth phase is accompanied by numerous formal and informal control measures, which will be discussed later in Chapter 6.6. Sometimes, it is preceded by a pilot phase including feasibility study, as stated by CO5, CO8 and DC4.
In the final fifth phase, executive internal stakeholders and external stakeholders like governmental institutions or financiers request some accountability from the operative actors. Thus, some evaluations and final reports are prepared. However, the final phase is less characterized by any control activities taken, but much more by what happens after the official end. Three options emerged during the analysis:

- Stakeholders undertake follow-up activities to examine the sustainability of the joint PPP activities,
- Stakeholders agree on a clear final end without any further engagement,
- Stakeholders decide to continue the PPP or to expand it.

The last alternative has been opted for quite often while it should be added that in these cases the PPPs were already set up from the outset in a way that facilitated this flexibility. The involved stakeholders either continue the PPP for an indefinite term, or the continuation is an actual expansion which was envisaged from the beginning. Two further options emerged from this:

- Extension of the same PPP activities in one country/region by geographic focus (roll out into one or more other countries/regions),
- Extension of PPP activities within one country/region by thematic focus.

The last alternative has been opted for if DCAs are involved, and those PPPs are split up into two or three major sections with separate budget and a duration of two to three years each. In this case, each of the major sections undergoes the phases three to five of the execution period while the preparatory and initial activities in phases one and two of the exploration period are only done once. Such an approach was chosen amongst others for the PPPs of CO3, CO5, CO10-1, DC1 and DC3:

> *Also das [Name der PPP] besteht aus drei Teilprojekten. Ein Projekt für [Zielland in Afrika], eins für [Zielland in Asien] und, wo wir aktiv sind, für [afrikanische Zielländer]. [...]. Weiterfinanzierung oder ein Weiterverlauf des Projekts ist in Diskussion, dass wir das tatsächlich nächstes Jahr nochmal verlängern. (CO10-1)*
> (Well, the [PPP name] is composed of three subprojects. One project for [target country in Africa], one in [target country in Asia] and [...], where we are active, for [African target countries]. [...]. Continued financing or a continuation of the project are being discussed so that we will extend it indeed once again next year.)

> *[CO13] ya metió [número] millones de dólares en la primera fase y estamos comprometiendo [número] más. En esta segunda fase ya estamos incorporando el tema [...] de viabilidad económica de alianzas. O sea ya estamos metiendo como un objetivo que se empieza vislumbrar cómo se va a sostener estas alianzas sin que estemos nosotros metiendo dinero. Pero en una primera etapa no está visualizada, nada más está visualizado [...] que probar el concepto. Y ahora que tenemos un concepto que es viable, que es atractivo, estamos buscando cómo a darle escala y cómo hacerlo entonces también económicamente viable y sostenible. (CO13-1)*
> [CO13] already put [number] million dollars in the first phase and we are committing to [number] more. In this second phase, we are already incorporating the issue of [...] financial viability of alliances. This means that we are setting as an objective that it shall become clear how these alliances will sustain without us putting money in. But this was not visualized in a first step, nothing else was visualized than proving the concept. And now we have a concept that is viable, which is attractive, we are seeking to scale it up and to make it financially viable and sustainable.)

The timeline, thus the duration of PPPs, is not only determined by contractual arrangements on the one side but also by external and internal influence factors on the other side. Part of this are **extrinsic and intrinsic risks** (Chapter 6.2.6) but also **control challenges and problems** as well as the **institutional environment**, which will be described in the Chapters 6.6.4 and 6.7. Keeping this in mind, several actors like CO1-1 underscore the importance of integrating time buffers and of remaining somehow flexible, despite defined deadlines:

> *Schon angestrebt, aber wenn gute Gründe dafür sprechen, dass Verzögerung eintritt, dann muss man die auch [...] entsprechend berücksichtigen. (CO1-1)*
> (It is intended, but if there are good reasons for delay, then you have to [...] consider them accordingly.)

> *Aber es ist ja nicht so, dass man zu einem Zeitpunkt X mit irgendwas fertig sein muss. Ich meine, ein definiertes Projektende bedeutet nicht, dass man im [MMYYYY] damit wirklich fertig sein muss. (CO1-2)*
> (But it is not such that you have to be done with something by a date X. I mean, a defined project end does not mean that you have to be done with that by [MMYYYY].)

In summary, a project phases and period structure does not always exist in PPPs for development but still seems to be quite common. Even the procedure tends to follow similar patterns and timelines although internal and external influence factors may cause uncertainties, delays or deviations from schedule. Moreover, project phases cannot not always clearly be distinguished from each other, in particular between initiation and design, because the type of the PPP and its origin play a pivotal role in this context.

6.3.3 Preparatory Actions and Planning Quality

The extents to which PPP stakeholders prepare for partnerships vary strongly between public and private sector organizations, but also among each of them because of the different previous PPP experiences (6.3.1.2). While newcomers like CO10 concede that they were not really prepared for partnership work, also more experienced actors like CO5, CO13-1 and DC1 were uncertain about how to prepare adequately because of the individuality of each partnership and the novelty of frequently associated actor constellations. CO13-1 describes his way of preparation as a kind of trial and error, while CO5 adds that his company did not offer special trainings for development cooperation. However, there is agreement among the interview partners that fundamental questions must be discussed very intensely at the beginning.

> *Ich glaube, man muss am Anfang sehr ausführlich und intensiv darüber sprechen, was am Ende dabei rauskommen soll. Was wollen wir erreichen? Wie wollen wir es erreichen? Mit welchen Mitteln wollen wir es erreichen? Wie begleiten wir das Projekt gemeinsam? Welche Rollen werden festgelegt? Wer ist noch daran beteiligt? (CO1-1)*
>
> (I believe that at the beginning you have to talk in much detail and intensely about what the outcome shall be. What do we want to achieve? How do we want to achieve it? By what means do we want to achieve it? How do we accompany the project jointly? Which roles are determined? Who else is participating?)

CO4 adds the consideration of the institutional environment in potential target countries including legislations and beneficial public financial support. This is why CO5, CO6, DC4 and DC5 recommend to carry out a sound analysis of the policy issue on scope, and to conduct baseline and feasibility studies before starting PPP projects. Despite any uncertainties DCAs seem to tackle partnerships in a quite structured manner. DC3 explains that the conception comprises an operation plan, which is subjected to critical reviews by colleagues and the management board to ensure quality, also called quality circle. The views and voices of beneficiaries and local stakeholders are considered as well. While IO5 adds that an operation plan *"[...] has to have the expected outputs in the whole results framework, which includes the indicators, the outputs, the activities, the budget, and that's monitored then."*, CO7 and CO13 strongly emphasize that the establishment of clear governance structures is fundamental for the initiation of partnerships. What matters more than the mere application of conceptual preparatory actions is the way they are executed. For example, some baseline studies and conceptions differ by the multidimensionality of their analysis. CO4 stresses the need to match the objectives, interests and strategies of the own planning with the benefits of targeted beneficiaries or of other affected stakeholders. DC5 explains that in the planning phase they did not only consider opinions of directly or indirectly affected stakeholders but also asked for presumably impartial views:

> *Nicht: Wie gehen wir die Länder an? Aber: Was bieten wir ihnen an? (CO4)*
> (Not: How do we tackle these countries? But: What can we offer them?)

> *Partimos desde cero, haciendo talleres con los actores para identificar si la creación de [nombre de la PPP] hace sentido o no. Entonces, hicimos un taller con el sector privado, con proveedores de equipo, con financiadores, con desarrolladores de proyectos de [enfoque del PPP]. [...]. Después hicimos un taller con el sector público, con las instituciones de gobierno relacionadas con la [enfoque del PPP]. [...]. Después hicimos otro con el sector académico y con las universidades, los bancos. (DC5)*
> (We started from zero, offering workshops with the actors to figure out whether the creation of [PPP name] makes sense or not. Hence, we organized a workshop with the private sector, with equipment providers, with financiers, with project developers of [PPP focus]. [...]. Then we held a workshop with the public sector, with governmental institutions related to the [PPP focus]. [...]. Then we offered another one with the academic sector and universities, the banks.

Moreover, DC5 states that they created some lines of action and work plans for each partner at an inaugural assembly. A way of institutionalizing the individual partnership preparation has been noted in the case of CO14:

> *We are just developing a tool to prepare ourselves for a new partnership. And this [...] tool is part of our newest strategy, which is on the developing stage. [...]. We have made efforts to try to compare some partnerships with other partnerships and try to [remark: quantify them in relative numbers and not monetarily], [...] whether it has a high value, a minimum value, or a low value in terms of reputation. So, when we see the different partnerships that we have within the reputation axis, we compare them between these three variables and we see that some of them are higher in value than others. (CO14)*

Consequences of insufficient preparation and planning were discussed by DC4 for an exemplary PPP project with multi-million USD budget where the DCA came on board during the implementation phase. The purpose was to improve the local people's access to a certain basic good in selected developing countries by providing affordable technologies. Thus, the assumption was that the targeted group of people could not afford existing commercial technologies, which proved to be wrong, according to DC4. Moreover, he bemoans the lack of diligence in the project proposal and shows astonishment that the project was finally approved despite inherent deficiencies:

> *Und da hat sich später herausgestellt, dass das einfach gar nicht der Fall ist. Das ist mal so eine Annahme gewesen, aber das hat nie jemand nachgeprüft, ob es denn wirklich daran liegt, dass die sich das nicht leisten können oder ob das ganz andere Gründe hat. Also es gab von vornherein schon verschiedene Design-Fehler [...]. Also diese dreiseitige Projektidee, die da mal ursprünglich eingereicht war, die hat natürlich nicht nur so ihre Mängel gehabt, was gewisse Grundannahmen anging, sondern die war eben auch überhaupt nicht ausgereift*

> *[...]. Ich meine, man kann natürlich ein [Betrag] Millionen-Projekt nicht auf drei Seiten planen. (DC4)*
>
> (And later it turned out that this is basically not the case. That has just been an assumption, but nobody has ever verified whether this is due to the fact that they cannot afford it or whether there are any other reasons. Thus, from the beginning, different design errors were made [...]. Well, this three-sided project idea, which had actually been submitted, not only had some deficiencies regarding some basic assumptions, but was basically not mature [...]. I mean, you cannot plan a [amount] multi-million project on three pages.)

In summary, all interview partners agree that appropriate preparation and planning are pivotal for the actual implementation and for partnerships in general. From their comments it can be concluded that the related activities extend over the phases one to three, which can last from a few months up to more than one year.

6.4 Budget and Resource Planning

This chapter describes various aspects of budget and resource planning in PPPs for development. It begins with an analysis of financing mechanisms and equity ownership and continues with different characteristics of resource planning. Moreover, it links the empirical observations from the interviews to the theoretically derived assumptions of the TCE (Chapter 4.2). Finally, it displays major cost factors in PPPs for development including potential for more efficient use of resources. All these elements serve the answering of **research question 2.1**.

6.4.1 Financing Mechanisms and Equity Ownership Structure

For PPPs exist diverse financing approaches that depend particularly on the underlying PPP type and vary by the concrete financial or non-financial contribution made by the involved stakeholders. In turn, this depends on the funding of the stakeholders as such. Directly involved private and public actors bear the main burden of the necessary resources, but third-party indirect financiers often play an important role. National governments do not fund only IOs on a regular basis but are also the main financiers and clients of DCAs. In specific partnerships, such as public tender-based research PPPs, funds occasionally flow to private sector firms as well, as stated by CO5. DC1 adds that NGOs and foundations often finance PPPs directly, or occasionally indirectly through DCAs. She adds that in the case of the NGOs the financing is provided mostly at local level and in the form of in-kind contribution. Thus, staff from the local NGOs assumes specific subtasks of the PPP. As stated in Chapters 6.2.2.3 and 6.3.1.4, fair financial burden-sharing is a fundamental requirement of PPPs and therefore influences the selection of concrete partners. Thus, in most PPPs public and private actors make contributions in equal shares, a fact, which is particularly requested by the public sector, as stated by DC1, DC3, and CO10-1 amongst others:

> *[...] der Kern ist [zuständiges Ministerium]-Finanzierung, und die wird eben zu mindestens 50% vom Beitrag von den privaten Unternehmen komplettiert, in-kind oder in cash. Das heißt, der Hauptbeitrag kommt eigentlich sowohl vom [zustän-*

> *digen Ministerium] als auch von den privaten Partnern. Und dann haben wir jetzt zwei Stiftungen mit in der Finanzierung [...]. (DC1)*
> ([...] the core is [ministry in charge] financing and this is matched by at least 50% from the private companies, either in-kind or in cash. This means that the actual main contribution comes from both the [ministry in charge] and also from the private partners. And now we also have two foundations involved in the financing [...].)

> *Wenn [DCA Partner] quasi 50 % liefert, müssen wir als private Partner die anderen 50 % liefern. Natürlich dann aufgeteilt zwischen allen Partnern. (CO10-1)*
> (If [DCA partner] actually provides 50%, we as private partners have to provide the remaining 50%. Of course, split up between all partners).

On an occasional basis, foundations, IOs and NGOs obtain resources from the private sector for specific thematic purposes or projects. Still, this does not seem to apply for actual PPPs where companies are really engaged in.

> *[...] our current income from private sector is quite minimal. So, mostly we are getting income from the Member States but we are a kind of working at expanding this. (IO5)*

Moreover, it should be noted that in the present context foundations are entities that are independent from companies. Some of the interviewed private sector firms have anchored their PPP activities in their own foundations. By nature, both DCAs and IOs receive the funding of their administration and business activities mainly from taxpayers while the private sector finances its PPP activities from regular business cash flows. An overview of the diverse finance structures of PPPs for development is given in Figure 41.

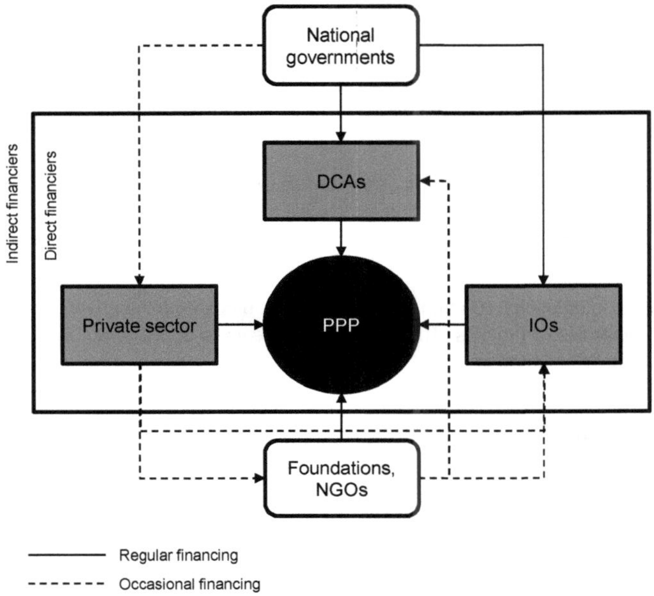

Figure 41: Finance structures of PPPs for development.

The financing mechanisms vary by the origin of the funding. One can distinguish between funds being directly allocated to a specific PPP and those serving other purposes as well (Table 50 and Table 51).

Most of the analyzed PPPs rely on co-financing mechanisms where all partners contribute a certain amount of resources, either in cash or in-kind. Thus, the resources are matched and joint ownership is taken. Others, like CO2 and IO6, make financial commitments but maintain separate equity ownership structures in the sense that each partner bears the costs for the individual PPP activities. This results from risk reduction considerations and from the rejection of the idea of an integrated governance structure. CO8, DC5 and DC6 told that in their partnerships the stakeholders pay a kind of membership fee which ranges from four-digit to six-digit US-Dollar amounts. Although it seems to be rather common that all partners pay the same fee, one interviewee explained that in his partnerships a distinction was made between core and regular partners, and the former were the main financiers being endowed with more decision rights.

Financing mechanism	Reference
Co-financing (each partner contributes X% of the overall budget/necessary resources (cash or in-kind)	*[...] wenn man Arbeitskraft teilt, in-kind Contributions, dass man sagt: "Okay, die [DCA Partner] stellt einen Ingenieur. Die [CO5] stellt einen Ingenieur." (CO5)* ([...] if you share labor force, in-kind contributions, that you say: "Okay, the [DCA partner] provides an engineer. The [CO5] provides an engineer.")

Financing mechanism	Reference
Independent financing of the own activities by each partner	*Wir übernehmen alle Kosten, die seitens [CO2] entstehen. [UN-Organisation] übernimmt die Kosten, die durch die Aufgaben seitens der [UN-Organisation] entstehen. [UN-Organisation] wird im Rahmen von [Name der PPP] vom [zuständigen Ministerium] finanziell gefördert. (CO2)* (We assume all costs that incur on the part of [CO2]. [UN organization] assumes the costs that incur by the activities of the [UN organization]. [UN organization] is financially promoted by the [ministry in charge] in the context of the [PPP name].) *We financed projects but never send [...] our personnel. Well, some companies they do that [...] but [...] it would be a little bit risky in my opinion because usually business does business. (IO6)*
Membership fee (fixed)	*Y ellos pagan una cuota para pertenecer a [nombre de la PPP]. Cada año se fija una cuota, ellos pagan una cuota y [nombre de la PPP] les brinda diferentes servicios, como talleres, información. (DC5)* (And they pay a fee for belongig to [PPP name]. Every year, there is fixed a fee, they pay a fee and [PPP name] provides them different services, such as workshops, information.)
Membership fee (sales-oriented)	*[...] umsatzorientierte Beitragsstaffel. Dass natürlich auch die ganz Großen mehr zahlen als die ganz Kleinen, aber es zahlt jetzt jeder [...]. (DC2)* ([...] sales-oriented contribution scale. Of course, the very big ones pay more than the very small ones but now everybody pays [...].)

Table 50: Direct financial allocations.

On the other hand, the sample comprises several examples of indirect financial allocation, such as credits/loans, ODA, public (research) funds and self-financing mechanisms. CO6 reports on a partnership for which a separate legal entity was created and endowed with a joint loan by the partners. The partnership entity generates continuous income, which finances the project corporation and the loan repayment. Thus, CO6 describes a PPP that is actually a mix of loan-based co-financing and self-financing while the latter is an uncertain mechanism. Like CO6, CO13 pursues a comparable approach, with the difference that the project initiator did not have to contribute almost a third of the total funding. Of course, the equity ownership structure complies with the funding proportions in this case.

Financing mechanism	Reference
Credits/loans	*Und dann wurde eine Projektgesellschaft gegründet. Diese Projektgesellschaft wurde mit einem Darlehen der beteiligten Unternehmen ausgestattet. (CO6)* (And then, a project corporation was founded. This project corporation was provided with a loan from the participating companies.)
ODA	*The contribution of the private sector to the developing countries, currently, is related to the contribution of ODA. ODA is*

Financing mechanism	Reference
	really insignificant because when you compare that to what is needed then you really have to start thinking. (IO5)
Public (research) funds	*[...] öffentlich geförderte Projekte waren, meistens aus Forschungstöpfen heraus [...]. (CO5)* ([...] public funded projects were, mostly by research funds [...].
Self-financing	*[...] distintas lineas de ingreso [...] como vincular las tarifas del operador de [enfoque del PPP] para que una fracción de esto vaya al [nombre de la PPP]. Entonces tienen un mecanismo recurrente. (CO13-2)* ([...] different income streams [...] like linking the tariffs of the [PPP focus] supplier so that a fraction of that goes to the [PPP name]. Thus, there is a recurring mechanism.)

Table 51: Indirect financial allocations.

The aforementioned approaches illustrate numerous possible financing mechanisms of PPPs. All of them have in common that no indefinite funding is intended but that both the public and the private sector consider their contributions as start-up financing. They emphasize that PPPs with indefinite duration need to be sustainably financed in the long run. The self-financing mechanisms, as described by CO6 and CO13, form possible options, but they basically build on existing business models with large-scale production and are therefore not transferable to all kinds of partnerships. That is why numerous interview partners underlined that the design of PPPs must rely on a business case.

6.4.2 Characteristics of Resource Planning

This chapter analyzes resource planning and approval procedures, their elements and specifics, as well as the demonstrated level of diligence and quality in doing that. In general, the procedures are strongly influenced by the financing mechanisms and by the equity ownership structure. For instance, in co-financed or membership fee-based partnerships, tight interorganizational resource planning and approval procedures are in place, besides the respective intraorganizational ones, while in independently financed PPPs these procedures seem to be followed rather isolated from each other and with fewer alignment. Two major approaches have been gathered from the interviews, which can be defined as upstream and downstream budget allocation (Figure 42).

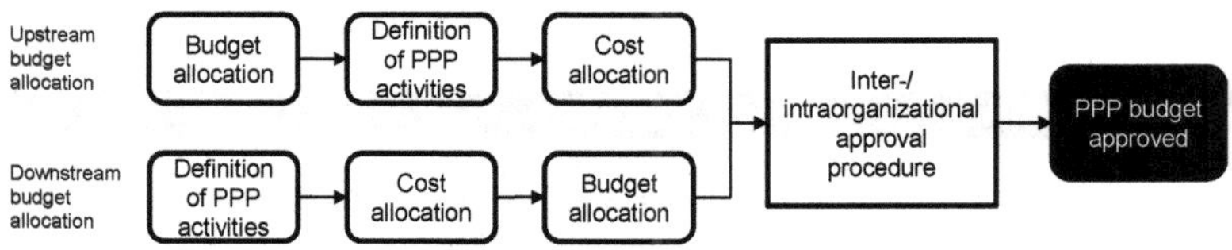

Figure 42: Resource planning and approval procedure.

In the first case, governmental entities aim to address a certain policy issue and allocate a certain budget for doing pertinent development activities linked to that, such as PPPs. Thus, the government engages a DCA or an IO to initiate a project and to jointly implement that with suitable private partners and other third-party actors.

> *Es gibt [...] andere Verfahren, wo [...] gerade bei diesen Partnerschaften [...] öffentliche Auftraggeber [...] häufiger kommen und sagen: "Mhm, wir haben ein Budget von Summe X für einen Zeitraum Y. Was könnt ihr denn mit diesem Geld in diesem Zeitraum zu diesem Thema machen?" Und dann ist es uns sozusagen überlassen, das Ganze zu planen und dann zu gucken, wenn ich [X] Millionen habe, was kann ich mit diesen [X] Millionen machen. So, und dann gibt es auch hier in der [DC2] nicht das eine Antragsverfahren oder nicht das eine Verfahren, wie wir planen. Es hängt am Ende dann immer von den Auftraggebern ab [...]. (DC2)*
>
> (There are [...] other procedures where [...] especially in these partnerships [...] public clients [...] often come and say: "Mhm, wir have a budget of amount X for a period Y. What can you do with this money in this period of time for that topic?" And then it is basically left to us to plan the whole thing and to look what I can do with these [X] million, if I have [X] million. Thus, there is no single application process or procedure for how we do the planning. At the end, it depends always on the clients [...].)

> *[...] [UN-Organisation] als UN-Institution bei sowas [...] immer in erster Reihe steht, wenn solche Mittel vergeben werden. [...] alle Regierungen der Welt sind ja über verschiedene Ministerien zum Teil auch gezwungen, [...] an UN-Institutionen Mittel zu vergeben. (DC4)*
>
> ([...] [UN organization] as UN institution is [...] always at the forefront when such resources are allocated. [...] through different ministries all governments are partially obliged [...] to allocate resources to UN institutions.)

Thus, the budget allocation takes place before the definition and planning of concrete PPP activities and allocation of costs. The second case occurs reversely and describes the downstream budget allocation procedure where the budget is calculated on the basis of the costs for defined PPP activities. In both scenarios, the approval procedure can occur within and/or between organizations. Still, in the first case, the government seems to be in a stronger position because the public side enters into negotiations with a usually non-negotiable budget and with relatively strict PPP requirements. Given an even balance between public and private contributions, both sides have to tailor their activities to a predetermined budget. In the second case, activities have to be clearly defined and costs be reasonably broken down because each party needs to receive internal approval at the end. Thus, budget negotiations can be tough. In any case, experienced staff like project managers and operational team members should be consulted for making realistic assessments and plannings.

> *[Anmerkung: Die Mitglieder] sind mit den Kostenpositionen [Anmerkung: zum Vorstand] hingegangen, haben gesagt: "Das kostet round about [X] Millionen Euro für drei Jahre [...]." So, dann gibt es natürlich großes Heulen und Zähne klappern. "Viel zu teuer und öh." Und dann fängt man eben an, ja, letztlich in einem Aushandlungsprozess das Ganze zu verhandeln, wo wir dann aber auch am Ende relativ schnell zu einem Ergebnis gekommen sind, weil wir [...] nachweisen konnten, dass die Kosten am Ende wirtschaftlich sind. Da stehen jetzt nicht irgendwelche Luftbuchungen für goldene Wasserhähne, First-Class Flüge, [...], sondern was wirklich sehr detailliert dann auch nachweisbar war. So, und dann*

sind wir am Ende zu einem Ergebnis gekommen, und dann haben wir gesagt: "So, das ist das Budget. Das sind die Aufgaben." (DC2)

([Remark: The members] we went with the cost items [remark: to the governance board] and said: "That costs round about [X] million euros for three years [...]." So, then there is a lot of screaming and chattering of teeth. "Way too expensive and öh." And then you simply start negotiating the whole thing, but where we got results quickly at the end because we [...] could demonstrate that the costs are efficient at the end. There are not any creative cost allocations for golden water taps, first class flights, [...], but it was really very detailed and also provable. Thus, we then obtained result and said: "So, this is the budget. That are the tasks.")

Usually, it's the project manager or the project team who basically goes through the different designs [...] a draft plan for the project, looks at what information is already there. If some needs assessments are needed? What are the objectives? What could be the targets? Those kinds of things, and it's really just a team effort to put a price tag on all those different elements. (IO7)

Private sector firms often calculate a business case in this context, as underlined by CO5. DC3 adds that even in a common budget the separation between public and private money must remain clear. In no case, budget and resource planning will be fully integrated because all project activities have cost implications so that at one point internal budget managers from each party have to give their approval. Some actors conduct continuous approval processes before releasing funds:

So what happens within [CO7]? You have someone who looks at the money. But this is the person who gets the bills from the organization. And they will then check with the programme manager inhouse to make sure that the milestones have been met. So, we do not release the funds until we know that, whatever we had committed, the partner is going to [remark: do what he is supposed to do]. Then we release the money. (CO7)

In this context, CO14 emphasizes that the rigour of approval processes increases with the requested budget amount. Moreover, CO10 underlines the little flexibility to request additional resources and therefore to adjust the budget once it is approved because the budget allocation to one project is aligned with those for numerous other projects. Factors that may influence the budgeting positively are price or demand guarantees while uncertainty over overall funding, such as in the case of some IOs, or over the number of members who finally join in can hamper the approval procedures.

Organisationen kommen häufig auf uns zu: "Könnt ihr uns das nicht preiswerter anbieten?", wenn es um Produkte geht. Dann habe ich immer gesagt: "Ja, können wir, wenn Ihr uns eine Garantie dafür gebt, wieviel Ihr pro Jahr abnehmt." Dann können wir ganz anders planen. (CO1-1)

(When it is about products, organizations often approach us: "Could you not offer that cheaper?". Then I always said: "Yes, we can, but only if you give us a guarantee of how much you demand annually." Then we can plan quite differently.)

[...] budget reductions and related financial constraints the UN organizations are facing, and which induce them to rely increasingly on resource mobilisation, extra-budgetary funding as well as non-staff personnel and related contractual arrangements for the discharge of organizational mandated work and core activities. (IO1)

With respect to the example by DC4 in terms of insufficient planning quality, which was quoted already in Chapter 6.3.3, he bemoans moreover the lack of sound needs assessment so that financing mechanism and resource allocation are not properly linked to the PPP's purpose.

> *[...] man hat am Anfang diese Zahl [XY] in den Raum geworfen, überhaupt keine Vorstellung gehabt, welches Förderinstrument überhaupt genutzt werden soll. [...] diese Ziele [...] waren völlig aus der Luft gegriffen und haben jeglicher Logik oder jeglicher Voruntersuchung entbehrt. (DC4)*
> ([...] at the outset, they presented this figure [XY], did not have any idea about which funding instrument should actually be used. [...] these targets [...] were simply plucked out of thin air and there was absolutely no logic or preliminary investigation.)

In summary, it seems that the budget planning and approval in PPPs for development is done duly in most cases and at the operative level, but the overall quality tends to depend very much on the financier's and management's diligence. DC2 reports that the approvers sometimes examine even small amounts and question every cost item, while others care about large positions only and are merely interested in the final sum. CO13 adds that financial viabiltiy became an explicit objective of their partnership. Moreover, they benchmark the draft budget against its expected impact upon the targeted beneficiaries. Hence, they try to allocate the total budget in a way that every activity or cost item receives the funding it needs for being implemented effectively.

6.4.3 Transaction Characteristics

While uncertainty is a transaction characteristic being addressed across different chapters in the results part, the behavioral characteristics will be touched upon in the governance Chapter 6.5. Hence, this chapter describes the presence of asset specificity and frequency of resource provision in PPPs.

6.4.3.1 Specificity of Resources

Specificity of resources basically means that the PPP partners customize the resources they contribute to specific needs of the joint partnership. Many of them do that while others try to build on their existing business or to generate synergy effects by experiences from, or investments in, ongoing or previous partnerships. The main motivation to tailor the amount, design and type of resources to certain PPPs basically results from the fact that the individual requirements of the partnership itself and/or the institutional environment leave no other option. This applies for public and private sector partners alike. Even actors, such as DCAs, which run by mandate numerous projects at the same time, are not prepared for tackling any kind of policy issue anywhere in the world at all times and struggle with standardizing their project management approaches. In this context, DC5 adds that performance indicators and benchmarks are used to be determined individually for every partnership.

> *Also wir haben in keinem der [Art der PPP] die [Produkte], wie sie bereits existieren, eins zu eins angewandt. Das wäre letztendlich ein klassischer Vertriebspro-*

zess gewesen. Wir haben immer was oben drauf gebastelt. Entweder [...] ein existierendes [Produkt] erweitert oder auf der grünen Wiese oft auch neue Sachen entwickelt [...]. (CO5)

(Well, in none of the [PPP type] we have applied the [products] as they already exist. At the end, this would have been a typical distribution process. We always put something on top. Either [...] enhancing an existing [product] but often also developing new things on the greenfield.)

[...] es gibt eben verschiedene Tools, derer man sich bedienen kann. Und für manche stehen auch [...] Excel-Vorlagen zur Verfügung. Ich habe ehrlich gesagt noch nie Vorlagen benutzt. Also am Ende sagt man dann doch meistens: "Nö, wir machen unser eigenes." (DC1)

([...] there are different tools we can use. And for some of them there are also [...] Excel templates available. Honestly, I have never used these templates. Because at the end you say most often: "No, we do our own one.")

[...] weil auch da jedes Projekt einfach anders ist. Wir müssen es [...] deswegen alleine anders aufziehen, weil wir pro Land andere Schwerpunkte haben und jeweils andere Strukturen haben. (DC3)

([...] because every project is basically different. Basically, we have to set it up [...] differently because we have different foci and different structures per country.)

So, somebody doesn't design for you externally [...] the project management. It's in partnership. The company and you need to work together because it's a joint project. (IO5)

In the context of external influence factors, CO5 adds that the contractual arrangements often do not allow private sector firms to build completely on existing technologies but require doing something from the scratch. Furthermore, CO4 remarks that diverging norms and standards for certain technologies in different markets and also different cultural aspects, such as positive and negative associations with certain colours, make customization unavoidable. However, some partnerships intend to harmonize pertinent norms and standards across national borders and therefore to decrease the degree of product standardization. This procedure can contribute to reducing TC and to improving resource efficiency. Moreover, CO3 and CO10-1 underline that a main challenge private firms are facing lies in the customization of regular high-priced products to the needs of PPPs for development, for which only a small fraction of the actual price can be charged, while at the end, a positive business case shall still be reached. To facilitate different private firms to partner with DCAs and IOs, some of them have set up specialized programmes designed for bigger and smaller companies from different sectors and going along with varying requirements.

What we do is that we have a range of possible programmes that we can propose to the partners that approach us. (IO6)

[...] different UN agencies, some banks, other entities who conduct rather rigorous due-diligence procedures. Of course, we apply it a little bit on a case-by-case basis. We cannot expect a small national company to have all the management systems in place as has a large multinational from a high-risk sector. (IO7)

In summary, the overall level of asset specificity seems to be high in PPPs for development. It is the higher the more partners pool and integrate their resources, and the lower the less synergy effects can be generated and results be used for other purposes. For example, the asset specificity is high if staff members dedicate full-time to a partnership and acquire specific knowledge while it is lower if the PPP work amounts only to a few hours per week.

6.4.3.2 Resource Provision Process

Frequency is a critical dimension of the TCE (Chapter 4.2.4) and is a vehicle to characterize resource provision processes in the context of PPPs. It forms an indicator of their size and complexity in terms of financial and geographic scope and number of partners. One aspect is availability. The more microcredits are granted, the more trainings are given to local stakeholders, or the higher the number of countries in which partnership activities have been rolled out the higher is the frequency of resource provision in PPPs. Higher frequency often implies large scale partnerships being implemented in several countries by numerous stakeholders involved and tends to be accompanied by a higher level of control complexity and need for commitment.

> *Este modelo es muy intensivo, es muy hands-on, o sea necesitas estar allí, poder articular los actores [...]. Lo hemos replicado [número de dos cifras] veces en la región [...] y hay aparte [número de dos cifras] fondos más que están en una etapa de diseño. (CO13-1)*
>
> (This model is very intensive. It is very hands-on. This means that you need to be there and to be able to coordinate the actors [...]. We replicated this a [two-digit number] of times in the region [...], and besides there is a [two-digit number] of more funds, which are in the design phase.)

Moreover, one can differentiate between internal and external resource provision. Any activities that are done by the involved partners themselves are part of the internal resource provision, while the external one encompasses any goods or services brought in by contracted third-party actors or not involved internal departments. Often they come into play in the implementation phase where they assume some project activities, such as training measures for local stakeholders or internal audit and monitoring tasks. But their competencies are also demanded in the preparation and design phase when experts assess the project feasibility, or at the end when impartial evaluators prepare an indepedent final report.

> *Und die Umsetzung erfolgt dann durch lokale NGOs, weil da kein [DC1] Personal hinreist. (DC1)*
>
> (And the implementation is done by local NGOs, no [DC1] personnel will travel there.)

> *So, sometimes it's done by the project manager, sometimes by a hired external consultancy [...] or sometimes it's done by that internal monitoring and evaluation unit. And then [...] control mechanisms, we have internal audits as well as external audits, too, sometimes. But the internal audits, they also are in place to make sure that the projects are implemented according to the rules and guidelines that we have [...]. So, in some national projects, we do have NGOs as implementing partners or certain components as well. (IO7)*

Sometimes, external resources are also used to relieve the project partners from tedious operational burdens, such as documentation work, who can then focus on management activities instead.

> *[...] hier arbeitet auch ein Berater, [...] der wird [...] immer für eine gewisse Zeit eingekauft, der viel schreibt, und wir geben halt auch unseren Input, was er schreiben soll bzw. wir korrigieren das dann eben. (CO4)*
> *([...] here is also working a consultant, [...] who is [...] always contracted for some time, who writes a lot, and we just give our input for what he is supposed to write, and we correct that, respectively.)*

> *Man kann diese Expertise auch outsourcen und [...] einen Gutachter beauftragen und eher das Management übernehmen. (DC3)*
> (You can also outsource this expertise and [...] hire an expert and instead assume more management tasks.)

In summary, it seems that many PPPs for development pursue a combined approach of internal and external resource provision for which frequency is a relevant indicator. External resources are used amongst others to promote compliant and effective MC processes and to therefore meet requirements of transparency and accountability.

6.4.4 Resource Efficiency

While the previous subchapters analyzed fundamental characteristics and procedural elements of budget and resource planning, this chapter complements these analyses by an exploration of the general understanding and perception of resource efficiency in the context of PPPs and by the identification of material cost factors. Furthermore, it reveals some reasons of inefficiencies and mentions proposals on cost reductions. Before being asked for cost factors and potential for cost reduction, the interview partners were consulted on their overall assessment of resource efficiency. While two interviewees answered that their engagement is cost-effective because of little invested resources, CO8 underlines that for him efficiency and effectiveness mean the achieving of agreed goals by the available resources. Thus, the understanding of resource efficiency differs, but also its perceptions.

> *So, I don't think issues of efficiency are such a problem. (IO5)*

> *Well, I would be unrealistic if I told you NO. Yes, I experienced [...] that [remark: resource inefficiency] at several levels but [...] in these PPPs [...]. It happens and it is there. (IO6)*

Moreover, the assessment of resource efficiency seems to pose challenges, even to larger organizations despite some first steps towards counteractions.

> *[...] this dashboard that we developed to measure what is the benefit from one partner and other partners, is a further step to try to measure that benefit. And eventually, I think we are missing to also compare the costs-benefits between the different partnerships. (CO14)*

Yeah, we really haven't done a comprehensive mapping of all the lessons learned from the different challenges or so [...]. I can't really give you a good scientific response on that one and on the main cost factors. It depends so much on the type of a project. (IO7)

In this context, CO13-2 remarks that at the beginning a partnership costs quite a lot, but once a suitable partnership model is found and configurated the resource efficiency starts improving. Both CO3 and DC2 state that the private sector's profit orientation leads to a more efficient use of resources in the sense that private actors questioned in detail every cost item somewhat stronger than the public sector and assessed for any type of activity whether it is needed or not, whether it contributes to the goal attainment or not. The reasons for lack of efficiency are manifold, but two major examples for that will be given here. In terms of resource allocation, there exist different ideas of how much resources are needed to implement certain activities, a fact, which can possibly be explained by the organizational differences of public and private sector. DC2 gives a pertinent example of the organization of major PPP-related events:

Wir machen [...] relativ große Veranstaltungen [...]. Für eine große Veranstaltung mit Ministerbeteiligung, mit Vorstandsbeteiligung, mit möglicherweise Demonstrationen vor der Tür, mit Organisation einer Pressekonferenz zu machen, [...] da sind ein bis zwei Personen für 2 bis 3 Monate komplett belegt halt. Und was kommt dann dabei raus? Eine Veranstaltung von einem Tag. Ganz viele der Unternehmen [...] sagen: "Ja, ich habe da eine Agentur, die macht mir das [...]. Was kostet euch denn die Agentur?" So, und dann kommen da ganz schnell sechsstellige Summen, die dann so eine Agentur auch mal für so eine Veranstaltung kostet. Ich sage: "Ja, das ist das, was wir alles selbst als [DC2] leisten müssen, weil wir keine Agentur haben. Oder ihr habt uns nicht das Geld gegeben, dass wir eine Agentur beauftragen können." (DC2)

(We make [...] relatively big events [...]. For the preparation of a big event with participation of ministers, of board members, possibly demonstrations before the door, with the organization of a press conference, [...] there are one or two persons completely occupied with for 2 to 3 months. And what is the outcome? An event of one day. Many of the companies [...] say: "Well, I have an agency which is doing that for me [...]. How much does it cost you?" And such an agency costs easily six-digit amounts for just one event. I say: "Yeah, that is what we as [DC2] have to do on our own because we have no agency. Or you did not give us the money for contracting an agency.")

Another corporate interview partner stresses the importance of selecting the right people and reports from negative previous experiences with academic, public and other private partners:

[...] wenn ich da die falschen Leute an Bord habe oder den falschen Partner auswähle, der nicht ein gemeinsames Ziel mit mir verfolgt, dann wird mein Personal wirklich schlecht eingesetzt, und der Return on Investment ist miserabel. Es gibt Beispiele, die ich da aus eigener Erfahrung gesehen habe, wo Seiten reportet wurden, was Leute angeblich an Zeit auf dieses Projekt verwendet haben. Das war lächerlich. Also da wurden Steuergelder wirklich missbraucht. (n/a)

([...] if I have the wrong people on board or select the wrong partner who does not pursue a joint goal together with me, then my staff will be employed badly and the return on investment is dreadful. There are examples from my own experience where pages have been reported on expenditure of time which people have allegedly dedicated to this project. That was ridiculous. Tax money was really misused there.)

A further interviewee harshly criticizes the way resources were used in partnerships with UN organizations and particularly refers to overhead costs that IOs charge in joint projects and which will be analyzed in more detail in Chapter 6.4.4.1:

> *[...] man hat aufgrund dieser ganzen Bürokratie und Administration eigentlich kaum Ressourcen, um wirklich Experten oder Knowhow für die Projekte seitens der [UN-Organisation] bereitzustellen. Das heißt, 95 % der Arbeit wird letztendlich von Partnern wie uns gemacht [...]. Und auf Seiten der [UN-Organisation] sind eigentlich kaum Leute, die fachlich mitarbeiten können oder dann auch die Zeit für so etwas haben [...]. Das ist jetzt zum Teil auch ein Einzelfall, aber das Projekt braucht die [UN-Organisation] nicht [...]. Die Hauptineffizienz ist einfach die Einschaltung oder Zwischenschaltung so einer UN-Institution [...]. Und dann [...] das Budget [...] für ein bis zwei [UN-Organisation] Mitarbeiter [...], die aber letztendlich gar nicht wirklich mitarbeiten und keine Entscheidungen treffen, sondern sich einfach nur einmal die Woche von mir updaten lassen, um dann wiederum eine kurze Email an das Ministerium zu schreiben. Also das sind sehr, sehr, sehr krasse Ineffizienzen, die da auf der Budgetseite auftreten. [...] ich will uns auch nicht ganz rausnehmen. Wir sind natürlich auch auf lokale, [...] nicht Mitarbeiter, aber Netzwerke angewiesen, wo auch nicht immer alles glatt läuft. Also, es gibt die Leute, mit denen man dann in diesen Ländern zusammenarbeitet, die verlangen auch eigentlich zu hohe Preise für das, was sie liefern [...]. Man ist aber letztendlich auf diese Leute angewiesen [...]. Da muss dann vielleicht auch hier und da ein paar Euro mehr bezahlen, auch wenn man weiß, dass die jetzt nicht unbedingt zehn Tage gearbeitet haben, sondern nur fünf. Also das ist sowas, da muss man dann einfach bei diesem internationalen Projektgeschäft, gerade in Entwicklungsländern, auch mal ein Auge zudrücken. (n/a)*
>
> ([...] because of all this bureaucracy and administration you actually have very little resources to really provide experts or knowhow from the [UN organization] to the projects. This means that 95% of the work will finally be done by partners like us [...]. And from the side of the [UN organization] there are hardly any people who could work substantively or who have time for that [...]. That is in parts an individual case, but the project does not need this [UN organization]. The main inefficiency is basically the involvement or intermediation of such an UN institution [...]. And then [...] the budget [...] for one to two [UN organization] employees [...] who do not really contribute and do not make any decisions but simply receive a weekly update from me for writing then a short email to the ministry. Thus, there are very very strong inefficiences on the budget side. [...] I do not want to exclude us. Of course, we depend also on local [...] not employees but networks where not everything is working smoothly either. There are people you collaborate with in these countries who charge actually too high prices for that what they are delivering [...]. But finally you rely on these people [...]. Then you have to pay maybe a few euros more here and there, even if you know that they did not work ten days but only five. Well, that is something in this international project business, especially in developing countries, where you just have to turn a blind eye.)

However, he remarks that his criticism relates to a problem of international law that cannot be resolved on a project basis and affects the UN System in general. In summary, the manifold experiences of resource inefficiency show that there seems to be abundant potential for more efficient use of resources in the sense of more accurate resource planning, partner selection, streamlining decision-making processes, etc. However, the question of resource efficiency also tends to be a matter of perception to a large extent.

6.4.4.1 Cost Factors

The interview partners were asked for factors which they see as the main cost drivers in their partnerships. Their responses were aggregated per type of interview partner (Table 52). Although in several interviews the responses actually related to other questions also implied cost factors, only those factors have been counted that were explicitly mentioned as such by the interview partners.

Interview partners	Private	Public		Total number of times mentioned
		DCA	IO	
Cost factors				
Staff (incl. work time, hiring and turnover)	x	x		9
Production (incl. any material and technology used)	x	x		5
General administration	x	x		4
Management/overhead expenses	x	x	x	3
Travel	x			3
Bureaucracy	x	x		2
Knowledge building/loss of knowledge	x			2
Distribution	x			1
Management control (in particular monitoring and evaluation)			x	1
Publicity work (incl. awareness campaigns and events)		x		1
Relationship building	x			1
Studies including scientific monitoring/support		x		1
Workshops	x			1

Table 52: Cost factors.

The dominant cost factors in most partnerships all form staff-related expenditures for own and external staff. This aspect was confirmed at least by the private sector and by DCAs.

> *[...] Personalkosten. Seien es unsere eigenen, seien es für externe Berater, Consultants oder Gutachter, aber das ist immer der größte Anteil und, ich denke mal, zwei Drittel. (DC1)*
>
> ([...] personnel costs. Whether for our own advisors or for external ones, consultants or experts, these always account for the largest share, I guess, two-thirds.)

Another factor, which is strongly related to personnel costs, in particular in terms of staff turnover, is knowledge building or loss of knowledge, respectively, which is paralleled by investments into new relationship building. In this context, CO12 remarks that insuffcient skills of one partner cause frictions and lead to higher TC.

> *[...] die Leute waren jetzt alle so drei, vier Jahre dabei, und das Team ist jetzt komplett ausgewechselt. Das Knowhow muss wieder neu aufgebaut werden. Das ist vielleicht etwas, wo der Knowhow-Transfer passiert, aber ich erkläre sehr viel schon zum dritten Mal [...]. Man kann ja von niemandem erwarten, dass er*

ständig dabei bleibt. Aber die People und Knowhow-Aufbau sind so die größten Kostentreiber. (CO4)

([...] all the people were there for about three, four years and the team has now been completely exchanged. The knowhow had to be built up again. Maybe this is something where knowhow transfer happens, but I explain many things already for the third time [...]. You cannot expect from anybody to stay forever. But people and knowhow building are the main cost drivers.)

Depending on the extent to which production capacities and technology are used, manufacturing costs gain a larger share but most interview partners confirmed that it remains well behind. An exception seems to be infrastructure projects which are highly intensive in physical resources. Furthermore, administration and bureaucratic procedures are generally perceived as important cost drivers. One factor that apparently is discussed controversially among PPP stakeholders is the adequacy of management fees or contributions margins, which IOs charge from project budgets in order to cover their so-called overhead costs.

Also, die UN kann meines Wissens nach zwischen 10 und 15 % des Projektbudgets einfach mal so abzwacken, um eben ihre ganzen Overhead-Kosten zu decken, um eben in dem Fall Büros in [UN Standort] auch mitzufinanzieren [...]. Und dann haben Sie natürlich in allen möglichen Ländern riesen Administrationen. Also, die UN ist ja erstmal so ein Selbstverwaltungsmonstrum. (n/a)

(Well, to my knowledge the UN can simply scrape up 10 to 15% from the project budget, just to cover their entire overhead costs, in this case to co-finance offices in [UN location] [...]. And then they have huge administrations in diverse countries. Thus, the UN is basically such a kind of bureaucratic monster.)

The biggest challenge with large organizations is the bureaucracy. So, you lose a lot of time and time is money. And the second thing, because of the bureaucracy, you lose a lot money on administrative costs because, you know, this goes to this one and goes to that one and so on. (CO7)

[...] we do have a management fee, kind of a thing. So, for every contribution that we receive we do take a general management fee of [one-digit number] %. So, that also applies for the private sector funding. (IO7)

Hence, the management fees seem to vary between IOs, and CO8 remarks that overhead costs are basically indirect costs from which projects also benefit. For instance, the partners can use existing local infrastructure (e.g. offices, telecommuniation), which IOs maintain in diverse countries, and therefore do not need to install their own ones just for project purposes. He looks at this cost factor less critically than other private sector actors and moreover adds that his company can invoice the labor time of working students from the cost position "overheads". IO7 highlights expenditures for MC measures, especially monitoring and evaluation for which they are used to allocate about 3% of the total project costs.

In summary, there are numerous cost factors in PPPs, and their relevance depends on the type of involved partners and on the employed resources. Still, staff-related expenditures seem to be clearly dominant in most PPP types. For precise analyes, detailed cost overviews would be needed but the researcher had no access to them.

6.4.4.2 Cost Reduction

On the basis of the aforementioned cost factors, several interview partners identified some potentials for cost reductions. On the private sector side, some actors call for more pragmatism in the operational procedures while CO3 recommends selecting partners that tend to work efficiently and therefore prevent major project management inefficiencies from the outset:

> *Wir mussten auch die [DCA Partner] gelegentlich überzeugen, dass man jetzt mit Ressourcen, auch gerade auf Unternehmensseite, gerade auch bei den kleineren Partnern, haushalten muss und jetzt nicht bei jedem Event erwarten kann, dass alle Partner vor Ort sind. Manchmal wird das halt nur [CO3] sein, die vor Ort sind, und die anderen Partner auch mit vertreten. Also dass sie einen gewissen, effizienten Pragmatismus walten lassen und nicht politische Vollständigkeit als Kriterium an den Tag legen. (CO3)*
>
> (Sometimes, we also had to convince the [DCA partner] to economize resources, in particular on the private sector side and especially with smaller partners. You cannot expect that all partners will be on-site for each event but that sometimes only [CO3] will be there and also represent the other partners. Thus, they exercise some kind of efficient pragmatism and do not apply political completeness as a criterion.)

The public sector especially calls for more alignment of work programmes between organizations and for more flexible application of rules and guidelines to different kinds of partnership so that existing organizational structures can be used more efficiently.

> *[Remark: Removing] duplicated responsibilities and resources for engaging with the private sector within the Secretariat. (IO1)*

> *[...] just by the fact of our presence [...] we cut the transaction costs. For example, a company wants to engage in [country XY]. We already exist there, we already have an office. So, the operation costs are really reduced. So, whatever they put in, in cash or in-kind, can really go to the directions. So, it's just being able to factoring the partnership modalities [...]. And we have our operating procedures, we have very tight, I think probably too tight, measures for monitoring and audit and all this. (IO5)*

Different views exist on the reduction of personnel costs. While CO5 sees the biggest saving potential in lowering personnel costs because they are the largest cost item, CO4 remarks that in his partnership much of the operational work is already done by cost-efficient young professionals. Moreover, the fact that often there are only few full-time posts in PPPs available, and that many actors accomplish the partnership work as part of their regular task portfolio, seems to reduce saving potentials in this area. More alignment of technology standards across national borders was also mentioned by CO4 and CO10-1 in the context of cost reduction and more efficient use of resources.

6.5 Governance and Control Pattern

This chapter serves the answering of **research question 2.1** and analyzes different governance structures in existing PPPs for development. Furthermore, it studies diverse governance levels and the level of cooperation in these partnerships. It makes reference to theory-oriented control types and categories of control mechanisms as well as to fundamental assumptions of the ACI and TCE. Therefore, it builds the basis for the in-depth analysis of MC in Chapter 6.6.

6.5.1 Governance Structures and Governing Bodies

This chapter discusses designs of governance structures including their material governing bodies. Instead of giving a general overview it makes this matter more tangible by comparing four examples of different governance structures for selected PPP types at an aggregated level.

1) Civic association & integrated partnership (Figure 43)
2) Multilateral alliance (Figure 44)
3) Strategic alliance, direct implementation work (Figure 45)
4) Strategic alliance, indirect implementation work (Figure 46)

The **first example** compiles the governance structures of two PPPs which can be classified as a combination of **civic association** and **integrated partnership**. In both cases, a membership-based separate legal entity had been created. The stakeholders comprise mainly private sector and public sector actors that with few exceptions originate from the same country. Academia, consultancies and NGOs also have a stake but play a minor role. All members have to pay a kind of membership fee and delegate representatives to the normative, executive and operational level. While the general assembly elects the management board and votes on fundamental activities and decisions, the management board coordinates, controls and executes diverse activities which are clustered into activity lines or working groups. Here, DCAs take a strong supporting function in the implementation through a PMO-like secretariat or technical advisory council. Their support tasks range from promoting internal and external communication to preparing decision bases for the executive level and counselling of the working groups. However, they can also embrace coordination functions if the management board delegates authority accordingly. Depending on the possibility and willingness to engage, the members second their own staff occasionally, temporarily or full-time to the different governing bodies to meet their membership obligations. Usually, some proportionality requirements apply to ensure that the compositions of the different bodies are fairly balanced (e.g. minimum number of delegates from firms, government, NGOs). Thus, the management board is either composed of people of equal rank or, for instance, of one president, one deputy, one treasurer and several assessors. The operational level usually consists of experts having expertise in the different activities, which are on scope of the partnership. Results are reported to the members and their internal stakeholders, such as executive board or minister. Despite the existence of hierarchies, this governance structure can be classified as hybrid because of the democratic participation rights at the normative level, which endow each member with equal voting rights.

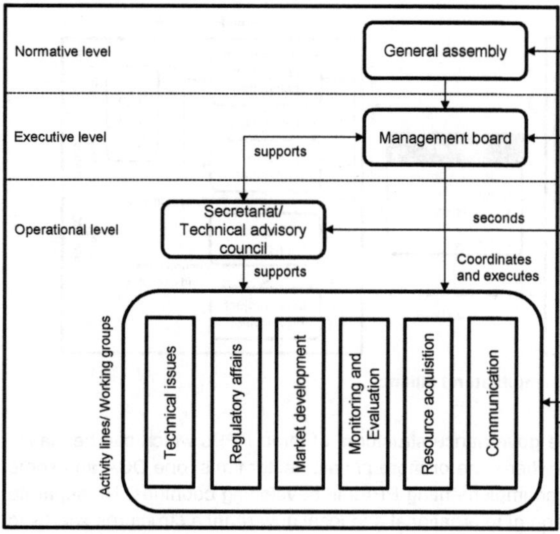

Figure 43: Governance structure – civic association and integrated partnership.

The **second example** displays the governance structures of two PPPs which can be classified as a **multilateral alliance** where numerous large private sector firms, IOs, governmental entities, DCAs and NGOs are partnering to harmonize policy and technology norms and standards across national borders. These partnerships often run under the auspices of global initiatives that were launched by IOs and national governments. Two cases of multilateral alliances have been identified, which are distinguished by their type of activities. While both are platforms of interorganizational dialogues, only one of them links their advocacy work to physical PPP activities on the ground. At the normative level, delegates of the different partners meet up annually to make fundamental decisions and to coordinate the programme of work with subordinated governing bodies. In the first case, the stakeholder representatives are often part of both project steering committee and task forces, while in the second case, the management committee is usually composed of CEOs and high-ranked leaders. They delegate decision-making rights to commissioners at the executive level who coordinate and monitor the operational work, in particular the local project work for which a project company is usually founded. A central secretariat supports the management and policy committee in its work. The representatives of the policy and project committee meet twice a year and hold monthly telephone conferences. By contrast, hierarchies are less distinctive in the first case, and are without physical activities. The PMO is staffed and managed by the IO partners and plays a central role at all three levels. It receives support by specialized staff that can provide advice on issues related to the substantive work of the partnership. Moreover, the project coordinaton between PMO, project steering committee and task forces seems to be relatively close and less formal and hierarchic than in the second case. The task forces meet usually once every three months or hold at least a formal telephone conference. Moreover, there is ample spontaneous communication going on. In both cases, formal reporting back to the internal stakeholders at the executive board level takes place once per year.

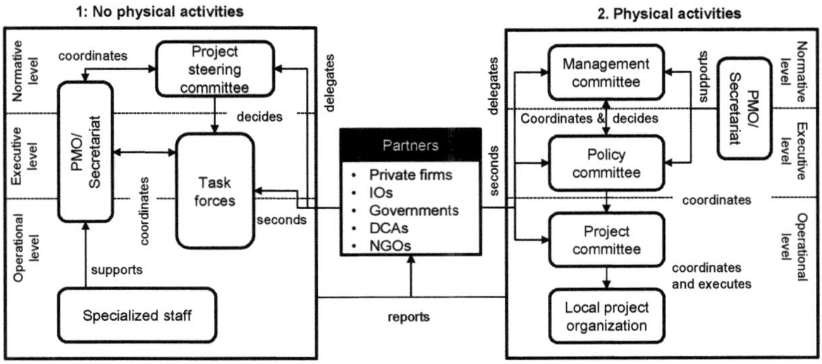

Figure 44: Governance structure – multilateral alliance.

The **third example** compiles the governance structures of three PPPs which can be classified as a **strategic partnership** where one or more private sector firms, one DCA and some local actors are jointly funding and implementing PPPs in developing countries. No separate legal entity is created. The creation of international and local governance structures seems to rely upon the number of partners involved. In the case of a bilateral partnership between one multinational company and one DCA, both actors assign staff to a global and a local project team. At the global level, each organization designates one coordinator who coordinates the collaboration between both entities but also manages internal processes. Moreover, they coordinate the joint work of a local project team, which is composed of representatives from both sides. However, these local actors only work part-time for the partnership. Thus, the corporate representive is mainly engaged in sales activities while the DCA one is also involved in other development commitments of his organization on the ground. In general, the governance structure is rather informal and communication takes place directly between the coordinators. By contrast, a multilateral partnership that comprises several multinational firms and includes NGOs and different local actors rests on a more formal governance structure, split up into steering committee and project comittee at international level while the local implementation is more left to local partners as compared to the bilateral cooperation form. The steering committee embraces all partners involved and often meets only once or twice per year while the remaining communication occurs by phone, Skype or email. This committee seeks to build consensus and defines the overall work programme. The project committee, in some PPPs also called core partner commitee, has a more operational but still managerial function and uses to meet more often, e.g. about every two to three months. Core partners have usually contributed more resources and assume more responsibility in the partnership. The project committee coordinates and monitors the implementing work that is done by partnering local private sector firms and NGOs, in some PPPs also called core implementing partners, but also liaises with the local governments to align the partnership work with institutional framework conditions. Depending on the degree of division of work, subcommittees might be created that are responsible for their own work packages and are headed by subproject managers. However, offside the formal governance structure, bilateral meetings often play a crucial role in coordination because at this informal level two or more partners harmonize their positions and interests in different subject matters before discussing them in committee sessions. To reduce graphical complexity, Figure 45 does not show any reporting lines but the monitoring is endorsed by milestone reports as well as intermediate and final reports between the different governing bodies and back to internal stakeholders, such as the executive boards.

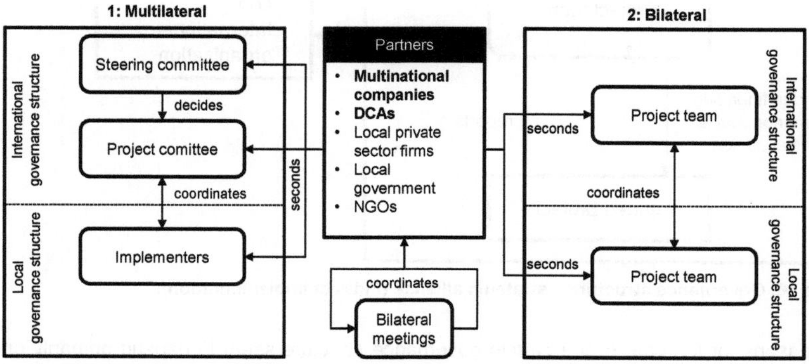

Figure 45: Governance structure – strategic alliance (direct implementation).

The **fourth example** displays the governance structure of one PPP which can be classified as a **strategic partnership** where a private sector firm and an IO collaborate in the financing of local projects that are pertinent to their business or mandate. They identify potential projects or call for applications in the first step. Then, they assess the feasibility of the projects and support the implementers in the project design and launch. Moreover, they accompany the projects along their implementation and provide the project staff with managerial and technical advice. They request some accountability from the responsible persons of the funded projects in terms of participation of joint events and reporting. The private sector firms and IOs monitor progress and results and summarize the overall achievements in final reports, which they have to submit to their internal stakeholders. There are no formal governance bodies in place, but the project team being composed of four people assumes managerial and operational tasks alike. Occasionally, further people from the two organizations support the project team but are not part of the governance structure. However, this PPP finances and supports projects in the field but does not have staff or any other kind of network in the countries of project implementation. Thus, the actual PPP work remains at the headquarter level.

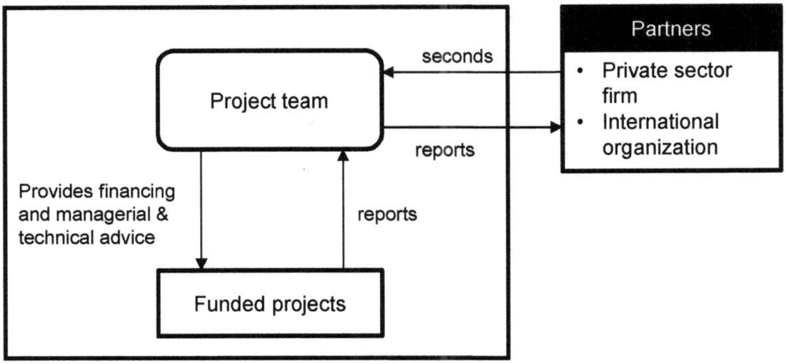

Figure 46: Governance structure – strategic alliance (indirect implementation).

The reasons for the choice of a certain governance structure seem to depend primarily on the type and number of partners involved, which are strongly related to the PPP type and level of complexity, but also on the individual preferences of the concrete actors doing the implementation.

> *Also [Name der ersten PPP] ist wesentlich formeller strukturiert [...], auch weil mehr Partner involviert sind [...]. Bei [Name der zweiten PPP] gab es zwei Koordinatoren, die quasi eine Standleitung zueinander hatten. Da gab es kein großes Gremium. Also, wir haben bewusst darauf verzichtet, weil wir sagten: "Wir wollen jetzt keine Steuerung durch Menschen, die sich auch nur einmal oder zweimal im Jahr mit sowas beschäftigen." Dafür ist es zu speziell. (CO3)*
>
> (Well, [name of the first PPP] is much more formally structured [...], also because more partners are involved [...]. For [name of the second PPP] there were two coordinators who had a kind of dedicated line with each other. There was not such a big committee. We relinquished that intentionally because we said: "We do not want a governance by people who only deal with that once or twice per year." It is too specific for that.)

> *Entonces, [...] los proyectos que estamos creando traen sus principios. [...] los [tipo del PPP] tienen que ser transparentes, inclusivos, independientes. [...] es una organización que tiene una estructura. Hay gente, hay un director, hay "staff", [...]. Entonces, es un ente donde tiene un board que es multi-sectorial y pues es bastante dependiente. (CO13-2)*
>
> (Well, [...] the projects that we are creating carry their principles. [...] the [PPP type] have to be transparent, inclusive, independent. [...] it is an organization which has a structure. There are people, there is a director, there is "staff", [...]. So, it is an entity that has a board which is multi-sectoral and therefore it is very dependent.)

> *In my view, if it's like a bilateral donor Member State, if they sit in the governance mechanism of the project initiative, if it's a strategic partner, they do have a say. But if it's not a key strategic partner, but a little bit less active collaboration with the company, they don't tend to be involved that much. But it depends a little bit on the project governance mechanism. Of course, the host government, where we operate, might have some say but what I know is that they don't tend to be so involved. (IO7)*

So, [...] we do not want to have like a very bureaucratic and rigid structure. (IO8)

On the public sector side exist moreover some overarching governing bodies, such as inter-bureau committees or project appraisal committees, which coordinate partnership work internally or assume control and approval functions for the project work. In summary, all the aforementioned examples of PPPs are mainly governed in a hybrid manner although existing formal governance structures indicate some hierarchies.

6.5.1.1 Partner-Specific Internal Governance Structures

Besides the overall governance structures of PPPs each partner maintains an internal project-related governance structure, which relies strongly on the internal departments involved and on the degree of decentralization (Chapters 6.1.3 and 6.1.4). These intraorganizational governance structures are connected with each other by interorganizational interfaces. In this context, DC1 urges the need for one fix focal point in each organization while DC4 describes his role as an interface node being the central contact person for several partners, not all of whom were directly in touch with each other. This is amongst other things typical of partnerships where governments engage their DCAs to do partnership work and channel most communication through them but barely get directly in touch with the private sector partners, for instance. Very much decentralized public and private organizations that maintain local organizational and staff presence strongly use this infrastructure as local governance mechanism for project implementation including MC. Furthermore, some IOs split their PPP activities into an operational and a strategic managerial component.

This [...] work [...] is being done actually by the technical division of [IO6]. We as Strategic [department name] will be in support of them and managing the partnership with the external stakeholders [...] but we do not enter into the practical work [...]. So, it has to do very much with the consolidation of the brand of [IO6]. You develop these partnerships [...] and you engage the stakeholders [...]. (IO6)

Usually, the country level takes the decision on those on their own. They sometimes might consult with us or the regional bureau, but those kinds of simple policy dialogue, these kinds of a little bit more informal partnerships happen all the time without any further engagement of other units, just the country office. [...] they will need to monitor the performance of the partners throughout the partnership. (IO7)

Similar to that, some DCAs possess a kind of modular project management system that is supported by IT-based tools. They support the organization in managing cooperations with private sector firms, in administering multiple parallel projects and provide tools and templates to exercise certain control functions, such as monitoring impact or progress. DC2 explains that usually one department takes the project lead from the DCA's side, but other departments such as an internal consulting unit, finance or HR are also part of the extended internal governance structure. The management board supports this tight internal cooperation by subjecting project concepts to an internal quality circle and provides feedback to its operational implementers. DC3 and DC5 stress that each partner should have an internal governance structure for making the overall PPP governance effective:

Dann ist sicherlich [...] von Seiten des Projektpartners ein gewisses Projektmanagement erforderlich, um die definierten Aktivitäten voranzubringen. (DC3)
(Then there is truly [...] a certain project management needed from the project partner's side for advancing the defined activities.)

Nosotros tenemos objetivos internos dentro de [DC5], donde sí tenemos [...] una análisis de impacto.
(We have some internal objectives within [DC5] where we have [...] an impact analysis.)

In summary, the effectiveness of governance structures in PPPs relies particularly on the existence of well-functioning intraorganizational governance structures on the one hand and interorganizational interfaces between the different partners.

6.5.1.2 Sharing of Responsibilities and Taking of Ownership

The responsibility of certain activities or large-scale project parts is either explicitly determined by contract or rather implicitly by special skills and expertise. CO2, CO4, CO6, DC4 and others comment that the specific knowhow and core competences partners possess in technology and markets, or the networks and contacts they maintain with certain countries, governments and people, determine the respective responsibilities:

Es wurde jetzt nicht gesagt "Du bist für das und das verantwortlich.", sondern es hat sich so rausgebildet. (CO4)
(They did not say "You are responsible of this and that.", but it simply developed.)

There are components then within the training that are closer to [private sector partner] and there are others that are closer to [IO8]. Sometimes, what we do is also splitting the responsibilities on specific topics. Let us say, maybe we focus on impact analysis, whereas [private sector partner] focuses in a session more on [...] leadership and fundraising. (IO8)

Moreover, an organization's mandate or formal governance structure including contractually defined management positions and work packages set a framework to the assignment of responsibilities to the respective partners. Those responsibilities can be broken down to milestones and single implementation activities, as stated by DC1.

Im Rahmen der Vertragserstellung wird das Personal benannt, das auf dem Projekt arbeitet. Die Arbeitspakete werden benannt. (CO8)
(Within the contract preparation is named the personnel that works on the project. Work packages are mentioned.)

Und jeder hat auch seine eigenen, klar definierten Aufgaben und auch Kompetenzen. (CO9-1)
(And everybody has his own clearly defined tasks and also competences.)

So, we are involved in that in more of a coordination role because we have the mandate to coordinate [several IOs] at country level. (IO5)

However, responsibilities are not necessarily fixed forever. In governance structures, where committee positions are filled by election on a rotating basis, public and private actors alternate in taking responsibility for certain activities, as underlined by DC6. However, CO6, DC2 and IO5 emphasize that the taking of ownership of the assigned tasks and responsibilites is the decisive factor in the end:

> *So, das ist das, was wir mit dem Vorstand vereinbart haben, wo wir eigentlich auch hinkommen müssen: Eine sehr viel stärkere Eigenverantwortung, noch nicht mal Selbstorganisation, aber Eigenverantwortung, Themen vorantreiben, etc., was viel, viel stärker von den Mitgliedern kommen muss. (DC2)*
> (So, this is what we have agreed with the board where we actually have to get to: a much stronger ownership, not even self-organization, but ownership, pushing certain issues, etc., what needs to be driven much much more by the members.)

Awareness of the respective strengths and weaknesses eases the sharing of responsibilities so that the taking of ownership can also mean leadership to some extent.

> *Es braucht immer eine Organisation, die ein Stück weit auch die Verantwortung übernimmt, die Sachen voranzutreiben. Das ist teilweise unterschiedlich verteilt. In vielen Fällen übernehmen wir hier einen großen Teil der Aktivitäten, die dann immer in enger Abstimmung mit den Partnern erfolgen. (CO1-1)*
> (There is always an organization needed which assumes the reponsibility of advancing the things to some extent. That is in parts differently distributed. In many cases we assume a big part of the activities, which are always implemented in close consultation with the partners.)

> *Entonces, reconocer las fortalezas y debilidades de cada organización es lo que te va a permitir también asignar mejor o de manera más eficiente las responsabilidades. (CO13-2)*
> (So, recognizing the strengths and weaknesses of every organization is what allows you to assign responsibilities better or in a more effcient way.)

In summary, operational and managerial responsibilites of PPP activities seem to be clearly defined and assigned in most partnerships while the taking of ownership could be improved in some cases.

6.5.1.3 Delegation of Authority

The degree of delegated authority and decision rights between superior and affiliated subordinated partners, as well as degree of intraorganizationally between managerial and operational staff, are strongly related to the sharing of responsibilities and the taking of ownership. In their capacity as contractor of national governments public actors like DCAs enjoy a high level of authority because the ministries in charge transfer most of managerial and operational responsibility to them. Despite some authority left to the DCAs, governments tend to set some strict requirements in terms of financing, reporting and accountability that frame the decision-making authority of the DCAs (Chapters 6.2.2.3 and 6.3.1.4). CO9-1 adds that in general clearly defined tasks and competences stipulate somebody's authority of decision-making. But sometimes very simple aspects are decisive. While CO1-1 points to the impossibilty of managing partnerships with a very decentralized structure and many local activities from headquarters level alone, CO11 stresses the importance of trust that prompts managers to delegate authority to lower levels. Both emphasize the need for efficient upwards reporting and communication:

> *We have a lot of power at operational level. And I would say, in this case it is really not top-down, but on the other way, bottom-up. They trust us. Our bosses trust us from both sides. (CO11)*

IO7 reports about a risk assessment tool that helps operational staff, being endowed with a high level of authority, to decide whether a higher ranked person should be consulted for final decision-making or not:

> *So, it's a tool for the different offices to assess the partner, think of the risks and benefits of the partnership and also whether they should be taking the decision on their own or whether they should include higher levels of the organization into the decision-making and also the risk management, should anything be questioned afterwards. (IO7)*

Efficiency and unequal skills and competences are further drivers of delegated authority and responsibilites. According to DC1, partners sometimes do neither have enough capacities nor willingness to fully engage. In this situation, it makes the PPP implementation easier and more efficient if a few people are entitled to decide and speak on the others‘ behalf.

> *Und es gibt Mitglieder [...], die sagen: "Wir haben überhaupt kein Interesse daran, uns irgendwie in diese ganze Diskussion [...] einzubringen und da mit der Regierung [...] zu verhandeln. Ihr macht genau das Richtige, und deswegen gebe ich einfach meine Stimme dazu." Beteiligen sich nicht an unseren Treffen, kommen nicht zu unseren Treffen [...], aber beteiligen sich darüber zu sagen: "Wir machen einfach bei euch mit, und ihr dürft auch in unserem Namen sprechen." (DC2)*
>
> (And there are members [...] who say: "We are not interested at all in contributing anyhow to all these discussions [...] and to negotiate [...] with the government. You are doing the right things and that is why I give my vote to that." They do not contribute to our meetings, do not participate at our meetings [...] but contribute by saying: "We simply cooperate with you and you are also allowed to speak on our behalf.")

In summary, delegation of authority is based on hierarchy but implies the shifting from a hierarchic to a more hybrid governance structure the more decision-making competences and responsibilites are transferred to subordinated partners, governing bodies or operational staff members. The extent and motivations of delegating authority are diverse and rely mainly on considerations of efficient controllability of PPP activities and on the willingness to take ownership.

6.5.1.4 Level of Complexity

Governance and the level of complexity stand in a reciprocal relationship because certain characteristics of governance structures increase complexity while complex partnerships also require an appropriate governance structure. Main drivers of complexity are the number and type of partners involved as well as the number of countries in which a partnership is rolled out.

> *Also, die relativ flach-hierarchische, bilaterale Zusammenarbeit hat natürlich Schnelligkeit und Effektivität oft auf ihrer Seite. Je größer und multipler die Partner, desto komplexer wird natürlich auch die Steuerung. (CO3)*
> (Well, the relatively low-hierarchic, bilateral cooperation benefits from promptness and effectiveness. The larger and more multiple the partners are the more complex becomes the governance.)

In addition, CO4 and CO5 point out that the complexity of contractual arrangements and the risk of non-compliance with them increase in larger partnerships with numerous actors involved. DC1 underscores that such multi-stakeholder PPPs require a decentralization of the governance structure:

> *Im Fall von [Name der PPP] haben wir auch eine Steuerungsstruktur, die ein bisschen komplexer ist, dadurch, dass wir eben ein globales Vorhaben sind, und die Struktur hat in den meisten Fällen so zwei Ebenen. Das heißt, wir haben eine Steuerungsstruktur vor Ort, mit den Leuten, die vor Ort sind, und wir haben eine Steuerungsstruktur auf internationaler Ebene, die dann eben die internationalen Partner auch zusammenbringt [...]. (DC1)*
> (In the case of [PPP name] we have a governance structure which is a little bit more complex because it is a global project and this structure is used to have two levels. This means that we have one governance structure on the ground with the people who are there, and we have another governance structure at global level that brings together the international partners [...].)

Moreover, CO8 and DC5 explain that quite diverging interests and too much voluntariness in the engagement make partnership governance more complex because conflicts between partners arise and the level of commitment is adversely influenced:

> *[...] en la mesa directiva hay gente muy valiosa, muy importante. Pero te digo, son personas que donan parte de su tiempo a su [nombre de la PPP] pero [nombre de la PPP] no les paga. Ellos tienen sus propias empresas, sus propios trabajos. Entonces, este tampoco les permite como dar una visión estratégica y decir, "Bueno, vamos a hacer esto, vamos a hacer el otro", porque no tienen el tiempo para hacerlo [...]. Esto lo hace muy muy complejo. (DC5)*
> ([...] in the executive board are very valuable and important people. But I tell you, these are people who donate part of their time to [PPP name] but [PPP name] does not pay them. They have their own companies, their own work. Hence, this does not allow them either to give a strategic vision and to say "Well, we do this one, we do that one" because they do not have the time to do that [...]. This makes it very very complex.)

Another aspect that is maybe not obvious for the other partners is the internal complexity one partner faces, and the many interfaces the lead department has to manage, in particular if the supply chain is affected.

> *[...] wir müssen das dann versuchen zu koordinieren, dass dann auch die Kollegen bei uns in der Produktion entsprechend das wieder einrichten können. Denn Sie können nicht einfach am Montag anrufen und sagen, dass Sie am Dienstag die Ware brauchen. Das geht nicht. (CO1-1)*

([...] we then have to try to coordinate this such that the colleagues in the production then can configure it. Because you cannot simply make a call on Monday and say that you need the product on Tuesday. This does not work.)

In summary, the very different reasons of governance complexity are hard to abolish. That is why CO13-1 emphasizes the need to adjust the MC design to the level of complexity of the governance structure:

> *[...] la estructura de gestión necesaria para [nombre de la PPP] es mucho más compleja y es mucho más robusta. O sea necesitamos diferentes niveles de control [...], tanto a nivel de ejecución [...] como es a nivel temático. (CO13-1)*
> ([...] the governance structure being necessary for the [PPP name] is much more complex and is much more robust. This means that we need different control levels [...], at both the execution level [...] and the thematic level.)

6.5.2 Governance Levels

This chapter analyzes in which way and to what extent the governance structures studied in Chapter 6.5.1 are established in practice. Here, the focus is placed on decision-making processes in conjunction with theoretical control patterns wherefore the way for an in-depth analysis of MC mechanisms in Chapter 6.6 will be paved. Another aspect that describes governance in practice is the level of cooperation whose analysis basically relies on the ACI theoretical framework. Hence, this chapter is generally very much inspired by the conceptual and theoretical basics from the Chapters 0 and 4.

The actual governance level in PPPs is of course influenced by the underlying governance structure, by the formal status different partners have, by their number, but also by the way governance is perveiced and by the conception of its own role. CO3 and CO10-1 emphasize that fewer partners involved make the governance less hierarchic although some stakeholders, such as third-party actors, have less of a say. Despite existing hierarchies and formal role assignment, CO1-1 recommends reflecting on the own role in a partnership:

> *Was hier, glaube ich, ganz wichtig ist zu sagen, das ist jedenfalls unser Prinzip: Wir verstehen uns nicht als Geldgeber. Wir verstehen uns als Partner. Deswegen heißt das ja auch Partnerschaft. (CO1-1)*
> (I believe what is very important to say is that this is at least our principle: We do not deem ourselves a donor. We conceive ourselves as a partner. That is why it is actually called partnership.)

Another statement by IO7 illustrates that the governance level might be a matter of perception in the end and does not necessarily coincide with the actual level:

> *We tend to be a little bit more hierarchical as far as I have observed. As mentioned, we consult a little bit more. We get maybe some more endorsement from different actors than they do [...]. It's not necessarily only us who can be [...] hierarchic and bureaucratic. Sometimes, it's also the companies, especially the big multinationals. (IO7)*

In summary, governance levels seem to be objective in theory but tend quite often to be subjective in practice. Thus, the actual governance level deviates from the formally established governance structure.

6.5.2.1 Decision-Making Processes

Governance structures form the infrastructural basis of decision-making processes, which are moreover characterized by formal and informal rules of procedure and other influence factors that are conducive or obstructive to these processes (Figure 47).

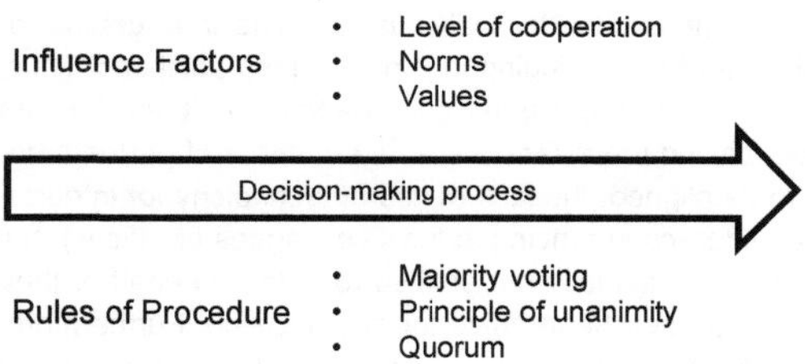

Figure 47: Characteristics of decision-making processes.

Decision-making has to do with **norms**, **values** and the **level of cooperation** with public and third-party actors, as stated by CO1-1:

> *[...] deswegen gehen wir nicht in die Rolle zu sagen: "Wir sind nur die, die den Scheck unterschreiben. Wir wollen mitgestalten." Und das sagen wir von Anfang an. Und wir respektieren auch entsprechend unseren Partner, [...] wir sind hier gleichberechtigt. Auch wenn wir ein Riesenunternehmen sind und ihr aus eurer Sicht eine kleine NGO. Und das hat etwas mit Respekt und Achtung zu tun. (CO1-1)*
>
> ([...] for this reason, we do not take the role of saying: "We are only the ones who sign the cheque. We want to actively shape." And this is something we say from the beginning. And we respect our partners accordingly, [...] we are among equals. Although we are a large company and you, from your point of view, a small NGO. And this has to do with respect and esteem.)

In general, the decision-making processes appear quite democratic. Several actors like CO6 and DC2 emphasize that their governing bodies apply the **principle of unanimity**. In other partnerships suffices the **majority vote** while CO4 adds that in his task forces at least 80% of the present members need to vote in favour for adopting a decision. The voting procedure is supervised by a chair and co-chair who are responsible for the protocol. In some cases a **quorum** is required. However, these procedures are not necessarily set in stone and can change over time.

> *[...] tiene sus procedimientos para la toma de decisión. Siempre tiene que ser aprobado por mayoría de votos [...]. Primero para que se pueda dar una decisión del comité, [...], tiene que haber quórum, es decir la mitad más uno. Entonces, esto sí lo que teníamos establecido y todo era por votación, por mayoría de voto.*

Después ya no. [...] hay un poco esta situación de que el presidente decide pero también el vicepresidente. Hay como [...] dentro este grupo de personas tres o cuatro que son un poco los que dicen, [...], los que toman la decisión. (DC5)

([...] it has its procedures for the decision-making. It always has to be approved by majority vote. First, so that the committee can make a decision, [...], it must have a quorum, that means the half plus one. Thus, that is what we had established and all that was by voting, by majority vote. Later on not anymore. [...] there is a little bit the situation that the president decides but the vice-president does so too. There are like [...] three or four in this group of people who are a bit like those who [...] make the decisions.)

Moreover, DC2 emphasizes that these formal procedures are important to hold actors accountable later on because democratically made decisions relying on clear rules exercise more pressure on implementation. However, there exists also some kind of informal decision-making processes. For instance, no one can hinder individual partners from getting together prior to an actual decision-making and from bringing in jointly aligned positions. Thus, decisions are often made bilaterally and offside the regular governance structures. Factors that can moreover complicate decision-making processes are a high number of partners because more individual interests need to be aligned, the lack of use of technology for integrating remotely located stakeholders (e.g. video-conferencing to local colleagues or offices), but also the presence of representatives who are actually not entitled to vote on behalf of their organization and therefore must confer with their head office for any decision. Furthermore, stakeholders that join in at a later stage after partnership initiation usually have to accept fundamental decisions which the remaining partners already made before. These decisions refer for instance to the design of the governance structure or the overall PPP objectives. Thus, they can only try to influence the remaining parts of the operational implementation in their interest. In summary, DC6 underlines that decision-making in general must be fair and consensus-oriented in the sense that the interests of all stakeholders are considered and that nobody is overreached.

[...] yo creo que lo importante en la toma de decisiones de la [tipo de PPP] es que sean decisiones que promuevan el crecimiento y las oportunidades para todos los miembros de [nombre de la PPP] sin discriminar y sin ser parciales [...]. Y todos son basadas en el consenso y pues en tratar de proveer las mejores condiciones para la mayoría o para todos los miembros de [nombre de la PPP]. (DC6)

([...] I believe that the important thing about the decision-making of the [PPP type] is that the decisions promote the growth and opportunities for all members of [PPP name] without being discriminatiory and without being partial [...]. And all are based on consensus when it is about providing the best conditions for the majority or for all members of [PPP name].)

6.5.2.2 Control Types

In Chapter 3.4, three major control types have been described, which typically occur in JV like partnerships with hybrid governance structures. Given the fact that most of the PPPs from the empirical sample tend to be governed in that way, the occurence and characteristics of dominant, independent and shared control will be analyzed in the following sections. All three control types are strongly related to the matter of governance structure including sharing of responsibility and delegation of authority.

6.5.2.2.1 Dominant Control

The general understanding of dominant control seems to imply a situation of strong power imbalance between public and private sector where the latter has to take on a subordinate role to the conditions of the public actor, whether it is an IO partner or the local government who have the final say at both operational and managerial level.

> *Das letzte Wort hat ja sowieso immer das Land oder die Region, die dann die Policy schreibt. Das war auch immer klares Commitment der [IO Partner] und jeglicher Partner, dass wir etwas vorschlagen, aber am Ende entscheidet das Land oder die Region, was da drin entsteht. Und auch danach dann. (CO4)*
> (The final say always has the country or the region, which is writing the policy. This has always been a clear commitment from the [IO partner] and from any other partners that we propose something but at the end the country or the region decides what happens there. And also afterwards.)

> *They basically describe the process which you are going to use, and they describe what the final performance is you are going to have. And so, they do not allow room for any innovation. (CO12)*

> *It's member states who are the bosses. We have accountability to member states and to the general public only, not to private sector entities. So, it's an engagement with clear rules but it's not an engagement amongst equals [...]. So, there are all kinds of engagements which vary very much in nature. But the commonality is that we keep the intergovernmental nature and the independence of the organization. We wouldn't go into a partnership of equals where we depend on them more than they depend on us. That's something we are simply not allowed to do. (IO3)*

However, other interview partners emphasizes that in their partnerships the decision-making is indeed left to the governing bodies which formalize the control structures and prevent the execution of dominant control by one specific partner. CO6 adds that in his partnership dominant control means that one company takes the lead for the project implementation and this goes along with increased responsibility. Thus, in contrast to the experiences of CO12, there seems to be a linear relationship between control and responsibility level. Still, actors like CO3 and DC2 experienced both situations in which other public and private sectors tried to exert dominant control:

> *Wenn das von einer Seite vorgeschrieben wird: "Jetzt war [Name der PPP] erfolgreich. Jetzt müsst ihr bitte noch diese drei Unternehmen dazu nehmen." Das würde nicht funktionieren. Das wurde leider viel zu oft auch gemacht, dass dann aus einer gewissen Anmaßung heraus [...] einer der Partner, sei es das Unternehmen oder sei es der öffentliche Sektor, einfach gesagt hat: "Das muss jetzt so funktionieren." So läuft es dann nicht. (CO3)*
> (If from one side it was prescribed: "[PPP name] was successful. Now you still have to accept these three companies." This would not work. But this was done way too often, that from a certain arrogance [...] one of the partners, whether it be the company or the public sector, simply said: "This has to work like that." But it does not work like that.)

> *Da kommen dann einzelne Vorstandsmitglieder oder einzelne Leute aus diesem [Steuerungsorgan] und verlangen dann auf einmal, dass das [PMO] das und das*

tut oder ohne es dann auch weiter abzusprechen, was später dann wieder zu Problemen führt. (DC2)

(Then there come in single board members or individual people from this [governing body] and request that the [PMO] does this or that without agreeing on that, what leads again to problems later on.)

In summary, dominant control works if all partners involved accept this as the way of how the governance structure including decision-making procedures shall be practiced and subordinate themselves accordingly. Otherwise it seems to simply cause conflicts.

6.5.2.2.2 Independent Control

A major characteristic of independent control is the separation of governance among actors within partnering organizations and between partners. While one IO interviewee comments that his organization hosts some partnerships but each of them with a separate governance, which is not integrated in the overall goverance structure of the organization, CO2 and CO3 stress that in their companies each partner controls the resources provided by themselves. Still, here too, alignment and coordination take place between the different public and private partners:

Und zwischen denen und uns hier, auf jeder Seite, hatten Abstimmungen stattgefunden. Wobei auch ganz klar gesagt werden muss: Die [DCA Partner] hat natürlich ihre Leute gesteuert, und wir haben unsere Leute gesteuert. Das heißt, wir haben immer einen Querabgleich gehabt [...]. Also will heißen: Independent, but not isolated steering of resources. (CO3)

(And between them and us coordination took place on each side. Also, what should be clearly said is: The [DCA partner] controlled their people and we controlled our people. This means we always had a cross check [...]. So, this means: Independent, but not isolated steering of resources.)

Other reasons of independent control are the opportunity for each partner to make use of the own strengths and the need for operational efficiency. CO6 explains that in his partnership the different private sector partners took responsibility and ownership of separate projects in different regions and markets to which they have special access or maintain traditionally close relationships:

Die Brasilianer sind dann stark in Südamerika engagiert [...]. Die Franzosen, [...], die haben ja traditionell auch einen Blick auf Afrika, aus alter historischer Verbundenheit. Also gibt's da schon gewisse Kontinuitäten. (CO6)

(The Brazilians are strongly engaged in South America [...]. The French, [...], traditionally take a look at Africa, resulting from historic links. Thus, there are certain continuities.)

In line with CO13, DC4 emphasizes that independent control requires delegated authority and is imperative to ensure smooth PPP implementation at the operational level. IO8 adds that higher decision-makers *"are not necessarily strictly involved into the project management"* itself.

"Wir, als eigentlicher Implementierer, als Projektmanager, müssen auch eine gewisse Flexibilität haben, was die Budgetverwendung angeht." Also, wir können

jetzt nicht wegen allen 100 Euro erstmal bei [IO Partner] anfragen. Dann geht das da drei Hierarchien hoch und runter [...]. Also wir haben uns [...] zusichern lassen, dass wir kleinere Budgets für bis zu [Bewilligungsgrenze], [...], dass wir die eigenverantwortlich und spontan und flexibel bewilligen können. (DC4)

("We as the actual implementer, as project manager, need to have a certain flexibility concerncing the use of budget." So, we cannot ask the [IO partner] for every 100 euros. Then this goes three hierachies up and down [...]. So, we seeked assurances that we can approve smaller budgets spontaneously, flexibly and on our own authority up to [approval limit].)

In summary, independent control is accompanied by clear separation of duties and resources, degrees of freedom in decision-making but ultimately requires alignment of individual actions. In line with the theoretical concept of independent control, most of the independently controlled partnerships had created no separate legal entity. However, this possibility should not be ruled out completely because in some partnerships independent and shared controls go hand in hand, for instance, if the overall governance structure is hybrid but individual partners take full responsibility of specific projects or projects tasks.

6.5.2.2.3 Shared Control

One fundamental characteristic of shared control is a consensus-oriented governance structure with governing bodies, which apply democratic decision-making procedures. CO4 and CO6 point to the high-level committee meetings where managers exercise top-down shared control, following the principle 'one man, one vote'. DC1 reports that the partners in his PPP consciously agreed on making decisions in consensus only because it improves their acceptance and the willingness to take ownership. Furthermore, the complexity of the governance structure requires that everybody has a say and that it is not about power play.

Wie werden Entscheidungen getroffen und werden Sie auch akzeptiert? [...] bei uns sagt das [zuständige Ministerium] ganz klar: "Wir sind zwar der Auftraggeber, aber unterwerfen uns in Anführungsstrichen sozusagen dieser Steuerungsstruktur des Vorstandes, weil, auch wenn wir das meiste Geld geben, es uns nichts bringt." De facto wäre es möglich, dass das [zuständige Ministerium] hier anruft und sagt: "Du machst bitte morgen das und das." Da haben sie eine ganz klare Weisungsmöglichkeit. [...] langfristig wird das Ganze nur funktionieren und nachhaltig sein, wenn die Mitglieder es tatsächlich von selber vorantreiben, auch die Themen vorantreiben. Es gibt [...] kein Mitglied und auch [...] kein Vorstandsmitglied, was immer zu 100% weiß, was da überall anders passiert. Müssen sie auch nicht. Die steuern das Ganze, und dann weiß es eben jeder für seine Verästelungen. (DC2)

(How are decisions made and how are they accepted? [...] in our case the [ministry in charge] clearly says: "Indeed, we are the client but in quotation marks we subordinate ourselves to this governance structure of the board because, although we give most of the money, it does not pay." In fact, it would be possible that the [ministry in charge] calls and says: "Tomorrow, you make this and that." There, they have a very clear opportunity to issue instructions. [...] in the long run, the whole thing will only work and be sustainable if the members proactively push it and also advance the topics. There is [...] no member and [...] no board member either that always knows 100% what happens elsewhere. And they do not need it. They control the whole thing and then everybody knows it for his part.)

But they [remark: private sector] can sit in the governance mechanisms. So, for example, in some of the new initiatives that we are planning, we do want them to be represented and we do want their voice to be heard, because they are more like private sector related initiatives, even for the credibility of the initiative and so that it interests the private sector. (IO7)

Other characteristics of shared control are relative low hierarchies where partners communicate actively and also spontaneously to coordinate their activities and demonstrate a high level of commitment. CO3 emphasizes that this works particularly well in bilateral cooperation, and CO1-1 underlines that it requires active participation by each partner. Moreover, respect is also paid to smaller partners, their ideas are seriously discussed, and the overall cooperation is target-oriented.

[...] dann kann man halt als normaler Partner [...] auch Vorschläge unterbreiten. Also, da muss ich sagen, gab es immer offene Diskussionen und eine [...] demokratische Entscheidungsfindung [...]. (CO5)

([...] then you can present ideas [...] also as a normal partner. To be honest, there have always been open discussions and a [...] democratic decision-making [...].)

[...] this is a really great cooperation because there are no hierarchies. We are now, we feel like a family. And this is why we do not need too much time to take a decision, we are open, and we always find very good solutions together. (CO11)

However, the shared control mechanisms based on the committee structure are significantly bypassed, or leveraged to some extent, if arrangements tend to be made bilaterally rather than negotiated in the committees.

[...] das eine ist eben sozusagen der offizielle Rahmen, in dem Dinge immer sehr respektvoll besprochen werden, aber die harten Details werden halt bilateral verhandelt. (CO8)

([...] the one thing is the formal level, so to say, where things are discussed always very respectfully, but the hard facts are negotiated bilaterally.)

Moreover, the balance of shared control can shift in those governance structures where committee and board members are elected for a certain term, but where the number of members or partners exceeds the number of available executive positions. Another limitation is that in some cases an IO's internal rules and guidelines or governmental influence inhibit the execution of shared control but require more authority for the public partner. Still, in summary, shared control seems to be a quite democratic governance mechanism that de facto levels off power distances among partners, promotes diversity of ideas and effective project implementation.

6.5.2.3 Categories of Control Mechanisms

As discussed in Chapter 3.4 and described for the present PPPs in Chapter 6.5.2.2, the three major control types can be further specified by three categories of control mechanisms, which are geared to the level of complexity and are classified according to either more formal or more informal orientation. Their occurence and characteristics in PPPs for development will be analyzed in the following sections.

6.5.2.3.1 Context-Oriented Control

Many of the partnerships falling into the category of context-oriented control maintain a global but decentralized governance structure whose stakeholders put strong emphasis on the active involvement of beneficiaries and local partners in any implementation activity. CO3 stresses that in his PPP clearly designated coordinators on each partner's side align their actions closely and are used to communicate rather informally and spontaneously.

> *Und zusammen mit den Business Ownern, mit den Prozessverantwortlichen der Partner oder den zukünftigen Kunden, [...] hat man dann entsprechend das prototypische [Produkt] designt. (CO5)*
> (And together with the business owners, with the process owners from the partners or the future clients, [...] they designed the prototypical [product] accordingly.)

CO8 speaks in this context of an "agile and iterative process" that includes the local partners from the "requirement analyses" to the final implementation. Moreover, IO7 emphasizes that high control complexity requires leaving much freedom of decision-making to the local level where the headquarters is consulted only for matters of overarching interest, such as the cooperation with potentially risky partners. A pronounced sharing of responsibilities is accompanied by little control tightness.

> *[...] there is a lot of division of responsibilities. There are some responsibilities that are given to junior staff, and they have decision or power on certain themes. When there is a problem, the problem may get at our level, at my level. And we just discuss, and some decisions are taken at my level. If the problem is a big problem, or an issue that may have a broader impact even outside [PPP name], then of course it elevates to senior management. (IO8)*

In summary, CO13-2 remarks that longstanding relationships and a proven record of success from joint previous business engagements or PPP activities promote context-oriented control while a high number and diversity of partners make it simply imperative.

6.5.2.3.2 Content-Oriented Control

The analyzed PPPs being most closely related to this category are neither subject to a low level of control complexity nor do they face very tight formal control measures. It should be noted that characteristics of all three categories can be found in a single partnership, depending on the project status, on the type and number of actors involved, and on the extent to which stakeholders really follow procedures as per governance structure. For instance, CO3 tells that in a follow-up partnership of the original PPP more formal control is applied, going along with more power of governing bodies. Thus, the control complexity is higher than usual. Still, they also continue informal communication and coordination processes:

> *Also [Name der Nachfolger-PPP] ist wesentlich formeller strukturiert. Da gibt es wesentlich, auch weil mehr Partner involviert sind, mehr Gremien, [...] Steuerungsausschuss, Telefonkonferenzen dieser Gremien. (CO3)*
>
> (Well, the [name of the follow-up PPP] is more formally structured. Also, because more partners are involved, more bodies exist, [...] steering committees, telephone conferences of these bodies.)

As described by CO4 or CO6, the top management can directly influence decision-making processes through the annual meetings of the board of directors, while CO7 emphasizes that adopting the role of a parent company allows to directly intervening in implementation processes. IO7 adds that also experiences and competences in partnership work determine the level of formal control in the same way as critical processes are relevant for the whole organization, such as risk assessment (Chapter 6.5.2.3.1):

> *So, back to the monitoring of the project, we would have up to four times a year tele-conferences with the project managers of the organizations like [PPP name]. So, they give us updates. We will attend some of their meetings if they are in [...]. When they pull together their stakeholders, we will go there to talk about our part and to hear what is going on. Just to keep an eye on things [...], but we are not implementing. We are just present. So, they know we are not just giving money and going away. (CO7)*

> *But then we have a lot of offices which are not so used to working with the private sector. So, they need a little bit more guidance and that can then be provided by the regional and headquarters units. (IO7)*

However, two more private sector actors reported from other not very complex partnerships that are framed by little control tightness and remain without much intervention by the executive bodies, which leave them a high degree of freedom in decision-making. In summary, the content-oriented control in practice is adjusted to the way control is exercised, but is still more flexible to use a customized mix of formal and informal MC mechanisms and is moreover applied to PPPs with higher levels of control complexity as well.

6.5.2.3.3 Consultation-Oriented Control

Consultation-oriented control seems to rely on close cooperation and intensive communication between governing bodies and operational project actors. For efficiency reasons, the coordination is sometimes confined to the headquarters or board level only, and control mechanisms, such as reporting lines, are therefore exercised from afar. The integration of existing sales and distribution staff into the PPP implementation is part of a control approach that is geared to a centralized rather than decentralized governance structure. However, this requires clear responsibilities and the acceptance of the corresponding decision-makers by all involved partners.

> *[...] wir hatten immer unseren Projektingenieur vor Ort, der auch Geschäftsführer der Projektgesellschaft war [...] und dort auch sehr gut vernetzt ist. Der hat regelmäßig berichtet. Es gab eine monatliche Telefonkonferenz, in der sich dann die beiden zuständigen [Projektmanager] mit dem Projektverantwortlichen vor Ort ausgetauscht haben. (CO6)*
> ([...] we always had our project engineer on the ground who also was the director of the project corporation [...] and has established an excellent network there. He reported to us on a regular basis. There was a monthly telephone conference where the two responsible [project managers] exchanged views with the local project owner.)

> *Da gibt es einen ganz klaren Ansprechpartner, und [Anmerkung: die Ergebnisse aus den Gesprächen mit diesem sind] [...] das, was wir dann auch abstimmen. Und das ist dann maßgeblich. Ich diskutiere solche Fragen jetzt nicht mit jedem einzelnen Mitglied, sondern wenn überhaupt, dann mit dem Vorstand und mit dem Auftraggeber [zuständiges Ministerium]. (DC2)*
> (There is a very specific contact person and [remark: the results from the conversations with him are] [...] that what we coordinate then. And that is decisive. I do not discuss such questions with every single member but with the board and with the client [ministry in charge].)

> *So, usually we have something like a project board and we do have a [...] project appraisal committee who needs to approve each new project [...] also provides a lot of feedback on the design of the project. (IO7)*

However, as mentioned before in Chapter 6.5.2.1, control can also be exercised through informal consultations outside the regular governance structure.

> *Also, es gibt einen formalen Abstimmungsprozess, und es gibt einen informellen. Das ist eigentlich auch in jeder Organisation so. [Anmerkung: Zum Zeitpunkt des] Termins, an dem sich alle zusammensetzen und [...] zu einem Ergebnis kommen wollen, ist das Ergebnis meistens [Anmerkung: bereits] abgesprochen. (CO8)*
> (Well, there is a formal coordination process and there is an informal one. This is actually in each organization like that. [Remark: On the date of the] meeting when all people come together [...] and want to reach a conclusion, the results have often been agreed [remark: already].)

In summary, consultation-oriented control in PPPs for development is process-oriented like in the theory, and formal rather than informal. Still, informal interorganizational consultations seem to be common in many partnerships and are important for the coordination of resource contributions and alignment of different interests.

6.5.2.4 Level of integration of Control Systems

Integration of control systems basically means the extent to which partners coordinate and share their control activities. It is strongly related to the governance structure but also to equity ownership and resource contribution. Four areas seem to be particularly relevant in this context, namely monitoring and performance measurement as well as management of human resources and event coordination. While DC5 tells from the existence of a joint impact model, CO7 regrets the absence of joint benchmarks and milestones:

> *We do it for ourselves within [CO7]. It is one of those things that I dream of. A few years, maybe a year from now or two [...], [remark that really depends] on the projects, [...] [remark: we will] benchmark [remark: the projects] against the industry. (CO7)*

> *Nosotros [...] tenemos un modelo de impactos donde nosotros analizamos cómo y si hemos logrado el objetivo o no lo hemos logrado. (DC5)*
> (We have an impact model where we analyze how and if we have achieved the objective or not.)

Monitoring activities seem to be undertaken often separately but sometimes jointly. At least, the lack of coordination may cause some trouble in the PPP implementation. Still, it should be noted that some activities only require individual monitoring. For instance, CO4 emphasizes that he had to monitor the use of own resources for internal purposes only and to report them to his superior accordingly.

> *Bei manchen Projekten ist das Monitoring auch so eine Sache, die stark beim Projektpartner liegt. Auf der anderen Seite ist das auch eine Sache, die auch die [DC3] natürlich nachverfolgt. Das Monitoring an sich kann geteilt werden, kann aber auch bei den Privaten liegen oder nur bei [DC3]. Das ist auch sehr unterschiedlich. (DC3)*
> (In some projects, the monitoring is a thing that strongly lies with the project partner. On the other side, it is also a matter that the [DC3] monitors. The monitoring as such can be shared, but can also lie with the privates or with [DC3] only. This is very different.)

> *It's sometimes a pain in the neck as well that they have their own monitoring templates and then you need to do several for different ones. (IO7)*

In terms of human resources management, most stakeholders maintain a separate equity ownership structure. Thus, each partner provides project staff or maintains his project team but does not finance someone jointly or second staff to another partner. As indicated in Chapter 6.2.5, CO4 represents an exception because for the first years of the PPP the company left an employee to the IO partner. Despite clear rules to prevent conflicts of interest (Chapter 6.2.2.3), the exchange of staff helps public and private sector to understand each other better and therefore contributes to integrating the respective control systems in PPPs:

> *[...] wir haben eine Kollegin, die war zufälligerweise auf Jobsuche, wollte sich weiterentwickeln, und man hat ihr eben angeboten, bei der [IO Partner] anzufangen. Also, man hat dann den [CO4]-Vertrag [...] nicht gekündigt, aber er ist eben auf still gesetzt worden. (CO4)*
> ([...] we had a colleague who was coincidentally looking for a new job, wanted to develop herself, and then she was offered to start working with the [IO partner]. Thus, the [CO4] contract was not terminated but was simply inactivated.)

Moreover, DC4 emphasizes that local colleagues in particular serve as interfaces with other local stakeholders and are therefore elements to build an integrated control system between partners but also between headquarter and local level in very decentralized governance structures. In summary, the level of integration of control systems is limited in most PPPs at the current stage. However, the experiences from the quoted interview partners revealed potential for better integration in the four very relevant areas of activity that were mentioned at the beginning of this chapter.

6.5.3 Level of Cooperation

This chapter focuses on the extent and quality of cooperation between PPP stakeholders. First, a general analysis addressing reasons and characteristics of high and low level of cooperation is conducted while the two subsequent subchapters make reference to some basics of the ACI and the TCE, namely actor orientations and opportunism, which are both specific indicators of the goodness of interorganizational cooperation. Regarding the general understanding of good cooperation, CO1-1, CO3, CO6 and IO8 explain that in their view partnerships should distinguish themselves by a high level of mutual respect and equality at eye-level where intercultural differences are a source of creativity rather than being perceived as an obstacle, and where people closely collaborate and can rely on each other. CO2 and DC1 praise the open, honest, collegial and constructive way of cooperation in their partnerships. CO11 even describes the PPP actors as a family. Thus, they all made predominantly positive experiences.

> *[...] we collaborate in a spirit of partnership. So, it is not that we put pressure on them or they put pressure on us [...]. So, we really try to work well together and in the mutual respect. And even we try to serve the interest of the partnership of course. (IO8)*

However, in the context of cooperation with local stakeholders CO5 remarks that in spite of overall positive results partnerships can produce winners and losers among local actors, for instance, the introduction of a new technology makes the beneficiaries more productive while other market participants loose competitiveness. This might be a source of conflicts. Other aspects that CO8, DC5 and IO8 define as characteristics of close cooperation are a very good match of complementary resources, are the creation of synergies between the different partners, and a good portion of pragmatism with respect to the achievement of common goals. Moreover, IO5 adds the exchange of staff as a sign of very good collaboration:

> *[...] and sometimes you even have exchange of staff. So, you can actually have a staff member from the private sector being seconded to the [IO5] team and working with them as a team. So, it really varies from sector to sector, from country to country, depending on the project. (IO5)*

Still, cooperative relations cannot necessarily be taken for granted. So, some interviewees made ambivalent experiences. Two of them bemoaned little involvement and interest of the public partner in the operational work while another one felt by contrast too much controlled. However, both see the reasons for this in the institutional nature of the public sector rather than in bad intentions of the concrete actors.

> *From the [IO partner] side there are three different persons, and I would say their role has been limited to be more like an advisor or a provider than a team or really work together. [...] the interactions are very limited. (CO14)*

> *I think the public sector always tried to maintain the lead. I mean, they control it, the project is where it is going to go. (CO12)*

[...] einmal pro Woche hat man ihm dann quasi freundlicherweise die Chance gegeben, das alles abzunicken, was wir hier so machen. Wir hätten [IO Partner] auch gerne mehr eingebunden [...]. Also, das war nicht so, dass wir das da an uns reißen wollten, ganz im Gegenteil. Wir hätten uns [...] viel mehr Input erhofft [...]. Also, ich habe jetzt [...] viel kritisiert, aber da geht es mehr um dieses Bürokratiemonster UN. Da geht es jetzt nicht unbedingt um die Leute, mit denen man zu tun hat. Also, die Zusammenarbeit war eigentlich gut, freundschaftlich und kooperativ. Das kann ich eigentlich nicht anders sagen. (n/a)

([...] once per week he was kindly given the opportunity to agree on all that what we have done. Actually, we would have liked to involve [IO partner] more [...]. So, it was not like that we wanted to usurp that, quite the contrary. We would have [...] expected much more input [...]. Well, I now have [...] criticized a lot, but it is more about this immense bureaucracy called UN. It is not necessarily about the people you are dealing with. Thus, the collaboration was actually good, friendly and cooperative. I cannot say anything different.)

However, CO14 remarks that there are different levels of interaction. Thus, interaction often takes place with counterparts from the other side only. Hence, private sector operational staff communicates with those from the public sector. The same applies to middle and executive management. In summary, the overall level of cooperation is very positive in most of the analyzed PPPs although there remains potential of closer cooperation and coordination in some partnerships.

6.5.3.1 Actor Orientations

On the basis of the five actor orientations of the ACI, the interview partners were asked to make a qualitative assessment of the overall level of cooperation in their respective partnerships (Chapter 4.1.2) and to consider different actor constellations for that, if appropriate. Although not all interview partners were in a position to make an assessment, tendencies still reveal. Most of them emphasize the cooperative nature of their partnerships while egoistic-rational behavior obviously appeared in some PPPs as well. An altruistic, competitive or hostile orientation is adopted relatively rarely (Table 53).

	Hostile	Competitive	Egoistic-rational	Cooperative	Altruistic
Companies	2	2	4	10	1
DCAs	1	0	1	5	1
IOs	0	1	0	1	1

Table 53: Scale-based assessment of actor orientations.
(Nominal frequency)

Several interview partners comment that they experienced situationally and over time two, three or even four of these behavior patterns in the same partnership. Notwithstanding, they emphasize that only cooperative behavior based on consensus is successful in the long run. Also, hostile behavior can vary and often depends very much on the concrete people involved and less on the represented organization as such.

Also, zum Großteil war es kooperativ, weil man immer versucht hat, einen Konsens zu finden [...]. Es gibt mehrere Beispiele. In sämtlichen Sitzungen, die wir da hatten bzw. haben, wo eben stark der eigene Nutzen hervorkommt. Und ich rede jetzt nicht nur von unseren [...] Mitwettbewerbern, sondern auch von NGOs, usw., die dann eben Vorstellungen haben, die beispiellose Sachen fordern, die eben einfach auch nicht möglich sind. Also um Ihre Frage zu beantworten, 80 % kooperativ, aber dann egoistisch-rational. (CO4)

(It was mostly cooperative because they tried to reach a consensus [...]. There are several examples. In numerous meetings that we had or have, from where the individual benefit strongly emerges. And I do not only talk about our [...] competitors but also about NGOs, etc., who had some kind of ideas, who claim unprecedented things, which were basically not possible. To answer your question, 80% cooperative, but then egoistic-rational.)

Und auch ablehnend, also Verweigerung, ja, zerstörerische Argumentationen, keine rationale Abwägung von Argumenten [...] aus verschiedenen Gründen. Und das war mal bei einem Partner so, und beim gleichen Partner war es dann wieder andersrum, je nachdem welche Person mitinvolviert war. (CO5)

(And also negative, also refusal, even destructive argumentations, no rational weighing of arguments [...] for different reasons. And this varied by the same partner, in dependence of the involved person.)

Several public and private actors unanimously underline that non-cooperative actors are usually detected quickly and at an early stage because cooperative behavior is pivotal for building trustful relationships without which large and complex partnerships with several diverse members would not work. CO8 emphasizes moreover that in his perception most partners consider their partnership activities as long-term investments and are not keen on quick benefits. Competitive and egoistic-rational actor orientations were noted both interorganizationally and intraorganizationally, even if these partners had to represent the interests of their fellow partners.

Kompetitives [Anmerkung: Verhalten] gab es [...] interessanterweise leider auch in der eigenen Firma. Das sollte eigentlich nicht der Fall sein, gab es aber auch, dass Gruppen kompetitiv gearbeitet haben, aber natürlich auch zwischen Partnern. (n/a)

(Interestingly competitive [remark: behavior] existed [...] regrettably also within the own company. Actually, that should not be the case, but it happened, that groups worked competitively, but of course between partners as well.)

Egoistisch-rational [...], es war oft auch klar, dass einzelne Personen hier nicht unbedingt vordergründig im Interesse des vertretenden Partners agieren, sondern auch egoistisch, mit eigenen Zielen. (CO5)

(Egoistic-reational [...], it was often obvious that single actors did actually not act necessarily in the interest of the partner they represented, but also followed their egoistic and own objectives.)

Furthermore, DC5 points to non-competitive orientations within sectors while CO12 underlines the opportunistic nature of competitive behavior. However, it still seems that some interview partners interpreted the terms *competitive* and *egoistic-rational* synonymously:

I think it was somewhere between cooperative and competitive. And so they are willing to work with each other, but they are also like, you know, "Well, if I do it this way, I may make a little bit more money than does my partner here". (CO12)

> *Entre el grupo del sector privado es cooperativo y competitivo, aquí dentro. Pero entre el sector privado y el sector público es cooperativo. (DC5)*
> (Within the private sector group it is cooperative and competitive, but between private sector and public sector it is cooperative.)

Altruism was noted for only a few partners, such as NGOs or some local stakeholders, because most organizations pursue clear business interests or have to fulfill a given mandate.

> *[...] jeder hatte seinen klaren Auftrag von seiner Organisation, die eine gewisse Zielvorstellung hatte. Auch wenn [DCA Partner] z.B. eine gewisse Zielvorstellung hat, dann steht dahinter auch ein Budget, dann steht dahinter auch ein Job, etc. Also, altruistisch würde ich jetzt bei einer NGO sehen, wo jeder irgendwie sagt: "Ich mache meinen Job, ohne irgendwie dafür Geld zu bekommen." Insofern sehe ich eigentlich [...] nur die Möglichkeit von entweder kooperativ oder egoistisch-rational. (CO8)*
> ([...] everybody had a clear mandate from his organization, which had certain objectives. Even if [DCA partner] also has certain objectives, where is a budget behind, where is a job behind, etc. Thus, I would see altruism for a NGO where everybody somehow says: "I do my job with getting any money for that." That is why I actually see [...] only the opportunity of either *cooperative* or *egoistic-rational.*)

> *Die [anderer DCA Partner] ist sicherlich nicht so altruistisch in ihrem Handeln wie [lokale Stakeholder]. Ich meine die [anderer DCA Partner] ist eine [Rechtsform des anderen DCA Partners], die verdienen letztendlich einen Haufen Geld damit. Die Leute, die ich von [lokale Stakeholder] vor Ort kennengelernt habe, das sind wirklich noch Leute, die von der Entwicklungshilfe überzeugt sind, und das ist einfach ihr Leben, und die stellen auch ihr eigenes Wohl unter das des Projekts. Und die machen das wirklich aus reiner Überzeugung, sehr altruistisch kann man sagen. (n/a)*
> (The [other DCA partner] is truly not as altruistic in its actions as the [local stakeholders]. I mean the [other DCA partner] is a [legal form of the other DCA partner] who earn a lot of money with that. The people I got to know from the [local stakeholders] on the ground, they are really people who are convinced of development cooperation and that is basically their life. They subject their own benefit to that one of the project. And they really do it by conviction, one can say very altruistic.)

In summary, CO13-2 concludes that only cooperative orientation forms a sustainable partnership model that can create benefits for all stakeholders. He argues that competitive, egoistic-rational and hostile behavior hinder the joint solution of common problems, which usually always arise during PPP implementation, while altruistic behavior would not sufficiently incentivize actors to invest and commit themselves as much as necessary to the partnership as such.

6.5.3.2 Causes and Risk of Opportunistic Behavior

Opportunism or opportunistic behavior is one of the two fundamental theoretical assumptions that connect the ACI with the TCE and is a driver of non-cooperative behavior in interorganizational relationships, such as PPPs (Chapter 4.2.3). This chapter reveals causes and risks of opportunistic behavior and presents counteractions to prevent or limit the consequences of this phenomenon. Figure 48 gives an overview of these aspects and shows when the risk of opportunistic behavior is high or low.

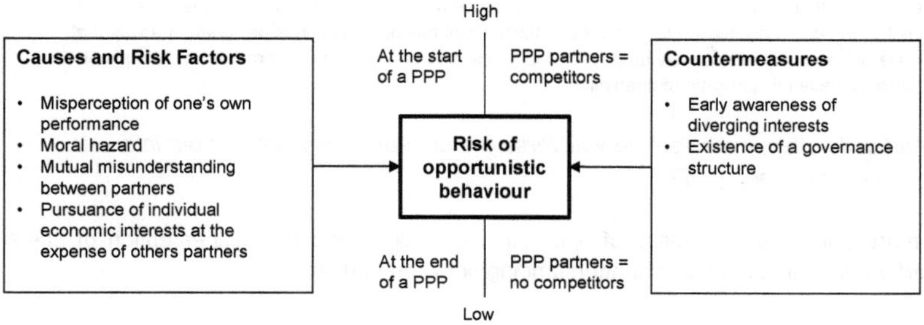

Figure 48: Risk of opportunistic behavior.

One main issue is the pursuance of individual economic interests at the expense of others partners, thus typifying an egoistic-rational actor's attitude where only the own gain matters. This risk is particularly high if regular market competitors are involved in a joint partnership. One private sector interviewee reported from a situation where the main competitor has been partner at the same time, advocating for intentionally lower quality requirements for the underlying product in order to increase the economic benefit. However, maximum efficiency and durability formed core objectives of this PPP so that this corporate partner's attempt infringed upon the goals of waste reduction and sustainability. An example of moral hazard is presented by CO12 in this context:

> *So, there is a cooperative ability to win the project, but then there is a competition inside each group to maximize their gain. (CO12)*

In addition, CO8 emphasizes by the subsequent comment that competitive behavior is very natural, while CO10-1 states that competitors can also well collaborate with each other if the concrete actors consider the partnership as a repeated game in which cooperation implies the highest outcome for everyone.

> *Was sicherlich immer eine Rolle bei so vielen Partnern spielt, auch vielen privaten Partnern, dass vielleicht eben doch im Hintergrund gewisse Konkurrenz eine Rolle spielt oder manche Partner eher miteinander können als andere. (CO8)*
> (What probably always matters with so many partners, also many private partners, is that a certain competition plays a role in the background or some partners can get along with each other better than others can.)

Moreover, CO6 points to the fact that the goverance structures can stop opportunistic behavior at an early stage, and IO7 underlines that early awareness of diverging interests cannot rule out moral hazard, but it can at least mitigate the risk of opportunism:

> *Natürlich gibt es dann immer wieder auch den Versuch die eigene Sichtweise und die eigenen Prioritäten […] in so einer Diskussion […] voranzubringen. Klar. Aber die Funktionsweise dieser Organisation ist so angelegt, dass das relativ*

schnell wieder so eingeordnet und einsortiert wird, dass man am Ende da doch kooperativ unterwegs ist. Einfach, weil wir dieses Einstimmigkeitsprinzip haben. (CO6)

(Of course, there is once in a while an attempt to move forward one's own view or one's own priorities [...] in such a discussion [...]. But the functioning of this organization is designed in a way that this is arranged again relatively quickly, so that in the end one is on a cooperative way. Simply because we have this principle of unanimity.)

And quite often, if they are very adverse, we do realize early on that our interests do not really meet. (IO7)

Other more unintentional causes of opportunistic behavior are the misperception of one's own performance and mutual misunderstanding between partners.

[...] el riesgo es que no haya un trabajo conjunto entre el sector privado y el sector público, que haya una separación y que no haya un entendimiento. [...] había dos personas que buscaban un poco más su beneficio pero terminaron entendiendo que era el beneficio para todos [...]. (DC5)

([...] the risk is that there is no joint collaboration between the private sector and the public sector, that there is a separation and that there is no understanding. [...] there were two people who were seeking a bit more for their own benefit, and they terminated by understanding that it was a benefit for all [...].)

[...] everybody thinks they are the bests [...] and they are not the bests. I mean [IO5] probably thinks "we do so well" and the private sector comes and thinks "what the hell are they doing!". People are already thinking about that. (IO5)

According to the experiences of CO9-1 and IO7, the risk of opportunism is highest at the beginning of a partnership when the different actors undergo a joint learning phase and try out what works and what does not work. CO8 comments that this behavior is reasonable because everyone enters into a partnership with a clear mandate and certain objectives that are henceforth negotiated and harmonized and in doing so, everybody needs to make some compromises. In the end, only those remain who expect an outcome that outweighs the sum of their compromises and investments as well as inherent risks.

Man kann vielleicht unterteilen, dass man sagt: "Am Anfang haben wir [...] opportunistischer agiert, waren so ein bisschen wie ein kleines Start-up und haben uns dies und das angeschaut." Und jetzt langsam, mit steigender Größe wird es "professioneller", in dem Sinne, dass wir arbeitsteiliger arbeiten, vielleicht mehr Ressourcen einbinden [...]. Wir versuchen einfach zu wachsen. (CO9-1)

(Maybe you can structure it by saying: "At the outset we have [...] acted more opportunistically, were such a kind of little start-up and were taking a look at this or that." And now slowly, with increasing size it becomes more "professional", in the sense, that we divide more labor perhaps integrate more resources [...]. We simply try to grow.)

In summary, this chapter touches upon elements of game theory but only mentions them without the intention of further theoretical discussion, which would go beyond the scope of the present work. In principle, opportunism is an issue in PPPs for development but a diligent partner selection at the beginning, the implementation of a formal governance structure, and the mere course of time help to prevent or mitigate the risk of opportunistic behavior.

6.6 Management Control

This chapter serves the answering of **research question 2.1** and forms the core part of the analysis of the empirical results. The structure of the present chapter is strongly geared to the control archetypes and typologies in Chapter 0 and therefore aims to contrast the conceptual and theoretical basics with the empirical evidence of the field research. It begins with some aspects of formal and informal control, encompassing behavior/results control and clan/social control, and continues with an analysis of the control extent/tightness and environmental factors which influence the MC in the PPPs on scope.

The importance of MC for project work and PPP implementation has been unanimously confirmed by all interview partners. They underline that MC helps to define specific goals and overall objectives, PPP activities and related milestones. Thus, it makes project management more feasible, as stated by DC5, and it is imperative to measure achievement of results, in particular if a large number of partners is involved.

> *[...] was die Rolle an Management Control betrifft, geht es darum, die Zielvorgaben optimal umzusetzen [...] Ergebniskontrolle, Budgeteinhaltung, Zeit spielen natürlich eine Rolle. Abhängigkeiten in Arbeitspaketen, das sind alles Dinge, die eine gute Projektsteuerung leistet. (CO5)*
> ([...] concerning the role of management control, it is about optimal implementation of target benchmarks [...]. Results control, budget compliance, time also play a role of course. Dependencies in work packages, all these are things which a good project control has to cover.)

> *[...] Steuerungsstruktur ist [...] ein wichtiges Element im Projektmanagement [...]. (DC1)*
> ([...] control structure is [...] an important element in project management [...].)

> *Management control has always a very important role to play. (IO1)*

In summary, CO5 stresses that common project control and management methods and procedures are often employed although they usually require customization to specific project needs and to the number and types of involved stakeholders.

6.6.1 Behavior and Results Control

This chapter gives an overview of different formal control structures and mechanisms that apply in PPPs for development. First, the performance orientation of the different public and private actors will be analyzed before considering the performance measurement as such, including benchmark indicators used in PPPs. Monitoring and reporting constitute two core elements of MC, and that is why they are analyzed separately. Finally, the use of behavior and results control will be put in the context of rules and guidelines which may frame the PPP implementation.

6.6.1.1 Performance Orientation

Different understandings of performance orientation imply diverging requirements and claims for performance measurement, and result in two major perspectives, one that advocates for more specific and measurable results, while the other one follows a looser impact-oriented approach. First of all, CO1-1 and DC2 call for a performance orientation that is fit for purpose, which basically means that the people involved develop awareness of the overall PPP setting including partnership-related and environmental challenges and local conditions as well as a sense of feasibility of intended activities. Thus, objectives and targets are supposed to be realistic and suitable and need to be customized for each PPP project individually. This requires an open mindset that allows making adjustments to the original planning and goal-setting in the course of the project.

> *Ja, ich meine, wenn Sie dann dort vor Ort sind, dann brauchen Sie halt mal für 50 Kilometer drei Stunden. Das muss man dabei alles berücksichtigen. Und das kriegen Sie bei Projekten nur dann mit, wenn Sie auch mal vor Ort waren und gesehen haben, wie die Verhältnisse sind. Und das wird häufig bei Projekten unterschätzt. (CO1-1)*
>
> (Well, I mean, when you are there on-site, you sometimes need three hours for just 50 kilometers. All that you have to remind. And you only get this if you have ever been on the ground and have seen what the conditions there are. This is something which is often underestimated in projects.)

> *Also, ich sage auch immer, was zählt, ist das Ergebnis. Wenn man irgendwie jetzt im Laufe der Umsetzung feststellt: "Mensch, auf die Art und Weise oder mit den und den Aktivitäten kommen wir da gar nicht hin," dann bin ich da total offen, auch zu sagen: "Dann machen wir es anders." Oder dann überlegen wir zusammen, dass wir die Aktivität dann nicht machen und eine andere Aktivität machen. Oder man kann auch irgendwie die Strategie ändern [...]. (DC1)*
>
> (Well, I always say, what matters is the result. If you recognize at one point during the implementation: "Gosh, in this way or by these activities we cannot make it," then I am totally open to say: "Then let us do it differently." Or we deliberate together whether to do not do the activity, or do another activity. Or you can also somehow change the strategy [...].)

In the context of impact-making, DC2 adds that they challenge every planned activity by its expected impact and contribution to the PPP's objectives. In his view, performance orientation implies that the process and control design promotes the quick achievement of good and viable results. However, there seem to exist diverging understandings of, claims of, and views on the use of rather specific quantitative versus looser qualitative performance measurement. Although the use of specific quantitative indicators is very common, critical voices remark the sometimes limited explanatory power of these indicators and the unavailability of baseline data, while CO5 emphasizes that cause-and-effect relationships are often hard to determine.

> *I mean if you say that [remark: a certain] percentage of the population knew about this problem [...], that's very quantitative, but is not yet changing [remark: the population's] behavior. [...] it's just an intermediate quantitative measure of awareness. (IO3)*

Usually, we do need to put quite sort of impact or target indicators and baselines in the projects. But quite often we do have the problem of not having proper baseline data [...]. So, it also takes quite a bit of resources to get the proper baseline and then to think what are sort of meaningful targets. (CO7)

Depending on the PPP type, the measurement approaches and the understanding of goal achievement, there tend to exist different ideas about partnership performance between public and private sector. Still, a few private sector interviewees acknowledged that in the development cooperation much focus is placed on very concrete and measurable project targets, which are prepared on the basis of homogenous criteria for all PPPs.

Natürlich sind wir jetzt wieder bei der Diskussion: Sagt [CO3] "Ja, das ist erreicht." oder sagt der [IO Partner]-Mann "Es ist erreicht."? [IO Partner] sagt: "Ja, ich habe die Signatures auf den Verträgen." Ich sage: "Ja, es ist jetzt aber noch nicht in jedem Land implementiert." (CO3)
(Of course, we are back to the discussion: If [CO3] says "Yes, that is achieved." or if the [IO partner]-guy says "It is achieved."? [IO partner] says: "Yes, I have got the signatures on the contracts." I say: "Yes, but it is still not yet implemented in every country.")

Und ansonsten ist mir eben auch aufgefallen, dass in der EZ eine sehr starke Wirkungsorientierung herrscht, die immer wieder anmahnt: "Wir müssen die Erträge, die Einkommen steigern. Wo stehen wir? Was machen wir hier?" Während in so einem Forschungsprojekt [...] reicht halt einfach mal ein Paper und ein Vortrag auf einer Konferenz, um die Vorgaben zu erfüllen. (CO5)
(And moreover noted that in the field of development cooperations dominates a very strong performance orientation, which urges again and again: "We have to increase the outcomes, the incomes. What do we stand for? What are we doing here?" While in such a research project [...] a paper or a presentation at a conference simply suffice to meet the requirements.)

We have to impose the milestones in a way. As I said before, the [IOs and NGOs] work differently [...]. They are helping [country XY]. But we want to see whom we have helped in [country XY]. They want to be seen doing good [...]. They do help the poor people. But [...] we granulate, we want to know whom we helped, [...] if we give a scholarship, which students got a scholarship and what happened to them afterwards. (CO7)

In summary, some interview partners assess the performance orientation of the other partners quite critically but there is common understanding across sectors about the necessity of effective performance measurement in PPPs, which must not necessarily be quantitative.

6.6.1.2 Elements of Performance Measurement

In conformity with the analysis of the overall performance orientation in the PPPs on scope, this chapter gives an overview of different performance measurement elements, which will be addressed in more detail in the following chapters. In particular, the private sector and DCAs have established numerous different tools and approaches of performance meausurement. Some of them are characteristic of certain partners, such as the business case focus and management incentives in the private sector, but the general impression is that all kinds of actors use a bundle of indicators and different complementary mechanisms to measure the performance of PPPs (Table 54).

Interview partners	Private	Public	
		DCA	IO
Elements of performance measurement			
Accounting and commercial calculations (business case)	x		
Baseline study (determination of target indicators) and endline study (target attainment control)	x	x	
Determination of minimum performance standards	x		
Evaluations	x	x	
Financial criteria (e.g. volumina)	x		
Key performance indicators (KPIs)	x		
Management incentives	x		
Milestone-monitoring		x	
Operation plan	x	x	
Regular meetings and workshops	x		
Results-based approach (actual results vs. expected output)			x

Table 54: Elements of performance measurement.

Some of them are individually determined by each partner but most of them are jointly agreed upon. For instance, the results-oriented operation plan is a tool where for each overarching objective subgoals and target values are determined, which in turn correspond to the expected results. If a PPP is rolled out in several places or countries these goals and targets are further broken down. One private sector interviewee stated that the remuneration of the involved actors depends to some extent on goal attainment in the PPP. However, some benchmark indicators form only means to an end, as stated by CO3. For instance, the number of delivered trainings or sold products is only a vehicle to approximate the number of people actually reached. Other factors like budget compliance do not say anything about whether an impact has been made or not. That is why CO14 points to the difficulty of formulating meaningful performance indicators. In a positive sense, CO1-1 adds that indicators hardly reflect multiplier effects so that the actual impact may exceed the measured performance:

> *Denn in diesen Communities ist der Austausch untereinander relativ hoch, und die lernen dann sozusagen voneinander, insbesondere in [...] abgelegenen Gebieten. Das gilt jetzt nicht für die großen Städte. (CO1-1)*
>
> (Because there is quite a lot of exchange amongst each other in these communities, and they learn from each other, particularly in [...] remote areas. This does not apply for the big cities.)

Some interviewees reported from too loose or insufficient performance measurement, which manifested itself in absence or shortcomings of performance indicators. DC6 states that they had some benchmarks, which were finally not quantified, while DC5 made the experience that initially agreed milestones and other indicators were disregarded from some point onwards when the focus of the PPP activities had shifted and concentrated on one specific line of activities. Moreover, DC4 bemoans that the performance measurement in his PPP was firstly not granular enough and secondly moderated over time:

> *[...] es gab eben nur ein großes Deliverable, einen großen Meilenstein [...]. Da gab es jetzt keine Zwischenschritte mehr, die gemonitort wurden [...]. Es gab natürlich ganz klar diese Ziele, aber die wurden im Projektverlauf immer weniger kommuniziert und immer weiter gesenkt. (DC4)*
> ([...] there was only one big deliverable, one big milestone [...]. There were no further intermediate steps, which were monitored [...]. Of course, there were these very clear goals, but they were less and less communicated and more and more decreased.)

In summary, both public and private sector pursue diverse performance measurement approaches that can measure and control the actual performance relatively well if they are used in a combined manner. Altogether, there exists no one-size-fits-all approach because objective performance measurement is hard to reach so that much of it is often left to individual interpretation in the end.

6.6.1.3 Benchmark Indicators

This chapter compares different benchmarking approaches applied to the PPPs on scope and analyzes the characteristics, but also strengths and weaknesses of qualitative and quantitative indicators. Table 55 gives an overview of diverse quantitative and qualitative benchmark indicators that have been mentioned by the different interview partners. Following a clustering approach by CO3, this table differentiates between impact-related core indicators and process indicators, which serve administrative purposes and are a means to an end.

	Benchmark indicators	Examples and specifications	Quantitative	Qualitative
Process indicators	Budget deviation	Within budget/budget overrun by x% or in absolute terms	x	
	Counseling sessions	Number	x	
	Countries or people reached (e.g. by a product, trainings, awareness campaign)	- Counseling/training delivered to x thousands of people - Engagement in x communities in the countries XYZ	x	
		Roll out of the PPP activities in x countries accomplished		x
	Meetings and workshops	Number	x	
	Memberships	- # of registrations - # of signatories that bind their production to certain upper emission limits or relinquish of the use of environmentally unfriendly ingredients in their supply chain	x	
	Time deviation	In nominal days or man-days	x	
	Trainings	X trainings à 90 minutes	x	
		Training accomplished (yes/no)		x
Core indicators	Acceptance of banking software	Number of transactions	x	
	Countries or people reached (e.g. by a product, trainings, awareness campaign)	- Outreach of x million beneficiaries by 20xx	x	
	Creation of a functioning PPP	- Creation of a product/service - Creation of a governance structure - Reaching economic viability		x
	Creation of decent jobs	Number of new jobs (differentiated by male/female)	x	
	Contribution to the SDGs	Contribution in currency XY to the SDGs	x	
	Development impact (e.g. knowledge transfer, improvement of living conditions/local production capacities)	Impact made (yes/no)		x
	Environmental impact	Reduction of CO2 emissions by X% or in tons	x	
	Health-related values	Improvement of the blood values of x%/absolute number of people, benchmarked against certain health parameters	x	
	Income increase	Income of target group increased on average by x%	x	
	Making value chains more sustainable	x% of the total value creation results from emission free production	x	
		Waste products can be fully recycled or used for other production purposes (yes/no)		x
	Marketability	Number of commercial clients for product XY	x	
		- Development of a business case accomplished - At least one external investor has decided to commercialize the outcome product XY of the PPP in country XY		x
	Products sold	Number of products sold/revenue	x	
		Availability on the ground (yes/no)		x
	Volumina of granted (micro-)credits	Amount and number	x	

Table 55: Overview of qualitative and quantitative benchmark indicators.

There exist diverging demands on the purpose of benchmarking and about the suitability of qualitative versus quantitative indicators. To start off, a quotation of CO1-1, who takes a slightly philosophical view when he points to the fact that the definition of benchmarks is strongly related to the question "what is an achievement?", makes clear that probably no kind of indicator can fully benchmark in numbers or qualitatively what the exact impact is that PPP activities have made:

> *Aber wenn ich sage: "Ich habe 10 Leuten über ein Projekt persönlich geholfen." Ist das ja auch schon ein Erfolg. Ja? Und da wir es hier immer mit Menschen zu tun haben, dürfen Sie diese Komponente nicht unterschätzen. Die können Sie nur in einer Projektformulierung nicht ausdrücken. Die können Sie auch schlecht messen, aber ich sage Ihnen mal bei dem, was ich bisher erlebt habe, bei Abschlussveranstaltungen, wenn dann irgendwie 10, 15, 20 Leute oder auch 30 Leute, die da sind, selber aufstehen, sich zu Wort melden und sagen: "Das und das war dabei für mich wichtig," ist das schon ein Wert. Der spielt im Gesamtprojekt unter den Aspekten, wie wir sie jetzt gerade diskutiert haben, eine sehr untergeordnete Rolle. Aber individuell kann das viel bewirkt haben, was wir gar nicht wissen, was daraus geworden ist. (CO1-1)*
>
> (But when I say: "I personally helped 10 people in a project." This is already a success, right? And as we are always dealing with people, you should not underestimate this component. You cannot express this by a project formulation alone. That is something you can just badly measure, but I tell you what I hitherto experienced during final events, when 10, 15, 20 people or even 30 people, who are there, stand up, take the floor and say: "This and that was important for me. This is already a value as such. For the aspects of the total project, as we just discussed them, that plays a really minor role. But individually this might have made a lot of impact, from which we do not know how it ended up.)

Moreover, CO5, DC2, and IO3 unanimously remark that benchmarks, such as improvement of the overall living conditions, relying on strong cause-and-effect relationships and being subject to multiple potential influence factors, are hard to measure because their contribution is almost not attributable. In line with IO5 and others, DC3 emphasizes that benchmark indicators are used to be specifically customized to each and every project, sometimes even for specific activities. One reason for this approach is the fact that budgets vary by project and also form constraints to potential monitoring activities so that the benchmarking design has to be adjusted to the given resources and therefore reflects the often high specificity of resources employed in this analysis. However, DC2 and DC3 stress that the indicators must be defined in a monitorable and verifiable way, in particular if intermediate or final impact assessments are executed by external evaluators.

The benchmark indicator, which has been mentioned by almost all interviewees, measures "impact", a kind of development impact in the respective fields of action (e.g. energy, health). This indicator sounds quite venerable but summarizes the dilemma that many stakeholders face in designing meaningful quantitative benchmarks. "Making impact" is easy to agree on, but it is little binding while the definition of "meaningful" is not an easy task either.

> *Wissen Sie, das Problem hier ist, wenn ich solche Ziele vorgebe: XY muss erreicht werden. Dann wird alles daran gesetzt, XY zu erreichen. Wie ich dahin komme, spielt dann gar keine Rolle mehr. Und ich muss ja, wenn ich Veränderungen erreichen will, völlig anders vorgehen. Ich brauche natürlich eine entsprechende Menge an Leuten, die ich damit erreiche. Aber mir hilft es nicht, wenn ich 10.000 erreiche und nichts erreicht habe. Und wenn ich 5.000 erreiche und was erreicht habe, ist mir das Ergebnis lieber. Deswegen gehe ich da auch dann lieber eher ergebnisoffen rein. (CO1-1)*

(You know, if I determine such goals the problem is: XY must be achieved. Then everything is done to achieve XY. How I get there does not matter anymore. And if I want to realize some changes, I have to proceed completely differently. Of course, I need a certain number of people, that I reach in this way. But it does not help me if I have reached 10,000 but have not achieved anything. Thus, I prefer to have reached 5,000 and have achieved something. That is why I like more to join in without prejudging the outcome.)

Allerdings ist da das Problem, es gibt einfach nicht die Rohdaten, um das valide zu messen, oder es gäbe sie, aber es wäre dann mit einem sehr großen Aufwand verbunden, tatsächlich dann diese Impact Studies so auszuführen, dass man valide Aussagen treffen könnte. Das heißt, man schaut sich das eher qualitativ an. Welche [Beiträge] haben wir [geleistet]? Was machen die [Zielgruppen] mit den [Ressourcen]? Passt vom Gefühl her die Story zu dem, was wir [...] erreichen möchten? (CO9-1)

(Although the problem is that there are basically not enough raw data to measure it validly, or they existed but this would imply quite a lot of effort to actually conduct these impact studies, for making valid statements at the end. That is why one tackles it rather qualitatively. What [contributions] did we [make]? What do the [target groups] make with the [ressources]? Does it feel like that the story fits to what we [...] want to achieve?

Our final goal is that the [beneficiaries] are actually growing and scaling up and impacting positively more and more people. It is not just, we do not have an internal benchmark of saying, "Okay, we are investing these and we want to get, we are investing 100 and we want to get 100 plus X". It is really more like the mission for [IO8] is accomplished when we see that the [beneficiaries] are actually scaling up and impacting more positively more people. (IO8)

Moreover, CO5 underlines that in cases of complex starting situations the actual creation of a PPP including governance structure and joint objectives can already be rated as an achievement. In her view, the definition of benchmark indicators can also occur in the form of a gradual process where indicators become more specific the more the PPP advances. Thus, benchmark indicators should be realistic and evolve over time because it is not reasonable to determine expected quantitative outcomes if the partners even struggle for agreeing on joint goals they are willing to commit to or to aim reaching x million people in country xy if the financing and support by local stakeholders are still uncertain.

However, most interviewees stressed that they cannot relinquish these quantitative benchmarks despite the difficulties of measuring them but that acceptance by every partner involved is imperative as well as complementarity between qualitative and quantitative indicators. That is why they follow some structured determination procedures.

[...] tratamos de crear métricas que satisfagan a los diferentes actores pero que en el mismo tiempo tengan la capacidad de ser medibles y alcanzables. (CO13-2)

([...] we try to create metrics that satisfy the different actors but have the capacity to be measurable and attainable at the same time.)

So, there were kind of qualitative and quantitative indications and [...] these programmes usually do not only touch the business where they are operating in, but they have a broader perspective. So, you also measure the outreach over your supply chain. What is the impact you have on a country? This is something that really is interesting for a company. (IO6)

So, usually we do have quite a bit of project management support from regional and headquarters level where they try to help the different offices to set meaningful target indicators. So that it's not only looking at the impact, that can mean anything, but looking at something a little bit more meaningful and measurable. (IO7)

It is not about benchmarks that we need to achieve. But there are clearly some quantitative aspects that we monitor. [...] their focus is on behavioral change in social impacts. So, it is also very difficult to be measured, but we try to monitor and then report on a number of people directly and indirectly impacted by the [beneficiaries]. (IO8)

In summary, there is some unanimity among both public and private interview partners that a mix of quantitative and qualitative benchmark indicators, which are customized to each individual PPP project, is most suitable to providing the necessary input for performance measurement activities. Therefore, it forms the basis of effective monitoring and meaningful reporting. Moreover, the process indicators are raised for administrative purposes and accountability towards the executive level, but they play a secondary role for the achievement of the actual PPP goals.

6.6.1.4 Monitoring

This chapter analyzes the characteristics of monitoring and the extent to which it is practiced in PPPs for development. Several interview partners unanimously emphasize the importance of monitoring as an element of MC that is imperative to enable effective project management and to make sure that progress is made in the PPP implementation. A monitoring framework can comprise diverse monitoring actions that are related to specific PPP activities, control the proper use of budget and financing mechanisms that focus on results control or on keeping partnership processes efficient and compliant (Table 56).

Monitoring type	Monitoring actions/foci
Activities	• Milestones monitoring (e.g. versus operation plan) • Preparation of monitoring reports • (Update) meetings and (telephone) conferences • Visits on the ground • Work packages per staff
Budget/finance	• Budget and resource appropriation • Monitoring of payout/transactions • Preparation of monitoring reports • Sales and expenses
Press	• Media coverage (extent of reporting, positive/negative/neutral

Monitoring type	Monitoring actions/foci
	reporting)
Processes	• Compliance with guidelines, rules and standards (internal/external audit) • (Update) meetings and (telephone) conferences
Results	• Achievement of benchmark indicators • Actual/target performance comparison • Preparation of monitoring reports

Table 56: Monitoring actions and foci per monitoring type.

Depending on the monitoring focus, pertinent actions can be done inhouse or be outsourced and provided by external evaluators or auditors accordingly. This depends also to some extent on the governance structure. While in decentralized structures the actors tend to be more prone to leave monitoring activities to third-partys, compared to those in centralized structures, also the opposite might take effect. The reason is that monitoring is one of the core elements of formal control so that despite a generally decentralized governance structure, the partners want to keep the monitoring centralized.

> *As we are a decentralized organization, monitoring of PPPs is so far also done mainly decentralized. However, with the introduction of my unit [...] in [month/year], it was acknowledged that a centralized monitoring is needed for PPPs. (IO2)*

> *We have like a structured team monitoring and evaluating our projects. So, that one is a whole unit of monitoring and evaluation in [...]. (IO5)*

> *So, sometimes it's done by the project manager, sometimes by a hired external consultancy [...] or sometimes it's done by that internal monitoring and evaluation unit. And then [...] we have internal audits as well as external audits, too, sometimes. But the internal audits, they also are in place to make sure that the projects are implemented, according to the rules and guidelines that we have. (IO7)*

Who has the ownership of monitoring depends on the level of integration of the control system and is usually agreed individually for each PPP, as stated by CO10 (Chapter 6.5.2.4). Like the benchmark indicators, monitoring seems to be very much customized so that even IT-based tools provide only a limited support. For most partnerships, relatively tight monitoring structures have been established with a broad control focus and clear reporting lines, in particular in resource-intensive PPPs in which also tax money is invested.

> *Wir [...] lassen uns entsprechende Dokumentationen über den Projektfortschritt schriftlich geben. Das ist auch dann im Vertrag so festgehalten. Häufig ist das auch damit verknüpft, ob eine nächste Zahlung ausgelöst wird. Es wird nur dann eine Zahlung erfolgen, wenn wir uns davon ein Bild gemacht haben, ob das Projekt auch wirklich vorangegangen ist und man dem Projektziel näher kommt und*

nicht befürchten müssen, dass nur fünf neue Landcruiser gekauft worden sind. (CO1-1)

(We [...] seek corresponding written documentations about the project progress. This is also stipulated by contract accordingly. Often this is also linked to the release of the next payment. A paying out will only happen if we got an idea of whether the project has really made progress and whether one got closer to the project goal and there is no reason to fear that only five new Landcruisers have been bought.)

[...] ist eigentlich immer eher so, dass man jetzt nicht so feste oder starre Tools benutzt, sondern sich eher an den Inhalten orientiert. (DC1)

([...] it is actually always more like that you do not use such fixed tools, but that you focus more on the contents.)

Es gibt leider/zum Glück in [DC2] nicht das eine Monitoring-Tool, wie ich bestimmte Sachen mache. De facto bastelt sich da jeder für jedes Vorhaben immer irgendwas zusammen. Also, wie steuern oder wie monitoren wir es? Auf der einen Seite haben wir unseren Operationsplan, wo wir einfach gucken, wie wir das Ganze machen. Dann haben wir ein paar wirkungsorientierte Indikatoren festgelegt, die wir dann versuchen zu erheben. (DC2)

(There is unfortunately/fortunately not that single monitoring tool in the [DC2] on how I have to do certain things. De facto, everybody puts anything together for every project. So, how do we control or monitor it? On the one side, we have our operation plan where we simply look how we do the whole thing. We have then determined a few results-oriented indicators that we then try to gather.)

In this context, CO3 adds that to-do lists and action lists including timeframe and completion status (red, yellow, green) are prepared for each country of operation. DC1 states that these monitoring results are then discussed internally, but also during committee meetings at local and international level, in order to assess if the milestones and expected results have been achieved, if adjustments to the planning and PPP activities need to be made, or if the project is within time and budget or not. Field visits on-site are one mechanism to review these activities, and take place particularly at the beginning of a PPP to promote smooth initiation of operations, and to ultimately examine the results before official conclusion. Thus, monitoring is time-bound in many cases (Figure 49).

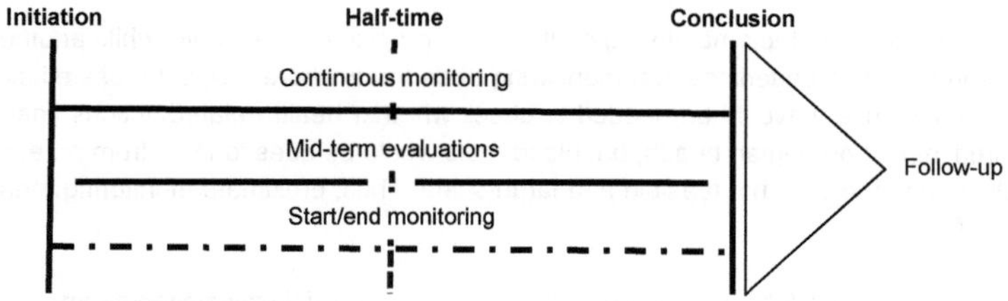

Figure 49: Time-bound monitoring approaches.

While some monitoring actions are done only at the beginning and the end of a PPP, some others are undertaken continuously, e.g. on a monthly or quarterly basis. Mid-term evaluations seem to be quite common and are often conducted by external experts. DC4 explains that they confine the monitoring to the achievement of major milestones, but do not review every intermediate step. In this context, IO7 emphasizes the tension between costly monitoring on the one hand and efficient use of resources on the other hand:

Die Arbeitspakete werden benannt. Und dann wird [...] die tatsächliche Arbeit, die erfolgt, [erfasst]. Die einzelnen Mitarbeiter erfassen das regelmäßig, [...] täglich, wöchentlich, monatlich, je nachdem wie ein Unternehmen das regelt. Bei uns würde ich eher monatlich sagen. (CO8)

(The work packages are named. And then is [...] [recorded] the actual work that is carried out. The different employees register this regularly, [...] daily, weekly, monthly, depending on how a company regulates these things. I would say that for us it is rather monthly.)

[...] Zwischenevaluierungen, wo wir [...] Gutachter [...] beauftragen, die dann zur Hälfte des Projekts eine Mid-Term-Evaluierung vornehmen [...], sodass man dann hier auch zusammen mit allen Partnern entscheiden kann: Was müssen wir jetzt verändern? Was ist nicht gut gelaufen? Was ist gut gelaufen? [...] an welchen Stellschrauben müssen wir drehen, damit wir unsere Projektziele noch in den nächsten ein bis zwei Jahren erreichen können? (DC3)

([...] interim evaluations where we [...] contract [...] experts who then conduct a mid-term evaluation at halfway of the project [...], so that we can decide with all partners together: What do we have to change now? What did not work well? What did work well? [...] what adjustments do we need to make for achieving our project goals in the next one to two years?)

[...] there is a monitoring of the results on a quarterly basis at least. I think we had monthly ones when I was managing some projects. So, it depends a little bit on the [private sector partners] as well. [...]. It's sometimes a pain in the neck as well that they have their own monitoring templates and then you need to do several for different ones. But usually, at least on a quarterly basis, at least one type of monitoring report needs to be put together. [...]. Then a lot of the projects are usually recommended that they would have mid-term evaluations to make sure that we gather the lessons and then [remark: make improvements in] the second half of the project. Usually, it's about half way the mid-term or a bit after. Sometimes, there is like an end-evaluation if there is a continuation project [...]. When I was managing projects and looking at some other projects, it was not done for every single project because it's quite costly, it's time-taking, but it's recommended. (IO7)

Others like IO6 concentrate their monitoring on the major project activities only, while another private sector interviewee underlines that monitoring ends there where it would cross ethical boundaries. For instance, it would be needed to check whether health-related actions finally had the desired impact on human health, but blood tests would be questionable from an ethical perspective and moreover not feasible at a large-scale. Thus, proximate monitoring measures must suffice.

Wir müssen also den letzten Wirkungsschritt [...] bis hin zur [Nachweisbarkeit im Blut] nicht gehen, weil ganz stark davon ausgegangen werden kann, wenn das jemand kauft, [...], dass er es dann auch verwendet. Und wenn es gekauft wird, dann weiß man, dass es auch im Grunde konsumiert wird. Und wenn es konsumiert wird, dann trägt es zur Verbesserung der Gesundheit bei. Das heißt, da haben wir im Grunde eine abgespecktere Version von Monitoring and Evaluation verwendet, dass wir [...] auf Coverage abgestellt haben. (n/a)

(Thus, we do not have to make the last measurement [...] up to the [traceability in the blood], because it may be strongly assumed that if somebody buys that, [...], he also will use it. And if it is used it contributes to improving health. This means that there we have basically used a light version of monitoring and evaluation, as we [...] focussed on coverage.)

Follow-up monitoring activities seem to take place at only one point in time and usually conclude with a final evaluation or final report. In particular companies seem to shift their focus once a project has been concluded so that their staff receives new tasks or is assigned to other projects, while CO5 underlines that this depends also very much on individual persons. Thus, DCAs and IOs are more likely to do some follow-up because they keep their governance structures and staff presense on the ground. Some actors like IO3 and IO5 maintain databases where they make learning and best practices from concluded PPPs available for the consideration by ongoing and future engagement managers.

In summary, the monitoring activities by both public and private sector are quite comprehensive. While there are no major differences in the diligence by which both sides practice monitoring, the private sector tends to place a stronger focus on financial monitoring while DCAs and IOs show a higher commitment to follow-up activities.

6.6.1.5 Reporting and Accountability

Different kinds of reports and their level of detail are basically the outcome documentation of the monitoring activities which are shared internally with the management and joint stakeholders or externally with public and private actors (Figure 50). The reporting frequency broadly coincides with the monitoring frequency (e.g. weekly, monthly, annually; Figure 49).

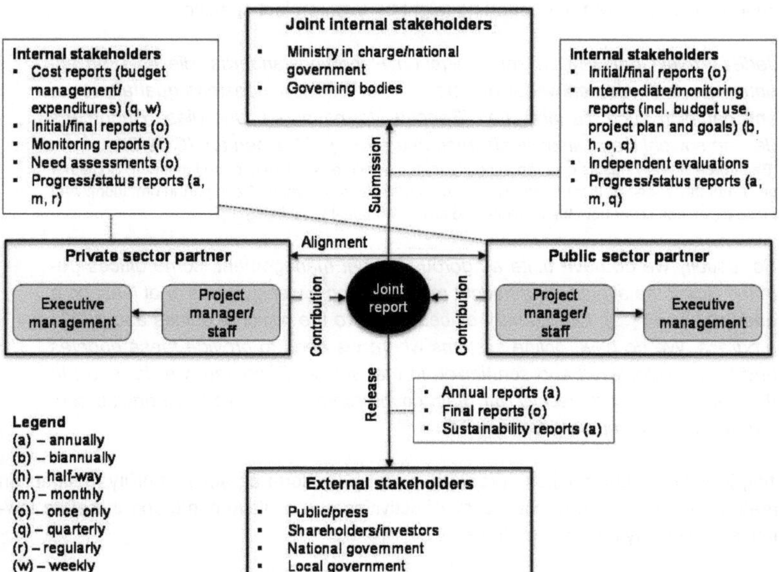

Figure 50: Reporting lines and frequencies.

Operational public and private project managers and staff usually report detailed processes but also core benchmark indicators, towards the respective executive management. There are no clear definitions of many report types, but the researcher noted that cost, monitoring and progress/status reports are often used synonymously. Depending on meaning, scope and governance structure, these reports are produced weekly, monthly or even annually. A regular reporting is quite common in PPPs with rather hybrid governance structure, and it basically means informal communication and coordination where ad-hoc reporting is common. At an aggregated level, these types of reports are also shared with the governing bodies or higher stakeholders, such as the ministry in charge that finances a PPP. In this case, an intermediate or monitoring report might link the use of resources to concrete implementation activities and achievements, while in reports at operational level all expenditures and man-days are listed in detail. Some report types like need assessments or initial and final reports are usually prepared only once. The latter is often released towards the press and local governments, too, or achievements get integrated into sustainability reports. One interview partner commented that for legal requirements her company has to prepare an annual report for the national government's consideration as well, although it is involved in the PPP itself. The reports for the external and joint internal stakeholders are mostly prepared in close cooperation and submitted by all partners together. However, the ownership of report preparation might vary between the partners because of diverging competences in writing them, or because of proximity to the respective stakeholders. Thus, specific reports, such as the sustainability report, have to be published by the private sector only, while the DCAs and IOs usually take the responsibility of reports going to the national governments. The level of detail and the inclusion of process and core benchmark indicators need to be target-oriented, but numerous interview partners confirmed that the executive level is often very much interested in getting specific information on the use of resources and implementation steps already made. In some cases, the reporting might be even project-specific.

> *Jedes Projekt hat wirklich seine eigenen Reportingstandards, die im [Vertrag] enthalten sind. Also entweder auf monatlicher Basis, mindestens quartalsweise, und natürlich auch die jährlichen [Berichtsinformationen]. Und diese Reportings decken sowohl die finanzielle als auch operative, [...] Sachen ab. (CO9-2)*
> (Each project really has its own reporting standards, which are included in the [contract]. So, either on a monthly basis, at least quarterly, and of course, also the yearly [reporting information]. And these reportings cover both the financial and also operational [...] things.)

> *So, usually we do have quite a rigorous budget management, some offices [remark: report the allocation of budget resources] on a weekly basis or at least on a quarterly basis [...]. Our country offices report to the regional offices about their progress. We do have online systems where we need to provide these updates and they are followed and scrutinized in that sense. Of course, we do report to the governments are usually our main counterparts, and if we have private sectors we can also report to them. (IO7)*

Reporting in general, but monitoring reports in particular, form an accountability mechanism that creates awareness and transparency of activities and achievements and therefore lowers bounded rationality between partners.

> *Und diese Monitoringberichte stellen wir unserem [Steuerungsorgan] halbjährlich vor. [...] das ist das, was wir auf der einen Seite gemacht haben. Das wissen sie*

im Normalfall sowieso, weil sie es ja beschlossen haben, dass wir dann da versuchen, da zu spiegeln, was das Ganze denn eigentlich bewirkt hat. [...] darüber wird dann auch der Mitgliederversammlung Bericht erstattet, dass die Mitglieder dann auch wieder wissen, was da war [...], was das [Steuerungsorgan] oder [...] sie alle gemeinsam dann eben auch leisten [...], weil [...] kein Mitglied und auch kein [Steuerungsorgan] [...] immer zu 100% weiß, was da überall anders passiert. (DC2)

(And we present these monitoring reports to our [governing body] biannually. [...] on the one side that is what we have done. Usually, they know that anyway because they agreed it, but then we try to reflect what the whole thing has effected. [...] the general assembly is then also informed about that, so that the members also know what happened [...] what the [governing body] or [...] they all together are performing [...] because [...] no member and no [governing body] either [...] always knows 100% what happens elsewhere.)

In addition, DC1 stresses the particular high level of accountability that stakeholders of stock companies request, while another DCA interviewee remarks that reporting cannot only form a cumbersome duty but even be counterproductive and cause mutual frustration if different organizational cultures and practices clash with one another:

Also, ich glaube, dass [...] [Namen zweier multinationaler] Unternehmen sind, die eben sehr im Fokus sind, [...] auch im Sinne von Shareholder-Value [...]. Die [...] immer wieder im Haus verteidigen müssen, warum wir [...] eine halbe Million in [Zielland] ausgeben [...]. Also, die stehen nochmal unter einem ganz anderen Rechtfertigungszwang als [...] ein mittelständisches Unternehmen, das sich durchaus auch mal das eine oder andere leisten kann und einfach sagt: "Wir finden das gut, und das ist eine tolle Sache. Deswegen machen wir das jetzt mal." (DC1)

(Well, I believe that [...] [name of two multinational] are companies which are very much in focus, [...] also in the sense of shareholder value [...]. They [...] have to defend internally again and again why we [...] spend half a million in [target country] [...]. Thus, they are under quite a different pressure to justify their positions more than [...] a medium-sized company, which can simply afford one or the other thing and simply says: "We like that and it is a great thing. That is why we are doing this now.")

[...] um es [...] den UN-Mittelverwendungslinien gerecht zu machen, hätten wir das eben so kompliziert für die [Begünstigen] machen müssen und da hätten wir das eigene Berichtswesen der [Begünstigten] und die Praktiken in der Bank so durcheinander würfeln müssen, [...] wo dann auch die lokalen Umsetzungspartner irgendwann gemerkt hätten: "Mein Gott, was tun wir uns hier eigentlich an mit dieser ganzen Bürokratie? Und bis vor fünf Monaten haben wir Kredite noch per Handschlag vergeben, bei so viel Mikrokrediten." [...]. Und jetzt auf einmal müssen wir hier massenweise Papierkram ausfüllen und Online-Reporting und hin und her. (n/a)

([...] in order to [...] meet the UN rules on the use of funds, we would have to make that complicated for the [beneficiaries] and we had to jumble the [beneficiaries'] own reporting that much, [...] where the local implementing partners noticed at one point: "Oh my gosh, why are we doing this? With all this bureaucracy, and five months ago, we still granted credits with a handshake, for such microcredits." And suddenly, we have to fill out massive paperwork and online reporting and all that.)

Others like DC6 state that they are not requested to provide specific reports but still they inform all their members in each assembly about progresses and results. In summary, in most

PPPs clear reporting lines and requirements on the publication frequency of the different types of reports exist. This goes along with the degree of accountability, which seems to be the higher the more hierarchic a governance structure is, and the more external stakeholders request information and have a say. However, there exist different understandings of the need and extent of reporting between stakeholder types and local versus international level, which interfere with internal rules and guidelines. These will be analyzed in the next chapter.

6.6.1.6 Rules and Guidelines

This chapter describes rules and guidelines on which PPPs are based, which frame the partnership implementation, and the use of which is either mandatory or voluntary. The former result from local or national legal requirements, from resolutions adopted by member states or from internal procedures being stipulated by the respective executive management. The latter are the most adequate practices or templates than can be used if appropriate. Regarding the necessity of rules and guidelines different views exist. While CO2 points to the need of compliance with standards and codes of conduct, IO1 emphasizes the importance of complementary interests and values. IO3 repeats that internal guidelines prohibit any kind of partnership with firms from the arms and tobacco industry.

> *UN-private sector cooperation needs to be based on common or mutually supportive objectives in accordance with the United Nations core values, objectives and principles. (IO1)*

According to CO4, the respective legislations in the countries of implementation influence the design of internal policy guides or guidance documents, which are updated regularly. These standards characterize different areas of MC, in particular the performance measurement including monitoring and reporting, where requirements are made on monitoring procedures or reporting frequencies. Part of that are for instance, procurement directives, lending guidelines, partner selection criteria, social and environmental standards, or simply some project management templates that have to be respected and followed, as stated by CO9-2, IO5, and others. IO7 remarks that her organization has implemented internal review procedures for rules and guidelines in order to examine their appropriateness and practicability. Thus, internal stakeholders at country, regional and headquarter level are consulted and asked for providing feedback on certain rules and guidelines. However, there are also critical voices on the necessity of rules and guidelines. While CO1-2 says that PPPs with recognized partners and joint objectives should work without any principles or codes of conduct, CO3 underlines that best practices guide are usually unable to address the individuality and complexity of partnerships:

> *Ich finde auch diese Toolbooks sind teilweise [...] nicht unbedingt hilfreich in jeder Hinsicht. Manchmal sind sie viel zu umfangreich. Manchmal fehlen ganz wesentliche Dinge. [...]. Es fühlen sich viele dazu berufen, darüber etwas zu schreiben, aus verschiedensten Ecken kommend. Sei es nun aus der eher unternehmensberatergetriebenen Zusammenführung von Unternehmen, sei es in Mergers oder Joint Ventures, sei es in öffentlichen-privaten Partnerschaften, wie man sie außerhalb des Entwicklungsbereiches sieht. [...]. Also, es ist ein sehr offenes Feld, und es ist am Ende doch ein relativ technischer und aber auch kreativer*

Prozess, bei dem man viel falsch machen kann, weil einfach eine gute Partnerschaft auf gerne mal 10 bis 15 entscheidenden Kriterien beruht. Und wenn es nur neun oder 14 sind [Anmerkung: im Toolbook], kann das schon zu viel Abweichung vom Idealfall sein und dann dazu führen, dass diese Partnerschaft nicht funktioniert. (CO3)

(In every regard, I find that parts of these toolbooks are [...] not really useful. Sometimes they are way too comprehensive. Sometimes fundamental things are missing. [...]. Many people feel called to write something about that, coming from very different corners, whether from the consulting-driven integration of companies, whether it is in mergers or joint ventures, whether it is in public-private partnerships as you see them outside the development area. [...]. So, it is a very broad field, and is still a relatively technical but also creative process in the end, where a lot of things can go wrong, because a good partnership can easily rely on even 10 to 15 decisive criteria. And when there are only nine or 14 [remark: in the toolbook], this can already be too much deviation from the optimum and may have the effect that this partnership does not work.)

In summary, there is no common sense on the use of rules and guideliness, unless they are not mandatory. Yet, it can be concluded that they should be prepared in close coordination between all actors involved and, in particular, operational implementers should be consulted to ensure their practicability.

6.6.2 Clan and Social Control

The following subchapters address diverse characteristics and fundamental areas of action of informal MC where clan and social control mechanisms are applied. It starts with an overview of typical control activities and of the way of how communication occurs between stakeholders in governance structures where informal MC is common. Moreover, it will be analyzed how clan and social control contribute to the alignment of diverging interests, what role this kind of control plays for conflict management, and how this is used in networking and knowledge management activities.

6.6.2.1 Control Activities and Communication

Social and clan control activities embrace primarily different kinds of social gatherings and events that serve the face-to-face communication between the different partners involved in a PPP, and therefore reflect to some extent ways on which governing structures and formal control structures are implemented and lived in practice. Table 57 gives an overview of different activities including the general occasions and purposes they have, and which are interdependent. Thus, different meetings or workshops take place for certain reasons while these reasons require in turn the organization of those gatherings.

Type of activity

- Board meetings
- Breakfast meeting
- Capacity-building trainings/ training workshops
- Client-contractor dialogues
- Congresses
- Field visits
- Inauguration/kick-off meeting
- Multilateral side events
- Other workshops
- Partner days
- Planning workshops
- Regular coordination meetings
- Strategy meetings
- Task force meetings
- Working group meetings

Occasion/purpose

- Ceremonies
- Decision-making
- Exchange of experiences and knowledge
- Monitoring
- Networking/relationship-building
- Opinion-forming
- Progress/status updates
- Reporting
- Strategy-building
- Training measures

Table 57: Social and clan control activities.

While some activities, such as breakfast meetings, congresses or multilateral side events (e.g. private sector sessions during high-level IO meetings, such as the UN General Assembly) intend to hold ceremonies, to nurture existing relationships or to promote networking and relationship-building including the exchange of experiences and knowledge, other activities result from the governance and control structure. For instance, board meetings or planning workshops at executive level or field visits, training sessions and working group meetings at operational level serve the implementation of decision-making processes, information-sharing or monitoring. High-level meetings often take place only once or twice per year, while at operational level task forces and working groups coordinate and get together regularly and sometimes spontaneously. It should be noted that diverse technical tools support web-based communication that does not require physical presence and is primarily used for ad-hoc operational coordination. Much communication is done by telephone, Skype or email. Moreover, the regularity of the activities is strongly correlated with the frequency of monitoring actions or reporting, and goes along with them. Thus, they also take place monthly, quarterly or only once, as in the case of kick-off meetings or final ceremonies.

The vast majority of the interviewees describe communication as a key social control mechanism that is practiced intensively and is accompanied by close cooperation between partners. CO1-1 emphasizes that frequent conversations are pivotal to make other partners feeling respected and equal in a PPP with big and small organizations. Moreover, CO2 explains that her company has designed joint communication strategies with the IO partner, and CO3 stresses that they decided for a dedicated communication line with clear focal points to promote ongoing exchange and coordination. Thus, the communication in most PPPs is very intensive because the project work simply requires that.

Also der Austausch ist sehr intensiv. Normal [...] einmal im Monat. Häufig kommt es zu 14-tägigen Telefonkonferenzen, weil die Fluktuation und die Vielfalt der Wünsche ansteigen. (CO1-1)

(Well, the exchange was very intensive. Normally, [...] once per month. Telephone conferences often take place every two weeks because the fluctuation and the diversity of the wishes increase.)

Einmal im Quartal, entweder war es ein Face-to-Face Meeting oder als Telefonkonferenz, wo wir uns eben zusammen telefoniert haben [...]. Aber sonst war es sehr viel ad hoc. (CO4)

(Once every three months, it was either a face-to-face meeting or telephone conference where we made joint calls [...]. But otherwise there was quite a lot ad-hoc.)

Und es gibt natürlich zwischen diesen [...] Treffen und diesem Gipfel einen regen Austausch von Emails und eine erkleckliche Zahl von Telefonkonferenzen. So wird es gesteuert. (CO6)

(And between these [...] meetings and this summit are taking place a lively exchange of emails and a considerable number of telephone conferences. This is the way it is conducted.)

CO8 remarks that local staff presence promotes the communication with local stakeholders, in particular with local governmental authorities. In this context, CO4 and DC4 underline the relevance of language and intercultural differences, which may ease or hinder communication with local actors. Like DC4, CO7 strongly emphasizes the necessity to communicate openly and honestly from the beginning, to set expectations clearly, and to say openly what the consequences of goal achievement or target shortfall are:

Also man ist sowieso immer per Du. Ist im Englischen ja auch nicht so schwer wie im Deutschen. Und man spricht offen und ehrlich, man schreibt offen und ehrlich. Man muss sich jetzt nicht nur mit Euer Ehren und Your Highness und große Exzellenz und so anreden, wie es ja dann gerade in [Kontinent] die Leute unter sich öfter machen, sondern einfacher Anruf, kurzer Smalltalk und dann kurz über das Geschäft geredet. Also Partnerschaft auf Augenhöhe, wenig hierarchisch. (DC4)

(Well, you are always on a first name basis with somebody. In English, it is simply not that difficult as in German. And one speaks openly and honestly, one writes openly and honestly. You do not have to address one another by 'your excellency' and 'your highness' as people especially in [continent] are used to do that, but a simple call, short smalltalk, and then briefly talked about the business. So, partnership at eye-level, little hierarchic.)

And then you need to talk to them [...] in the beginning much more often and then less as the project progresses, but you need to have your finger on the pulse of the time, in the sense that they know that this is not a guaranteed partnership for 20 years. You say that you do this as a pilot partnership for years, and a year from now we talk again if this still makes sense. If it does not make sense for you or for us, we stop it. If we are willing to scale up, we scale up. If we need to scale down, we scale down. So it is the frank way of working together. So, the partners understand where they are with you. For us that works best. (CO7)

Moreover, CO14 adds that speaking the same language can also imply sharing joint values and objectives, which facilitate communication and project work:

> *I think the conversation with [IO partner] has actually been very fluent, because we speak the same language and we agree with the same values and purposes when it comes to a specific project [...]. So, I think, I have better conversations with those guys than with [name of a partnership with mainly NGOs being involved], for instance, which is an NGO. (CO14)*

In summary, frequent and close personal interactions based on face-to-face meetings or verbal communication by phone or internet form important mechanisms to complement or replace behavior, and results control mechanisms. Communication can be rather formal or informal, depending on the spontaneity of the interactions, but usually it is a mix of a fixed number of meetings or calls per year and ad-hoc exchanges.

6.6.2.2 Alignment of Diverging Interests

This chapter addresses reasons of diverging interests between PPP stakeholders and shows informal control approaches for aligning interests by making use of clan and social control mechanisms. CO7, DC1 and DC2 situate the reasons mainly in the corporate culture between public and private sector where business interests of the latter might conflict with the overarching political interests that DCAs and IOs pursue. Moreover, insufficient awareness of PPP work, lack of mutual understanding and uncertainty are sources of diverging interests. The involvement of competitors and third-party actors may further complicate the alignment of interests, but is sometimes needed to solve a policy issue.

> *Also, da sind wir, glaube ich, schon diejenigen gewesen, [DC1], die da gepusht haben, weil vielleicht für die Unternehmen zum Teil ganz andere Ergebnisse zählen. Also, ich glaube unternehmensintern ist es einfach so, dass da eher Verkaufszahlen interessieren. [...]. Für die sind einfach andere Regionen geschäftlich interessanter. [...] dass den Unternehmen nicht so bewusst war: "Mensch, so ein Planungsworkshop [...] ist ja richtig verbindlich." Also da sagt man jetzt nicht mal so irgendwas, sondern das machen wir dann hinterher auch. (DC1)*
>
> (Well, I believe that we have been the ones, [DC1], who pushed there because for the companies very different results may matter in certain cases. So, I believe that within the companies sales numbers are more interesting. [...]. For them, other regions are commercially simply more interesting. [...] that the companies were not aware of: "Gosh, such a planning workshop [...] is really binding." So, it is not like just saying anything, but at the end of the day we really do that.)

> *Also, eine operative Partnerschaft mit einem Business-Case muss Konkurrenten immer denklogisch trennen [...]. Also, man sollte jetzt nicht drei Konkurrenten auf ein Projekt loslassen. Das wird in der Regel nur funktionieren, wenn man ein [...] Collective-Action-Problem adressieren möchte, wie z.B. Korruption. Anti-Korruption funktioniert nur, wenn alle mitmachen. Da muss man Konkurrenten an einen Tisch bringen. (CO3)*
>
> (So, an operative partnership with a business case always has to separate competitors from a logical point of view [...]. So, you should not release three competitors to a joint project. This will usually work only if you [...] want to address a collective action problem, such as corruption. Anti-corruption only works if all people participate. There you have to bring competitors to the table.)

Aber andererseits muss man dann immer die Mitte finden. Und die finde ich halt mit manchen NGOs 0,0. (CO4)

(But on the other side. you always need to find the middle. And with some NGOs I find that 0.0)

That is why DC1 and DC2 unanimously stress that no partner should keep calm about the real interests out of a false sense of modesty, but that clear and honest communication is imperative to verify the compatibility of diverging interests. Still, CO3 and CO10 were initially a little bit reserved regarding the clear communication of business interests because of little or none PPP experience and of potentially negative reactions by the public sector, in particular by the ministry in charge.

Ich glaube [...] die Unternehmen sollten da mit ihren Interessen ehrlich sein. [...] das [zuständige Ministerium] sagt so: "Wir haben das Interesse." Und die Privaten müssten sagen: "Okay, wir haben das Interesse. Und da ist ein Bereich, wo sich das überlappt, und da müssen wir reingehen." Und wenn es diesen Überlappungsbereich nicht gibt, dann sollte man auch so ehrlich sein und sagen: "Ja, der ist nicht gegeben." (DC1)

(I believe [...] the companies should be honest regarding their interests. [...] the [ministry in charge] says: "We have this interest." Und the privates must say: "Okay, we have that interest. Und there is an area where it overlapps and there we have to go in." And if this overlapping area does not exist, you should be honest and say: "Well, it is not given.")

According to DC3, the underlying negotiation processes can take months and be very exhausting. Concepts and ideas are played back and forth in a ping-pong manner. However, the basis of a PPP is established by such a procedure where these concepts and ideas are continuously refined, and diverging interests and proposals are therefore aligned in the end. In line with CO3, she adds that the entire communication has to be done at eye-level and in a respectful manner. CO6 and DC2 remark that discussions and negotiation processes are often tough but are necessary to obtain results which are really accepted by all partners at the end. Moreover, DC2 emphasizes the necessity to reflect critically and continuously during PPP implementation whether there is still enough overlapping of interests, or not, and to make adjustments if appropriate. For achieving this, DC2 applies a Harvard approach like IO5 as well:

Und das [...] läuft bei uns immer unter verhandeln nach der Harvard-Methode, dass man [...] versucht, Interessensüberschneidungen herzustellen, dass jeder erstmal seine Interessen äußert. [...]. Und Interessen übereinander zu bringen, ist sehr viel einfacher als Standpunkte miteinander in Einklang zu bringen, weil Standpunkte sind eigentlich ja nicht verhandelbar. [...] wir [...] versuchen [...] über die Interessen zu kommen und sagen: "Was ist denn euer Interesse?" Und dass man das eben versucht zu verbinden. Und das ist ein ständiger Diskussions- und Aushandlungsprozess. (DC2)

(And this [...] runs for us always under negotiating by applying the Harvard method, that we [...] try to create overlaps of interest, that first of all everybody expresses his interests. To align interests is much easier than harmonizing standpoints because standpoints are actually not negotiable. [...] we [...] try [...] to come from the interests and say: "What is your interest?" And then one tries to connect. And that is a continuous negotiation process.)

They already have an advisory counsel for the private sector, and they did start it together with Harvard University [...], looking at issues from the perspective of the private sector. (IO5)

CO13-2 and DC5 share the experiences of DC2 and IO5, whereas DC5 emphasizes the close cooperation with the national government, which consults the PPP actors before laws affecting the PPP implementation are enacted. Negotiations between partners take place at different levels, in operational working groups as well as at high level in the governing bodies. However, CO8 underlines that hard details or critical negotiation items are often deliberated offside the regular communication channels and platforms. Moreover, the public sector acknowledges that the private sector usually needs to have business cases for PPPs.

[...] Implementierung [...] im Feld [...]. Viele dieser Partner sind im Grunde genommen ihren regulären Geschäftstätigkeiten nachgegangen und haben sich aber gewisse Tätigkeiten anrechnen lassen können. Da gab es so eine Art Matching-Prinzip. Da gibt es so unterschiedliche Modelle. Je nachdem wie nah das an der kommerziellen Tätigkeit ist, desto weniger kann man anrechnen. (CO8)
([...] implementation [...] in the field [...]. Many of these partners basically continued their regular business activities but could get credited certain activities. There was such a kind of matching principle. There are different models. Depending on how close they are to the commercial activity, one may get credited less.)

Die [DCA Partner] sagt auch ganz klar: "Das muss ja für euch auch wirtschaftlich irgendwo Sinn machen. Also wozu Geld reinstecken, wenn ihr am Ende nur Geld reinsteckt und es euch nicht hilft am Ende etwas Nachhaltiges daraus zu machen." (CO10-1)
(The [DCA partner] says very clearly: "That must somehow make economic sense for you. Thus, why to invest if you only put in money, but in the end it does not help you to make something sustainable out of it.")

In summary, both CO1-2 and DC6 underline the importance of communication and trust as informal control mechanisms that promote the alignment of diverging interests because formal controls, even stipulated by contract, can anticipate potential conflicts only to a limited extent:

Also was [CO1-1] mit gegenseitigem Vertrauen beschrieben hat, also, es gibt ein gemeinsames Interesse. Und die Idee, vertraglich irgendwelche Interessenskonflikte im Vorfeld schon zu formulieren und auszuschließen, die gibt es [...] gar nicht so unbedingt. (CO1-2)
(So, what [CO1-1] described by mutual trust, so, there is a mutual interest. And the idea of formulating contractually any conflicts of interest already in advance, this does [...] not necessarily exist.)

[...] la conciliación se ha dado mediante la comunicación. El sector público esté abierto a escuchar al sector privado, que puedan llegar a acuerdos beneficios para ambas partes. (DC6)
([...] the conciliation was done by means of communication. The public sector is open to listen to the private sector in order to reach beneficial agreements for both sides.)

6.6.2.3 Conflict Management

This chapter analyzes sources of conflicts as well as pertinent prevention and resolution mechanisms. Most interview partners tell that there are or were no major conflicts in their partnerships. Still, the sources are very similar to the reasons of diverging interests among partners and comprise also differences in the corporate cultures between public and private sector, high number of partners involved, insufficient communication and coordination, insufficient awareness of PPP work, and lack of mutual understanding. However, CO8 mentions that quite often interpersonal problems cause conflicts, which have no structural or PPP-inherent origin at all, so that bilateral conversations instead of formal procedures can form an alternative.

> *[...] the different organizational cultures getting together in a partnership might be a source of conflict, i.e., business-oriented vs. bureaucracy. (IO1)*

To prevent and resolve conflicts, different public and private actors have implemented formal or informal mechanisms. CO2, CO3, CO9 and DC2 point out that continuous dialogue but also pragmatism and the willingness to tackle problems already when they emerge contribute to preventing conflicts to a large extent:

> *Probleme identifizieren wir [...] gemeinsam mit unserem Partner und arbeiten stetig daran, unsere [...] Projekte zu verbessern. (CO2)*
> (We identify problems [...] together with our partner and work continuously on [...] improving our projects.)

> *[...] das ist auch die Schönheit von PPP-Maßnahmen, dass man sich gegenseitig ein wenig erzieht, um es mal so zu sagen. Und die Stärken der Sektoren, wenn der Dialog funktioniert, zur Anwendung bringt und bestimmte Marotten und Schwächen, die vielleicht auch bestehen, ein bisschen nach hinten stellt. (CO3)*
> ([...] this is also the beauty of PPP measures, that you educate one another a little bit, to say it this way. And to let the strengths of the sectors take effect, if the dialogue works, and to place certain quirks or weaknesses, which might exist, in the rear.)

Some actors like IO7 have established formal conflict resolution mechanisms while CO1, CO8 and CO13-2 state that delegating the problem to an upper level, but also democratic decision-making procedures where the PMO or third-party actors like NGOs exercised a moderating influence on the conflicting parties, helped to settle disputes in the past:

> *[...] we also have stakeholder response mechanisms [...] in place. So, if, for example, a community is not happy with the partnership initiative that we have, they do have an official and transparent way of raising a concern to the headquarter level, who then looks at the complaints, or the concerns and questions. [...]. In the contracts [...] it's defined what the mechanisms are. That's standard language in the legal templates (IO7)*

> *La forma de resolución fue realmente una cuestión [nota: de decisión] de mayoría. Quien toma un rol más activo en el tema de mediación es actores neutros como [socio NGO]. Nosotros difícilmente podemos tener una confrontación directa porque somos una organización privada que tiene un objetivo muy claro*

de creación de valor. Entonces, una postura de nosotros muy firme de confrontar no sería buena para el propio desarrollo de un proceso colaborativo. Entonces, quien hace la labor de ser intermediarios son organizaciones neutras y [...] intentas hacer mecanismos de resolución de problemas y toma de decisiones para que a la hora que haya un enfrentamiento sea muy claro el camino que tengas que seguir. (CO13-2)

(The mode of resolution was really a question of majority [remark: voting]. Those who take a more active role in the matter of mediation are neutral actors like [NGO partner]. We can hardly have a direct confrontation because we are a private organization that has a clear objective of value creation. Hence, a firm position from our side would not be good for the development of a collaborative process as such. Thus, who does the work of being intermediaries are the neutral organizations and [...] you try to design problem resolution and decision-making mechanisms so that at the moment when a conflict happens it is very clear which way you have to go.)

Only two interviewees reported from severe conflicts and incidents, which finally entailed the termination of the partnerships. In the first case, one DCA and the partnering IO assessed the prospects of the PPP completely differently. The interviewee explained that his DCA did not see any chance to reach the project objectives while the IO wanted to revise the project design and adjust the targets to the reality. He stated that these would have been completely contrary to the actual ones. Thus, the ministry in charge finally cancelled the project and therefore terminated the PPP. In the second case, personal dispute caused the PPP's termination.

A mí me tocó una vez en [país europeo] una gran pelea, en una reunión de la [nombre de la PPP] de allá de [país europeo], donde alguien de la [nombre de la PPP], del sector privado, dijo cosas terribles del gobierno y el hombre del gobierno se enojó, se salío, se fue y allá la [actividad del PPP] está parada en [país europeo]. No hay más [actividad del PPP]. [...]. Todos los beneficios que tenían nos quitaron. Entonces, ahí hay un descontento del sector privado y se están peleando constantemente. (DC5)

(A big dispute happened to me once in [European country], in a meeting of the [PPP name] from there in [European country], where somebody from the [PPP name], from the private sector, said terrible things about the government, and the man from the government got annoyed, went out, left, and the [PPP activity] was stopped then in [European country]. There is no [PPP activity] anymore. [...]. They took away from us also the benefits they had. Hence, there is a discontent from the private sector's side, and they constantly argue about this.)

In summary, most public and private actors try to early prevent any emergence of conflicts. A few of them have implemented formalized resolution procedures while the majority channels problems through existing governance structures. However, if the partners' positions are diametrically opposed, or relationships are sustainably charged or even destroyed, whether it be at personal or institutional level, conflicts might cause the termination of the PPP.

6.6.2.4 Networking and Knowledge Management

Networking and knowledge management are two elements of informal control whose tight linkage is crucial for the long-term orientation and implementation of PPPs. CO1-1 and CO8 stress that networks are platforms that facilitate different stakeholders to exchange ideas and experiences as well as to learn from each other, to raise awareness of difficulties, and to sound cooperation opportunities. Thus, networks serve as door opener and forerunner of joint PPP projects.

> *Wo man sich [...] in dem Netzwerk genau über solche Erfahrungen austauscht. [...] es muss ja nicht jeder diese Erfahrung aufs Neue machen, sondern profitiert ja von dem, was auch andere wissen. [...] deswegen ist dieses langjährige, parallele Netzwerken [...] so wichtig, weil [...] ein großes [Unternehmen] nicht einfach nur als potentieller Geldgeber herumläuft, sondern gemäß seiner Expertise auch an bestimmten Stellen aktiv sein möchte, und so bildet sich das dann in unseren Partnerschaften auch tatsächlich ab. (CO1-1)*
> (Where you [...] exchange such experiences in the network. [...] not everybody must make this experience anew but benefits from what others know. [...] that is why this longstanding, parallel networking is [...] so important, because [...] a large [company] does not simply walk around as a potential donor, but wants to be active at some points in accordance with its expertise and that is indeed reflected by our partnerships.)

In particular, DCAs usually maintain comprehensive networks with diverse public and private actors across the globe, which they built up through hundreds of projects in different thematic areas. Traditionally, they have good access to local governmental authorities wherefore DCAs are valuable vehicles for private sector firms to establish contact with political decision-makers in developing countries whose support and goodwill is imperative for doing business there. CO8 remarks in this context that recommendations are important elements in big networks for making business, while CO9-2 highlights that taking the public sector on board of joint projects implies having a meter on the pulse of political developments because actors like DCAs are used to possessing comprehensive regional expertise on markets, local conditions and culture:

> *[...] profitiert man davon, dass wir die öffentliche Hand mit im [Name der PPP] haben, somit auch ein Ohr in Afrika mit in der politischen Diskussion haben. Man weiß, wo sich gewisse politische Gespräche vielleicht gerade befinden, was so die Richtungen sind, auf was man achten muss [...]. Man ist [...] vernetzt mit [...] Internationalen Organisationen. Das heißt, man kann sich auch untereinander austauschen. (CO9-2)*
> ([...] we benefit from having the public authorities in the [PPP name], so that we also have an ear for the political discussions in Africa. You know where certain political discussions are going on right now, what the tendencies are, and where you have to take care of [...]. You are [...] connected with [...] international organizations. This means that you can exchange experiences.)

For this reason, public partners often take responsibility of initiating and maintaining the local networks in PPPs, as stated by IO7, because they possess the knowhow and some standardized procedures for doing that. Moreover, existing networks or policy platforms are often the source of PPPs (Chapter 6.3.1.1). CO4 noted an increasing staff rotation between members of his PPP-related network where private sector actors are hired by IOs or move to NGOs. However, the disadvantage of much staff rotation is the loss of knowledge whose rebuilding is costly in terms of time and money (see quotation from CO4 in Chapter 6.4.4.1). That is why CO8 has created knowledge-sharing platforms and data management systems, and IOs like IO3, IO5, and IO6 promote knowledge-sharing and collect feedback from previous and ongoing PPPs to gather expertise for future engagements:

We have since 15 years a system where each and every engagement we have with private sector [remark: is stored]. (IO3)

[...] partnerships [...] are like case studies through which we learn, and then we share this knowledge with other country offices. [...] we share from these best practices. And even from here, we can view the way the due diligence works, for example. What are the delays? Where are the bottlenecks? Where are the challenges? And from there, we make suggestions of how this can be further improved. (IO5)

[...] try very much to focus on creating synergies among organizations, so that they can also benefit from the exchange of expertise and leverage this case that they have in common. (IO6)

However, regarding the actual level of knowledge transfer between public and private actors diverse experiences exist. While DC4 negates any real exchange between his DCA and the involved IO, CO14 describes knowledge-sharing as the core purpose of the PPP in which his company is participating:

We also share with them, because one of the biggest contributions from [PPP name] is the knowledge and the dissemination of good practices when it comes to develop social businesses. So, I think they are also accessive to knowledge and to experience directly from the field experience, to develop those publications that would be part of the contribution for [IO partner]. So, I think that is the mutual benefit. (CO14)

Hence, knowledge management also relies on the efficient coordination and involvement of internal departments in the PPP work (Chapter 6.1.3). In turn, networking also implies knowledge-sharing and the matching of complementary skills and resources. In summary, networking and knowledge management are interdependent informal control mechanisms and imperative for long-term oriented PPPs and their smooth implementation.

6.6.3 Control Extent and Control Focus

This chapter forms the empirical counterpart to the theoretical consideration of control archetypes in Chapter 0. First of all, characteristics of control extent and tightness will be discussed, followed by an analysis of some contractual MC elements. In practice, a tight control extent and a broad control focus manifest themselves in the form of strict and diligent MC procedures, which are stipulated by contract, and for which each partner takes ownership, also involving different internal stakeholders. This affects in particular critical aspects like the design of the contractual arrangements or resource planning and approval, which go along, for instance, with tight monitoring activities and quality control (see quotation from CO7 in Chapter 6.4.2). However, standardization can relieve the bureaucratic burdens to some extent.

[...] when it has to do with money, it is more restricted. [...] it is more rigorous the way that the high-level is measuring the partnership. If there is money in be-

tween, it means that there will be attention in the partnership, there will be more control or a kind of due diligence. (CO14)

Die Projekte durchlaufen auch bei uns einen strengen Qualitätsprozess und eben auch mit Überprüfung durch das Management Board [...] und auch von [Anmerkung: erfahrenen] Kollegen [...]. (DC3)
(Our projects undergo a strict quality process and include examination by the management board [...] and also by [remark: experienced] colleagues [...].)

[...] the legal office within [IO7] always needs to approve every single change and some clauses are non-negotiable [...]. But these kinds of things and how they can use our logo, all that is standard text in the legal templates. (IO7)

In PPPs with loose control criteria and narrow control focus, for instance, where no local governance structure exists, consultation-oriented control from afar is required, as reported by CO6 from a management perspective (Chapter 6.5.2.3.3). From a more operational perspective, DC4 explains that the responsible IO exercises little control and only requests a brief update once per week. More generally, IO7 emphasizes the need for an appropriate and targeted control extent (see quotation from IO7 in Chapter 6.4.3.1). In this context, CO6 adds that the control extent is diminished once the implementation processes are established and well-coordinated so that the level of uncertainty decreases. Complementary to this, CO12 remarks that the monitoring tightness and focus are situation-oriented and vary by the actual performance. Hence, if benchmark indicators are not met, MC is broader and tighter.

6.6.3.1 Contractual Controls and Formalization of Management Control Practices

Contractually stipulated controls and formalized MC practices support rather tight control regimes with broad control focus. This affects in particular the determination of implementation steps, the governance structure design, monitoring activities, reporting, and the sharing of responsibilities and decision-making processes. While in case of DC2 a fundamental set of rules, which clearly stipulates the governance structure and defines how all partners shall cooperate, has been established, CO13-2 points to a model with binding bilateral contracts between the partners and a non-binding governance manual. This still works because of a high level of commitment being demonstrated by all partners.

[...] se tiene un manual de gobernanza que prácticamente detalla toda la operación de como funciona la plataforma pero [...] no es un acuerdo que se haga vinculante. Sí, se firma, se acuerda, se trabaja entre todos en conjunto y al final esto es lo que está rigiendo el comportamiento. Sin embargo la cuestión vinculante es bilateral entre [socio NGO], [CO13], y con el [socio IO]. [...] términos de gobernanza y esto está en los estatutos legales de la organización. (CO13-2)
([...] we have a governance manual, which basically details the whole operation of how the platform works but [...] it is not a binding agreement. Yes, we sign, we agree, we work all together and this is what is governing the behavior at the end. Still, the binding matter is bilateral between [NGO partner], [CO13], and with the [IO partner]. [...] governance terms, and that is in the legal statutes of the organization.)

CO1-1 states that they stipulate milestones, and therefore implementation steps, including related monitoring and progress reporting by contract. In addition, CO8 and IO6 underline that reporting is a binding and serious formal MC mechanism:

> *Wir monitoren auch die Projekte und lassen uns auch entsprechende Dokumentationen über den Projektfortschritt schriftlich geben. Das ist [...] im Vertrag so festgehalten (CO1-1)*
> (We also monitor the projects and request written documentations about the project progress. That is [...] stipulated by contract.)

> *[...] reading through the final report [...] is not just like reading but it is also a sort of like checking, what they are writing. So, it is not just that we take it for granted what they send us. (IO6)*

The importance of the early definition of roles and responsibilities in PPPs was stressed by CO6, where CO6 and IO6 add that those capacities and the taking of ownership manifest in their respective PPP contracts. Based on this, CO4 points to the formalization of decision-making procedures including minimum participation by members, while CO8 adds that formal procedures are often complemented by informal coordination processes (Chapters 6.5.2.1 and 6.6.2.2). Moreover, he mentions external auditors as a control mechanism whose approval of cost items and billing or budgeting processes is often formally required by contract. Despite any formalized contractual controls, CO3, CO10-1, and DC2 unanimously confirm that in practice partnerships often operate more pragmatic and informal so that the way of getting to the objectives is rather flexible, because many rules apply mainly in conflict situations:

> *[...] die Verträge sind harte Kollaborationsverträge, wo drin steht, dass man sich in einem gewissen Umfang verpflichtet, sich zu engagieren. Die Einzelheiten sind darin nicht festgelegt. Also, es ist nicht festgelegt, wer was in welchen Umfang macht. Das heißt, die Flexibilität hat man rechtlich schon. Ich meine, es ist einfach deshalb nicht durchsetzbar, weil es eine no-win-Situation wäre. (CO3)*
> ([...] the contracts are tight collaboration contracts which stipulate the commitment to engagement to some extent. The details are not determined in there. So, it is not determined who does what to which extent. This means that there is flexibility from a legal perspective. I mean, it is simply not enforceable because it would be a no-win situation.)

> *Wir [...] als [DC2] haben [...] mit dem [zuständigen Ministerium] [...] einen sehr formalisierten Rahmen. Das ist das, wie es formal zu sein hat. Und ganz häufig funktioniert es viel, viel besser. Da braucht man diesen ganzen formalisierten Rahmen gar nicht, wenn der Auftraggeber zufrieden ist und wir [...] als Auftragnehmer [...] die Standardregeln einhalten [...]. Das greift ja immer nur in Konfliktfällen [...]. (DC2)*
> (We [...] as [DC2] have [...] a very formalized framework [...] with the [ministry in charge]. This is like it has formally to be. And quite often it works much much better. There you do not need this formalized framework at all, if the client is satisfied and we [...] as contractor [...] comply with the standard rules. This applies usually in conflict situations only.)

Moreover, too much formalized MC might be counterproductive in some fields like monitoring or reporting, as stated by IO5 and by one DCA interviewee in Chapter 6.6.1.5, whose quotation has been kept anonymous.

And we have our operating procedures, we have very tight, I think probably too tight, measures for monitoring and audit and all this. (IO5)

In summary, the contractual arrangements of many PPPs clearly define MC activities to be done and formalize how they shall be executed. Notwithstanding, the stakeholders of most PPPs tend to leave enough flexibility to enable pragmatic project work that is able to react to unexpected developments or to reassign tasks and responsibilities if necessary and if all partners agree with that. The simple reason is that it is the achievement of objectives that matters in the end.

6.6.3.2 Contractual Safeguardings

The necessity of contractual safeguardings in PPPs was emphasized by most interview partners. Public sector entities like IO1 and IO3 stress the need to protect the UN's independence, integrity and reputation (including name and emblem), while the private sector seems to be concerned mostly about intellectual property rights. This is a concern that DCAs often acknowledge and consider for the contract design, in the sense that certain clauses are deleted, amended, or new paragraphs included if the business fundamentals of the private partner are otherwise seriously threatened.

Und das ist ein hohes Risiko bei vielen der Organisationen, die auch Partnerschaften nicht als eine Art Innovationsprozess begreifen, wo jeder [...] irgendwo die Balance zwischen Replizierung und Schutz des Innovators sieht, weil [...] Aufwand am Anfang entsteht und Ertrag dann erst später [...]. Deswegen gibt es Intellectual Property, [...] wo Investitionen oder Return on Investment in eine faire Balance gebracht werden. (CO3)
(And this is a high risk in many of the organizations, which do not consider partnerships as a kind of innovation process, where everybody [...] sees the balance somewhere between replication and protection of the innovator, because expenditures arise in the beginning and revenue just later [...]. That is why intellectual property exists, [...] where investments or return on investment are brought in a fair balance.)

Nonetheless, DCAs insist on public access to the outcome of PPPs which are partially financed by public funds.

Wir haben zu den Eigentumsrechten am geistigen Eigentum eine Klausel. Alles, was gemeinschaftlich finanziert wird, soll auch der Gemeinschaft oder öffentlich zugänglich bleiben [...], ist aber auch mit bestimmten Firmen, die [...] für Technologien arbeiten und die davon leben, dass das eben nicht öffentlich bekannt ist, natürlich ein Verhandlungsfaktor. (DC3)
(We have a clause on the property rights of the intellectual property. Everything, which is jointly financed, shall remain accessible to the community or to the public [...]. Still, this is a negotiation issue for certain companies, [...] which work for technologies, and rely on the condition that those things are not disseminated in the public.)

For this reason, CO5 agrees with the partnering DCA that the property rights will be left to the DCA, insofar as his company does not commercialize the project results from the PPP. Others like CO4 share only information which the public partner could use from the outset.

> *[...] in den Verträgen waren natürlich die negativen Eventualitäten angesprochen und entsprechend abgesichert [...]. Da ist zum Beispiel eine Klausel drin, [...], wenn wir die Projektergebnisse nicht kommerziell verwerten, [...] dann gehen die Rechte an die [DCA Partner] über, sodass die [DCA Partner] das an einen Dritten weitergeben könnte, um kommerziell ausgewertet zu werden. [...] das ist so ein spezifischer Punkt, wo die EZ-Zusammenarbeit sehr klar war. Wenn öffentliche Steuergelder fließen und [CO5] daraus nichts Kommerzielles macht, dann gehen die Rechte über. (CO5)*
>
> ([...] negative eventualities were addressed and assured accordingly in the contracts [...]. For instance, there is a clause, [...], if we do not commercialize the project results, [...] then the rights will be transferred to the [DCA partner], so that the [DCA partner] could pass them on to a third-party for commercializing them. [...] and this is such a specific point where the development cooperation was very clear. If public tax money is used and [CO5] does not make anything commercial out of it, then the rights are transferred.)

Concerns on issues like the infringement of intellectual property do not only accompany the actual PPP implementation but arise already before contracts are concluded. That is why so-called secrecy agreements might be concluded in order to impede the release of confidential information during the initial negotiations (Chapter 6.1.5.3.1). One private sector interviewee adds that government guarantees, which ensure a certain minimum demand for specific products, enable firms to do reliable product planning and therefore to agree on PPP conditions being beneficial for the public DCA or IO partner (Chapter 6.4.2). Moreover, CO6 and IO7 highlight that their contractual safeguardings include clauses on conflict resolution and the course of law in the terms and conditions, in the event of difficulties and dispute which would require legal action. CO13-2 remarks that contractual safeguardings serve the protection of the governance structure and of the decision-making processes against individual opportunism. For this reason, CO9-1 agreed on transparency clauses to diminish information asymmetries:

> *[...] cuando tu creas [...] la gobernanza, lo que haces es blindar el proceso de toma de decisiones para que alguien no pueda hacer un uso individual o un uso que beneficia un interés personal [...]. (CO13-2)*
>
> ([...] when you create [...] the governance, what you are doing is that you armour the decision-making process so that someone cannot make an individual use or a use that benefits a personal interest [...].)

> *Natürlich gibt es da Informationsasymmetrien. Natürlich will ein [Begünstigter] uns bestimmte Sachen vorenthalten, und wir haben uns eben [...] vertraglich bestimmte Rechte zusichern lassen, damit wir eben Moral Hazard vermeiden [...]. (CO9-1)*
>
> (Of course, there are information asymmetries. Of course, a [beneficiary] wants to deprive us of certain things and that is why we [...] seeked certain legal assurances in order to avoid moral hazard [...].)

However, DC1 states that sanctioning is neither really formalized nor actually possible because law enforcement is very difficult in PPPs which usually are of transnational nature. Hence, in the worst case scenario, the joint activities terminate abruptly and all partners stop their contributions. In summary, the interview partners demonstrate awareness of the need to protect their own resources and interests by contract. Still, they also see the limitations of legal possibilities so that they tend to focus on key issues like intellectual property rights and invest instead more efforts in the prevention of conflicts and contractual infringement than in downstream sanctioning.

6.6.4 Environmental Factors

This chapter analyzes the practical influence of diverse environmental factors on MC, which form a fundamental element of the conceptual control archetypes and typologies of IORs including PPPs and JVs (Chapter 0, Figure 18). First of all, control challenges in PPPs for development are discussed, followed by an analysis of the relevance of intercultural influences and differences in organizational cultures for MC. Moreover, control problems and potential measures to counteract them are presented. The special role that trust and risk basically play for the control archetypes and for the concept of typologies has already been demonstrated in Chapter 3.6. For this reason, MC aspects of trust and risk management will be discussed in the present chapter as well.

6.6.4.1 Control Challenges

This chapter summarizes major impact factors which the interview partners perceived hitherto as challenging for project managment and control in their respective partnerships. Finding the right balance between commercial interests and the added value of development cooperation, was mentioned by DC3, while IO1 sees moreover potential imbalances in partnerships emanating from a broad spectrum of participants and diverging regional development. This concurs with potential misunderstandings and intercultural challenges or differences in the organizational culture because public and private sector entities differ by their ways of thinking and therefore have different approaches to joint policy issues. DC2 and IO3 remark that it is challenging to promote mutual understanding and develop mutual awareness of what the respective partners are able to perform:

> *Problem am Anfang ist tatsächlich, alle unter einen Hut zu kriegen, und dann auch unter diesem Hut zu behalten und ständig sozusagen um Verständnis für die Position des anderen zu werben. Das [zuständige Ministerium] oder die [nationale Regierung] tickt einfach anders, als alle unsere anderen Unternehmen das tun. (DC2)*
>
> (The initial problem really is to find the right balance, and then to keep the balance and to promote all the time understanding for the position of the others. The [ministry in charge] or the [national government] simply think differently than do all our other companies.)

> *We have often the misunderstanding of private sector entities on what [IO3] can and can not do. (IO3)*

Intercultural differences, but moreover organizational differences, manifest themselves in diverging understandings of hierarchies, time horizons, or in the perceived level of professionalism. CO13-2 argues that these aspects can be challenging for trust building between partners:

> *[...] the culture is different [...]. Quite often they do not have the professional approach towards funds, how to track money and compliance and all of these things [...] and also that things take [...] very, very long. [...] if we decide to stop something, we can stop it now. We do not have to go through many, many bodies until you can get a final agreement. [...] an UN-organization [...] they are very hierarchical and they are very demanding, because they think [...] companies and all that owe them something. So, it is a different way of working together. And you cannot exercise power over them. You know, even when the things that they are doing are not exactly what you agreed upon, it is very difficult to challenge them. (CO7)*

> *[...] el lenguaje y la cultura de las administraciones también es un reto. Sobretodo cuando son de distintos sectores. [...] al inicio el nivel de confianza es un reto en alianzas de este tipo. No porque tengas una desconfianza inmediata en el socio sino por el entendimiento de los propios conceptos. Es decir, te das cuenta que la palabra "gestión", la palabra "planeación" o "estrategia" o cualquier tipo de concepto es entendido de una forma muy distinta en otras organizaciones [...]. Entonces, [...] entender distinto las cosas cuando te vas al resultado, pues llegas a caminos completamente diferentes. (CO13-2)*
> ([...] the language and the culture of the administrations are also a challenge. Especially, if they are from different sectors. [...] the trust level of this type of alliances is a challenge in the beginning. Not because you have immediate distrust in the partner but for the understanding of your own concepts. This means, you are aware of the term "control", the word "planning" or "strategy" or any other type of concept is understood very differently in other organizations [...]. So, [...] understanding the things differently brings you to completely different ways when you get to the results.)

Together with CO12, CO13-1 notes morever that gaining public actors willing to make changes and to adjust structures is very complicated because priorities others than the joint incentive of making revenue and turnover prevail for them:

> *[...] cuando vienes del sector privado, una de las primeras cosas que te da shock es lo complicado que es mover estructuras hacia una misma dirección. Y esto es porque la alineación de incentivos es mucho más complicada. O sea en una compañia todo el mundo tiene el mismo incentivo que es de generar ganancias, es de tener un buen desempeño económico. Entonces, es más fácil mover a toda la estructura a un mismo lugar. Puede haber una diferencia de opiniones en cómo llegar allá pero por lo menos esto es la visión. (CO13-1)*
> ([...] when you come from the private sector, one of the first things that schocks you is to realize how complicated it is to move structures in the same direction. And that is because the alignment of incentives is much more complicated. This means, in a company everybody has the same incentive which is making profit, it is having a good economic performance. Hence, it is easier to move the whole structure to the same place. There might be different opinions about how to get there but the vision remains the same.)

For resource planning, CO10-1 stresses the challenge to align different project ideas originating from public and private partners with a limited budget available, while DC5 mentions the difficulty to find qualified but affordable external staff for filling vacancies of paid full-time positions in the governance structure. Moreover, she identified external and internal communication as a challenge for PPP implementation because of the governance board's initial hesitance and reservation of sharing relevant information with both its own partners and external stakeholders. Insufficient availability of proper baseline data was bemoaned by IO7, while CO14 mentions difficulties in convincing his senior management of the value of the PPP engagements for the company.

In summary, control challenges related to resource planning and governance have been indirectly addressed in previous chapters already, while issues of intercultural and organizational differences as well as serious control problems will be analyzed in the following subchapters.

6.6.4.2 *Influences of Organizational Culture*

This chapter shows influences of public and private organizational cultures on PPP implementation and analyzes implications for MC resulting from them. Therefore, it specifies some of the control challenges mentioned in Chapter 6.6.4.1. Figure 51 provides an overview of some influences of public and private organizational cultures.

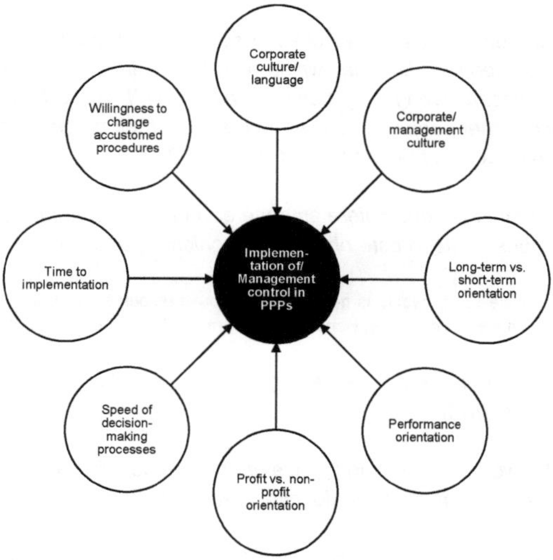

Figure 51: Influences of public and private organizational cultures.

In a very general manner, IO1 points to fundamental differences between the UN System and private sector, which should be considered by MC because they might be a source of conflict, as stated before (Chapter 6.6.2.3).

> *Organizational cultural differences (i.e. UN bureaucracy vs. more dynamic private organizations) as well as regional diversities in the context of partnerships [...] should be taken into consideration when establishing control and management responsibilities within a partnership and mixed (private and UN participated) control/management mechanisms should be put in place when necessary. (IO1)*

In particular, the **speed of decision-making processes**, the **performance orientation**, the **time it takes to implement joint PPP activities**, and the **unwillingness to change accustomed procedures** seem to be bemoaned by the private sector, especially in PPPs with IOs, while IOs state that companies are basically too much **profit-oriented** and do not see the whole picture the public sector is responsible for. By contrast, CO4 criticizes that the UN System works rather **short term-oriented**, while CO5 acknowledges that IOs and also local governments adopt by mandate a macroeconomic perspective instead of focussing on the private sector's microeconomics:

> *[...] der öffentliche Dienst ist vielleicht weniger geeignet, um wirklich vor Ort Hands-on-Implementierung voranzutreiben. Das mache ich vielleicht eher mit den privatwirtschaftlichen Partnern, die einen echten Mehrwert darin sehen, um Geld damit zu verdienen. (CO5)*
> ([...] the public sector is maybe less suitable for really advancing hands-on implementation on the ground. Maybe I do this better with private partners who see a real added value in doing that in order to earn money.)

> *The public sector viewed it as, "If we change something, it is different than our normal standard procedure". And they would almost view it as [...] what we have been doing in the past is wrong. [...] they were not driven by cost. I mean, as far as they saw, it was other people's money and therefore their career was a higher risk than the excess-Dollars that they would spent. (CO12)*

> *Porque el sector privado lo que quiere es generar recursos económicos. [...] y el sector gobierno pues no tiene este objetivo. El gobierno pues tiene otro objetivo social. (DC5)*
> (Because what the private sector wants is generating economic resources. [...], and the governmental sector does not have this objective. Hence, the government has another social objective.)

> *And that's a difference in the private sector, you have one bottom line, we have multiple bottom lines. (IO3)*

> *The private sector works so fast and [...] we need to do due diligence and its taking three months but they think it should take three days. (IO5)*

> *That private sector is not used to consulting the government [...]. They just do identify an area and want to ABC and that's it, without thinking further. But, we kind of need to hold back a little bit and think it through first before sending a ton of mobile phones in a country that might crash the networks in an emergency situation or things like that. (IO7)*

CO13-2, DC1 and DC3 remark that private sector firms think by nature in shorter timeframes and more in margins because they have to generate the resources for PPP engagements on their own. DC4 adds that the public sector's strong accountability to the taxpayers is one reason why funding is often subjected to very strict due diligence procedures before it is released.

> *[...] ein Unternehmen muss ja seinen Umsatz und seinen Gewinn selbst erwirtschaften. Und wir bekommen die Aufträge und setzen sie um. Das ist, glaube ich, schon mal auch eine andere Denke. (DC3)*
> ([...] a company has to generate its revenue and profit on its own. And we receive orders and implement them. I think that is indeed another way of thinking.)

Furthermore, CO4, IO6 and IO7 perceive the **different languages which public and private sector speak**, as one major challenge that is related to the organizational culture. CO4 attributes this in particular to the diplomatic language used by IOs and also expresses his astonishment about the **cult of personality** that seems to be practiced around high-ranked people in some organizations:

> *Ich bilde mir ein, ein bisschen Englisch zu können, aber das ist eine Sprache, die ich nicht verstehe, extrem kompliziert geschrieben. (CO4)*
> (In my mind, I am able to speak decent English, but this is a language which I do not understand, extremely complicated written)

> *[...] maybe the most important thing I have learned in these years, one word: It's Language! The role that I also have here is really putting together two worlds that speak a different language, and I am in the middle. Because the real challenge with public-private partnerships is really putting together two worlds. You have a lot of challenges in speaking together. (IO6)*

That is why CO3 urges public and private actors to acquire a deep understanding of handling PPPs and of the intraorganizational structure of the respective partners in order to better understand what does work in a partnership and what does not. In DC3's view, this is a long process that takes a major part of the PPP work. For this reason, she recommends meeting up regularly for enhancing mutual understanding and for learning one another's language. However, despite some general cultural clashes that obviously exist between the public and private sector's way of working, CO14 and DC6 did not identify significant differences which would hamper the PPP work:

> *I think actually with [IO partner] the conversation has been very fluent, because we speak the same language and we agree on the same values and purposes when it comes to a specific project [...]. (CO14)*

Moreover, IO8 deems interorganizational differences being enriching experiences for both parties involved, while IO6, knowing very well both professional worlds, stresses the necessity of simply accepting some cultural differences if actors from different sectors collaborate:

> *So, that has a hierarchy, but it's part of the game. If you want to enter into a partnership with the UN you need to know that. Still, if you're an UN agency you need to know that the private sector has its own conduct. And it's usually quicker than the one of the UN. (IO6)*

Although interorganizational differences between public and private sector seem to be an important concern to be taken into account by MC, several interview partners like DC2, CO6 and CO8 report on **cultural differences between actors of the sampe type**, but also on intraorganizational differences which have MC implications for the whole partnership (e.g. in terms of management and meeting culture or delegation of authority):

> *[…] er [kam] halt regelmäßig eine Dreiviertelstunde zu spät ins Meeting […]. So Sachen […] haben schon genervt, und ich bin da auch ein sehr rationaler, methodisch denkender Mensch, der sich schon mal aufregt, wenn eine Telefonkonferenz anberaumt wurde, in Outlook akzeptiert wurde und derjenige taucht nicht auf, und dann muss ich ihm wieder hinterher telefonieren. Also, das sind so Sachen, die habe ich bei mir im Team ungern toleriert, und die fand ich bei Partnern auch immer nervig, die eine andere Meetingkultur haben. (CO5)*
> ([…] he [was] regularly delayed by 45 minutes for the meeting […]. Such things […] were really annoying and in this regard I am a very rational, methodically thinking person, who gets upset if a telephone conference was scheduled, was accepted in Outlook, and then he does not show up so that I have to call after him again. These are such things which I disliked to tolerate in my team, and I always found them very annoying on the side of partners who have another meeting culture.)

> *Das spielt eine Rolle, dass natürlich Managementkulturen völlig unterschiedlich sind. In der Regel sehr hierarchisch. Verantwortung hin und her geschoben. Dass es eine flache Hierarchie gibt, ist in Afrika eher seltener, finde ich. Dann wiederum vielleicht bei Internationalen Organisationen genau das Gegenteil. Hoher Grad an Flexibilität und Eigenverantwortung […]. Das hängt sehr stark von den Partnern ab. (CO8)*
> (It does in fact matter that there are completely different management cultures. Usually, very hierarchical. Reponsibiltiy is shifted back and forth. Flat hierarchies rarely exist in Africa, I think. But then, it might be just the opposite in international organizations. High degree of flexibility and self-responsibility […]. That depends very much on the partners.)

Similar to DC2, CO6 reports that the different companies send delegates employed at **different hierarchy levels** and endowed with different **decision-making competencies** to project management meetings. Thus, while some representatives have the power of acting pragmatically and making decisions on their companies' behalf, others have to seek approval for every step by their headquarter. Therefore, he recommends that representatives develop a sense of common management culture. CO8 remarks the importance of appropriate internal anchoring of the PPP work:

> *Sie haben auch ganz unterschiedliche Managementstile. Die einen sind partizipativer unterwegs. Bei den anderen ist das eher top-down. (CO6)*
> (They also have very different management styles. Some of them are more participative. With others it is rather top-down.)

> *[…] aber wir sind […] auch nicht DAS Unternehmen [CO8], sondern ich bin der Mitarbeiter einer Abteilung bei der [CO8] von ganz vielen […]. Wenn ich […] einen "Salee" von uns zur [DCA Partner] losschicke, dann hat der eine andere Erwartungshaltung und kennt das Thema vielleicht gar nicht. (CO8)*
> ([…] but we are […] not THE company [CO8] either, but I am an employee from one department of several ones within [CO8]. If I […] send a "salee" from us to [DCA partner], then he might have another expectation and perhaps does not know the subject matter at all.)

> *Wenn ich mir [Unternehmenspartner A] angucke, vollkommen hierarchisch, es gibt kaum einen Mitarbeiter, der Entscheidungen treffen kann. Der muss alles im Detail jeweils mit seiner Führung abstimmen, und es wird immer die Rechtsabtei-*

lung einberufen [...]. [...] als Gegensatz [Unternehmenspartner B] [...], wo alle Mitarbeiter ein Höchstmaß oder, was ich wahrnehme, ein sehr, sehr hohes Maß an Entscheidungsmöglichkeiten haben, [...] an Selbstbestimmung, [...] an Eigenverantwortlichkeit. (DC2)

(When I look at [company partner A], fully hierarchical, there is barely any employee who can make decisions. He has to align everything in detail with his management and the legal department is always involved [...]. [...] by contrast [company partner B] [...], where all employees have high degree or, what I perceive, have a very very high degree of decision-making power, [...] of autonomy, [...] of self-responsibility.)

CO3 and CO11 stress the importance of openmindedness, which implies the willingness to learn from each other, and IO8 recommends to put "[...] different points of view on the tables and [...] take a decision based on that.":

Und wenn man dann auf etwas beharrt, weil man glaubt, dass man das braucht und meint, das geht, das geht aber auf gar keinen Fall, weil es rechtlich, politisch, moralisch, organisationsinteressensseitig nicht opportun oder gar unmöglich ist, dann kann man dadurch eine Partnerschaft ruinieren, ganz schnell. (CO3)

(And if you insist on something because you believe that you need it or that it works, but it does not work at all because it is legally, politically, morally or with regard to the organizations' interests not opportune or even impossible, then you can thereby destroy a partnership very quickly.)

This is why IO7 appeals to the partners' stamina, and in this spirit, CO13-2 emphasizes that their today's governance structure and set of management controls form the outcome of a long alignment procedure and is therefore a combination of public and private management approaches, for instance, in terms of performance measurement for the determination of benchmark indicators. Still, interorganizational differences may lead to the failure of PPPs. One DCA interviewee sees the reason for that mainly in the project management and monitoring.

Understanding what it really takes to work in partnership, it can be a little bit of a painful process for both. [...]. Some of them do get frustrated with the process, and then the partnership does not happen, but a lot of them do also understand and appreciate the effort that it takes. (IO7)

Minor interorganizational cultural differences, which still reflect very diverging ways of thinking, are reported by DC2 and CO4. The latter bemoans that presumably stricter duty travel policies on his company's side and simplified visa procedures for international civil servants from IOs clash if the public sector wants to arrange at short note a meeting in any country without visa waiver for ordinary citizens. In the same context, DC2 emphasizes that the whole communication with the partners involved and the entire organization of duty travels is done by himself without support from any secretariat. Moreover, he notes very diverging handlings of the compensation of overtime work, so that he urges all partners to mutually respect the specifics of other organizational cultures and to be flexible in adapting to the needs of others.

[...] die [IO Partner] können [...] überall hinreisen. Ich muss mir halt meistens ein Visum besorgen. [...] ich muss hier auch meine Reisekosten verteidigen, und solche Sorgen hat man da anscheinend nicht. (CO4)

([...] the [IO partner] can [...] travel everywhere. I mostly have to request a visa. [...] I also have to defend my travel expenses and such worries obviously do not exist there.)

Ich sage: "Nein, ich habe keine Sekretärin. [...] ich habe jetzt kein Vorzimmer, was irgendwie für mich die Anrufe entgegen nimmt." Was bei ganz vielen Unternehmen immer weniger, aber tatsächlich doch der Fall ist. Und das sind dann so Kleinigkeiten, wenn es irgendwie um [...] Reisen geht. Ich organisiere meine Reise von A bis Z selbst. [...] eine Kollegin von [Unternehmenspartner] sagte: "Ja, in meinem Vertrag steht, dass alle Überstunden mit dem Gehalt abgegolten sind." Eine Mitarbeiterin von einem mittelständischen Unternehmen sagte: "Naja, meine Arbeitszeit hat heute Morgen begonnen, als ich mein Auto am Bahnhof abgestellt habe und endet nachher, wenn ich wieder in mein Auto am Bahnhof steige." [...] Kollegin von [NGO Partner] sagte: "Ja, wenn wir mal mehr arbeiten, dann nehmen wir irgendwann einfach mal einen freien Tag, und dann ist das auch okay." [...] da müssen dann einfach alle [...] mit umgehen und da auch flexibel sein, was die auch mittlerweile alle verstanden haben. (DC2)

(I say: "No, I have no secretary. [...] I have no outer office which receives the calls for me." This still holds true for many companies, but less and less. And there are such minor details when it is about [...] traveling. I organize my journeys completely on my own. [...] a colleague from [company partner] said: "Yes, in my contract is stipulated that any overtime is compensated by the salary." An employee from a medium-sized company said: "Well, my working time has begun this morning when I dropped my car at the station and finishes later when I get in my car again." [...] a colleague from [NGO partner] said: "Yes, if we work one day, then we take a day off later on, and that is okay then." [...] all of them simply must [...] deal with that and also be flexible, what meanwhile everybody has understood.)

In summary, there are diverse influences of diverging organizational cultures on MC, which the interview partners perceived as tedious, or even as a burden, and which are addressed by informal social control measures, such as flexibility, intensive communication, openmindedness or willingness to learn from each other. Still, as CO12 also notes, mutual prejudices prevailing from the private sector's side about the public sector and vice-versa seem to be confirmed by some quotations. For instance, it is questionable whether the public sector is by nature more bureaucratic than the private sector. Statements, such as those made by DC2, paint a rather differentiated picture in this regard.

6.6.4.3 Intercultural Influences

Intercultural differences matter for MC because speaking the same language and originating from the same cultural environment create familiarity and therefore form connecting elements. Both CO5 and IO8 confirm that those links make it easier to build relationships between partners and facilitate communication because collaborating abroad and talking about private topics, such as the recent results from the domestic soccer league, bring people together and might be crucial for efficient PPP implementation. CO3, CO4, CO5 and DC4 unanimously emphasize that any kind of business or cooperation is in many societies very much relationship-based, whether in Africa, Asia or the Middle East. That is why much investment in relationship-building at eye-level and in the individual capacity to act on the international stage is imperative in their view. Everybody's willingness to personally adapt to local circumstances is assumed.

Unternehmen gehen vielleicht manchmal politisch etwas unsensibel vor, vielleicht auch kulturell unsensibel. Da ist die [DCA Partner] unheimlich stark. Die auch immer wieder darauf hinweist, dass man mit den Partnern vor Ort extensive Dialoge führen muss, dass da eigene Reisen nötig sind, um mit den Partnern vorher zu klären, was dieses Projekt will [...]. (CO3)

(Companies may sometimes act in a politically insensive manner, maybe even culturally insensitve. In this regard, the [DCA partner] is pretty strong. They always point to the need for extensive dialogues with the partners on-site, and for separate journeys that are necessary in order to agree with them in advance about the project's aims [...].)

Wichtig ist natürlich, dass man co-partizipatorisch vorgeht und hier nicht [...] einfach was ausrollt und glaubt, man kann die Weisheit von der deutschen Welt eins zu eins übertragen. (CO5)

(It is important to proceed in co-participative manner and to not [...] simply roll out anything and believe that one can transfer the wisdom from the German world one-to-one.)

Moreover, intercultural differences also impact upon organizational cultures. For instance, in many countries and in rural areas in particular, business is done with a handshake and does not rely on bureaucracy and the filling in of forms. Thus, to gain the local stakeholders' acceptance of the PPP partners' rules of procedure, respect of people's culture, history and traditions is indispensable. Awareness of ethno-political tensions resulting from former suppressions or wars helps to understand and control conflicts and to customize the governance structure as well as formal and informal control mechanisms in order to mitigate those tensions. CO4 reports in this context from a kick-off meeting where the alignment of interests and any decision-making was severly interfered with the historical tensions between the home countries of the participating African partners.

Die [Anmerkung: Zusammenarbeit] muss auf Augenhöhe und wenig hierarchisch und partnerschaftlich stattfinden [...] denn in Ländern Asiens, Ländern Afrikas, die ja zum Teil immer noch kolonialisiert werden oder zumindest lange unter den Europäern gelitten hatten, ist man natürlich sehr, sehr kritisch, wenn da die Leute aus Europa und den USA kommen. Und wenn man da nicht vom ersten Tag an mit großem Lächeln und mit ein bisschen Späßchen und viel Freude und viel Offenheit klar macht, dass man sich auf Augenhöhe begegnet, dann ist das Projekt von vorneherein eigentlich zum Scheitern verurteilt. (DC4)

(The [remark: cooperation] must be at eye-level and little hierarchical and take place in partnership [...] because in Asian countries, in African countries, which are partially still colonialized or had at least suffered from the Europeans for a long period of time, people are very, very critical if people from Europe and the USA show up. And if you do not encounter them from the first day on with a broad smile, some jokes, much pleasure and much openness for making clear to face one another at eye-level, then the project is actually doomed to fail from the outset.)

However, the diplomatic environment of IOs and other cultures in general hold many pitfalls. One private sector interviewee reports about a situation where his superior made a blunder because the jokes where misinterpreted by partners. As a consequence, the relationship is sustainably damaged. Thus, he urges the necessity of demonstrating intercultural sensitivity in PPPs and of choosing another tone and style towards foreign partners, compared to the way you might be communicating with your staff or people from your native culture.

Mein Boss hat sich da halt extremst [Anmerkung: den Mund] verbrannt und leider habe ich darunter jetzt immer noch zu leiden, hat halt auch die Firma in den Au-

gen des [Partners] verbrannt. Und das ist halt, wenn man sich [Anmerkung: der kulturellen Unterschiede] nicht bewusst ist und meint: "Ich kann so sein, wie ich jetzt [Name des Interviewpartners] gegenüber jeden Tag bin", weil ich verstehe, dass das jetzt ein Witz ist und verstehe, wenn es ein Hinweis ist, dass ich mehr tun soll." (n/a)

(My boss extremely [remark: put his foot in it] and I still suffer from that, he also scorched the company in the [partner's] eyes. And this happens if you are not aware of [remark: the cultural differences] and believe: "I can be like as I face [name of the interviewee] every day", because I understand that this is supposed to be a joke and understand the hint that I shall do more.)

Hence, a key learning that several interview partners gathered from their multicultural PPP engagements is the need to base project management and control on the principle of intercultural sensitivity. CO8 adds that many members of his PPP's project team on-site held degrees in social or political sciences, rather than in engineering or natural sciences, although the PPP was about technology transfer. This is because strong intercultural differences between the implementers and the beneficiaries required strong social skills for raising people's interest in technology and for convincing them to adopt it. Moreover, he remarks that intercultural diversity is part of the organizational DNA of most PPPs for development. In this vein, CO5, CO13-2, CO14, and IO8 emphasize that by nature most companies, DCAs, and IOs have a very multicultural staff composition, so that the individuals' mindset, sympathy and differences in the organizational culture impact upon MC including conflict potential, and these elements prevail over intercultural differences:

Al final [...], [CO13] se está volviendo en una compañia global más que mexicana y las organizaciones con las que estamos son internacionales también. (CO13-2)

(Finally [...], [CO13] is becoming a global company, more than a Mexican, and the organizations we are working with are international as well.)

I think the people who are in this space of international development are very open and very multicultural and they are always open to new different cultures. (CO14)

[...] you can work with two people from the same country, but the mindset is totally different. [...] we are working in a professional environment. [...] the thing that would bring us together [...] is the fact that we both speak [language], but we can still be in a position of looking at the problem to be solved in a totally different way because she works for [company partner] and I work for [IO8]. Therefore, I think what characterizes the most [...] is the place where we work for, rather than where we come from, in this particular context. (IO8)

In summary, intercultural influences matter for MC, not only because they impact on the exertion of MC, but, even more importantly, the selection of suitable formal and informal controls contributes to mitigating and preventing intercultural conflicts and to paving the way for multilateral collaboration and the implementation of PPPs. Still, finally, the personal chemistry between the concrete actors involved must fit.

6.6.4.4 Trust

This chapter analyzes the general level of trust in the PPPs on scope and looks on the relationship between trust and MC in practice. Moreover, it focuses on trust building mechanisms and makes therefore reference to the theoretical foundation in Chapter 3.6.1.
At the beginning of a partnership it is important to create mutual trust between all partners involved, regardless of their size or type, as stated by CO1, DC2 and others. Moreover, CO2 and CO8 emphasize that this process should be accompanied with open and honest dealings with each other, based on a constructive performance attitude, mutual respect and transparency. Otherwise, a PPP will not really start working.

> *The trust is really a key element because partnerships are hard work and you don't go that way unless you trust that it's a worthy initiative in that sense. (IO7)*

In addition, CO3 perceives the creation of trust in large-scale PPPs with numerous partners as very challenging, while CO4 underlines that with major competitors being also involved in the partnership fully trustful relationships will never be possible. Moreover, trust is not necessarily a static phenomenon that increases continuously the longer partners collaborate. The risk of decreasing trust is particularly high in partnerships with a high-level of initial trust, which may emanate from previous experiences or the partner's reputation.

> *So, the risk is to have this sort of descending curve where you start with a huge trust. In the sense that you usually have to deal with both an UN agency and on the other side a private sector actor that has been screened and is considered as valued. [...]. This trust sometimes falls when bureaucracy starts because business has its own way dealing with things, its own timetable, its own agenda [...] and the UN has another. (IO6)*

Both positive previous experiences and other partners' goodwill prompt public and private sector to enter into joint PPPs. In existing partnerships, already participating actors with good reputation can serve as carriers for attracting further partners because the involvement of the former is a kind of quality seal standing for reliability. This takes even more effect if the potential partners originate from the same country and are embedded in the same institutional environment to a large extent.

> *Ich denke, [DCA Partner] ist ein sehr starker Partner gewesen, weil [Anmerkung: es] eine deutsche Entwicklungsorganisation ist, mit der man auch vertrauensvoll langfristig ein Projekt aufsetzen kann. Wir waren uns ziemlich sicher, dass, wenn [DCA Partner] einsteigt, es auch ein sehr verlässlicher Partner sein wird. (CO3)*
> (I think, [DCA partner] has been a very strong partner because [remark: it] is a German development agency, with which one can setup a long-term project in a trustful manner. We were pretty sure, if [DCA partner] joins in, it will be a reliable partner.)

Most interview partners describe the relationships with the other partners as trustful, from both public and private side. However, a few critical voices have been noted in the context of trust and communication. Reasons of little trust or distrust are different understandings of the same subject matter, according to CO13-2, and possible prejudices that CO12 perceives in his supplier role on the public sector's side:

> *The level of trust [...] is very low because the agencies think the contractor is just going to build the minimum amount as possible and will find every string, every way in the book to cut costs, which means that the agency will be left with a sub-standard product. [...] from [CO12]'s perspective we have had some hardship getting into a lot of these teams, because they view us as the source of leaks. (CO12)*

> *[...] creo que el nivel de confianza se podría ver afectado no por una desconfianza en sí sino por un nivel de entendimiento distinto. (CO13-2)*
> ([...] I believe that the trust level could be seen affected not by distrust as such but by a different level of understanding.)

In summary, trust is a basic requirement for good partnership work and most PPPs rely on trustful relationships. However, trust-building requires a good portion of emotional intelligence and continuous maintenance efforts from all partners, given its extremely fragile nature.

6.6.4.4.1 Relationship between Trust and Management Control

This chapter analyzes the relationship between trust and MC, based on the conceptual dimensions of trust (Chapter 3.6.1.2). In general, DC1 emphasizes the importance of trust and cooperative interaction for MC, while IO2 remarks that the partner selection follows in large parts a trust-based control approach and therefore makes reference to **competence trust**. In this sense, trust in the competencies and reputation of the respective public partner prompts CO2 and CO8 to enter into a joint PPP with him:

> *[DCA Partner] sind halt ein trusted Adviser für Regierungen seit vielen Jahren und haben international einen guten Ruf [...]. (CO8)*
> ([DCA partner] have simply been trusted advisers for governments for many years and have a good reputation globally [...].)

For doing MC in practice, CO9-2, DC4 and DC4 underline that **contractual trust** is imperative because themselves are unable to monitor every activity acomplished by their counterparts and to verify all information received from them. Thus, PPP implementation requires reciprocal honesty and loyalty.

> *Gleichermaßen vertraut das Board natürlich sehr stark auf die [IO Partner]. [...]. Die können nicht auf täglicher Basis gucken, was [CO9] macht. Es gibt ein Reporting, aber natürlich muss ein gewisses Vertrauen da sein, wie wir die tägliche Arbeit umsetzen [...]. [...] das ist auch beidseitig da. (CO9-2)*
> (At the same time, the board trusts of course very much in the [IO partner]. [...]. They cannot look on a daily basis what [CO9] is doing. There is a reporting, but obviously there must be certain trust in how we implement our daily work [...]. [...] that is given from both sides.)

> *[...] aber letztendlich kommt es bei solchen Projekten viel, viel auf Vertrauensbasis an, [...] weil man gar nicht alles so mikromanagementmäßig überwachen kann [...]. (DC4)*

([...] but finally it depends very very much on the trust basis, [...] because you cannot monitor everything in a micro management way.)

The creation of **goodwill trust** can take some time because, as CO10-1 stated, at the beginning of the PPP they did not know well the respective interests and objectives of the other partners. Still, in line with the observations of Das and Teng (2001a) and of Emsley and Kidon (2007), they built up goodwill trust quickly because another private sector partner, with whom longstanding and trustful business relationships already existed, provided CO10 with goodwill-related information and therefore helped to overcome information asymmetries and to remove concerns. DC2 adds that increased goodwill trust makes MC more efficient in the sense that social control replaces formal control mechanisms, e.g. in terms of communication. Moreover, IO7 shows the reciprocal relationship between MC and trust:

> *Und gesteigertes Vertrauen hilft da, dass man auch mal zum Telefon greift, dass man nicht alles immer nur schriftlich macht, sich dann auch tatsächlich darauf verlassen kann, etc. (DC2)*
>
> (And increasted trust helps that sometimes one also picks up the phone, that not everything is only done in written form, and that you can indeed rely on that, etc. [...].)
>
> *So, if it's a smooth partnership in a way you have a good team, who is uninterrupted, you have good delivery and if every partner does what he has promised to do. That tends to increase the trust, I would say. But if there are challenges in implementing [...] [remark: Management Control], either side, that does influence the trust to some extent. (IO7)*

However, goodwill trust is fragile and might deteriorate if the management does not make enough efforts to keep a high level of trust, as stated by IO6, or creates information asymmetry.

> *Ahora, [nota: lo que afecta la relación] de los socios mismos del sector privado con la mesa directiva, yo no la diría desconfianza pero [...] es como [...] descontento de: "Oye, es que no estás informando adecuadamente, o sea no estoy enterado de qué estás haciendo o cómo lo estás haciendo." (DC5)*
>
> (Now, [remark: concerning the relationship] of the private sector members themselves with the governance board I would not say that it is distrust but [...] it is like [...] dissatisfaction with: "Hey, it is that you are not informing adequately, so I am not aware of what you are doing or how you are doing it.")

A shift from goodwill trust to **vertical trust** has been noted by IO8 who argues that, once confidence in the partners' integrity and commitment to the joint interests and objectves is established, authority and ownership tend to be delegated to the operational level, going along with less control. IO6 adds that the path for getting there is often difficult because the alignment process of diverging interests may obstruct the creation of trust to some degree. Similar experiences have been made by CO11 and DC2 as well (see quotation from CO11 in Chapter 6.5.1.3).

> *[...] relationships are based on trust and how much you believe in the person, who is managing the project, is able to do. So, I would say it also evolved a little bit with the time. It has not always been the same. [...] when you see that their*

> *work is very good, you can like give more trust and also decision power to the person who works for you. (IO6)*

In the context of **system trust**, CO6 emphasizes that similar organizational cultures contributed to trust building, while DC6 perceives the reliability of the governance structure as very conducive to that:

> *[...] es un alto nivel de confianza, sobretodo por la parte de seguridad y de confiabilidad que ha aportado el comité coordinador a la [nombre de la PPP]. (DC6)*
> ([...] it is a high trust level, especially from the aspect of security and reliability, which the coordination commitee has contributed to the [PPP name].)

In summary, there is a viceversa relationship between trust and control in practice as well. If the conditions of the different aforementioned trust dimensions are fulfilled the trust level is high, as stated by CO14, who indicated that his company trusts blindly in the IO partner regarding the joint PPP activities. However, IO2 stresses that too much trust may infringe the adherence to internal rules of procedure if it replaces fix formal control mechanisms (e.g. due diligence in terms of partner selection).

6.6.4.4.2 Trust-building Mechanisms

This chapter clusters several control mechanisms, which contribute to achieving the different dimensions of trust that have been presented in Chapter 6.6.4.4.1.

- **Communication and meetings**: Several interview partners highlight the importance of clear and open communication of their opinions and interests in combination with regular meetings as contributors to trust building. DC3 adds that this implies active listening to the needs and interests of the partners as well.

  > *Das Vertrauen entsteht über die Zeit, und Vertrauen hat etwas damit zu tun, ob ich meinen Partner akzeptiere und respektiere und ich ihm zutraue, es umzusetzen. Und das entwickelt sich eben aus den entsprechenden Gesprächen und Treffen. (CO1-1)*
  > (Confidence emerges over time, and trust has to do with the question of whether I accept and respect my partner and if I trust him to implement it. And this evolves from the corresponding conversations and meetings.)

  > *So, I think trust is also sometimes built by talking honestly about the challenges. So, it's not a whole deal break [...] in that sense, but quite often it can increase trust to openly discuss [...]. (IO7)*

  Moreover, CO7 emphasizes the importance of face-to-face communication, whereas DC2 adds that in the first months and years of their PPP much time was dedicated to the facilitation of personal encounters in order to reduce prejudices resulting from previous experiences between private sector firms and NGOs. In this regard, CO7 and DC2 make reference to the next category of trust building mechanisms.

- **Confidentiality and transparency**: Like CO6, DC2 highlights the importance of confidential communication in order to tear down interpersonal barriers and to reduce prejudices, which both hamper honest communication between partners. CO8 remarks in this context that competitors are often sceptical towards joint partnerships, so that transparency is crucial in his view for prompting collaboration. Such transparency can be reached by setting up a clear governance structure and by agreeing on milestones, timelines and criteria of a successful partnership, according to CO7 and CO13-2. In the end, initially distrustful partners become often aware of the numerous overlaps of interest.

  [...] die regelmäßigen Treffen auf der CEO-Ebene [...] [Anmerkung: finden] [...] unter Ausschluss der Öffentlichkeit dann statt. Insofern gibt es da eine freie Diskussion, und das ist auch das, was die Vorstandsvorsitzenden in der Regel sehr, sehr schätzen, also den freien Meinungsaustausch [...]. (CO6)
  ([...] the regular meetings at CEO level [...] [remark: take place] [...] in camera. Thus, there is a free discussion, and that is what the CEOs usually appreciate very much, so the free exchange of opinions [...].)

  [...] es hat auch ganz viel kleinere Treffen gegeben, wo nur [Anmerkung: wenige] Leute dabei waren [...], teilweise absolut vertraulich, dann manchmal mit diesen Chatham House Rules, wo vorher vereinbart war, worüber wir sprechen, dann aber eigentlich alle in diesen Hintergrundgesprächen [...] gemerkt haben: "Naja, eigentlich wollen wir ja alle das gleiche oder haben sehr ähnliche Ziele [...]." (DC2)
  ([...] there have also been many smaller meetings where only [remark: a few] people participated [...], partially absolutely confidential, sometimes with these Chatham House Rules, where it has been agreed before what we will talk about. But then, all of them noticed in these background discussions [...]: "Well, actually we all want the same thing or have very similar goals [...].")

- **Connections and existing relationships**: PPPs being composed of DCA, and IO partners with existing relationships to local governments and good reputation in certain target countries, capitalize on some leap of faith which can catalyze the trust building between involved private sector and local stakeholders, according to DC4 and IO7. On the other side, CO10-1 describes the longstanding business relationships with another private firm as the reason why they trusted this firm to get on board of an existing partnership and therefore to contribute complementary resources. In the event of distrust or lack of connections, a third-party, such as NGO, can help to build linkages including trust. CO13-1 points to the Halo Effect for defining this phenomenon.

  Y creo que hay un tema que, muy sinceramente va metido con el tema de reputación que te da el Halo Effect. Es de una organización que es un tercero que está enfocado en el medio ambiente que está diciendo: "Estas soluciones realmente están luchando por el medio ambiente". (CO13-1)
  (And there is a topic which is honestly very much related to the matter of reputation that gives the Halo Effect. It is from an organization which is a third-party that is focussing on the environment and saying: "These solutions are really fighting for the environment.")

- **Culture and language**: In DC3's view, the public sector's ability to understand the language of the private sector and viceversa is pivotal to build trust between them. From an intercultural perspective, CO8 stresses the same origin and nationality as mechanism for facilitating the creation of trust. However, CO13-2 argues that the creation of a new, PPP-specific culture being independent from the respective individual organizational cultures is decisive at the end.

In summary, all these mechanisms seem to contribute to trust building. What they have in common is that they basically all rely on personal relationships between individual actors. For this reason, CO4 describes frequent staff turnover, such as replacement of project managers, as one of the major obstacles to the maintenance of a high trust-level because after each change trust must be rebuilt.

6.6.4.5 Management of Control Problems

This chapter first gives an overview of major control problems which the interview partners have identified for their PPP projects, and describes their roots and consequences. In the second step, risk management and control measures are addressed because many extrinsic and intrinsic risks are related with control problems or are even their driving factors. That is why the present subchapter on risk management and control is integrated in the MC section of the results analysis and not in Chapter 6.2.6.

6.6.4.5.1 Control Problems and Consequences

An overview of major control problems is given by Table 58. The control problems are ranked by their frequency of mention and go hand in hand with an indication of the pertinent interview partners. Moreover, suggested or taken countermeasures and reactions to tackle the control problems are presented. **Unfulfilled expectations**, **misaligned goals and interests**, as well as **diverging priorities** were recognized as the most pressing control problems in PPPs for development. DC2 and IO7 note that some private sector firms tend to perceive the public partners as a kind of service provider, in particular, if they pay fix financial contributions to the joint partnership. Morever, CO7 and DC1 experienced that awareness of diverging interests often arises at a late stage of PPP implementation.

> *[...] jedes Mitglied denkt [...] verständlicherweise [...]: "Naja, ich zahl da ja jetzt irgendwie so einen Mitgliedsbeitrag, und dann habe ich da irgendwie jemanden [im Steuerungsorgan] und der muss dann auch irgendwie für mich tätig werden." [...]. Wir können keine individuelle Beratung für jedes mitgliederspezifische Einzelproblem machen. (DC2)*
>
> ([...] each member thinks [...] understandably [...]: "Well, I pay such a kind of membership fee and then I have somehow someone [in the governing body] who must take action for me." [...]. We cannot make an individual counselling for every member-specific single problem.)

> *[...] in one case a private sector entity provided us funding and they expected us to be like a consultancy. So, those kinds of situations where the rules of the game are not clear and expectations are something different, those can result in challenges. And then sometimes these kinds of circumstances [...] might cause delays in projects. We are very used to the challenges that come from operating with the [remark: local] public sector. [...]. We are quite used to it but private sector isn't always. (IO7)*

That is why CO3 calls for continuous consensus-building about the amount and programme of work and stresses the necessity of joint priority setting and placed emphasis on common interests. Both, CO3 and DC4, argue that one or more **partners' insufficient experiences or competences** in the subject matter, or in PPP work as such promote these discrepancies.

Control problems	Mentioned by	Frequency	Suggested and/or taken countermeasures/reactions
Divergence/misalignment of expectations, goals, interests and priorities	CO3, CO5, CO7, CO10, CO14, DC1, DC2, IO6, IO7	9	- Clear delineation and definition of mandate and PPP setting - Continuous consensus-building about the amount and programme of work - Demonstration of greater commitment by the partners - Early and honest communication of interests, goals and expectations - Implementation of strict and common monitoring procedures with the partners - Increased attention from the company's top management on progress and achievements (→ tighter internal reporting requirements) - Joint priority setting and emphasis on common interests - Willingness to make compromises and to prioritize the successful PPP implementation over the full assertion of individual interests
Lack of commitment/lack of support from the partner(s)	CO4, CO5, DC4, DC5, IO7	5	- Increasing the personal exchange between partners and closer coordination (e.g. by face-to-face meetings or by phone) - Replacement of voluntary staff by a full-time and paid manager and team - Taking of leadership/ownership by the more committed partner(s)
Lack of (resource) efficiency/planning; Mismatch of project design with actual goals	CO4, CO5, CO7, DC4, IO8	5	- Alignment of the project design (including project phases and activities) with the goals to be reached - Due diligence and closer coordination with the other partners in the design phase (e.g. common definition of realistic assumptions that shall underlie the PPP) - Internal reassignment/organizational merger of responsibilities - Performance-based payment of financial contributions - Planning for the exit from a partnership (clear start/end date) - Premature termination of the PPP
Misunderstandings/ underestimation of (the complexity of) PPP work and egoism	CO8, DC2, IO7, IO8	4	- Continuous and open discussions - Demonstration of greater commitment and active seeking of clarification in the event of lack of clarity - Setting of rules of the game that are clear to everybody
Staff turnover/leaving of focal points	CO4, CO10, DC5, IO8	4	- Demonstration of commitment and perseverance by the remaining partners
Bad data availability/ comparability of data and lack of forecast mechanisms (e.g. for product demand forecast and resource planning)	CO1, IO7	2	- More frequent telephone conferences for supply vs. demand coordination (every two weeks) - Partial product delivery, if necessary - Use of mobile tools and technologies for data collection and progress monitoring
Bureaucracy (e.g. decision-making or project staff recruiting procedures)	CO12, IO8	2	- Change of mentality in the public sector (e.g. admission of more flexibility in project planning and increase of openmindedness)
Geographic conditons hamper effective control	CO1, CO9	2	- Consideration of (external) risks that are hard to address by MC (e.g. civil war, natural disasters) → diversification of PPP activities - Establishment of mobile teams (technical implementation of PPP activities and monitoring) - Flexibility, pragmatism and willingness to align with given local economic, political and social conditions

Control problems	Mentioned by	Frequency	Suggested and/or taken countermeasures/reactions
Lack of an effective governance structure	CO13, DC5	2	- Invitation of all members to meeting sessions of the governance board - Reassignment of responsibilities and shifting the focus on each partner's core competencies - Replacement of voluntary staff by a full-time and paid manager and team (being specialized in finance, marketing, project design, etc.)
Lack of (internal) communication	DC5, IO6	2	- Implementing strict and common monitoring procedures with the partners - Invitation of all members to meeting sessions of the governance board - Preparation of a regular bulletin to be circulated to all partners involved
Lack of (keeping) trust	IO6, IO7	2	- Implementing strict and common monitoring procedures with the partners
Lack of (PPP) experiences/competencies	CO3, DC4	2	- Intensification of knowledge exchange between public and private partners - Willingness to learn from each other
Lack of priority on policy and non-compliance (intraorganizationally)	IO2, IO3	2	- Centralization of monitoring - Establishment of an accountability framework
Lack of results or of visible outcome (e.g. because of long ramp-up phase)	CO3, DC2	2	- Demonstration of the business case behind the PPP towards the executive management - Improvement of the affordability for small and medium-sized companies to engage and join an existing PPP - Intensification of knowledge exchange between public and private partners
Unclear/inconsistent requirements for PPP work (e.g. regarding benchmarking and performance measurement)	CO7, IO2	2	- Centralization of monitoring - Establishment of an accountability framework - Harmonization of benchmark indicators and performance measurement approaches between partners
Duplication of/lack of clarity about duties and responsibilities	IO1	1	- Provision of more substantive mandates by member states concerning PPP engagements - Specification of the program of work of the UN System regarding PPP engagements - Streamlining of reporting lines to the executive management
Failure/inappropriateness of the MC design (e.g. its costs exceed its benefits, cost-efficient monitoring is impossible; failure of due diligence)	n/a	1	- Assessment of MC measures by their expected efficiency and effectiveness prior to their implementation - Cap the administration and MC costs (especially for monitoring) to X% of the total project budget - More diligent MC in the preparation, initiation and design phase - Redirection of financial resources to PPP projects with a more efficient MC design
High workload and time limits	CO8	1	- Conduction of a priority setting for a bench of activities or options, which all might be reasonable
Information asymmetries	CO9	1	- Inclusion of contractual safeguardings in PPP contracts to prevent moral hazard (e.g. documentation obligations)
Lack of strategic vision	DC5	1	- Hiring of a paid manager and team who can dedicate full-time to the PPP work and support the creation of a joint strategic vision
Opportunistic behaviour	CO9	1	- Inclusion of contractual safeguardings in the PPP contract to prevent moral hazard (e.g. documentation obligations)
Too little local presence	CO9	1	- Increase of the general local presence on the ground - Increase of the involvement of colleagues based in existing local or regional offices
Uncertainty	CO8	1	- Flexibility and willingness to adjust the PPP to changes and amendments
Unreliable and unstable funding (regarding UN organizations)	IO1	1	- Replacement of voluntary contributions by more assessed contributions from member states

Table 58: Control problems and countermeasures/reactions.

Furthermore, CO3 and DC2 underline that the aforementioned problems become particularly evident if it takes a long time until results are measurable or visible. That is why CO3 stresses the need of intense knowledge exchange between public and private partners and of working out the business case behind a PPP in order to demonstrate the connectability of business and development cooperation. For achieving better results, he urges public actors to provide support measures to small- and medium-sized company, whose specific knowhow is needed, but which would otherwise hesitate to join PPPs for development, because of the inherent risks and financial burdens. **Lack of commitment** has been bemoaned by both public and private sectors. This perception results, for instance, from a low level of cooperation (see quotation from DC4 in Chapter 6.5.3) or differences in meeting cultures, which might be rooted in the respective organizational culture (see quotation from CO5 in Chapter 6.6.4.2). A governance structure, where all positions are filled voluntarily by the partners involved, might be vulnerable to insufficient commitment. That is why DC5 advocates for the creation of paid management and operational positions where people dedicate their full time to the PPP work. Here, DC5 makes reference to two further control problems, **lack of an effective governance structure** and **lack of (internal) communication**, which have also been noted by CO13-2 and IO6, respectively. To relieve deficiencies in appropriate communication DC5 started to invite all members to governing body sessions, while CO13-2 tries to improve the governing structure's effectiveness by assigning responsibilities according to core competencies:

> *[...] la falta de una estructura de conducción, una estructura de implementación de acciones. [...] esto es su principal problema. (DC5)*
> ([...] the abscence of a governance structure, an structure for implementation of actions. [...] that is its main problem.)

> *Y estamos intentando movernos a un modelo de gestión que es distinto [...]. [...] se empieza a enfocar más al "core" [...] donde tienen más "expertise" mientras que esta responsabilidad se asigna al alguien más [...]. Entonces, sí hay una cuestión de evolución en la cuestión de como manejas el proyecto. (CO13-2)*
> (And we are trying to move to a governance model that is different [...]. [...] one begins to focus more on the "core" [...] where they have more "expertise" while this responsibility is assigned to somebody else [...]. Hence, there is in fact a question of evolution in the question of how you manage a project.)

Other major control problems are the **lack of (resource) efficiency and planning**, being associated with a mismatch between project design and actual goals on the one side, and **misunderstandings or underestimations of the complexity of PPP work** on the other side. That is why DC4 emphasizes the importance of framing the first three PPP phases by continuous due diligence activities, and of tightly coordinating them with all partners for finally obtaining solid project designs. CO7 adds that clear milestones including fixed start and end dates and a solid financial situation of each partner are imperative. Otherwise, PPPs might be terminated prematurely, as happened in one case.

> *For instance, [PPP name], we did not plan for the exit [...], how to exit a programme like that. We created a dependency. That is why I am saying, "It is very crucial to make sure that the partner has other money." [...]. Another thing that is important is that you have a clear start and an end state of a project, even if it is for 20 years. You have to say, you know, "2020 we are going to stop this" [remark: assuming 2000 as starting year]. And then you backtrack to say, "What are the milestones that should have been achieved to declare this project for you as success?" But everybody knows in June 2020 this thing is going to stop. That is really one of the most important things to put in place. (CO7)*

Actual resource inefficiencies, but also their perception, are related to the misunderstanding of the complexities that are inherent to PPP work. This, for instance, might refer to the underestimation of the costs of certain PPP activities, or to the expectation that those activities happen faster (see quotation from DC2 in Chapter 6.4.4). To counteract these problems, IO7 advocates for continuous and open communication, for detailed explanations of the reasons of complexities, and for setting clear rules of the game:

> *[...] when you work on big policy changes and national systems, it can also result sometimes in delays and slow progress to some extent. So, sometimes the private sector might expect that things happen faster, or we can just bypass some of the national actors or so. [...] I think even if there are delays, if we discuss those openly, [...] they do see the value in continuing when we discuss. (IO7)*

Both CO4 and CO10-1 mourn the **frequent staff turnover** in IOs and DCAs, which is particularly critical if focal points are leaving and new relationships need to be built up. That hampers or can even stop the PPP implementation for some time. This problem becomes even more severe if bureaucracy procedures delay the recruitment of new staff, as stated by IO8. While CO12 calls for more openmindedness and flexibility from the public sector's side, IO8 remarks that PPP work requires both public and private partners to accept each other's organizational specifics to a large extent and to demonstrate commitment and perseverance even in difficult situations:

> *[...] the recruitment-system within in the UN is not necessarily very, very fast because of many other reasons of internal checks and it is a different reality. Someone cannot get recruited in one day. So, I think there were like a couple of months where from [IO8] side [...] the main person responsible was to be recruited. I think that it took a little bit longer than what [private sector partner] would have expected. [...]. To some extent, there is always a degree of bureaucracy of procedures to be respected [...] kind of like things that are given for granted when you work with someone within this central organization. (IO8)*

The **lack of retaining trust** and **existing inherent prejudices** that need to be overcome as well as **internal non-compliance with rules of procedure** are control problems named by IOs only.

> *[...] we have quite often the lack of trust, that we still do have a lot of colleagues who are very suspicious about the private sector. (IO7)*

> *[...] a culture of non-compliance can be observed throughout the organization. (IO2)*

> *We have currently the lack of priority on policy [remark: and the problem] that people are too much afraid of engaging because they don't know what is allowed and what is not. (IO3)*

Unclear or inconsistent requirements for PPP work, such as for performance measurement, can intensify these problems, as stated by CO7 and IO2. To tackle these issues, IO2 and IO6 advocate for stricter formal MC, such as tighter and centralized monitoring and the establishment of an accountability framework. CO7 calls for a harmonization of performance measurement practices to make sure that achievements are benchmarked by the same criteria:

> *So, for me, the secret is to keep them very strictly monitored. Monitored means also having procedures of common control or approaches with the partners. (IO6)*
>
> *[...] when you take numbers it is easy to say, "500 people trained". [...]. We know that. [...] we are still struggling to find the best way because the staff that all the companies show is the same staff. They say, "500 people trained" or "500 students went so school" and all that. But it does not mean anything. After these students are finished, they have no jobs. [...] or whatever it is. So, it is very difficult to benchmark. (CO7)*

More in general, DC3 mentions intermediate or mid-term evaluations as proper mechanisms to identify control problems. However, the **lack of proper data availability** or **difficult geographic conditions**, named by CO1, CO9 and IO7, can hamper effective control including monitoring and require the partners' willingness and flexibility to adapt to given conditions:

> *[...] in [...] a lot of the countries that we operate in, the data is a big issue. So, getting good quality data can be really really challenging. [...] work with some companies to develop mobile tools, using mobile technology, to monitor progress of the initiatives and those kinds of new ways of gathering data. [...] it's not always that we have an easy way of comparing data from a year to another and monitoring our progress in that sense. (IO7)*

Thus, social control in the form of increased personal communication and coordination might replace formal MC in situations, where it is hardly applicable. The remaining control problems in Table 58 have been explicitly mentioned by one interview partner only. For instance, one DCA interviewee bemoans the **inappropriateness of the MC design**, which is either not viable or the costs would exceed the benefits:

> *Und dann ging aber das große Problem los. Monitoring, wie Sie es hier ansprechen. Ja, erzählen Sie dann mal der Bank, wenn sie das Geld schon hat, dass sie doch dann bitte jetzt einmal die Woche einen Bericht schicken soll, wie diese Mittel verwendet wurden. Also da lässt dann aber die Lust des Sacharbeiters deutlich nach, da jede Woche wiederum in seinen Filialen rumzutelefonieren, wer denn jetzt wie viele Mittel davon verbraucht hat. Und das ist dann auch wiederum so eine Sache, ja, man hat es nicht mehr so wirklich in der Hand, wenn das Geld erstmal weg ist. Dann kriegt man irgendeinen Bericht. Kann es nicht wirklich nachvollziehen. Also man müsste ja letztendlich dann in ganz [Zielland] rumlaufen und gucken ob diese Anlagen auch gebaut wurden. (n/a)*
>
> (And then the big problem took effect. Monitoring, as you address it here. Well, tell the bank, when they already have the money, that they shall start sending a report once per week, showing how these resources have been used. Then the responsible person's mood starts decreasing, to call every branch every week and to ask who has used how many resources. And the other thing is that you cannot really control the money anymore, once it has been paid out. Then you get any kind of report that you cannot really understand. Actually, you would have to walk around in the whole [target country] and look whether the industrial plants have really been built.)

Thus, he concludes that MC design needs to strike the right balance between expenditures for the actual project activities and administration including MC, while the latter is supposed to support the PPP implementation and not viceversa. To prevent information asymmetries and opportunistic behavior, CO9 relies on contractual safeguardings (see quotation from CO9 in Chapter 6.6.3.2).

In summary, there exists a broad range of control problems in PPPs for development, which are often interrelated, being perceived by public and private sector actors alike. Except for one PPP, the control problems in all remaining PPPs have been overcome or will be tackled by the countermeasures listed in Table 58. However, they should be interpreted as possible solutions rather than as universal solutions for the respective underlying control problem because their severity and interrelation with other control problems is likely to vary by partnership. Thus, different combinations of countermeasures are required.

6.6.4.5.2 Risk Management and Control

Diverse extrinsic and intrinsic risks affect PPPs over their lifetime and potentially hamper their successful implementation (Chapter 6.2.6). The responsibility of risk management and control is the taking of suitable measures to prevent, or at least mitigate, these risks and therefore to protect a PPP. The interviews revealed that they take phase-oriented risk management and control measures which are either integrated in the structural design of partnerships or applied before and during its implementation (Figure 52 and Table 59).

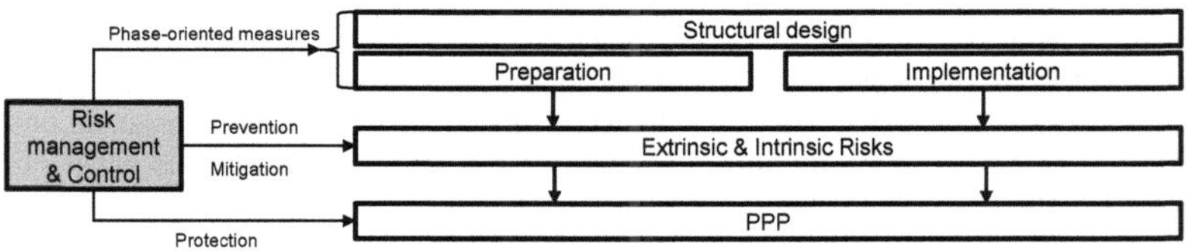

Figure 52: Lifetime- and phase-oriented risk management and control.

For the **structural design** of PPP, several actors defined red lines or exclusionary criteria that impede any partnership or lead to sanctioning, e.g. restrictions on the partner selection (CO7) and on the level of cooperation (IO3) or no admission of product placement (DC1). Usually, this is associated with tight contractual arrangements including monitoring during the **implementation**.

> *We have a catalogue of risks as, for instance, we do not support individuals. If someone wants to build a school in Africa, we do not even want to discuss with them because we think: "What makes you think you can build a school in Africa? Did you talk to the government? Did you talk to the people? Do the people want that, or is it your ego that is driving you?" We do not ask those questions. We just do not get involved. [...]. Even when we support the [IO partner] or [PPP name], we know exactly what the money is going to be used for. So, we always make sure we only get into contracts when we know that we really get hands on to a*

certain extent to the project. And the fund is for that project, not a general support. (CO7)

So, we don't associate our name and emblem. We do engage, we do dialogue, we do collaborate but we don't [remark: enter into partnerships] amongst equals with private sector. (IO3)

Usually, we do also recommend that our offices would deal with at least exclusionary criteria of the risk assessment before they start discussing with the company. (IO7)

Larger private sector firms tend to diversify their PPP activities, for instance, rolling out partnership activities in several countries and involving several partners with redundant skills and competences in order to reduce depedencies. In this context, CO5 recommends to allocate work packages for which each partner has to take responsibility:

[...] wir haben von Anfang versucht uns ein bisschen breiter aufzustellen. Das war auch insbesondere ein Wunsch von der [CO3], mehr als ein oder zwei Länder anzugehen. Auch wenn das für die [DCA Partner] mehr Aufwand und Risiko bedeutet, hat sich doch gezeigt, dass sich in dem einen oder anderen Land einfach politische Risiken auch realisiert haben. (CO3)
([...] from the outset we tried to position ourselves a bit broader. It was also the particular desire of the [DCA partner] to tackle more than one or two countries. Even if that implied more effort and risk for the [DCA partner], it became evident that in one or the other country political risks materialized.)

Also, es gab immer wieder [...] große Risiken bezüglich der Abhängigkeit, wie gut ein Partner jetzt auch die aufgetragenen Aufgaben ausführt. Deswegen hatten wir dann auch zunehmend versucht, abgeschlossene, in sich autarke Arbeitspakete für uns zu definieren [...], weil die Abhängigkeit von Partnerbeiträgen immer ein Risiko war, insbesondere wenn man einen Arbeitspaket-Leader hatte, der schlechte Arbeit abgeliefert hat. Dann konnte man als einzelner Partner auch so viel investieren wie man wollte, die Ergebnisse waren dann immer noch schlecht. (CO5)
(Sometimes, there were [...] huge risks regarding the dependency of how well a partner performed the tasks he was responsible for. That is why we increasingly tried to define self-contained, autonomous work packages [...] because the depedency from partner contributions was always a risk, in particular when you had a work package leader who delivered bad work. Then, you as a single partner could invest as much as you wanted, the results still remained bad.)

[...] die Idee war, eine Partnerschaft mit einer Organisation wie der [UN-Organisation] oder der [UN-Organisation] zu schließen, die da sehr stark aufgestellt sind und viel mehr Erfahrung haben. Und ich denke, so wurden die Risiken auf der Sozial- und Umweltseite dezimiert. (CO9-2)
([...] the idea was to partner with an organization like the [UN organization] or the [UN organization], which are strongly positioned there and have much more experience. And I think that is how the environmental and social risks were reduced.)

Many interview partners strongly stress the necessity of conducting a due diligence and a sound risk assessment in the **preparation** but also doing continuous risk analysis during partnership implementation. In this context, public actors like DC1, IO1 and IO3 call for financial disclosure and transparency at the beginning, but also for transparent procedures along the project implementation in order to avoid risks, such as conflicts of interest. They request that relevant IO staff be checked for potential personal conflicts of interest, or that private sector firms demonstrate their creditworthiness.

> *[...] we try to mitigate by doing the proper due diligence and continuous risk management, following the partner also after we have done the screening. (IO7)*

IO5 adds that this applies also for looser partnerships, based on MoUs, and that the due diligence is undertaken by independent reviewers to ensure impartiality. Despite the general tendency of centralized review and evaluation, IO7 emphasizes that local offices are still requested to do a separate risk assessment and to take responsibility:

> *Each office that initiates partnerships, they are also required to do risk management from their side, which comes with the benefit that it helps them to understand the partner that they want to work with, instead of externalizing that risk management to some other units within the organization. (IO7)*

For a kind of soft risk mitigation, DC2 recommends to provide some guidance to private sector partners, especially if they possess hitherto limited experience in PPP and the subject matter. Tighter risk control is taken by CO7 who links the release of funding tranches to the achievement of specific milestones:

> *So that is also with milestones for us, this means, when we sign the contract we give 25 % of the money. Then they go and start to do whatever. And six months from now we have to see what has been done, based on what we agreed. And when everything is done and you need to do the second tranche [...], we will pay the next money for them to go and do whatever we have agreed. So, we go like that. So, that is how we pay. We never give money in advance, [...], to say, "For the next five years go and do that." That never works. (CO7)*

	Interview partners	CO1	CO3	CO5	CO6	CO7	CO8	CO9	DC1	DC2	DC3	IO1	IO2	IO3	IO5	IO7	Total
Risk management and control measures																	
Structural	Definition of exclusionary criteria					x			x					x		x	4
	Diversification		x				x										2
	Tight contractual arrangements and credible sanctioning						x							x			2
	Joint values and objectives											x					1
	Risk preparedness										x						1
Preparation	Due diligence/risk assessment	x						x			x			x	x	x	6
	Financial disclosure and transparency										x	x					2
	Sound partner selection							x						x			2
	Careful target country selection				x												1
	Definition of work packages and taking of responsibility			x													1
	Involvement of all involved and affected stakeholders	x															1
	Sound project design	x															1
Implementation	Continuous risk analysis and management				x											x	2
	Monitoring	x				x											2
	Commitment	x															1
	Guidance									x							1
	Performance-based resource allocation					x											1
	Transparent procedures												x				1

Table 59: Overview of risk management and control measures.

Many extrinsic and intrinsic risks eventually emerge to actual control problems. For instance, intrinsic risks, such as adverse influences from bureaucracy, lack of commitment and staff turnover, became real and required countermeasures to manage them. The questions of why the risk management and control measures in Table 59 did not fully avert them, or to which extent they prevented at least more severe consequences, cannot be reasonably answered on the basis of the given interview data. Still, the overlapping of many risk management and control measures with the countermeasures from Table 58, such as due diligence and risks assessment, tight monitoring and the emphasis on joint interests and objectives, leads to the conclusion that upstream and downstream MC activities complement each other with respect to the point in time of contract conclusion. That is why the present subchapter on risk management and control is integrated in the MC section of the results analysis and not in Chapter 6.2.6.

6.6.5 Control Effectiveness

The last part of the results analysis of MC in PPPs for development is dedicated to the effectiveness of the MC measures and characteristics that have been presented in the previous subchapters. This analysis has been carried out by means of the interviewees' perception of the actual level of commitment and contract compliance as well of the de facto contract enforceability in the scrutinized PPPs on scope.

6.6.5.1 Commitment

The overall level of commitment seems to be perceived as quite positive by most interview partners. Intrinsic motivation and the willingness to assume responsibility are characteristics of the level of commitment, which actors like CO1, CO4, CO8 and DC2 note on their partners' side but also claim for themselves. CO1-1 and CO12 add that partners approach one another and declare their willingness to collaborate in the interest of common objectives:

> *Ich bin wahrscheinlich ein bisschen altmodisch gestrickt. Wenn ich sowas unterschreibe, dann mache ich auch mit. Und wenn Sie jetzt in unseren Web-Auftritt schauen, wir spielen das fast gar nicht. Für uns ist das halt selbstverständlich. Ich kann mir vorstellen, dass andere Firmen da ein bisschen anders agieren. (CO4)*
> (Probably, I am a little bit old-fashioned. If I sign such a thing, I also join in. If you look at our web presence, we almost do not talk about it. For us, this is simply natural. I can imagine other companies to act a little bit different in this regard.)

> *Well, I think the commitment to getting the project done is pretty high on both sides. Both sides want to get it done. (CO12)*

> *[Wir] haben dann auch das Glück, da auch Partner und Unternehmen zu haben, die gesagt haben: "Wir machen uns gemeinsam mit euch auf diese Reise, und wir müssen da eben auch alle gemeinsam lernen." (DC2)*
> ([We] are fortunate to have partners and companies which said: "We make the journey together with you and we all have to learn jointly.")

Moreover, CO6 was amazed by the 'espirit de corps' in his PPP where partners place much emphasis on unanimity of governing body decisions and support one another if someone's project activities face problems:

> *Also, da gibt es schon so einen Geist, dass man hier an einem Strang zieht. Wenn wir gemeinsam gesagt haben: "Wir machen dieses Projekt", und [...] es gilt auch immer Einstimmigkeit. (CO6)*
> (Well, there is actually such a kind of spirit that you act in concert. If we have commonly said: "We do this project", and [...] there always applies unanimity.)

DC1 and DC2 calls for awareness-building of what commitment actually means because they experienced repeatedly that the partners did not recognize the binding nature of governing body decisions. In this vein, DC1 also emphasizes the importance of thinking about how diverging interests and objectives can be aligned because, as IO5 stated, commitment requires complementary and overlapping goals. Other determinants of commitment are the time elapsed or speaking the same language, which may increase the partners' willingness to augment the own contributions.

> *Wir hatten sehr zuverlässige Partner. Wir hatten sehr zuverlässige Partner, die aber nicht selbstständig waren. Wir hatten sehr selbstständige Partner, wo sich die wirtschaftlichen Interessen sehr schnell verändert haben, die für ein halbes Jahr ein super Partner waren und dann eigentlich quasi nicht mehr. Das hatten wir irgendwie alles. Aber ich denke, je länger man zusammenarbeitet, die gleiche Sprache spricht, desto mehr hat man ein Vertrauensverhältnis. (CO8)*
> (We had very reliable partners. We had very reliable partners, but who did not work independently. We had very independent partners whose economic interests changed very fast, who were great partners for half a year and then actually not anymore. We had kind of all of that. But I think the longer you collaborate, speaking the same language, the more you have a trustful relationship.)

> *El nivel de compromiso ha sido bastante bueno desde inicio. No diría que el compromiso está aumentando, creo que más bien son las apuestas que están haciendo las instituciones cada vez más grande a la plataforma. Y esto es pues buena señal de que están a bordo del proyecto, que están dispuestos a dar más. (CO13-2)*
> (The level of commitment has been pretty good from the outset. I would not say that the commitment has increased, I believe that the contributions, which the institutions make to the platform, are becoming bigger and bigger every time. And this is then a good signal that they are on board of the project, that they are ready to give more.)

With respect to CO8's comment, CO10-1 argues that misunderstandings and lack of communication can induce shrinking interest in joint PPP work and therefore decrease the level of commitment. Moreover, CO8 and CO10-1 consider high staff turnover as an obstacle to keeping commitment. Most interviewees observed a balanced commitment between public partners. However, DC5 notes a stronger private sector commitment, as compared to that of the local government, because the latter was not in a position to make financial contributions. Still, they actively engaged in meetings of the governing bodies. CO10-1 adds that the inclusion of local partners promoted the overall level of commitment by all partners. Resource inefficiencies and unfulfilled promises are characteristics and drivers of low commitment alike because if one party perceives low commitment on the other partner's side, trust might be destroyed and that partner tends to reduce its commitment, too (see quotation from CO5 in Chapter 6.4.4). Thus, decreasing commitment by one partner can trigger a downward spiral of the overall level of commitment. According to CO4, commitment in the form of gestures of symbol politics and promises is harmful to high levels of commitment and trustful relationships as well. That is why CO1 and CO7 emphasize the importance of active engagement in terms of continuous exchange of opinions, discussions and control, especially monitoring:

> *[...] when we do a contract, we make sure that the people deliver what they have committed to do. We do not do like other organizations that just give money. We are more involved in the project. [...] we talk to the people, we go and visit them, we follow up, we check on milestones, we adapt. So, it is a different way of working. (CO7)*

In summary, the demonstration of commitment by all partners to a joint PPP is essential for its implementation because governing structures and related MC measures rely on the full acceptance and support by all of them. Without commitment PPPs do not work. However, commitment is a quite vulnerable attitude whose level starts deteriorating once it is no longer demonstrated by all partners to the same extent.

6.6.5.2 Contract Compliance and Enforceability

The overall level of contract compliance seems to be high rather than low, although IO3 bemoans frequent compliance issues upon which the MC in IO4's organization places its major focus. CO4 argues that even opposite views and diverging interests never raised doubts about the contract compliance by the other partners. IO7 adds that diligent partner selection procedures are used to filter out potentially unreliable partners and CO7 emphasizes the good PPP experiences which his company has had with large globally known IOs:

> *Contract compliance [...] I think, in general it's quite good. Of course, we have had cases where a company has started a partnership and then, when the market changed, they withdrew. But we don't hear that many. [...] I would say, [...] in a way the partnership negotiation process is already sort of painful enough so that it leaves the non-serious actors out to some extent. (IO7)*

> *[...] it is easier to work with them because they are big and you do not have to worry about non-compliance [...], because they are an internationally recognized organization (CO7)*

Both CO9-2 and CO13-2 agree that PPP contracts should stipulate as far as possible clear objectives, clear assignment of roles and responsibilities and clear performance expectations that are linked to incentive schemes because these are suitable mechanisms to promote contract compliance, according to their experience. However, CO5 concludes that contract compliance is strongly related to commitment and is finally partner-dependent. He argues that contracts are actually unnecessary and compliance can be largely taken for granted if all partners' willingness to commit is high and sufficient commonality of interests is given:

> *[...] was Vertragstreue und Engagement, Verpflichtung angeht, [Anmerkung: ist es] sehr stark partnerabhängig. Ist der politische Wille da, da was gemeinsam zu machen? Haben wir eine gemeinsame, überlappende Agenda? Wenn das erkennbar war, dann war man sich sicher, man braucht diese Vertragsklauseln nicht. Man findet irgendeinen Weg, um sich zu verständigen. (CO5)*
> ([...] concerning contract compliance and commitment, [remark: it is] very much partner-dependent. Is there political will to do something together? Do we have a common, overlapping agenda? If this was recognizable, then you could be sure not to need these contract clauses. You find a way to communicate.)

By contrast to contract compliance, the overall level of contract enforceability seems to be low, despite the existence of sanction clauses for the event of non-compliance of contractual obligations in many PPP contracts. One reason is 'force majeure', as CO1-1 calls it, that PPP partners face in developing countries with fragile political stability and unreliable legal systems. Thus, law enforcement is quite often limited in those countries. CO9-2 and DC1 agree with this assessment and recommend conducting a thorough analysis of local legal conditions before implementing PPP activities in critical countries, such as in Africa:

> *[…] natürlich setzen wir gewisse Mindestmaßstäbe, dass wir eine English Law Documentation haben und somit auch einen Gerichtsstandort möglichst festsetzen wollen, aber ich glaube, im schlimmsten Fall muss man sich dann doch den lokalen Gegebenheiten unterwerfen. Man wird nicht alles durchsetzen können. Ja, das ist ein Risiko, was [Name der PPP] trägt. Deswegen muss man sich da auch mit den lokalen Rechtsgegebenheiten auseinandersetzen. (CO9-2)*
> ([…] of course we set certain minimum standards, that we have an English Law Documentation and therefore determine preferably a place of jurisdiction as well, but I believe that in the worst case you have to bow to the local situation. You will not be able to enforce everything. Yes, this is a risk, which the [PPP name] bears. That is why you also have to deal with the local legal conditions.)

Another aspect is the reasonableness of law enforcement in terms of PPPs. CO3 argues that PPP contracts are probably rarely enforced in the event of disputes and non-compliance because once PPP contracts need to be enforced the idea of partnership is undermined and the level of commitment is likely to drop to the minimum level possible:

> *Also, gesagt wird immer von PPP, dass diese Verträge nicht rechtlich 'enforceable' sind. Rein rechtlich betrachtet sind sie es wohl. Man muss wohl unterscheiden zwischen ‚wäre rechtlich durchsetzbar' und ‚wird nicht rechtlich durchgesetzt'. Ich kann mich jetzt an keinen öffentlichen Fall erinnern, wo jemand verklagt wurde: "Er möge bitte seine PPP-Beiträge erbringen." Ich weiß auch nicht, wie sinnvoll es ist, Partner zu einer Zusammenarbeit zu zwingen. Ich meine auch, dass es reputationsseitig für beide Partner wahrscheinlich kein Gewinn wäre, sich gegenseitig zu verklagen […]. (CO3)*
> (Well, it is always said about PPPs that these contracts are not legally enforceable. From a purely legal point of view, probably they are. Probably, you need to differentiate between legally enforceable and not being legally enforced. I cannot remember any public case where somebody was sued: "Please, could he provide his PPP contributions." Moreover, I do not know how reasonable it is to compel partners to cooperate. I also think that it would not be beneficial to sue each other, from a reputational point of view.)

In situations where, for instance, some partners do not make the agreed contributions or misuse other partners' corporate design (e.g. logo), the other partners suspend their contributions, too, (DC1) or the legal office sends cease-and-desist letters (IO3). Thus, the terminability of PPP contracts is basically given. Still, DC1 remarks that in the event of non-compliance, the contracts' terms and conditions do not forsee more far-reaching sanctions, such as financial penalties. However, CO13-2 states that they can actually not enforce certain behavior by other partners, and DC2 confesses that currently the possible sanctions are rather limited, and that is why in his PPP has been set up a process to work out approaches for better contract enforceability:

> *Also die Mitglieder verpflichten sich […] bestimmte Ziele zu erreichen und sollten wir da feststellen, dass diese Ziele nicht erreicht werden, diskutieren wir aktuell Sanktionsmöglichkeiten. Schmeißen wir die […] wieder raus? Müssen die Strafzahlungen leisten? Was auch immer. Es ist komplett offen. Sozusagen werden wir da tatsächlich nochmal ein höheres Maß an Verbindlichkeiten einführen, weil*

im Moment, wenn jemand das Ziel nicht erreicht, dann sagt man: "Ja, nicht erreicht." Und was wir dann machen sollen, wissen wir aktuell nicht. (DC2)
(Well, the members commit to [...] the achievement of certain objectives and if we noted that these goals have not been reached, we are currently discussing possible sanctions. Shall we [...] chuck them out again? Do they have to make financial penalities? You name it. It is completely open. We will introduce indeed a higher level of obligation because at the moment, if somebody does not reach the goal, we say: "Yes, not achieved." And currently we do not know what to do then.)

CO6 differentiates between the actual partners involved and external third-party actors. In his view, rules to respect apply for both groups alike, but core partners should collaborate in a family-like manner and be able to relinquish on threatening with sanctions. By contrast, he makes very clear to be willing to take legal action if external partners behave non-compliant or breach the contract.

In summary, external conditions and the reasonableness of seeking law enforcement in PPPs limit the enforceability of underlying contracts. At least concerning the cooperation with core partners, litigations and sanctions do not seem to be appropriate means of reaching PPP implementation because when those options are taken into account the level of commitment and trust tends to be low already. Finally, both elements are important determinants of the proper functioning of PPPs (Chapters 6.6.4.4 and 6.6.5.1).

6.7 Institutional Environment

This chapter is related to the ACI approach in Chapter 4.1 and serves the answering of **research question 2.1**. It analyzes first in which regard different institutional levels affect the implementation of PPPs, and then deals with institutional constraints and the role of governmental authorities. At the end, the interview partners' endeavours to expand PPP activities and their perception of the influence of global institutions will be illuminated.

6.7.1 Institutional Levels

This chapter connects the matter of governance structures with the analysis of the institutional environments in which the studied PPPs are embedded, an approach that has been pursued before at theoretical level by Petersen (2011) and Van Kersbergen and Van Waarden (2004) in particular (Chapter 2.1.2). Institutional level means either global, regional, or local in this context. The local one can be further broken down to federal, state, and municipal level (Figure 53).

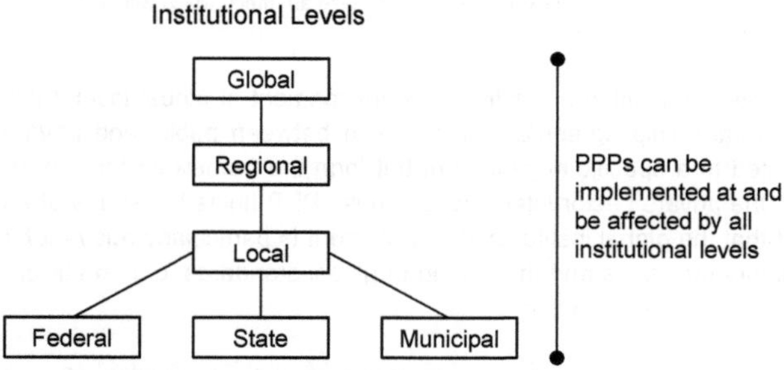

Figure 53: Overview of different institutional levels.

For instance, IO5's organization is running PPP projects at all three levels because an organizational structure that is composed of regional and country offices besides the headquarters enables them to implement a broad range of partnerships addressing diverse policy issues. For some private actors, the global presence of IOs and DCAs is associated with familiarity with different institutional environments is indeed a selection criterion because issues like communicable diseases can be combatted only through transnational cooperation only as these diseases do not stop at national boarders. One private sector interviewee adds that for this reason the cooperation with NGOs is often confined to local national activities. Moreover, CO9-2 remarks that IOs might exert some political influence on the institutional environment for enabling it to implement the PPP, while CO5 experiences that the collaboration with DCAs was more effective than with IOs:

> *[...] wenn [...] [Anzahl an] internationale Organisationen [...] zusammen [...] etwas finanzieren, dann profitieren wir natürlich auch von, ich will jetzt nicht sagen, dem Schutz, aber den politischen Möglichkeiten einer solchen Institution. (CO9-2)*
> ([...] if [...] [number of] international organizations [...] finance something [...] together, then we also benefit from, I would not call it protection, but the political opportunities of such an institution.)

DC1 states that the influence of the institutional levels might vary over time. For instance, local stakeholders might be involved only when the exploratory phases and the design phase have been concluded. Thus, the importance of the institutional environment shifts from global to local level in the course of the PPP implementation. Moreover, PPPs can contribute to building an institutional environment at local level, as stated by CO13-2:

> *[...] am Anfang [...] muss man die öffentliche Seite gar nicht unbedingt mitnehmen. Das ist eine [Art der PPP]. Die funktionieren auch erstmal ohne öffentliche Seite. Wir haben die zunehmend eingebunden. Also sie sind jetzt sehr viel stärker mit drin als am Anfang noch. (DC1)*
> ([...] at the beginning [...] you do not necessarily have to involve the public side. That is a [PPP type]. These work initially without the public side. We involved them stepwise. So, now they are much more integrated than they were at the beginning.)

> *Es una organización que va a llenar gaps institucionales sobre el mercado, que van a hacer un efecto, que van a catalizar a qué otros actores empiecen a entrar en movimiento. (CO13-2)*

(It is an organization which will fill institutional market gaps that will make an effect, which will catalyze other actors to start taking action as well.)

PPPs are predominantly embedded within an institutional environment at global level if IOs are involved or high-level partnership agreements are closed between public and private entities, which are not related to a specific engagement but form the framework for interorganizational cooperation. One private sector interviewee, whose PPP holds the status of an UN observer, emphasized that the global institutional environment is particularly relevant for PPPs that deal with regulatory questions and the setting of global standards, e.g. in the energy sector in terms of CO2 emissions‘ reduction.

> *It deals in terms of priorities because governments set the agenda of priorities, of course, or the implementation of the SDGs. And going down, a UN agency needs to stick to those priorities and try to have programmes that are implemented on those priorities. So, you need to ensure coherence. [...]. You need to be within the framework. (IO6)*

However, CO2, CO3 and IO5 remark that operational PPP implementation takes mostly place at country level because many PPP activities have a regional or local focus, even if they are planned and executed by international actors. IO7 lists a broad range of activities in this context:

> *[...] our role at country level: national planning and policy, reform work, creating the enabling environment, advocacy, building capacity, being there to convene public-private dialogue, implementing direct projects on value chain development or risk mitigation [...] or brokering different partnerships. So, in a way the private sector is a key stakeholder in all these fields and our work areas, in a way does link it very strongly to all these themes. (IO7)*

DC3 adds that her organization is instructed by the ministry in charge to be active at the micro level only, thus operational implementation work at local level. Finally, local governments decide whether they adopt certain standards as defined by the PPP actors, or whether they admit PPP activities only under certain conditions (see quotation from IO7 in Chapter 6.2.5). If PPPs emerge as a consequence of public tenders, the institutional level and environment are therefore already determined:

> *PPP findet vor allen Dingen vor Ort statt, d.h. die Regierungen müssen in den Ländern entscheiden, ob sie [Standards für zugrundeliegendes Produkt] definieren wollen und das im Grunde auch durch nationale Gesetze umsetzen. (CO3)*
> (PPP take place primarily on the ground, which means that governments have to decide in their countries whether they want to define [standards for underlying product] and basically implement them by national legislation.)

> *Meistens ist es Länder- oder Regioneninitiative, dass eben dann Tenders ausgeschrieben werden. (CO4)*
> (The calling for tenders results mostly from a country or regional initiative.)

In summary, a PPP's institutional level, and therefore its institutional environment, are determined to a large extent by the policy issue being addressed, by the types of actors involved, and by the geographic scope which it takes.

6.7.2 Institutional Constraints

This chapter analyzes institutionally driven constraints that public and private actors face during the creation and implementation of joint PPPs for development. It differentiates between formal and informal institutional constraints. What both have in common is that they can be hardly influenced by the PPP actors.

6.7.2.1 Formal Constraints

Most formal constraints result from legal rules and regulations, which restrict PPP implementation by their application or non-application either way. One IO interviewee remarks that especially normative IOs defining global standards for certain policy areas regulate many industry sectors. Moreover, the UN System's member states set rules and guidelines for PPP activities. These limit the flexibility of IOs to adapt themselves on preferences and needs of the private sector partners, especially in terms of contractual arrangements and goal alignment.

> *It's strict. It's an agenda and you should stick to that if you really want to reach the SDGs. I mean, if you disperse you kind of dilute energies, messages. [...]. An UN agency has to have a clear clean message, and all the activities need to be kind of consolidated around that. (IO6)*

> *[...] sometimes we do run into problems that a company cannot sign our templates and we cannot sign their templates. That they want us to follow a certain national law and as an entity we cannot do that. So, sometimes we then need to find an alternative arrangement. For example, a company then enters into a partnership with another entity that we work with, rather than directly with us, because of these kinds of limitations. [...]. To some extent, it can be a little bit cumbersome, but in another perspective it's also quite understandable because we are set up as we are because of our Member States. And we cannot really deviate from that for many reasons. (IO7)*

At national or local level, institutional constraints are mainly imposed by the respective governments whose political support and legislations are decisive for the practical feasibility of PPP projects, as stated by DC1. Governments subject products like drugs or technologies to comprehensive approval processes and set high requirements to their permission, independent of whether they are exclusively designed for PPP activities or not.

> *[...] die Ansprüche von Zulassungsbehörden sind weltweit in den letzten 10 Jahren deutlich gestiegen. [...]. Das heißt, dieser Aufwand ist riesengroß geworden,*

was ja auch gut und vernünftig ist, die Wirksamkeit und insbesondere auch die Verträglichkeit eines Medikaments zu dokumentieren. (n/a)

([...] the requirements of the regulatory authorities significantly increased globally in the last 10 years. [...]. That means that this effort became tremendous, which is basically good and reasonable for documenting the effectiveness and compatibility of drugs.)

Moreover, they may constrain PPP engagements in general, as noted by CO14. Another interviewee adds that in some regions governments define by principle and for political reasons other standards than their neighbouring countries and therefore increase institutional constraints and transaction costs for the PPP implementation.

I think here in Mexico there is another challenge, which is the government because [...] international agencies cannot put money if the government is not giving them the permission to put it in some specific project in the country. (CO14)

Restriction on harzardous substances. Da gibt es eben auch Vorschriften, die eingehalten werden müssen, die umgesetzt werden müssen. Die kommen von Länderregierungen bzw. von der Europäischen Union [...]. Das passiert jetzt übrigens gerade in den arabischen Gebieten. [...]. Bildlich gesprochen: "Ich, Saudi-Arabien, will nicht die gleiche Policy haben wie die Vereinigten Arabischen Emirate. Ich, Jordanien, will es anders haben als die [...] und ich brauche ein [Produkt]-Label so, grün, blau, rot." (n/a)

(Restriction on hazardous substances. There are simply regulations to be respected and implemented. They come from national governments or the European Union [...]. This happens particularly in the Arab region. [...]. In metaphorical terms: "Me, Saudi Arabia, do not want to have the same policy as the United Arab Emirates. Me, Jordan, want to have it differently compared to them [...] and I need a [product] label like this, green, blue, red.")

CO9-2 adds that some uncertainty and bounded rationality may exist on either side if a certain product is still very new and no legal coverage is granted by extant rules and regulations. Thus, the lack of user experiences challenges governments and subordinated public authorities to adjust or extend the legislation to new products, while companies in turn may not know how to tackle the approval process. However, DC4 remarks that issues of troublesome regulations and legislation can usually not be resolved within the project setting of PPPs, where DC1 adds that law enforcement is often limited in developing countries. Thus, institutional boundaries simply have to be accepted, and PPP partners must deal with them in the best possible way. Still, in some cases, PPP might also serve as a kind of advisory council to the government, and therefore may influence the determination of institutional constraints in different ways.

[...] estamos atravesando una reforma energética en el país. [Tipo de energía] fue considerada [...] para un mercado de certificados de energía. Entonces, la [nombre de la PPP] tiene que dar opiniones, tiene que dar su postura para el gobierno de qué opina de esto [...]. Entonces, allí es donde los socios y la mesa directiva aportan conocimientos. (DC5)

([...] we are going through an energy reform in the country. [Energy type] was considered [...] for an energy certificate market. Hence, the [PPP name] has to give opinions, has to give its position to the government about what we think of this [...]. So, there it is where the members and the executive board contribute knowledge.)

More in general, CO3 states that formal constraints are not negative per se because an institutional framework provides some guidance to PPP implementation and may therefore ease the coordination between the stakeholders:

> *[...] Notwendigkeit von standardisierten Rahmenbedingungen oder rechtlichen Rahmenbedingungen für diese Art von Public-Private Partnerships. (CO3)*
> ([...] necessity of standardized framework conditions or legal conditions for this kind of public-private partnerships.)

Thus, standards produce clarity, and therefore, they enable actors like CO10 to develop products without uncertainty of non-compliance with rules and regulations. However, standards increase the complexity of PPP implementation and reduce the resource efficiency if all countries, where a PPP is rolled out, define their own national standards, which therefore form an impediment. By contrast, transnational standards promote far-reaching impacts by PPP work including higher resource efficiency, as stated by CO10-2. Still, the public sector's institutional possibilities are often limited to monitoring at a large scale whether all actors fully comply with certain rules and regulations.

> *[...] das kann man bei den zehn großen Unternehmen von staatlicher Seite relativ gut kontrollieren, aber bei den tausenden von kleinen Unternehmen, kann es die staatliche Seite eben nicht mehr kontrollieren. (DC1)*
> ([...] you can control that for the ten large companies relatively well from the public side, but for the thousands for small companies, the public side simply cannot control it anymore.)

For the case of Germany, the country of origin of most of the interviewees, DC2 remarks that German legislations did neither promote nor hamper PPP implementation. In summary, formal constraints exert a considerable influence on PPPs for development. They set boundary conditions to PPP designs and to the way of implementation, but rarely inhibit the actual creation of this kind of public-private cooperation. Moreover, formal constraints can even have positive implications if they are equally applied to the concerned stakeholders and therefore create binding and reliable rules of game for all and diminish uncertainties about the institutional environment.

6.7.2.2 Informal Constraints

Many of the informal constraints that PPPs are facing relate strongly to extrinsic risks (Chapter 6.2.6.1) and to environmental influence factors (Chapter 6.6.4). Political influences, such as civil wars, strikes or elections in fragile countries, contribute to the design of institutional environments as much as cultural, economic and social differences do. DC3 and DC4 make clear that the socio-economic development level of countries is essential for the decision of implementing certain PPP activities in a certain country or not, because PPPs as such can provide only limited preparatory work for creating a sufficiently enabling environment. Depending on the subject matter, they need to be able to build on fundamental infrastructure. For instance, if a banking and microfinance sector is almost absent in country XY and reliable technology for electronic banking is not available, PPPs that rely on cashless resource allocation and the use of advanced hardware and software are hard to implement. On the other side, countries that have already made too much progress on a certain policy issue may also drop out of the grid because either governments dispose of enough skills and resources to tackle the policy issue on their own, or the market is already sufficiently attractive for the private sector to dare starting its own business operations there. DC3 adds that low corruption, economic growth and an enabling investment climate attract many private sector actors to engage especially in Africa, while CO5 remarks that strong local presence of competitors, or even their active involvement in a joint PPP, might reduce private partners' willingness to invest. However, private sector firms also face social constraints in the sense of environmental, moral responsibility. For instance, limited monitorability of impact is accepted to avoid interference with the personal rights of the beneficiaries (see quotation from "n/a" in Chapter 6.6.1.4), or take-back processes are implemented for technologies that contain toxic chemicals and through which uncontrolled waste disposal shall be prevented. CO6 experienced the vulnerability of the ecosystem as a major risk, which therefore forms a boundary to PPP activities that must not be crossed under any circumstances. Moreover, trade-offs might arise between technological efficiency and affordability constraining the design of products whose dissemination is actually intended by the PPP.

> *[...] bestimmte Technologien bringen jetzt halt die und die Effizienz, und Sie wollen ja jetzt auch nicht die Bevölkerung vor die Nase stoßen, dass sie nur noch teuerste Technologie kaufen müssen. (CO4)*
> ([...] certain technologies generate this or that efficiency, but you do not want to offend the population either, so that they have to buy the most expensive technology only.)

Some more invisible constraints result from public perceptions and opinions concerning the role the private sector should, or should not, play in development cooperation, as stated by CO8. Moreover, CO1-1 remarks that certain industries enjoy little esteem and confidence from the civil and public side, especially from NGOs, so that the existence of some kind of bogeymen informally constrains opportunities for PPP cooperation.

> *[...] in der klassischen, reinen NGO-Welt sind wir auch eher jemand, der völlig anders gesehen wird. Das heißt, wir müssen auch mal über unser Verhalten, unsere Beiträge die Brücken bauen, damit die Leute auch ein bisschen [...] ihr Feindbild ändern und sagen: "Ja, macht eigentlich Sinn, mit denen zusammenzuarbeiten. Die können auch was beitragen. Die haben Werte, die uns helfen." (CO1-1)*
> ([...] in the classical, mere NGO world, we are something that is seen completely differently. Thus, through our behavior, our contributions, we have to build bridges so that the people [...] change their attitude a little bit, and say: "Yes, actually, it makes sense to cooperate with them. They can contribute something. They have values that help us.")

> *[...] kritischen Stimmen [...] kommen meistens gar nicht aus den Ländern, sondern eher hier aus Deutschland, also gerade auch so eben Bundestag oder NGOs. (n/a)*
> ([...] critical voices [...] do not come primarily from the countries, but rather from Germany, especially from the Bundestag or NGOs.)

In summary, informal institutional constraints tend to be less rigid and restrictive towards PPP implementation than are the formal ones. However, they are more fundamental by nature and are harder to shift or overcome because some of them, such as the political situation, are exogenously given and cannot be influenced by PPP stakeholders in the way regulations and standards can be in the reverse case.

6.7.3 Role of Governmental Authorities

This chapter is dedicated to the concrete roles that governments and their authorities play for the implementation of PPPs for development. In the subsequent subchapters, specific measures of support, impediment and accountability taken by governmental actors will be presented. The governmental role for PPPs as such is defined by several factors, but foremost by the ideological support provided for combatting the underlying policy issue and by the extent to which governments share interests and objectives inherent to a partnership. This applies especially for IOs which rely to a high degree on governmental support, in the sense of funding and mandate, as stated by IO2. In this regard, CO4 and DC5 note a high level of governmental commitment, mainly from the Western community.

> *Yo creo que el gobierno tiene muy claro las metas de las Naciones Unidas. O sea este gobierno se ha comprometido para disminuir el cambio climático [...]. En este sentido, yo creo que el país está muy consciente de qué se debería hacer. (DC5)*
>
> (I believe that the government is very aware of the goals of the United Nations. This means that this government is committed to diminishing the climate change [...]. In this sense, I believe that the country is well aware of what it should do.)

National or local governments play a particularly strong role if they hold an active membership in a partnership or are represented in advisory or supervisory councils, as in the case of CO6 and DC5. Certainly, the private sector generally seeks proximity to public decision-makers in the way that they practice systematic relationship-building and networking because a government's political orientation is quite important for the business opportunities that companies have in a country. This can be quite difficult in countries where archaic structures prevail in the actual political system, and village elders are the de facto authorities in some places. Thus, the actual governmental authorities often have no say in such regions.

> *Die Erfahrung mit den [Teams] in [afrikanisches Land]. Dieses [Team] kann nicht so ohne weiteres in ein Dorf fahren, sondern die schicken, und das ist wirklich so, einen Tag vorher den Späher hin, und der kündigt an, dass morgen das und das kommt: "Bist du einverstanden?". Wenn der sagt: "Ich bin einverstanden", dann darf der einreisen. Und Sie müssen sich das wirklich wie im Film vorstellen. Der sitzt dann da auf seinem Stuhl, Thron, und sagt dann: "Ja" oder "nein". (CO1-1)*
>
> (The experience with the [teams] in [African country]. This [team] cannot simply enter a village, but they send, and this is really like that, a scout one day before, and he announces that tomorrow will come this and that: "Do you agree?". If he says: "I agree", then you can enter. And you need to imagine this like in a movie. He is sitting there on his chair, throne, and then says: "Yes" or "no".)

However, DC2 experienced that all kind of relationship building can be worthless if a new government with objectives very different from the previous one comes into power. That is why a PPP's nature may change quite a lot over time, in the sense that the partnership's objectives need to be harmonized with the new government's interests. CO13-2 concludes that governments are sometimes quite active or even dominant, or passive and reluctant to PPPs, depending on the respective institutional environment. The same applies for the private sector. Nonetheless, CO13-2 argues that the government's role should not be overrated in the sense that not too much responsibility of either support or impediment should be shifted to the public authorities. In summary, he concludes that PPP work is the responsibility of the whole society:

> *Creo que sería injusto decir que las autoridades tienen que hacer algo en particular para provocar este tipo de alianzas. Porque el concepto alrededor de lo que estamos buscando, que es la sostenibilidad o algunos mencionan como creación de valor compartido, es algo que se tiene que mover de manera conjunta [...]. Entonces, no creo que sea solo un cambio en el que la autoridad tenga que poner ciertos incentivos para invertir en este tipo de acciones sino creo que también es un cambio de la propia sociedad en la cuestión de a que asignan valor [...]. [...] empresas también tienen que entender que el valor no solamente está en la parte económica sino está en muchos otros lados. Entonces, se me haría difícil decir que el gobierno tiene que hacer ciertas acciones para detonarlo. Creo que es una cuestión de toda la sociedad. (CO13-2)*
>
> (I believe that it would be injust to say that the authorities have to do someting particular for stimulating this type of alliances. Because the concept being around is what we are looking for, which is the sustainability, or some also mention shared value creation, it is something that we have to move forward together [...]. Thus, I do not believe that it is only a change in which the government must put certain incentives for investing in this kind of actions, but I also believe that it is a change of the own society in the question of what we attribute value to [...]. [...] companies also have to understand that value is not only something economic but has many different characteristics. So, it would be difficult for me to say that the government must take certain actions for launching it. I believe this is a question of the whole society.)

6.7.3.1 Support and Impediment

The support and impediment to PPP initiatives can be provided and exercised by either the home state(s) of the companies and DCAs or by the governmental authorities in the target countries. Even if goverments do not actively support a PPP by either funding or political involvement, it is at least necessary to obtain their permission for undertaking partnership activities which are backed by the local legislation, as argued by CO5 and DC4. As mentioned in Chapter 6.6.2.4 already, DCAs and IOs may act as important door openers towards local authorities. Still, IO8 remarks that not only the name "United Nations" but also good branding reputation of the private sector partner can be helpful to receive necessary public support in the target countries.

> *[...] wir waren natürlich auch auf den politischen Support angewiesen. Also, in beiden Ländern waren vorab alle relevanten Ministerien informiert. [...]. Und da hat [IO Partner] auch eine gute und große Rolle gespielt, dass [...] eben die Türen bei den Ministerien geöffnet wurden. Die Ministerien vor Ort haben dann natürlich aktiv nichts gemacht, aber es war natürlich wichtig, sich den Segen von denen zu holen [...]. (DC4)*
>
> ([...] we relied of course upon the political support. So, in both countries all relevant ministries have been informed before. [...]. And [IO partner] played there a good and big role, that they actually opened the doors to the ministries. The ministries on-site did not actively do anything, but it was certainly important to obtain their blessing.)

Many interviewees like CO8 and DC1 feel very well-received and supported in the target countries. CO9-2 tells that some countries promote international investments very much, and

CO10-1 experienced that authoritarian attitudes initially used to evolve to cooperation at eye-level where both sides want to learn from each other. Thus, the public authorities started asking, for instance, how the economic and legal framework conditions should be designed for better meeting the needs of the industry concerned. However, such collaborative relationships require strong investments in trust building and the demonstration of respect to the local culture and people.

> *Also von den [...] Regierungsorganisationen oder Regierungsinstitutionen, die es direkt betraf, waren die Stakeholder durch die [Name der PPP] eigentlich sehr gut eingebunden [...]. Insofern kann ich da jetzt von keinem Fall berichten, wo uns [...] eine Behörde oder eine Regierung Steine in den Weg gelegt hätte. (CO8)*
>
> (The stakeholders from the [...] directly affected governmental organizations or institutions were actually very well involved by the [PPP name] [...]. For this reason, I cannot report of any case where [...] an authority or government would have placed obstalces in the way.)

In other cases, as stated by CO4, countries gladly joined PPPs officially and proactively and took ownership for implementing the partnership's objectives in their respective countries. He adds that their motivation can be explained amongst others by the fact that some countries would otherwise have no opportunity to meet the SDGs and commitments they have made to the United Nations, in the context of the Post-2015 Development Agenda. Especially, the governments of wealthier Western countries tend to contribute cash resources and therefore to finance PPPs to a large extent. While DC5 appreciates the fact that high-ranked people occupied positions of the PPP's governance board and of pertinent governmental advisory councils at the same time, wherefore constant contacts and exchanges with the authorities could be achieved, other actors wish to receive more political guidance and support from their own government for the PPP activities in the target countries.

> *Bei allem, was den ganzen Dialog irgendwie mit [Zielländern] angeht, würde ich mir von der Bundesregierung deutlich stärker wünschen, dass sie da sehr, sehr viel deutlicher Flagge zeigt und sagt: "Das ist das, was wir von euch erwarten. Das ist auch das, was wir nicht wollen." Da tun sie sich aber auch ein bisschen schwer. (n/a)*
>
> (In everything concerning the whole dialogue with the [target countries] I would appreciate much more engagement by the federal government and that it says: "That is what we expect from you. That is what we do not want." In this regard, they are struggling a little bit.)

Very diverse experiences in PPPs dealing with the same subject matter were made by CO13-2 whose company received full support or even total rejection in two different countries:

> *Tienes países como Panamá donde el sector público es quien que está empujando el [enfoque de la PPP] y está incitando que organizaciones privadas se unen. Y también tienes lugares como Venezuela donde estábamos tratando de crear [enfoque de la PPP] y nos dijeron "esto es ilegal por las leyes que nosotros tenemos" y simplemente formó un obstáculo que terminó con el [nombre de la PPP]. (CO13-2)*
>
> (You have countries like Panama where the public sector is the one who is pushing the [PPP focus] and is animating private sector organizations to unite. And you also have places like Venezuela

where we were trying to create [PPP focus] and they told us "it is illegal because of the laws we have", and this simply formed an obstacle which terminated the [PPP name].)

In this context, CO1-1 points to cultural aspects where the international PPP partners perceive certain attitudes by the authorities as obstructive, but they simply have to cope with them:

Und ich sage mal, in Afrika ticken die Uhren immer noch mal anders. [...] wenn die Behörde nicht arbeitet, warten Sie einfach mal 3 Monate, bis Sie die Genehmigung haben. Das heißt, das muss man dann flexibel [...] adjustieren. (CO1-1)
(And I may say, clocks may tick somewhat differently in Africa. [...] if an authority is not working, you simply wait 3 months until you get the permission. Thus, you have to flexibly [...] adjust.)

Moreover, others like CO10-1 and DC1 emphasize changes of government as well as bureaucracy and unclear responsibilities to be major obstacles to operational PPP implementation:

Mein Eindruck [...] ist, dass sich so mit dem Ministerwechsel insgesamt die Haltung gegenüber der Privatindustrie doch so ein bisschen beruhigt hat, verhaltener ist. Also der [Name des Ministers] war da sehr engagiert, was die Förderung von der Privatwirtschaft und die Einbeziehung der Privatwirtschaft anbetrifft, und der jetzige Minister ist da sehr viel verhaltener. (n/a)
(My impression [...] is that through the change of minister the general attitude towards the private sector has calmed down a little bit, being more reserved. The [minister's name] was very much engaged in the promotion of the private sector and the involvement of the private sector, and the current minister is much more reserved in this regard.)

[...] Fälle, wo dann die Zuständigkeiten zwischen verschiedenen Behörden in dem Land nicht klar sind. Da sagt der eine: "Ja, nein, wir wollen das nicht machen." Oder die anderen sagen: "Wir wollen das nicht machen." Oder das Gegenteil ist der Fall. Dann sagen beide: "Nein, da muss aber unser Stempel drauf." [...]. Also das sind Sachen, die manchmal Verzögerungen reinbringen [...]. (DC1)
([...] cases, where the sharing of responsibility between different authorities is not clear in a country. One says: "Yes, no, we do not want to make that." Or the others say: "We do not want to make it." Or the contrary is the case, then both say: "No, our stamp must be put on that." [...]. These are things which cause delays sometimes [...].)

Four interview partners bemoan trade restrictions affecting their PPP activities. For instance, DC1 explains that the target country allows the import of necessary products for experimental purposes only but not at a large scale. This circumstance counteracts the generation of a sustainable business case, making the whole PPP become unattractive for the private sector partners. That is why another DCA interviewee calls his own government to emphasize more its role in supporting PPPs and to link them much more strongly than before to concrete demands towards the recipient countries.

[...] diese Währung "Projekte", nenne ich sie mal, ist natürlich immer was, was der Bundesregierung und auch Unternehmen und am Ende auch uns [...] deutlich bessere [...] Eintrittspforten bietet, dass wir vielleicht sagen [...]: "Die Bundesregierung macht ja jetzt zehn Projekte, um [...] zu fördern [...]." Da sind wir nochmal deutlich besser [...] in der Lage, auch Forderungen zu stellen. Und das ist mit vielen dieser Länder eben ein ständiges Geben und Nehmen. Und ich glaube, dass

die Bundesregierung da die letzten Jahre, für den Bereich, ein bisschen wenig gegeben hat. (n/a)

([...] this currency "projects", I may call it like this, is always something that offers much better [...] entry gates to the federal government, but also to companies, and finally to us, that we may say [...]: "The federal government is doing there ten projects in order [...] to promote [...]." Then, we are in a much better [...] position to also make demands. And in many countries, this is a kind of give-and-take. And I believe that the federal government has given a little bit too less for this area in the last years.)

Moreover, CO9-2 and CO10-1 criticize restrictions on foreign currency export and special taxes on the PPP activities as significant impediments in the past. CO12 adds that another major bureaucratic obstacle is diverging legislations within one country, e.g. between diverse federal states, while pointing out that municipal governments' power over awarding concessions are challenging for PPPs that rely on access to certain natural resources. In summary, governmental support and impediment translate formal institutional constraints into action or non-action taken by public authorities at country level. Both the existence and abscence of actions by public actors can be conducive or obstructive to PPP implementation.

6.7.3.2 Accountability

In PPPs, accountability can be manifold so that IO1 considers the same in connection with transparency as core principles upon which partnerships should be built. Especially IOs are strongly held accountable by member states and through formalized intergovernmental bodies. IO2 links this circumstance to the expectation that also private sector firms will subordinate themselves to such hierarchies if they want to partner with his organization.

We have an intergovernmental mandate, and [...] if you look at the principles, they clearly say that [remark: partnership engagement] must be confirmative with the intergovernmental nature. It's Member States who are the bosses. We have accountability to Member States and to the general public only, not to private sector entities. (IO2)

Also, the PPP activites of DCAs might be exposed to critical questions and reviews by governmental institutions, tedious procedures, which are still reasonable from CO3's point of view.

Es gibt manchmal schon relativ konkrete Anfragen aus irgendwelchen Kommissionen oder häufig auch von Mitgliedern aus dem [Parlament] [...] üblicherweise eher von der Linken [...]. [...]. Nicht speziell jetzt für [Name der PPP], aber generell: "Wie arbeiten Sie mit Privaten im Bereich Landwirtschaft?" oder: "Setzen Sie [Chemikalie] ein?" (n/a)

(Sometimes, there are relatively concrete enquiries from any commissions or often also from members of the [Parliament] [...] usually more from the leftist [...]. [...]. Not with particular reference to [PPP name], but in general: "How do you collaborate with the privates in the field of agriculture?" or "Do you use [chemical product]?")

Wenn jemand Geld für bestimmte Ergebnisse gibt, dann ist ein gewisser Respekt vor diesem Geldgeber ja allen gut angeraten, und dann sollte man auch im

Grunde [...] liefern [...]. Das ist völlig in Ordnung, und das sollte man weder unter- noch überschätzen. (CO3)

(If somebody gives money and for certain results, then a certain respect to the donor is well recommended to everybody, and then one should basically [...] deliver [...]. This is absolutely fair and should be neither under- nor overestimated.)

However, this kind of request of accountability might also emanate from local stakeholders who made negative experiences with stakeholders from abroad.

In [country XY] people are more demanding. They want to know exactly what you want to do, and all that because they are mindful of abuse from external companies. So, you really have to have your staff together. They do not just accept anything and everything just because you give money. (CO7)

In summary, CO6 appreciates accountability in the form of clear expectations because it does not only exert pressure on the PPP partners to make achievements, but also empowers them to actively influence framework conditions in their interest:

Natürlich gibt es eine Erwartungshaltung der Politik und auch Internationaler Organisationen, dass von uns da Vorschläge kommen, wie man es denn da machen kann. Welche Technologien brauchen wir? Welche Rahmenbedingungen brauchen wir? Das wird dann aber auch gehört. (CO6)

(Of course, there are clear expectations from politics and also from international organizations that we make suggestions on what to do. Which technologies do we need? Which framework conditions do we need? But this is then also heard.)

6.7.4 Expansion of PPP Activities

In the light of predominantly positive previous experiences from PPPs, the vast majority of the interview partners declared their willingness to maintain the current level of partnership engagement, or to change and expand it. While CO2 and CO11 stress their companies' motivation to deepen the cooperation in their respective existing PPP but not to engage in other partnerships, CO6, DC6 and IO7 declare their fundamental interest in enhancing PPP engagements, but under specific conditions. They unanimously advocate for more integrated multi-stakeholder PPPs instead of small-scale partnerships that comprise only a few of the relevant stakeholders because policy issues like renewable energy use gained in increasing importance for economics, politics and civil society gained in recent years. For instance, DC6 argues that projects on efficient use of resources should not concentrate on one resource type only, such as renewable energy generation, but reminds of interdependencies between different resource types, and therefore also takes into account impacts on human resources (in terms of labor supply) or water supply. IO7 stresses the private sector's innovative capacities, so that IO1 and IO3 underline the clear interest in enhancing PPP cooperation and to reach out into other sectors, with a few exceptions:

I think, increased partnerships means multi-stakeholder partnerships. So, it's not necessarily one-on-one partnerships between us and a specific company but more multi-stakeholder initiatives in that sense. [...]. And if we look at the donor landscape as well, a lot of them are keen to also have private sector engaged in the programmes they fund, looking at how we use private sector innovations, how we use private sector as a delivery mechanism in a way. There is a lot of interest in challenging funds or having these kinds of private sector-led initiatives and solutions for the normal development context […]. (IO7)

I believe that the UN could benefit from partnering with media companies, promoting and communicating more actively our vision and UN values as well as with information technology companies that could help the UN to better manage knowledge. Evidently, the UN should stay more systematically far away from those companies dealing with arms, alcohol, tobacco and other products posing serious reputational risks. (IO1)

CO13-2 imagines the banking and finance sector to be a stronger catalyzer of resources in the future, which may stimulate the creation of new PPPs, because not only the public sector faces budget constraints. While DCAs commonly are contracted by their national government for specific projects with a given budget, including PPPs, the willingness of the private sector to invest is limited even if PPPs proved to be successful, as stated by CO14. Thus, DCA's expansion of PPPs depends to a large extent on the resources being allocated by their ministry in charge.

[…] el sector financiero en cualquiera de las actividades que estamos haciendo sería un actor bastante bien recibido. […]. Todo el sector financiero tiene un montón de capacidad de mover recursos y meter servicios a la cuestión del mercado. Entonces, tenemos que agarrar escala […]. Pues jalar recursos de [nota: socios] bilaterales o de gobiernos. […]. Entonces, las entidades financieras tienen un rol bastante fuerte en esto. (CO13-2)

([…] in any of the activities we are doing, the financial sector would be a very well received actor. […]. The whole financial sector has abundant capacities to move resources and to put services on the market. Hence, we have to scale up […]. So, pulling resources from [remark: bilateral] partners or governments. […]. Thus, the financial entities have quite a strong role in this.)

The company is allocating and investing in this, but, you know, the capacity is limited to the amount of [CO14] is willing to put every year in these projects. So, as there are no other entities, investors put in more money so that we could scale up or reach the double of the [beneficiaries] that we are reaching so far. (CO14)

However, IO5 remarks that PPPs require other approaches for interorganizational engagement than hitherto practiced in joint projects with DCAs or governmental authorities in emerging and developing countries. She advocates for selling PPPs as a kind of marketable product to private sector actors in order to increase the overall volume of PPP activities:

We are thinking about products or product offers because we think that most of the product offers that we have are tailored for governments. So, we are looking at what we haven't […] because you cannot work with the private sector the same way you work with the government. There has to be a shift. […]. A product offer is for example that you want to work on a water project in [target country], and we want the private sector to partner with us. How do you offer this to them? How do you package it? You cannot just put in a proposal the way we do it for governments and submit. It needs to be packaged differently for the private sec-

tor. So, they want to be attracted [...], and to work and be really willing to come and partner with us and actually sit down and implement it. (IO5)

If the PPP implementation proved to be successful in one country, an option of expansion consists in the possibility of extending the duration and thematic focus of the ongoing partnerhsip, or of rolling out the same activities in other countries. This approach was followed amongst others by CO1 and CO10 who appreciate very much the fact that they could rely on the same partners who maintained similar infrastructures in other countries as well, wherefore TC were reduced, especially during the first three phases (Chapter 6.3.2). Thus, no costly search for new partners and investments in relationship- and trust-building were necessary. Notwithstanding, the expansion of PPP activities tends to be a gradual and time-consuming process. CO10-1 explains that current expansion strategies rely in his company's case on the development from mere supplier relationships with IOs to joint research PPPs. He still remarks that this process requires both an internal and external change of mind because if clients got to know you hitherto as supplier only, it may take some time until they accept you as partner at eye-level. Moreover, their own management needs to be convinced by the benefits of certain PPP projects. This most often takes some time, too, because PPPs usually do not belong to the core business of the companies. That is why an executive board wants to first see positive results from smaller engagements before the budget for more comprehensive and closer cooperation with public actors like IOs is released. One private sector interviewee adds that some kind of risk-mitigating guarantees given by his own national government may encourage mid-size companies in particular to engage more in PPPs, and therefore to make investments in developing countries where hitherto no or only very little business operations are going on. In summary, CO1-1 appeals to all PPP stakeholders to keep some curiosity and openmindedness towards new potential PPPs because many opportunities might not be forseeable yet:

Und das, was wir in Zukunft bereit sind zu tun, wissen wir zum Teil noch gar nicht, weil gerade ganz viel Neues entsteht. Also, wir brauchen neue und [...] innovative Partnerschaften. Und wie genau die aussehen sollen, wissen wir zum Teil selber noch nicht. Das ist noch ganz offen. (CO1-1)

(And what we are willing to do in the future, we do not know yet, because currently many new things are arising. So, we need new and [...] innovative partnerships. And we do not even know yet how they will look like in detail. That is still unknown.)

6.7.5 Influence of Global Institutions

This chapter concentrates on the influence of global institutions, in the form of public organizations, multi-stakeholder initiatives and policy guidelines, and on the creation and design of PPPs for development. First, the influence of the UN and other global initiatives and platforms will be illuminated before in the second step the interviewees' expectations on the transition from the MDGs to the SDGs will be compared.

6.7.5.1 *UN and other Global Initiatives and Platforms*

The UN System as well as global initiatives and policy platforms in their sphere of influence were named by the interview partners as most influential drivers of PPPs for development. While IO1 calls the UN Global Compact initiative an important catalyst of public-private co-operation, IO2 and IO4 highlight the role of DCAs, member states, non-governmental actors or supranational institutions in creating PPPs:

> *[...] the Global Compact Office considers openly itself as an example of partnership machinery between the UN and the private sector, a voluntary initiative pursuing two objectives: mainstreaming the "Ten Global Compact Principles" in business activities around the world [...] and catalyzing actions in support of broader UN goals, such as the MDGs. (IO1)*

> *From my observations, philanthropic foundations, such as the Bill and Melinda Gates Foundation, as well as other international or national organizations in the development field, such as the EU or the DFID[15], play an important stake in the steering and control of projects. (IO2)*

IO4 remarks that IOs are particularly endorsed in their endeavours of PPP creation by Anglo-Saxon countries, such as the USA or the United Kingdom, or also by Brazil and China in the context of South-South Cooperation. But impulses for PPPs can also emanate intraorganizationally, as stated by an IO interviewee who reports on the results of an internal staff survey among offices around the world:

> *I think it was about 90% that said that also their governments see that there is a strong national interest in developing the private sector and engaging the private sector to different national level work as well. [...] a lot of offices said that they see it fundamental for the country to develop in an inclusive way that private sector is a key stakeholder. [...]. But, of course, capacity in that is also key. So, we need to pay a lot of attention to the internal capacity development and putting the enablers in place in that sense that we can implement what we said to do. Looking at the survey, looking at different messages coming from different offices, and also from the responses from the private sector [remark: stating] that they are more keen to engage [remark: in PPPs], I would assume it leads to increasing partnerships. (n/a)*

Several private sector actors said that their partnership activities were strongly guided by conventions and policy platforms, such as COP21[16] or UNFCCC[17], or by norm-setting standards being issued by UN Specialized Agencies in the field of health-related matters. Others, like CO7 and DC3, stress that their PPP concepts are always attuned to promoting the implementation of the SDGs, or formerly MDGs, and that they show which activities contribute to the achievement of which goal:

---

[15] DFID: Department for International Development (department of the United Kingdom government)
[16] COP21: 21st annual session of the Conference of the Parties (2015 UN Climate Change Conference)
[17] UNFCCC: United Nations Framework Convention on Climate Change

> *For us, it is really important that everything we do can be brought back to the goals, to say, "Yes, we see the MDGs. This is what we want to do, and this is our contribution." [...] if you are going to the Dow Jones Sustainability reporting, all our things are based on the MDGs. (CO7)*

In summary, one private sector interviewee appeals to the public sector to overcome existing prejudices and calls upon all relevant stakeholders of PPPs to tightly collaborate in order to make global institutions, such as the SDGs, effective:

> *[...] also, es gibt ja eine Menge pharmakritischer NGOs, aber tatsächlich ist ja gerade mit diesen globalen Initiativen* die Frage verbunden, ob *dieses Weltbild nicht komplett überholt ist, also angesichts dieser neuen Sustainable Development Goals. Ich meine, wenn man die erreichen will, dann müssen alle zusammenarbeiten. (n/a)*
> ([...] there are lots of NGOs being critical of the pharmaceutical industry, but especially for these global initiatives arises the question of whether this worldview is not completely outdated, with respect to these new Sustainable Development Goals. I mean, if we want to achieve them, we all have to collaborate.)

6.7.5.2 Transition from MDGs to SDGs

The adoption of the MDGs in the year 2000 marked the formalization of a development agenda for the UN System and its Member States and defined eight overall goals to be achieved by 2015. Especially the eighth goal "Global Partnership for Development" and the subordinated targets 8.E and 8.F requested public actors, such IOs and national governments including DCAs, to promote public-private cooperation, e.g. in the form of PPPs. In 2015, the MDGs were replaced by the SDGs which apply to all Member States alike. Compared to the MDGs, the SDGs were not defined for developing countries only. Moreover, the SDGs are much more comprehensive than the MDGs as they comprise 17 goals and 169 targets where public-private cooperation is a cross-cutting issue affecting all goals. That is why this chapter is dedicated to the expectations the interview partners derive from the transition from the MDGs to the SDGs, and to the implications they see for their respective PPPs. Regardless of any positive or negative expectations or implications for their own work, the vast majority of the interview partners takes the transition very serious, especially because the SDGs now contain specific targets, as stated by CO1. CO3 and CO5 underline that the importance of the SDGs lies in their framework character which encourages PPP stakeholders to strive for new actor constellations in order to address policy issues of common interest and relevance, even if the measurable impact on the operational work might be limited:

> *Es ist wichtig, diese Sustainable Development Goals zu haben, so wichtig wie es war, Millennium Goals zu haben. Sie sind halt internationaler Leitfaden für alle Akteure. Sie sind für die verschiedenen Sektoren auch eine Klammer, unter der sich jeder versammeln kann. Vom Wechsel von MDGs zu SDGs erwarte ich für uns jetzt spezifisch keine große Veränderung [...]. [...] das Thema wird dadurch weiteren Auftrieb erhalten und ist weiter aktuell und wird bestimmt auch nicht weniger Ressourcen generieren. (CO3)*

(It is important to have got these Sustainable Development Goals, as important as it has been to have Millenium Goals. They are basically an international guideline for all actors. They are for the different sectors also a bracket through which everybody can gather together. From the transtion from the MDGs to the SDGs, I do not expect any major change for us [...]. [...] the topic will be given additional boost and continue to be on the agenda, and it will certainly not generate less resources.)

Es geht ja eigentlich jetzt auch darum, die globalen Probleme, die alle betreffen, gemeinsam anzugehen, und [...] da muss man neue Konstellationen denken, neue Partnerschaften, die vielleicht bisher noch nicht auf der Agenda waren, insbesondere was eben Nord-Süd-Kooperationen angeht. [...] die globalen Probleme sind so breit und so komplex, da hat fast jeder was im Portfolio, was er einbringen kann. (CO5)

(It is actually about tackling altogether the global problems which affect all of us, and [...] there we have to conceive new constellations, new partnerships, which hitherto might not have been yet on the agenda, especially regarding North-South cooperations. [...] the global problems are so broad and so complex that almost everybody has something in his portfolio that he might contribute.)

Positive expectations are expressed by CO4, DC1, DC2, DC3, IO2 and others. However, actors like DC2 and DC4 assume that the SDG's influence takes effect in the political arena first, because governments must enhance public-private cooperation to achieve the SDGs, but limited implications for the operational PPP activities are expected in the short-to-medium run. In the long run, political decisions taken by national governments with respect to the SDGs may cascade down and therefore affect PPPs as well. Like CO13-2, CO4 expects development banks in particular, such as the World Bank Group, to provide more funding to PPP-based activities, and therefore to raise more countries' serious interest in joining the initiative in which his company participates.

Das wird sich schon auswirken. Alleine wenn ich auf die letzten Millennium Development Goals schaue, dann hat das ganz klar eine Auswirkung gehabt. Alles, was die Länder machen und alles das, was die Geber auch machen, muss sich dem nachordnen, und muss sich da anpassen, muss sich rechtfertigen. Und ich erwarte, dass das jetzt für die Sustainable Development Goals genauso sein wird. [...] es gibt ja irgendwie viel mehr Ziele als vorher. Von daher ist es vielleicht noch detaillierter. (DC1)

(That will make impacts. If I just look at the recent Millennium Development Goals, then they had a clear impact. Whatever countries are doing, and whatever donors are making, has to get subordinated to them and has to align and has to justify itself.)

[...] als [Name der PPP] selbst wird uns das relativ wenig helfen, weil diese Ziele dann doch irgendwie teilweise zu abstrakt sind und irgendwie zu weit vom Kerngeschäft der einzelnen Unternehmen. (DC2)

([...] for the [PPP name] as such it will of relatively little help because some of these goals are still somehow too abstract and somehow too far away from the core business of the respective companies.)

[...] auf unsere Arbeit [...] sehe ich keine direkte Verbindung, dass sich dadurch irgendwie strukturell was in dem Programm ändert. [...]. Also, es ist eher so, dass wir [...] unsere einzelnen Projektziele natürlich [...] darauf ausrichten, dass wir die formulierten Ziele mit unterstützen. (DC3)

([…] I do not see any direkt link […] to our work […] that it will change structurally anything in the programme. […]. It is rather such that we […] will gear our single project goals […] in a way that we also support the defined goals.)

Si logramos hacer una conexión muy clara y mucho más directa [nota: entre los objetivos de los socios y los SDGs] hay todo un acceso a financiamiento que puede ser bastante útil. Pero […] creo que no se ha dado completamente esta alineación que estamos buscando. (CO13-2)

(If we reach to create a very clear and much more direct connection [remark: between the objectives of the partners and the SDGs], there will be an access to financing which could be quite helpful. But […] I believe that this alignment we are looking for has not been completely given yet.)

IO6 welcomes the stronger binding nature of the SDGs, and IO7 already notes more openness in her organization towards engagement with the private sector. In this spirit, CO14 expects more serious engagements as well as closer collaboration and communication with the public sector from the transition to the SDGs:

[…] MDGs were kept too flexible at the end of the day. So, that's why they were not able to achieve the goals. Now, there is a more pragmatic approach. (IO6)

Sometimes, some of the offices actually don't really engage with the private sector […]. So, obviously we have a little bit less interaction with them but now there is an increasing amount of offices, that I see, that say: "We do need to support and we want training and more technical skills-building". So, I think with the SDGs the private sector is much broader on the agenda. And from the government's side, the governments are increasingly more interested. (IO7)

[…] the private sector was not taken into consideration in the past. I think this is the first time in an international development agenda that the private sector is formally invited to get engaged. So, in the first place, my expectation is the society agenda is more open to see private sector doing something because in the past. […] everyone when [CO14] was participating in a forum or an event, especially locally, people were like, "What is [CO14] doing here? […] my expectation is also to create frameworks or to create a common language to communicate what the private sector is contributing with this agenda, because […] I think, there are still many companies asking why they should be engaging with SDGs. And I expect more frameworks or more communication from these organizations to engage the private sector. I think the private sector has the capabilities to really bring value to the global efforts. (CO14)

However, scepticism was similarly voiced by both public and private actors who definitely do not await implications for their operational PPP work, because the overarching objectives being pursued by the SDGs are basically not different from the MDGs, as stated by CO9-2. In this regard, IO2 and IO8 remain cautious in their impact assessment of the SDGs, prompting one private sector interviewee to draw a slightly optimistic conclusion:

There is certainly more talk of partnerships, we have to fill it with substance. And especially for the large global companies, they have to shift from the corporate social responsibility […]. […] we are more interested in their change of behavior and we put it explicitly that we engage with private sector entities in order to change their behavior. (IO2)

I think it is more like an internal thing within the UN. [...] for [PPP name], I do not think it will be impacted by this transition. Of course, [...] we definitely keep in mind the overall fit within the SDGs, but in operational matters nothing [...] will dramatically change. (IO6)

Naja, böse formuliert, können sich doch jetzt schon die heute 30- bis 40- Jährigen darauf freuen, dass sie 2030 die Ziele für 2050 formulieren. (n/a)
(Well, rudely worded, the today's people in their thirties to forties can already look forward to preparing in 2030 the goals for 2050.)

In summary, most interview partners do not expect significant impacts from the SDGs on their actual PPP operations as these goals remain very much high-level, despite more goals and more concise targets. Notwithstanding, many of them await the SDGs to serve as catalyzer for raising intraorganizational awareness of the relevance of partnership engagements and to increase the overall political legitimation of PPPs.

6.8 Critical Success Factors

This chapter discusses CSFs that the interview partners identified for their partnerships, analyzes which implications these factors have for MC and how the awareness of them can contribute to improving the MC of PPPs for development. While the Chapters 6.8.1 and 6.8.2 serve the answering of **research question 2.2**, the Chapter 6.8.3 refers to **reseach question 3**. Regarding the question of what "success" actually means, different ideas exist, and for many interview partners it was difficult to give precise answers. Most actors, such as DC1 and IO3, expect clear and measurable results which create a sustainable impact:

Also, Erfolg ist, wenn wir die Indikatoren erreichen, [...] wenn wir das, was wir uns zum Ziel gesetzt haben, auch erreichen. [...] ein Aspekt von Erfolg, den man auf längere Sicht sehen würde, wäre eben [...] Nachhaltigkeit. (DC1)
(Well, success is if we achieve the indicators, [...] if we reach the objectives that we have set ourselves. [...] one aspect of success, which you would see in the long run, is sustainability.)

Partnership is successful if it delivers results [...]. Partnership is a failure if either it doesn't deliver results, it means if there is not a benefit, or if some of the risks become true, even if you deliver results but at the price of whitewashing or bluewashing, as it is called with the UN association, of undue influence, of reputational damage to us [...]. So, the failure can be on both sides, the lack of the benefits and the materialization of the risks. (IO3)

Sustainable impact is not a clearly defined term. Still, several actors like CO5, CO13-2 and IO7 emphasize that this impact is characteristic of successful partnerships. It means positive results for the society and the targeted beneficiaries but also for the stakeholders involved, such as economic returns for the private sector. In additon, CO1-1 and CO1-2 advocate for a differentiated definition of success which places strong focus on future achievements and therefore accepts intermediate failures as part of natural learning processes:

> *[...] selbst wenn man sagt: "Man erreicht nicht das, was man ursprünglich mal vorhatte." Sie haben sozusagen Zusatzgewinne [...]. Das sind nämlich Aspekte, die dabei häufig vergessen werden. (CO1-1)*
> ([...] even if you say: "You do not achieve what you have actually envisaged." You have such a kind of additional gains [...]. These are aspects which are often left behind.)

> *[...] dem Erkenntnisgewinn für die Gemeinschaft [...]. Also selbst ein Projekt, was sich am Ende als nicht erfolgreich erwiesen hat, bedeutet vielleicht, dass andere bestimmte Fehler nicht machen werden. (CO1-2)*
> ([...] the gain of knowledge for the society [...]. Even a project, which did not prove to be successful at the end, might imply that certain other errors will not be made.)

In the following subchapters an overview will be given of extrinsic and intrinsic success factors to see how those for the PPPs for development of this study agree or complement with others found in previous studies (Chapter 2.3).

6.8.1 Extrinsic Factors

Like in Chapter 2.3.1, one distinguishes between **economic**, **legal/political** and **social** success factors. Moreover, an enabling economic environment, in conjunction with active and passive political support, is pivotal for successful PPP implementation (Table 60). While active political support can be reached through systematic relationship building with governmental authorities (sometimes also called "lobbying"), passive political support relies mainly on the simple acceptance of the PPP activities and is linked to legal certainty and a clear regulatory framework.

> *Und es hat auch sicherlich zum Erfolg von [Name der PPP] beigetragen, ganz gezielt auf rechtliche Rahmenbedingungen für partnerschaftliches Engagement seitens der [DCA Partner] einzuwirken. (CO3)*
> (And the exertion of active influence on the legal framework conditions for partnership engagement by [DCA partner] has truly contributed to the success of [PPP name].)

> *[...] [Nombre del PPP] es exitosa porque se ha logrado posicionar entre el gobierno y realmente el gobierno toma en cuenta las opiniones de [Nombre del PPP]. Esto es muy muy positivo y es muy exitoso. (DC5)*
> ([...] [PPP name] is successful because it achieved to position itself inside the government, and the government really takes the opinions of [PPP name] into consideration. That is very very positive and it is very successful.)

Different aspects of strong societal support were emphasized by DC2 as a CSF, including awareness- and trust-building. This applies especially for PPPs going along with a high potential reputational risk, which can become apparent if badly managed, as stated by CO6.

> *Ich glaube, für uns ist ein Erfolgsfaktor, dass [...] es uns gelungen ist, auch über die Mitgliedschaft hinaus ein hohes Maß an Vertrauen und Offenheit und Aner-*

> *kanntheit aufzubauen. [...] wir werden letztlich von allen Akteuren wahrgenommen. (DC2)*
>
> (I believe that one success factor for us is that we [...] succeeded in building up a high level of trust and openness and recognition also beyond the membership. [...] we are finally perceived by all actors.)

Interview partner:		CO1	CO3	CO4	CO6	DC2	DC5	DC6	Total
Extrinsic factors									
Economic	**Success factors**								
	Favorable market conditions						x		1
Legal/Political	**Success factors**								
	Clearly defined regulatory framework						x		1
	Legal certainty							x	1
	Lobbying		x						1
	Political support						x		1
Social	**Success factors**								
	Education and knowledge transfer	x							1
	Enthusiasm			x					1
	Public awareness					x			1
	Public confidence					x			1
	Public recognition					x			1
	Obstacles								
	Management of reputational risk				x				1

Table 60: Extrinsic factors.

In summary, the raised extrinsic CSFs do not substantially deviate from those surveyed by the literature review, even if their naming slightly differs.

6.8.2 Intrinsic Factors

This chapter gives an overview of the intrinsic CSFs which were mentioned by the interview partners, and clusters them in line with the four-level structure in Chapter 2.3. In this regard, it also compares major differences between the findings from the literature review and the empirical results from the present field study as well as explains the implications for MC for some CSFs.

6.8.2.1 Intrinsic Factors – Interpersonal CSFs

In line with Chapter 2.3.2.1, the interpersonal CSFs are clustered by the four categories **management**, **relationship characteristics**, **team behavior** and **general**, while the latter only contains obstacles (Table 61). Management support and team behavior, based on the willingness to closely collaborate and to implement joint PPP activities in a focused manner, are perceived as decisive for a partnership's success, and thereby these features coincide with the findings from the literature review. More generally spoken, a good level of intrinsic motivation coupled with some passion forms even an additional catalyzer of success, but may lead equally quickly to failure if absent. All the more, cooperation at eye-level and inter-cultural openess are crucial (see quotation from DC4 in Chapter 6.6.4.3).

Also ich denke, dass es wichtig war, auf unserer Seite hier jemanden zu haben, der sieben, acht Jahre Erfahrung im öffentlich-privaten Dialog und mit Multi-Stakeholder Partnerschaften hat, und viele [DCA Partner]-Partnerschaften bei anderen Unternehmen oder auch hier im Hause haben deshalb nicht funktioniert, weil der Dialog nicht funktioniert hat. [...]. Es erfordert eine enorme Dialogkultur und eine Implementierungskultur. Das braucht meiner Meinung nach auch einfach ein hohes emotionales Commitment der Partner zur Sache. Das ist auf jeden Fall sehr hilfreich. (CO3)

(Well, I think that it was important for us to have somebody who has seven, eight years of experience in public-private dialogue and with multi-stakeholder partnerships, and many [DCA partner] partnerships with other companies, but also with us, did not work because the dialogue did not work. [...]. It requires an enormous dialogue culture and implementation culture. In my view, the partners also need a high emotional commitment to the subject matter. That is at least very helpful.)

Und irgendwann war dann das Projekt [...] gestorben [...], weil einfach alle Partner vor Ort die Motivation verloren hatten. (n/a)

(And at one point then, the project [...] died [...], because all partners on-site had simply lost motivation.)

And there is one person in [private sector partner], [...], the passion is there, but there is also the person on higher level in [private sector partner] that really likes and believes in the project. [...]. So, that is definitely a very much important aspect to take into account in determining why this is a successful partnership. [...] I would say to summarize really like the fact that [remark: the PPP] is really well perceived within [private sector partner]. [...] the patron of this initiative within [private sector partner] is very much on board. (IO8)

However, no CSFs were mentioned more often than trust and medium-to-long-term commitment as essential elements of PPP relationships. On the other side, the lack of trust forms a serious obstacle to successful PPP implementation. This confirms the findings from the literature review. That is why CO1-1 and CO10-2 name mutual trust building one of the predominant tasks at the beginning of a partnership and underline that this applies for any kind of PPP, insofar as trustful relationships have not been established by previous cooperation.

[...] ein wesentlicher Erfolgsfaktor war [...] gegenseitiges Vertrauen. Also, man konnte sich auf den Partner verlassen, also jetzt gerade unser öffentlicher Partner, die [DCA Partner]. Das ist ein über viele Jahre entstandenes und immer ge-

lebtes Vertrauen. Das hat sicherlich dazu beigetragen, dass wir erfolgreich waren, dass die andere Seite auch immer mitgedacht hat: "Was ist für euch jetzt gerade noch wichtig?" (CO8)

([...] a material success factor was [...] mutual trust. Thus, one could rely on the partner, especially our public partner, the [DCA partner]. This trust has been built and practiced over many years. This has surely contributed to being successful, that the other side always followed in the sense: "What is currently still important for you?")

El compromiso de los actores, tanto del sector público como del sector privado. (DC5)

(The commitment by the actors, from both the public and the private sector.)

So, I think it's mainly the problem that we have quite often the lack of trust, that we still do have a lot of colleagues who are very suspicious about the private sector. (IO7)

In this regard, DC1, IO6 and others plead for communicating openly and honestly their own interests and expectations to prevent distrust and to overcome previous negative experiences and prejudices, as stated by DC2. CO12 concludes that all this requires everybody's willingness to get involved with another partner:

I think, initially, it's important to speak the same language and to set the expectations right. (IO7)

I think it is the willingness to be open to new ideas, the comfort-level, [...]. The ability to actually sit down and learn about it. I think most of the PPP-projects I worked on, [...] are going so fast and doing everything. The agencies themselves do not spend any time on trying to learn about some other things being proposed to them, [...] you know, it is easier to say no than yes. (CO12)

In summary, the identified interpersonal intrinsic CSFs confirm basically those success factors surveyed by the literature review. Still, it seems that in PPPs for development more importance is attributed to factors being associated with interorganizational and intercultural differences as well as with the building of longstanding relationships between public and private actors.

		Interview partner:	CO1	CO2	CO3	CO4	CO5	CO6	CO8	CO9	CO10	CO12	CO14	DC1	DC2	DC4	DC5	IO6	IO7	IO8	Total
Intrinsic factors - interpersonal																					
		Success factors																			
Interpersonal	Management	Leadership and management support			x															x	2
Interpersonal	Management	Internal buy-in																	x	x	2
Interpersonal	Management	Continuous relationship management																	x		1
Interpersonal	Relationship Characteristics	Trust	x	x					x	x	x		x								6
Interpersonal	Relationship Characteristics	Commitment			x	x		x									x		x		5
Interpersonal	Relationship Characteristics	Open, honest and effective communication (e.g. consultations)								x				x			x	x	x		5
Interpersonal	Relationship Characteristics	Openness (towards new ideas)										x				x					2
Interpersonal	Relationship Characteristics	Alignment of expectations																	x		1
Interpersonal	Relationship Characteristics	Cooperation on eye-level														x					1
Interpersonal	Relationship Characteristics	Fun and humor														x					1
Interpersonal	Relationship Characteristics	Low hierarchies														x					1
Interpersonal	Relationship Characteristics	(Mutual) understanding																x			1
Interpersonal	Relationship Characteristics	Reliability							x												1
Interpersonal	Relationship Characteristics	Speaking the same language																	x		1
Interpersonal	Relationship Characteristics	Transparency		x																	1
Interpersonal	Team Behavior	Implementation culture/ working in a focused manner			x	x											x				3
Interpersonal	Team Behavior	Cooperation/ cooperative behavior					x							x							2
Interpersonal	Team Behavior	Dialogue culture			x																1
Interpersonal	Team Behavior	Willingness to consider the other partner's interest							x												1
Interpersonal	Team Behavior	Willingness to learn and listen										x									1
Interpersonal	General	Motivation and passion				x										x				x	3
Interpersonal	General	Existing previous experiences			x						x										2
Interpersonal	General	Commitment from the benficiaries of a PPP																		x	1
Interpersonal	General	Persistence					x														1
Interpersonal	General	Personal contacts with government									x										1
Interpersonal	General	Personal drive				x															1
		Obstacles																			
Interpersonal	General	Distrust/lack of trust													x				x		2
Interpersonal	General	Dialogue does not work			x																1
Interpersonal	General	Lack of personal drive				x															1
Interpersonal	General	Negative previous experiences													x						1
Interpersonal	General	Prejudices													x						1

Table 61: Intrinsic CSFs – Interpersonal factors.

6.8.2.2 *Intrinsic Factors – Inherent/Structural CSFs*

Compared to the inherent/structural CSFs surveyed by the literature review in Chapter 2.3.2.2, different characteristics of risk management are neither perceived as success factors nor as obstacles (Table 62). Two categories called **management control** and **general** have been included instead, while emphasis is placed on **goal alignment**, **responsibility sharing** and **strategy** alike. The obstacles are more precisely differentiated by lack of **responsibility sharing and clear mandate** as well as **institutional and other deficiencies.** Several public and private interviewees underline that the definition and sharing of clear and common goals at the outset, combined with a clear strategy and strong performance orientation, pave the way for successful PPP implementation later on:

> *Die Ziele müssen realistisch sein, die Ressourcen müssen ausreichend sein. (CO3)*
>
> (The goals must be realistic, the resources must suffice.)

> *The success of the project stands and falls with clear goals, where it is clear that you know what you want, they know what you want, and you are the right partner for them, or they are the right partner for you. That would determine the success. (CO7)*

> *[…] was wir richtig gemacht haben, da eine glasklare Strategie zu haben, sehr klare Ziele zu haben. Und dass sich das dann auch immer sehr einfach bemessen lässt: Trägt es dazu bei oder trägt es dazu nicht bei? (DC2)*
>
> ([…] what we did right is to have a very clear strategy, very clear goals. So that is then easy to measure: Does it contribute or does it not contribute?)

While CO2 calls for a clear delineation of PPP work from commercial activities, CO8, DC1 and DC3 explicitly stress the importance of having a business case behind each partnership. They link this to the taking of ownership and commitment, two buzzwords they expect to be filled with substance.

> *[…] generell ist es wichtig, dass der private Partner so ein Ownership hat. Also, dass es nicht etwas ist, was er aus altruistischen Gründen tut […], sondern es muss tatsächlich ein kommerzieller Gedanke dahinter sein, oder auch ein Business Case, dass er da auch seine Interessen verfolgen kann. Wenn er das nicht kann, dann wird er das Projekt unter Umständen auch nicht so engagiert mit uns gemeinsam durchführen und schon gar nicht, wenn wir dann draußen sind. Nach [Anzahl an] Jahren sind wir spätestens raus, und damit das [Anmerkung: Engagement] gegeben ist, ist es ganz wichtig, dass er diesen Business Case hat. Und dann meinte ich aber mit Ownership, dass er den [Anmerkung: Projekt-] Antrag auch schreibt bzw. auch in der Konzeption aktiv beteiligt ist […]. Es geht nicht, dass ich dann mit meinen tollen Visionen aus der EZ reingehe und das alles alleine mache und ihn dann am Ende bitte, das zu unterschreiben, […] und wir damit ein Projekt haben. Aber dieses Projekt ist dann quasi ohne Leben, ohne Commitment, ohne Ownership. Dieser Prozess, dieses Kennenlernen, und dass er dann auch selbst schreibt und mitformuliert, ist ganz wichtig, weil nur so ist man auch Teil des Ganzen und fühlt sich als Owner des Projekts. (DC3)*

([...] generally it is important that the private partner takes such a kind of ownership. Thus, this it is not something what he/she is doing for altruistic reasons [...], but it must in fact be a commercial idea behind, or also a business case, so that he/she can pursue his/her interests. If he/she cannot do that, he/she might not conduct the project that actively together with us, even once we are out. After [number of] years we are out at the latest, and to make sure that the [remark: commitment] is given, it is important that he/she has this business case. And by ownership I mean that he/she also writes the [remark: project] application or also actively contributes to the conception [...]. It does not work that I bring in my great visions from the development cooperation, but do it all alone and just ask him/her to sign in the end, [...] and that we then have a project by this. But this project then actually is without energy, without commitment, without ownership. This process of getting to know each other, and the need that he then also writes and formulates is very important because only by doing this you feel to be part of the whole thing and you feel like owner of the project.)

In terms of MC, the relevance of networking and knowledge sharing is associated with the consideration and matching of complementary skills and competences and was highlighted by several interview partners, especially from the private sector. It may contribute to the creation of an improved, more efficient MC culture and structure, as stated by CO13-2:

[...] ein weiterer Erfolgsfaktor ist natürlich einfach dieser Zugang zu einem Netz von Experten auf einem Gebiet, wo man ja selbst nicht der Experte ist [...]. Da hilft es natürlich, mit Leuten zusammenzuarbeiten, die seit Jahrzehnten in diesem Umfeld Projekte implementieren. Und andersherum bringen wir natürlich wieder das letzte Knowhow bezüglich [Kernkompetenz] mit. [...] diese breite Ansammlung von Expertise, die so ein Setting mit sich bringt, ist sicherlich ein wichtiger Faktor und die damit zusammenhängenden Kontakte auch einfach. (CO8)

([...] another success factor simply is this acess to a network of experts in one area, where oneself is not an expert [...]. Of course, it helps to collaborate with people who have been implementing projects in this environment for decades. On the other side, we bring in the most recent knowhow regarding [core competency]. [...] this broad concentration of expertise, which is associated with such a setting, surely is an important factor as well as the inherent contacts.)

[...] we share our knowhow, what we have as [CO11]. [...] we have managerial thinking. We have a network. [...]. What they have, they have also a great network. (CO11)

La fortaleza está en que cada uno de los socios que está sentando en la mesa tiene capacidades diferentes y esto hace que una iniciativa sea enriquecida con multiples perspectivas. Esto es creo que sería la fortaleza más grande. El hecho de enriquecer con perspectivas y el enriquecer con conocimiento y con las redes que cada uno de las organizaciones tiene [...]. [...] desde métricas que se modifican para tener una eficiencia más clara, desde una perspectiva privada donde el [socio] tiene que acercarse a nuestro entendimiento y nosotros al de ellos hasta el cambio en todo un proceso como el project management que le tienes que entregar a alguien más. Entonces, el hecho de que haya estas diferencias y estas fortalezas al final empieza a crear una nueva cultura que va a permear en todo, no solo en el proceso de management sino en el proceso de medición, de monitoreo, etc. (CO13-2)

(The strength is that each member who is sitting in the board has different capacities, and that is what enriches an initiative with multiple perspectives. I believe that this would be the biggest strength. The fact of enrichment by perspectives, and the enrichment by knowledge and by the networks that each organization has [...]. [...] from the metrics being modified for having clearer efficiency, from a private perspective where the [partner] has to approach our understanding and we do theirs, up to the total change of a process like the project management that you have to hand over to somebody else. Hence, the fact that there are these differences and these strengths begins to ultimately create a new culture which penetrates everything, not only the management process but also the process of benchmarking, of monitoring, etc.)

In this context, DC5 and DC6 add that the involvement of renowned experts from the partnership's field of action, such as former politicians, and the positioning of the PPP as one that is open to new stakeholders being interested in the underlying subject matter, as well as the increasing institutionalization of the partnership as such, formed additional CSFs. Other actors like CO3 and CO4 underline that successful PPPs rely on a clear and effective MC and project management structure as well as upon an efficient inter- and intraorganizational project coordination. All this requires skilled managerial and operational staff, but also an effective risk management that covers the whole set of MC mechanisms in a PPP, pursuant to CO3 and CO7:

Clear, clear risk management in all those things will determine if the programme will succeed or fail. (CO7)

Otherwise a PPP might be doomed to fail from the beginning, as stated by DC4. That is why his organization dedicates very much time and energy to doing thorough work in the initiation, preparation and design phase in order to prevent a later situation where the project design and structure reveals to be unsuitable, resulting in frustration on all sides and in the loss of taxpayers' money if the partnership fails at the end. Furthermore, a coherent MC and project design requires clearly defined roles and responsibilities, which should be embedded within an accountability and regulatory framework, according to CO6, IO1 and IO2. The latter recommends linking such a framework to the requirement that each partner specifies the risks he/she is facing and for whose analysis he/she will be held accountable. With respect to accountability, IO3 remarks that his organization will install a benchmark on transparency to prevent silo structures including information asymmetry where partners do not actively communicate and even deprive one another of relevant information. Moreover, coherence and continuity in the sense of keeping a common understanding and vision about the PPP work and activities are pivotal in the whole PPP implementation, as stated by CO5:

Also, bevor man irgendeine Partnerschaft oder ein Projekt eingeht, muss irgendwie ein gemeinsames Verständnis, eine gemeinsame Vision existieren. Da kann man schon im Vorfeld oft sehen, ob das da ist. Haben die beteiligten Partner hier wirklich durchdacht, was wir vorhaben? Natürlich ist auch oft das persönliche, eigene Engagement entscheidend. Es gab oft Fälle, in denen die Projektakquise von anderen Personen durchgeführt wurde, als die Umsetzung. Und dann sozusagen, wenn wir nicht die Person hinter der Idee haben, wird es schon schwieriger, dass da auch eine erfolgreiche Umsetzung erfolgt. (CO5)

(Well, before one enters into any partnership or project, a common understanding, a joint vision must somehow exist. Often you can see in advance if that is given. Did the involved partners really think thoroughly about what we are planning to do? Of course, the personal, your own engagement is often decisive. There were often cases in which the project acquisition was undertaken by different people than for the implementation. And to say so, if I do not have people being commited to the idea, it gets more difficult to achieve a successful implementation.)

Also, die Erfolgsfaktoren waren ein gemeinsames Verständnis der Projektpartner, wie ich ein gutes Projekt organisiere, klare Verteilung von Verantwortung, Rechten und Pflichten. [...]. Das ist das Ausschlaggebende. (CO6)

(Well, the success factors were a common understanding between the project partners of how to organize a good project, clear assignment of responsibility, rights and duties. [...]. That matters.)

For this purpose, IO1 remarks that *"[...] regional specifics and priorities need to be taken into consideration for PPP initiatives, [...]"*. At the end, it matters that the awareness of CSFs in terms of project management and control is accompanied by the willingness to make amendments. CO7 stresses that this awareness *"[...] determines what you do because once you identify challenges or when you identify things that need to be changed, then you have to do something. You know, like for instance, you can say, "Okay, the platform they are using is outdated. We need to find a new platform." So, who finds a new platform? How much will it cost, and who pays for it because it was not budgeted or planned for whom?"*. On the other side, the project management and control structure do not necessarily change a lot if framed by clear rules of procedure. Just the way they are practiced might evolve over time:

> *Projektmanagement war ziemlich vordefiniert. Ich meine, wir haben klare Prozesse, wie wir ein Projekt zu managen haben, die [DCA Partner] auch. Und das war sozusagen die institutionelle [...] Grundlage. Ja, vielleicht habe ich dann mal einfach schnell eine E-Mail geschrieben und [...] nicht erst lange überlegt, [...], sondern [...] direkt [...]. [...] das ist das Ergebnis von Vertrauen und von der langjährigen Zusammenarbeit auf verschiedenen Ebenen. [...]. Es wurde pragmatischer oder direkter. (CO8)*
>
> (Project management was pretty much predefined. I mean, we have very clear processes for how we have to manage a project, the [DCA partner] as well. And that was basically the institutional [...] basis. Well, maybe I just wrote simply a quick email and [...] not thinking long time about it, [...], but [...] directly [...]. [...] that is the result of trust and of longstanding cooperation at different levels. [...]. It became more pragmatic or direct.)

> *Was wir jetzt feststellen können ist, dass [...] man bestimmte Themen einfach auf dem kleinen Dienstweg bespricht. [...] die Reaktionsgeschwindigkeit wurde vielleicht erhöht, um auf bestimmte Themen zu reagieren, gegenüber der Anfangszeit, wo sich alles noch einspielen musste. (CO9-1)*
>
> (What we notice is that [...] the communication for certain topics passes through inofficial channels. [...] the response time on certain topics might have increased, compared to the beginning, where everything still needed to get attuned to each other.)

In summary, the identified inherent/structural intrinsic CSFs coincide with numerous success factors gathered from the literature review and complement them. Still, it seems that in PPPs for development stronger emphasis is placed on success factors related to the institutional environment and to aspects of responsibility sharing.

Interview partner:			CO1	CO2	CO3	CO4	CO5	CO6	CO7	CO8	CO9	CO10	CO11	CO13	CO14	DC1	DC2	DC3	DC4	DC5	DC6	IO1	IO2	IO8	Total
Intrinsic factors - inherent/structural																									
Inherent/Structural		**Success factors**																							
	Definition	Definition of a common goal	x						x																2
		Clear delineation from commercial activities		x																					1
	Goal Alignment	Clear and realistic goals			x				x								x								3
		Sharing common goals					x								x					x					3
		Business case														x		x							2
		Clear expectations		x					x																2
		Commercial interest								x								x							2
		Consideration of mutual interests			x				x																2
	Management Control	(Strong) network(ing) and knowledge sharing								x	x	x	x		x					x				x	7
		Consideration and matching of complementary skills and competences			x					x	x	x		x										x	6
		Clear (project) control structure						x								x									2
		Adaptive system	x																						1
		Clear predictability		x																					1
		Clear risk management							x																1
		Continuity					x																		1
		Measurability of performance															x								1
		Priority setting																				x			1
		Sufficient resources			x																				1
	Responsibility Sharing	Clear and shared duties and responsibilities						x			x	x													3
		Taking of ownership																x		x					2
		Effective organizational structure				x																			1
	Strategy	Clear strategy														x	x								2
		Institutionalization and market positioning of the partnership																			x				1
		Shared vision					x																		1
	General	Common understanding					x	x	x																3
		Consideration of regional specifics and priorities																				x			1
		Managerial thinking											x												1
		Openness to accept new partners																			x				1
		Skilled staff			x																				1
		Obstacles																							
	Responsibility Sharing and Clear Mandate	Imprecision of the mandate/unclear focus																		x		x			2
		Duplication of responsibilities																				x			1
		Lack of clearly defined roles and responsibilities within an accountability framework																					x		1
		Unclear internal positioning																				x			1
	Institutional and other deficiencies	Absence of a regulatory framework in general																				x			1
		Lack of a regulatory and institutional framework for activities funded by extra-budgetary resources																				x			1
		Lack of a long-term strategy																				x			1
		Structural lack of control and commitment				x																			1
		Unsuitable PPP design and structure																	x						1

Table 62: Intrinsic CSFs – Inherent/Structural factors.

6.8.2.3 *Intrinsic Factors – Procedural CSFs*

Compared to the procedural CSFs surveyed by the literature review in Chapter 2.3.2.3, the interview partners place much less emphasis on cost and legal aspects which are generally relevant factors of successful PPP implementation. That is why no corresponding categories have been created for the procedural CSFs. In the literature, high importance was attributed to *competitive, efficient and transparent procurement processes*, a success factor which could not be identified in the empirical sample at all. This might be explained by the fact that infrastructure-like PPPs with the private sector in a supplier role formed the dominant PPP type in the past (Chapter 2.2.1.1.1). Most importance was attached to **governance and MC** aspects in terms of operational PPP implementation. Both public and private interviewees deem strong *performance orientation* including clear milestones and concrete result expectations pivotal for the success of partnerships while especially the private sector points to the necessity of *adequate alignment of diverging interests* and *continuous monitoring and evaluation* of PPP activities, based on ongoing and intense communication between all actors.

> *Clear milestones. What will success look like? What are the timelines? How much will it cost? What happens if it costs more than that? Regular meetings and updates, face-to-face at least once a year, every six months a tele-conference. You know, if there are changes, inform each other, adapt and change. (CO7)*

> *[...] the fact that [...] working with the private sector counterpart is even more challenging because [...] the private sector might read things in a different way, so it can have like a little bit raise the bar from the UN side in pushing a little bit harder. And this is something that, I believe, it is another aspect of success. (IO8)*

> *[...] aber es sind halt auch viele politische Interessen zugegen, und man muss sich da halt auch mit beschäftigen und investieren, Leute miteinzubinden, Kommunikation, gemeinsame Auftritte, die nicht schon mittelbar zur Zielerreichung führen, aber es ist einfach nötig, dass man hier ein bisschen über das Projektgeschehen hinausguckt. Und das sind so die Faktoren, die das Ganze zum Erfolg oder Misserfolg führen. (CO5)*
>
> ([...] but there are also many political interests present, and you have to deal with that and invest, involve people, communication, joint presentations, which do not directly contribute already to goal achievement, but it is simply necessary to look a little bit beyond the project activities. And these are the factors which are decisive for success or failure of the whole thing.)

> *Und so ein ganzes Programm kann nur funktionieren, wenn ein entsprechendes Monitoring da ist. Das heißt, die [technische Anlage] kann [operieren], aber wenn sie keiner kontrolliert, dann macht sie es morgen nicht mehr. Das heißt, auf Regierungsebene muss also entsprechend geschult sein und Ressourcen geschaffen werden, dass das Monitoring da ist. (CO10-1)*
>
> (And such a program can only work if corresponding monitoring is in place. This means, the [technical facility] can [operate], but if nobody controls it, it will not do that tomorrow anymore. Thus, the governmental level must be schooled accordingly, and resources for monitoring need to be provided.)

However, successful procedures are sometimes not continued if a partner who has taken a lead role before suddenly withdraws.

[El proyecto] [...] estaba diseñado muy en la manera como [DC5] trabaja, con planes de acción, con indicadores, con milestones, con una estrategia muy clara de qué se quiere lograr cada año, qué acciones van a hacer, o sea con un plan de trabajo anual. Y esto funcionó un poco mientras [DC5] estuvo allí. Después nosotros decidimos, cuando ya no formabamos parte más del comité coordinador, dejar esto a su manera. Entonces, ellos ya no tienen más un plan de trabajo anual. (DC5)

([The project] [...] was designed very much in the way like [DC5] works, with action plans, with indicators, with milestones, with a very clear strategy what to achieve every year, which actions to take, so with an annual work plan. And that worked somehow while [DC5] was there. After that, when we were not part of the coordinating committee anymore, we decided to leave it to them. So, they do not have an annual work plan anymore.)

Furthermore, CO1-1 and IO3 stress the importance of *effective project coordination and management*, based on clear operation plans and decision-making procedures. CO4 add that *good leadership* and *efficient reporting lines* are crucial to always reaching their target audience in a timely manner. In this regard, reporting does not only mean bottom-up, but also top-down, and also refers to the communication between operational and executive staff at their respective levels. In this vein, he underlines that the steering committee of his PPP deliberates on structural and procedural amendments once CSFs have been identified.

And then it's a question of the management of the partnership. If everything goes well, every condition is fulfilled, but it's badly managed, it doesn't deliver results either. (IO3)

Others like CO2 call for *compliance with standards and codes of conduct* or the actual *separation of defined duties and responsibilities*, such as CO9-2, while DC4 names *lack of financial predictability* in conjunction with *uncertainty* as serious obstacles for making the **actual processes** of operational PPP **implementation** successful:

Irgendwann nach einem halben Jahr haben dann auch die Partner vor Ort [...] gesagt: "Wir haben die Schnauze jetzt voll. Dürfen wir denn jetzt hier [PPP Aktivität ausführen] oder nicht? Dürfen wir denn eure Mittel verwenden oder nicht? Wir laufen hier rum, machen Marketing, versprechen allen [Begünstigten], [...]. Stimmt das denn jetzt noch oder nein?" Und wir mussten denen dann eben immer erzählen: "Ja, tut uns leid. Ist noch alles on hold [...]." (DC4)

(Some time after half a year, also the partners on the ground [...] said: "We are upset. Are we allowed to [executing PPP activity] or not? Are we allowed using your resources or not? We are running around here, make marketing, make promises to all [beneficiaries], [...]. Is this still true or not anymore?" And we always had to tell them: "Well, we apologize. Everything is still on hold, examination.")

In summary, the identified procedural intrinsic CSFs complement those from the literature review by shifting the focus to partnerships that are mostly governed in a hybrid manner because PPPs with the private sector in a supplier role tend to be more hierarchical with the public sector in the lead, from the partner selection at the beginning to the final assessment and evaluation at the end.

		Interview partner:	CO1	CO2	CO3	CO4	CO5	CO7	CO9	CO10	CO14	DC4	DC5	IO1	IO3	IO6	IO7	IO8	Total
Intrinsic factors - Procedural																			
		Success factors																	
Procedural	Governance and Management Control	Performance orientation (e.g. clear milestones and concrete results)						x					x			x		x	4
		Adequate alignment of diverging (political) interests			x		x				x								3
		Continuous monitoring and evaluation	x	x						x									3
		Effective coordination and management of project activities	x												x				2
		Following a joint communication strategy		x			x												2
		Regular and reasonable reporting of PPP activities		x		x													2
		Compliance with standards and codes of conduct		x															1
		Flexibility															x		1
		Regular meetings						x											1
		Relationship-building					x												1
	Planning and Implementation	Capacity to deliver and implement												x					1
		Conscientious planning and preparatory actions	x																1
		Finding the right implementation pace															x		1
		Separation of defined duties and responsibilities							x										1
		Obstacles																	
	Actual processes	Lack of effective partner and project selection												x					1
		Lack of financial predictability										x							1
		Lack of follow up of engagements												x					1
		Lack of formal regular and independent performance evaluation												x					1
		Lack of measurement for the 8th MDG on partnership												x					1
		Uncertainty										x							1

Table 63: Intrinsic CSFs – Procedural factors.

6.8.2.4 Intrinsic Factors – General CSFs

This chapter embraces CSFs of overarching nature which do not clearly fit into one of the previous clusters of intrinsic factors. Compared to those gathered from the extant literature, no finance-related success factors or obstacles were identified from the interview sample. In terms of PPP **implementation**, CO1-1 reminds us to continuously reflect our own actions and to be willing to learn and make necessary adjustments, while CO2 and CO5 recommend concentrating on core competencies and not losing sight of the adoption of the PPP activities in the field:

> *Es muss [...] die Offenheit bei Themen da sein, die auftauchen, die so vorher nicht adressiert wurden und als neue Herausforderung auf den Tisch kommen, dass man dann gemeinsam nach Lösungen sucht, ohne grundsätzlich den Projektrahmen zu sprengen. (CO1-1)*
>
> (There must be [...] openness towards topics that pop up, but have not been addressed before and are put as new challenge on the table, to look together for solutions, without going basically beyond the project scope.)

> *Die Adoption [Anmerkung: der Lösungen] im Feld war uns immer wichtig [...]. Wie viele Leute erreiche ich? Wird sie wirklich adoptiert, die Lösung? Wird sie gelebt? Ist der Mehrwert nachweisbar, und wird der von den Betroffenen gesehen? Dann, wenn ich das alles mit "ja" beantworten kann, habe ich einen Erfolg. Und dann habe ich auch eine Zukunftsaussicht. Und wenn das im Gegenteil eben nicht der Fall ist, [...], dann scheitert das Ganze halt. (CO5)*
>
> (The adoption [remark: of the solutions] in the field has always been important for us [...]. How many people do I reach? Is the solution really adopted? Is it practiced? Is the added value measurable, and do the beneficiaries see it? If I can answer all this by "yes", I am successful. And then I also have future prospects. And if this is otherwise not the case, [...], the whole thing fails.)

For IO7, all this **requires** a good portion of *appetite for risk,* and she recommends close cooperation with beneficiaries of PPP initiatives. Like CO14, she also places emphasis on mutual satisfaction in the sense of *shared value* as basis of successful partnerships for development because *unclear cost-benefit relationships* might be harmful. In case of PPPs with strong decentralized governance structure, *taking ownership by local stakeholders* and the *knowledge of micro challenges* on the ground were identified by IO1 as CSFs.

> *And a little bit of an appetite for risk [...] because in partnerships we tend sometimes to be a little bit too risk-averse and sometimes we don't get the best results because we are too risk-averse instead of risk-aware. [...] getting the buy-in from others, not only between [IO7] and the private sector entity. Especially, the community who [...] is working to improving and kind of co-designing the initiative. (IO7)*

> *[...] the mutual value that must be this shared value. It does not matter if it is economical value or something more intangible, but somehow both [remark: public and private side] should recognize that there is a value from this partnership. And it is not necessary to be very explicit, but everyone in the partnership should be feeling that he is winning something. [...]. So, [...] if the cost-benefit is not clear for the company nor for the ally, it will die, it will be finished. (CO14)*

From a more **general** perspective, CO7 and CO11 perceive good *reputation*, accompanied by *credibility* and *strong corporate brands*, as an important foundation of successful PPPs. Obstacles, which CO4, CO8 and DC2 hitherto faced, are insufficient *awareness-building* of the sense of urgency to resolve the different policy issues that are underlying their PPPs, but are also too much *staff turnover* and perceived *narrow-mindedness* in terms of performance orientation on side of third-party actors. DC2 adds that low awareness of the policy issue to be addressed, in conjunction with a relatively small number of members and little financial contributions, requires keeping the national government as client and main financier on board of the PPP:

> *Ja, eben, die enge Sicht z.B., wie ich vorher schon öfters erwähnte, die die NGOs haben. "Ich muss CO_2 einsparen, egal zu welchem Preis. Und wenn das Produkt für den Kunden in [Zielland], zum Beispiel, unbezahlbar wird." [...] aber Hauptsache es ist eingespart, und ich kann was ausrechnen. Das finde ich halt etwas zu kurz. (CO4)*
>
> (Well, the narrow view, for instance, which NGOs have as I mentioned a couple of times before already. "I have to save CO_2, no matter the price. And even if the products become unaffordable for the client in [target country], for instance." [...] but at least it is saved and I can calculate something. That is a bit too narrow-minded in my view.)

> *Und da ist es uns nicht gelungen, denen deutlich den Mehrwert aufzuzeigen, dass wir dann sagen: "Wir können nur als [Art der PPP], und wenn wir das alle gemeinsam machen, tatsächlich etwas bewirken. Ihr als Einzelunternehmen, [...] ihr werdet niemals in der Lage sein, mit [lokale öffentliche und private Stakeholder in verschiedenen Ländern] ausführlich in den Dialog zu gehen, was ihr denn eigentlich noch haben wollt." Und das ist uns bislang nicht gelungen. Sozusagen die, die eigentlich alle unsere Ziele erfüllen und das machen, zur Mitarbeit zu bewegen. (DC2)*
>
> (And there we did not manage to show them the value added, so that we then say: "We can only make an impact, as a [PPP type], if we do it all together. You as single companies, [...] you will be never in a position to enter into intense dialogue with [local public and private stakeholders in different countries]." This is something that we have not achieved yet. In other words, to prompt them to cooperate and to meet all our objectives.)

In summary, the identified general intrinsic CSFs complement rather than confirm those success factors from the literature review, placing more emphasis on success factors and obstacles, which affect the actual implementation, than on formal requirements and financing aspects.

		Interview partner:	CO1	CO2	CO4	CO5	CO7	CO8	CO11	CO14	DC2	IO1	IO7	Total
Intrinsic factors - general														
		Success factors												
General	Implementation	Ability of self-reflection	x											1
General	Implementation	Adoption in the field				x								1
General	Implementation	Awareness-building									x			1
General	Implementation	Buy-in from outside											x	1
General	Implementation	Continuous learning and making adjustments	x											1
General	Implementation	Focusing on core competencies		x										1
General	Implementation	Satisfaction towards the partnership											x	1
General	Implementation	Shared value								x				1
General	Requirement	Credibility and reputation					x		x					2
General	Requirement	Appetite for risk											x	1
General	Requirement	Knowledge of micro challenges										x		1
General	Requirement	Local ownership										x		1
General	Requirement	Strong brands							x					1
		Obstacles												
General	General	Adverse development impact											x	1
General	General	Dissatisfaction towards the partnership											x	1
General	General	Frequent staff turnover						x						1
General	General	Narrow-mindedness			x									1
General	General	Unclear cost-benefit relationship								x				1

Table 64: Intrinsic CSFs – General factors.

6.8.3 Potential for Improvement of Management Control

This chapter makes no reference to any specific extrinsic or intrinsic CSFs, but illuminates different aspects of MC where the interview partners identified potential for improvement. While some actors like CO6 and CO8 declare to be quite satisfied with the way MC is currently working in their respective PPPs, many others create linkages between risks, controls problems or CSFs and potential for improvement. This refers especially to characteristics of formal MC. Placing strong emphasis on performance orientation and sustainable outcomes, CO7 urges first of all **more careful selection of PPP projects** and partners, while DC5 underlines the **necessity of involving all relevant stakeholders** in a partnership. This might go hand in hand with a **more comprehensive local presence**, as stated by CO9. It applies in particular to PPPs which imply quite a lot of decentralized partnership work on the ground, but still keep a centralized governance structure:

> *I personally think that organizations should not blindly give money. [...]. They should not give money and say, "Go and do whatever you think is best." They should really partner with organizations and monitor the project and really be interested in the outcome [...] because if you are not interested in the outcome, it never goes right, for nobody. Because the partner also feels that you do not care, you just want to get rid of money. You know, it is for me really crucial that the corporate world gets involved. Do not throw money at problems. [...] try to find solutions that are long-term because sometimes you can even cause more harm than good. (CO7)*

In this vein, IO1 and IO7 call for a **more balanced risk management** which weighs risks up against opportunities in terms of PPP activities and intended outcomes as well as PPP strategies. However, CO12 perceives the risk-sharing between public and private partners as mostly unfair because in his view the public sector tries to unduly transfer risks to the private sector without paying properly for that. Thus, he recommends that the public sector simply **accepts certain risks being hard to mitigate**, but at least realizes that operational risks over the lifetime of PPP project cannot be fully outsourced to private actors without also delegating full authority and control to them. From his contractor perspective, he advocates moreover for a **budget and resource planning process based on the total cost of ownership approach**.

> *I mean from a financial aspect, quite a lot of the selection processes are set up. They are still set up based on a minimization of the initial cost. [...]. They [remark: the public clients] have given you the design, and it is set up, so what the biggest driver is the lowest initial cost. And then these guys built-in a bunch of access management fees and stuff that they are going to have to pay for, you know, they maintain [infrastructure focus] over a long period of time. If they actually based selections on total cost of ownership, you know, I think that would help do this. (CO12)*

Apart from a cost focus that is stronger related to the total cost of ownership of PPPs, there are some more interview partners who see potential for making the project management and processes more efficient in the sense that they occur more tool-based, are accompanied by measurable benchmarks, but still leave enough flexibility to react to unexpected events. In this regard, CO4 wishes to have a **higher level of control tightness** in his partnership and agrees with CO12's aspiration to **strengthen the influence of project management approaches and tools from the private sector**. Public and private actors like CO5, CO12 and IO1 recommend making **more concerted efforts for identifying commonalities** in terms of developing mechanisms and frameworks of coordination, evaluation, monitoring and reporting, which are compatible with the individual intraorganizational requirements and the respective institutional environments, in short, to **make MC more coherent and fit for purpose**:

> *Also, ich würde mir stark ein Projektmanagement [...] mit dementsprechenden Tools wünschen. [...]. Das heißt jetzt nicht, dass ich irgendwelche wöchentlichen*

Log-Listen ausgefüllt haben möchte, aber ein schönes Protokoll, usw. Eine ein bisschen akkuratere, disziplinierter Arbeitsweise würde ich mir hier wünschen, [...], das ist jetzt keine Kritik [...], das sind halt Sachen, die ich ein bisschen anders machen würde. [...] ich würde mir [...] effizienteres Projektmanagement wünschen und natürlich wir als Industrie, dass mehr auf uns gehört wird. [...]. Messbarere KPIs würde ich mir auch wünschen. Ich weiß, wir haben die KPIs, und natürlich ist eine Unterschrift "messbar". Aber Sie wissen ja auch, dass eine Unterschrift auf einer Absichtserklärung schnell getätigt ist. (CO4)

(Well, I would very much wish a project management [...] with corresponding tools. [...]. This does not mean that I want to have filled out log lists on a weekly basis, but an appropriate protocol, etc. A little more accurate and disciplined working procedure would be desirable, [...], this is no criticism [...], but these are simply things which I would do a bit differently. [...] I would wish a more efficient, effective project management and of course as industry partners that our voice is more often heard. [...]. Measurable KPIs would also be desirable. I know, we have these KPIs and a signature is indeed "measurable". But you also know that a signature is quickly placed on a letter of intent.)

Ja, also was oft vielleicht nicht immer ganz klar ist, ist die Ausgestaltung der Ergebnisse. Da gibt es vielleicht zwischen Organisationen und Partnern unterschiedliche Vorstellungen. Bei der UN sind es vielleicht eher diese Leitfäden, diese Frameworks, die da als Ergebnis rauskommen sollten. [...] als privatwirtschaftliches Unternehmen ist aber wirklich auch der kommerzielle Nutzen [...] entscheidend. Man muss als [CO5] vielleicht auch gewisse Rückschritte machen, was die Nutzung technischer Tools angeht, wenn ich dann mit reinen EZ-Organisationen zu tun habe versus ich habe mit [...] Partnern aus dem technischen Umfeld zu tun. (CO5)

(Well, what is often maybe not very clear is the design of the results. Maybe there exist different ideas between organizations and partners. For the UN guidelines, these frameworks might be the expected outcome. [...] as a private sector company the commercial benefit is actually [...] pivotal. In terms of the use of technical tools, we as [CO5] we may have to step back to a certain extent if working with pure development cooperation agencies versus dealing with [...] partners from the technical environment.)

Given its core value and worldwide visibility, the United Nations are priviledged and targeted partners for the business [...] activities and dual interests (both for good corporate citizenship and increased profit making through cause-marketing). At the same time, the private sector considers the UN's complex, time-consuming, legal processes and burdensome bureaucracy as a serious impediment to establishing sound partnerships. The "miracle formula" would be finding the right balance between the necessity to safeguard the UN independence, integrity and reputation/image, and the need to promote, through greater pragmatism and proper flexibility, successful partnerships that would advance the organization's universal goals without the UN loosing their soul. [...] establish a multi-agency and multi-disciplinary task force to revise thoroughly the current Guidelines for cooperation with the private sector, harmonize their application across the system (with an emphasis on strict selection criteria), to simplify and streamline legal requirements for partnerships, in accordance with the UN core values, principles and activities. On that basis, mechanisms/frameworks of coordination, reporting, evaluation and monitoring should be developed to ensure and improve effective management, transparency and accountability for the establishment of partnerships in a way that any affiliation of a company to the UNGC will not automatically be considered/perceived as sufficient guarantee or "green light" for entering into partnership with such participating company. (IO1)

However, DC4 remarks that the project partners' hands are often tied because the frameworks, guidelines or rules of procedure, which the PPP work of DCAs and IOs is based on, are determined by national laws or international resolutions which cannot be amended on a project basis. Thus, the institutional environments set limitations in this regard. Still, mechanisms of informal control show abundant potential for improvement. Much emphasis was placed on **more awareness-raising campaigns** and **improved communication of joint achievements and personal interests**, both internally and externally. In this vein, learning effects might be more easily reached in consecutive PPPs with previous partners, as stated by DC1:

Wo wir selber besser werden müssen, ist definitiv das ganze Thema Kommunikation und wie kommunizieren wir eigentlich unsere Erfolge. Und wie gelingt es uns, dann einfach auch noch viel mehr tatsächlich zu bewirken? [...]. Und dieses ganze Thema Kommunikation ist ganz sicher was, [...] wo ich mir auch von allen Mitgliedern und auch von meinem [Steuerungsorgan] eigentlich mehr erhoffe, dass die da selber deutlich mehr tätig werden und sich nicht immer nur auf uns verlassen. (DC2)

(What we definitely have to improve is the whole matter of communciation, and how we actually communicate our successes. And how do succeed in making even much more impact? [...]. And the whole issue of communication is definitely something, [...] where I actually expect also more engagement from all members, but also from my [governing body] and that they do not always rely on us alone.)

Ich denke, [...] ein Lerneffekt wäre, wenn man jetzt mit den gleichen Partnern zukünftige Vorhaben hätte. Ich glaube, den privaten Partnern wäre klarer, dass sie sich auch von Anfang an mehr einbringen müssen, also auch ihre Interessen mehr einbringen müssen. Also, nicht zu denken: "Ja, unsere Interessen, die kriegen wir dann schon noch unter." Sondern, dass die von Anfang an stärker sagen müssen: "So, hier haben wir ein Interesse. Und das wollen wir. Und das wollen wir nicht." (DC1)

(I think [...] a learning effect would also be to have projects with the same partners in the future. I believe that the private partners would be more aware of the need to contribute from the outset, also to advocate more for their interests. Just not thinking: "Well, our interests, we will still get them somehow included." But that they need to say much more strongly from the outset: "Well, here we have a stake. And that is what we want. And that is what we do not want.")

While DC6 advocates for **more formal incentives set by the public sector** to win more private companies for the matter of concern, CO14 and IO2 recommend pursuing **more trust-based control** and demonstrating **more mutual empathy** in this regard. IO6 concludes that this altogether might result in augmented taking of ownership:

Pues, yo creo que promover la adopción de esta tecnología en instituciones del sector público, pues también ayudaría a incrementar el número de proyectos que también pues se incrementara el número de instituciones que realizan las certificaciones en cuanto a [tecnología]. Y promover la formación de técnicos y de mano de obra especializada en el ámbito de la [enfoque del PPP]. Pues, [...] mejorar [...] el financiamiento a los proyectos de [enfoque del PPP]. (DC6)

(Well, I believe that promoting the adoption of this technology by institutions of the public sector would then also help to increase the number of projects, which then would also increase the number of institutions that realize the certifications regarding the [technology]. And promote the capacity-building of technicians and of specialized labor forces and in the area of the [PPP focus]. Then, [...] improve [...] the financing of the projects on [PPP focus].)

I wish I could have some more empathy from the different partners. [...] I do not know who should be more empathic with whom, if partner companies with international development agencies or international development agencies with companies. Sometimes I think we are pursuing different things. I mean, [CO14] is a company [...] pursuing to achieve more families, to increase the portfolio and the international agency seems like they are pursuing this, but not with multinational companies. (CO14)

In my opinion, the "trust-based" management control, which appears to be in place, leaves a lot of room for improvement. (IO2)

You need to have good programmes to sell that are relevant and attract the interest of companies and foundations. Because the programmes are coherent to what they do. So, they feel ownership. They should feel ownership, of course. So, this is what we will strategically try to kind of develop. And there should be partnerships that help [IO6], and this is what we will do, to consolidate the brand of [IO6]. (IO6)

Furthemore, CO12, DC3 and DC5 stress the importance of **knowledge management and information sharing** in the spirit of good and trustful cooperation for promoting effective MC that is unbiased by information asymmetries and distrust, which are both drivers of bounded rationality and potential opportunism. This applies in particular in the event of frequent staff turnover and little experience in public-private cooperation.

[...] sometimes there are certain teams that would look at [contractors] as they are going to be the leads and they did not give you very much information and you could not do much for them. Other teams brought us all the way in and [...] were the ones we actually helped the most and got success with changing specifications for the agencies, so the more they would bring us in, the better everything turned out for all members of the team. (CO12)

[...] dieses Aufarbeiten der Lessons-learned kommt tatsächlich immer zu kurz. Da ist vereinzelt dieses Wissen, also bei den einzelnen Personen, natürlich Projektwissen [...]. Aber da müsste man [...] diese Erfahrung nochmal besser oder noch mehr aufarbeiten, wirklich für die anderen Mitarbeiter und auch für die Partner [...], weil natürlich auch Leute wechseln [...] oder dann aus dem Unternehmen rausgehen [...]. Und dann geht alles verloren. (DC3)

([...] this processing of the lessons learned often comes off badly. Partially, there is this specific knowledge, with the single persons, project knowledge of course [...]. But actually one should [...] process these experiences much better or much more, for the other employees but also for the partners [...], because people also change [...] or then leave the company [...]. And then everything gets lost.)

> *[...] ellos no conocen los instrumentos de cooperación público-privada que maneja también la ONU, que manejamos nosotros. Entonces, me parece que lo primero es que ellos conozcan este tipo de proyectos y luego los inviten que participen y salgan beneficiados. Finalmente, es un beneficio para ellos. (DC5)*
> ([...] they do not know the instruments of public-private cooperation, which also the UN is applying, that we are applying. Hence, it seems to me that first they need to get to know this type of projects and then we invite them to participate and make profit. Finally, it is a benefit for them.)

In summary, both public and private actors see potential for improvement for formal MC, especially in the field of project management, performance measurement and monitoring. However, they recognize that changes or flexibilizations of MC practices face boundaries where the institutional environment has clearly determined what the rules of procedure are. This is why many of them advocate for replacing or complementing formal MC by informal control mechanisms if suitable and feasible. Finally, all the suggestions for improvement revolve around the question of how mutual understanding and the level of cooperation can be improved such that all the partners' interests are appropriately addressed and the common objectives of resolving the underlying policy issue are met.

7. Overall Assessment and Discussion

In the preceding chapter, material results from the empirical field study have been presented to answer the research questions RQ1, RQ2.1 and RQ2.2. Fundamentals of MC in IORs, JVs and PPPs and a combined approach composed of the ACI and the TCE served as conceptual and theoretical foundation of this study. Based on this framework, have been developed the interview guides (Chapter 5.2.2.1), analyzed the collected data, and structured the presentation of results (Chapter 5.3). In this vein, this chapter will first of all present a short wrap-up of central findings from Chapter 0, then discuss the theoretical contributions of the results, and conclude with the way and extent to which theoretical characteristics of the ACI and TCE manifest themselves in the different findings. However, despite its strong theoretical foundation, the present research work is very much practice-oriented. That is why in the next step conclusions on implications are not only drawn for MC research but special emphasis is placed on summarizing findings that might be considered by decision-makers in PPPs for development. This supports the answering of research question RQ3 by converting the research findings into practical recommendations. The findings presented in Chapter 6.8 are particularly relevant for that. Moreover, the limitations of this study in conjunction with the need and potential for future research in the underlying research field are shown. This doctoral work concludes with some final remarks and an outlook.

7.1 Summary of the Research Approach and Central Results

The starting point of the present study was the finding that there is abundant literature on MC in diverse kinds of infrastructure PPPs in different countries and regions in the world, but very little research work has been carried out that deals with aspects of MC in PPPs for development. The extant pertinent literature primarily adopted a business-ethical rather than a business case-oriented perspective and considered institutional framework conditions only to a limited extent. The literature review revealed the dominance of new institutional theories in serving as theoretical framework for especially empirical studies on PPPs, JVs or IORs/IFRs. Finally, a combined framework composed of ACI and TCE was found to be suitable for building the theoretical basis of the present study. The theoretical assumptions and characteristics of the ACI and the TCE influenced the formulation of the research questions and served as reference framework for designing and structuring the interview guides, the results analysis and the subsequent discussion in Chapter 7.3. Such a procedure is recommended by Bogner et al. (2014, p. 33).

The research results rely upon data from a qualitative field study. Data have been collected through 28 interviews with experts from companies, IOs and DCAs as part of a multinational sample. The results analysis as such was a multi-stage and computer-assisted process where verbatim transcription of tape recordings, the creation of coding categories and finally the coding of textual data formed time-consuming but imperative steps. A due quality assessment demonstrated reliability and validity of the data and, thus, of the chosen research approach. A brief summary of central results is given in the following paragraphs that are clustered by the research questions.

T. S. Konrad, *Management Control in Public-Private Partnerships*,
Schriften zu Wirtschaftsprüfung, Steuerlehre und Controlling,
https://doi.org/10.1007/978-3-658-22868-2_7

RQ1: What are key characteristics of PPPs between DCAs/IOs and the private sector to be taken into account by management control?

Before analyzing the design of MC in PPPs for development and inherent CSFs, a stocktaking of the basic characteristics and the general partnership setting was necessary. The interview results reflect the enormous diversity of the analyzed PPPs that all consist of private sector firms and IOs and/or DCAs. Moreover, they often involve some more stakeholders, such as academic institutions, NGOs or philanthropic foundations, and address a broad range of policy issues related to sustainable development. Neither a clear qualification profile for PPP work nor a clear job profile could be identified, so that the concrete actors often carry out operational and managerial tasks alike. Most of the PPPs for development correspond to one of the PPP types that rely on a hybrid governance structure. The design of the legal arrangements tends to be adjusted to the governance level and underlines the long-term orientation of most PPPs. These legal arrangements are kept as formal as necessary, and as flexible as possible. The level of decentralization turned out to be high in many partnerships, especially on the public side where IOs and DCAs maintain global organizational structures including permanent local staff.

The motivation for creating PPPs originates predominantly from business-related extrinsic factors, such as the complementation of resources, lobbying, market development, polishing of image and reputation, reduction of environmental impact, or securing of resources. While companies link these factors to their main motivation for doing and improving core business, DCAs and IOs set up PPPs with the aim to fulfill mandates which governments impose on them. Obviously, individual motivations imply individual objectives that all partners involved pursue through their engagement. However, the individual objectives must be compatible with the overall objectives and targets of PPPs. That is why public and private actors generally link their objectives to clear expectations of PPPs, notably in terms of the achievement of common goals and the existence of common interests, clear communication of expectations and predictability, mutual benefit, as well as professional competences and commitment.

The private sector has increasingly recognized the strategic nature of PPPs for development for consolidating the core business activities, and therefore private sector firms do not only contribute skills and competences but also financial and in-kind resources to joint partnerships with international governmental actors. What matters is less the kind and amount of resources that every party puts in, but much more important is the complementarity of sufficient resources to facilitate the achievement of objectives. Nevertheless, the financial expenses related to the resource contributions are generally not only fairly shared between the different partners involved but also adjusted to the benefits and risks that are associated with a certain PPP. Regarding the identified extrinsic and intrinsic risks, public actors pointed to the danger of reputational damage emanating from some industries while private actors bemoaned frequent staff turnovers and bureaucracy in the public sector. Both sides perceive diverse kinds of political risks which must be accepted to some extent, and imply that PPPs for development generally require some risk appetite by all partners.

RQ2.1: How is management control in PPPs between DCAs/IOs and the private sector designed?

PPPs for development evolve from initiatives that are equally taken by both public and private sectors through different channels. Regardless of the existence or absence of any previous partnership experience, and no matter what the PPP type is, both public and private actors usually undertake diligent, multi-stage partner selection procedures including risk assessment and apply various hard and soft selection criteria. The same level of due diligence was observed for resource planning and approval processes. The PPP implementation generally splits up into an exploratory and an execution section, for which subordinated project phases have been identified. However, this structure reflects a conceptual pattern rather than a universally applicable phase model because, in practice, project phases are often hard to clearly delineate from each other. The resource endowment of PPPs for development relies on either joint or separate funding, provided by equal or diverging shares from public and private actors, while the magnitude of necessary financing is geared to the main cost factors, comprising especially staff and production. Most interview partners emphasized that any kind of partnership requires a sustainable self-financing mechanism and should be based on a business case at the best.

Four exemplary governance structure designs were analyzed in depth, namely civic association & integrated partnership, multilateral alliance, and two forms of strategic alliances. Together they represent the governance structure designs of most partnerships that are included in the sample and have in common that they are primarily governed in a hybrid manner with slight tendency to some hierarchies. The level of cooperation among partners is mostly high, and interactions between them are mainly of cooperative nature although some egoistic-rational behavior comes into play from time to time. The mix of formal and informal control mechanisms is used for compiling each PPP individually and is attuned to making the chosen governance structure work efficiently. In general, it seems that PPP partners try to apply as much formal control as necessary, but as little as possible. That is why the importance of informal social and control mechanisms was stressed by the vast majority of the interview partners. A well-balanced set of MC mechanisms including clear responsibility sharing enables actors to master the often complex PPP work and to cope with environmental factors, such as intercultural and organizational influences, but also control challenges and problems. Sometimes, the latter remain insurmountable and lead to early termination or ultimate failure of a partnership, for instance in the event of corruptive or fraudulent activities by one partner. Nevertheless, these cases seem to happen rarely because many efforts are put into diligent partner selection on the one hand, and on governance structures and control mechanisms that promote democratic decison-making and effectively prevent opportunistic behavior on the other hand. The institutional environment defines the cornerstones of the arena of interaction of PPPs for development. Indeed, PPPs often aim to reach changes and shiftings of the institutional environment, particularly those partnerships which tackle issues of norm- and standard-setting in policy areas, such as energy or health. Still, in the end, the institutional constraints often have to be taken for granted, particularly the informal ones. These constraints must be considered for the design of the governance structure and MC.

7.2 Implications for Practitioners

This chapter summarizes implications for practitioners on the basis of the findings gathered from the empirical results and briefly depicts the feedback obtained from the interviewees with respect to the communicative validation.

7.2.1 Recommendations for Management Control Design in PPPs for Development

The results from Chapter 6.8 serve as source of input for recommendations for improving the MC design in existing and future PPPs for development. Therefore, these results form the basis for discussion of the research questions RQ2.2 and RQ3.

RQ2.2: What are critical success factors (CSFs) of PPPs between DCAs/IOs and the private sector?

RQ3: How should management control in PPPs between DCAs/IOs and the private sector be designed in order to promote successful implementation and to avert adverse influences?

First of all, Figure 54 gives an overview of all CSFs that were mentioned at least three times by any of the three groups of interview partners who often linked these factors to suggestions for improvement of MC in their respective PPPs.

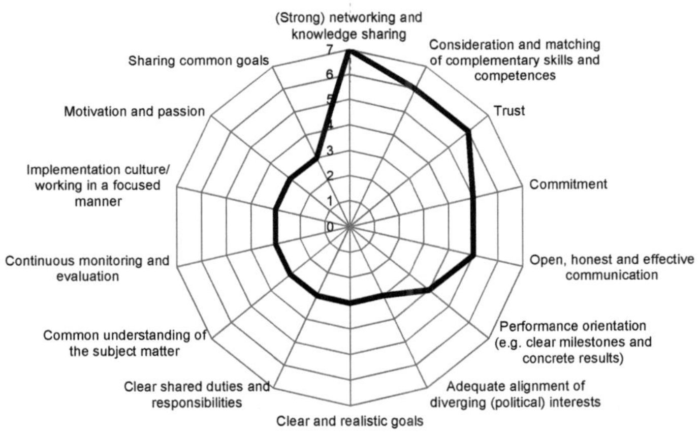

Figure 54: Most frequently mentioned critical success factors.

In addition, the identified risks, the institutional environment and control problems should be considered for the design of the governance structure and MC because the latter often proved to be CSFs with a negative sign. However, not all CSFs become important at the same time. Deliberations on the governance structure to choose, and on the level of MC to apply, typically do not start before the initiation phase where cost estimations are made and drafts of the contractual arrangements are prepared. In this sense, Figure 55 depicts the linkage of the most frequently mentioned CSFs to phase-oriented governance and control activities.

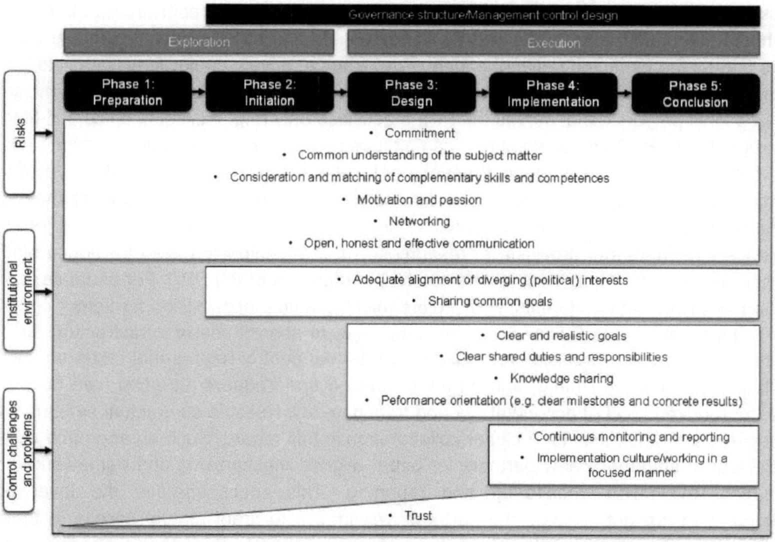

Figure 55: Phase-oriented consideration of critical success factors for governance structure and management control design.

It is imperative that all actors of a PPP demonstrate a continuously high level of **commitment** which is linked to the ability and willingness to endure difficult situations and to overcome control challenges and problems jointly. Moreover, the demonstration of commitment helps to prevent control problems, such as misunderstandings or misaligned expectations, goals and interests, and can therefore avert concerns of opportunistic behavior. Strong commitment is characteristic of effective social control, but it does not work without a high level of **open and honest communication** using the most suitable communication channels efficiently. Although internal hierarchies and time-consuming internal decision-making processes sometimes require more formal communication and coordination, the decision-making authority should be delegated such that at operational level informal communication can largely replace formal communication processes. In the implementation phase at the latest, operational actors must be allowed to directly contact their counterparts from the other partners instead of having to formally route their request through the executive management level. This applies particularly for decentralized governance structures where the local staff has the best knowledge of the local conditions and sometimes has to make decisions shortly. A good portion of intrinsic **motivation and passion** shown by the concrete actors involved lends additional credence to the demonstrated commitment. It is imperative that all partners build a **common understanding** of the policy issue to be addressed, and of what PPP work means to them, in order to prevent, amongst others, the aforementioned control problems which also take effect in the event of insufficient commitment. Due to the fact that unanticipated difficulties or changing environmental conditions may require a PPP's reorientation, this common understanding must be kept up-to-date throughout the PPP's lifetime. In the context of PPPs for development, **networking** is closely related to the matching of **complementary skills and competences**. Thus, any public or private organization that wants to address a certain policy issue and/or invest in sustainable business opportunities through a PPP should select partner/s by the degree of compatible and complementary skills and resources and by the expected network effects. For instance, private sector firms with little geographical decentralization of their business activities, hesitating to make significant investments in a local presence that serves the PPP's activities only (e.g. individual office, full-time staff designated to PPP implementation), can increase their outreach by partnering with IOs or DCAs that maintain a large global presence of local and regional offices. In the light of a recommended budget and resource planning process relying more on the principle of sharing the total costs of ownership, PPP actors may seek a stronger integration of their internal governance structures and provision of resources at the decentralized level to reduce staff and other overhead costs, at least for the contractual duration of the PPP. For example, despite the risk of conflict of interests, PPP actors might examine possibilities for tighter cooperation in terms of joint staff financing, staff exchange, or shared use of infrastructure such as office and production facilities, vehicles. A tight formal control regime that relies on joint rather than individual monitoring, and on more detailed and frequent reporting, can help to ensure the required level of accountability and transparency. Reliable contractual safeguarding measures form the basis for a closer collaboration in this regard. Such an approach supports the call of some interview partners for better aligned mechanisms and frameworks of coordination, evaluation, monitoring and reporting. This could improve the level of **knowledge sharing** but requires the partners' willingness to grant mutual access to their respective networks. Hence, **networking** is inseparably linked to **knowledge sharing** and viceversa, but the latter tends to effectively take place not before contract conclusion because of confidentiality and intellectual property concerns, thus not until the beginning of the design phase. In this regard, PPP actors should decide as early as possible if and how the PPP could continue after its official conclusion. This means that they have to develop a vision for the long-term existence of their partnership. That refers amongst others to legal questions of property rights and ownership and applies in particular to situations where a partnership proved to be economically viable with an underlying sustainable business case and faces limited extrinsic risks. In this scenario, the public sector can start to disengage operationally while the involved private sector firms have to invest in local branches and extend their business activities.

Before a PPP can turn out to be successful a few more CSFs should be considered. Already in the first consultations and during the negotiations in the initiation phase much emphasis should be placed on the **alignment of diverging interests**. Though partners may pursue their individual interests, these must not oppose the overall objectives of the partnership and must be honestly communicated to the partners for enabling an alignment if necessary. Reluctance to do this was noted on the private sector side, but the empirical results revealed that the public sector generally appreciates this frankness. The public sector is mostly also interested in creating a business case because otherwise a PPP rarely goes beyond being a subsidized institution.

In the next phase, the harmonized overall goals and interests should be converted into **clear and realistic measurable objectives** that are embraced by a strong **performance orientation** which relies on clear milestones and concrete expected results. These CSFs must manifest themselves in design activities like the definition of benchmarks or work plans, and also in the resource allocation to formal control measures, such as **monitoring** and **reporting**. From the experiences of the interview partners, it can be concluded that the potential for improvement lies in more cost-efficient and target-oriented monitoring and reporting which could be reached by e.g. increasing the magnitude of corresponding activities, removing duplicated activites, or abandoning activities that do not produce sufficient, or qualitatively satisfying, information for control and decision-making. The real level of commitment, motivation and performance orientation becomes apparent as of the implementation phase because these three factors are pivotal for making effective another CSF, namely the creation of an **implementation culture** where all partners involved act in concert for achieving the common objectives.

Several interview partners called for more trust-based control, and, indeed, **trust** seems to be the success factor which more than any other CSF is of cross-cutting nature. Trustful relationships tend to be built over time and cannot be assumed as given from the beginning, unless the same actors know each other from previous joint engagements already. Nevertheless, a certain leap of faith that matures to real trust should be granted by all partners as of phase one for preparing the interpersonal basis for the first joint activities in the initiation and design phase. In general, the ability and willingness to trust and to build trust is pivotal across all phases, but at the latest when phase four begins, a good level of trust should have been reached for enabling successful PPP implementation. Given the cross-cutting and likewise fragile nature of trust, which is maybe even the most central social control mechanism, PPP actors should act in all phases in the spirit of the other identified CSFs because their achievement tends to strongly contribute to building and keeping a good level of trust.

In summary, the CSFs and the potential for improving MC, which were mentioned in Chapter 6.8, hold true for PPPs to varying extents because, ultimately, all partnerships and their actors are individual entities. Still, their phase-oriented consideration may contribute to designing the governance structure and MC for making a PPP for development a success.

7.2.2 Results from the Communicative Validation

The time-consuming and selective acquisition phase in conjunction with the serious interest of most interview partners in the subject matter as such, and in the empirical results in particular, is also manifested in the feedback obtained on the communicative validation presentation. This presentation included central results from the interviews and therefore provides answers to the RQ1, RQ2.1 and RQ2.2. The overall feedback underpins the practical value added of the empirical results which were basically understandable and did not require further explanation.

> *He leído los resultados que me has compartido, éstos me parecen muy interesantes y totalmente acordes con las diferentes realidades de los proyectos PPP. Por mi parte, no tendrían ninguna aclaración u observación. (DC5)*
>
> (I read the results that you shared with me, they appear very interesting to me and totally in accordance with the different realities of the PPP projects. From my side, there would not be any need for clarification.)

Moreover, one interviewee asked for the possibility to present some of the results on occasion of an annual strategy meeting that is attended by all partners involved in the concerned PPP:

> *Wir haben [...] einen Strategiedialog, wie es mit dem [Name der PPP] weitergehen soll, und ich könnte mir vorstellen, dass es ganz spannend wäre, einige Ihrer Ergebnisse [...] einmal zu präsentieren, damit wir auch von anderen lernen. (DC1)*
>
> (We are having [...] a strategy dialogue on how to continue with the [PPP name] and I could imagine that it would be quite interesting [...] once to present some of your results so that we can also learn from others.)

In summary, these comments underline the commonly observed willingness among the interview partners to learn from other partnerships.

7.3 Conclusions on Theoretical Characteristics of ACI and TCE

The intergrated theoretical framework composed of ACI and TCE forms the backbone of the whole study and therefore requires a comparison of the ACI's and TCE's theoretical assumptions with the empirical results. As both Broweleit (2014) and Endenich (2012) noted on the basis of review studies from Ferreira and Merchant (1992) and Scapens and Bromwich (2010, p. 280 f.), the accounting community attaches growing attention to theory-based discussion of results in empirical studies for assessing the scientific relevance of empirical results. That is why the following two subchapters discuss the way and extent to which the results reflect theoretical characteristics of the ACI and TCE.

7.3.1 Manifestation of ACI-related Characteristics

In line with Figure 20 in Chapter 4.1, this chapter focuses on the ACI's major elements, namely **actor constellations/orientations**, **modes of interaction**, and **institutional setting**. As described by Mayntz and Scharpf (1995, p. 44) at the conceptual level, this study shows that actors from private sector, IOs and DCAs come together in diverse constellations, as manifested in the form of different PPP types and contractual arrangements (Chapters 6.1.5.2 and 6.1.5.3), to resolve public policy issues of joint interest which they otherwise would not be able to address. This has been theorized by March and Olsen (1989, p. 43) and Scharpf (1997, p. 69) and is underlined by the quotes from CO3 and IO5 in Chapter 6.2.1.1. The results in Chapters 6.2.2.2 and 6.2.5 support the idea of March and Olsen and Scharpf that close collaboration and complementarity are crucial in PPPs while rivalries and diverging interests and objectives counteract common goals, implying that high levels of mutual respect and confidence in each other's willingness to reach these goals are imperative. For this reason, the interview partners were asked to rate the overall level of cooperation of the **actor constellations** in their respective PPP by making use of the actor orientation scale according to Mayntz and Scharpf (1995, p. 57). In most of the analyzed PPPs, the involved actors demonstrated a cooperative attitude and serious conflicts hitherto barely arose. Thus, in accordance with the definition given by Scharpf (1997, p. 72), the level of potential conflict is low in the actor constellations chosen by the considered PPPs for development.

Regarding the **modes of interaction**, unilateralism can be ruled out as an applicable institutional arrangement for PPPs for development. Due to their international and multi-stakeholder character, these PPPs are influenced by diverse institutional environments, and the fact that partners usually rely on cooperative behavior and on individual skills and competences makes *unilateral actions* impossible to work (Table 23 in Chapter 4.3.2). One infrastructure PPP with a related market-based governance structure is included in the sample where the public partner makes decisions irrespective of the needs and concerns of the private one. The private sector interviewee said that this kind of unilateral action made a long-term cooperation impossible in the end (see quotation from CO12 in Chapter 6.5.2.2.1). By contrast, the existence of the three remaining modes of interaction, according to Scharpf (1997, p. 93), has been observed in the sample. *Majoritarian voting* is quite common, whether forming the democratic basis of regular decision-making processes in especially large membership-based PPPs, or serving for conflict management (Chapters 6.5.2.1 and 6.6.2.3). And indeed, the governance structures of all PPPs are based on *negotiated agreements*, which can either be tight or rather loose, depending on the PPP type. However, the negotiation process is not confined to the initial conclusion of PPP contracts, but is a form of interaction that happens continuously because contracts can hardly address any contigencies which might occur during PPP implementation. Thus, through a partnership's governing bodies, the partners make decisions that result from upstream or parallel negotiations because individual diverging interests and objectives might be concerned and need to be aligned (Table 23 in Chapter 4.3.2). Nevertheless, *hierarchical direction* is not uncommon either. The extent and possibility of majoritarian voting and negotiation power at operational level largely depend on the delegation of authority by the superiors of each partnering organization. Hierarchical direction as phenomenon of hierarchic governance structures results from power imbalance, where for instance the IO partner sets the arena of interaction and transaction (Chapter 4.3.1), or one or more partners assume more responsibility and take more ownership than others and, in return, claim more dominant control rights (Chapter 6.5.2.2.1). Thus, hierarchical direction is consciously accepted by the subordinated partners and does not seem to happen unexpectedly.

Both definition approaches of **institution** or **institutional setting** take effect in the case of the analyzed PPPs for development (Chapter 4.1.5). However, the definition by North (2005, p.22) considering the institutional environment as a set of formal and informal rules, norms and boundaries proves to be more pertinent to the PPPs for development, not least because PPPs are not only influenced by institutional framework conditions, but many of them intend to change these in their favour (e.g. PPPs dealing with the setting of energy, health or technology standards). Figure 56 gives a schematic view of the linkages which the sample's PPPs revealed to maintain with institutional settings.

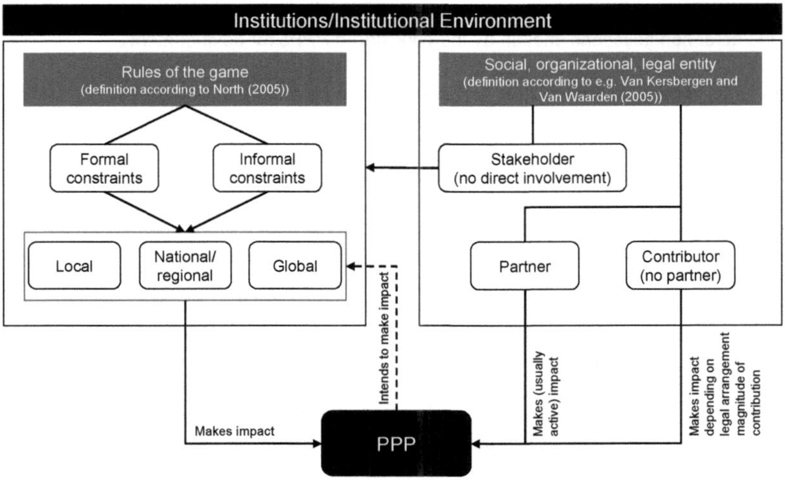

Figure 56: Approaches to defining and understanding institutions and the institutional environment.

Indeed, all partners, whether private sector, IO or DCA, represent some kind of organizational and legal entity and usually make an active impact on the PPP they are involved in. The individual influence varies according to the established governance structure which in most cases was of hybrid or hierarchical nature. In hybrid ones, all partners have more or less the same level of influence, while hierarchical ones allow a few partners to exercise more power than, or over, others. Nevertheless, the definition of *institutions* in its narrow sense, according to Van Kersbergen and Van Waarden (2005), refers mostly to stakeholders, such as local, national or international governmental actors, who are either not directly involved in a PPP or make contributions but do not actively commit to a partnership. The latter is typical of those partnerships where national governments charge DCAs to seek the creation and implementation of PPPs in their political interest. Thus, these national governments commonly provide funding to the PPP, but do not act as active partners (Chapter 6.4.1). However, they often have a strong say because they link their funding to concrete activities and make non-negotiable demands for the design of the PPP contract. In this regard, Williamson's differentiation between a macroanalytic and a microanalytic perspective in terms of the definition of institutions becomes blurred (Chapter 4.1.4). Moreover, his approach to taking an institutional environment as exogenously given cannot be fully supported with respect to the analyzed PPPs for development. Indeed, many interview partners acknowledged that the *rules of the game* being subject to formal and informal institutional constraints are often invariable and therefore set boundaries to PPP implementation. This applies in particular to informal constraints, such as the level of human development or the political stability in countries of PPP operations, which are therefore accepted as exogenously given (Chapter 6.7.2.2). By contrast, PPPs in the form of a multilateral or strategic alliance often aim to harmonize different national norms and standards across national borders (e.g. energy, health), or launch a new technology in cooperation with local actors depending on approval by the target country's governmental authorities. In both cases, the PPP actors try to stimulate a change of the institutional environment in favour of reaching the partnership's objectives. To this end, a reciprocal relationship between PPP and institutional environment is created. The power balance in this reciprocal relationship seems to rely on the political and economic strengths of the concrete PPP partners on one side and on the government's active and passive support and impediment to the PPP implementation on the other side (Chapters 6.7.3.1 and 6.7.3.2). This is why many private sector interviewees frankly declared their special motivation in partnering with DCAs and IOs through the global network of good contacts which the latter maintain with diverse governmental authorities in national states, and through their facilitator role. Hence, the more PPP actors exert influence on norms, rules and regulations at local, regional, or global level, the more they evolve to institutions in the sense of North (2005). This leads to the conclusion that neither the institutional setting nor the actors' personal expectations, perceptions and preferences with respect to politics remain necessarily static over the course of the PPP implementation period (Chapter 4.1.4). Furthermore, the idea that an institutional environment cannot finally determine the actors' concrete actions or outcomes of interaction is supported by the empirical findings on PPPs for development. On the one side, institutional constraints often leave enough flexibility to the design of operational PPP implementation, despite the difficulties they are causing for PPP actors. On the other side, outcomes of PPP activities largely rely on suitable and effective governance structures going along with commitment of partners who trust each other and support joint objectives without demonstrating opportunistic behavior. With respect to Scharpf's proposition of four clusters of institutional settings, the results reflect all settings apart from *anarchic minimal institutions*, and let assume that one mode of interaction can be embedded in one or more institutional settings (cf. Scharpf (1997), p. 46 f.). For instance, the hybrid governance structure of multilateral and strategic alliances aiming to change global norms and standards usually relies on strong *joint-decision systems* including annual and/or intra-year *assemblies* (Table 23 in Chapter 4.3.2). Being part of those alliances often means becoming member by acceptance of membership conditions (e.g. regular participation, payment of membership fee), and, in return, public and private members obtain access to a large *network* of stakeholders in their policy area or industry of interest. Thus, a hybrid governance structure on the one side, and a clear mandate by member states conferred to the partnering IOs on the other side, characterize institutional settings that are both hierarchical and non-hierarchical at the same time. This example shows that a PPP's internal governance structure is closely related to the institutional environment, and vice versa, and the theoretical characteristics of the ACI help to explain this linkage. Nevertheless, this example also demonstrates that one PPP type, or one type of governance structure, does not necessarily follow one specific mode of interaction or fit into one specific institutional setting. This awareness supports the view of Richardson and Kilfoyle (2009) who argue that alliances and networks being governed in a hybrid manner could still adopt multiple forms of cooperation over the course of their duration (Chapter 4.3.2).

7.3.2 Manifestation of TCE-related Theoretical Assumptions

This chapter addresses the question of how TCE-related assumptions manifest themselves in the empirical results of this study. With this focus in mind, neither the general existence of TC in PPPs will be questioned, nor the existence of a relationship between TC and MC will be discussed. These aspects were studied by theorists, such as Ronald Coase and Oliver Williamson, and were confirmed by numerous empirical studies on MC in PPPs, JVs, and IORs in the past (Chapters 2.2.1.2, 4.2.1 and 4.2.2). The empirical results have shown that all PPPs for development are based on the exchange and merger of different kinds of resources, and in this regard they support the assumption put forward by VdM and Vosselman (2000) and Vosselman (2002) that all transactional relationships contain some MC mechanisms (Chapter 4.2.2). Sources and drivers of TC are manifold and vary by type and governance structure of each PPP; they are strongly linked to the major cost factors identified for PPPs for development, and have been addressed throughout the results section (Chapter 6.4.4.1). With respect to the relationship between TC and MC, Dekker (2004), Nicholson (2006) and others argue that control challenges and problems are main drivers of TC that require suitable mixtures of formal and informal controls to counteract them and to reduce TC (Chapter 4.2.2). The entire Chapter 6.6 is dedicated to giving an overview of formal and informal MC instruments being applied in the PPPs on scope. Chapters 6.6.4.1 and 6.6.4.5 describe what type of control challenges and problems the interview partners have hitherto faced and what countermeasures they have taken. Moreover, all interview partners demonstrated much awareness of cost factors and underscored the need to generate as much value for money as possible. Governance structure and MC instruments were selected and customized for each PPP individually. Hence, it can be concluded that they all aim to decrease TC in their respective PPPs as far as possible, seeking a cost-efficient mix of effective formal and informal control mechanisms. Chapters 6.5.2.2 and 6.5.2.3 show which control types and which formal and informal control mechanisms have been chosen and observed in which situations. The specific formal and informal control instruments are presented in Chapters 6.6.1 and 6.6.2. Therefore, the need for a sound analysis of the relationship between TC and MC, as requested by Cäker and Siverbo (2011), Dekker (2004), Langfield-Smith (2008), Marques et al. (2011), and Vosselman and VdM (2009), has been addressed in Chapter 4.2.2. Furthermore, in the same chapter Covaleski et al. (2003) and Speklé (2001) point to different kinds of risks, such as opportunistic behavior, while Anderson and Dekker (2005) and Chalos and O'Connor (2005) consider TC as the result of misaligned transaction characteristics and the contract structure. That is why they advocate for the implementation of contractual controls amongst other measures. Their concerns have been addressed in a results overview of control measures against extrinsic and intrinsic risks taken in PPPs for development, as well as by analyzing contractually formalized control practices and safeguardings (Chapters 6.6.3 and 6.6.4.5.2). A detailed discussion of how bounded rationality, opportunism, and other transaction characteristics manifest themselves in the empirical results is presented in the next chapter. It is followed by a brief discussion of governance characteristics of TCE.

7.3.2.1 Behavioral and Transaction Characteristics

The results show that bounded rationality and opportunism, but also uncertainty (including complexity), asset specificity, and frequency are critical issues in PPPs for development that are interlinked and need to be addressed. Mitigating them is of major relevance for the design of governance structures and the selection of a set of formal and informal control mechanisms (Figure 57).

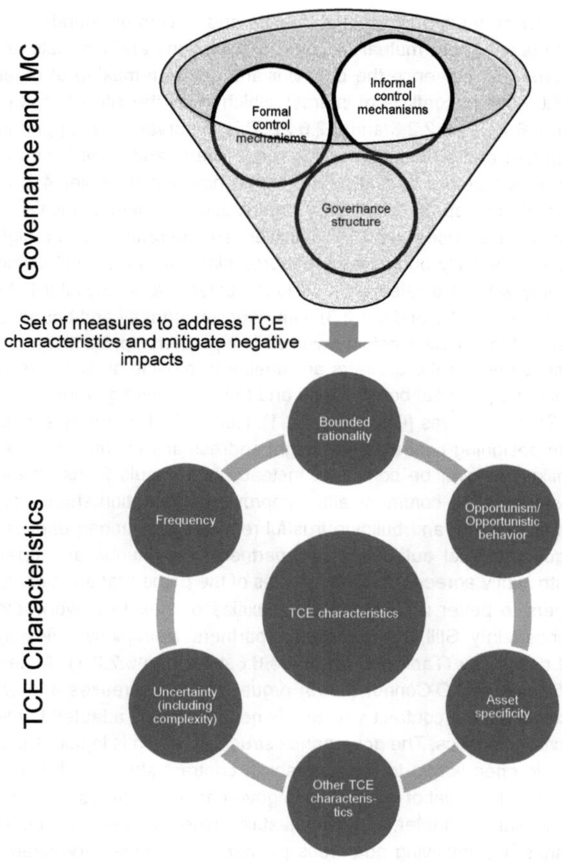

Figure 57: Interconnections between governance and MC and TCE characteristics.

One major concern of the **bounded rationality** assumption is the incompleteness of contracts resulting from the lack of availability of all pertinent information. This issue was definitely observed in the sample, emanating from the contractual arrangements. **Uncertainty** about how to do PPP work and the underestimation of its **complexity** were quoted as control problems by several interview partners (Table 58 in Chapter 6.6.4.5.1). Except for supply contracts, PPP stakeholders do not even endeavour to reach complete contracts, whether they are rather loose or tight. In line with observations made by Vosselman (2002) and Williamson (1987), the results allow to conclude that PPP stakeholders are aware of the incompleteness and imperfection of information. Therefore, they act as rationally as possible, such that they oppose complexity and uncertainty to a high level of flexibility towards the inclusion of new information in decision-making once it is available, no matter what the underlying type of contract might be (Chapters 4.2.3 and 6.1.5.3.2).

The responses from the interview partners suggest that causes and drivers of bounded rationality are, for instance, uncertainty about mutual outcome expectations and interests, as well as about incentive-structures that influence the behavior and decision-making of other partners. This uncertainty might result in conflicts of interest, which imply the intrinsic risk of opportunistic behavior (Chapters 6.2.2.2, 6.2.2.3 and 6.2.6.2). This observation is supported by experiences from Dekker (2004) and further accounting researchers, and underlines the issue that bounded rationality exists before and after contract conclusion (Chapter 4.2.3). Furthermore, many interview partners reported that their organizations, whether private or public, often had limited previous experiences with PPP activities, and therefore faced a high level of uncertainty which made especially budget and resource planning quite challenging for them. That is why uncertainty was also rated as a serious obstacle to successful PPP implementation (Chapters 6.1.3, 6.4.2, 6.4.3 and 6.8.2.3). However, uncertainty and bounded rationality are not only confined to the concrete actors involved in a partnership, but they turn even into formal institutional constraints if the partners are unable to provide sufficient relevant information and to convince the potential beneficiaries and the concerned governmental authorities of supporting the PPP's objectives (Chapter 6.7.2.1). Hence, PPP partners should not dedicate too much effort to designing contracts that might address any eventualities because these contracts are unlikely to ever be complete. Instead, they should focus on the reduction of uncertainty by fostering clear communication, improving information sharing towards internal and external stakeholders, and building trustful relationships among partners and between beneficiaries, governmental authorities and partners. Continuous and open discussions, in combination with jointly agreed and binding rules of the game that are clear to everybody, enable PPP partners to better understand complexities of their PPP work and therefore reduce the level of uncertainty. Still, this requires the partners‘ willingness to flexibly adjust the PPP to changes, if necessary (Table 58, Chapters 6.6.4.5.1 and 6.7.2.1). Anderson and Dekker (2005) and Chalos and O'Connor (2005) argue that TC increases and organizational performance decreases if the contract structure is not adequately adapted to the magnitude of the transaction characteristics. The governance structure, which is legally stipulated at least in broad outline, is often linked to a partnership's contract structure. For this reason, one chapter is dedicated to the level of complexity in governance structures (Chapter 6.5.1.4). As summarized in the same chapter, large multi-stakeholder partnerships being implemented in several countries and involving numerous partners, who have very diverse interests and moreover face comprehensive internal coordination efforts, are subject to a generally high level of governance and control complexity. This favours the occurence of bounded rationality and the upsurge of feelings of uncertainty among the partners.

On the basis of the empirical results, the following section discusses ways of opposing uncertainty among partners and presents practical aspects for designing MC. First, it was observed that contracts of PPPs tackling complex policy issues tend to have longer durations or allow more flexibility for extension. Therefore, ex-ante TC for PPP preparation and initiation can be decreased because preparatory procedures, such as the partner selection, are costly and time-consuming (Chapter 6.3.1.3). Moreover, PPPs displaying a high level of control complexity often rely on governance structures that favour a shared and content-oriented control model with a mix of formal and informal control mechanisms to keep organizational performance high and costs for control activities as low as possible (Chapters 6.5.2.2.3 and 6.5.2.3).

The behavioral assumption of the TCE, **opportunism/opportunistic behavior** is strongly related to the **asset specificity** of transactions, and so both characteristics are evaluated together (Chapter 4.2.4). Generally, the results support the ideas of Baudry and Chassagnon (2010) and of Ghosal (1996) that opportunism depends on the attitude and commitment of individuals and that it can vary over time. Nevertheless, it should be added that these behavioral characteristics tend to be strongly influenced by external factors for which individuals cannot be held fully accountable. For instance, for competing companies it is hard to trust and to closely cooperate in joint partnerships. Moreover, both public and private actors have to represent and defend the interests and objectives of their respective organizations. Unintentional causes, such as the misperception of one's own performance and mutual misunderstanding, aggravate the risk of opportunism. The sum of these facts endorses the appeal of Covaleski et al. (2003) to sensitize PPP actors for that risk and thus to implement preventive control mechanisms from the outset (Chapters 4.2.3, 6.5.3.1 and 6.5.3.2). It seems that the risk of opportunistic behavior is highest at early stages of a partnership but is often mitigated quickly by effective formal control mechanisms, or it simply diminishes the more PPP partners know and trust one another. Kamminga and VdM (2007) drew a causal relationship between control complexity, information asymmetry, and opportunistic behavior. They argue that a high level of control complexity increases the risk of occurrence of the other two factors, especially in hybrid governance structures (Chapter 4.2.3). The empirical results nurture the idea that PPPs with global governance structures are more complex and more difficult to control the more partners are involved and the more stakeholders are affected. Nevertheless, little evidence has been found that supports the assumption of Kamminga and VdM (2007). Indeed, the level of control complexity in multilateral alliances is by nature higher than in PPPs composed of just two parties. However, control complexity is not an exogenous phenomenon to be taken for granted. The results rather show that lean governance and decision-making structures within each partner's internal organization form the first step to curb control complexity. The second step refers to the actual PPP, and is the creation of a governance structure that is as little complex as possible, being complemented by a suitable mix of formal and informal MC (Chapter 6.5.1.4). Hence, it is very much the partners' responsibility to deal with the reasons of complexity and to counteract them by setting up a governance structure and devising a MC design strategy that prevent and avert harmful consequences of the causal relationship, as outlined by Kamming and VdM (2007).

Although opportunism was quoted neither as a major control problem nor as a major obstacle to PPP work, its causes and drivers were rated high in both cases (Chapters 6.6.4.5.1, 6.8.2.1 and 6.8.2.2). This observation is backed by the scale-based assessment of actor orientations (Chapter 6.5.3.1). The outcome of this assessment does not only serve as a determinant of the level of cooperation, but it can also be considered as an indicator of the degree and risk of opportunism in PPPs. While *hostile* actor orientation is a clear indicator of opportunistic behavior, *competitive* and *egoistic-rational* attitudes point to an increased risk of the same. However, the fact that the majority of the interviewees rated the level of cooperation in their partnerships as *cooperative* allows one to conclude that opportunism is not a major issue in the analyzed PPPs for development. Several interview partners noted the existence of contractual safeguardings as well as increased information sharing and knowledge management to be crucial (Chapters 6.6.3.2 and 6.8.3). In this regard, the findings of this study support the idea that effective mitigation and prevention of opportunism including the risk of its occurence are CSFs for PPPs, as argued by Dekker (2004) and Groot and Merchant (2000) (Chapter 4.2.3).

As concluded in Chapter 6.4.3.1, the overall level of **asset specificity** in the analyzed PPPs for development is high because all partners contribute specific skills and resources. Several interviewees emphasized that the governance structure and the employed control mechanisms are actually customized for each PPP, despite attempts of standardization. Nevertheless, the results do not back the positive correlation between asset specificity and the risk of opportunism, as assumed by Baudry and Chassagnon (2010), Covaleski et al. (2003), Reeves (2008), and VdM and Vosselman (2000), because opportunism is not a major issue in most PPP as stated before (Chapter 4.2.4). Maybe this can be explained by the fact that these researchers refer to more hierarchic PPP models where one partner represents the contracting party while the PPPs considered for this study rely primarily on hybrid governance structures. Hence, hybrid governance obviously works also for partnerships with an asset specificity that is above intermediate level. Indeed, PPPs terminating prematurely cause high investment losses for the partners, but on the one hand this happens rarely, and on the other hand much emphasis is placed on establishing sustainable financing mechanisms of PPPs and rolling them out in other countries or places (Table 18). Thus, for the underlying sample, the empirical findings do not corroborate the concerns of high risk of opportunism and investment losses related to a high level of asset specificity.

The critical dimension of **frequency** has been investigated by analyzing the resource provision processes in PPPs for development (Chapter 6.4.3.2). Large-scale PPPs, such as multilateral alliances, with comprehensive project activities in different countries imply a high transaction volume and frequency, and are typically characterized by a multi-tier governance structure (Figure 44). In this regard, the empirical findings endorse the assumption that high volume PPPs with frequent resource provision require elaborated governance structures. However, frequency is the critical parameter that is least pertinent to the present study among the transaction characteristics, so that the focus of the empirical results does not permit a wider-ranging discussion.

Regarding formal MC, a selection of behavior and results controls has commonly been used in all analyzed PPPs. By monitoring PPP activities and preparing different kinds of reports based on that, relevant information for external and internal stakeholders is generated and disclosed. These control measures contribute to alleviating bounded rationality and uncertainty by creating transparency of PPP activities and their achievements. The extent and focus of these controls tend to be adapted to the level of uncertainty at a certain stage and can therefore vary over the course of the PPP implementation (Chapter 6.6.3). However, they can also render decision-making even more complex (Chapters 6.6.1.4 and 6.6.1.5). Rules and guidelines on MC procedures may give ideas on how to design MC in PPPs, but these are usually too complex to apply a common set of predefined MC mechanisms to them, as suggested by best practice patterns (Chapter 6.6.1.6). The results also show that durable partnerships do not work without informal MC mechanisms being complementary to the formal ones that are used in a specific PPP for development. This observation endorses the idea of social embeddedness of transactions to reduce TC and to prevent opportunism, as suggested by VdM and Vosselman (2000) (Chapter 4.2.3). Trust is one of the most important but also one of the most unstable informal control mechanisms being used to encounter bounded rationality and to reduce information asymmetry. It is intertwined with other control mechanisms, such as communication, knowledge sharing, or networking, which all rely on information sharing. Without trust, information is unlikely to be exchanged and information asymmetry to be lowered or removed. Trust is unstable in the sense that it is particularly vulnerable to intrinsic risks, control problems, and basically to any kind of opportunistic behavior. Moreover, it requires continuously high investments in good interpersonal relationships. Once trust is lost it is costly to rebuild it, if at all possible (Chapter 6.6.4.4.1). This tight linkage to MC may explain why trust is one of the most frequently mentioned CSF (Chapter 6.8.2.1). When asked in the light of the individually identified CSFs for the potential of improvements in their PPPs, several interviewees made some suggestions, but many of them saw no major need for fundamental adjustments or changes of their governance structures and MC mechanisms (Chapter 6.8.3). This observation allows one to conclude that the analyzed PPPs are predominantly governed and controlled in an effective manner. In only one reported case, a combination of bounded rationality, opportunism and uncertainty led to the early termination of a PPP for development (Chapter 6.1.5.4).

In summary, the TCE's behavioral and transaction characteristics hold true for the research focus of this study and manifest themselves in the empirical results and support the outcome from previous research. However, some findings are not compatible with the previously identified characteristics of the TCE's behavioral assumptions and critical dimensions. Therefore, these findings enhance existing knowledge and reveal opportunities for further research activities.

7.3.2.2 Governance Characteristics

This chapter discusses the governance characteristics of the TCE, according to Oxley (1997), as well as the attributes and considerations derived from the three major types of governance structures: hierarchic, hybrid, and market-oriented, pursuant to Williamson (1996, p. 105) (Chapter 4.2.5). In view of Oxley's assertions, they are partially supported by the empirical findings. Most of the analyzed PPPs are based on a hybrid governance structure and are often designed in a JV-like manner, especially in multilateral and strategic alliances. Usually, there exist clear decision-making procedures and reporting lines including regular monitoring activities which are complemented by comprehensive clan and social control measures (Chapters 6.5.1 and 6.6.2.1). This evidence sustains Oxley's assertion of market-oriented governance structures. By contrast, the results are less indicative of support for the first two assertions. Almost all analyzed PPPs are cross-boundary and consist of a multinational set of partners. In particular, membership-based multilateral alliances are very big in terms of the number of partners involved. Still, there is no clear indication that their governance structures are necessarily more hierarchic. It seems that for every PPP exists an individual undefined critical threshold of partners which necessitates delegation of authority and decentralized decision-making in order to make partnership work efficiently and effectively. While far-reaching and strategic decisions tend to be made at the highest governance level in a democratic manner between high-level representatives from all partners, much authority is left to the implementing actors at operational level. Such an approach is followed notably by large multinational firms and international organizations that maintain comprehensive decentralized organizational structures including staff presence in the target countries of PPP operations (Chapter 6.1.4). So, even if a governance structure formally relies on a hierarchical design, it still might be practiced in a hybrid manner (Chapter 6.5.1.4). This can be explained by the fact that PPP work is very much relationship-based and therefore depends on personal contacts between local representatives of the partners and local stakeholders, such as governmental authorities. In this vein, IO interviewees said in terms of partner selection that the executive management indeed reserves the right to refuse any partnership, but in practice delegates the authority of the selection procedure including risk assessment to the field staff at country and regional level and concentrates more likely on high-level flagship partnerships (Chapter 6.3.1.3). By contrast, the area of work that is managed quite hierarchically across all PPP types is budgeting and resource planning. Several public and private interview partners bemoaned the often too specific resource allocation that impedes a more flexible shifting of budget among PPP activities in the course of changing priorities (Chapter 6.5.2.2.2). These often result from an unstable institutional environment with volatile economic, political and social conditions on the one side, and from unforseeable opportunities and challenges arising during PPP implementation on the other side (Chapters 6.7.4 and 6.8.2.2). Hence, Oxley's first two assertions tend to hold true for certain areas of work, such as partner selection and resource planning, rather than for cross-boundary multi-stakeholder PPPs in general.

With respect to the three considerations that were derived from the work of Williamson (1996, p. 105) (Table 20), only some limited conclusions can be drawn for the second and third one, which primarily refer to market-based transactions and incentive intensity, but cannot be discussed appropriately because of too few data generated. Only one analyzed PPP worked in a market-based governance structure. Moreover, the present study tackled the matter of incentive schemes not so much at the level of individuals but at more aggregated level in the sense of what objectives do a company, DCA, or IO pursue by a certain PPP engagement, what outcome expectations do they have, and what motivates them to demonstrate commitment towards PPPs. In this vein, the results support Williamson's consideration that mutual incentive structures should be clear to all partners from the beginning to prevent conflicts of interest and opportunism. In the context of contract compliance and enforceability some interviewees felt the urge to stipulate objectives, responsibilities and performance expectations as far as possible by contract, and to link inherent incentive schemes which are framed by a mix of formal and informal MC mechanisms (Chapter 6.6.5.2). Lack of awareness of incentive structures is equal to bounded rationality and implies high risk to turn into conflicts of interests (Chapter 6.2.2.3). Nevertheless, the focus of the thesis study and the kind of results obtained do not allow concluding that in more market-based transactions the incentive intensity is stronger than in others. What seems to hold true is that much emphasis is placed on fair incentive intensity so that benefits and risks of partnerships are well-balanced, a claim that is met in most of the analyzed PPPs (Chapter 6.2.6.3). PPP partners usually try to align different incentive structures as far as possible in the initiation and preparation phase to avoid the need of implementing rigid contractual arrangements. That is why informal control mechanisms, such as intense communication and the building of trustful relationships, are deemed pivotal for the coordination of diverging interests (Chapter 6.6.3.2). This observation backs Williamson's third consideration to some extent. No supporting evidence is found for the first consideration because many interview partners are aware of the impossibility of reaching complete contracts, and they design them intentionally less detailed and rigid than they could, as discussed in Chapter 7.3.2.1.

In summary, the TCE's governance characteristics proved to be relevant for explaining findings from the sample. Nevertheless, the empirical results provide less supporting evidence to them than to the behavioral assumptions and critical dimensions discussed in Chapter 7.3.2.1. In particular, the theoretical considerations according to Williamson (1996, p. 105) seem to be hardly applicable to the mainly hybrid-governed PPPs for development because they reflect rather competitive market-based customer-supplier transactional relationships. Therefore, the findings point to potential for future research.

7.3.3 Contribution to and Implications for Management Control Research

Qualitative field research stands at the crossroad of making a meaningful contribution to MC research and delivering applicable recommendations for action to practitioners who might even have participated in a research study (cf. Lamnek and Krell, 2010, p. 159 ff.; Silverman, 2010, p. 419 f.). Thus, the present work faces dual accountability towards enhancing MC research in terms of PPPs, JVs, and IORs/IFRs, but also towards the interview partners. Merchant and Van der Stede (2006) bemoaned the burden of time management which accounting researchers often dedicate to proving the significance of empirical results for making a credible contribution of theory, but that they lose sight of the compatibility of their findings with the demands in the real world, especially because field research deals with the examination of real phenomena (cf. Atkinson and Shaffir, 1998). That is why they urge other accounting researchers to focus more on the practical relevance of empirical results. On the other side, Ferreira and Merchant (1992) raised the issue of often insufficient linkage between field study results and their contribution to advancing the current state of knowledge and the underlying theories. In addition, Ahrens and Chapman (2006) stressed the strong theoretical nature of qualitative field research. Bearing in mind these requests for the present study, Chapter 7.2 provides a summary of essential practical implications as concluded from the overall results in Chapter 0. Following Endenich (2012, p. 299 ff.), who also pointed to the challenge of dual accountability, the analysis of the theoretical contribution to accounting research is likewise divided into three categories, namely the *theoretical frameworks*, *methodologies*, and *geographical scopes* as applied in previous research. Since the quantitative literature review in Chapters 2.2.1.2.2 to 2.2.1.2.4 has been structured in the same way, the described categorization is reasonable.

Theoretical frameworks: The choice of a mixed theoretical approach being composed of the ACI and TCE expands that literature which uses a theoretical framework for discussing empirical results. Furthermore, no other study was found which hitherto used ACI and TCE in a combined manner in order to analyze any kind of PPP, JV or IOR/IFR. None of the considered articles on PPPs for development used the TCE (Chapter 2.2.3). The TCE in its current form was mainly shaped by Oliver Williamson and was adopted and further developed by many previous studies in the area of MC research (cf. Berry et al., 2009; Speklé, 2001; Vosselman and VdM, 2009). Although Williamson (1996, p. 4 f.) also ascribes to the TCE a macroanalytic and a microanalytic component, he accepts the first one, namely the institutional environment, as given and confines his theoretical focus to the micro-level (Chapter 4.1.5). This is the main difference between Williamson's analysis and the present study. This work intends to strengthen the macroanalytic perspective by matching the ACI with the TCE. The reason for this is that the purpose of different PPPs for development, dealing with policy issues related to the harmonization of norms and standards, is to bring about changes of the institutional environment. The present study's main contribution at the theoretical framework level is twofold: 1) it shows the practical applicability and relevance of the ACI approach, according to Fritz Scharpf, for PPPs, such as those for development, and 2) it expands the comprehensive extant TCE-based research on MC in JVs and IORs/IFRs performed notably by Dutch scholars, such as Dekker (2004, 2008), Kamminga and VdM (2006), VdM and Vosselman (2000) or Vosselman and VdM (2009), to PPPs (Chapters 2.2.2.2 and 2.2.2.3).

Methodologies: By applying a field study research design, the present work has chosen an approach which few pertinent studies have hitherto made use of before, but which still proved to be suitable for accounting research (cf. Lillis and Mundy, 1999; Smith, 2015, p. 146 f.; Chapters 2.2.1.1.3 and 2.2.1.2.3). As stated in 5.1.2, Hopwood (1983), Dekker (2016) and other accounting researchers see the strength of field research in its contribution to providing knowledge that helps to better understand the context and institutional environment of accounting activities. In this regard, the chosen methodology is attuned to the underlying theoretical framework because the idea of the combined ACI-TCE approach is the consideration of the institutional environment of PPPs for development for the discussion of their governance structure and MC design. Complementary to the field research design, this study also relies on the conduction of interviews as a proven method of data collection. Finally, the choice of a qualitative research design results from the consideration of the strengths and weaknesses of the diverse possible quantitative and qualitative methods. That is why Flick et al. (2013, p. 326 f.) recommend researchers to select a research design including data collection methods which they deem most adequate to work on the research subject (cf. Endenich, 2012, p. 301). Following their postulate, the interview-based collection of empirical data generated in-depth insights in the existence, extent and functioning of MC in PPPs for development. Hence, the present study differs from previous studies in the way that the institutional environment has been explicitly considered for both the theoretical and the methodological setup.

Geographical scopes: While previous studies often focused on a certain country or region, the present work adopted a subject matter-oriented international perspective. By considering PPP experiences from Germany, Mexico and Switzerland, it complements extant literature by data from countries which hitherto had not received much attention according to the findings from the literature review (Figure 11 in Chapter 2.2.1.2.4). However, it must not be seen as a study on comparative management accounting, such as the work by Brandau (2010) or Endenich (2012), because country-driven specifics of MC and the influence of intercultural differences represent only a small part of the overall analysis of MC in PPPs for development. By contrast, it does not follow the approach by Stadtler and Probst (2012) either who also interviewed experts from diverse global PPPs for development, but without geographic anchoring. The main challenge of determining the geographical scope of this kind of PPPs is their global character. This applies in particular for global policy platforms, processed by PPP types such as multilateral alliances. Moreover, the opinions of interviewees from IOs cannot be linked to a specific geographical origin. Finally, the present study's focus is most proximate to the approach chosen by Kolk et al. (2008) who used Dutch multinational firms as starting point for their selection of PPPs for development with global outreach. Most corporate interviewees from the present study originate from Germany. However, to avoid a too strong national bias, the PPP experiences from Mexican and Swiss company and DCA representatives were also considered in the sample. The determination of minimum requirements for the companies and DCAs, for their representatives, and also for commonalities of the economic, legal and political framework conditions of these countries ensures comparability (Chapter 5.2.1.1).

The understanding of this study's contribution of theory and of the way it is tied up to suitable methodologies and previous geographic scopes allows deriving implications for future research on MC in PPPs for development (Figure 58).

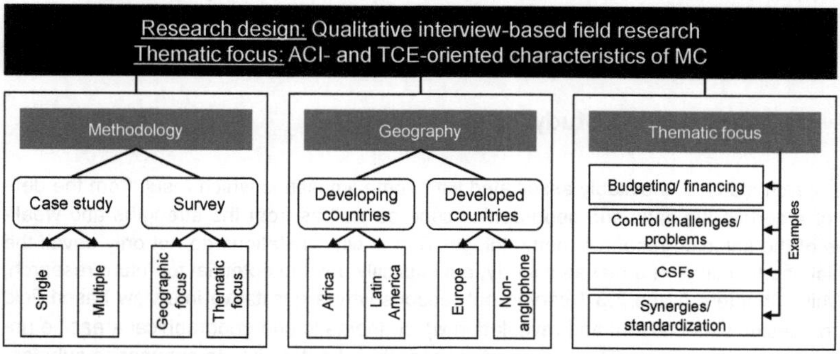

Figure 58: Areas of potential future research.

One option would be the conduction of single or multiple case studies for one or several PPPs to gain even more in-depth knowledge of the functioning of MC in partnerships for development. In the event of empirical and interview-based case studies, the challenge will be to find interviewees who are willing to share insights into their organizations and to reveal their employers's identity (cf. Halinen and Törnroos, 2005; Scapens, 1990). Alternatively, a survey at a larger scale could be done to examine the representative nature of the results obtained in the present study (cf. Lillis and Mundy, 2005). It could either take a geographic focus and consult PPP experiences on various MC issues from one or few countries or otherwise analyze selected MC topics, such as performance measurement or budgeting/financing, in various countries or regions. Although the present study includes experiences from Mexico, both Africa and Latin America remain regions that have received little attention by PPP-related accounting research, compared to Asia where particular emphasis was hitherto placed on China and India (Chapter 2.2.1). This research gap could be overcome as part of two- or multi-country studies that embrace developing or emerging countries and developed European or non-anglophone countries to adjust the perspective distortion which might have arisen from the previous geographical emphasis on Australia, UK or USA. Regarding thematic foci, there is abundant potential especially for application-oriented MC research, for instance, the identified control challenges and problems form natural points of departure for thorough cause analyses including the development of customized governance and MC structure and the consideration of the CSFs (cf. Broadbent and Laughlin, 2008; Carbonara and Pellegrino, 2014). The many CSFs raised by the present study and the numerous previous studies also serve as starting points for in-depth qualitative research (cf. Osei-Kyei and Chan, 2015; Yuan et al., 2009). Two other exemplary topics which stir PPP actors are the financing mechanisms of PPPs for development and the identification of opportunities for using synergy effects from standardized procedures across different partnerships. Thus, there remains much research potential for creating more sustainable PPP financing mechanisms, an opinion expressed by the public sector interviewees in particular, and for elaborating suitable templates and procedures which promote cost-efficient standardizations and improve the compatibility of different PPP activities (e.g. PPP creation, resource allocation, performance measurement), but still allow dealing with the individual character of most partnerships (e.g. institutional constraints, varying contributions that the same IO or DCA makes in different PPPs in dependence of the private sector partner's skills and competences). Hence, in summary, the empirical results of the present study, in conjunction with the identified potential for further research, underline the relevance of accounting research in the field of MC in PPPs for development.

7.4 Limitations of the Study

Any research study is unevitably associated with some limitations which result from the definition of a certain thematic and geographic scope as well as from the strengths and weaknesses of the selected research methodology. That is why limitations do not only unveil the potential shortcomings of a research study, but implicitly point to potential for future research, too. While Chapters 0 and 7.3.3 carved out reasons why a qualitative interview-based field research design was chosen, and revealed in which thematic and geographical areas lie untapped opportunities for prospective investigations, this chapter aims to summarize substantial limitations related to the content and to the employed theoretical framework and methodology.

7.4.1 Specific Limitations related to the Content and to the Selected Theoretical Framework

The theoretical framework of any research study goes along with certain assumptions, which refer to selected phenomena of the reality. Therefore, theoretical frameworks represent one source of limitations. Hence, the theoretical frame of any research study should be critically evaluated (cf. Flick et al., 2013). As the one-size-fits-all model is unlikely to exist, a combined mixed-theory approach comprising ACI and TCE was chosen to facilitate a more substantive analysis of the empirical results (cf. Benito et al., 2008; Dekker, 2003). Despite the dominance of the TCE in MC research related to PPPs, JVs, and IORs/IFRs, the literature review showed the reasonable employment of other theories in the past, too (cf. Meira et al., 2010; Chapter 2.2.1.2.2). For instance, the principal-agent theory might be suitable to serve future more in-depth research of thematic areas, such as the alignment of diverging interests or incentive structures of the involved PPP partners, which the present thesis has addressed but not discussed in much detail (cf. Benito et al., 2008). In this vein, a major content-related limitation is the preference given to thematic breadth instead of depth for the examination of MC in PPPs for development. This approach inhibits a profound discussion of the empirical results, but is owed to the very little existing knowledge of that matter. Thus, the broad overview provided by this study has revealed many starting-points for prospective research. Such a broad focus on MC in conjunction with a combined theoretical framework required an explorative instead of a hypotheses-based analysis procedure including less specified research questions, as formulated in this study (cf. Brandau, 2010, p. 145).

7.4.2 Specific Limitations related to the Methodology Applied

Exploratory, interview-based field research was undertaken to collect qualitative data for the present study on PPPs for development. The main limitations of such an approach comprise the absence of generalizability and statistical representativeness of the empirical results. That is why the results allow formulating statements with respect to tendencies only, instead of making universal conclusions for the population of all existing and past PPPs (cf. Gibbert et al., 2008; Gläser and Laudel, 2010, p. 27 f.; Maxwell, 2013, p. 137 f.; Mayring, 2016, p. 23 f.). Regarding the sampling strategy, preference was given to depth over breadth because of the very little previous knowledge about the design of MC in PPPs for development, and for gaining a more differentiated overview of MC designs in different types of these PPPs (cf. Moll et al., 2006, p. 377; Patton, 2009, p. 227 f.). The lack of generalizability of the results does not only limit the transferabiltiy of the findings to other PPPs for development but also to other kinds of PPPs. However, some results, such as the findings on the CSFs, are compatible with those from previous studies (Chapter 7.3). Thus, it is not unlikely that the empirical results from the present study also manifest themselves in other kinds of PPPs, and this would support the idea that transferability is given to some extent (cf. Maxwell, 2013, p. 137). Basically, the present empirical results can be interpreted as a first stocktaking of how MC in PPPs for development looks like in practice, and they therefore pave the way for putting forward hypotheses which can be examined by future more in-depth case studies or quantitative surveys. These could help to obtain more in-depth insights, and to facilitate conclusions on causal relationships because potential causalities hitherto remained undetected, or could not be verified statistically (cf. Borchardt and Göthlich, 2009, p. 36; Gläser and Laudel, 2010, p. 28; Scapens, 1990). Although the present empirical results are even more universal than those from case studies tend to be, an issue which cannot be negated is the fact that the data was collected at a certain point of time, and no longitudinal examination over a longer time period took place. This is another parameter which inhibits the generalizabilty of the results (cf. Kornacker, 2014, p. 412). This limitation is counteracted by the minimum pertinent PPP experience which the interview partners had to fulfill so that their explanations are usually based on long-term observations (Chapter 5.2.1.1).

Other material limitations affect the interview preparation and conduction. First of all, a balanced sampling of PPPs including interview partners and environmental factors is pivotal because it determines, or can at least affect, the content and quality of the empirical results and should therefore be aligned with the research questions (cf. Bogner et al., 2014, p. 34 f.). For empirical field studies, the economic and political environment proved to play a strong role, a notion which was particularly raised by comparative management accounting in the past. However, a researcher has only limited control over such disruptive factors from outside (cf. Broweleit, 2014, p. 340; Endenich, 2012, p. 308). The different multinational PPPs for development considered in the present thesis are embedded in diverse economic environments. This issue has been implicitly addressed by asking the interview partners for institutional constraints they are or were facing, and for CSFs of their PPPs. The latter revealed political stability and sound economic environment to be crucial for a partnership's success (Chapter 6.8.1). Further potential disruptive factors are age, gender, national origin, or personal attitudes, which have been widely neglected. Instead, emphasis was placed on the level of pertinent experience to ensure an appropriate quality level of the interview responses. This is reflected by the selection criteria being applied to the cohort of interview partners (Chapter 5.2.1.1). These criteria promote comparability of their pertinent PPP experiences.

Hence, the heterogenous academic backgrounds among the interview partners, and the heterogeneity of the positions they held, should not be seen as shortcomings but as a contribution to forming a basis for the formulation of generalizing hypotheses in future research (cf. Bogner et al., 2014, p. 31).

Qualitative studies like the present one, based on purposive instead of random sampling, run the risk of being subject to a *self-selection bias* (cf. Patton, 2009, p. 230; Söhnchen, 2009, p. 138). In the present context this would mean that interviewees from only those companies, IOs, and DCAs are willing to share their experiences whose PPPs including the implemented governance and MC structure are functioning well. This kind of bias may distort results in the sense that it promotes a largely positive interpretation of a subject matter. And indeed, only one failed PPP was included in the sample. However, adverse impact from this limitation is mitigated by the willingness of most interview partners to learn from the experiences of the others, from which many interview partners drew their motivation to participate in this study. That is why the vast majority of them also critically reflected on the strengths and weakenesses of their respective PPPs during the interviews. A further limitation is the non-consideration of experiences from beneficiaries of the PPPs and other pertinent stakeholder groups, such as NGOs or national government representatives. They were excluded in order to keep the focus on the directly interacting partners from the private sector and from IOs/DCAs (cf. Henke, 2016, p. 306 f.; Müller, 2013, p. 351 f.). Still, a holistic approach that includes the voices of all relevant stakeholders would be reasonable to pursue as part of in-depth case studies.

Moreover, a good preparation of interview-based field work requires a quality interview guide which is decisive for the quality and kind of data which form the input that is considered for the answering of the research questions in Chapter 4.5 (cf. Gläser and Laudel, 2010, p. 142 ff.; Helfferich, 2011, p. 28 f.). Another potential reason of criticism in this context is the multilingualism of this thesis whose results rely on English, German, and Spanish language interviews that were conducted by the author, a German native speaker. Moreover, it was him who translated the interview guides while not all English language interviews were given by native speakers. Still, to ensure proper translation and interpretation, and to limit the *interviewer bias* at an early stage, pretests were undertaken with respect to the German and English language interview guides (cf. Kaya, 2009, p. 52; Lillis, 1999; Chapter 5.2.1.2). For the Spanish ones, fellow researchers from the EGADE Business School in Monterrey/Mexico, were consulted. The early provision of the interview guides enabled the interview partners to prepare themselves appropriately. Moreover, a complete translation of German and Spanish interview transcripts into English was not deemed reasonable because the content analysis of the results could be undertaken irrespective of the interview language, and therefore authenticity of the statements maintained (cf. Boucoiran, 2010, p. 170; Kruse et al., 2012, p. 64). Finally, it is neither possible nor desirable to design all-embracing interview guides because of time limits and boundaries set by the chosen research focus. Moreover, too strict interview guides, or the posing of too many closed questions, foster the risk of self-fulfilling prophecy so that desired answers instead of new knowledge may be produced. That is why a semi-structured interview design was selected for which the pretest formed a core quality assurance mechanism (cf. Bortz and Döring, 2006, p. 311; Helfferich, 2010, p. 168 f., 180; Krippendorff, 2004, p. 40 f.). In terms of the interview conduction, the authenticity and sincerety of answers from interview partners are hard to examine (cf. Bortz and Döring, 2006, p. 327; Miles and Huberman, 2014, p. 312 f.). To prevent this limitation to some extent, strict confidentiality was assured to the interview partners, prompting several of them to share insights which should not be further communicated, neither internally nor externally, but which were still very valuable for contextualizing the interviewees' answers properly (cf. Bogner et al., 2014, p. 89 ff.; Patton, 2009, p. 406).

The creation of categories and the coding of the interview data are both subject to a high level of subjectivity and can therefore undermine the reliability and validity of empirical results (Chapter 5.3.2). Suitable quality assurance measures revealed that external and internal validity as well as reliability of the results are given so that a good fit of the system of categories and of the codes can be assumed. The feedback from the communicative validation allows concluding that the level of authenticity of the responses from the interviewees is high (cf. Flick, 2014, p. 495; Mayring, 2016, p. 120; Chapters 5.3.3.2 and 7.2.2). In summary, the adherence to the thresholds of the aforementioned quality criteria allows drawing the conclusion that certain methodological limitations are uncritical issues in the present study (cf. Miles and Huberman, 2014, p. 310 ff.).

7.5 Conclusion and Outlook

The present study on MC in PPPs for development provides an aggregated overview of existing governance structures and MC mechanisms in different types of these partnerships and discusses the empirical results from the theoretical perspective of the ACI and TCE. It focuses on the collaboration between international governmental actors, namely IOs and DCAs, and the private sector, and links the demand for a substantive contribution of theory to the derivation of implications for practitioners (cf. Ferreira and Merchant, 1992; Merchant and Van der Stede, 2006). In this spirit were formulated the underlying research questions which close the identified research gap and form the guideline throughout the entire study, especially for the empirical work (cf. Maxwell, 2013, p. 75; Ryan et al., 2002, p. 153; Chapter 4.5). Moreover, this study acknowledges the often global and interdisciplinary character of PPPs for development and is therefore designed as an international field study. It goes along with a qualitative research design in the wake of which 28 interviews were conducted with representatives from multinational private sector firms, IOs, and DCAs. The data collection took place in several countries and embraces pertinent experiences from both the executive and the operational level. Because of the integrated approach to strongly linking theory and practice, and comparing to extant literature, which has hitherto barely focused on PPPs for development and which often neither relies on empirical data nor on a sound theoretical foundation, this study provides a comprehensive and substantive overview of governance structures and MC mechanisms (Chapters 6.5 and 6.6). Therefore, it enhances existing management accounting and control research on PPPs, JVs, and IORs/IFRs in geographical, methodological and theoretical terms.

Every PPP has its particular characteristics, challenges, and problems which a field study can consider only to a limited extent so that the value added of this study relies on the aggregation of the manifold experiences from different partnerships wherefore it provides a good amount of evidence for formulating generalizing hypotheses that can be verified by quantitative research in the future. Moreover, the broad range of PPP topics presented in the results overview, ranging from the general setting as well as preparation, resource endowment, and implementation of PPPs to governance and formal and informal MC or institutional aspects, shows the remaining abundant potential for future research, whether as part of in-depth case studies or large-scale surveys, to reach better generalizability of the findings from this study (Chapter 0). The research focus could be narrowed to certain elements of formal and informal MC, as done by previous research with respect to risks or trust in PPPs for instance (cf. Das and Teng, 2001a; Emsley and Kidon, 2007; Langfield-Smith, 2008; Vélez et al., 2008). The use of other pertinent theories or theoretical approaches beyond the dominant TCE might help to detect and explain hitherto unknown phenomena or causalities. The variation of the geographical scope and the inclusion of the perspective from other stakeholders, such as NGOs and local beneficiaries, can contribute to increasing the generalizability and validity of the present results (cf. Kolk et al., 2008; Singh and Prakash, 2010). Altogether, there are multiple opportunities for future research that could address this study's limitations mentioned in Chapter 7.4. The interviewees' willingness to learn from each other and their positive feedback on the communicative validation encourage such research (Chapter 7.2.2). In this vein, the conclusion and outlook are finally not summed up better than by voices from international leaders of the public and private sector world. Both Klaus Schwab from the World Economic Forum (WEF) and Ban Ki-moon in his capacity as UN Secretary-General at that time emphasized at the 2016 annual meeting of the WEF the role which public-private cooperations in general, and PPPs in particular, play for addressing global challenges such as climate change. Their following statements rest on the 2015 Paris Agreement and on the SDGs which had been adopted by the UN General Assembly in the same year:

> *"[...] for the first time the non-political stakeholders in business and elsewhere were integrated into the process, and this helped secure a successful outcome. But now we have to go from declaration to implementation, and this is where Davos can serve as a platform". [...] I have never before been so excited, because today there are so many issues, so many challenges for which the WEF's role in promoting public-private partnership is ideally suited. I would say the need for cooperation between governments and non-public actors has never been as great as it is now."* (Klaus Schwab, founder and executive chairman of the WEF)[18]

> *"The Paris Agreement will reinforce climate action and make important contributions to realizing the Sustainable Development Goals. [...]. Governments and the private sector must to align their investment and infrastructure decisions with the goal to limit temperature rise well below 2 degrees, even 1.5 degrees Celsius. The Paris Agreement gives the private sector an unprecedented opportunity to create clean energy, climate resilient economies. [...]. I will work to help strengthen the action agenda and public-private partnerships."* (Ban Ki-moon, UN Secretary-General from 2007 to 2016)[19]

Hence, the need for creating and successfully implementing PPPs for development is unbroken, and MC forms a core element of coordination of the various public and private actors.

---

[18] Quotation gathered from an interview of The Telegraph with Klaus Schwab on the 16th of January 2016 on the occasion of the imminent 2016 annual meeting of the WEF: http://www.telegraph.co.uk/finance/financetopics/davos/12103375/Davos-must-confront-a-world-at-a-tipping-point.html (by Warner, 2016).

[19] Quotation gathered from a speech held by Ban Ki-Moon on the 21st of January 2016 during a plenary session of the 2016 annual meeting of the WEF: https://www.un.org/sg/en/content/sg/statement/2016-01-21/secretary-generals-remarks-world-economic-forum-plenary-session-new (by United Nations Secretary-General, 2016).

The findings and recommendations from this study stand by for the decision-makers' consideration of further development of existing and the creation of future partnerships.

8. Annex

8.1 Complementary Tables

Author (year of publication)	Journal category
Abdul-Aziz (2012)	Engineering & Management
Acar et al. (2008)	Public Administration & Public Management
Acerete et al. (2011)	Accounting
Acquaah (2009)	General Management & International Business
Almarri (2017)	Engineering & Management
Anderson and Dekker (2005)	General Management & International Business
Andon (2012)	Accounting
Andrews et al. (2015)	Public Administration & Public Management
Appuhami et al. (2011)	Accounting
Appuhami and Perera (2016)	Accounting
Babatunde et al. (2012)	Engineering & Management
Baiman and Madhav (2002)	Accounting
Baker (2003)	Accounting
Benito et al. (2008)	Accounting
Berry et al. (2009)	Accounting
Bloomfield (2006)	Public Administration & Public Management
Boersma et al. (2003)	General Management & International Business
Boland et al. (2008)	Accounting
Bovaird (2004)	Public Administration & Public Management
Brinkerhoff and Brinkerhoff (2011)	Public Administration & Public Management
Broadbent and Laughlin (2008)	Accounting
Broadbent and Guthrie (2008)	Accounting
Broadbent and Laughlin (2003a)	Accounting
Broadbent and Laughlin (2003b)	Accounting
Broadbent and Laughlin (2004)	Accounting
Budäus and Grüb (2007)	Public Administration & Public Management
Burke and Demirag (2015)	Accounting
Caglio and Ditillo (2008)	Accounting
Cäker and Siverbo (2011)	Accounting
Carbonara and Pellegrino (2014)	General Management & International Business
Chalos and O'Connor (2005)	Accounting
Chalos and O'Connor (2004)	Accounting
Chan et al. (2010a)	Engineering & Management
Chan et al. (2010b)	Engineering & Management
Chen et al. (2009)	General Management & International Business
Chen et al. (2013)	Development & Non-profit
Cheung et al. (2012)	Engineering & Management

T. S. Konrad, *Management Control in Public-Private Partnerships*,
Schriften zu Wirtschaftsprüfung, Steuerlehre und Controlling,
https://doi.org/10.1007/978-3-658-22868-2

Author (year of publication)	Journal category
Choi and Beamish (2004)	General Management & International Business
Chou and Pramudawardhani (2015)	Performance & Project Management
Chung (2016)	Accounting
Chung and Hensher (2015)	Accounting
Coletti et al. (2005)	Accounting
Cooper and Slagmulder (2004)	Accounting
Das and Teng (2001a)	General Management & International Business
Das and Teng (2001b)	General Management & International Business
Dekker (2003)	Accounting
Dekker (2004)	Accounting
Dekker (2008)	Accounting
Dekker (2016)	Accounting
Demirag et al. (2011)	Accounting
Demirag et al. (2012)	Accounting
Donada and Nogatchewsky (2006)	Accounting
El-Gohary et al. (2006)	Performance & Project Management
Emsley and Kidon (2007)	Accounting
English et al. (2010)	Accounting
English and Baxter (2010)	Accounting
Forrer et al. (2010)	Public Administration & Public Management
Froud (2003)	Accounting
Georgieva et al. (2012)	General Management & International Business
Gerstlberger and Schneider (2013)	Public Administration & Public Management
Giacobbe and Booth (2009)	Accounting
Grimsey and Lewis (2002a)	Accounting
Grimsey and Lewis (2002b)	Performance & Project Management
Grimsey and Lewis (2005)	Accounting
Groot and Merchant (2000)	Accounting
Gupta and Chandra (2013)	General Management & International Business
Hakansson and Lind (2004)	Accounting
Hayllar (2010)	Public Administration & Public Management
Henderson and McGloin (2004)	Public Administration & Public Management
Henjewele et al. (2013)	Engineering & Management
Hodge and Greve (2007)	Public Administration & Public Management
Hwang et al. (2013)	Performance & Project Management
Isidor et al. (2015)	General Management & International Business
Jacobson and Choi (2008)	Public Administration & Public Management
Jamali (2004)	Public Administration & Public Management
Jiang et al. (2011)	General Management & International Business
Johnson and Korsgaard (2002)	General Management & International Business
Kamminga and VdM (2007)	Accounting
Kamminga and VdM (2006)	General Management & International Business
Kaufmann and O'Neill (2007)	General Management & International Business

Author (year of publication)	Journal category
Keating and Keating (2013)	Organizational Studies
Khoday (2007)	Public Administration & Public Management
Kivilä et al. (2017)	Performance & Project Management
Klijn and Teisman (2003)	Public Administration & Public Management
Kolk et al. (2008)	General Management & International Business
Koppenjan (2005)	Public Administration & Public Management
Koppenjan and Enserink (2009)	Public Administration & Public Management
Krause (2014)	Public Administration & Public Management
Langfield-Smith (2008)	Accounting
Langfield-Smith and Smith (2003)	Accounting
Larimo et al. (2016)	General Management & International Business
Le Nguyen et al. (2015)	General Management & International Business
Li B. et al. (2005)	Engineering & Management
Li J. et al. (2009)	General Management & International Business
Li P. et al. (2013)	Accounting
Liu J. (2014)	Performance & Project Management
Liu X. (2014)	General Management & International Business
Loosemore and Cheung (2015)	Performance & Project Management
Luo (2007)	General Management & International Business
Makino et al. (2007)	General Management & International Business
Mantecon et al. (2016)	Performance & Project Management
Marques et al. (2011)	Accounting
Martin and Halachmi (2012)	Public Administration & Public Management
McQuaid and Scherrer (2010)	Public Administration & Public Management
Meschi (2005)	General Management & International Business
Meschi and Riccio (2008)	General Management & International Business
Miller et al. (2008)	Accounting
Moilanen (2007)	Accounting
Mota and Moreira (2015)	Performance & Project Management
Mouritsen and Thrane (2006)	Accounting
Ng et al. (2007)	General Management & International Business
Nicholson et al. (2006)	Accounting
Osei-Kyei and Chan (2015)	Performance & Project Management
Owens et al. (2013)	General Management & International Business
Park et al. (2015)	General Management & International Business
Petersen (2011)	Public Administration & Public Management
Pongsiri (2002)	Public Administration & Public Management
Pothukuchi (2002)	General Management & International Business
Poulton and Macartney (2012)	Development & Non-profit
Rahaman et al. (2010)	Accounting
Rangel and Galende (2010)	Public Administration & Public Management
Reed and Reed (2009)	Development & Non-profit
Reeves (2008)	Public Administration & Public Management
Richardson and Kilfoyle (2009)	Accounting

Author (year of publication)	Journal category
Richter (2004)	Development & Non-profit
Samii et al. (2002)	Development & Non-profit
Schäferhoff et al. (2009)	General Management & International Business
Schepper et al. (2015)	Performance & Project Management
Sciulli (2008)	Accounting
Shaoul et al. (2012)	Accounting
Shen et al. (2006)	Performance & Project Management
Singh and Prakash (2010)	Public Administration & Public Management
Stadtler and Probst (2012)	General Management & International Business
Stafford et al. (2010)	Accounting
Sturchio (2008)	Development & Non-profit
Sukoco (2016)	General Management & International Business
Tang L. et al. (2010)	Performance & Project Management
Teisman and Klijn (2002)	Public Administration & Public Management
Tomkins (2001)	Accounting
Torres and Pina (2001)	Accounting
Trafford and Proctor (2006)	Public Administration & Public Management
Meira et al. (2010)	Accounting
Utting and Zammit (2009)	Development & Non-profit
VdM and Kamminga (2015)	Accounting
VdM and Scapens (2008)	Accounting
VdM and Vosselman (2000)	Accounting
VdM and Vosselman (2006)	Accounting
Van der Stede (2003)	Accounting
Van Ham and Koppenjan (2010)	Public Administration & Public Management
Vélez et al. (2008)	Accounting
Verweij (2015)	Performance & Project Management
Vosselman and VdM (2009	Accounting
Waring et al. (2013)	Public Administration & Public Management
Watson (2003)	Accounting
Wettenhall (2007)	Public Administration & Public Management
Yang et al. (2013)	Public Administration & Public Management
Yuan et al. (2009)	Engineering & Management
Zhang Y. and Li (2001)	General Management & International Business
Zhang Y. and Rajagopalan (2002)	General Management & International Business

Table 65: Total list of reviewed articles.

Journal	Number of articles	VHB JQ3 Ranking	ABS 2015	Publishing house
Abacus	1	B	3	Wiley
Accounting and Business Research (ABR)	1	B	3	Taylor & Francis
Accounting Forum (AF)	2	C	3	Wiley
Accounting, Auditing and Accountability Journal (AAAJ)	5	B	3	Emerald
Accounting, Organizations and Society (AOS)	18	A	4*	Elsevier
Asian Review of Accounting (ARA)	1	-	2	Emerald
Australian Accounting Review (AAR)	6	C	2	Wiley
Australian Journal of Public Administration (AJPA)	1	No ranking	-	Wiley
Construction Management and Economics (CME)	2	-	2	Taylor & Francis
Contemporary Accounting Research (CAR)	2	A	4	Wiley
Corporate Governance (CG)	1	C	3	Emerald
Critical Perspectives on Accounting (CPA)	6	B	3	Elsevier
Development *(Remark: peer-reviewed journal)*	1	-	-	The Company of Biologists Ltd
Engineering, Construction and Architectural Management (ECAM)	1	-	1	Emerald
European Accounting Review (EAR)	3	A	3	Taylor & Francis
European Management Journal (EMJ)	3	B	2	Elsevier
European Management Review (EMR)	1	B	3	Wiley
Financial Accountability & Management	1	C	3	Wiley
Financial Management	1	B	3	Wiley
Halduskultuur – Administrative Culture (HAC) *(Remark: peer-reviewed journal)*	1	-	-	Haldus-kultuur
International Business Review (IBR)	6	B	3	Elsevier
International Journal of Organizational Analysis (IJOA)	1	-	-	Emerald
International Journal of Productivity and Performance Management (IJPPM)	1	C	1	Emerald

Journal	Number of articles	VHB JQ3 Ranking	ABS 2015	Publishing house
International Journal of Project Management (IJPM)	12	C	2	Elsevier
International Journal of Public Sector Management (IJPSM)	8	C	1	Emerald
International Review of Administrative Sciences (IRAS)	1	C	3	SAGE
International Studies Review (ISR)	1	-	-	Wiley
Journal of Accounting and Organizational Change (JAOC)	2	B	2	Emerald
Journal of Business Ethics (JBE)	1	B	3	Springer
Journal of Business Research (JBR)	2	B	3	Elsevier
Journal of Construction Engineering and Management (JCEM)	1	-	2	American Society of Civil Engineers
Journal of Contingencies & Crisis Management (JCCM)	1	-	-	Wiley
Journal of Engineering, Project and Production Management (JEPPM)	1	-	-	Association of Engineering, Project, and Production Management
Journal of Facilities Management (JFM)	2	-	-	Emerald
Journal of Financial Management of Property and Construction (JFMPC)	1	-	-	Emerald
Journal of International Accounting Research (JIAR)	1	B	2	American Accounting Association
Journal of International Business Studies (JIBS)	3	A	4*	Palgrave Macmillan
Journal of International Financial Markets, Institutions and Money (JIFMIM)	1	-	3	Elsevier
Journal of International Management (JIM)	5	B	3	Elsevier
Journal of Management in Engineering (JME)	1	-	2	American Society of Civil Engineers
Journal of Strategy and Management	1	C	-	Emerald
Journal of World Business (JWB)	1	B	4	Elsevier
Management Accounting Rese-	12	A	3	Elsevier

Journal	Number of articles	VHB JQ3 Ranking	ABS 2015	Publishing house
arch (MAR)				
Management International Review (MIR)	1	B	3	Springer
Management Research Review (MRR)	1	C	1	Emerald
Management Science (MS)	1	A+	4*	informs (Institute for Operations Research and the Manage-ment Sciences)
Managerial Finance (MF)	1	-	1	Emerald
Organization Studies (OS)	1	A	4	SAGE
Public Administration (PA)	2	B	4	Wiley
Public Administration and Development (PAD)	1	No ranking	2	Wiley
Public Administration Quarterly (PAQ)	1	C	-	SPAEF
Public Administration Review (PAR)	7	B	4	Wiley
Public Money and Management (PMM)	4	C	2	Taylor & Francis
Public Management Review (PMR)	2	B	3	Taylor & Francis
Review of European, Comparative & International Environmental Law (RECIEL)	1	-	-	Wiley
Strategic Management Journal (SMJ)	4	A	4*	Wiley
The Accounting Review (AR)	1	A+	4*	American Accounting Association
The American Review of Public Administration (ARPA)	1	C	-	SAGE
The British Accounting Review (BAR)	2	C	3	Elsevier
World Development (WD)	2	-	3	Elsevier
Zeitschrift für öffentliche und gemeinwirtschaftliche Unternehmen (ZÖGU)	1	C	-	Nomos

Table 66: Reviewed journals including number of reviewed articles.
(Source: VHB JOURQUAL 3 ranking, Academic Journal Quality Guide 2015 ranking and name of the publishing house)

Journal	VHB JQ3 Ranking
Behavioral Research in Accounting	B
Business Ethics Quarterly	B
International Journal of Accounting	B
Journal of Accounting and Economics	A+
Journal of Accounting Research	A+
Journal of Management Accounting Research	B
Review of Accounting Studies	A

Table 67: Reviewed accounting journals without usable results.
(Source: VHB JOURQUAL 3 ranking)

Methods	Number of articles
Interviews, Multiple Cases	6
Archival, Interviews, Single Case	6
Conceptual, Single Case	5
Interviews, Single Case	4
Archival, Interviews, Multiple Cases	4
Interviews, Survey	3
Conceptual, Survey	3
Conceptual, Interviews, Multiple Cases	3
Interviews, Multiple Cases, Survey	2
Conceptual, Interviews	2
Archival, Interviews, Observations, Single Case	2
Archival, Interviews, Multiple Cases, Survey	2
Archival, Conceptual, Multiple Cases	2
Archival, Conceptual, Interviews, Single Case	2
Interviews, Observations, Single Case	1
Interviews, Observations, Multiple Cases	1
Conceptual, Multiple Cases	1
Conceptual, Interviews, Survey	1
Archival, Survey	1
Archival, Interviews, Observations	1
Archival, Interviews	1

Table 68: Reviewed articles with mixed method research design by frequency.

Methods	Number of articles
Archival, Interviews, Single Case	5
Interviews, Multiple Cases	4
Interviews, Single Case	3
Archival, Conceptual, Multiple Cases	2
Archival, Interviews, Multiple Cases	2
Archival, Conceptual, Interviews, Single Case	2
Conceptual, Interviews, Multiple Cases	2
Interviews, Observations, Multiple Cases	1
Conceptual, Single Case	1
Archival, Interviews, Observations, Single Case	1
Conceptual, Survey	1
Archival, Interviews, Multiple Cases, Survey	1

Table 69: MC-centered articles with mixed method research design by frequency.

Number	Name or type of publication	Year	Author(s)
1	JEPPM	2017	Almarri
2	JFM	2012	Babatunde et al.
3	JCEM	2004	Chan et al.
4	JCEM	2010a	Chan et al.
5	JME	2010b	Chan et al.
6	SMJ	2009	Chen D. et al.
7	IJPM	2015	Chou and Pramudawardhani
8	AOS	2004	Dekker
9	AOS	2008	Dekker
10	JCEM	2002	Glagola and Sheedy
11	AOS	2000	Groot and Merchant
12	MRR	2013	Gupta et al.
13	Non-journal publication	2006	Hardcastle et al.
14	IJPM	2013	Hwang et al.
15	IJPSM	2008	Jacobson and Ok Choi
16	IJPSM	2004	Jamali
17	SMJ	2002	Johnson et al.
18	EMJ	2006	Kamminga and VdM Kooistra
19	MAR	2008	Langfield-Smith
20	MAR	2003	Langfield-Smith and Smith
21	CME	2006	Leiringer
22	Monography	2003	Li B.
23	CME	2005a	Li B. et al.
24	MAR	2013	Li P. et al.
25	IBR	2008	Meschi and Riccio
26	IJPM	2015	Mota and Moreira
27	IJPM	2015	Osei-Kyei and Chan

Number	Name or type of publication	Year	Author(s)
28	AME	2002	Peng and Shenkar
29	JCEM	2006	Tang W. et al.
30	IJPSM	2006	Trafford and Proctor
31	AOS	2008	Vélez et al.
32	CME	2009	Yuan et al.
33	JCEM	2005	Zhang X.
34	IBR	2001	Zhang Y. and Li
35	JIBS	2002	Zhang Y. and Rajagopalan
36	RE	2010	Zhao et al.

Table 70: Publications numbered by source.
(Table 66 for journal abbreviations)

Category	Aggregate Actors	Collective Actors				Corporate Actors
		Coalition	*Club*	*Movement*	*Association*	
Action	Individual	Joint	Joint	Joint	Joint	Organization
Purpose	Individual	Individual	Individual	Collective	Collective	Organization
Resources	Individual	Individual	Collective	Individual	Collective	Organization
Decisions	Individual	Agreement	Voting	Consensus	Voting	Hierarchical

Table 71: Overview on types of actors as per ACI.
(Source: Scharpf (1997), p. 57)

	Institutional Setting			
	Anarchic Field	*Network*	*Association*	*Organization*
Unilateral action	x	x	x	x
Negotiated agreement	(x)	x	x	x
Majority vote	-	-	x	x
Hierarchical direction	-	-	-	x

Table 72: Modes of Interaction.
(Source: Scharpf (1997), p. 47)

8.2 Exemplary Interview Guide (for companies)

Interview Questions

Preface

Dear Mr./Mrs.,

The present research project explores and compares management control in Public-Private Partnership (PPP) projects between International Organizations/agencies of development cooperation and the private sector and intends to identify critical success factors of those projects.
If desired, we will be very happy to provide you with a compilation of the major results and findings after completion of the research project.

General information:

- This interview guide and the information generated through the interview serve research purposes only.
- We explicitly assure you that all information obtained from you will be treated strictly **confidential**.
- All your comments and responses will be anonymized in a way that rules out traceability to a certain person and/or company/organization. For **anonymization** purposes a coding method will be applied.
- The interview will be recorded on tape and transcribed afterwards (subject to your approval). Both tape records and transcriptions will be used project-internally only and will not be accessible to third parties. The tape records will be deleted after project completion.

Notices to answer the questions:

- In case that you do not feel in a position to answer a question for any reason, you can refuse to respond without justification.
- Your participation is voluntary.

Definition "Management Control": Management control comprises all measures and mechanisms that ought to control actions, behavior and processes of actors involved in a partnership and to influence them in a certain direction. Moreover, management control is supposed to avert harmful impacts upon the partnership and to support achievement of objectives. With respect to PPPs management control refers in particular to project control, project management and project monitoring.

Section 1: Profile of the Interviewee

1.1 Interviewee profile

- Current job position (job title) and responsibilities
- Length of employment in this position
- Educational background (e.g. field of study)
- Have you ever been working for an agency of development cooperation/for an international organization before?

1.2 Profile of the partnership project

1.2.1 Please name a few basic information of the partnership

- Type of contract/legal framework
- Length of contract
- Departments involved
- Financiers
- Project volume

1.2.2 What is your company's overall strategy concerning the cooperation with international organizations (e.g. objectives)?

Section 2: General Discussion

2.1 What are the main objectives of the partnership and what was your company's motivation to create or enter into this partnership?

2.2 How did you prepare for the partnership? What have been the major project phases of the partnership?

2.3 What contributions does your company make to the partnership (e.g. skills and competences, financial and non-financial resources)? What is the public sector partner contributing?

2.4 How is the budget and resource planning process for the partnership designed (planning process between your company and your public sector partner and approval process within your company)?

2.5 What are the main cost factors in the partnership project? Do you see potential for more efficient use of resources? If so, where?

2.6 What are generally the key risks of partnerships with international organizations, from your experience? How do you address these risks?

Section 3: Project Control, Project Management and Project Monitoring

3.1 Which role does management control play in the partnership from your point of view?

3.2 How are the project management/organization and project monitoring in your partnership designed?

3.3 What are the benchmarks of the partnership (qualitative and quantitative)? How do you measure their achievement?

3.4 Which contractual safeguarding clauses apply to your partnerships (e.g. protection of intellectual property rights, dispute resolution mechanisms)? How do you try to ensure contract compliance and to promote your partner's commitment to joint objectives?

3.5 How do you assess the influence of intercultural differences and of differences in the organizational culture on the partnership implementation in general?

3.6 How would you generally describe the level of trust in your partnership projects?

3.7 What have been major project control/project management problems, according to your experience?

Section 4: Institutional Embedding and Partnership Implementation

4.1 How would you describe the institutional environment of the partnership?

- External influences/institutional constraints
- Role of (local) authorities/governmental agencies in partnership implementation (insofar they are not involved in the partnership as such)

4.2 How would you characterize the decision-making processes in the partnership (before the background of defined responsibilities)? How would you describe the interaction between the project partners?

4.3 How do you assess the level of cooperation between the involved partners? Which of the following behavior patterns concerning the interaction between you and your public partners did you observe?

- *Altruistic* (own benefit does not matter)
- *Cooperative* (mutual benefit matters)
- *Competitive* (delta between own and others' benefit matters)
- *Egoistic-rational* (own benefit only matters)
- *Adverse* (loss of others is equal to own benefit)

Section 5: Critical Success Factors

5.1 How would you define success and failure of partnerships projects (before the background of expectations, anticipated challenges and difficulties, etc.)?

5.2 What are critical success factors of your partnership? Which factors/obstacles adversely impact on these partnerships?

Section 6: Final Comments

6.1 How should management control develop further in future partnerships with international organizations, from your point of view?

6.2 What changes and differences do you expect for your company's partnership activities in course of the transition from the MDGs to the SDGs?

8.3 Exemplary Description of the Research Study

technische universität
dortmund

Management Control in Public-Private Partnerships between International Organizations/ Development Cooperation Agencies and the Private Sector
(Working title)

Practice-oriented PhD project by the Department of Management Accounting and Control, TU Dortmund University

Key words: Critical success factors (CSF), development cooperation agency (DCA) international organization (IO), management control (MC), public-private partnership (PPP), private sector

Study objectives
1. Contribute to the identification of management control patterns being applied in PPPs between IOs/ DCAs and the private sector
2. Provide new evidence on critical success factors and on suitable management control mechanisms to be implemented in terms of IO/ DCA-related PPP initiatives

Your contribution

- Sharing your experiences in common partnerships (ongoing or concluded) with IOs/ DCAs, related to our research objectives (focus on management control)
- Providing experienced colleagues for an interview who are/were involved in joint partnership initiatives
- Remark: We do not set restrictions to the academic/technical background of your colleague(s).

Your benefits

- You contribute to a current interdisciplinary research topic with international focus
- You may benefit from the partnership experience of other firms or IOs/ DCAs facing similar challenges like you
- If desired, you can obtain research results in a condensed manner for your interest and consideration after research project completion

Why you? How did we come across you?

Your comprehensive stakeholder engagement and commitment to diverse global partnership activities for promoting sustainable development has particularly raised our special interest. We expect your partnership experiences from the collaboration with various public but also other private actors to make a valuable contribution to our present research project.

Content of the study

Research questions

Type	Research question
Design of MC systems	How is management control in IO/ DCA-related PPPs designed? a) By means of which measures and mechanisms efficient and effective control is sought to be ensured? b) Which resources, risks and responsibilities are employed/ shared? How is maximum control kept?
CSF	What are key success factors of PPPs between IOs/ DCAs and the private sector?
Impact of MC systems	How should management control in IO/ DCA-related PPPs be designed in order to promote the partnership's success and to avert harmful influences?

Background

Challenge	Problem
Societal	Social needs and global challenges (e.g. poverty eradication, climate change, urbanization) require (international) cooperation between different actors (e.g. governments, private sector, NGOs).
Sectoral	Increasing involvement of the private sector in the provision of public services.
Managerial	PPPs are complex inter-organizational forms of cooperation, which pose challenges to management control as control and governance tool: 1) Several actors with different institutional frameworks, 2) Partial transfer and therefore loss of control over resources, information sovereignty and responsibilities, 3) Quantitative performance measurement is difficult to implement

Methodology

Characteristics	Implementation
Research approach	Qualitative interview-based field study
Multi-stakeholder perspective	Semi-structured interviews with 20-30 experts from private sector firms and IOs/ DCAs being involved in pertinent PPPs for development
Field study	Gathering of experiences from several partnership projects
Expertise	Private sector and IO/ DCA experts should have gained pertinent experience in the implementation of joint PPP projects, regardless academic/ technical background
Complements	Overarching partnership experiences of senior experts from IOs and from public development cooperation entities complement the sample

Contact person TU Dortmund University: Thomas Konrad, M.Sc.

Permanent address information
TU Dortmund University
Faculty of Business, Economics and Social Sciences
Dep. of Management Accounting and Control
Vogelpothsweg 87
D-44227 Dortmund/ Germany

Current contact details
Phone: xxx
Email: xxx

8.4 List of Codes from MAXQDA

The coding of the interviews has been conducted across the three groups of interview partners: private sector, IOs and DCAs. Insofar as the aggregated code frequency of the meta categories does not match with the sum of the code frequency of the sub categories, this difference results from the fact that single codes have been directly assigned to the meta category.

Meta codes	Sub codes: 1. Level	2. Level	3. Level	4. Level	5. Level	Specifications and key questions	Code frequency
Basics							**337**
	Stakeholder						0
		Stakeholder types involved				Different types of private and public actors involved in a PPP	31
			Number stakeholders			Size of a PPP in terms of the number of stakeholders involved	5
			Number internal staff			Staff provided by each stakeholder for a PPP	10
		People involved					0
			Job description and responsibilities			Specific position of the interview partner	38
			Qualification for PPP work			Academic and (previous) professional experiences	29
			Dedication to PPP work			- Motivation - Workload	14
			Local staff presence for PPP			- International staff sent to the field - Contracting of local staff	16
		Departments involved				Department(s) taking ownership for the specific PPP activities	26
		Internal support				- Additional departments supporting the PPP activities - Management support	12
		Degree of internationalization/ Decentralization				Balance between PPP actvities conducted at HQ level or in the field	14
	PPP Characteristics						0
		PPP types				Different kinds of partnerships, ranging from hierachy- to market-based	29
		Purpose/policy issues				Problem tackled by the PPP (e.g. climate change)	28
		Legal contract					23
			Loose			Contract is little binding	17
			Tight			Contract is detailed and specific	12
		Duration and year of initiation				-	15
		Durability				- Short-/medium-/long-term orientation of the PPP - Stability factors	11
		Financial volume				in EUR or USD	7
Partnership Setting							**448**
	Motivation						0

Meta codes	1. Level	2. Level	3. Level	4. Level	5. Level	Specifications and key questions	Code frequency
		Extrinsic				General external factors motivating stakeholders to engage in PPP activities	7
			Directly business-driven			Explicitly communicated business interests	21
			Indirectly business-driven			Implicitly communicated business interests	15
		Intrinsic				Factors without direct business purpose motivating stakeholders to engage in PPP activities	10
	Objectives						0
		Own Objectives/other Stakeholders' objectives				- Objectives being generally pursued by engagement in PPP activities - Awareness of the other partners' objectives	35
		Mutual expectations/Goal alignment				- Expectations placed on the PPP - Compatibility of diverging expectations and objectives	35
		Strategic/Non-Strategic				Nature of the objectives	21
		Conflicts of interest/trade offs				Reasons for and awareness of conflicts of interest	14
	Requirements					Fundamental requirements stakeholders pose to PPP activities	24
	Strategy						0
		Existence, Duration and Nature				Basic characteristics of PPP strategies	19
		Elements				Implementation of PPP strategies	18
	Contributions						0
		Kinds of resources				- Origin of resources - Resources particularly needed	16
			Skills and Competences			- Core competencies - Public vs. private sector competencies	26
			Financial			- Cash and non-cash contributions - Conditions for financial contributions	16
			In-Kind			Tangible and intangible in-kind resources	16
		Complementary/ Overlapping				Complementarity of the different kinds of resources	26
	Risk Management and Control						0
		Risk Categories				-	1
			Extrinsic			External risks which cannot or can only hardly be influenced by the PPP stakeholders	30
			Intrinsic			PPP-inherent risks that the PPP stakeholders can influence	36
		Risk Control				Measures to address, prevent and mitigate extrinsic and intrinsic risks	41
		Balance between Benefits and Risks				Balance level and influence factors	21
Preparation and Implementation							**210**
	Partner Selection						0
		Origin of the initiative				Initiator/s of a PPP	22

Meta codes	1. Level	2. Level	3. Level	4. Level	5. Level	Specifications and key questions	Code frequency
		Characteristics and Procedure				General characteristics and selection procedure	30
		Selection Criteria				- Internally vs. externally driven criteria - Hard vs. soft criteria	37
		Previous Experiences				- Existence of previous experiences with the selected partner(s) - Influence of previous experiences on partner selection	23
	Preparatory Actions					- Level of preparation for a PPP - Extent and kinds of preparatory actions taken	33
	Planning Quality					- Due diligence elements - Examples of insufficient planning (quality)	21
	Project Phases					- Different kinds of project phases in PPPs - Reasons of the chosen phase structure	44
Budget and Resource Planning							**187**
	Financing Mechanism					- Different kinds of financing mechanisms - Financing differentiated by public vs. private sector - Conditions and restrictions of the different financing mechanisms	35
	Equity Ownership/Separation of Resources					Separation of ownership in a PPP	15
	Resource Planning						0
		Planning and Approval Procedure				Procedural steps and level of autonomy	24
		Planning Quality				Quality assurance mechanisms and planning deficiencies	11
	Transaction Characteristics						0
		Specificity of Resources Employed/Synergy Effects				- Reasons for the use of specified/customzied resources - Extent to which resources are specified - Synergy effects between two or more ongoing/previous PPP projects	25
		Resource Provision Process (Frequency & Outsourcing)				- Frequency: meaning in the context of PPPs - Outsourcing: characteristics and reasons	19
	Resource Efficiency					Level of resource efficiency and need for improvement	25
		Cost Factors				Main cost factors and cost drivers	24
		Cost Reduction				Cost reduction approaches and measures	9
Governance and Control Pattern							**321**
	Governance Structure					-	16
		Governing Bodies				Different kinds of governing bodies	26
		Partner-specific internal project-related structure				Characteristics and internal processes	35
		Sharing of Responsibilities and Taking of Ownership				- Criteria for the determination of responsibilities - Degree of formalization of responsibilities	36

Meta codes	Sub codes: 1. Level	2. Level	3. Level	4. Level	5. Level	Specifications and key questions	Code frequency
		Delegated Decision Rights				- Reasons for the delegation of decision rights - Challenges and boundaries	19
		Level of Complexity				Reasons and characteristics of governance complexity	17
	Governance Level					Factors that influence the chosen governance level	7
		Decision-Making Processes				- Formal and informal rules of procedure - (Perceived) level of hierarchy	12
			Control Type				0
				Dominant		- General understanding of the different control types - Areas and extent of use of the different control types - Differences between theory and practice	15
				Independent			12
				Shared			24
			Categories of Control Mechanisms				0
				Context-oriented		- Reasons and conditions for the use of the three categories of control - Extent of use of the different control mechanisms	8
				Content-oriented			7
				Consultation-oriented			12
			Level of Intergration of Control Systems (between Partners)			Extent to which the control systems of the different partners involved are integrated	9
		Level of Cooperation				- General understanding of partnership - Drivers and obstacles of cooperation	27
			Scale-based assessment			Five types: hostile, competitive, egoistic-rational, cooperative, and altruistic	26
			Risk of non-cooperative behavior/ opportunism			Reasons for non-cooperative behavior and opportunism	13
Management Control							**766**
	Control Mechanisms						0
		Behavior and Results Control					0
			Performance Measurement				0
				Performance Orientation		- Understanding of performance measurement - Demand on performance measurement	19
					Specific	Characteristics and elements of specific vs. loose performance orientation	20
					Loose		8
				Benchmark Indicators		- Demand on benchmarking - Determination of benchmark indicators and challenges	25
					Qualitative	- Reasons for using qualitative/quantitative benchmarks - Types of qualitative/quantitative benchmark indicators	9
					Quantitative		26
			Monitoring			Existence, extent, focus, relevance, and understanding of monitoring	23
				Regular Activi-		Monitoring elements, procedures, and tools	27

Meta codes	Sub codes: 1. Level	2. Level	3. Level	4. Level	5. Level	Specifications and key questions	Code frequency
				ties			
				Follow-Up Activities		Evaluation and impact assessment activities	11
			Reporting			-	9
				Accountability		- External/internal reporting lines/structures - Types of reports	23
				Level of Detail/Use of benchmark indicators		- Details/information included in reports - Demand for detailed reporting	22
			Rules and Guidelines			Commitment to, reasons for, and use of (internal) rules and guidelines	21
		Clan and Social Control (Interaction between partners)					0
			Activities			Types and regularity of social activities	30
			Communication			Characteristics of personal and non-personal communication activities	33
			Alignment of Diverging Interest and Objectives			- Reasons for diverging interests - Characteristics/mechanisms of the alignment process	36
			Conflict Management			- Conflict incidents and their consequences for MC - Countermeasures/instruments/mechanisms of conflict resolution	22
			Networks			Relevance and benefits of networks	14
			Knowledge management/ sharing			Knowledge management/sharing mechanisms, processes and obstacles	10
	Control Extent/tightness					-	12
		Contractual controls and formalization of MC Practices				- Formal control mechamisms vs. MC in practice - (Mandatory) control elements as per contract - Need for formalized MC	23
		Contractual Safeguardings				- Areas to protect/safeguarding elements - Sanctioning mechanisms	20
	Environmental Factors						0
		Control challenges				Challenges MC is facing in practice	23
		Influences of Organizational Culture					0
			Influences of Organizational Culture in general			- Fundamental differences in the organizational culture of different partners - Awareness of interorganizational differences	37
			Implications for MC			Consequences of different organizational cultures for MC	29
		Intercultural Influences					0
			Intercultural Influences in general			Characteristics of intercultural differences	16
			Implications for MC			Consequences of intercultural differences for MC	13
		Trust					0
			Trust in general			General meaning of trust for PPPs	27
			Impact of Trust on MC			- Relationship between trust and MC - Trust as MC mechanism - Challenges of trust in the context of MC	15

Meta codes	1. Level	2. Level	3. Level	4. Level	5. Level	Specifications and key questions	Code frequency
			Trust-building Mechanisms			Different formal and informal control mechanisms	19
		Control Problems					0
			Problems and their Roots			- Cause-and-effect relationship - Public vs. private sector perception	49
			Countermeasures/ Reaction (consequences for MC)			Adjustment of formal/informal control mechanisms and other actions	29
	Control Effectiveness					-	7
		Contract Enforceability				Opportunities and ways of enforcing contracts	16
		Contract Compliance				- Control focus on compliance - Determinants of non-compliance - Compliance issues	11
		Commitment				- Level/understanding of commitment - Determinants/drivers of commitment - Reasons for/consequences of lack of commitment	25
Institutional Environment							**198**
	Institutional Levels					-	6
		Micro level (local, national, regional)				- Institutional focus of PPP activities - Relevance of the institutional level for PPP activities - Institutional restrictions	9
		Macro level (international)					5
	Institutional Constraints						0
		Formal - legal (laws, policies, regulations)				Different kinds of formal/informal institutional constraints and their implications for the implementation of PPPs	25
		Informal - economic/ethical/political/societal					21
	Role of Governmental Authorities						15
		Support and Promotion				- Ways in which governmental authorities support/impede PPP implementation actively/passively	19
		Impediment					12
		Accountability				- Accountability in practice and nature of accountability - Governmental institutions which request accountability	9
	Expansion of PPP activities					- Areas and potential partners for expanding PPP activities - Conditions and aspects to consider for expanding PPP activities	30
	Influence of Global Institutions						0
		UN and other global initiatives and platforms				Intergovernmental platforms, governments, NGOs, etc.	14
		Transition from MDGs to SDGs (expectations/				- Positive/negative/neutral expectations - Implications for own PPP activities	33

Meta codes	1. Level	2. Level	3. Level	4. Level	5. Level	Specifications and key questions	Code frequency
		implications)					
Critical Success Factors							**193**
	Definition of Critical Success Factors					Approaches of defining success with respect to PPPs	11
	Extrinsic factors					Economic, legal, political and social factors	9
	Intrinsic factors						0
		Interpersonal				Factors related to the collaboration between the stakeholders involved	35
		Inherent/structural				Factors related to the fundamental setup of the PPP	47
		Procedural				Factors related to the implementation of the PPP	23
		General				Other factors	17
	Implications of CSFs for MC					Affected fields of and learnings/consequences for MC	20
	Potential for improvement					Diverse suggestions for improving MC in PPPs	31
Total							**2660**

9. Bibliography

Abdul-Aziz, A.-R. (2012). Control mechanisms exercised in Malaysian housing public-private partnerships. *Construction Management and Economics*, *30* (1), 37–55.

Abernethy, M. A., & Lillis, A. M. (1995). The impact of manufacturing flexibility on management control system design. *Accounting, Organizations and Society*, *20* (4), 241–258.

Abernethy, M. A., Lillis, A. M., Brownell, P., & Carter, P. (2001). Product diversity and costing system design choice: field study evidence. *Management Accounting Research*, *12* (3), 261–279.

Acar, M., Chao Guo, & Kaifeng Yang. (2008). Accountability When Hierarchical Authority Is Absent: Views From Public-Private Partnership Practitioners. *The American Review of Public Administration*, *38* (1), 3–23.

Acerete, B., Stafford, A., & Stapleton, P. (2011). Spanish healthcare public private partnerships: The 'Alzira model'. *Critical Perspectives on Accounting*, *22* (6), 533–549.

Acquaah, M. (2009). International joint venture partner origin, strategic choice, and performance: A comparative analysis in an emerging economy in Africa. *Journal of International Management*, *15* (1), 46–60.

Adler, P. S. (2001). Market, Hierarchy, and Trust: The Knowledge Economy and the Future of Capitalism. *Organization Science*, *12* (2), 215–234.

Ahrens, T., & Chapman, C. S. (2004). Accounting for Flexibility and Efficiency: A Field Study of Management Control Systems in a Restaurant Chain. *Contemporary Accounting Research*, *21* (2), 271–302.

Ahrens, T., & Chapman, C. S. (2006). Doing qualitative field research in management accounting: Positioning data to contribute to theory. *Accounting, Organizations and Society*, *31* (8), 819–841.

Ahrens, T., & Chapman, C. S. (2007). Management accounting as practice. *Accounting, Organizations and Society*, *32* (1-2), 1–27.

Ahrens, T., & Dent, J. F. (1998). Accounting and Organizations: Realizing the Richness of Field Research. *Journal of Management Accounting Research*, *10*, 1–39.

Almarri, K. (2017). Critical Success Factors for Public Private Partnerships in the UAE Construction Industry: A Comparative Analysis between the UAE and the UK. *Journal of Engineering, Project, and Production Management*, *7* (1), 21–32.

Almquist, R., Grossi, G., van Helden, G. J., & Reichard, C. (2013). Public sector governance and accountability. *Critical Perspectives on Accounting*, *24* (7-8), 479–487.

Alvesson, M., & Deetz, S. (2000). *Doing critical management research. SAGE series in management research*. London, Thousand Oaks, New Delhi: SAGE Publications.

Anderson, S. W., & Dekker, H. C. (2005). Management Control for Market Transactions: The Relation Between Transaction Characteristics, Incomplete Contract Design, and Subsequent Performance. *Management Science*, *51* (12), 1734–1752.

Anderson, S. W., Glenn, D., & Sedatole, K. L. (2000). Sourcing parts of complex products: evidence on transactions costs, high-powered incentives and ex-post opportunism. *Accounting, Organizations and Society*, *25* (8), 723–749.

Andon, P. (2012). Accounting-related research in PPPs/PFIs: present contributions and future opportunities. *Accounting, Auditing & Accountability Journal*, *25* (5), 876–924.

Andrews, R., Esteve, M., & Ysa, T. (2015). Public–private joint ventures: Mixing oil and water? *Public Money & Management*, *35* (4), 265–272.

T. S. Konrad, *Management Control in Public-Private Partnerships*,
Schriften zu Wirtschaftsprüfung, Steuerlehre und Controlling,
https://doi.org/10.1007/978-3-658-22868-2

Appuhami, R., & Perera, S. (2016). Management controls for minimising risk in public-private partnerships in a developing country. *Journal of Accounting & Organizational Change*, *12* (3), 408–431.

Appuhami, R., Perera, S., & Perera, H. (2011). Management Controls in Public-Private Partnerships: An Analytical Framework. *Australian Accounting Review*, *21* (1), 64–79.

Arevalo, J. A., & Fallon, F. T. (2008). Assessing corporate responsibility as a contribution to global governance: the case of the UN Global Compact. *Corporate Governance: The international journal of business in society*, *8* (4), 456–470.

Arrow, K. (1969). The Organization of Economic Activity: Issues Pertinent to the Choice of Market versus Non-market Allocations. *Analysis and Evaluation of Public Expenditures: The PPP System*, *1*, 47–64.

Atkinson, A. A., & Shaffir, W. (1998). Standards for Field Research in Management Accounting. *Journal of Management Accounting Research*, *10*, 41–68.

Babatunde, S. O., Opawole, A., & Emmanuel Akinsiku, O. (2012). Critical success factors in public-private partnership (PPP) on infrastructure delivery in Nigeria. *Journal of Facilities Management*, *10* (3), 212–225.

Baiman, S., & Rajan, M. V. (2002). Incentive issues in inter-firm relationships. *Accounting, Organizations and Society*, *27* (3), 213–238.

Baker, C. R. (2003). Investigating Enron as a public private partnership. *Accounting, Auditing & Accountability Journal*, *16* (3), 446–466.

Baldwin, C. Y. (2007). Where do transactions come from? Modularity, transactions, and the boundaries of firms. *Industrial and Corporate Change*, *17* (1), 155–195.

Ball, A., & Craig, R. (2010). Using neo-institutionalism to advance social and environmental accounting. *Critical Perspectives on Accounting*, *21* (4), 283–293.

Baudry, B., & Chassagnon, V. (2010). The close relation between organization theory and Oliver Williamson's transaction cost economics: a theory of the firm perspective. *Journal of Institutional Economics*, *6* (4), 477–503.

Baumgarth, C., & Koch, J. (2009). Inhaltsanalyse. In C. Baumgarth (Ed.), *Empirische Mastertechniken. Eine anwendungsorientierte Einführung für die Marketing- und Managementforschung* (1st ed., pp. 131–166). Wiesbaden: Gabler.

Beck, A. C., Campbell, D., & Shrives, P. J. (2010). Content analysis in environmental reporting research: Enrichment and rehearsal of the method in a British–German context. *The British Accounting Review*, *42* (3), 207–222.

Benito, B., Montesinos, V., & Bastida, F. (2008). An example of creative accounting in public sector: The private financing of infrastructures in Spain. *Critical Perspectives on Accounting*, *19* (7), 963–986.

Bennett, E., James, S., & Grohmann, P. (2000). *Joint Venture Public-Private Partnerships for Urban Environmental Services*. PPPUE Working Paper Series. New York, *Volume II*.

Berding, K. (2011). *Controlling in Sportverbänden. Schriftenreihe Sportökonomie in Forschung und Praxis: Bd. 13*. Hamburg: Verlag Dr. Kovač.

Berry, A. J., Coad, A. F., Harris, E. P., Otley, D. T., & Stringer, C. (2009). Emerging themes in management control: A review of recent literature. *The British Accounting Review*, *41* (1), 2–20.

Berry, A. J. (1994). Spanning Traditional Boundaries. *Leadership & Organization Development Journal*, *15* (7), 4–10.

Bevir, M., & Richards, D. (2009). Decentring Policy Networks: A Theoretical Agenda. *Public Administration*, *87* (1), 3–14.

Bloomfield, P. (2006). The Challenging Business of Long-Term Public-Private Partnerships: Reflections on Local Experience. *Public Administration Review*, *66* (3), 400–411.

Boehle, M. (2014). *Wirkungsorientierter Haushalt für Kommunalverwaltungen: Ansätze zur organisationsübergreifenden Wirkungssteuerung am Beispiel der Hilfen zur Erziehung in der Kinder- und Jugendhilfe*. *Schriftenreihe Schriften zum betrieblichen Rechnungswesen und Controlling: Bd. 128*. Hamburg: Verlag Dr. Kovač.

Boersma, M. F., Buckley, P. J., & Ghauri, P. N. (2003). Trust in international joint venture relationships. *Journal of Business Research*, *56* (12), 1031–1042.

Bogner, A., Littig, B., & Menz, W. (2014). *Interviews mit Experten: Eine praxisorientierte Einführung*. *Qualitative Sozialforschung*. Wiesbaden: Springer VS.

Boland, R. J., Sharma, A. K., & Afonso, P. S. (2008). Designing management control in hybrid organizations: The role of path creation and morphogenesis. *Accounting, Organizations and Society*, *33* (7-8), 899–914.

Borchardt, A., & Göthlich, S. E. (2009). Erkenntnisgewinnung durch Fallstudien. In S. Albers, D. Klapper, U. Konradt, A. Walter, & J. Wolf (Eds.), *Methodik der empirischen Forschung* (pp. 33–48). Wiesbaden: Gabler Verlag.

Bortz, J., & Döring, N. (2006). *Forschungsmethoden und Evaluation: Für Human- und Sozialwissenschaftler ; mit 87 Tabellen* (4., überarb. Aufl.). *Springer-Lehrbuch Bachelor, Master*. Heidelberg: Springer-Medizin-Verl.

Boucoiran, T. (2010). *Einfluss nationaler Kultur auf das Controlling: Eine Exploration deutscher und französischer Controllingpraxis aus Sicht deutscher Unternehmen*. *Schriftenreihe Schriften zum betrieblichen Rechnungswesen und Controlling: Bd. 87*. Hamburg: Verlag Dr. Kovač.

Bovaird, T. (2004). Public–Private Partnerships: from Contested Concepts to Prevalent Practice. *International Review of Administrative Sciences*, *70* (2), 199–215.

Brandau, M. (2010). *International vergleichendes Controlling: Empirische Ergebnisse einer Feldstudie in Brasilien und Deutschland*. *Schriftenreihe Schriften zum betrieblichen Rechnungswesen und Controlling: Bd. 86*. Hamburg: Verlag Dr. Kovač.

Brandau, M., Hoffjan, A., & Wömpener, A. (2014). The globalisation of a profession: Comparative management accounting in emerging and developed countries. *European Journal of International Management*, *8* (1), 73.

Brinkerhoff, D. W., & Brinkerhoff, J. M. (2011). Public-private partnerships: Perspectives on purposes, publicness, and good governance. *Public Administration and Development*, *31* (1), 2–14.

Broadbent, J., Gill, J., & Laughlin, R. (2008). Identifying and controlling risk: The problem of uncertainty in the private finance initiative in the UK's National Health Service. *Critical Perspectives on Accounting*, *19* (1), 40–78.

Broadbent, J., & Guthrie, J. (2008). Public sector to public services: 20 years of "contextual" accounting research. *Accounting, Auditing & Accountability Journal*, *21* (2), 129–169.

Broadbent, J., & Laughlin, R. (2003a). Public private partnerships: an introduction. *Accounting, Auditing & Accountability Journal*, *16* (3), 332–341.

Broadbent, J., & Laughlin, R. (2003b). Control and legitimation in government accountability processes: the private finance initiative in the UK. *Critical Perspectives on Accounting*, *14* (1-2), 23–48.

Broadbent, J., & Laughlin, R. (2003c). The Development of Contracting in the Context of Infrastructure Investment in the UK: The Case of the Private Finance Initiative in the National Health Service. *International Public Management Journal*, *6* (2), 173–198.

Broadbent, J., & Laughlin, R. (2004). Forum: Public-Private Partnerships: PPPs: Nature, Development And Unanswered Questions. *Australian Accounting Review*, *14* (33), 4–10.

Broadbent, J., & Laughlin, R. (2005). The Role of PFI in the UK Government's Modernisation Agenda. *Financial Accountability and Management, 21* (1), 75–97.

Broweleit, T. (2014). *Risikomanagement in Nonprofit-Organisationen: ein empirischer Vergleich zwischen Deutschland und Großbritannien.* Techn. Univ., Diss.--Dortmund, 2014.

Bruns, W. J., Jr., & McKinnon, S. M. (1993). Information and Managers: A Field Study. *Journal of Management Accounting Research, 5,* 84–108.

Budäus, D., & Grüb, B. (2007). Public Private Partnership: Theoretische Bezüge und praktische Strukturierung. *Zeitschrift für öffentliche und gemeinwirtschaftliche Unternehmen, 30* (3), 245–272.

Bundesgesetzblatt. 2005. Gesetz zur Beschleunigung der Umsetzung von Öffentlich Privaten Partnerschaften und zur Verbesserung gesetzlicher Rahmenbedingungen für Öffentlich Private Partnerschaften. *Bundesanzeiger* 2676.

Burke, R., & Demirag, I. (2015). Changing perceptions on PPP games: Demand risk in Irish roads. *Critical Perspectives on Accounting, 27,* 189–208.

Burns, T. R., Baumgartner, T., & DeVille, P. (1985). *Man, decisions, society: The theory of actor-system dynamics for social scientists. Studies in cybernetics: v. 10.* New York: Gordon and Breach Science Publishers.

Caglio, A., & Ditillo, A. (2008). A review and discussion of management control in inter-firm relationships: Achievements and future directions. *Accounting, Organizations and Society, 33* (7-8), 865–898.

Cäker, M., & Siverbo, S. (2011). Management control in public sector Joint Ventures. *Management Accounting Research, 22* (4), 330–348.

Carbonara, N., & Pellegrino, R. (2014). PPP for public infrastructure in Italy: opportunity and challenges. *Managerial Finance, 40* (11), 1078–1094.

Chalos, P., & O'Connor, N. G. (2004). Determinants of the use of various control mechanisms in US–Chinese joint ventures. *Accounting, Organizations and Society, 29* (7), 591–608.

Chalos, P., & O'Connor, N. G. (2005). The Perceived Effect of Accounting Controls on U.S.-Chinese Joint Venture Transaction Costs and Performance. *Journal of International Accounting Research, 4* (2), 53–73.

Chan, Albert P. C., Chan, Daniel W. M., Chiang, Y. H., Tang, B. S., Chan, E. H. W., & Ho, K. S. K. (2004). Exploring Critical Success Factors for Partnering in Construction Projects. *Journal of Construction Engineering and Management, 130* (2), 188–198.

Chan, Albert P. C., Lam, Patrick T. I., Chan, Daniel W. M., Cheung, E., & Ke, Y. (2010a). Critical Success Factors for PPPs in Infrastructure Developments: Chinese Perspective. *Journal of Construction Engineering and Management, 136* (5), 484–494.

Chan, Albert P. C., Lam, Patrick T. I., Chan, Daniel W. M., Cheung, E., & Ke, Y. (2010b). Potential Obstacles to Successful Implementation of Public-Private Partnerships in Beijing and the Hong Kong Special Administrative Region. *Journal of Management in Engineering, 26* (1), 30–40.

Chen, D., Park, S. H., & Newburry, W. (2009). Parent contribution and organizational control in international joint ventures. *Strategic Management Journal, 30* (11), 1133–1156.

Chen, J., Chen, Ted Hsuan Yun, Vertinsky, I., Yumagulova, L., & Park, C. (2013). Public-Private Partnerships for the Development of Disaster Resilient Communities. *Journal of Contingencies and Crisis Management, 21* (3), 130–143.

Chenhall, R. H. (2003). Management control systems design within its organizational context: findings from contingency-based research and directions for the future. *Accounting, Organizations and Society, 28* (2-3), 127–168.

Cheung, E., Chan, A. P., & Kajewski, S. (2012). Factors contributing to successful public private partnership projects. *Journal of Facilities Management, 10* (1), 45–58.

Choi, C.-B., & Beamish, P. W. (2004). Split management control and international joint venture performance. *Journal of International Business Studies, 35* (3), 201–215.

Chou, J.-S., & Pramudawardhani, D. (2015). Cross-country comparisons of key drivers, critical success factors and risk allocation for public-private partnership projects. *International Journal of Project Management, 33* (5), 1136–1150.

Chua, W., Mahama, H., & Dirsmith, M. (2007). The Effect of Network Ties on Accounting Controls in a Supply Alliance: Field Study Evidence. *Contemporary Accounting Research, 24* (1), 47–92.

Chung, D. (2016). Risks, Challenges and Value for Money of Public-Private Partnerships. *Financial Accountability & Management, 32* (4), 448–468.

Chung, D., & Hensher, D. (2015). Risk Management in Public-Private Partnerships. *Australian Accounting Review, 25* (1), 13–27.

CIA. (2016). The World Factbook. Retrieved from https://www.cia.gov/library/publications/resources/the-world-factbook/, on 31st of July 2017.

Coase, R. H. (1937). The Nature of the Firm. *Economica, 4* (16), 386–405.

Coase, R. H. (1960). The Problem of Social Cost. *Journal of Law and Economics, 3* (Oct. 1960), 1–44.

Coase, R. H. (1998). The New Institutional Economics: Papers and Proceedings of the Hundred and Tenth Annual Meeting of the American Economic Association (May, 1998). *The American Economic Review, 88* (2), 72–74.

Coleman, J. S. (1974). *Power and the structure of society* ([1st ed.]). *Fels lectures on public policy analysis*. New York: Norton.

Coletti, A. L., Sedatole, K. L., & Towry, K. L. (2005). The Effect of Control Systems on Trust and Cooperation in Collaborative Environments. *The Accounting Review, 80* (2), 477–500.

Cooper, R., & Slagmulder, R. (2004). Interorganizational cost management and relational context. *Accounting, Organizations and Society, 29* (1), 1–26.

Costa, E., Ramus, T., & Andreaus, M. (2011). Accountability as a Managerial Tool in Non-Profit Organizations: Evidence from Italian CSVs. *VOLUNTAS: International Journal of Voluntary and Nonprofit Organizations, 22* (3), 470–493.

Covaleski, M. A., Dirsmith, M. W., & Samuel, S. (1996). Managerial Accounting Research: The Contributions of Organizational and Sociological Theories. *Journal of Management Accounting Research, 8*, 1–35.

Covaleski, M. A., Dirsmith, M. W., & Samuel, S. (2003). Changes in the institutional environment and the institutions of governance: extending the contributions of transaction cost economics within the management control literature. *Accounting, Organizations and Society, 28* (5), 417–441.

Das, T. K., & Teng, B.-S. (2001a). Trust, Control, and Risk in Strategic Alliances: An Integrated Framework. *Organization Studies, 22* (2), 251–283.

Das, T. K., & Teng, B.-S. (2001b). A risk perception model of alliance structuring. *Journal of International Management, 7* (1), 1–29.

Dekker, H. C. (2003). Value chain analysis in interfirm relationships: a field study. *Management Accounting Research, 14* (1), 1–23.

Dekker, H. C. (2004). Control of inter-organizational relationships: evidence on appropriation concerns and coordination requirements. *Accounting, Organizations and Society, 29* (1), 27–49.

Dekker, H. C. (2008). Partner selection and governance design in interfirm relationships. *Accounting, Organizations and Society, 33* (7-8), 915–941.

Dekker, H. C. (2016). On the boundaries between intrafirm and interfirm management accounting research. *Management Accounting Research, 31*, 86–99.

Demirag, I., Khadaroo, I., Stapleton, P., & Stevenson, C. (2011). Risks and the financing of PPP: Perspectives from the financiers. *The British Accounting Review, 43* (4), 294–310.

Demirag, I., Khadaroo, I., Stapleton, P., & Stevenson, C. (2012). The diffusion of risks in public private partnership contracts. *Accounting, Auditing & Accountability Journal, 25* (8), 1317–1339.

Demsetz, H. (1967). Toward a Theory of Property Rights. *The American Economic Review, 57* (2), 347–359.

Diekmann, A. (2016). *Empirische Sozialforschung: Grundlagen, Methoden, Anwendungen* (10. Aufl.). Reinbek bei Hamburg: rowohlts enzyklopädie im Rowohlt Taschenbuch Verlag.

Donada, C., & Nogatchewsky, G. (2006). Vassal or lord buyers: How to exert management control in asymmetric interfirm transactional relationships? *Management Accounting Research, 17* (3), 259–287.

Doty, D. H., & Glick, W. H. (1998). Common Methods Bias: Does Common Methods Variance Really Bias Results? *Organizational Research Methods, 1* (4), 374–406.

Eisenhardt, K. M. (1989). Building Theories from Case Study Research. *Academy of Management Review, 14* (4), 532–550.

El-Gohary, N. M., Osman, H., & El-Diraby, T. E. (2006). Stakeholder management for public private partnerships. *International Journal of Project Management, 24* (7), 595–604.

Emsley, D., & Kidon, F. (2007). The Relationship between Trust and Control in International Joint Ventures: Evidence from the Airline Industry. *Contemporary Accounting Research, 24* (3), 829–858.

Endenich, C. (2012). *Comparative Management Accounting: Ein Vergleich der Controllingforschung und –praxis in Deutschland und Spanien.* Wiesbaden: Gabler Verlag.

Endenich, C., Brandau, M., & Hoffjan, A. (2011). Two Decades of Research on Comparative Management Accounting - Achievements and Future Directions. *Australian Accounting Review, 21* (4), 365–382.

English, L. M., Guthrie, J., Broadbent, J., & Laughlin, R. (2010). Performance Audit of the Operational Stage of Long-Term Partnerships for the Private Sector Provision of Public Services. *Australian Accounting Review, 20* (1), 64–75.

English, L., & Baxter, J. (2010). The Changing Nature of Contracting and Trust in Public-Private Partnerships: The Case of Victorian PPP Prisons. *Abacus, 46* (3), 289–319.

Eschenbach, R., Horak, C., & Furtmüller, S. (2007). Rechnungswesen und Controlling in NPOs. In C. Badelt (Ed.), *Handbuch der Nonprofit Organisation. Strukturen und Management* (4th ed., pp. 340–361). Stuttgart: Schäffer-Poeschel.

Ferreira, L. D., & Merchant, K. A. (1992). Field Research in Management Accounting and Control: A Review and Evaluation. *Accounting, Auditing & Accountability Journal, 5* (4).

Finger, H. (2014). *Ausgestaltung und Kontingenzfaktoren des Investitionscontrollings bei Übertragungsnetzbetreibern: Eine empirische Untersuchung zum Management Accounting Change. Schriftenreihe Schriften zum betrieblichen Rechnungswesen und Controlling: Bd. 117.* Hamburg: Verlag Dr. Kovač.

Finger, K. M. (2015). ICC OPEN MARKETS INDEX. Retrieved from https://iccwbo.org/publication/icc-open-markets-index-3rd-edition-2015/, on 31st of July 2017.

Firth, M. (1996). The diffusion of managerial accounting procedures in the People's Republic of China and the influence of foreign partnered joint ventures. *Accounting, Organizations and Society*, *21* (7-8), 629–654.

Flick, U. (2014). *Qualitative Sozialforschung: Eine Einführung* (7. Aufl.). *Rororo Rowohlts Enzyklopädie*. Reinbek bei Hamburg: Rowohlt Taschenbuch Verlag.

Flick, U., Kardorff, E. v. v., & Steinke, I. (Eds.). (2013). *Qualitative Forschung: Ein Handbuch* (10. Aufl.). Reinbek bei Hamburg: Rowohlt Taschenbuch Verlag.

Forrer, J., Kee, J. E., Newcomer, K. E., & Boyer, E. (2010). Public-Private Partnerships and the Public Accountability Question. *Public Administration Review*, *70* (3), 475–484.

Froud, J. (2003). The Private Finance Initiative: risk, uncertainty and the state. *Accounting, Organizations and Society*, *28* (6), 567–589.

Früh, W. (2011). *Inhaltsanalyse: Theorie und Praxis* (7., überarb. Aufl.). *UTB: Vol. 2501*. Konstanz: UVK-Verl.-Ges.

Früh, W. (2015). *Inhaltsanalyse: Theorie und Praxis* (8., überarb. Aufl.). *UTB: Vol. 2501*. Konstanz, München: UVK Verl.-Ges..

Georgieva, D., Jąndik, T., & Lee, W. Y. (2012). The impact of laws, regulations, and culture on cross-border joint ventures. *Journal of International Financial Markets, Institutions and Money*, *22* (4), 774–795.

Gerdes, S. (2011). *Strategic management accounting in information technology: An analysis of the implementation of strategic techniques as tools in information systems*. Techn. Univ., Diss.--Dortmund, 2011. *Controlling und Management/Controlling and Management: Vol. 43*. Frankfurt am Main: Lang.

Geringer, J. M., & Hebert, L. (1989). Control and Performance of International Joint Ventures. *Journal of International Business Studies*, *20* (2), 235–254.

Gerstlberger, W. D., & Schneider, K. (2013). Outsourcing and concession models as door opener for public-private partnerships in the European health sector? *International Journal of Public Sector Management*, *26* (7), 554–575.

Ghoshal, S., & Moran, P. (1996). Bad for Practice: A Critique of the Transaction Cost Theory. *Academy of Management Review*, *21* (1), 13–47.

Giacobbe, F., & Booth, P. (2009). Controlling International Joint Ventures: An Investigation of Australian Parent Partners. *Australian Accounting Review*, *19* (2), 103–116.

Gibbert, M., Ruigrok, W., & Wicki, B. (2008). What passes as a rigorous case study? *Strategic Management Journal*, *29* (13), 1465–1474.

Gidman, P., Blore, I., Lorentzen, J., & Schuttenbelt, P. (1995). *Public Private Partnerships in Urban Infrastructure Services* (UMP Working Paper Series No. 4). Nairobi, pp. 1–11.

Glagola, C. R., & Sheedy, W. M. (2002). Partnering on Defense Contracts. *Journal of Construction Engineering and Management*, *128* (2), 127–138.

Gläser, J., & Laudel, G. (2010). *Experteninterviews und qualitative Inhaltsanalyse: Als Instrumente rekonstruierender Untersuchungen* (4. Aufl.). *Lehrbuch*. Wiesbaden: VS Verlag für Sozialwiss.

Gomes, E., Barnes, B. R., & Mahmood, T. (2016). A 22 year review of strategic alliance research in the leading management journals. *International Business Review*, *25* (1), 15–27.

Grimsey, D., & Lewis, M. K. (2002a). Accounting for Public Private Partnerships. *Accounting Forum*, *26* (3&4), 245–270.

Grimsey, D., & Lewis, M. K. (2002b). Evaluating the risks of public private partnerships for infrastructure projects. *International Journal of Project Management*, *20* (2), 107–118.

Grimsey, D., & Lewis, M. K. (2005). Are Public Private Partnerships value for money? Evaluating alternative approaches and comparing academic and practitioner views. *Accounting Forum, 29* (4), 345–378.

Groot, T. L., & Merchant, K. A. (2000). Control of international joint ventures. *Accounting, Organizations and Society, 25* (6), 579–607.

Grossman, S. J., & Hart, O. D. (1986). The Costs and Benefits of Ownership: A Theory of Vertical and Lateral Integration. *Journal of Political Economy, 94* (4), 691–719.

Guest, G., Bunce, A., & Jonhson, L. (2006). How Many Interviews Are Enough? An Experiment with Data Saturation and Variability. *Field Methods, 18* (1), 59–82.

Gupta, A., Chandra Gupta, M., & Agrawal, R. (2013). Identification and ranking of critical success factors for BOT projects in India. *Management Research Review, 36* (11), 1040–1060.

Håkansson, H., & Lind, J. (2004). Accounting and network coordination. *Accounting, Organizations and Society, 29* (1), 51–72.

Halinen, A., & Törnroos, J.-A. (2005). Using case methods in the study of contemporary business networks. *Journal of Business Research, 58* (9), 1285–1297.

Hall, P. A., & Taylor, Rosemary C. R. (1996). Political Science and the Three New Institutionalisms. *Political Studies, 44* (5), 936–957.

Hamilton, W. H. (1919). The Institutional Approach to Economic Theory. *The American Economic Review, 9* (1), 309–318.

Hardcastle, C., Edwards, P.J., Akintoye, A. and Li, B. (2006). Critical success factors for PPP/PFI projects in the UK construction industry: a critical factor analysis approach. In T. S. Ng (Ed.), *Public Private Partnerships: Opportunities and Challenges* (pp. 75–83). Pokfulam.

Hayllar, M. R. (2010). Public-Private Partnerships in Hong Kong: Good Governance – The Essential Missing Ingredient? *Australian Journal of Public Administration, 69* (S1), 99–119.

Heinze, J. (2012). *Regierungskommunikation in Deutschland.* Wiesbaden: VS Verlag für Sozialwissenschaften.

Helfferich, C. (2011). *Die Qualität qualitativer Daten: Manual für die Durchführung qualitativer Interviews* (4. Aufl.). Wiesbaden: VS Verlag für Sozialwissenschaften/Springer Fachmedien Wiesbaden GmbH Wiesbaden.

Henderson, J., & McGloin, E. (2004). North/South infrastructure development via cross-border PPP mechanisms. *International Journal of Public Sector Management, 17* (5), 389–413.

Henjewele, C., Fewings, P., & D. Rwelamila, P. (2013). De-marginalising the public in PPP projects through multi-stakeholders management. *Journal of Financial Management of Property and Construction, 18* (3), 210–231.

Henke, A. (2016). *Beschaffungscontrolling preisvolatiler Rohstoffe: Eine empirische Analyse unter besonderer Berücksichtigung von Gasversorgungsunternehmen. Schriftenreihe Schriften zum betrieblichen Rechnungswesen und Controlling: Bd. 144.* Hamburg: Verlag Dr. Kovač.

Himme, A. (2009). Gütekriterien der Messung: Reliabilität,Validität und Generalisierbarkeit. In S. Albers, D. Klapper, U. Konradt, A. Walter, & J. Wolf (Eds.), *Methodik der empirischen Forschung* (pp. 485–500). Wiesbaden: Gabler Verlag.

Hodge, G. A., & Greve, C. (2007). Public-Private Partnerships: An International Performance Review. *Public Administration Review, 67* (3), 545–558.

Holsti, O. R. (1969). *Content analysis for the social sciences and humanities.* Reading Mass. u.a.: Addison-Wesley.

Hood, C. (1990). J. G. March and J. P. Olsen Rediscovering Institutions: The Organizational Basis of Politics, New York, Free Press, 1989. *Journal of Public Policy, 10* (03), 349.

Hopf, C. (2013). Qualitative Interviews - ein Überblick. In U. Flick, E. v. Kardorff, & I. Steinke (Eds.), *Qualitative Forschung. Ein Handbuch* (10th ed., pp. 349–360). Reinbek bei Hamburg: Rowohlt Taschenbuch Verlag.

Hopper, T., & Powell, A. (1985). Making Sense of Research into the Organizational and Social Aspects of Management Accounting: A Review of its Underlying Assumptions [1]. *Journal of Management Studies, 22* (5), 429–465.

Hopwood, A. G. (1983). On trying to study accounting in the contexts in which it operates. *Accounting, Organizations and Society, 8* (2-3), 287–305.

Hurrle, B., & Kieser, A. (2005). Sind Key Informants verlässliche Datenlieferanten? *Die Betriebswirtschaft, 65* (6), 584–602.

Hwang, B.-G., Zhao, X., & Gay, Mindy Jiang Shu. (2013). Public private partnership projects in Singapore: Factors, critical risks and preferred risk allocation from the perspective of contractors. *International Journal of Project Management, 31* (3), 424–433.

Irvine, H. (2003). Trust me! A personal account of confidentiality issues in an organisational research project. *Accounting Forum, 27* (2), 111–131.

Isidor, R., Schwens, C., Hornung, F., & Kabst, R. (2015). The impact of structural and attitudinal antecedents on the instability of international joint ventures: The mediating role of asymmetrical changes in commitment. *International Business Review, 24* (2), 298–310.

Ivanova, M., Gordon, D., & Roy, J. (2007). Towards Institutional Symbiosis: Business and the United Nations in Environmental Governance. *RECIEL, 16* (2), 123–134.

Jacobson, C., & Ok Choi, S. (2008). Success factors: public works and public-private partnerships. *International Journal of Public Sector Management, 21* (6), 637–657.

Jamali, D. (2004). Success and failure mechanisms of public private partnerships (PPPs) in developing countries: Insights from the Lebanese context. *International Journal of Public Sector Management, 17* (5), 414–430.

Jiang, M. S., Chu, R., & Pan, Y. (2011). Anticipated duration of international joint ventures: A transaction cost perspective. *Journal of International Management, 17* (2), 175–183.

Johnson, J. P., Korsgaard, M. A., & Sapienza, H. J. (2002). Perceived fairness, decision control, and commitment in international joint venture management teams. *Strategic Management Journal, 23* (12), 1141–1160.

Jones, C., Hesterly, W. S., & Borgatti, S. P. (1997). A General Theory of Network Governance: Exchange Conditions and Social Mechanisms. *Academy of Management Review, 22* (4), 911–945.

Kaid, L. L., & Wadsworth, A. J. (1989). Content analysis. In P. Emmert & Barker L. L. (Eds.), *Communications. Measurement of communication behavior* (pp. 197–217). New York: Longman.

Kamminga, P., & van der Meer-Kooistra, Jeltje. (2006). Parents' Contribution and Management Control of Joint Ventures. *European Management Journal, 24* (2-3), 226–235.

Kamminga, P. E., & van der Meer-Kooistra, Jeltje. (2007). Management control patterns in joint venture relationships: A model and an exploratory study. *Accounting, Organizations and Society, 32* (1-2), 131–154.

Kaplan, R. S. (1984). The Evolution of Management Accounting. *The Accounting Review, 59* (3), 390–418.

Kaplan, R. S. (1986). The role for empirical research in management accounting. *Accounting, Organizations and Society, 11* (4-5), 429–452.

Kaufmann, J. B., & O'Neill, H. M. (2007). Do culturally distant partners choose different types of joint ventures? *Journal of World Business, 42* (4), 435–448.

Kaya, M. (2009). Verfahren der Datenerhebung. In S. Albers, D. Klapper, U. Konradt, A. Walter, & J. Wolf (Eds.), *Methodik der empirischen Forschung* (pp. 49–64). Wiesbaden: Gabler Verlag.

Keating, B., & Keating, M. (2013). Private firms, public entities, and microeconomic incentives. *International Journal of Organizational Analysis, 21* (2), 176–197.

Kenis, P., & Schneider, V. (1987). The EC as an international corporate actor: Two case studies in economic diplomacy. *European Journal of Political Research, 15* (4), 437–457.

Khoday, K. (2007). Mobilizing Market Forces to Combat Global Environmental Change: Lessons from UN? Private Sector Partnerships in China. *Review of European Community & International Environmental Law, 16* (2), 173–184.

Kieser, A., & Walgenbach, P. (2007). *Organisation* (5., überarb. Aufl.). Stuttgart: Schäffer-Poeschel.

Kim, J., & Mahoney, J. T. (2005). Property rights theory, transaction costs theory, and agency theory: an organizational economics approach to strategic management. *Managerial and Decision Economics, 26* (4), 223–242.

King, N. (1994). The qualitative research interview. In C. Cassell & G. Symon (Eds.), *Qualitative methods in organizational research. A practical guide* (pp. 14–36). London: Sage.

Kivilä, J., Martinsuo, M., & Vuorinen, L. (2017). Sustainable project management through project control in infrastructure projects. *International Journal of Project Management.*

Klaes, M. (2000). The History of the Concept of Transaction Costs: Neglected Aspects. *Journal of the History of Economic Thought, 22* (02), 191.

Klenke, K. (2008). *Qualitative research in the study of leadership* (1. ed.). Bingley: Emerald.

Klijn, E.-H., & Teisman, G. R. (2003). Institutional and Strategic Barriers to Public—Private Partnership: An Analysis of Dutch Cases. *Public Money and Management, 23* (3), 137–146.

Kolk, A., van Tulder, R., & Kostwinder, E. (2008). Business and partnerships for development. *European Management Journal, 26* (4), 262–273.

Koppenjan, J. F.M. (2005). The Formation of Public-Private Partnerships: Lessons from Nine Transport Infrastructure Projects in The Netherlands. *Public Administration, 83* (1), 135–157.

Koppenjan, Joop F. M., & Enserink, B. (2009). Public-Private Partnerships in Urban Infrastructures: Reconciling Private Sector Participation and Sustainability. *Public Administration Review, 69* (2), 284–296.

Kornacker, J. (2014). *Budgeting under the impact of contextual factors: Empirical evidence from German multinational enterprises in China. Schriftenreihe Schriften zum betrieblichen Rechnungswesen und Controlling: Bd. 127.* Hamburg: Verlag Dr. Kovač.

Krause, T. (2014). A contingency framework on partnership risk. *International Journal of Public Sector Management, 27* (4), 317–333.

Krippendorff, K. (2004). *Content analysis: An introduction to its methodology* (2. ed.). Thousand Oaks, Calif.: SAGE Publ.

Kromrey, H. (2006). *Empirische Sozialforschung: Modelle und Methoden der standardisierten Datenerhebung und Datenauswertung* (11., überarb. Aufl.). *UTB: Vol. 1040.* Stuttgart: Lucius & Lucius.

Kruse, J., Bethmann, S., Eckert, J., Niermann, D., & Schmieder, C. (2012). In und mit fremden Sprachen forschen. Eine empirische Bestandsaufnahme zu Erfahrungs- und Handlungswissen von Forschenden. In J. Kruse, S. Bethmann, D. Niermann, & C. Schmieder (Eds.), *Qualitative Interviewforschung in und mit fremden Sprachen. Eine Einführung in Theorie und Praxis* (pp. 27–68). Weinheim: Beltz Juventa.

Kuckartz, U. (2010). *Einführung in die computergestützte Analyse qualitativer Daten* (3., aktualisierte Aufl.). Wiesbaden: VS Verl. für Sozialwissenschaften.

Kuckartz, U. (2014). *Qualitative Inhaltsanalyse. Methoden, Praxis, Computerunterstützung* (2. Aufl.). *Juventa Paperback*. Weinheim, Bergstr: Beltz Juventa.

Kuckartz, U. (2016). *Qualitative Inhaltsanalyse. Methoden, Praxis, Computerunterstützung* (3., überarb. Aufl.). s.l.: Beltz Juventa.

Kuckartz, U., Dresing, T., Rädiker, S., & Stefer, C. (2008). *Qualitative Evaluation: Der Einstieg in die Praxis* (2., aktualisierte Aufl.). Wiesbaden: VS Verlag für Sozialwissenschaften.

Kvale, S. (2007). *Doing Interviews*. London, England: SAGE Publications, Ltd.

Kvale, S., & Brinkmann, S. (2009). *Interviews: Learning the craft of qualitative research interviewing* (2. ed.). Los Angeles: Sage.

Lamnek, S., & Krell, C. (2010). *Qualitative Sozialforschung* (5., vollständig überarbeitete Aufl.). Weinheim: Beltz J.

Langfield-Smith, K. (2008). The relations between transactional characteristics, trust and risk in the start-up phase of a collaborative alliance. *Management Accounting Research*, *19* (4), 344–364.

Langfield-Smith, K., & Smith, D. (2003). Management control systems and trust in outsourcing relationships. *Management Accounting Research*, *14* (3), 281–307.

Larimo, J., Le Nguyen, H., & Ali, T. (2016). Performance measurement choices in international joint ventures: What factors drive them? *Journal of Business Research*, *69* (2), 877–887.

Le Nguyen, H., Larimo, J., & Ali, T. (2015). How do ownership control position and national culture influence conflict resolution strategies in international joint ventures? *International Business Review*.

Leiringer, R. (2006). Technological innovation in PPPs: Incentives, opportunities and actions. *Construction Management and Economics*, *24* (3), 301–308.

Li, B. (2003). *Risk Management of construction public private partnership projects* (Ph.D. thesis).

Li, B., Akintoye, A., Edwards, P. J., & Hardcastle, C. (2005a). Critical success factors for PPP/PFI projects in the UK construction industry. *Construction Management and Economics*, *23* (5), 459–471.

Li, B., Akintoye, A., Edwards, P. J., & Hardcastle, C. (2005b). Perceptions of positive and negative factors influencing the attractiveness of PPP/PFI procurement for construction projects in the UK. *Engineering, Construction and Architectural Management*, *12* (2), 125–148.

Li, B., Akintoye, A., Edwards, P. J., & Hardcastle, C. (2005c). The allocation of risk in PPP/PFI construction projects in the UK. *International Journal of Project Management*, *23* (1), 25–35.

Li, J., Zhou, C., & Zajac, E. J. (2009). Control, collaboration, and productivity in international joint ventures: theory and evidence. *Strategic Management Journal*, *30* (8), 865–884.

Li, P., Tang, G., Okano, H., & Gao, C. (2013). The characteristics and dynamics of management controls in IJVs: Evidence from a Sino-Japanese case. *Management Accounting Research*, *24* (3), 246–260.

Lillis, A. M. (1999). A framework for the analysis of interview data from multiple field research sites. *Accounting and Finance*, *39* (1), 79–105.

Lillis, A. M., & Mundy, J. (2005). Cross-Sectional Field Studies in Management Accounting Research—Closing the Gaps between Surveys and Case Studies. *Journal of Management Accounting Research*, *17* (1), 119–141.

Linder, S. H. (1999). Coming to Terms With the Public-Private Partnership: A Grammar of Multiple Meanings. *American Behavioral Scientist, 43* (1), 35–51.

Liu, J., E.D. Love, P., Smith, J., Regan, M., & Sutrisna, M. (2014). Public-Private Partnerships: a review of theory and practice of performance measurement. *International Journal of Productivity and Performance Management, 63* (4), 499–512.

Liu, X., Vredenburg, H., & Steel, P. (2014). A Meta-analysis of Factors Leading to Management Control in International Joint Ventures. *Journal of International Management, 20* (2), 219–236.

Loosemore, M., & Cheung, E. (2015). Implementing systems thinking to manage risk in public private partnership projects. *International Journal of Project Management, 33* (6), 1325–1334.

Luo, Y. (2007). Private control and collective control in international joint ventures. *Management International Review, 47* (4), 531–566.

Maher, M. E. (1997). Transaction cost economics and contractual relations. *Cambridge Journal of Economics, 21* (2), 147–170.

Makino, S., Chan, C. M., Isobe, T., & Beamish, P. W. (2007). Intended and unintended termination of international joint ventures. *Strategic Management Journal, 28* (11), 1113–1132.

Mantecon, T., Song, K., & Luo, H. (2016). The Control and Performance of Joint Ventures. *Financial Management, 45* (2), 431–465.

March, J. G., & Olsen, J. P. (1989). *Rediscovering institutions: The organizational basis of politics.* New York: The Free Press.

March, J. G., & Simon, H. A. (1976). *Organisation und Individuum: Menschl. Verhalten in Organisationen. Führung, Strategie, Organisation : Ser. 3: Bd. 3.* Wiesbaden: Betriebswirtschaftlicher Verlag Gabler.

Marques, L., Ribeiro, J. A., & Scapens, R. W. (2011). The use of management control mechanisms by public organizations with a network coordination role: A case study in the port industry. *Management Accounting Research, 22* (4), 269–291.

Martin, M. H., & Halachmi, A. (2012). Public-Private Partnerships in Global Health: Addressing Issues of Public Accountability, Risk Management and Governance. *Public Administration Quarterly, 36* (2), 189–237.

Maxwell, J. A. (2013). *Qualitative research design: An interactive approach* (3. ed.). *Applied social research methods series: Vol. 41.* Los Angeles, Cal.: Sage.

Mayer, H. O. (2013). *Interview und schriftliche Befragung: Grundlagen und Methoden empirischer Sozialforschung* (6., überarb. Aufl.). *Sozialwissenschaften 10-2012.* München: Oldenbourg.

Mayntz, R., & Scharpf, F. W. (1995). Der Ansatz des akteurzentrierten Institutionalismus. In *Mayntz, Scharpf (Hg.) 1995 – Gesellschaftliche Selbstregelung und politische Steuerung* (pp. 39–72).

Mayring, P. (2015). *Qualitative Inhaltsanalyse: Grundlagen und Techniken* (12., überarb. Aufl.). *Beltz Pädagogik.* Weinheim: Beltz.

Mayring, P. (2016). *Einführung in die qualitative Sozialforschung* (6. Aufl.). s.l.: Beltz.

McQuaid, R. W., & Scherrer, W. (2010). Changing reasons for public–private partnerships (PPPs). *Public Money & Management, 30* (1), 27–34.

Meira, J., Kartalis, N. D., Tsamenyi, M., & Cullen, J. (2010). Management controls and inter-firm relationships: a review. *Journal of Accounting & Organizational Change, 6* (1), 149–169.

Menard, C. (2005). A New Institutional Approach to Organization. In C. Menard & M. M. Shirley (Eds.), *Handbook of New Institutional Economics* (pp. 281–318). Berlin/Heidelberg: Springer-Verlag.

Menard, C., & Shirley, M. M. (2005). Introduction. In C. Menard & M. M. Shirley (Eds.), *Handbook of New Institutional Economics* (pp. 1–18). Berlin/Heidelberg: Springer-Verlag.

Merchant, K. A., & Manzoni, J. F. (1989). The Availability of Budget Targets in Profit Centers: A Field Study. *The Accounting Review, 64* (3), 539–558.

Merchant, K. A., & Van der Stede, W. A. (2006). Field-Based Research in Accounting: Accomplishments and Prospects. *Behavioral Research in Accounting, 18* (1), 117–134.

Merchant, K. A., & Van der Stede, W. A. (2012). *Management control systems: Performance measurement, evaluation and incentives* (3rd ed). Harlow, England, New York: Financial Times/Prentice Hall.

Merkens, H. (2013). Auswahlverfahren, Samling, Fallkonstruktion. In U. Flick, E. v. v. Kardorff, & I. Steinke (Eds.), *Qualitative Forschung. Ein Handbuch* (10th ed., pp. 286–299). Reinbek bei Hamburg: Rowohlt Taschenbuch Verlag.

Meschi, P.-X. (2005). Environmental uncertainty and survival of international joint ventures: the case of political and economic risk in emerging countries. *European Management Review, 2* (2), 143–152.

Meschi, P.-X., & Riccio, E. L. (2008). Country risk, national cultural differences between partners and survival of international joint ventures in Brazil. *International Business Review, 17* (3), 250–266.

Miles, M. B., Huberman, A. M., & Saldaña, J. (2014). *Qualitative data analysis: A methods sourcebook* (Edition 3). Los Angeles, London, New Delhi, Singapore, Washington DC: Sage.

Miller, P., Kurunmäki, L., & O'Leary, T. (2008). Accounting, hybrids and the management of risk. *Accounting, Organizations and Society, 33* (7-8), 942–967.

Mjoen, H., & Tallman, S. (1997). Control and Performance in International Joint Ventures. *Organization Science, 8* (3), 257–274.

Moilanen, S. (2007). Knowledge Translation in Management Accounting and Control: A Case Study of a Multinational Firm in Transitional Economies. *European Accounting Review, 16* (4), 757–789.

Moll, J., Major, M., & Hoque, Z. (2006). The Qualitative Research Tradition. In Z. Hoque (Ed.), *Methodological issues in accounting research. Theories, methods and issues* (pp. 375–398). London: Spiramus.

Monette, D., Sullivan, T., & DeJong, C. (2013). *Applied social research: A tool for the human services*: Cengage Learning.

Mota, J., & Moreira, A. C. (2015). The importance of non-financial determinants on public–private partnerships in Europe. *International Journal of Project Management, 33* (7), 1563–1575.

Mouritsen, J., & Thrane, S. (2006). Accounting, network complementarities and the development of inter-organisational relations. *Accounting, Organizations and Society, 31* (3), 241–275.

Müller, F. (2013). *Unternehmensplanung von Flughäfen unter dem Einfluss der Entgeltregulierung. Schriftenreihe strategisches Management: Bd. 144*. Hamburg: Verlag Dr. Kovač.

Müller, N. A. (2016). *Asset Management in der Wasserversorgung: Dyadische empirische Analyse unter besonderer Berücksichtigung der Schnittstelle zum Controlling. Schriftenreihe strategisches Management: Bd. 190*. Hamburg: Verlag Dr. Kovač.

Naderer, G., & Balzer, E. (2011). *Qualitative Marktforschung in Theorie und Praxis: Grundlagen - Methoden - Anwendungen* (2., überarb. Aufl.). Wiesbaden: Gabler Verlag/Springer.

Neu, D. (1991). Trust, contracting and the prospectus process. *Accounting, Organizations and Society, 16* (3), 243–256.

Ng, P. W.-K., Lau, C.-M., & Nyaw, M.-K. (2007). The effect of trust on international joint venture performance in China. *Journal of International Management, 13* (4), 430–448.

Nicholson, B., Jones, J., & Espenlaub, S. (2006). Transaction costs and control of outsourced accounting: Case evidence from India. *Management Accounting Research*, *17* (3), 238–258.

Nooteboom, B., Berger, H., & Noorderhaven, N. G. (1997). Effects of Trust and Governance on Relational Risk. *Academy of Management Journal*, *40* (2), 308–338.

North, D. C. (1986). The New Institutional Economics. *Journal of Institutional and Theoretical Economics*, *142* (1), 230–237.

North, D. C. (1990). *Institutions, institutional change, and economic performance. The Political economy of institutions and decisions*. Cambridge, New York: Cambridge University Press.

North, D. C. (1994). Economic Performance Through Time. *The American Economic Review*, *84* (3), 359–368.

North, D. C. (1996). *Institutions, Organizations and Market Competition* (Economic History). Washington University, St. Louis.

North, D. C. (2005). Institutions and the Performance of Economies Over Time. In C. Menard & M. M. Shirley (Eds.), *Handbook of New Institutional Economics* (pp. 21–30). Berlin/Heidelberg: Springer-Verlag.

O'Neill, J. (2001). Building Better Global Economic BRICs. *Global Economics Paper* (66). Retrieved from http://www.goldmansachs.com/our-thinking/archive/archive-pdfs/build-better-brics.pdf, on 31st of July 2017.

Osborne, S. P. (2006). The New Public Governance? *Public Management Review*, *8* (3), 377–387.

Osei-Kyei, R., & Chan, A. P. (2015). Review of studies on the Critical Success Factors for Public–Private Partnership (PPP) projects from 1990 to 2013. *International Journal of Project Management*, *33* (6), 1335–1346.

Ostrom, E. (2005). Doing Institutional Analysis: Digging Deeper Than Markets and Hierarchies. In C. Menard & M. M. Shirley (Eds.), *Handbook of New Institutional Economics* (pp. 819–848). Berlin/Heidelberg: Springer-Verlag.

Ostrom, E., Gardner, R., & Walker, J. (1994). *Rules, games, and common-pool resources*. Ann Arbor: University of Michigan Press.

Otley, D. (1994). Management control in contemporary organizations: Towards a wider framework. *Management Accounting Research*, *5* (3-4), 289–299.

Otley, D., Broadbent, J., & Berry, A. (1995). Research in Management Control: An Overview of its Development. *British Journal of Management*, *6* (1), 31–44.

O'Toole, L. J. (1995). Rational Choice and Policy Implementation: Implications for Interorganizational Network Management. *The American Review of Public Administration*, *25* (1), 43–57.

Ouchi, W. G. (1979). A Conceptual Framework for the Design of Organizational Control Mechanisms. *Management Science*, *25* (9), 833–848.

Ouchi, W. G. (1980). Markets, Bureaucracies, and Clans. *Administrative Science Quarterly*, *25* (1), 129–141.

Owens, M., Palmer, M., & Zueva-Owens, A. (2013). Institutional forces in adoption of international joint ventures: Empirical evidence from British retail multinationals. *International Business Review*, *22* (5), 883–893.

Oxley, J. E. (1997). Appropriability Hazards and Governance in Strategic Alliances: A Transaction Cost Approach. *Journal of Law, Economics, and Organization*, *13* (2), 387–409.

Park, C., Vertinsky, I., & Becerra, M. (2015). Transfers of tacit vs. explicit knowledge and performance in international joint ventures: The role of age. *International Business Review*, *24* (1), 89–101.

Parkhe, A. (1991). Interfirm Diversity, Organizational Learning, and Longevity in Global Strategic Alliances. *Journal of International Business Studies, 22* (4), 579–601.

Parkhe, A. (1993). "Messy" Research, Methodological Predispositions, and Theory Development in International Joint Ventures. *Academy of Management Review, 18* (2), 227–268.

Patton, M. Q. (1987). *How to Use Qualitative Methods in Evaluation*. Beverly Hills, CA: Sage.

Patton, M. Q. (2009). *Qualitative research & evaluation methods* (3. ed.). Thousand Oaks, Calif.: Sage.

Peng, M. W., & Shenkar, O. (2002). Joint venture dissolution as corporate divorce. *Academy of Management Executive, 16* (2), 92–105.

Pessali, H. F. (2006). The rhetoric of Oliver Williamson's transaction cost economics. *Journal of Institutional Economics, 2* (01), 45.

Petersen, O. H. (2011). Multi-Level Governance of Public-Private Partnerships: An Analysis of the Irish Case. *Halduskultuur – Administrative Culture, 12* (2), 162–188.

Petring, A. (2007). Fritz W. Scharpf, Games Real Actors Play. Actor-centered Institutionalism in Policy Research, Boulder 1997. In S. Kailitz (Ed.), *Schlüsselwerke der Politikwissenschaft* (pp. 421–424). Wiesbaden: VS Verlag für Sozialwissenschaften.

Pongsiri, N. (2002). Regulation and public-private partnerships. *International Journal of Public Sector Management, 15* (6), 487–495.

Pothukuchi, V., Damanpour, F., Choi, J., Chen, C. C., & Ho Park, S. (2002). National and Organizational Culture Differences and International Joint Venture Performance. *Journal of International Business Studies, 33* (2), 243–265.

Poulton, C., & Macartney, J. (2012). Can Public–Private Partnerships Leverage Private Investment in Agricultural Value Chains in Africa? A Preliminary Review. *World Development, 40* (1), 96–109.

Przyborski, A., & Wohlrab-Sahr, M. (2010). *Qualitative Sozialforschung: Ein Arbeitsbuch* (3., korrigierte Aufl.). *Lehr- und Handbücher der Soziologie*. München: Oldenbourg.

Qu, S. Q., & Dumay, J. (2011). The qualitative research interview. *Qualitative Research in Accounting & Management, 8* (3), 238–264.

Rahaman, A. B., Neu, D., & Everett, J. (2010). Accounting for Social-Purpose Alliances: Confronting the HIV/AIDS Pandemic in Africa . *Contemporary Accounting Research, 27* (4), 1093–1129.

Rangel, T., & Galende, J. (2010). Innovation in public–private partnerships (PPPs): the Spanish case of highway concessions. *Public Money & Management, 30* (1), 49–54.

Reed, A. M., & Reed, D. (2009). Partnerships for Development: Four Models of Business Involvement. *Journal of Business Ethics, 90* (S1), 3–37.

Reeves, E. (2008). The Practice of Contracting in Public Private Partnerships: Transaction Costs and Relational Contracting in the Irish Schools Sector. *Public Administration, 86* (4), 969–986.

Resch, K., & Enzenhofer, E. (2012). Muttersprachliche Interviewführung an der Schnittstelle zwischen Sozialwissenschaft und Translationswissenschaft.: Relevanz, Grundlagen, Herausforderungen. In J. Kruse, S. Bethmann, D. Niermann, & C. Schmieder (Eds.), *Qualitative Interviewforschung in und mit fremden Sprachen. Eine Einführung in Theorie und Praxis* (pp. 80–100). Weinheim: Beltz Juventa.

Rhodes, R. A. W. (1996). The New Governance: Governing without Government. *Political Studies, 44* (4), 652–667.

Richardson, A. J., & Kilfoyle, E. (2009). Accounting in markets, hierarchies and networks: The role of accounting in the transnational governance of postal transactions. *Accounting, Organizations and Society, 34* (8), 939–956.

Richter, J. (2004). Public–private Partnerships for Health: A trend with no alternatives? *Development, 47* (2), 43–48.

Richter, R., & Furubotn, E. G. (2003). *Neue Institutionenökonomik: Eine Einführung und kritische Würdigung* (3., überarb. und erw. Aufl). *Neue ökonomische Grundrisse*. Tübingen: Mohr Siebeck.

Ring, P. S., & Van De, A. H. (1994). Developmental Process of Cooperative Interorganizational Relationships. *Academy of Management Review, 19* (1), 90–118.

Rockart, J. (1982). The changing role of the information systems executive: a critical successfactors perspective. *Sloan Management Review, 23* (1), 3–13.

Roslender, R., & Hart, S. J. (2003). In search of strategic management accounting: Theoretical and field study perspectives. *Management Accounting Research, 14* (3), 255–279.

Rössler, P. (2010). *Inhaltsanalyse* (2., überarb. Aufl.). *UTB Basics: Vol. 2671*. Konstanz, Stuttgart: UVK-Verl.-Ges.

Ryan, B., Scapens, R. W., & Theobald, M. (2002). *Research method and methodology in finance and accounting* (2. ed.). London: Thomson.

Sako, M. (1992). *Prices, Quality and Trust. Interfirm Relations in Britain and Japan*. Cambridge: Cambridge University Press.

Samii, R., Van Wassenhove, L. N., & Bhattacharya, S. (2002). An Innovative Public–Private Partnership: New Approach to Development. *World Development, 30* (6), 991–1008.

Sartorius, K., & Kirsten, J. (2005). The boundaries of the firm: why do sugar producers outsource sugarcane production? *Management Accounting Research, 16* (1), 81–99.

Scapens, R. W. (1990). Researching management accounting practice: The role of case study methods. *The British Accounting Review, 22* (3), 259–281.

Scapens, R. W. (1994). Never mind the gap: towards an institutional perspective on management accounting practice. *Management Accounting Research, 5* (3-4), 301–321.

Scapens, R. W., & Bromwich, M. (2010). Management Accounting Research: 20 years on. *Management Accounting Research, 21* (4), 278–284.

Schäferhoff, M., Campe, S., & Kaan, C. (2009). Transnational Public-Private Partnerships in International Relations: Making Sense of Concepts, Research Frameworks, and Results. *International Studies Review, 11* (3), 451–474.

Scharpf, F. W. (1997). *Games real actors play: Actor-centered institutionalism in policy research. Theoretical lenses on public policy*. Boulder, Colo.: Westview Press.

Scharpf, F. W. (2000). *Interaktionsformen: Akteurzentrierter Institutionalismus in der Politikforschung. UTB für Wissenschaft Uni-Taschenbücher Politikwissenschaft: Vol. 2136*. Opladen: Leske + Budrich.

Schepper, S. de, Haezendonck, E., & Dooms, M. (2015). Understanding pre-contractual transaction costs for Public–Private Partnership infrastructure projects. *International Journal of Project Management, 33* (4), 932–946.

Schlichting, T. (2013). *Controllingverständnis und Planungssysteme in internationalen Konzernen: Eine deutsch-spanische Perspektive. Schriftenreihe Schriften zum betrieblichen Rechnungswesen und Controlling: Bd. 113*. Hamburg: Verlag Dr. Kovač.

Schmidt, C. (2013). Analyse von Leitfadeninterviews. In U. Flick, E. v. v. Kardorff, & I. Steinke (Eds.), *Qualitative Forschung. Ein Handbuch* (10th ed., pp. 447–455). Reinbek bei Hamburg: Rowohlt Taschenbuch Verlag.

Sciulli, N. (2008). Public private partnerships: an exploratory study in health care. *Asian Review of Accounting, 16* (1), 21–38.

Seal, W., Cullen, J., Dunlop, A., Berry, T., & Ahmed, M. (1999). Enacting a European supply chain: a case study on the role of management accounting. *Management Accounting Research*, *10* (3), 303–322.

Shaoul, J., Stafford, A., & Stapleton, P. (2012). Accountability and corporate governance of public private partnerships. *Critical Perspectives on Accounting*, *23* (3), 213–229.

SHCP. (2004) Acuerdo por el que se establecen las Reglas para la realización de proyectos para prestación de servicios. *Diario Oficial*.

Shen, L.-Y., Platten, A., & Deng, X. P. (2006). Role of public private partnerships to manage risks in public sector projects in Hong Kong. *International Journal of Project Management*, *24* (7), 587–594.

Shepherd, A. (2000). Governance, Good Government and Poverty Reduction. *International Review of Administrative Sciences*, *66* (2), 269–284.

Silverman, D. (2010). *Doing qualitative research: A practical handbook* (3. ed.). Los Angeles: SAGE Publ.

Simon, H. A. (1959). Theories of Decision-Making in Economics and Behavioral Science. *The American Economic Review*, *49* (3), 253–283.

Singh, A., & Prakash, G. (2010). Public–Private Partnerships in Health Services Delivery. *Public Management Review*, *12* (6), 829–856.

Smith, M. (2015). *Research methods in accounting* (3. ed.). Los Angeles: Sage.

Söhnchen, F. (2009). Common Method Variance und SingleSource Bias. In S. Albers, D. Klapper, U. Konradt, A. Walter, & J. Wolf (Eds.), *Methodik der empirischen Forschung* (pp. 137–152). Wiesbaden: Gabler Verlag.

Speklé, R. F. (2001). Explaining management control structure variety: a transaction cost economics perspective. *Accounting, Organizations and Society*, *26* (4-5), 419–441.

Stadtler, L., & Probst, G. (2012). How broker organizations can facilitate public–private partnerships for development. *European Management Journal*, *30* (1), 32–46.

Stafford, A., Acerete, B., & Stapleton, P. (2010). Making concessions: Political, commercial and regulatory tensions in accounting for European roads PPPs. *Accounting and Business Research*, *40* (5), 473–493.

Stoker, G. (1998). Governance as theory: five propositions. *International Social Science Journal*, *50* (155), 17–28.

Sturchio, J. L. (2008). Business engagement in public programs: the pharmaceutical industry's contribution to public health and the millennium development goals. *Corporate Governance: The international journal of business in society*, *8* (4), 482–489.

Sukoco, B. M. (2016). The effects of relatedness, number of partners, and learning on equity contributions in joint ventures. *Journal of Strategy and Management*, *9* (2), 156–171.

Tang, L., Shen, Q., & Cheng, E. W. (2010). A review of studies on Public–Private Partnership projects in the construction industry. *International Journal of Project Management*, *28* (7), 683–694.

Tang, W., Duffield, C. F., & Young, D. M. (2006). Partnering Mechanism in Construction: An Empirical Study on the Chinese Construction Industry. *Journal of Construction Engineering and Management*, *132* (3), 217–229.

Teisman, G. R., & Klijn, E.-H. (2002). Partnership Arrangements: Governmental Rhetoric or Governance Scheme? *Public Administration Review*, *62* (2), 197–205.

Tomkins, C. (2001). Interdependencies, trust and information in relationships, alliances and networks. *Accounting, Organizations and Society*, *26* (2), 161–191.

Torres, L., & Pina, V. (2001). Public private partnership and private finance initiatives in the EU and Spanish local governments. *European Accounting Review*, *10* (3), 601–619.

Trafford, S., & Proctor, T. (2006). Successful joint venture partnerships: public-private partnerships. *International Journal of Public Sector Management*, *19* (2), 117–129.

UIA. Yearbook of International Organizations. Retrieved from http://www.uia.org/yearbook, on 31st of July 2017.

UN. (2000). United Nations Millennium Declaration (A/RES/55/2).

UN. (2015a). *Taking stock of the global partnership for development. MDG Gap Task Force report: Vol. 2015*. New York: United Nations.

UN. (2015b). Transforming our world: the 2030 Agenda for Sustainable Development (A/RES/70/1).

United Nations Secretary-General. (2016). Secretary-General's remarks at World Economic Forum Plenary Session: "The New Climate and Development Imperative" [as prepared for delivery]. Retrieved from https://www.un.org/sg/en/content/sg/statement/2016-01-21/secretary-generals-remarks-world-economic-forum-plenary-session-new, on 31st of July 2017.

Utting, P., & Zammit, A. (2009). United Nations-Business Partnerships: Good Intentions and Contradictory Agendas. *Journal of Business Ethics*, *90*, 39–56.

Vaivio, J. (2008). Qualitative management accounting research: Rationale, pitfalls and potential. *Qualitative Research in Accounting & Management*, *5* (1), 64–86.

Van der Meer-Kooistra, J., & Kamminga, P. E. (2015). Joint venture dynamics: The effects of decisions made within a parent company and the role of joint venture management control. *Management Accounting Research*, *26*, 23–39.

Van der Meer-Kooistra, J., & Scapens, R. W. (2008). The governance of lateral relations between and within organisations. *Management Accounting Research*, *19* (4), 365–384.

Van der Meer-Kooistra, J., & Vosselman, E. G. (2000). Management control of interfirm transactional relationships: the case of industrial renovation and maintenance. *Accounting, Organizations and Society*, *25* (1), 51–77.

Van der Meer-Kooistra, J., & Vosselman, E. G. (2006). Research on management control of interfirm transactional relationships: Whence and whither. *Management Accounting Research*, *17* (3), 227–237.

Van der Stede, W. A. (2003). The effect of national culture on management control and incentive system design in multi-business firms: evidence of intracorporate isomorphism. *European Accounting Review*, *12* (2), 263–285.

Van Ham, H., & Koppenjan, J. (2010). Building Public-Private Partnerships: Assessing and managing risks in port development. *Public Management Review*, *3* (4), 593–616.

Van Kersbergen, K., & van Waarden, F. (2004). 'Governance' as a bridge between disciplines: Cross-disciplinary inspiration regarding shifts in governance and problems of governability, accountability and legitimacy. *European Journal of Political Research*, *43*, 143–171.

Vanberg, V. (1982). *Markt und Organisation: Individualistische Sozialtheorie und das Problem korporativen Handelns. Die Einheit der Gesellschaftswissenschaften: Bd. 31*. Tübingen: J.C.B. Mohr.

Vélez, M. L., Sánchez, J. M., & Álvarez-Dardet, C. (2008). Management control systems as inter-organizational trust builders in evolving relationships: Evidence from a longitudinal case study. *Accounting, Organizations and Society*, *33* (7-8), 968–994.

Verweij, S. (2015). Producing satisfactory outcomes in the implementation phase of PPP infrastructure projects: A fuzzy set qualitative comparative analysis of 27 road constructions in the Netherlands. *International Journal of Project Management*, *33* (8), 1877–1887.

Vosselman, E. G. (2002). Towards horizontal archetypes of management control: a transaction cost economics perspective. *Management Accounting Research, 13* (1), 131–148.

Vosselman, E. G., & van der Meer-Kooistra, J. (2009). Accounting for control and trust building in interfirm transactional relationships. *Accounting, Organizations and Society, 34* (2), 267–283.

Waring, J., Currie, G., & Bishop, S. (2013). A Contingent Approach to the Organization and Management of Public-Private Partnerships: An Empirical Study of English Health Care. *Public Administration Review, 73* (2), 313–326.

Warner, J. (2016). Davos must confront a world at a tipping point: The founder of the World Economic Forum says global leaders need to adapt to ever-faster change. Retrieved from http://www.telegraph.co.uk/finance/financetopics/davos/12103375/Davos-must-confront-a-world-at-a-tipping-point.html, on 31st of July 2017.

Watson, D. (2003). The Rise and Rise of Public Private Partnerships: Challenges for Public Accountability. *Australian Accounting Review, 13* (31), 2–14.

Wettemann, U. (2012). Übersetzung qualitativer Interviewdaten zwischen Translationswissenschaft und Sozialwissenschaft. In J. Kruse, S. Bethmann, D. Niermann, & C. Schmieder (Eds.), *Qualitative Interviewforschung in und mit fremden Sprachen. Eine Einführung in Theorie und Praxis* (pp. 101–120). Weinheim: Beltz Juventa.

Wettenhall, R. (2007). ActewAGL: a genuine public-private partnership? *International Journal of Public Sector Management, 20* (5), 392–414.

Williams, O. F. (2014). The United Nations Global Compact: What Did It Promise? *Journal of Business Ethics.*

Williamson, O. E. (1973). Markets and Hierarchies: Some Elementary Considerations. *American Economic Review, 63* (2), 316–325.

Williamson, O. E. (1979). Transaction-Cost Economics: The Governance of Contractual Relations. *Journal of Law and Economics, 22* (2), 233–261.

Williamson, O. E. (1987). Transaction cost economics: The Comparative Contracting Perspective. *Journal of Economic Behavior & Organization, 8* (4), 617–625.

Williamson, O. E. (1990). *Die ökonomischen Institutionen des Kapitalismus: Unternehmen, Märkte, Kooperationen. Die Einheit der Gesellwissenschaften: Bd. 64.* Tübingen: J.C.B. Mohr.

Williamson, O. E. (1991). Comparative Economic Organization: The Analysis of Discrete Structural Alternatives. *Administrative Science Quarterly, 36* (2), 269–296.

Williamson, O. E. (1993a). Calculativeness, Trust, and Economic Organization. *The Journal of Law and Economics, 36* (1), 453–486.

Williamson, O. E. (1993b). Transaction Cost Economics and Organization Theory. *Industrial and Corporate Change, 2* (1), 107–156.

Williamson, O. E. (1996). *The mechanisms of governance.* New York: Oxford University Press.

Williamson, O. E. (1998). Transaction Cost Economics: How It Works; Where It is Headed. *De Economist, 146* (1), 23–58.

Williamson, O. E. (1999). Public and private bureaucracies: A Transaction Cost Economics Perspectives. *Journal of Law, Economics, and Organization, 15* (1), 306–342.

Williamson, O. E. (2010). Transaction Cost Economics: The Natural Progression. *American Economic Review, 100* (3), 673–690.

Wimmer, R. D., & Dominick, J. R. (2009). *Mass Media Research: An Introduction* (8th ed., Int. ed.). Australia: Gardners Books.

Woods, N. (2000). The Challenge of Good Governance for the IMF and the World Bank Themselves. *World Development*, *28* (5), 823–841.

World Bank. (2016). Public-Private Partnerships Laws/Concession Laws. Retrieved from https://ppp.worldbank.org/public-private-partnership/legislation-regulation/laws/ppp-and-concession-laws, on 31st of July 2017.

Wright, L. L. (2004). The Need For International Qualitative Research. In B. J. Punnett & O. Shenkar (Eds.), *Handbook for international management research* (2nd ed., pp. 49–67). Ann Arbor, Mich.: Univ. of Michigan Press.

Wrona, T. (2006). Fortschritts- und Giitekriterien im Rahmen qualitativer Sozialforschung. In S. Zelewski & N. Akca (Eds.), *Fortschritt in den Wirtschaftswissenschaften* (1st ed., pp. 189–216). s.l.: DUV Deutscher Universitäts-Verlag.

Yang, Y., Hou, Y., & Wang, Y. (2013). On the Development of Public-Private Partnerships in Transitional Economies: An Explanatory Framework. *Public Administration Review*, *73* (2), 301–310.

Yin, R. K. (2014). *Case study research: Design and methods* (5th ed.). Los Angeles: Sage Publications Ltd.

Young, S. M. (1999). Field Research Methods in Management Accounting. *Accounting Horizons*, *13* (1), 76–84.

Yuan, J., Zeng, A. Y., Skibniewski, M. J., & Li, Q. (2009). Selection of performance objectives and key performance indicators in public–private partnership projects to achieve value for money. *Construction Management and Economics*, *27* (3), 253–270.

Zhang, X. (2005). Critical Success Factors for Public–Private Partnerships in Infrastructure Development. *Journal of Construction Engineering and Management*, *131* (1), 3–14.

Zhang, Y., & Li, H. (2001). The control design and performance in international joint ventures: a dynamic evolution perspective. *International Business Review*, *10* (3), 341–362.

Zhang, Y., & Rajagopalan, N. (2002). Inter-partner Credible Threat in International Joint Ventures: An Infinitely Repeated Prisoner's Dilemma Model. *Journal of International Business Studies*, *33* (3), 457–478.

Zhao, Z.-Y., Zuo, J., Zillante, G., & Wang, X.-W. (2010). Critical success factors for BOT electric power projects in China: Thermal power versus wind power. *Renewable Energy*, *35* (6), 1283–1291.

MIX
Papier aus verantwortungsvollen Quellen
Paper from responsible sources
FSC® C105338

FSC
www.fsc.org

If you have any concerns about our products,
you can contact us on
ProductSafety@springernature.com

In case Publisher is established outside the EU,
the EU authorized representative is:
Springer Nature Customer Service Center GmbH
Europaplatz 3, 69115 Heidelberg, Germany

Printed by Libri Plureos GmbH
in Hamburg, Germany